# Management

## Books by Peter F. Drucker

THE TEMPTATION TO DO GOOD

THE LAST OF ALL POSSIBLE WORLDS

THE CHANGING WORLD OF THE EXECUTIVE

TOWARD THE NEXT ECONOMICS

MANAGING IN TURBULENT TIMES

ADVENTURES OF A BYSTANDER

THE UNSEEN REVOLUTION

MANAGEMENT: TASKS, RESPONSIBILITIES, PRACTICES

MEN, IDEAS, AND POLITICS

TECHNOLOGY, MANAGEMENT, AND SOCIETY

THE AGE OF DISCONTINUITY

THE EFFECTIVE EXECUTIVE

MANAGING FOR RESULTS

LANDMARKS OF TOMORROW

AMERICA'S NEXT TWENTY YEARS

THE PRACTICE OF MANAGEMENT

THE NEW SOCIETY

CONCEPT OF THE CORPORATION

THE FUTURE OF INDUSTRIAL MAN

THE END OF ECONOMIC MAN

# Management
## Tasks
## Responsibilities
## Practices

# PETER F. DRUCKER

**PERENNIAL LIBRARY**

Harper & Row, Publishers, New York
Grand Rapids, Philadelphia, St. Louis, San Francisco
London, Singapore, Sydney, Tokyo, Toronto

A hardcover edition of this book was published by Harper & Row, Publishers, Inc.

MANAGEMENT: TASKS, RESPONSIBILITIES, PRACTICES. Copyright © 1973, 1974 by Peter F. Drucker. All rights reserved. Printed in the United States of America. No part of this book may be used or reproduced in any manner whatsoever without written permission except in the case of brief quotations embodied in critical articles and reviews. For information address Harper & Row, Publishers, Inc., 10 East 53rd Street, New York, N.Y. 10022. Published simultaneously in Canada by Fitzhenry & Whiteside Limited, Toronto.

First HARPER COLOPHON edition published 1985.

Library of Congress Cataloging in Publication Data

Drucker, Peter Ferdinand, 1909-
    Management : tasks, responsibilities, practices.

    (Harper colophon books ; CN/1207)
    "Abridged & revised version."
    Bibliography: p.
    Includes index.
    1. Management. I. Title.
HD31.D773   1985     658.4     84-48157
ISBN 0-06-091207-3 (pbk.)

91 92 93 94 95 MPC 10

# Contents

# Preface:
# Management as Profession and Commitment

As a subject management is multidimensional. It is first a discipline in its own right. It is a young discipline; modern organizations are barely a century old, and management arose with them. But while there is still a great deal we do not know, we know that management is not just common sense. It is not just codified experience. It is, at least potentially, an organized body of knowledge. This book tries to present what we know so far. But it also tries to present the much larger body of our "organized ignorance"—that is, the areas in which we know that we need new knowledge in which we can define what we need, but in which we do not as yet possess the knowledge. Yet practicing managers cannot wait. They have to manage as the problems and needs arise. This book therefore attempts to develop approaches to the areas of our ignorance; to think through policies, principles and practices; to accomplish the managerial tasks. This book tries to equip the manager with the understanding, the thinking, the knowledge, and the skills for today's and also tomorrow's job.

Management is tasks. Management is a discipline. But management is also people. Every achievement of management is the achievement of a manager. Every failure is the failure of a manager. People manage, rather than "forces" or "facts." The vision, dedication, and integrity of managers determines whether there is management or mismanagement.

This book therefore focuses on the manager as a person. It focuses on what people do and what people achieve. Yet it always tries to integrate people and tasks. For the tasks are objective and impersonal. It is "managers" who perform. But it is "management" that determines what is needed and what has to be achieved.

Management is work. Indeed it is the specific work of a modern society, the work that distinguishes our society from all earlier ones. For management is the work that is specific to modern organization and makes modern organization perform. As work, management has its own skills, its own tools, its own techniques. Many of these are discussed in this book—a few in some detail.

But management is also different work from any other. Unlike the work of the physician, the stonemason or the lawyer, management must always be done in an organization—that is, within a web of human relations. The manager, therefore, is always an example. What he does is important. But equally important is who he is—far more important than it is with respect to the physician, stonemason or even lawyer. Only the teacher has the same twofold dimension, the dimension of skill and performance, and the dimension of personality, example and integrity. In this book, therefore, there is equal stress on the manager's tasks and on his character.

This book and its approach have been developed and tested in more than thirty years of teaching management to many different kinds of students in colleges, universities, and executive programmes and seminars. But the subject matter of the book itself has largely been developed out of nearly forty years of working closely with managers on all levels as a consultant, with managers in large and small businesses, and with managers in government agencies, in hospitals and in schools. Most of this experience has been in America, and with American businesses and public service institutions—although I have worked also with managements of businesses and nonbusinesses alike outside the United States, especially in Great Britain, Western Europe, Japan, and Latin America. The book therefore tries to include what every manager needs to know—but in a form in which it is also accessible to people who themselves have not yet worked as managers or even as employees in managed institutions. The user of this book can therefore be sure of two things: everything in the book has been developed in management practice and found both effective in it and central to it; and everything has been tested by students of management and found to be meaningful to them, as well as easily accessible.

Peter F. Drucker

Claremont, California
New Year's Day, 1985

# Management

# INTRODUCTION

# FROM MANAGEMENT BOOM TO MANAGEMENT PERFORMANCE

---

*The emergence of management in this century may have been a pivotal event of history. It signaled a major transformation of society into a pluralist society of institutions, of which managements are the effective organs. Management, after more than a century of development as a practice and as a discipline, burst into public consciousness in the management boom that began after World War II and lasted through the 1960s. What has the boom accomplished? What have we learned? And what are the new knowledges we need, the new challenges we face, the new tasks ahead, now that the management boom is over?*

# 1

# The Emergence of Management

*The Society of Institutions—From 1900 to 1970—The Employee Society—
The Need for New Social and Political Theory—Management: The Organ
of Institutions—Responsibility the Essence—From Business Society to Plu-
ralist Society—Why Business Management Has to Be the Focus—Business
Management the Exemplar—Business Management the Success Story—
The Emergence of Management a Pivotal Event*

During the last fifty years, society in every developed country has become
a society of institutions. Every major social task, whether economic performance or health care, education or the protection of the environment, the
pursuit of new knowledge or defense, is today being entrusted to big organizations, designed for perpetuity and managed by their own managements.
On the performance of these institutions, the performance of modern society—if not the survival of each individual—increasingly depends.

Only seventy-five years ago such a society would have been inconceivable.
In the society of 1900 the family still served in every single country as the
agent of, and organ for, most social tasks. Institutions were few and small.
The society of 1900, even in the most highly institutionalized country (e.g.,
Imperial Germany), still resembled the Kansas prairie. There was one
eminence, the central government. It loomed very large on the horizon—
not because it was large but because there was nothing else around it. The
rest of society was diffused in countless molecules: small workshops, small
schools, the individual professional—whether doctor or lawyer—practicing
by himself, the farmer, the craftsman, the neighborhood retail store, and so
on. There were the beginnings of big business—but only the beginnings.

And what was then considered a giant business would strike us today as very small indeed.

The octopus which so frightened the grandparents of today's Americans, Rockefeller's giant Standard Oil Trust, was split into fourteen parts by the U.S. Supreme Court in 1911. Thirty years later, on the eve of America's entry into World War II, every single one of these fourteen Standard Oil daughters had become at least four times as large as the octopus when the Supreme Court divided it—in employment, in capital, in sales, and in every other aspect. Yet, among these fourteen there were only three major oil companies—Jersey Standard, Mobil, and Standard of California. The other eleven were small to fair-sized, playing little or no role in the world economy and only a limited role in the U.S. economy.

While business has grown in these seventy years, other institutions have grown much faster. There was no university in the world before 1914 that had much more than 6,000 students—and only a handful that had more than 5,000. Today the university of 6,000 students is a pygmy; there are even some who doubt that it is viable. The hospital, similarly, has grown from a marginal institution to which the poor went to die into the center of health care and a giant in its own right—and also into one of the most complex social institutions around. Labor unions, research institutes, and many others have similarly grown to giant size and complexity.

In the early 1900s the citizens of Zurich built themselves a splendid City Hall, which they confidently believed would serve the needs of the city for all time to come. Indeed, it was bitterly attacked by conservatives as gross extravagance, if not as megalomania. Government in Switzerland has grown far less than in any other country in the world. Yet the Zurich City Hall long ago ceased to be adequate to house all the offices of the city administration. By now, these offices occupy ten times or more the space that seventy-five years ago seemed so splendid—if not extravagant.

## The Employee Society

The citizen of today in every developed country is typically an employee. He works for one of the institutions. He looks to them for his livelihood. He looks to them for his opportunities. He looks to them for access to status and function in society, as well as for personal fulfillment and achievement.

The citizen of 1900 if employed worked for a small family-type operation; the small pop-and-mom store employing a helper or two; the family household; and so on. And of course, the great majority of people in those days, except in the most highly industrialized countries—such as Britain or Belgium—worked on the farm.

Our society has become an employee society. In the early 1900s people asked, "What do you do?" Today they tend to ask, "Whom do you work for?"

We have neither political nor social theory for the society of institutions and its new pluralism. It is, indeed, incompatible with the political and social theories which still dominate our view of society and our approach to political and social issues. We still use as political and social model what the great thinkers of the late sixteenth and seventeenth centuries, Bodin, Locke, Hume, and Harrington, codified: the society which knows no power centers and no autonomous institution, save only one central government. Reality has long outgrown this model—but it is still the only one we have.

A new theory to fit the new reality will be a long time coming. For new theory, to be more than idle speculation and vague dreaming, must come after the event. It codifies what we have already learned, have already achieved, have already done. But we cannot wait till we have the theory we need. We have to act. We have to use the little we know. And there is one thing we do know: management is the specific organ of the new institution, whether business enterprise or university, hospital or armed service, research lab or government agency. If institutions are to function, managements must perform.

The word "management" is a singularly difficult one. It is, in the first place, specifically American and can hardly be translated into any other language, not even into British English. It denotes a function but also the people who discharge it. It denotes a social position and rank but also a discipline and field of study.

But even within the American usage, management is not adequate as a term, for institutions other than business do not speak of management or managers, as a rule. Universities or government agencies have administrators, as have hospitals. Armed services have commanders. Other institutions speak of executives, and so on.

Yet all these institutions have in common the management function, the management task, and the management work. All of them require management. And in all of them, management is the effective, the active organ.

The institution itself is, in effect, a fiction. It is an accounting reality, but not a social reality. When this or that government agency makes this ruling or this decision, we know perfectly well that it is some people within the agency who make the ruling or the decision and who act for the agency and as the effective organ of the agency. When we speak of General Electric closing a plant, it is not, of course, General Electric that is deciding and acting, it is a group of managers within the company.

Georg Siemens, who built the Deutsche Bank into the European continent's leading financial institution in the decade between 1870 and 1880 (see Chapter 49, "Georg Siemens and the Deutsche Bank"), once said,

"Without management, a bank is so much scrap, fit only to be liquidated." Without institution there is no management. But without management there is no institution. Management is the specific organ of the modern institution. It is the organ on the performance of which the performance and the survival of the institution depend.

## Management Is Professional

We further know that management is independent of ownership, rank, or power. It is objective function and ought to be grounded in the responsibility for performance. It is professional—management is a function, a discipline, a task to be done; and managers are the professionals who practice this discipline, carry out the functions, and discharge these tasks. It is no longer relevant whether the manager is also an owner; if he is, it is incidental to his main function, which is to be a manager. Eiichi Shibusawa's Confucian ideal of the "professional manager" in the early days of modern Japan (see Chapter 2) has become reality. And so has Shibusawa's basic insight that the essence of the manager is neither wealth nor rank, but responsibility.

## From Business Society to Pluralism

The rhetoric of the New Left talks of our society as being a big-business society. But this is as outdated as the rhetoric of the New Left is altogether. Society in the West *was* a business society—seventy-five years ago. Then business was, indeed, the most powerful of all institutions—more powerful even than some governments. Since the turn of the century, however, the importance of business has gone down steadily—not because business has become smaller or weaker, but because the other institutions have grown so much faster. Society has become pluralist.

In the United States in the 1970s, no businessman compares in power or visibility with the tycoons of 1900, such as J. P. Morgan, John D. Rockefeller, or—a little later—Henry Ford. Few people today even know the names of the chief executive officers of America's biggest corporations; the names of the tycoons were household words. Not even the largest corporation today can compare in power and even in relative wealth with those tycoons who could hold the U.S. government for ransom.

It makes little sense to speak of the "military-industrial complex." The high level of defense spending in the United States has for many years been an economic depressant. It would make more sense to speak of the "military-university complex." No business today—in fact, no business in American history—has a fraction of the power that today's big university has. By granting or denying admission or the college degree, the university grants or denies access to jobs and livelihoods. Such power no business—and no other institution—ever had before in American history. Indeed, no earlier institution would ever have been permitted such power.

In Europe things are only slightly different. Business careers have become respectable to a degree unknown in 1900. They have gained equality with careers in government, in academic life, or in the military—all of which ranked socially much higher seventy-five years ago. But still there is no one in French business today whose influence and power can compare with that of the DeWendel family of steelmakers in the France of the Third Republic, or with the power which a few families of the Haute Banque exercised through their control of the Banque de France and of French money and credit policy. There is no businessman and no business enterprise in Germany today that can compare in power and influence with the Krupps and other steel barons of 1900, or with I. G. Farben in the 1920s. There is no business executive in today's England who can compare in power and influence with the merchant banking families who, almost down to the 1930s, ran the Bank of England and, through it, the British Treasury, as family fiefs.

Of all contemporary societies, Japan can most nearly be described as a business society. Business management has greater influence in Japan than in any other developed country. But even in Japan, there is no business manager today and no business enterprise whose power and influence stand comparison with the power and influence which the great Zaibatsu concerns of 1900 or 1920—Mitsubishi, Mitsui, Sumitomo, and Yasuda—exerted on economy and society alike.

In the United States of 1900, almost the only career opportunity open to the young and ambitious was business. Today there are untold others, each promising as much (or more) income, and advancement as rapid as a career in business.

Around the turn of the century, whatever of the gross national product did not go to the farmer went in and through the private business economy. The nonbusiness service institutions, beginning with government, accounted probably for no more than 10 percent of the nonfarm gross national product of the United States at the turn of the century and up till World War I. Today, while farming has largely become a business, more than half of the gross national product goes to or through service institutions which are not businesses and which are not held accountable for economic performance nor subject to market test.

Well over a third of the gross national product in the United States today goes directly to governments, federal, state, and local. Another 3 to 5 percent goes to nongovernmental schools, that is, private and parochial, including the nongovernmental colleges and universities. Another 5 percent of GNP, that is, two-thirds of the total health-care bill, is also nongovernmental, but also nonbusiness. On top of this, there is a great variety of not-for-profit activities, accounting maybe for another 2 to 5 percent of gross national product. This adds up to 50 or perhaps as much as 60 percent of the GNP which does not go to the business sector but to, or through, public-service institutions.

Indeed, while the New Left talks of the big-business society, its actions show a keen awareness that business is not the dominant institution. Every period of public unrest since the end of the Napoleonic Wars began with uprisings against business. But the revolt against authority that swept the developed countries in the sixties centered in the institutions—especially the university—which were most esteemed by yesterday's radicals and which were, so to speak, the good guys of organization thirty or forty years ago.

The nonbusiness, public-service institutions do not need management less than business. They may need it more.

There is growing concern with management in nonbusiness institutions.

Among the best clients of the large American management consulting firms these last ten or fifteen years have been government agencies such as the Department of Defense, the city of New York, or the Bank of England. When Canada in the late sixties first created a unified military service, with army, navy, and air force all combined, the first conference of Canadian generals and admirals was not on strategy; it was on "management by objectives." The venerable orders of the Catholic Church are engaged in organization studies and in management development, with the Jesuits in the lead.

A generation or two ago, the German civil service knew that it had the answers. But now, the city of Hamburg—long known for its excellence in public administration—has created a management center for its civil service and has made management the responsibility of one of the senior members of the city's government. Even the British civil service has been reorganized with the objective of introducing "management."

An increasing number of students in advanced management courses are not business executives but executives from hospitals, from the armed services, from city and state governments, and from school administrations. The Harvard Business School even runs an increasingly popular advanced management course for university presidents.

The management of the nonbusiness institutions will indeed be a growing concern from now on. Their management may well become the central management problem—simply because the lack of management of the public-service institution is such a glaring weakness, whether municipal water department or graduate university.

And yet, *business management is the exemplar.* And any book on management, such as this one, has to put business management in the center.

## Why Business Management Has to Be the Focus

One reason is history. Business enterprise was the first of the modern institutions to emerge. From the beginning, that is, from the emergence of the railroads and the "universal banks" as large businesses in the late nineteenth century, business enterprise was unmistakably a new and different institution rather than an outgrowth of older ones, as were apparently government agency, university, hospital, and armed service. There was, of course, concern about management in other institutions.* But until recently it was sporadic and undertaken usually in connection with an acute problem and confined to it. But the work on management in business and industry was from the beginning meant to be generic and continuous.

Another reason why the study of management to this day has primarily been a study of business management is that so far the economic sphere alone has measurements both for the allocation of resources and for the results of decisions. Profitability is not a perfect measurement; no one has even been able to define it, and yet it is a measurement, despite all its imperfections. None of the other institutions has measurements so far. All they have are opinions—which are hardly an adequate foundation for a discipline.

The most important reason for focusing on business management is that it is the success story of this century. It has performed within its own sphere. It has provided economic goods and services to an extent that would have been unimaginable to the generation of 1900. And it has performed despite world wars, depressions, and dictatorships.

The achievement of business management enables us today to promise—perhaps prematurely (and certainly rashly)—the abolition of the grinding poverty that has been mankind's lot through the ages. It is largely the achievement of business management that advanced societies today can afford mass higher education. Business both produces the economic means to support this expensive undertaking and offers the jobs in which knowledge can become productive and can be paid for. That we today consider it a social flaw and an imperfection of society for people to be fixed in their opportunities and jobs by class and birth—where only yesterday this was the natural and apparently inescapable condition of mankind—is a result

*The work of Elihu Root as Secretary of War on the organization of the General Staff of the U.S. Army is an American example; the work of Adickes and Micquel as big-city mayors and ministers of the Crown on local government in Germany is another; both were done between 1900 and 1910.

of our economic performance, that is, of the performance of business management. In a world that is politically increasingly fragmented and obsessed by nationalism, business management is one of the very few institutions capable of transcending national boundaries.

The multinational corporation brings together in a common venture management people from a great many countries with different languages, cultures, traditions, and values, and unites them in a common purpose. It is one of the very few institutions of our world that is not nationalistic in its world view, its values, and its decisions; but truly a common organ of a world economy that, so far, lacks a world polity.

It is also business management to which our society increasingly looks for leadership in respect to the quality of life. Indeed, what sounds like harsh criticism of business management tends often to be the result of high, perhaps unrealistically high, expectations based on the past performance of business management. "If you can do so well, why don't you do better?" is the underlying note.

This book will discuss performance in the nonbusiness service institution at considerable length—a whole section of four chapters is devoted to it. I will stress again and again that managing the service institution is likely to be the frontier of management for the rest of this century. But the foundation of any work on management has to be business management.

The emergence of management may be the pivotal event of our time, far more important than all the events that make the headlines. Rarely, if ever, has a new basic institution, a new leading group, a new central function, emerged as fast as has management since the turn of the century. Rarely in human history has a new institution proven indispensable so quickly. Even less often has a new institution arrived with so little opposition, so little disturbance, so little controversy. And never before has a new institution encompassed the globe as management has, sweeping across boundaries of race and creed, language and traditions, within the lifetime of many men still living and at work.

Today's developed society, sans aristocracy, sans large landowners, even sans capitalists and tycoons, depends for leadership on the managers of its major institutions. It depends on their knowledge, on their vision, and on their responsibility. In this society, management—its tasks, its responsibilities, its practices—is central: as a need, as an essential contribution, and as a subject of study and knowledge.

# 2

# The Management Boom and Its Lessons

*The Management Boom—How the Management Boom Began—Its Spread —Its End—What Have We Learned?—Management a Generic Function —Management a Discipline—But Not "Technocracy"—Management Is Culturally Embedded—Management Is Polycentric—The Changed Management World—The Roots and History of Management*

"The management boom is over; the time for management performance has come." This, it is safe to predict, will be management's slogan for the rest of this century.

For twenty-five years, from the end of World War II to the end of the 1960s, a management boom swept over the entire world. Management, an obscure interest of a mere handful of people before World War II, became a worldwide concern. The management boom reached every country in the world, excepting perhaps only Communist China. It permanently changed society and economy—and above all, management. It created an awareness of management and its role, functions, and work which will remain with us.

But the management boom also raised new challenges for management, created new tasks and new problems. The management boom, as all booms must, has come to an end. The tasks which it left behind are ahead of us. Now is the time, therefore, to ask what the management boom has accomplished and what its lessons are.

Before World War II management was the concern of a tiny band of "true believers," mostly consultants and professors. Very few practicing managers paid any attention, though Alfred P. Sloan at General Motors,

11

Robert E. Wood at Sears, Roebuck, and Chester Barnard at the American Telephone Company—to mention some prominent Americans—were significant exceptions.* But even Barnard's colleagues at the Telephone Company showed no interest in what they considered his hobby. Few managers at that time would have even realized that they practiced management; and concern with management as a field of study, as a discipline, and as a social function was practically nonexistent.

The most extensive management library brought together before the days of World War II was the collection of the American consultant and management scholar Harry Hopf (1882–1949). Now preserved in the Advanced Management Institute of the General Electric Company in Crotonville, N. Y., it contains several thousand volumes. But even though management was Hopf's own interest, there are no more than sixty or seventy volumes that properly could be called management. The rest are accounting, taxation, engineering, and the like. Yet, the Hopf library contained everything written on management in any language (except Japanese) until the 1940s.

While Harvard had already begun to teach management, most other business schools of the time, American as well as European, were still either schools of commerce or, as in the case of the more progressive and sophisticated (e.g., New York University), schools of accounting, banking, and finance. They were schools of business skills. Management was either not taught at all or taught only in the form of production engineering or personnel.

## How the Management Boom Began

The change from neglect of management to, first, awareness of and then to stress on management came as a result of World War II. It was, above all, the performance of American manufacturing industry during the war that drew attention to management (though the performance of British managers during the same period merits far more attention than it has received). As a result, interest in management as a practice, as a discipline, but also as a focus of social, economic, and ethical concern began to attract growing interest in the United States.

The management boom, however, was triggered by a non-American. Sir Stafford Cripps (1889–1952), Chancellor of the Exchequer in Britain's first postwar Labour government, was a convinced socialist. But it was Cripps who conceived of management as the force that could restore the British economy and could provide the impetus for its growth and performance. It was Cripps who invented the productivity teams of British businessmen

*On these men and others, see "Note: The Roots and History of Management," p. 21.

and managers who were being sent to the United States to learn the secrets of management. It was Cripps who, by doing so, convinced the world—including many Americans—that management was an American invention.

A few years after the start of the exchange of productivity teams between Britain and America, the Marshall Plan was mounted, and management received a central place in it. The Marshall Plan set out to mobilize management for economic and social reconstruction. The success of the Marshall Plan made management a best seller. Suddenly everybody talked management, everybody studied management.

It was not much later that the Japanese followed the West. The Japanese first talked of a management boom when, after 1950, Japanese government and Japanese business, regaining autonomy after years of American occupation, began systematically to work on rebuilding the Japanese economy. They seized upon management as the central force and the critical factor.

Concern with management rapidly spread to the developing countries. In India and in Brazil, in the newly independent countries of Africa, and in Southeast Asia management associations were formed, management schools came into being, management began to become a major focus of governmental as well as of business concern.

Eventually the management boom reached the communist world. One communist country after another in Europe—beginning with the heretic Yugoslavs and followed by the Poles, the Hungarians, and the Czechs—set up management schools and management institutes, began to translate Western, especially American, management books, and began to teach management as the solution to economic stagnation. Ultimately even the Soviet Union succumbed. In 1969–70 it created two advanced management schools and simultaneously began—though with great hesitation—to talk about setting up autonomous managements in the major industries and major business enterprises.

## Management in the Developing Countries

The impact of the management boom on the developing countries may have been even greater than on the developed ones. Economic and social development means, above all, management. It became clear fairly early in the post-World War II period that management is the crucial factor in economic and social development. It was obvious that the economist's traditional view of development as a function of savings and capital investment was not adequate. Indeed, savings and capital investment do not produce management and economic development. On the contrary, management produces economic and social development, and with it savings and capital investment. It became apparent that, as a popular slogan in

Latin America has it, the developing countries are not underdeveloped, they are undermanaged.

Interest in management spread rapidly throughout the developing countries. Management schools, management institutes, and management societies were formed in Bombay, in Mexico, in West Africa, as well as in Turkey and Iran.

There were notable successes: the rapid development of Brazil; the rapid development of the noncommunist Chinese countries, that is, of Hong Kong, Singapore, and Taiwan; the rapid development of so poor and backward a peasant country as Iran; all are traceable to the impact of management. Management underlies the rapid growth of Mexico. And management also accounts for the great advances made in Colombia. Indeed, in many of these countries, pioneering work in management was being done, e.g., by the group organized by and around the Technical University in Monterey, Mexico, and by the group organized by and around the Universidad del Valle in Cali, Colombia.

Wherever rapid economic and social development took place after World War II, it occurred as a result of systematic and purposeful work on developing managers and management.

Yet, it also became increasingly clear, during this period, that the development of management and managers in most of the developing countries was not proceeding fast enough to generate adequate development, especially in view of the explosive growth of population. It also became clear that we do not yet know how to transfer the knowledge of management, its discipline, its vision, and its values, to new and different societies and cultures. And, the one transfer mechanism which effectively channels management competence into developing countries, the multinational corporation, proved (as will be discussed in Chapter 59, "The Multinational Corporation") ambiguous and controversial.

The task of transferring management knowledge and management competence from the developed countries to the developing ones, the task of generating entrepreneurial and managerial energies fast enough to satisfy the expectations of the developing world, still remains as one of the major tasks ahead.

Before World War II all the books on management filled no more than a modest shelf. By the late sixties American publishers alone brought out each year several hundred management titles— four or five times as many in one year as there had been written altogether in all the years before World War II.* Before World War II only Harvard taught management; by the

_____
*Management books have achieved the impossible: they have become best sellers—e.g., Alfred P. Sloan, Jr.'s *My Years with General Motors* (Doubleday, 1964). Even satires on

late sixties the number of business schools teaching management all over the world probably numbered well in the hundreds. Advanced management education was almost totally unknown before World War II. Nobody in the 1970s can count the number of advanced management courses, advanced management seminars, special schools, special institutes, staff colleges, and other institutions concerned with the professional formation and advanced training of managers all over the world.

## The End of the Management Boom

The management boom, as all such booms must, overreached itself and came to an end. The first sign—and this too is typical of a boom—was the appearance of books that prophesied that the management boom would last forever. In 1967 the American economist J. Kenneth Galbraith predicted in a worldwide best seller, *The New Industrial State* (Houghton Mifflin, 1967), that professional management in big corporations, armed with all the tools of modern management techniques, had become invincible and incapable of being displaced by any force—such as stockholders or governments. This prediction appeared at the moment when professional managers began to be unseated right and left by the takeover-raiders promising "asset management," with the full and enthusiastic support of the supposedly docile and impotent stockholders.

A year later another best seller on management by the French journalist-politician, Jean-Jacques Servan-Schreiber, *Le Défi Américain,* English translation, *The American Challenge* (Atheneum, 1968), predicted that American management was taking over the world (or at least Europe), and that there was a "management gap" between America and Europe which made American domination all but inescapable fate. This prediction appeared—and was greeted worldwide with tremendous headlines—at the very moment when the European economy began to forge ahead of America and when the American economy was forced on the defensive by the Europeans and the Japanese.

By 1970 the Galbraiths and Servan-Schreibers had begun to sound naïve. The management boom was over. It did not end with a crash or a bust. Indeed, there were few outward signs that anything had happened.

Only in Great Britain was there substantial unemployment of managers. And that reflected the generally depressed state of the British economy and the cresting wave of mergers and takeovers in Britain. But management

---

management have become best sellers, such as Robert Townsend's *Up the Organization* (Knopf, 1970). These books have been read by the general public even though they are replete with recondite and obscure management terms and management clichés which a few years ago only a handful of initiates would have understood.

consulting firms that had sharply expanded in the late sixties suddenly found their sales far below expectations. Yet firms that had been more conservative and had spent their resources on building quality rather than on adding staff continued to do extraordinarily well, in respect to both billings and fees. Such management programs, management books, and management speakers who had something to say continued in high demand; indeed, around 1970 nonbusiness managements, e.g., of public-service institutions, greatly stepped up their attendance at management programs, their buying of management books, and their use of management speakers. But the users became far more discriminating and demanding. Applications to business schools and to advanced management courses continued to climb; the students, however, were becoming quite critical of curriculum and teaching performance.

What happened was that the mystique of management was suddenly gone. One reason may have been the dollar crisis of 1971, which must have convinced even the least observant that there was no management gap. Another reason may have been the business debacles of that period—Penn Central and Lockheed in the U.S., Rolls-Royce in England—which made professional management look somewhat less than heroic. But the main reason was surely that managers themselves suddenly realized that management is challenge and work rather than a panacea, and that management techniques, no matter how sophisticated, are not magic spells. Above all, managers everywhere realized that the foundation on which the management boom had been based, that is, the knowledge acquired in the long years of obscurity before World War II, had been outpaced by new developments. New knowledge, new basic approaches, and new understanding, it was beginning to be seen, were needed. And those the management boom could not supply.

While it has run its course, the management boom has nevertheless permanently changed the world's economic and social landscape. There is no return to the period of management innocence, of management ignorance, and of management obscurity, that is, to the period before World War II and before the boom. Above all, the awareness of management as a force, as a function, as a responsibility, and as a discipline will remain. It is the one permanent result of the management boom. It is also the most important result.

## What Have We Learned?

What have we learned in these twenty-five years? Especially, what have we learned that should enable us to tackle the demands of the new era, the era of management performance?

The first thing is that management, that is, the organ of leadership, direction, and decision in our social institutions, and especially in business enterprise, is a *generic function* which faces the same basic tasks in every country and, essentially, in every society. Management has to give direction to the institution it manages. It has to think through the institution's mission, has to set its objectives, and has to organize resources for the results the institution has to contribute. Management is, indeed, J. B. Say's "entrepreneur" and responsible for directing vision and resources toward greatest results and contributions.

In performing these essential functions, management everywhere faces the same problems. It has to organize work for productivity, it has to lead the worker toward productivity *and* achievement. It is responsible for the social impact of its enterprise. Above all, it is responsible for producing the results—whether economic performance, student learning, or patient care —for the sake of which each institution exists.

## Management as a Discipline

This means, above all, that managers practice management. They do not practice economics. They do not practice quantification. They do not practice behavioral science. These are tools for the manager. But he no more practices economics than a physician practices blood testing. He no more practices behavioral sciences than a biologist practices the microscope. He no more practices quantification than a lawyer practices precedents. He practices management.

One implication is that there are specific managerial skills which pertain to management, rather than to any other discipline. One of these is communications within organizations. Another is the making of decisions under conditions of uncertainty. And there is also a specific entrepreneurial skill: strategic planning.

As a specific discipline, management has its own basic problems, its own specific approaches, its own distinct concerns. A manager who understands the discipline of management will still be an effective—and may even be a first-rate—manager with no more than minimum competence in managerial skills and tools. A man who knows only the skills and techniques, without understanding the fundamentals of management, is not a manager; he is, at best, a technician.

Management is a practice rather than a science. In this, it is comparable to medicine, law, and engineering. It is not knowledge but performance. Furthermore, it is not the application of common sense, or leadership, let alone financial manipulation. Its practice is based both on knowledge and on responsibility.

## Technocracy Is Not Enough

The management boom has proven that the manager must be more than a "technocrat." He cannot be confined to his discipline, cannot be content with mastery of his skills, his tools, and his techniques. Management is not culture-free, that is, part of the world of nature. It is a social function. It is, therefore, both socially accountable and culturally embedded.

General Motors may well be the best illustration of the inadequacy of the technocrat concept of management. In the technocrat's terms, that is, in terms of company performance, whether measured by market standing, by profit, or by productivity, General Motors in the post-World War II period has been an outstanding success. But at the same time, General Motors has been a resounding failure in public opinion, in politics, in its standing in the public esteem. Instead of reaping the rewards for its success as a technocrat, that is, as a business manager, General Motors has been forced on the defensive.*

The manager has to be a craftsman. His first duty is, indeed, to make his institution perform the mission and purpose for the sake of which it exists —whether this be goods and service, learning, or patient care. But this is not enough. Any institution exists for the sake of society and within a community. It, therefore, has to have impacts; and one is responsible for one's impacts. In the society of institutions of the developed countries, the leadership groups, that is, the managers of the various institutions, also have to take social responsibility, have to think through the values, the beliefs, the commitments of their society, and have to assume leadership responsibility beyond the discharge of the specific and limited mission of their institutions. This responsibility creates a major new challenge—and raises the most difficult problems, both of management and of political theory and practice. But it has become a fact.

## Management and Its Society

Management is an objective function, determined by the tasks, that is, it is a discipline. And yet it is culturally conditioned and subject to the values, the traditions, the habits of a given society.† The management boom

*For a further discussion of this, see the prologue and the epilogue to the 1972 reissue of my study of General Motors, *Concept of the Corporation*, originally published in 1946.

†A non-Western scholar, the Japanese Chie Nakane, has seen this much more clearly than any Westerner—precisely because the Japanese tradition is not a Western tradition, whereas management is distinctly a Western concept. See her book, *Japanese Society* (University of California Press, 1970).

owes a great deal of its force to the fact that management is not value-free.

The excitement over management in continental Europe, for instance, was in large measure the result of the promise that management would change cultural and social traditions. Management in the Europe of the fifties was, so to speak, the counterculture, which was welcomed, especially by the young and educated, as the battering ram to level the ramparts of privilege and of the class structure, and with them, the obstacles to opportunities which emphasis on birth, wealth, or elite education (e.g., in France) had put in the path of the able individual.

The excitement was even more pronounced in the communist world. There management promises truly to be a major political and cultural force against the establishment. Though surely an oversimplification, the developments of the sixties in the Soviet bloc can largely be explained in terms of the dynamics of management and their impacts on communist ideology and organization.

In the Russian satellite countries management was, to a large extent, the rallying cry of those who opposed the imposition of an alien, that is, Russian, system on their country. The communist reformers, first in Yugoslavia, then in Hungary, and finally, in Czechoslovakia, demanded managerial autonomy; that demand was at the center of their opposition to Stalinism. In part, of course, their motives were economic. But in equal measure, they looked to management as a force to reform government and society. Management to them embodied specifically Western values: the value of individual responsibility, the value of autonomy, respect for the individual. Management, precisely because it is not a political program but a social and economic function, became their hope for the preservation of their culture and society in the Western tradition.

For this reason too, management has become highly controversial in the Soviet Union and a potential threat to the Stalinist legacy of totalitarian despotism. When the Czechs proceeded to make their managers autonomous, the Russians felt that they had to move in their troops and tanks to stamp out this heresy; their own regime at home could not have survived such a development. For this reason, any movement toward management, no matter how badly needed to restore the Russian economy's capacity for growth and performance, is being resisted every inch of the way by all the entrenched forces of the Russian bureaucracy, and also of the Russian tradition. Management, one might suspect, rather than the "intellectuals," is the central threat to the Russian system. Management is, in effect, the "internal contradiction" of Communism. Marx was absolutely right when he attacked, well over a hundred years ago, the "utopian socialists" as antisocialists. Their emphasis on manager and entrepreneur as central, dynamic forces in society is, indeed, incompatible with the dictatorship of the proletariat.

The great question ahead of China, after Mao is gone, will certainly be the question of management and managers. Without facing up to this question, China may not be able to sustain economic growth or political cohesion. If it decides for bureaucracy—that is, for the Stalinist path—it can postpone this decision for a couple of decades, though probably only at a price in human lives, in terror, in suffering, and in spiritual debasement similar to that which Russia has had to pay for Stalinism. If it accepts management and managers, China will, however, equally have turned its back on Mao. The one thing that is unlikely is Mao's plan to have neither the monolithic government apparatus nor the autonomous and responsible manager.

It is also clear—though it may sound contradictory—that the more management can use the traditions, values, and beliefs of a society, the more it will accomplish. The management boom, while it put into question social and cultural traditions, also strengthened them. At the height of the boom, in the early and mid-sixties, there was a good deal of talk about the Americanization of the world, and especially, the Americanization of management. To be sure, insofar as management and managers have come to recognize that they face the same tasks, they have come to resemble each other. But the management boom has also been used to strengthen differences and different ways.

Whether today's Japan is westernized or whether the westernization is just a surface phenomenon enabling Japan to be even more Japanese than ever is not within the scope of this book (or within the competence of its author). But there is little doubt that Japanese management has not become westernized. It has accepted management concepts. It has eagerly grasped tools and techniques. It has listened. But it has used management, its concepts, its tools and techniques to remain Japanese. And only to the extent to which the concepts and tools of management enable the Japanese institution—whether business enterprise or government agency—to retain and to strengthen basic Japanese values have they been adopted.

Neither have European basic concepts in respect to management been overturned by the management boom. Top-management structure, for instance, has remained very much the same in Germany, in France, and in Italy. Only in Great Britain has there been a change in which the formerly undifferentiated board of directors has become divided into executive members, that is, top management in the American sense of the word, and nonexecutive members, that is, the supervisory group.

Career ladders too have been affected only to a slight degree.

In France a man still gets to the top in a big company by graduating from one of the *grandes écoles,* especially the École Polytechnique, going to work for the government as a generalist and then, twenty-five years later and with the rank of *inspecteur de finance,* moving directly into top management in business. In Germany the two parallel career ladders, as an engineer in highly specialized technical work and as a graduate in law (or perhaps, economics) in unspecialized staff work, still dominate. In Great Britain the best starting point for a top-management position is still accounting.

The one change has been the addition of marketing as a career ladder. But it is perhaps symptomatic that in Great Britain, where marketing has become most respectable, the marketing people in top-management positions tend to have made their careers in the British subsidiaries of American companies.

The management boom also left untouched the relationship between business and government in major countries. If anything, it has accentuated traditions: those of an adversary relationship in the U.S.; of the mercantilist tradition in continental Europe; of the *Ie,* the "extended family," in Japan, and of the "club" in Britain. (On this important topic see Chapter 27.)

By restoring the capacity of Europe and Japan to grow, the management boom has brought out clearly that management is not American. There is no American challenge. Just as the world of the 1970s has become polycentric in its politics and polycentric in its economics, so it has become polycentric in its management. We now know that all of us—Americans, Europeans, Japanese, and many others—have to learn management from each other.

## Note: The Roots and History of Management

Some recent writers on management seem to believe that the management boom invented, or at least discovered, management. This, needless to say, is nonsense. Management, both as a practice and as a field of thought and study, has a long history. Its roots go back almost two hundred years.

Management, one might say, was discovered before there was any management to speak of. The great English economists, from Adam Smith (1723–1790) to David Ricardo (1772–1823) to John Stuart Mill (1806–1873), including their successor and antagonist, Karl Marx (1818–1883), knew no management. To them the economy was impersonal and objective. As a modern exponent of the classical tradition, the Anglo-American Kenneth Boulding (b. 1910) phrases it, "Economics deals with the behavior of commodities, rather than with the behavior of men." Or, as with

Marx, impersonal laws of history were seen to dominate. Man can only adapt. Man can, at best, optimize what the economy makes possible; at worst, he impedes the forces of the economy and wastes resources. The last of the great English classical economists, Alfred Marshall (1842–1924), did indeed add management to the factors of production, land, labor, and capital. But this was a half-hearted concession. Management was still, even to Marshall, an extraneous factor, rather than central.

From the beginning there was a different approach which put the manager into the center of the economy and which stressed the managerial task of making resources productive. J. B. Say (1767–1832), perhaps the most brilliant economist produced by France—or for that matter by continental Europe—was an early follower of Adam Smith and the propagandist for *The Wealth of Nations* in France. But in his own works the pivot is not the factors of production. It is the entrepreneur— a word Say coined—who directs resources from less productive into more productive investments and who thereby creates wealth. Say was followed by the "utopian socialists" of the French tradition, especially François Fourier (1772–1837) and that eccentric genius, the Comte de Saint-Simon (1760–1825). At that time there were no large organizations and no managers, but both Fourier and Saint-Simon anticipated developments and "discovered" management before it actually came into being. Saint-Simon in particular saw the emergence of organization. And he saw the task of making resources productive and of building social structures. He saw managerial tasks.

It is for their stress on management as a separate and distinct force, and one which can act independently of the factors of production as well as of the laws of history, that Marx vehemently denounced the French and gave them the derisory name of "utopians." But it is the French—and above all, Saint-Simon—who, in effect, laid down the basic approaches and the basic concepts on which every socialist economy has actually been designed. No matter how much the Russians today invoke the name of Marx, their spiritual ancestor is Saint-Simon.

In America too management was early seen as central. Alexander Hamilton's (1757–1804) famous "Report on Manufactures" starts out with Adam Smith, but then Hamilton gave emphasis to the constructive, purposeful, and systematic role of management. He saw in management, rather than in economic forces, the engine of economic and social development; and in organization, the carrier of economic advance. Following him, Henry Clay (1777–1852) with his famous "American system" produced what might be called the first blueprint for systematic economic development.

A little later, an industrialist in Scotland, Robert Owen (1771–1858), actually became the first manager. In his textile mill in Lanark, Owen, in the 1820s, first tackled the problems of productivity and motivation, of the relationship of worker to work, of worker to enterprise, and of worker to management—to this day key questions in management. With Owen, the manager emerges as a real person, rather than as an abstraction, as in Say, Fourier, Saint-Simon, Hamilton, and Clay. But it was a long time before Owen had successors.

## The Emergence of Large-Scale Organization

What had to happen first was the rise of large-scale organization. This occurred simultaneously—around 1870—in two places. In North America the transcontinental railroad emerged as a managerial problem. On the continent of Europe, the "universal bank"—entrepreneurial in aim, national in scope, and with multiple headquarters—obsoleted traditional structures and concepts and required management.

One response was given by Henry Towne (1844–1924) in the United States, especially in his paper *"The Engineer as Economist."* Towne outlined what might be called the first program for management. He raised basic questions: effectiveness as against efficiency; organization of the work as against the organization of the plant community, that is, of the workers; value set in the marketplace and by the customer as against technical accomplishment. With Towne begins the systematic concern with the relationship between the tasks of management and the work of management.

At roughly the same time, in Germany, Georg Siemens (1839–1901), in building the Deutsche Bank into the leading financial institution of continental Europe, first designed an effective top management, first thought through the top-management tasks, and first tackled the basic problems of communications and information in the large organization (on Siemens see Chapter 49).

In Japan, Eiichi Shibusawa (1840–1931), the Meiji statesman turned business leader, in the seventies and eighties first raised fundamental questions regarding the relationship between business enterprise and national purpose, and between business needs and individual ethics. He tackled management education systematically. Shibusawa envisioned the professional manager first. The rise of Japan in this century to economic leadership is largely founded on Shibusawa's thought and work.

A few decades later, in the years before and after the turn of the century, all the major approaches to modern management were fashioned. Again the developments occurred independently in many countries.

In the 1880s Frederick W. Taylor (1856–1915), the self-taught American engineer, began the study of work. It is fashionable today to look down on Taylor and to decry his outmoded psychology, but Taylor was the first man in the known history of mankind who did not take work for granted, but looked at it and studied it. His approach to work is still the basic foundation (on this see Chapter 17). And, while Taylor in his approach to the worker was clearly a man of the nineteenth century, he started out with social rather than engineering or profit objectives. What led Taylor to his work and provided his motivation throughout was first the desire to free the worker from the burden of heavy toil, destructive of body and soul. And then it was the hope to break the Iron Law of wages of the classical economists (including Marx) which condemned the worker to economic insecurity and to enduring poverty. Taylor's hope—and it has largely been fulfilled in the developed countries—was to make it possible to give the laborer a decent livelihood through increasing the productivity of work.

Around the same time in France, Henri Fayol (1841–1925), head of a coal mine which for its time was a very large company, first thought through organization structure and developed the first rational approach to the organization of enterprise: the functional principle. In Germany, Walter Rathenau (1867–1922), whose early training had been in a large company (the German equivalent of the General Electric Company, AEG, founded by his father, Emil [1838–1915], but developed in large part under the supervision of Georg Siemens), asked: "What is the place of the large enterprise in a modern society and in a modern nation? What impact does it have on both? And, what are its fundamental contributions and its fundamental responsibilities?" Most present questions of the social responsibilities of business were first raised and thought through by Rathenau in the years before World War I. Also in Germany, at the same time, the new discipline of *Betriebswissenschaft* was developed by such men as Eugen Schmalenbach (1873–1955). The management sciences developed since —managerial accounting, operations research, decision theory, and so on —are largely extensions, though in the main, unconscious ones, of the *Betriebswissenschaft* of those years before World War I. And in America, German-born Hugo Muensterberg (1863–1916) first tried to apply the social and behavioral sciences, and especially psychology, to modern organization and management.

## The First Management Boom

After World War I there came what might be called the first management boom. It was sparked primarily by two of the most highly respected statesmen of the period, the American Herbert Hoover (1874–1964) and the Czech Thomas J. Masaryk (1850–1937). Hoover, the Quaker engineer, had vaulted to worldwide prominence by applying principles of management to the first massive foreign-aid operation in history: the feeding of hundreds of thousands of starving people: first, before America's entry into World War I in his Belgian Relief Operation, and then after the end of World War I in the relief operations in Central and Eastern Europe. But it was Masaryk, the historian, who had become the first president of the new Czech Republic, who conceived the idea that management would be able to restore the economies of Europe after their destruction by war—an idea that then found its realization twenty-five years later in the Marshall Plan after World War II. These two men founded the international management movement and tried to mobilize management as a major social force.

But the period between the two World Wars was not congenial to such an idea. It was a period of stagnation, a period in which the highest goal which any national government or any economy—except the United States—could conceive was a return to prewar, that is, a restoration of what had been. It rapidly became a world in which mounting political, social, and economic tensions paralyzed will as well as vision.

## The Work of the Twenties and Thirties

The first management boom fizzled out. Its high hopes were replaced by frustration. Yet behind the apparent stagnation work went on. It was in those years that the foundations for the sweeping management boom of the post-World War II period were put in place.

In the early twenties, Pierre S. du Pont (1870–1954) at the Du Pont Company, followed by Alfred P. Sloan, Jr. (1875–1966) at General Motors, first developed the organization principle for the new "big business," the principle of decentralization. Du Pont and, even more, Sloan also first developed systematic approaches to business objectives, to business strategy, and to strategic planning. Also, in the United States, Sears, Roebuck—led first by Julius Rosenwald (1862–1932) and then by Robert E. Wood (1879–1969)—built the first business to be based on the marketing approach. In Europe shortly thereafter, the architects of the Dutch-English merger that resulted in the Unilever Companies designed what to this day may well be the most advanced structure for the multinational corporation and came to grips also with the problem of multinational business planning and multinational marketing.

The discipline of management was also further developed. In the United States there were the successors to Taylor, the husband and wife team of Frank and Lillian Gilbreth (1868–1924, 1878–1972), and Henry Gantt (1861–1919). In Great Britain Ian Hamilton (1853–1947), reflecting on his experiences as a military leader during World War I, realized the need to balance formal structure and the policies that give "soul" to an organization. Two Americans, Mary Parker Follett (1868–1933) and Chester Barnard (1886–1961), first studied the process of decision-making in organizations, the relationships between formal and informal organizations, and the role and function of the executive. Cyril Burt (1883–1972) in England and the Australian Elton Mayo (1880–1949), working at Harvard, developed, respectively, industrial psychology and human relations and applied each to enterprise and management.

Management as a discipline also began to be taught in the interwar years. The Harvard Business School first began in the thirties to teach courses in management—though still mainly in production management. And the Massachusetts Institute of Technology started, at the same time, advanced management work with young executives in mid-career.

The American James McKinsey (1889–1937) and the Englishman Lyndall F. Urwick (b. 1891) started management consulting, that is, consulting no longer confined to technical problems, but dealing with fundamental management concerns such as business policy and management organization. Urwick also classified and codified the work on the structure of management and on the function of the executive that had been done until that time.

# 3

# The New Challenges

There were seven conceptual foundations to the management boom: (1) scientific management of work as the key to productivity; (2) decentralization as a basic principle of organization; (3) personnel management as the orderly way of fitting people into organization structures (which included such things as job descriptions, appraisals, wage and salary administration, but also "Human Relations"); (4) manager development to provide today for the management needs of tomorrow; (5) managerial accounting, that is, the use of analysis and information as the foundation for managerial decision-making; (6) marketing; (7) finally, there was long-range planning.

Each of the seven was practiced successfully well before the management boom got going (as discussed in the "Note: The Roots and History of Management" at the conclusion of the preceding chapter). The management boom, in other words, refined, added, modified—but created little. It made accessible to managers everywhere what, up to then, had been the arcane knowledge of a few experts. It made into general practice what, till then, had been the rare exception.

### The Need for New Knowledge in the Foundation Areas

By the late sixties or early seventies it was becoming clear that the knowledge on which the management boom was founded no longer sufficed. Even in most of the foundation areas there emerged needs for new knowledge, particularly with respect to productivity, organization design and structure, and the management of people. Scientific management could no longer deliver increased productivity. In every country there was a productivity crisis resulting in severe inflationary pressures.

In retrospect it is becoming apparent that the great productivity increases of the post-World War II period in Western Europe and Japan were only partially the result of better management. The main cause was the movement of very large numbers of people from areas and employments of low productivity, e.g., marginal subsistence farming in Sicily, in Spain, and in Japan's mountainous north, into high-productivity employment in industry. Without such massive migration the productivity gains of these growth areas would probably have been quite modest. But these migrations are over. In Western Europe the limit of absorptive capacity for guest workers has clearly been reached. In Japan there is not much population left in marginal farming. From now on productivity gains in these countries will have to be achieved by making existing workers more productive in existing jobs.

At the same time the demands on economic performance that can be satisfied only through higher productivity are escalating. Affluence, for instance, everybody "knew" (and many still believe) would greatly reduce the demand for economic performance. Once we knew how to produce material goods, the demand on the economic function in society would surely lessen. Instead we are confronted with a rising tide of human expectations. When President Kennedy coined this phrase in the early sixties, he had in mind the explosive growth of demands for economic rewards and satisfactions on the part of the poor, the underdeveloped countries of the world. But affluence has released a similar rising tide of human expectations among the remaining poor of the developed countries, whether American Negro or Sicilian peasant. And the affluent themselves are escalating their demands for economic performance faster than their own capacity to perform. The educated young people, contrary to the headlines in the popular press, show little sign of diminished demand for the traditional economic goods and services (even though traditional economic theory—the so-called Engel's Law—would have predicted such a drop). They show, in addition, an insatiable appetite for new services and new satisfactions—for education, for health care, for housing, or for leisure.

Equally new, and perhaps even more costly, is the demand for a clean environment. It too was a luxury until now. That the masses of yesterday, in city slum or sharecropper's shanty, enjoyed clean air, clean streets, safe water, and wholesome unadulterated food is nostalgic delusion.

Every one of these new expectations and demands requires massive economic efforts. Every one of them absorbs economic resources on a grand scale. Every one of them presupposes, above all, an economic surplus beyond anything the economy has ever produced before. To satisfy these demands requires, in other words, a far higher level of productivity.

We know what is needed. First the traditional approach focuses on only one factor of productivity: labor. But productivity is the output of all three factors of production: land, labor, and capital, in balance. Even in respect to the productivity of labor, we have taken only the first step: the analysis of individual pieces of work. We need to understand the principles of production so as to put work together into the most productive process. And we need to harmonize the very different requirements and logics of work and worker.

## Beyond Decentralization

Decentralization is the best principle of organization design *where it fits*. But the specifications for its application are fairly stringent. It fits the business for which it was originally designed: manufacturing, with distinct markets for distinct product lines. It fits few nonmanufacturing businesses perfectly or even adequately. And it does not fit manufacturing businesses such as the process industries (e.g., aluminum or steel), where the same process produces a variety of products with an infinity of overlapping markets.

Decentralization, we have further learned, is the best principle for the task of operating an ongoing business. It does not answer the organizational demands of the innovating task. And it is not enough, by itself, to organize the top-management task.

As a result of our experience we are looking at new—and so far still largely experimental—design principles: the task force team; simulated decentralization; the systems organization. They are far from satisfactory, so far. But their emergence bespeaks a great need for new models of organization design.

We know that the model which the management boom took to be the universal one is only a partial model, and in fact no longer the ruling model. The management boom was, in all areas, based on work done in and with manufacturing companies, companies that essentially had one product or one product line, operated within one national market, and which predominantly employed manual labor. The model, in other words, was General Motors.

Increasingly the dominant institutions to be managed and organized, even in the business field, are not manufacturing companies, not single-product companies operating in one country or one market alone, not companies employing primarily manual labor. They are businesses in the service industries—banking or retail businesses, and nonbusinesses such as hospitals and universities. They are multiproduct, multitechnology, multi-market businesses. They are multinational businesses. And increasingly, the central human resources are not manual workers—skilled or unskilled—but knowledge workers: company presidents but also computer programmers; engineers, medical technologists, hospital administrators, salesmen and cost accountants; teachers, and the entire employed educated middle class which has become the center of population gravity in every developed country. In other words, the model of yesterday is becoming less and less pertinent. But we do not, so far, have a new model.

## From Personnel Management to the Leadership of People

Finally, we know that we will have to go beyond personnel management. We will have to learn to lead people rather than to contain them.

Our traditional approaches fall into three categories. In part they are philanthropic: the desire to look after the needs, the housing, the health care, the welfare of people who cannot look after themselves. In part the traditional approaches are procedural: to handle in an orderly fashion the recurrent chores connected with the employment of people. In large mea-sure, finally, the traditional approaches aim at preventing and curing trou-ble; they see in people, above all, potential threats.

The traditional approaches are needed. They are, however, not enough. Beyond them we will have to learn to look on people as resource and opportunity rather than as problem, cost, and threat. We will have to learn to lead rather than to manage, and to direct rather than to control.

## The New Demands

While in important areas the old approaches and the old knowledge have been outgrown, demands have appeared in entirely new areas which only a few people at the start of the management boom even divined, let alone studied. Some of the fundamental assumptions on which the management boom based itself—the assumptions of all the work on management during the past century—are being put into doubt by new developments demand-ing new vision, new work, and new knowledge.

## The Entrepreneurial Manager

For three-quarters of a century management has meant primarily managing the established, going business. Entrepreneurship and innovation, while mentioned in many management books, were not seen as central from 1900 till today. From now on, management will have to concern itself more and more with creating the new in addition to optimizing the already existing. Managers will have to become entrepreneurs, will have to learn to build and manage innovative organizations.

We face a period of innovation such as the one in which the modern industrial economy was born in the last half of the nineteenth century. Then, in the fifty years between the end of America's Civil War and the outbreak of World War I, a new major invention made its appearance on average every fifteen or eighteen months. Each soon spawned new businesses and entirely new industries. Practically all the industries that we consider "modern" today, including aircraft and electronics, grew out of these inventions of the late nineteenth and early twentieth centuries. Economic growth right through the period of reconstruction after World War II was carried primarily by technologies that had been fully developed by the time World War I broke out, and by the four large industries built on these technologies: steel, the automobile, scientific agriculture, and organic chemistry. Now we face another period of major technological change in which the thrust of economic and industrial development will come from industries based on new, twentieth-century technologies and their development.

In sharp contrast to the late nineteenth century, much of the new technology will have to be developed and, above all, will have to be applied in and by already existing businesses. In the late nineteenth century the archetype was the inventor, a Siemens, a Nobel, an Edison, an Alexander Graham Bell, who worked by himself, at most with a few assistants. Even then successful application of an invention very rapidly led to the emergence of an enterprise. But it was not the enterprise that had to generate the new. These days increasingly it will be the existing, often large organization to which we will have to look for innovation—for the simple reason that both the trained people and the money needed to develop the new are concentrated in existing and usually large organizations. Management will therefore have to learn to run, at one and the same time, an existing managerial organization and a new innovative organization.

The need for social innovation may be even greater than for technical innovation. Social innovation has played as large a part in social and economic change and development as technical innovation. The needs of our society—the need for rapid social and economic development in the poor two-thirds of the world; the needs of our big cities; the needs of the environment; the need for productivity in education and health care—all these are opportunities for social innovation by business and business managers. They are opportunities for the entrepreneur, and as such offer challenges to, and make demands on, the knowledge, the skill, the performance of management.

## Multi-Institutional Management

The management boom was a boom in *business* management, and most management work of the preceding century centered in managing a business.

Now we know, however, that all our institutions need management.

This would have been heresy only a few years ago (as it still is in England and France to a good many managers in businesses and service institutions alike). Running a business and administering a public-service institution, e.g., a hospital, were then seen as being poles apart. The mission and purpose of an institution does indeed make a basic difference. Nothing is less likely to cure the managerial ills of the public-service institution than the attempt to make its management "businesslike" (on this see Chapters 11 through 14). But then, an investment banking firm also requires management that is different from that of a steel mill or of a department store. And the manager in public-service institutions faces the same tasks as the manager in a business: to perform the function for the sake of which the institution exists; to make work productive and the worker achieving; to manage the institution's social impacts and to discharge its social responsibilities. These are managerial tasks. Public-service institutions equally face the challenge of innovation, and have to manage growth, diversity, and complexity. And we do know, as said before, that a central management need is to make the nonbusiness, the service institution, manageable and managed for performance.

## Knowledge and Knowledge Worker

A primary task of management in the developed countries in the decades ahead will be to make knowledge productive. The manual worker is yesterday—and all we can fight on that front is a rearguard action. The basic capital resource, the fundamental investment, but also the cost center of a developed economy, is the knowledge worker who puts to work what he has learned in systematic education, that is, concepts, ideas, and theories, rather than the man who puts to work manual skill or muscle.

Taylor put knowledge to work to make the manual worker productive. His industrial engineer was one of the first knowledge workers employed in the manufacturing process. But Taylor himself never asked the question What constitutes "productivity" with respect to the industrial engineer who applies "scientific management"? As a result of Taylor's work, we could define what productivity is with respect to the manual worker; we still cannot answer what productivity is with respect to the industrial engineer, or to any other knowledge worker. The measurements which give us productivity for the manual worker, such as the number of pieces turned out per hour or per dollar of wage, are irrelevant if applied to the knowledge worker. There are few things as useless and unproductive as the engineering department which with great dispatch, industry, and elegance turns out the drawings for an unsalable product. Productivity with respect to the knowledge worker is, in other words, primarily quality.

One thing is clear: making knowledge productive will bring about changes in job structure, careers, and organizations as drastic as those which resulted in the factory from the application of scientific management to manual work. The entrance job—that is, the job that first introduces the man or woman with high formal education to the adult world of work and experience—will have to be changed drastically to enable the knowledge worker to become productive. For it is abundantly clear that knowledge cannot be productive unless the knowledge worker finds out who he is himself, what kind of work he is fitted for, and how he works best. There can be no divorce of planning from doing in knowledge work. On the contrary, the knowledge worker must be able to plan himself. Present entrance jobs, by and large, do not make this possible. They are based on the assumption—valid to some extent for manual work but quite inappropriate to knowledge work—that an outside expert such as the industrial engineer or the work-study specialist can objectively determine the one best way for any kind of work to be done. For knowledge work, this is simply not true. There may be one best way, but it is heavily conditioned by the individual and not entirely determined by physical, or even by mental, characteristics of the job. It is temperamental as well.

## Multinational and Multicultural Management

There is need for business managements to be multinational. Economically the world, and especially the developed world, has become one market. And the underdeveloped, the poor, countries differ from the developed ones only in their inability to afford what they would like to have. In terms of its demands, its appetites, and its economic values, the whole world has become one global shopping center, however divided it may be politically.

The multinational enterprise which optimizes productive resources, market opportunities, and talents beyond and across national boundaries is thus a normal, indeed a necessary, response to economic reality.

But all these developments introduce complexity into management well beyond what earlier generations had to deal with. For management is also a culture and a system of values and beliefs. It is also the means through which a given society makes productive its own values and beliefs. Management may well be considered the bridge between a civilization that is rapidly becoming worldwide and a culture which expresses divergent traditions, values, beliefs, and heritages. Management must become the instrument through which cultural diversity can be made to serve the common purposes of mankind. At the same time, management increasingly is not being practiced within the confines of one national culture, law, or sovereignty but multinationally. Indeed, management is becoming an institution—so far, almost the only one—of a genuine world economy.

Management, we now know, has to make productive the values, aspirations, and traditions of individuals, community, and society for a common productive purpose. If management does not succeed in putting to work the specific cultural heritage of a country and of a people, social and economic development is unlikely to take place. This is, of course, the great lesson of Japan—and the fact that Japan managed, a century ago, to put to work her own traditions of community and human values for the new ends of a modern industrialized state explains why Japan succeeded while every other non-Western country has so far failed. Management will have to be considered both a science and a humanity, both a statement of findings that can be objectively tested and validated, and a system of belief and experience.

Within the individual country, especially the developed country, business is rapidly losing its exceptional status as we recognize that it is the prototype of the typical, universal, social form, the organized institution requiring management. Beyond the national boundary, however, business is rapidly acquiring the same exceptional status it no longer has within the individual developed country. Beyond the national boundary, business is rapidly becoming the exception, and the one institution which expresses the reality of a world economy and of a worldwide knowledge society.

We need to learn how to harmonize in one institution and in one management both the need for managerial unity across national boundaries, that is, in a common world economy, and the need for cultural diversity.

## Management and the Quality of Life

Because our society is rapidly becoming a society of organizations, all institutions, including business, will have to hold themselves accountable for the quality of life and will have to make fulfillment of basic social values, beliefs, and purposes a major objective of their continuing normal activities rather than a social responsibility that restrains or that lies outside of their normal main functions. Institutions will have to learn to make the quality of life compatible with their main tasks. In the business enterprise, this means that the attainment of the quality of life will have to be considered an opportunity to be converted by management into profitable business.

This will apply increasingly to fulfillment of the individual. It is the organization which is today our most visible social environment. The family is private rather than communal—not that this makes it any less important. The community is increasingly in the organization. It will be the job of management to make the individual's values and aspirations redound to organizational energy and performance. It will simply not be good enough to be satisfied—as industrial relations and even human relations traditionally have been—with satisfaction, that is, with the absence of discontent. Perhaps one way to dramatize this is to say that we may, within another ten years, become far less concerned with manager development as a means of adapting the individual to the demands of the organization and far more with management development to adapt the organization to the needs, aspirations, and potential of the individual.

We also know that management creates economic and social development. Economic and social development is the *result* of management.

Japan a hundred years ago was an underdeveloped country by every material measurement. But it very quickly produced management of great competence, indeed, of excellence. Within twenty-five years Meiji Japan had become a developed country, and, indeed, in some aspects, such as literacy, the most highly developed of all countries. We realize today that it is Meiji Japan—rather than the traditional models of the economist: eighteenth-century England or nineteenth-century Germany—which is the model of development for the underdeveloped world.

Wherever we have contributed only the economic factors of production, especially capital, we have not achieved development. In the few cases where we have been able to generate management energies we have generated rapid development. Development, in other words, is a matter of human energies rather than of economic wealth. And the generation and direction of human energies is the task of management. Management is the mover and development is a consequence.

More important even than the new tasks, however, may be management's new role. Management is fast becoming the central resource of the developed countries and the basic need of the developing ones. From being the specific concern of business, i.e., the economic institution of society, management and managers are becoming the distinctive organs of developed society. What management is and what managers do will, therefore—and properly—become increasingly a matter of public concern rather than a matter for the experts. Management will increasingly be concerned as much with the expression of basic beliefs and values as with the accomplishment of measurable results. It will increasingly stand for the quality of life of a society as much as for its standard of living.

There are many new tools of management the use of which we will have to learn, and many new techniques. There are a great many new and difficult tasks. But the most important change for management is that the aspirations and values and the very survival of society in the developed countries will come to depend on the performance, the competence, the earnestness, and the values of their managers. The task of the next generation is to make productive for individual, community, and society the new organized institutions of our new pluralism. And that is, above all, the task of management.

# PART ONE

## THE TASKS

---

*Management is an organ of an institution; and the institution, whether a business or a public service, is in turn an organ of society, existing to make specific contributions and to discharge specific social functions. Management, therefore, cannot be defined or understood—let alone practiced—except in terms of its performance dimensions and of the demands of performance on it. The tasks of management are the reason for its existence, the determinants of its work, and the grounds of its authority and legitimacy.*

# 4

# The Dimensions of Management

*Management Is an Organ—It Exists Only in Contemplation of Performance—The Three Primary Tasks: Economic Performance; Making Work Productive and the Worker Achieving; Managing Social Impacts and Social Responsibilities—The Time Dimensions—Administration and Entrepreneurship—Efficiency and Effectiveness—Optimization and Innovation—The Specific Work of Management: Managing Managers—Focus on Tasks*

---

Business enterprises—and public-service institutions as well—are organs of society. They do not exist for their own sake, but to fulfill a specific social purpose and to satisfy a specific need of society, community, or individual. They are not ends in themselves, but means. The right question to ask in respect to them is not, What are they? but, What are they supposed to be doing and what are their tasks?

Management, in turn, is the organ of the institution. It has no function in itself, indeed, no existence in itself. Management divorced from the institution it serves is not management.

What people mean by bureaucracy, and rightly condemn, is a management that has come to misconceive itself as an end and the institution as a means. This is the degenerative disease to which managements are prone, and especially those managements that do not stand under the discipline of the market test. To prevent this disease, to arrest it, and, if possible, to cure it, must be a first purpose of any effective manager—but also of an effective book on management.

The question, What is management? comes second. First we have to define management in and through its tasks.

There are three tasks, equally important but essentially different, which management has to perform to enable the institution in its charge to function and to make its contribution:

—the specific purpose and mission of the institution, whether business enterprise, hospital, or university;
—making work productive and the worker achieving;
—managing social impacts and social responsibilities.

## 1. Purpose and Mission

An institution exists for a specific purpose and mission, a specific social function. In the business enterprise this means economic performance.

With respect to this first task, the task of specific performance, business and nonbusiness institutions differ. In respect to every other task, they are similar. But only business has economic performance as its specific mission. It is the definition of a business that it exists for the sake of economic performance. In all other institutions, hospital, church, university, or armed services, economics is a restraint. In business enterprise economic performance is the rationale and purpose.

A whole section of this book (Chapters 11, 12, 13 and 14) is devoted to the performance of the nonbusiness, the public-service, institutions. But the emphasis of this book is on business enterprise and the task of economic performance. While by no means the only task to be discharged in society, it is a priority task, because all other social tasks—education, health care, defense, and the advancement of knowledge—depend on the surplus of economic resources, i.e., profits and other savings, which only successful economic performance can produce. The more of these other satisfactions we want, and the more highly we value them, the more we depend on economic performance of business enterprise.

Business management must always, in every decision and action, put economic performance first. It can justify its existence and its authority only by the economic results it produces. A business management has failed if it fails to produce economic results. It has failed if it does not supply goods and services desired by the consumer at a price the consumer is willing to pay. It has failed if it does not improve, or at least maintain, the wealth-producing capacity of the economic resources entrusted to it. And this, whatever the economic or political structure or ideology of a society, means responsibility for profitability. (On the functions of profit see Chapter 6, p. 71.)

The first definition of business management is that it is an economic organ, the specifically economic organ of an industrial society. Every act, every decision, every deliberation of management, has economic performance as its first dimension.

## 2. Productive Work and Worker Achievement

The second task of management is to make work productive and the worker achieving. Business enterprise (or any other institution) has only one true resource: man. It performs by making human resources productive. It accomplishes its performance through work. To make work productive is, therefore, an essential function. But at the same time, these institutions in today's society are increasingly the means through which individual human beings find their livelihood, find their access to social status, to community and to individual achievement and satisfaction. To make the worker achieving is, therefore, more and more important and is a measure of the performance of an institution. It is increasingly a task of management.

Organizing work according to its own logic is only the first step. The second and far more difficult one is making work suitable for human beings —and their logic is radically different from the logic of work. Making the worker achieving implies consideration of the human being as an organism having peculiar physiological and psychological properties, abilities, and limitations, and a distinct mode of action. It implies consideration of the human resource as human beings and not as things, and as having—unlike any other resource—personality, citizenship, control over whether they work, how much and how well, and thus requiring responsibility, motivation, participation, satisfaction, incentives and rewards, leadership, status, and function.

Management, and management alone, can satisfy these requirements. For workers, whether machine tenders or executive vice-presidents, must be satisfied through their achievement in work and job—that is, within the enterprise; and management is the activating organ of the enterprise.

## 3. Social Impacts and Social Responsibilities

The third task of management is managing the social impacts and the social responsibilities of the enterprise. None of our institutions exists by itself and is an end in itself. Every one is an organ of society and exists for the sake of society. Business is no exception. Free enterprise cannot be justified as being good for business. It can be justified only as being good for society.

The first new institution to emerge after antiquity, the first institution of the West, was the Benedictine monastery of the sixth century. It was not founded to serve community and society, however. On the contrary, it was founded to serve exclusively its own members and to help them toward their own salvation. Therefore, Saint Benedict removed his monastery from human society and into the wilderness. He was not particularly afraid that his monks would yield to the temptations of the world. He saw a greater danger: that they would be concerned with the world, take responsibility for it, try to do good, and be forced to take leadership.

Unlike the Benedictine monastery, every one of our institutions today exists to contribute outside of itself, to supply and satisfy nonmembers. Business exists to supply goods and services to customers, rather than to supply jobs to workers and managers, or even dividends to stockholders. The hospital does not exist for the sake of doctors and nurses, but for the sake of patients whose one and only desire is to leave the hospital cured and never come back. The school does not exist for the sake of teachers, but for the students. For a management to forget this is mismanagement.

No institution can, therefore, exist outside of community and society as the Benedictine monastery, unsuccessfully, tried. Psychologically, geographically, culturally, and socially, institutions must be part of the community.

To discharge its job, to produce economic goods and services, the business enterprise has to have impacts on people, on communities, and on society. It has to have power and authority over people, e.g., employees, whose own ends and purposes are not defined by and within the enterprise. It has to have impact on the community as a neighbor, as the source of jobs and tax revenue, but also of waste products and pollutants. And, increasingly, in our pluralist society of organizations, it has to add to its fundamental concern for the quantities of life, i.e., economic goods and services, concern for the quality of life, that is, for the physical, human, and social environment of modern man and modern community.

This dimension of management is inherent in the work of managers of *all* institutions. University, hospital, and government agency equally have impacts, equally have responsibilities—and by and large have been far less aware of them, far less concerned with their human, social, and community responsibilities than business has. Yet, more and more, we look to business management for leadership with regard to the quality of life. Managing social impacts is, therefore, becoming a third major task and a third major dimension of management.

These three tasks always have to be done at the same time and within the same managerial action. It cannot even be said that one task predominates or requires greater skill or competence. True, business performance comes first—it is the aim of the enterprise and the reason for its existence. But if work and worker are mismanaged there will be no business performance, no matter how good the chief executive may be in managing the business. Economic performance achieved by mismanaging work and workers is illusory and actually destructive of capital even in the fairly short run. Such performance will raise costs to the point where the enterprise ceases to be competitive; it will, by creating class hatred and class warfare, make it impossible in the end for the enterprise to operate at all. And, mismanaging social impacts eventually will destroy society's support for the enterprise and with it the enterprise as well.

Each of these three tasks has a primacy of its own. Managing a business has primacy because the enterprise is an economic institution; but making work productive and workers achieving has importance precisely because society is not an economic institution and looks to management for the realization of basic beliefs and values. Managing the enterprise's social impacts has importance because no organ can survive the body which it serves; and the enterprise is an organ of society and community.

In these areas also, there are neither actions nor results except of the entire business (or university, or hospital, or government agency). There are no "functional" results and no "functional" decisions. There is only business investment and business risk, business profit and business loss, business action or business inaction, business decision and business information. It is not a plant that pollutes; it is Consolidated Edison of New York, the Union Carbide Corporation, the paper industry, or the city's sewers.

Yet, work and effort are always specific. There is tension, therefore, between two realities: that of performance and that of work. To resolve this tension, or at least to make it productive, is the constant managerial task.

## The Time Dimension

One complexity is ever-present in every management problem, every decision, every action—not, properly speaking, a fourth task of management, and yet an additional dimension: time.

Management always has to consider both the present and the future; both the short run and the long run. A management problem is not solved if immediate profits are purchased by endangering the long-range health, perhaps even the survival, of the company. A management decision is irresponsible if it risks disaster this year for the sake of a grandiose future. The all too common case of the great man in management who produces startling economic results as long as he runs the company but leaves behind nothing but a sinking hulk is an example of irresponsible managerial action and of failure to balance present and future. The immediate economic results are actually fictitious and are achieved by paying out capital. In every case where present and future are not both satisfied, where their requirements are not harmonized, or at least balanced, capital, that is, wealth-producing resource, is endangered, damaged, or destroyed.

Today we are particularly conscious of the time dimension in respect to the long-range impact of short-run economic decisions on the environment and on natural resources. But the same problem of harmonizing today and tomorrow exists in all areas, and especially with respect to people.

The time dimension is inherent in management because management is concerned with decisions for action. And action always aims at results in the future. Anybody whose responsibility it is to act—rather than to think or to know—commits himself to the future.

There are two reasons why the time dimension is of particular importance in management's job, and of particular difficulty. In the first place, it is the essence of economic and technological progress that the time span for the fruition and proving out of a decision is steadily lengthening. Edison, in the 1880s, needed two years or so between the start of laboratory work on an idea and the start of pilot-plant operations. Today it may well take Edison's successors fifteen years. A half century ago a new plant was expected to pay for itself in two or three years; today, with capital investment per worker twenty times that of 1900, the payoff period often runs to ten or twelve years. A human organization, such as a sales force or a management group, may take even longer to build and to pay for itself.

The second peculiar characteristic of the time dimension is that management—almost alone—has to live always in both present and future.

A military leader, too, knows both times. But traditionally he rarely had to live in both at the same time. During peace he knew no "present"; the present was only a preparation for the future war. During war he knew only the most short-lived "future"; he was concerned with winning the war at hand. Everything else he left to the politicians. That this is no longer true in an era of cold wars, near wars, and police actions may be the single most important reason for the crisis of military leadership and morale that afflicts armed services today. Neither preparation for the future nor winning the war at hand will do any longer; and as a result, the military man has lost his bearings.

But management always must do both. It must keep the enterprise performing in the present—or else there will be no enterprise capable of performing in the future. And it has to make the enterprise capable of performance, growth, and change in the future. Otherwise it has destroyed capital —that is, the capacity of resources to produce wealth tomorrow.

The only thing we know about the future is that it is going to be different. There may be great laws of history, great currents of continuity operating over whole epochs. But within time spans of conscious decision and action —time spans of years rather than centuries—in which the managers of any institution operate, the uncertainty of the future is what matters. The long-run continuity is not relevant; and anyhow, it can be discerned only in retrospect and only in contemplation of history, of how it came out.

For the manager the future is discontinuity. And yet the future, however different, can be reached only from the present. The greater the leap into the unknown, the stronger the foundation for the takeoff has to be. The time dimension endows the managerial decision with its special characteristics. It is the act in which the manager integrates present and future.

## Administration and Entrepreneurship

There is another dimension to managerial performance. The manager always has to *administer*. He has to manage and improve what already exists and is already known. But he also has to be an *entrepreneur*. He has to redirect resources from areas of low or diminishing results to areas of high or increasing results. He has to slough off yesterday and to render obsolete what already exists and is already known. He has to create tomorrow.

In the ongoing business markets, technologies, products, and services exist. Facilities and equipment are in place. Capital has been invested and has to be serviced. People are employed and are in specific jobs, and so on. The *administrative* job of the manager is to *optimize* the yield from these resources.

This, we are usually told, especially by economists, means *efficiency*, that is, doing better what is already being done. It means focus on costs. But the optimizing approach should focus on *effectiveness*. It focuses on opportunities to produce revenue, to create markets, and to change the economic characteristics of existing products and markets. It asks not, How do we do this or that better? It asks, Which of the products really produce extraordinary economic results or are capable of producing them? Which of the markets and/or end uses are capable of producing extraordinary results? It then asks, To what results should, therefore, the resources and efforts of the business be allocated so as to produce extraordinary results rather than the "ordinary" ones which is all efficiency can possibly produce?

This does not deprecate efficiency. Even the healthiest business, the business with the greatest effectiveness, can well die of poor efficiency. But even the most efficient business cannot survive, let alone succeed, if it is efficient in doing the wrong things, that is, if it lacks effectiveness. No amount of efficiency would have enabled the manufacturer of buggy whips to survive.

Effectiveness is the foundation of success—efficiency is a minimum condition for survival *after* success has been achieved. Efficiency is concerned with doing things right. Effectiveness is doing the right things.

Efficiency concerns itself with the input of effort into *all* areas of activity. Effectiveness, however, starts out with the realization that in business, as in any other social organism, 10 or 15 percent of the phenomena—such as products, orders, customers, markets, or people—produce 80 to 90 percent of the results. The other 85 to 90 percent of the phenomena, no matter how efficiently taken care of, produce nothing but costs (which are always proportionate to transactions, that is, to busy-ness).

The first administrative job of the manager is, therefore, to make effective the very small core of worthwhile activities which is capable of being effective. At the same time, he neutralizes (if he does not abandon) the very large penumbra of transactions: products or staff activities, research work or sales efforts, which, no matter how well done, will not yield extraordinarily high results (whether they represent the realized opportunities of the past, mere busy-ness, or unfulfilled hopes and expectations of the past, that is, the mistakes of yesterday).

The second administrative task is to bring the business all the time a little closer to the full realization of its potential. Even the most successful business works at a low coefficient of performance as measured against its potential—the economic results that could be obtained were efforts and resources marshaled to produce the maximum yield they are inherently capable of.

This task is not innovation; it actually takes the business as it is today and asks, What is its *theoretical optimum?* What inhibits attainment thereof? Where (in other words) are the limiting and restraining factors that hold back the business and deprive it of the full return on its resources and efforts?

One basic approach—offered here by way of illustration only—is to ask the question What *relatively minor changes* in product, technology, process, market, and so on, would significantly improve or alter the economic characteristics and results of this business? (This is similar to the vulnerability analysis of the modern systems engineers.)

In making steel these vulnerabilities—the factors that hold the economic results of the steel industry way below the theoretical potential of industry and process—might, for instance, be the need, in present steel technology, to create high heats three times, only to quench them three times. For the most expensive thing to produce are temperatures, whether heat or cold. In the electrical apparatus business one vulnerability might well be the habit of public-utility customers to have each generating turbine designed as if it were a unique product rather than assembled as one of a large number and according to standard performance specifications. Another vulnerability might be the habit of the public-utility customers to order turbines when money-market rates are low, which then creates expensive fluctuations in demand and production schedules. If these two habits could be changed, large generating turbines might well come down 40 to 50 percent in cost. In life insurance, to give one more example, a central vulnerability might be the high cost of the individual sale. A way to overcome this vulnerability and to realize the potential of the business somewhat more fully might be either statistical selling—elimination of the expensive personal selling efforts—or enrichment of the sales channel, for instance, by selling financial planning (including all other investment instruments, such as investment trust certificates), rather than only life insurance.

These examples are cited to show that a relatively minor change does not necessarily have to be easy to make. In fact, we may not know how to do it. But it is still minor, for the business would remain essentially as it is now, yet would have different economic results. And while the illustrations show clearly that these changes may require innovation, they are not, in themselves, innovations. They are primarily modifications of the existing business.

At the same time, inherent in the managerial task is entrepreneurship: making the business of tomorrow. Inherent in the task is innovation.

Making the business of tomorrow starts out with the conviction that the business of tomorrow will be and must be different. But it also starts out —of necessity—with the business of today. Making the business of tomorrow cannot be a flash of genius. It requires systematic analysis and hard, rigorous work *today*—and that means by people in today's business and operating within it.

The specific job of entrepreneurship in business enterprise is to make today's business capable of making the future, of making itself into a different business. It is the specific job of entrepreneurship in the going business to enable today's already existing—and especially today's already successful —business to remain existing and to remain successful in the future.

Success cannot, one might say, be continued forever. Businesses are, after all, creations of man which have no true permanence. Even the oldest businesses are creations of recent centuries. But a business enterprise must continue beyond the lifetime of the individual or of the generation to be capable of producing its contributions to economy and to society. The perpetuation of a business is a central entrepreneurial task—and ability to do so may well be the most trenchant and definitive test of a management.

## The Work of the Manager

Each of these tasks and dimensions has its own skills, its own tools, its own requirements. But the total management task requires their integration. And this too requires specific work and its specific tool. The tool is management; and the work is managing managers.

The tasks—economic performance; making work productive and the worker achieving; managing social impact and social responsibilities; and doing all this in a balance between the demands of today and the demands of tomorrow—are the things in which the public at large has a stake. The public has no concern with—and only mild interest in—what managers have to do to accomplish their tasks. It rightly is concerned with performance. But managers must be concerned with the means to the accomplishment of their tasks. They must be concerned with managerial jobs, with the work of the manager, with the skills he needs, and with his organization.

Any book of management that does not begin with the tasks to be performed misconceives management. Such a book sees management as something in itself, rather than as a means to an end. It fails to understand that management exists only in contemplation of performance. It treats management as an independent reality, whereas management is an organ which derives existence, identity, and justification from the function it serves. The focus must be on the tasks.

To start out discussing management with the work of the manager or with managerial organization—as most books on management do—is the approach of the technocrat, who soon degenerates into a bureaucrat. But it is even poor technocracy. For, as will be stressed again and again in this book, management work, management jobs, and management organization are not absolutes, but are determined and shaped by the tasks to be performed. "Structure follows strategy" is one of the fundamental insights we have acquired in the last twenty years. Without understanding the mission, the objectives, and the strategy of the enterprise, managers cannot be managed, organizations cannot be designed, managerial jobs cannot be made productive.

# Business
# Performance

We do not yet have a genuine theory of business and no integrated discipline of business management. But we know what a business is and what its key functions are. We understand the functions of profit and the requirements of productivity. Any business needs to think through the question What is our business and what should it be? From the definition of its mission and purpose a business must derive objectives in a number of key areas; it must balance these objectives against each other and against the competing demands of today and tomorrow. It needs to convert objectives into concrete strategies and to concentrate resources on them. Finally, it needs to think through its strategic planning, i.e., the decisions of today that will make the business of tomorrow.

# 5

## Managing a Business: The Sears Story

*What Is a Business and How Is It Managed?—How Sears, Roebuck Became a Business—Rosenwald's Innovations—Inventing the Mail-Order Plant—General Wood and Sears's Second Phase—Merchandise Planning and Manager Development—Sears's Third Phase: From Selling to Buying to Procurement—Class Markets and Mass Markets—The Challenges Ahead*

There are hundreds, if not thousands, of books on the management of the various functions of a business—production, marketing, finance, engineering, purchasing, personnel, public relations, and so forth. But what it is to manage a business, what management is supposed to do and how it should be doing it, are subjects which are rarely discussed.

This oversight is no accident. It reflects the absence of both a tenable theory of business enterprise and an adequate discipline of management. Therefore, rather than theorizing, we shall first look at the conduct and behavior of an actual business enterprise. There is no better illustration of what a business is and what managing it means than one of America's most successful enterprises: Sears, Roebuck and Company.

With sales in excess of $10 billion, Sears is the largest retailer in the world. It is by far the most profitable retail business anywhere and altogether one of the most profitable companies in the American economy, by any yardstick. Only Marks & Spencer in Great Britain can compare with Sears in terms of success (see Chapter 8). But, Marks & Spencer is not only much smaller—barely one-tenth of Sears; it also admittedly owes much of its success, especially in its earlier years, to imitating Sears.

Sears, Roebuck has also been a major growth company, even though its industry, the retail business, is, of course, old and well established, and totally lacking in the glamour of high technology or scientific innovation. No other business in America, not even General Motors, has shown such a consistent and sustained growth pattern since before the turn of this century.

Sears is also a political phenomenon that deserves study. In an age of consumerism, Sears would seem to be a prime target for consumer attacks. Yet there has been no or little criticism. Sears controls, through majority ownership, or through ownership of a substantial minority of the stock, the manufacturers of 60 percent of the merchandise it sells. It would seem a prime target for antitrusters and a glaring example of concentration of economic power. Yet there has never been mention of an antitrust investigation of Sears, let alone an antitrust suit.

The typical case studied in business schools is a case of failure, or at least of problems. But one can learn more from successes. It is far more important to know the right thing to do than to know what to avoid doing.

Sears became a business around the turn of the century with the realization that the American farmer represented a separate and distinct market. Separate because of his isolation, which made existing channels of distribution virtually inaccessible to him; distinct because of his specific needs, which, in important respects, were different from those of the city consumer. While the farmer's purchasing power was individually low, it represented a tremendous, almost untapped, buying potential in the aggregate.

To reach the farmer, a new distribution channel had to be created. Merchandise had to be produced to answer his needs and wants. It had to be brought to him at low price, and with a guarantee of regular supply. He had to be given a warranty of reliability and honesty on the part of the supplier, since his physical isolation made it impossible for him to inspect merchandise before delivery or to obtain redress if cheated.

To create Sears, Roebuck as a business required analysis of customer and market, and especially of what the farmer considered "value." Furthermore, it required major innovation in a number of distinct areas.

First, it demanded systematic "merchandising," that is, the finding and developing of sources of supply for the particular goods the farmer needed, in the quality and quantity he needed and at a price he could pay. Second, it required a mail-order catalog capable of serving as adequate substitute for the shopping trips to the big city the farmer could not make. For this reason, the catalog had to become a regular publication, rather than an announcement of spectacular bargains at irregular intervals. It had to break with the entire tradition of selling by mail and learn not to high-pressure the farmer into buying by exaggerated claims, but to give him a factual description of the goods offered. The aim had to be to create a permanent customer by convincing him of the reliability of the catalog and of the company behind it; the catalog had to become the "wish book" for the farmer.

Third, the age-old concept of *caveat emptor* had to be changed to *caveat vendor*—the meaning of the famous Sears policy of "your money back and no questions asked."* Fourth, a way had to be found to fill large quantities of customer orders cheaply and quickly. Without the mail-order plant, conduct of the business would have been physically impossible.

Finally, a human organization had to be built—and when Sears, Roebuck started to become a business, most of the necessary human skills were not available. There were, for instance, no buyers for this kind of operation, no accountants versed in the new requirements of inventory control, no artists to illustrate the catalogs, no clerks experienced in the handling of a huge volume of customer orders.

Richard Sears gave the company his name. He understood the needs of the customer; and he brilliantly improvised to satisfy these needs. But it was not he who made Sears, Roebuck into a business enterprise. In fact, Richard Sears's own operations could hardly be called a business. He was a shrewd speculator, buying up distress-merchandise and offering it, one batch at a time, through mail advertising. Every one of his deals was a complete transaction in itself which, when finished, liquidated itself and the business with it. Sears might have made a lot of money for himself. But his way of operating could never have founded a business, let alone perpetuate it. Indeed his success almost bankrupted him as it pushed his company far beyond the limit of his managerial capacity. His company was about to go under when he sold it to a total outsider, the Chicago clothing merchant Julius Rosenwald (1862–1932).

Between 1895, when he took control, and 1905, when the Chicago mail-order plant was opened, Rosenwald made a business enterprise out of Sears. He analyzed the market, began the systematic development of merchandise sources, and invented the regular, factual mail-order catalog and the policy of "satisfaction guaranteed or your money back." He built the productive human organization, and gave management people a maximum of authority and full responsibility for results. Later he gave every employee an ownership stake in the company, bought for him out of profits. Rosenwald is the father not only of Sears, Roebuck but of the distribution revolution which has changed the world economy in the twentieth century and which is so vital a factor in economic growth.

*Customers, I am given to understand, actually return less merchandise to Sears than to most of the large American department stores—it's the basic policy and what it expresses that makes the difference.

Only one basic contribution to the early history of Sears was not made by Rosenwald. The Chicago mail-order plant was designed by Otto Doering in 1903. Five years before Henry Ford's it was the first modern mass-production plant, complete with the breakdown of all work into simple repetitive operations, with an assembly line, conveyor belt, standardized, interchangeable parts—and, above all, with planned plant-wide scheduling.*

On these foundations, Sears had grown by the end of World War I into a national institution; its "wish book" was the only literature, besides the Bible, to be found in many farm homes.

The next phase of the Sears story begins in the mid-twenties. Just as the first chapter was dominated by one man, Julius Rosenwald, the second chapter was dominated by another, General Robert E. Wood (1879–1969). When Wood joined Sears, the original Sears market was changing rapidly. The farmer was no longer isolated; the automobile had enabled him to go to town and to shop there. He no longer formed a distinct market but was, largely thanks to Sears, rapidly modifying his way of life and his standard of living to conform to those of the urban middle class.

At the same time a vast urban market had come into being that was, in its way, as isolated and as badly supplied as the farmer had been twenty-five years earlier. The low-income groups in the cities had outgrown both their subsistence standards and their distinct lower-class habits. They were acquiring the money and the desire to buy the same goods as the middle and upper classes. The country was rapidly becoming one big homogeneous market—but the distribution system was still one of separate and distinct class markets.

Wood had made this analysis even before he joined Sears. Out of it came the decision to switch Sears's emphasis to retail stores—equipped to serve both the motorized farmer and the city population.

A whole series of innovations had to be undertaken to make this decision viable. To the finding of sources of supply and to the purchase of goods from them, merchandising had to add two new major functions: the design of products and the development of manufacturers capable of producing these products in large quantity. Class-market products—for instance, refrigerators in the twenties—had to be redesigned for a mass market with limited purchasing power. Suppliers had to be created—often with Sears money and Sears-trained management—to produce these goods. This also required another important innovation: a basic policy for the relations between Sears and its suppliers, especially those who depended on the company's pur-

*There is a persistent legend at Sears that Henry Ford before he built his own first plant visited and carefully studied the then brand-new Sears mail-order plant.

chases for the bulk of their business. Merchandise planning and research and the systematic building of hundreds of small suppliers capable of producing for a mass market had to be invented. They are as basic to mass distribution in Sears's second phase as mail order and catalogs were in its first, and they were as distinct a contribution to the American economy.

Retail selling also meant getting store managers. Mail-order selling did not prepare a man for the management of a retail store. The greatest bottleneck for the first ten or fifteen years of Sears's retail operation—almost until World War II—was the shortage of managers. The most systematic innovations had to be in the field of manager development; and the Sears policies of the thirties became the starting point for all the work in manager development now going on in industry.

Expansion into retail selling also meant radical innovations in organization structure. Mail-order selling is highly centralized; retail stores cannot be run from headquarters two thousand miles away. They must be managed locally. Only a few mail-order plants were needed to supply the country; Sears today has over a thousand stores, each with its own market in its own locality. A decentralized organization structure, methods of managing a decentralized company, measuring the performance of store managers, and maintaining corporate unity with maximum local autonomy—all these had to be devised to make retail selling possible. And new compensation policies had to be found to reward store managers for performance.

Finally, Sears had to innovate in store location, architecture, and physical arrangement. The traditional retail store was unsuited for the Sears market. It was not just a matter of putting the Sears store on the outskirts of the city and of providing it with an adequate parking lot. The whole concept of the retail store had to be changed. In fact, few people even at Sears realize how far this innovation has gone and how deeply it has influenced the shopping habits of the American people as well as the physical appearance of our towns. The suburban shopping center which appeared in the fifties as a radical innovation in retail selling is but a logical extension of the concepts and methods developed by Sears during the thirties.

The basic decisions underlying the expansion into retail stores were taken in the mid-twenties; the basic innovations had been made by the early thirties. This explains why Sears's volume of business and its profits grew right through the Depression and World War II.

In 1954 General Wood retired, though he retained influence in the company for another ten years. No other long-term dominant chief executive has emerged to replace him. Since Wood's retirement Sears has been run by a small team of men, a chairman, a president, and an executive vice-president. Without exception, these members of the top team retire after five to seven years in office rather than, like Rosenwald or Wood, holding power for twenty or thirty years.

The changes these successor managements brought about are almost as profound as those wrought by Rosenwald and Wood. They also redefined Sears's business. Under General Wood, Sears was moving from being a seller to being a buyer. Under his successors, Sears has redefined itself as a maker for the American family. Increasingly the emphasis is on Sears as the informed, responsible producer who designs for the American family the things it needs and wants. Today Sears's capital investment probably centers in the manufacturing plants it owns and controls—even though retail-store expansion has been pursued vigorously.

Sears again and again changed the definition of its market in line with the shifting patterns of the American population. Rosenwald made available mass goods to a new, emerging mass market. Wood made available to this mass market what earlier had been class-market goods, e.g., kitchen appliances. In the last twenty years Sears has shifted to a view of the American market in which there is no class market any more; it now operates on the assumption that the American middle class is, in its economic behavior, actually an upper class. Sears has thus greatly widened its product scope. Of course, Sears still carries appliances in its stores—and they probably are still the largest-selling product category. Sears has, however, also become the world's biggest diamond merchant, one of the country's biggest booksellers, and a large buyer and seller of original art objects, such as drawings, prints, and paintings.

General Wood had taken Sears into automobile insurance, which he rightly considered just as much an automobile accessory as brake lining or windshield wipers. His successors have added property insurance of all kinds. They have added a mutual fund to serve the new mass-capital market. They have gone into the travel business, and so on. In other words, Sears no longer defines its business as goods. It is defined as the needs, wants, and satisfactions of the American middle-class family.

Julius Rosenwald and, far more aggressively, General Wood had moved into controlling key manufacturers as the only way to make sure of the quality Sears needed, of the quantities its tremendous distribution system required, and of the lowest possible price for the customers. This is still the rationale given at Sears for ownership or control of manufacturing sources. But it would probably be more correct to describe the source relationship of Sears, Roebuck of today as procurement rather than as buying. The emphasis has steadily shifted toward a long-range strategy which anticipates what tomorrow's American family will be and what it will require, and then designs and develops the appropriate products or services. Sears today may be the first truly marketing-focused manufacturing business in the U.S., practicing what most manufacturing businesses so far only preach, that is, the total marketing approach. To this marketing strategy, focused on creating the sources of supply rather than on selling products to the

public, Sears owes both its tremendous growth in sales and its profitability.
Yet Sears today faces new challenges which will require innovation and strategic thinking fully as much as the developments of the past.
From the beginning Sears has been keenly aware of basic population trends in the United States. Wood's favorite management tool was a "little black book" full of population statistics and population projections. Julius Rosenwald, too, had built his business on population analysis and population trends. The Sears policy, all along, has been to find the majority market and to convert it into a true mass market.

There may be a market shift ahead in America, and Sears may not be strategically positioned for it. By the mid-1970s the young educated families, whose breadwinners make their living as knowledge workers, will dominate the American market. Even if Sears can transfer to them the special relationship it has had with their parents, the blue-collar workers of the big industrial cities, Sears does not make, buy, or sell in the areas in which their needs may be greatest and their spending likely to go up the fastest. Sears is still primarily thing-focused, primarily a maker, buyer, and seller of manufactured goods. The young educated families have a healthy appetite for goods; but in their spending behavior and values, they are upper-upper rather than upper class, even if their incomes are only average. This means that the major growth areas in their budgets may not be goods but information and education, health care, travel and leisure, reliable financial advice and services, and guidance on job and career choices. These, too, are wants and needs of the American family; these, too, are areas in which the American family needs an informed and responsible buyer. But these, by and large, are not areas in which Sears has established itself as the responsible maker and buyer.

Sears, further, has always looked upon its market as homogeneous. Sears has not been bothered by the fact that minority segments of the market were not its customers. Neither the very poor nor the very rich shop at Sears. But it has taken for granted that the bulk of the population buys the same merchandise, considers the same things of value, and altogether shares a common economic profile and a common economic psychology. This may no longer be true. There are signs that the American market is fragmenting into a number of big segments with significant differences in buying behavior and economic values between them. For such a development, Sears would seem to be quite unprepared.

Sears began in the forties to expand beyond the American frontier, into Canada, then into Latin America. In the sixties it went into Spain. It has acquired minority interests in retail stores in other European countries. There are persistent rumors that it plans to expand into Japan. But so far, Sears is still an American rather than a multinational business. It will have to face up to a difficult and risky decision. If it stays American, it faces the serious possibility of a steady slowdown in its growth and profitability as nongoods become increasingly important in the family budget of the American middle class. If it decides to become truly multinational, Sears would have to choose in what countries and markets the Sears mass-marketing approach can make the greatest contribution. It would then have to think through what policies—from store design to merchandising to the structure of the relationship to foreign countries, their governments, their manufacturers, their investors—this would require. And Sears would undoubtedly have to learn to apply the same basic approaches and principles quite differently in different markets and different cultures.

If Sears wants to maintain its leadership position and its capacity to grow, it faces major new challenges and may have to redefine what its business is, where its markets are, and where innovations are needed.

The right answers are always obvious in retrospect. The basic lesson of the Sears story is that the right answers are likely to be anything but obvious *before* they have proven themselves. "Everybody knew" around 1900 that to promise "satisfaction guaranteed or your money back" could bring only financial disaster to a retailer. "Everybody knew" around 1925 that the American market was sharply segmented into distinct income groups, each buying different things in different places. "Everybody knew"—as late as 1950—that the American consumer wanted to shop downtown, and so on.

Even more important as a lesson from the Sears story is the knowledge that the right answers are not the result of brilliance or of "intuition." Richard Sears had both—and failed. The right answers are the result of asking the right questions. And this in turn requires hard, systematic work to understand what a business is and what "our" business is.

# 6

## What Is a Business?

*Business Created and Managed by People, Not by Forces—The Fallacy of Profit Maximization—Profit: An Objective Condition of Economic Activity, Not Its Rationale—The Purpose of a Business: To Create a Customer—The Two Entrepreneurial Functions: Marketing and Innovation—The Marketing Revolution in America, Europe, and Japan—Marketing Not a Specialized Activity—IBM as an Example—Consumerism, the "Shame of Marketing"—From Selling to Marketing—The Enterprise as the Organ of Economic Growth and Development—Innovation as an Economic Function—As a Dimension of the Total Business—The Productive Utilization of All Wealth-Producing Resources—What Is Productive Labor?—Knowledge, Time, Product-Mix, Process Mix, and Organization Structure as Factors in Productivity—Making Knowledge Productive—The Functions of Profit— Profit as a Social Responsibility—How Much Profit Is Required?—Business Management a Rational Activity*

---

The Sears story shows that a business enterprise is created and managed by people and not by forces. Economic forces set limits to what management can do. They create opportunities for management's action. But they do not by themselves determine what a business is or what it does. Nothing could be sillier than the oft-repeated assertion that "management only adapts the business to the forces of the market." Management not only has to find these forces, it has to create them. It took a Julius Rosenwald seventy-five years ago to make Sears into a business enterprise, and a General Wood twenty-five years later to change its basic nature and thus insure its growth and success during the Depression and World War II. Now another management generation will have to make new decisions that will determine whether Sears is going to continue to prosper or to decline, to survive or eventually to perish. And that is true of every business.

Another conclusion is that a business cannot be defined or explained in terms of profit. Asked what a business is, the typical businessman is likely to answer, "An organization to make a profit." The typical economist is likely to give the same answer. This answer is not only false, it is irrelevant.

The prevailing economic theory of business enterprise and behavior, the maximization of profit—which is simply a complicated way of phrasing the old saw of buying cheap and selling dear—may adequately explain how Richard Sears operated. But it cannot explain how Sears, Roebuck or any other business enterprise operates, nor how it should operate. The concept of profit maximization is, in fact, meaningless.

Contemporary economists realize this; but they try to salvage the theorem. Joel Dean, one of the most brilliant and fruitful of contemporary business economists, still maintains the theorem as such. But this is how he defines it:

> Economic theory makes a fundamental assumption that maximizing profits is the basic objective of every firm. But in recent years, profit maximization has been extensively qualified by theorists to refer to the long run; to refer to management's rather than to owners' income; to include non-financial income such as increased leisure for high-strung executives and more congenial relations between executive levels within the firm; and to make allowance for special considerations such as restraining competition, maintaining management control, warding off wage demands, and forestalling anti-trust suits. The concept has become so general and hazy that it seems to encompass most of men's aims in life.
>
> This trend reflects a growing realization by theorists that many firms, and particularly the big ones, do not operate on the principle of profit maximizing in terms of marginal costs and revenues. . . .*

A concept that has "become so general and hazy that it seems to encompass most of men's aims in life" is not a concept. It is another way of saying, "I don't know and I don't understand." A theorem that can be maintained only when qualified out of existence has surely ceased to have meaning or usefulness.

The danger in the concept of profit maximization is that it makes profitability appear a myth. Anyone observing the discrepancy between the theory of profit maximization and the reality, as portrayed by Joel Dean, would be justified in concluding that profitability does not matter—the conclusion actually reached by John Kenneth Galbraith in *The New Industrial State.*†

Profit and profitability are, however, crucial—for society even more than

---

*Joel Dean, *Managerial Economics* (Prentice-Hall, 1951), p. 28.
†Houghton Mifflin, 1967.

for the individual business. Yet profitability is not the purpose of but a limiting factor on business enterprise and business activity. Profit is not the explanation, cause, or rationale of business behavior and business decisions, but the test of their validity. If archangels instead of businessmen sat in directors' chairs, they would still have to be concerned with profitability, despite their total lack of personal interest in making profits. This applies with equal force to those far from angelic individuals, the commissars who run Soviet Russia's business enterprises, and who have to run their businesses on a higher profit margin than the wicked capitalists of the West.

The first test of any business is not the maximization of profit but the achievement of sufficient profit to cover the risks of economic activity and thus to avoid loss.

The root of the confusion is the mistaken belief that the motive of a person—the so-called profit motive of the businessman—is an explanation of his behavior or his guide to right action. Whether there is such a thing as a profit motive at all is highly doubtful. It was invented by the classical economists to explain the economic reality which their theory of static equilibrium could not explain. There has never been any evidence for the existence of the profit motive. We have long since found the true explanation of the phenomena of economic change and growth which the profit motive was first put forth to explain.

It is irrelevant for an understanding of business behavior, profit, and profitability whether there is a profit motive or not. That Jim Smith is in business to make a profit concerns only him and the Recording Angel. It does not tell us what Jim Smith does and how he performs. We do not learn anything about the work of a prospector hunting for uranium in the Nevada desert by being told that he is trying to make his fortune. We do not learn anything about the work of a heart specialist by being told that he is trying to make a livelihood, or even that he is trying to benefit humanity. The profit motive and its offspring maximization of profits are just as irrelevant to the function of a business, the purpose of a business, and the job of managing a business.

In fact, the concept is worse than irrelevant: it does harm. It is a major cause for the misunderstanding of the nature of profit in our society and for the deep-seated hostility to profit which are among the most dangerous diseases of an industrial society. It is largely responsible for the worst mistakes of public policy—in this country as well as in Western Europe—which are squarely based on the failure to understand the nature, function, and purpose of business enterprise. And it is in large part responsible for the prevailing belief that there is an inherent contradiction between profit and a company's ability to make a social contribution. Actually, a company can make a social contribution only if it is highly profitable. To put it crudely, a bankrupt company is not likely to be a good company to work for, or likely to be a good neighbor and a desirable member of the community—no matter what some sociologists of today seem to believe to the contrary.

## The Purpose of a Business

To know what a business is we have to start with its *purpose*. Its purpose must lie outside of the business itself. In fact, it must lie in society since business enterprise is an organ of society. There is only one valid definition of business purpose: *to create a customer*.

Markets are not created by God, nature, or economic forces but by businessmen. The want a business satisfies may have been felt by the customer before he was offered the means of satisfying it. Like food in a famine, it may have dominated the customer's life and filled all his waking moments, but it remained a potential want until the action of businessmen converted it into effective demand. Only then is there a customer and a market. The want may have been unfelt by the potential customer; no one knew that he wanted a Xerox machine or a computer until these became available. There may have been no want at all until business action created it—by innovation, by credit, by advertising, or by salesmanship. In every case, it is business action that creates the customer.

It is the customer who determines what a business is. It is the customer alone whose willingness to pay for a good or for a service converts economic resources into wealth, things into goods. What the business thinks it produces is not of first importance—especially not to the future of the business and to its success. The typical engineering definition of quality is something that is hard to do, is complicated, and costs a lot of money! But that isn't quality; it's incompetence. What the customer thinks he is buying, what he considers value, is decisive—it determines what a business is, what it produces, and whether it will prosper. And what the customer buys and considers value is never a product. It is always utility, that is, what a product or service does for him. And what is value for the customer is, as we shall see (in Chapter 7), anything but obvious.

The customer is the foundation of a business and keeps it in existence. He alone gives employment. To supply the wants and needs of a consumer, society entrusts wealth-producing resources to the business enterprise.

## The Two Entrepreneurial Functions

Because its purpose is to create a customer, the business enterprise has two—and only these two—basic functions: marketing and innovation. Marketing and innovation produce results; all the rest are "costs."

Marketing is the distinguishing, unique function of the business. A business is set apart from all other human organizations by the fact that it *markets* a product or a service. Neither church, nor army, nor school, nor state does that. Any organization that fulfills itself through marketing a product or a service is a business. Any organization in which marketing is either absent or incidental is not a business and should never be managed as if it were one.

The first man in the West to see marketing clearly as the unique and central function of the business enterprise, and the creation of a customer as the specific job of management, was Cyrus H. McCormick (1809–1884). The history books mention only that he invented a mechanical harvester. But he also invented the basic tools of modern marketing: market research and market analysis, the concept of market standing, pricing policies, the service salesman, parts and service supply to the customer, and installment credit. He had done all this by 1850, but not till fifty years later was he first widely imitated even in his own country.

In the Far East marketing arose even earlier—also without finding imitators for a very long time. Marketing was invented in Japan around 1650 by the first member of the Mitsui family to settle in Tokyo as a merchant and to open what might be called the first department store. He anticipated by a full 250 years basic Sears, Roebuck policies: to be the buyer for his customers; to design the right products for them, and to develop sources for their production; the principle of your money back and no questions asked; and the idea of offering a large assortment of products to his customers rather than focusing on a craft, a product category, or a process. He also saw that the social changes in his country at that time had created a new class of potential customers, an urbanized new gentry and a new bourgeoisie. On these foundations he and his successors not only built what is to this day Japan's largest retail business, the Mitsukoshi chain of department stores. They also built one of the largest of Japan's manufacturing, trading, and financial combines, the Mitsui Zaibatsu.

The economic revolution of the American economy since 1900 has in large part been a marketing revolution. Creative, aggressive, pioneering marketing is still far too rare in American business—few businesses are even abreast of the Sears of 1925, let alone of the Sears of 1970. Yet fifty years ago the typical attitude of the American businessman toward marketing was "the sales department will sell whatever the plant produces." Today it is increasingly, "It is our job to produce what the market needs." However deficient in execution, the attitude has by itself changed our economy as much as any of the technical innovations of this century.

In Europe selling was not really accepted as a core function of business until well after World War II. Export sales were highly valued—a holdover from eighteenth-century mercantilism which considered domestic consumption to be antisocial but selling abroad highly patriotic and meritorious (a good bit of this belief still lingers on in Japan and underlies Japanese government attitudes and policies).

But selling was undignified. Before 1914 an export sales manager could get an officer's commission in the Prussian Army; he was a "gentleman." But a domestic sales manager was unacceptable and despised. As late as 1950 there were big Italian companies whose export sales managers sat on the board of directors as members of top management while no one, literally, was responsible for domestic sales—even though the domestic market accounted for 70 percent of the company's business.

This traditional European social prejudice against market, customer, and selling was, by the way, an important reason for the popularity of cartels in Europe. No one needs to worry about markets and sales—at least not in the short run—if an industry divides up the business through a tidy, tight cartel.

The shift from this attitude to one which considered marketing as a central business function—though perhaps not yet as *the* central function of business—is one of the main reasons for Europe's explosive recovery since 1950.

The marketing approach was first introduced into Europe in the twenties by an English retail chain, Marks & Spencer. Despite Marks & Spencer's success—in less than fifteen years, from 1920 to 1935, the firm became Europe's largest, fastest-growing, and most profitable retailer—few followed it until well after World War II. Since then the marketing revolution has swept Europe—leading practitioners are such companies as Philips in Holland, Unilever, and Fiat.

In Japan, similarly, few imitated Mitsui. The marketing revolution in Japan perhaps did not start until Sony, a brash newcomer, began to market in the 1950s, first in Japan, then worldwide. Until then most Japanese businesses were product-oriented rather than market-oriented, but they learned amazingly fast. The economic success of Japan in the world markets since the fifties, and with it the Japanese economic miracle, rests squarely on an acceptance of marketing as the first function of business and its crucial task.

Marketing is so basic that it cannot be considered a separate function (i.e., a separate skill or work) within the business, on a par with others such as manufacturing or personnel. Marketing requires separate work, and a distinct group of activities. But it is, first, a central dimension of the entire business. It is the whole business seen from the point of view of its final result, that is, from the customer's point of view. Concern and responsibility for marketing must, therefore, permeate all areas of the enterprise.

Among American manufacturing companies the outstanding practitioner of the marketing approach may well be IBM; and IBM is also the best example of the power of marketing. (See the discussion of IBM's near-miss in Chapter 60.) IBM does not owe its meteoric rise to technological innovation or product leadership. It was a Johnny-come-lately when it entered the computer field, without technological expertise or scientific knowledge. But while the technological leaders in the early computer days, Univac, GE, and RCA, were product-focused and technology-focused, the punch-card salesmen who ran IBM asked: "Who is the customer? What is value for him? How does he buy? And, what does he need?" As a result, IBM took over the market.

## From Selling to Marketing

Despite the emphasis on marketing and the marketing approach, marketing is still rhetoric rather than reality in far too many businesses. "Consumerism" proves this. For what consumerism demands of business is that it actually market. It demands that business start out with the needs, the realities, the values of the customer. It demands that business define its goal as the satisfaction of customer needs. It demands that business base its reward on its contribution to the customer. That after twenty years of marketing rhetoric consumerism could become a powerful popular movement proves that not much marketing has been practiced. Consumerism is the "shame of marketing."

But consumerism is also the opportunity of marketing. It will force businesses to become market-focused in their actions as well as in their pronouncements.

Above all, consumerism should dispel the confusion which largely explains why there has been so little real marketing. When managers speak of marketing, they usually mean the organized performance of all *selling* functions. This is still selling. It still starts out with "our products." It still looks for "our market." True marketing starts out the way Sears starts out —with the customer, his demographics, his realities, his needs, his values. It does not ask, "What do we want to sell?" It asks, "What does the customer want to buy?" It does not say, "This is what our product or service does." It says, "These are the satisfactions the customer looks for, values, and needs."

Indeed, selling and marketing are antithetical rather than synonymous or even complementary.

There will always, one can assume, be need for some selling. But the aim of marketing is to make selling superfluous. The aim of marketing is to know and understand the customer so well that the product or service fits him and sells itself.

Ideally, marketing should result in a customer who is ready to buy. All that should be needed then is to make the product or service available, i.e., logistics rather than salesmanship, and statistical distribution rather than promotion. We may be a long way from this ideal. But consumerism is a clear indication that the right motto for business management should increasingly be, "from selling to marketing."

## The Enterprise as the Organ of Economic Growth and Development

Marketing alone does not make a business enterprise. In a static economy there are no business enterprises. There are not even businessmen. The middleman of a static society is a broker who receives his compensation in the form of a fee, or a speculator who creates no value.

A business enterprise can exist only in an expanding economy, or at least in one which considers change both natural and acceptable. And business is the specific organ of growth, expansion, and change.

The second function of a business is, therefore, *innovation*—the provision of different economic satisfactions. It is not enough for the business to provide just any economic goods and services; it must provide better and more economic ones. It is not necessary for a business to grow bigger; but it is necessary that it constantly grow better.

Innovation may result in a lower price—the datum with which the economist has been most concerned, for the simple reason that it is the only one that can be handled by quantitative tools. But the result may also be a new and better product, a new convenience, or the definition of a new want.

The most productive innovation is a *different* product or service creating a new potential of satisfaction, rather than an improvement. Typically this new and different product costs more—yet its overall effect is to make the economy more productive.

The antibiotic drug costs far more than the cold compress which is all yesterday's physician had to fight pneumonia. The computer costs far more than an adding machine or a punch-card sorter, the typewriter far more than a quill pen, the Xerox duplicator far more than a copy press or even a mimeograph copier. And, if and when we get a cancer cure, it will cost more than even a first-class funeral.

The price of the product is thus only one measurement of the value of an innovation, or of economic process altogether. We may relate price to unit output, i.e., price of a drug to the saving it produces in days of hospital stay and in added years of working life. But even that is hardly adequate. We really need a value measurement. What economic value does innovation give the customer? The customer is the only judge; he (or she) alone knows his (or her) economic reality.

Innovation may be finding new uses for old products. A salesman who succeeds in selling refrigerators to Eskimos to prevent food from freezing would be as much of an innovator as if he had developed brand-new processes or invented a new product. To sell Eskimos a refrigerator to keep food cold is finding a new market; to sell a refrigerator to keep food from getting too cold is actually creating a new product. Technologically there is, of course, only the same old product; but economically there is innovation.

Above all, innovation is not *invention*. It is a term of economics rather than of technology. Nontechnological innovations—social or economic innovations—are at least as important as technological ones. (On this see Chapter 61, "The Innovative Organization.")

However important the steam engine was as an invention, two nontechnological innovations have had as much to do with the rise of modern economy: the mobilization of purchasing power through bank credit, and the application of probability mathematics to the physical risks of economic activity, that is, insurance. The innovation of limited liability and the subsequent development of the publicly owned limited-liability company were of equal importance. And installment credit (or as the British call it more accurately, hire purchase) has equal impact. It makes it possible to pay for the means to increase production out of the future fruits of the investment. It thus enabled the American farmer in the nineteenth century to buy the implements that made him productive and to pay for them after he had obtained the larger crop at lower cost. And this also makes installment credit a powerful dynamo of economic development in today's poor, underdeveloped countries.

In the organization of the business enterprise innovation can no more be considered a separate function than marketing. It is not confined to engineering or research but extends across all parts of the business, all functions, all activities. It cannot be confined to manufacturing business. Innovation in distribution has been as important as innovation in manufacturing; and so has been innovation in an insurance company or in a bank.

The leadership in innovation with respect to product and service has traditionally been focused in one functional activity which is responsible for nothing else. This has been particularly true for businesses with heavy engineering or chemical technology. In an insurance company, too, a special department charged with leadership responsibility for the development of new kinds of coverage may be in order; and there might well be other such departments charged with innovation in the organization of sales, the administration of policies, and the settling of claims. Yet another group might work on innovation in investing the company's funds. All these are the insurance company's business.

But—as discussed in more detail in Chapter 61—the best way to organize for systematic, purposeful innovation is as a business activity rather than as functional work. At the same time, every managerial unit of a business should have responsibility for innovation and definite innovation goals. It should be responsible for contributing to innovation in the company's product or service; in addition, it should strive consciously to advance the art in the particular area in which it is engaged: selling or accounting, quality control or personnel management.

Innovation can be defined as the task of endowing human and material resources with new and greater wealth-producing capacity. Innovation is particularly important for developing countries. These countries have the resources. They are poor because they lack the capacity to make these resources wealth-producing. They can import technology. But they have to produce their own social innovations to make imported technology work.

To have realized this was the great strength of the founders of modern Japan a century ago. They deliberately kept their country dependent on the West's technology— a dependence that remained until very recently. But they channeled their energies and those of their people into social innovations that would enable their country to become a strong modern society and economy and yet retain its distinct Japanese character and culture.

Innovation is thus crucial to economic development. Indeed, economic development is, above all, an entrepreneurial task.*

Managers must convert society's needs into opportunities for profitable business. That, too, is a definition of innovation. It needs to be stressed today, when we are so conscious of the needs of society, schools, health-care systems, cities, and environment. These needs are not too different in kind from those which the nineteenth-century entrepreneur converted into growth industries—the urban newspaper and the streetcar; the steel-frame skyscraper and the school textbook; the telephone and pharmaceuticals. The new needs similarly demand the innovating business.

## The Productive Utilization of Wealth-Producing Resources

The enterprise must utilize wealth-producing resources to discharge its purpose of creating a customer. It is, therefore, charged with productive utilization of these resources. This is the administrative function of business. In its economic aspect it is called productivity.

Everybody these last few years has been talking productivity. That greater productivity—better utilization of resources—is both the key to a

*On this see the essay by a South American educator and businessman Reinaldo Scarpetta, "Management Education as a Key to Social Development," in *Preparing Tomorrow's Business Leaders Today,* edited by Peter F. Drucker (Prentice-Hall, 1969).

high standard of living and the result of business activity is not news. And everyone knows by now that the scourge of modern economies, uncontrolled inflation, is a deficiency disease caused by inadequate productivity. But we actually know very little about productivity; we are, indeed, not yet able to measure it.

Productivity means that balance between *all* factors of production that will give the greatest output for the smallest effort. This is quite different from productivity per worker or per hour of work; it is at best distantly and vaguely reflected in such traditional standards.

These standards are still based on the eighteenth-century tenet that manual labor is, in the last resort, the only productive resource; manual work the only real effort. The standards still express the mechanistic fallacy —of which Marx, to the permanent disability of Marxian economics, was the last important dupe—that all human achievement could eventually be measured in units of muscle effort. Increased productivity in a modern economy is never achieved by muscle effort. It is always the result of doing away with muscle effort, of substituting something else for the laborer. One of these substitutes is, of course, capital equipment, that is, mechanical energy.*

At least as important, though unnoticed until very recently, is the increase in productivity achieved by replacing manual labor, whether skilled or unskilled, by knowledge, resulting in a shift from laborers to knowledge workers, such as managers, technicians, and professionals.

A little reflection will show that the rate of capital formation, to which economists give so much attention, is a secondary factor. Someone must plan and design the equipment—a conceptual, theoretical, and analytical task—before it can be installed and used. The basic factor in an economy's development must be the rate of "brain formation," the rate at which a country produces people with imagination and vision, education, and theoretical and analytical skills.

However, the planning, design, and installation of capital equipment is only a part of the increase in productivity through the substitution of brain for brawn. At least as important is the contribution made through the direct change of the character of work from one requiring the manual labor, skilled and unskilled, of many people, to one requiring theoretical analysis and conceptual planning without any investment in capital equipment.

This contribution first became evident in the 1950s in the analysis of the productivity gap between American and European industry. Studies—e.g.,

---

*Here we now have available the careful studies of Simon Kuznets (of the University of Pennsylvania and of Harvard) to show the direct relationship in United States industry between investment in capital equipment and increases in productivity.

by the Stanford Research Institute and by the Organization for Economic Cooperation (OEC)—showed clearly that the productivity differential between Western Europe and the United States was not a matter of capital investment. In many European industries productivity was as much as two-thirds below that of the corresponding American industry, even though capital investment and equipment were equal. The only explanation was the lower proportion of managers and technicians and the poor organization structure of European industry with its reliance on manual skill.

In 1900 the typical manufacturing company in the United States spent probably no more than $5 or $8 on managerial, technical, and professional personnel for every $100 in direct-labor wages. Today there are many manufacturing industries where the two items of expenditure are equal—even though direct-labor wage rates have risen proportionately much faster. Outside of manufacturing, transportation, and mining, e.g., in distribution, finance, insurance, and the service industries (that is, in two-thirds of the American economy), the increase in productivity has been caused primarily by the replacement of labor by planning, brawn by brain, sweat by knowledge.

The greatest opportunities for increasing productivity are surely to be found in knowledge work itself, and especially in management. The vocabulary of business—especially of accounting—in relation to productivity has become so obsolete as to be misleading. What the accountant calls productive labor is manual workers tending machines, who are actually the least productive labor. What he calls nonproductive labor—all the people who contribute to production without tending a machine—is a hodgepodge. It includes pre-industrial, low-productivity brawn labor like sweepers; some traditional high-skill, high-productivity labor like toolmakers; new industrial high-skill labor like maintenance electricians; and industrial high-knowledge personnel like foremen, industrial engineers, and quality control men. Finally, what the accountant lumps together as overhead—the very term reeks of moral disapproval—contains what should be the most productive resource, the managers, researchers, planners, designers, innovators. It may also, however, contain purely parasitical, if not destructive, elements in the form of high-priced personnel needed only because of malorganization, poor spirit, or confused objectives, that is, because of mismanagement.

We need a concept of productivity that considers together all the efforts that go into output and expresses them in relation to their result, rather than one that assumes that labor is the only productive effort. But even such a concept—though a big step forward—would still be inadequate if its definition of effort were confined to the activities measurable as visible and direct costs, that is, according to the accountant's definition of, and symbol for, effort. There are factors of substantial if not decisive impact on productivity that never become visible cost figures.

First there is knowledge—man's most productive resource if properly applied, but also the most expensive one, and totally unproductive, if misapplied. The knowledge worker is, of necessity, a high-cost worker. Having spent many years in school, he also represents a very high social investment.

Then there is time—man's most perishable resource. Whether men and machines are utilized steadily or only half the time will make a difference in their productivity. There is nothing less productive than idle time of expensive capital equipment or wasted time of highly paid and able people. Equally unproductive may be cramming more productive effort into time than it will comfortably hold—for instance, the attempt to run three shifts in a congested plant or on old or delicate equipment.

The most productive—or least productive—time is that of the manager himself. Yet it is usually the least known, least analyzed, least managed of all factors of productivity.*

Productivity is also a function of the product mix, the balance between various combinations of the same resources. As every manager should know, differentials in the market values of various combinations are rarely proportional to the efforts that go into making up the combinations. Often there is barely any discernible relationship between the two. A company turning out a constant volume of goods with unchanging materials and skills requirements and a constant amount of direct and indirect labor may reap fortunes or go bankrupt, depending on the product mix. Obviously this represents a considerable difference in the productivity of the same resources—but not one that shows in costs or can be detected by cost analysis.

There is also an important factor which I would call "process mix." Is it more productive for a company to buy a part or to make it, to assemble its product or to contract out the assembly process, to market under its own brand name through its own distributive organization or to sell to independent wholesalers using their own brands? What is the company good at? What is the most productive utilization of its specific knowledge, ability, experience, reputation?

Not every management can do everything, nor should any business necessarily go into those activities which seem objectively to be most profitable. Every management has specific abilities and limitations. Whenever it attempts to go beyond these, it is likely to fail, no matter how inherently profitable the venture.

People who are good at running a highly stable business will not be able to adjust to a mercurial or a rapidly growing business. People who have

*On this see my book, *The Effective Executive* (1966), especially Chapter 1.

grown up in a rapidly expanding company will, as everyday experience shows, be in danger of destroying the business should it enter upon a period of consolidation. People good at running a business with a foundation in long-range research are not likely to do well in high-pressure selling of novelties or fashion goods. Utilization of the specific abilities of the company and its management and observance of these specific limitations is an important productivity factor. Conglomerates may optimize the productivity of capital, but they will have rather low productivity—and inherently poor results—in other equally important areas.

Finally, productivity is vitally affected by organization structure and by the balance among the various activities within the business. If a lack of clear organization causes managers to waste their time trying to find out what they are supposed to do rather than doing it, the company's scarcest resource is being wasted. If top management is interested only in engineering (perhaps because that's where all the top men came from) while the company needs major attention to marketing, it lacks productivity; the resulting damage will be greater than could be caused by a drop in output per man-hour.

These factors are additional to the factors accountants and economists usually consider, namely, productivity of labor, capital, and materials. They are, however, fully as important.

We therefore not only need to define productivity so as to embrace all these factors affecting it, but also need to set objectives that take all these factors into account. We must develop yardsticks to measure the impact on productivity of the substitution of capital for labor, and of knowledge for both—and means to distinguish between creative and parasitical overhead, and to assess the impact on productivity of time utilization, product mix, process mix, organization structure, and the balance of activities.

Not only does individual management need adequate concepts and measurements for productivity, the economy needs them. Their lack is the biggest gap in our economic statistics and seriously weakens all economic policy. It frustrates our attempts to fight depression and inflation alike.

## The Functions of Profit

Profit is not a cause but a result—the result of the performance of the business in marketing, innovation, and productivity. It is a needed result, serving essential economic functions. Profit is, first, the test of performance—the only effective test, as the communists in Russia soon found out when they tried to abolish it in the early twenties (though they coyly called it the capital fund and avoided the bad word profit until well into the 1950s). Indeed, profit is a beautiful example of what engineers mean when they talk of the feedback such as underlies all systems of automated production: the self-regulation of a process by its own results.

Profit has a second function which is equally important. It is the premium for the risk of uncertainty. Economic activity, because it is activity, focuses on the future; and the one thing that is certain about the future is its uncertainty, its risks. The word "risk" itself is said to mean "earning one's daily bread" in the original Arabic. It is through risk-taking that any businessman earns his daily bread. Because business activity is economic it always attempts to bring about change. It always saws off the limb on which it sits; it makes existing risks riskier or creates new ones.

As the Sears story showed, the future of economic activity is a long one; it took fifteen or twenty years for basic Sears decisions to become fully effective, and for major investments to pay off. "Lengthening the economic detour" has been known for a hundred years to be a prerequisite to economic advance. Yet while we know nothing about the future, we know that its risks increase in geometric progression the farther ahead we commit ourselves to it.

Profit and profit alone can supply the capital for tomorrow's jobs, both for *more* jobs and for *better* jobs.

Again it is a definition of economic progress that the investment needed to create new and additional jobs increases.

Today's accountant or engineer does not make a better living than his grandfather on the farm because he works harder. He works far less hard. Nor does he deserve a better living because he is a better man. He is the same kind of human being as grandfather was, and grandfather's grandfather before him. He can be paid so much more and yet work so much less hard because the capital investment in him and his job is infinitely greater than that which financed his grandfather's job. In 1900, when grandfather started, capital investment per American farmer was at most $5,000. To create the accountant's or engineer's job, society first invests at least $50,000 in capital and expenses for school and education. And then the employer invests another $25,000 to $50,000 per job. All of this investment that makes possible both additional and better jobs has to come out of the surplus of economic activity, that is, out of profits.

And finally profit pays for the economic satisfactions and services of a society, from health care to defense, and from education to the opera. They all have to be paid for out of the surplus of economic production, that is, out of the difference between the value produced by economic activity and its cost.

Businessmen these days tend to be apologetic about profit. This is a measure of the dismal job they have done explaining profit—above all to themselves. For there *is* no justification and no rationale for profit as long as one talks the nonsense of profit motive and profit maximization.

No apology is needed for profit as a necessity of economy and society. On the contrary, what a businessman should feel guilty about, what he should feel the need to apologize for, is failure to produce a profit appropriate to the economic and social functions which profit, and only profit, can develop.

Walter Rathenau (1867–1922), the German executive, statesman, and social philosopher, who thought more deeply than any other Westerner of his time about the social responsibility of business, proposed replacing the word profit with responsibility. Profit, to be sure, is not the whole of business responsibility; but it is the first responsibility. The business that fails to produce an adequate profit imperils both the integrity of the resources entrusted in its care and the economy's capacity to grow. It is untrue to its trust.

At the very least, business enterprise needs a *minimum* of profit: the profit required to cover its own future risks, the profit required to enable it to stay in business and to maintain intact the wealth-producing capacity of its resources. This required minimum profit affects business behavior and business decision—both by setting limits and by testing their validity. Management, in order to manage, needs a profit objective at least equal to the required minimum profit, and yardsticks to measure its profit performance against this requirement. (For further discussion see Chapters 8 and 9.)

What, then, is managing a business? It follows from the analysis of business activity as the creation of a customer through marketing and innovation that managing a business must always be entrepreneurial in character. There is need for administrative performance. But it follows the entrepreneurial objectives. Structure follows strategy.

It also follows that managing a business must be a creative rather than an adaptive task. The more a management creates economic conditions or changes them rather than passively adapts to them, the more it manages the business.

But an analysis of the nature of a business also shows that management, while ultimately tested by performance alone, is a rational activity. Concretely this means that a business must set objectives that express what is desirable of attainment rather than (as the maximization-of-profit theorem implies) aim at accommodation to the possible. Once objectives have been set by fixing one's sights on the desirable, the question can be raised what concessions to the possible have to be made. This requires management to decide what business the enterprise is engaged in, and what business it should be engaged in.

# 7

# Business Purpose and Business Mission

*The Theory of the Business—The Fallacy of the* Unternehmer—*Why a Theory of the Business Is Needed—Especially in Today's Knowledge Organization—"What Is Our Business?" Neither Simple nor Obvious—Theodore Vail and the Telephone Company—Top Management's First Responsibility—Failure to Define Business Purpose and Business Mission a Major Cause of Business Frustration and Business Failure—Why "What Is Our Business?" Is So Rarely Asked—The Need for Dissent—The Customer Defines the Business—Who Is Our Customer?—Customer and Consumer —The Carpet-Industry Story—Where Is the Customer?—What Does He Buy?—What Is Value to the Customer?—There Are No Irrational Customers—The Economist's Concept of Value—What Is Price?—When to Ask, "What Is Our Business?"—Most Important: When a Business Is Successful —"What Will Our Business Be?"—The Importance of Population Trends —Changes in Economy, Fashion, and Competition—Anticipating Innovation—The Consumer's Unsatisfied Wants—"What Should Our Business Be?"—The Need for Planned Abandonment*

---

Every one of the great business builders we know of—from the Medici and the founders of the Bank of England down to IBM's Thomas Watson in our day—had a definite idea, had, indeed, a clear theory of the business which informed his actions and decisions. A clear, simple, and penetrating theory of the business rather than intuition characterizes the truly successful entrepreneur, the man who not just amasses a large fortune but builds an organization that can endure and grow long after he is gone.

The individual entrepreneur does not need to analyze his concepts and explain his theory of the business to others, let alone spell out the details. He is in one person thinker, analyst, and executor. Business enterprise, however, requires that the theory of the business be thought through and spelled out. It demands a clear definition of business purpose and business mission. It demands asking, "What is our business and what should it be?"

Unlike the single entrepreneur, business enterprise requires continuity beyond the life span of a man or of any one generation. It cannot, like the merchant-adventurer of old, engage in one venture at a time which is fully liquidated before the next venture is begun. It has to commit resources to an ever-longer future; it is in itself the result of commitments of the past and has, therefore, commitments to the past and to the future—an established organization, established policies, past decisions, investments, facilities, products, markets, and above all, people. Unless grounded in a theory of the business, these commitments cannot be made rationally. They are bound to splinter resources. And unless grounded in a theory of the business, these commitments cannot be reviewed and revised rationally. There is no way to determine that a change is needed unless results can be held against expectations derived from such a theory of the business.

Today's theory of the business always becomes obsolete—and usually pretty fast. Unless the basic concepts on which a business has been built are, therefore, visible, clearly understood, and explicitly expressed, the business enterprise is at the mercy of events. Not understanding what it is, what it represents, and what its basic concepts, values, policies, and beliefs are, it cannot rationally change itself. How rapidly even the most brilliant entrepreneurial idea can obsolesce the history of Henry Ford shows—with only fifteen years between an entrepreneurial idea that literally transformed economy and society and its obsolescence. (See Chapter 29, "Why Managers?")

Only a clear definition of the mission and purpose of the business makes possible clear and realistic business objectives. It is the foundation for priorities, strategies, plans, and work assignments. It is the starting point for the design of managerial jobs and, above all, for the design of managerial structures. Structure follows strategy. Strategy determines what the key activities are in a given business. And strategy requires knowing "what our business is and what it should be."

## The Fallacy of the *Unternehmer*

Insofar as the literature of management and economics has paid attention to the theory of the business, it has dealt with it as a need of the man at the top—or at most of a small top-management group.

The German tradition is most explicit on this point. The *Unternehmer,* that is, the top man and especially the owner-manager, alone knows what the business is all about and alone makes entrepreneurial decisions. Everybody else is essentially a technician who carries out prescribed tasks. No one but the *Unternehmer* needs to understand the mission and purpose of the business. Indeed, no one really should know and understand; *Unternehmertum*—entrepreneurship—is a mystique that better be kept hidden from the uninitiated, i.e., ordinary managers and professionals.

While only the Germans have formalized the traditional concept, it is subconsciously assumed by top-management people everywhere in the West (though not in Japan). This may have been adequate in the nineteenth-century business in which there were a few men at the top who alone made decisions, with all the rest manual workers or low-level clerks. It is a dangerous misconception of today's business enterprise.

In sharp contrast to the organizations of the past, today's business enterprise (but also today's hospital or government agency) brings together a great many men of high knowledge and skill, at practically every level of the organization. But high knowledge and skill also mean decision-impact on how the work is to be done and on what work is actually being tackled. They make, by necessity, risk-taking decisions, that is, business decisions, whatever the official form of organization. And the computer does not alter this fact. In fact, it makes the decisions of top management even more dependent on the decision input from lower levels—which is what then becomes the data of the computer.

When the computer first came in, in the early fifties, we heard a good deal about the imminent disappearance of the middle manager. Instead, the fifties and sixties brought in all developed countries a tremendous growth of middle managers. And, unlike traditional middle managers, the new middle people are largely decision-makers rather than executors of decisions made on high. (On this see Chapter 35, "From Middle Management to Knowledge Organization.")

As a result, decisions affecting the entire business and its capacity to perform are made at all levels of the organization, even fairly low ones. Risk-taking decisions—what to do and what not to do; what to continue work on and what to abandon; what products, markets, or technologies to pursue with energy and what markets, products and technologies to ignore —are in the reality of today's business enterprise (especially the large one) made every day by a host of people of subordinate rank, very often by people without traditional managerial title or position, e.g., research scientists, design engineers, product planners, and tax accountants.

Every one of these men bases his decisions on some, if only vague, theory of the business. Every one makes assumptions regarding reality, both inside and outside the business. Every one assumes that certain kinds of results are wanted and that other kinds are not particularly desirable. Every one knows, e.g., that "lowering the price of our product does not create new demand," or that "we do this" but "do not do that." Every one, in other words, has his answer to the question "What is our business and what should it be?" Unless, therefore, the business itself—and that means its top management—has thought through the question and formulated the answer—or answers—to it, the decision-makers in the business, all the way up and down, will decide and act on the basis of different, incompatible, and conflicting theories of the business. They will pull in different directions without even being aware of their divergences. But they will also decide and act on the basis of wrong and misdirecting theories of the business.

Common vision, common understanding, and unity of direction and effort of the entire organization require definition of "what our business is and what it should be."

### "What Is Our Business?"—Never Obvious

Nothing may seem simpler or more obvious than to know what a company's business is. A steel mill makes steel, a railroad runs trains to carry freight and passengers, an insurance company underwrites fire risks, a bank lends money. Actually, "What is our business?" is almost always a difficult question and the right answer is usually anything but obvious.

One of the earliest and most successful answers was worked out by Theodore N. Vail (1845–1920) for the American Telephone and Telegraph Company (also known as the Bell System) almost seventy years ago: "Our business is service." This sounds obvious once it has been said. But first there had to be the realization that a telephone system, being a natural monopoly, was susceptible to nationalization and that a privately owned telephone service in a developed and industrialized country was exceptional and needed community support for its survival. Second, there had to be the realization that community support could not be obtained by propaganda campaigns or by attacking critics as "un-American" or "socialistic." It could be obtained only by creating customer satisfaction. This realization meant radical innovations in business policy. It meant constant indoctrination in dedication to service for all employees, and public relations which stressed service. It meant emphasis on research and technological leadership, and it required financial policy which assumed that the company had to give service wherever there was a demand, and that it was management's job to find the necessary capital and to earn a return on it. The United States would hardly have gone through the New Deal period without a serious attempt at telephone nationalization but for the careful analysis of its own business that the Telephone Company made between 1905 and 1915.

Vail's definition served his company for two-thirds of a century, up into the late 1960s; it may have been the longest-lived answer to the question "What is our business?" That the American railroads never thought their way through to any definition of their business is surely a major reason for the perpetual crisis in which they have floundered since World War I, and for the almost complete lack of community support that is their greatest weakness.

In retrospect all of Vail's answers were obvious, if not trite. But not only did it take years to work them out, each was heresy when first propounded and bitterly resisted throughout the company. Vail was fired from his position as general manager in the late 1890s when he dared propose to his top management that the question "What is our business?" be asked. He was called back, a decade later, when the consequences of the lack of an answer had become painfully evident—that is, when the Bell System, operating without clear definition of its mission and purpose, had drifted into severe crisis and was threatened by government takeover.

The answer to the question "What is our business?" is the first responsibility of top management. Indeed, one sure way to tell whether a particular job is top management or not is to ask whether its holder is expected to be concerned with, and responsible for, answering this question. Only top management can make sure that this question receives the attention it deserves and that the answer makes sense and enables the business to plot its course and set its objectives.

That business purpose and business mission are so rarely given adequate thought is perhaps the most important single cause of business frustration and business failure. Conversely, in outstanding businesses such as the Telephone Company or Sears, success always rests to a large extent on raising the question "What is our business?" clearly and deliberately, and on answering it thoughtfully and thoroughly.

But there are reasons why managements shy back from asking the question; the first is that the question causes controversy, argument, and disagreement.

To raise the question always reveals cleavages and differences within the top-management group itself. People who have worked side by side for many years and who think that they know each other's thoughts suddenly realize with a shock that they are in fundamental disagreement.

## The Need for Dissent

Most managements shrink back from these disagreements as divisive and painful. But deciding "What is our business?" is a genuine decision; and a genuine decision *must* be based on divergent views to have a chance to be a right and an effective decision. (See Chapter 37, "The Effective Decision.") The answer to the question "What is our business?" is always a choice between alternatives, each of which rests on different assumptions regarding the reality of the business and its environment. It is always a high-risk decision. It always leads to changes in objectives, strategies, organization, and behavior.

This is far too important a decision to be made by acclamation. In the end there must, of course, be a decision. But it must be a decision based on conscious choice of alternatives rather than on suppression of different and dissenting opinions and points of view.

Indeed, to bring these dissents out into the open is in itself salutary. It is a big step toward management effectiveness. It enables the top-management group to work together precisely because each member is cognizant of fundamental differences within the group, and, therefore, far more likely to understand what motivates his colleagues and what explains their behavior. Conversely, hidden or half-understood disagreements on the definition of one's business underlie many of the personality problems, communication problems, and irritations that tend to divide a top-management group.

The main reason why it is important to bring out dissents within the top-management group on the question "What is our business?" is that there is *never one right answer*. The answer never emerges as a logical conclusion from postulates or from "facts." It requires judgment and considerable courage. The answer rarely follows what "everybody knows." It should never be made on plausibility alone, never be made fast, never be made painlessly.

## Method Rather Than Opinions

Another reason why managements fail to ask "What is our business?" is their reluctance to listen to opinions. And everyone has an opinion on "what our business is." Managements, however, quite rightly dislike debating societies and bull sessions.

There is need for a method for defining "what our business is." Opinions are, of course, needed—and anyhow are unavoidable. But they need to be focused on a specific, central issue to become productive.

With respect to the definition of business purpose and business mission, there is only one such focus, one starting point. It is the customer. The customer defines the business.

A business is not defined by the company's name, statutes, or articles of incorporation. It is defined by the want the customer satisfies when he buys a product or a service. To satisfy the customer is the mission and purpose of every business. The question "What is our business?" can, therefore, be answered only by looking at the business from the outside, from the point of view of customer and market. What the customer sees, thinks, believes, and wants, at any given time, must be accepted by management as an objective fact and must be taken as seriously as the reports of the salesman, the tests of the engineer, or the figures of the accountant. And management must make a conscious effort to get answers from the customer himself rather than attempt to read his mind.

Management always, and understandably, considers its product or its service to be important. If it did not, it could not do a good job. Yet to the customer, no product or service, and certainly no company, is of much importance. The executives of a company always tend to believe that the customer spends hours discussing their products. But how many housewives, for instance, ever talk to each other about the whiteness of their laundry? If there is something badly wrong with one brand of detergent they switch to another. The customer only wants to know what the product or service will do for him tomorrow. All he is interested in are his own values, his own wants, his own reality. For this reason alone, any serious attempt to state "what our business is" must start with the customer, his realities, his situation, his behavior, his expectations, and his values.

### Who Is the Customer?

"Who is the customer?" is the first and the crucial question in defining business purpose and business mission. It is not an easy, let alone an obvious question. How it is being answered determines, in large measure, how the business defines itself.

The consumer, that is, the ultimate user of a product or a service, is always a customer. But he is never *the* customer; there are usually at least two—sometimes more. Each customer defines a different business, has different expectations and values, buys something different. Yet, all customers have to be satisfied in the answer to the question "What is our business?"

The power of the question "Who is the customer?" and the impact of a thoughtful answer to it are shown by the experience of the carpet industry in the United States since World War II.

The carpet industry is an old one, with little glamour and little sophisticated technology. Yet it was a conspicuous marketing success in the American economy of the post-World War II period. For thirty years, until well into the early fifties, the industry had been in a steady, long-term, and apparently irreversible decline. Then, within a few years, the industry completely reversed the trend. Even "good" houses built before the fifties had, as a rule, no more than a cheap rug in the living room. Today, even low-cost homes—including most mobile homes—have wall-to-wall carpeting of fair quality in all rooms, kitchen and bathrooms included. And the home buyer is spending an increasing share of his housing dollar on carpeting.

Floor covering is one of the very few means to alter the appearance and comfort of a home, especially of a cheap and small one. This message had been broadcast by the rug and carpet manufacturers for decades, without the slightest effect on actual customer behavior. The rug and carpet industry achieved its success only when it stopped persuasion and hard selling, and instead thought through the questions "Who is our customer and who should he be?"

Traditionally the rug and carpet manufacturer had defined his customer as the homeowner, and especially as the family buying its first home. But at that stage, the young couple has no money left over for luxuries. They postpone buying rugs—and this means they are not likely to buy them at all. The industry realized, as a result of asking "Who is our customer, and who should he be?" that it must succeed in making the mass builder its customer. It therefore had to make it profitable for the mass builder to incorporate rugs and carpets into the new home at the time of building. This meant switching from selling individual rugs and carpets to selling wall-to-wall carpeting. In the traditional home the builder had to lay expensive and fully finished floors. Wall-to-wall carpeting can be put over cheap and unfinished flooring—resulting in a better house at lower cost to the builder.

The industry further realized that it must enable the new homeowner to pay for floor covering as part of the monthly payment on the mortgage, rather than expecting him to pay a substantial sum at a time when he is already short of cash. It therefore worked hard at getting the lending agencies, and especially the government agencies insuring home mortgages (such as the Federal Housing Administration), to accept floor covering as part of the capital investment in the house and thus as part of the mortgage value. Finally, the industry redesigned its product to enable the building contractor to act as the informed buyer for his customer, the homeowner. Today home buyers are offered a great variety of patterns and colors, but essentially only three qualities: "good," "better," and "best." The difference among them amounts to very little in the monthly mortgage payment, with the result that most homeowners order at least the "better" carpeting.

As this story shows, the right anwer to the question "Who is the customer?" is usually that there are several customers.

Most businesses have at least two. The rug and carpet industry has both the contractor and the homeowner for its customers. Both have to buy if there is to be a sale. The manufacturers of branded consumer goods always have two customers at the very least: the housewife and the grocer. It does not do much good to have the housewife eager to buy if the grocer does not stock the brand. Conversely, it does not do much good to have the grocer display merchandise advantageously and give it shelf space if the housewife does not buy.

Some businesses have two customers unconnected with each other. The business of an insurance company can be defined as selling insurance. But an insurance company is also an investor. In fact, it can well be defined as a channel that conducts the savings of the community into productive investments. An insurance company needs two definitions of its business, as it has to satisfy two separate customers. Similarly, a commercial bank needs both depositors and borrowers. It cannot be in business without either. Both, even if they are the same person or the same business, have different expectations and define the business of the bank completely differently. To satisfy only one of these customers without satisfying the other means that there is no performance.

One of the great strengths of Vail's definition of Bell Telephone's business was the acceptance in it of two separate customers: the telephone subscriber and the regulating agencies of the various state governments. Both had to be given service. Both had to be satisfied. Yet, they had widely different concepts of value, wanted and needed different things, and behaved quite differently.

There are also businesses in which economically there is only one customer while strategically—in terms of buying decision—there are two or more.

One of the reasons why IBM has been so successful in the computer business is that it realized early that entirely different people in a company have to buy a computer if there is to be a sale. The people who use the computer (which largely means accounting and financial people) have to buy it. But top management also has to buy. And so do the people who are to use the computer as their information tool, that is, operating managers. From the beginning, therefore, IBM has sold all these groups and has thought through what each looks for, needs to know, considers value, and how each can be reached.

Practically everyone who makes and sells equipment faces a similar situation. While the paper company pays the bill, the process engineer in the paper mill, the paper chemist in the laboratory, and the purchasing agent are all separate customers, each buying something different when they buy the same equipment or the same chemicals; each, above all, buying in different ways and reached through different channels.

It is also important to ask "Where is the customer?" One of the secrets of Sears's success in the 1920s was the discovery that its old customer was now in a different place: the farmer had become mobile and was beginning to buy in town. This made Sears realize early—almost two decades before most other American retailers—that store location is a major business decision and a major element in answering the question "What is our business?"

American leadership in international banking in the last twenty years is not primarily the result of superior resources. It is largely the result of asking, "Where is the customer?" As soon as the question was asked, it became clear that the old customers, the American corporations, were going multinational and had to be served from a multitude of locations all over the world rather than from New York or San Francisco headquarters. The resources for serving the new multinational customers did not come from the United States but from the international market itself, and, above all, from Europe and the Eurodollar market.

The next question is, "What does the customer buy?"

The Cadillac people say that they make an automobile, and their business is called the Cadillac Motor Division of General Motors. But does the man who spends $7,000 on a new Cadillac buy transportation, or does he buy primarily prestige? Does the Cadillac compete with Chevrolet, Ford, and Volkswagen? Nicholas Dreystadt, the German-born service mechanic who took over Cadillac in the Depression years of the thirties, answered: "Cadillac competes with diamonds and mink coats. The Cadillac customer does not buy 'transportation' but 'status.' " This answer saved Cadillac, which was about to go under. Within two years or so, it made it into a major growth business despite the Depression.

## What Is Value to the Customer?

The final question needed to come to grips with business purpose and business mission is: "What is value to the customer?" It may be the most important question. Yet it is the one least often asked.

One reason is that managers are quite sure that they know the answer. Value is what they, in their business, define as quality. But this is almost always the wrong definition.

For the teenage girl, for instance, value in a shoe is high fashion. It has to be "in." Price is a secondary consideration and durability is not value at all. For the same girl as a young mother, a few years later, high fashion becomes a restraint. She will not buy something that is quite unfashionable. But what she looks for is durability, price, comfort and fit, and so on. The same shoe that represents the best buy for the teenager is a very poor value for her slightly older sister.

Manufacturers tend to consider this as irrational behavior. But the first rule is that there are no irrational customers. Customers almost without exception behave rationally in terms of their own realities and their own situation. High fashion is rationality for the teenage girl; her other needs

—food and housing—are, after all, still taken care of by her parents, as a rule. High fashion is a restraint for the young housewife who has to budget, who is on her feet a great deal, who has "her man," and who no longer goes out every weekend.

The customer never buys a product. By definition the customer buys the satisfaction of a want. He buys value. Yet the manufacturer, by definition, cannot produce a value. He can only make and sell a product. What the manufacturer considers quality may, therefore, be irrelevant and nothing but waste and useless expense.

Another reason why the question "What is value to the customer?" is rarely asked is that the economists think they know the answer: value is price. This is misleading, if not actually the wrong answer.

Price is anything but a simple concept, to begin with. Then there are other value concepts which may determine what price really means. In many cases, finally, price is secondary and a limiting factor rather than the essence of value.

Here are some examples to illustrate what price might mean to different customers:

Electrical equipment such as fuse boxes or circuit breakers are paid for by the homeowner but selected and bought by the electrical contractor. What is price to the electrical contractor is not the manufacturer's price for the product. It is the price of the manufacturer plus the cost of installation —for that, of course, is price to his customer, the homeowner. Contractors are notoriously price-conscious. Yet, a high-priced make of fuse boxes and circuit breakers is the market leader in the U.S. To the contractor this line is actually low-priced because it is engineered to be installed fast and by relatively unskilled labor.

Xerox owes its success, to a large extent, to defining price as what the customer pays for a copy rather than what he pays for the machine. Xerox, accordingly, has priced its machines in terms of the copies used. In other words, the customer pays for the copy rather than for the machine—and, of course, what the customer wants are copies rather than a machine.

In the American automobile industry, where most new cars are sold in trade against a used car, price is actually a constantly shifting configuration of differentials between the manufacturer's price for a new car and prices for a second-hand and third-hand used car, a third-hand and fourth-hand used car, and so on. And the whole is further complicated on the one hand by constantly changing differentials between the amount a dealer will allow on a used car and the price he will ask for it, and on the other hand by the differences in running costs between various makes and sizes. Only advanced mathematics can calculate the real automobile price.

For products and services, price can be determined—as distinct from undifferentiated commodities such as copper of a certain purity—only by understanding what is value to the customer. As the Xerox example shows, it is up to the manufacturer or supplier to design the pricing structure which fits the customer's value concept.

But price is also only a part of value. There is a whole range of quality considerations which are not expressed in price: durability, freedom from breakdown, the maker's standing, service, etc. High price itself may actually be value—as in expensive perfumes, expensive furs, or exclusive gowns.

Here are two examples:

In the early days of the Common Market, two young European engineers opened a small office with a few hundred dollars, a telephone, and a shelf full of manufacturers' catalogs of electronic components. Within ten years they had built a large and highly profitable wholesale business. Their customers are the industrial users of electronic equipment such as relays and machine controls. The young engineers manufacture nothing. The components which they supply can be obtained, often at a lower price, directly from the manufacturer. But these young engineers relieve the customer of the tedious chore of finding the right component part. They need only be told the kind of equipment, the manufacturer, the model number, and the part that needs replacement—a condenser, for instance, or a microswitch. They then immediately identify the specific part needed. They also know what parts made by other manufacturers can be used for a job. They therefore can tell a customer what he needs, give him immediate service, often on the same day, and yet keep their inventory low. Expertise and speedy service is value to the customer for which he is perfectly willing to pay a substantial premium. "Our business is not electronic parts," said one of the young men, "it is information."

An American company making lubricating compounds for heavy earth-moving equipment such as is used by highway builders has long had a reputation for the quality of its products. Yet it could not gain more than a very small share of the market, as it competed against every major petroleum company. It then asked the question "What is value to the customer?" The answer was "to keep very expensive machinery operating without breakdowns." One hour down-time may cost a construction company more money than it could possibly spend on lubricating compounds in the course of an entire year. The company usually works against a deadline and risks penalty payments if it misses it. As a result of this seemingly obvious insight, the lubricating compound manufacturer no longer sells lubricating compounds. Instead he offers to pay the owner of heavy earth-moving equipment the full cost of any hour of down-time caused by lubricating failure. The only condition attached to this offer is that the construction company adopt and follow a maintenance program designed by the manufacturer's service representatives which, of course, prescribes the company's lubricating compounds. The company formerly had to price its products below those of the major petroleum companies; no customer now even asks, "What do you charge for your lubricating compounds?"

What about such concepts of value on the part of the customer as the service he receives? There is little doubt, for instance, that the American housewife today buys appliances largely on the basis of the service experience she or her friends and neighbors have had with other appliances sold under the same brand name. The speed with which she can obtain service if something goes wrong, the quality of the service, and its cost have become major determinants in the buyer's decision.

What a company's different customers consider value is so complicated that it can be answered only by the customers themselves. Management should not even try to guess at the answers—it should always go to the customers in a systematic quest for them.

The marketing approach outlined here will not, by itself, result in a definition of the purpose and mission of a business. For many businesses the approach will raise more questions than it answers. This is true of the business which has as its basic core of unity a common technology rather than a common market. (See Chapter 57, "Building Unity Out of Diversity.") Examples are chemical companies but also commercial banks. Similarly, process businesses—e.g., steel companies or aluminum refiners—need much more than one market definition to define their business. Of necessity, their products go into an infinity of markets, serve a multitude of customers, and have to satisfy a great variety of value concepts and value expectations.

Yet even such businesses should start their attempt to ask "What is our business?" by first asking, "Who are our customers? Where are they? What do they consider value?" A business—and for that matter, any institution—is determined by its contribution; everything else is effort rather than result. What the customer pays is revenue; everything else is cost. The approach from the outside, that is, from the market, is only one step. But it is the step that comes before all others. It alone can give understanding and thereby replace opinions as the foundation for the most fundamental decision that faces every management.

## When to Ask "What Is Our Business?"

Most managements, if they ask the question at all, ask "What is our business?" when the company is in trouble. Of course, then it *must* be asked. And then asking the question may, indeed, have spectacular results and may even reverse what appears irreversible decline—as shown by the example of Vail's work at Bell Telephone and of the reversal of the carpet industry's long-term downward trend.

The success of General Motors also resulted from asking "What is our business?" when the company was floundering. When Alfred P. Sloan, Jr., became president in 1920, GM was in deep trouble and barely viable. Sloan's definition of the purpose and mission of GM, and his development of both strategy and structure from this definition, gave GM leadership and outstanding profitability within three years or less.*

To wait until a business—or an industry—is in trouble is playing Russian roulette. It is irresponsible management. The question should be asked at the inception of a business—and particularly for a business that has ambitions to grow. Such a business better start with a clear entrepreneurial concept.

One successful example is the Wall Street firm which in the sixties rose to leadership in the American securities market. Donaldson, Lufkin, and Jenrette (DLJ) was founded by three young men right out of business school. They had little except an idea. Yet the firm rose within five or six years to seventh place among Wall Street houses. DLJ then became the first Wall Street firm to sell its shares to the public and started the long-overdue change of the New York Stock Exchange from a private club to a service institution. It was the first firm to do something about Wall Street's need to broaden its capital base, which thoughtful people had seen for thirty years. "Our business," the founders of DLJ said, "is to provide financial services, financial advice, and financial management to the new 'capitalists,' the institutional investors such as pension funds and mutual funds." In retrospect, this definition was obvious: right answers always are. By 1960 it had become quite clear that these new institutional investors were rapidly becoming the dominant force in the American capital market and the main channel through which individuals were directing their savings into the capital market. Yet at the time at which this answer was given, it went counter to everything the rest of Wall Street knew.

The man who decides to become his own boss may not have to ask, "What is my business?" If he, for instance, mixes up a new cleaning compound in his garage and starts peddling it from door to door, he needs to know only that his mixture does a superior job in removing stains. But when the product catches on; when he has to hire people to mix it and to sell it; when he has to decide whether to keep on selling directly or through retail stores—department stores, supermarkets, hardware stores, or all three; what additional products he needs for a full line—then he has to ask and

*On Sloan's work, see his book, *My Years with General Motors* (Doubleday, 1964), and my book, *Managing for Results* (1964).

to answer the question "What is my business?" Otherwise, even with the best of products, he will soon be back wearing out his own shoe leather peddling from door to door.

The most important time to ask seriously "What is our business?" is when a company has been successful. To understand this has been the great strength of Sears, Roebuck. It is also one of the secrets of the success of Marks & Spencer in Great Britain. (See the next chapter.) And not to have understood this is a major reason for the present crisis of American schools and American universities.

Success always obsoletes the very behavior that achieved it. It always creates new realities. It always creates, above all, its own and different problems. Only the fairy story ends "They lived happily ever after."

It is not easy for the management of a successful company to ask, "What is our business?" Everybody in the company then thinks that the answer is so obvious as not to deserve discussion. It is never popular to argue with success, never popular to rock the boat.

The ancient Greeks knew that the penalty for the hubris of success is severe. The management that does not ask "What is our business?" when the company is successful is, in effect, smug, lazy, and arrogant. It will not be long before success will turn into failure.

The two most successful American industries of the 1920s were anthracite coal mines and railroads. Both believed that God had given them an unshakable monopoly forever. Both believed that the definition of their business was so obvious as to eliminate all need for thought, let alone for action. Neither need have tumbled from its leadership position—the anthracite industry into total oblivion—had their managements not taken success for granted.

Above all: when a management attains the company's objectives, it should always ask seriously, "What is our business?" This requires self-discipline and responsibility. The alternative is decline.

## "What Will Our Business Be?"

Sooner or later even the most successful answer to the question "What is our business?" becomes obsolete.

Theodore Vail's answer was good for almost two-thirds of a century. But by the late 1960s it became apparent that it was no longer adequate; the telephone system was no longer, as in Vail's days, a natural monopoly. Alternative ways of telecommunication were rapidly becoming possible. By the late sixties it had also become apparent that the traditional definition of the telephone as an instrument to transmit voice messages had become inadequate, both because of the rapid growth in data transmission over telephone wires and because of the increasing possibility of transmitting visual images together with the voice. Vail's simple and elegant definition of the business of the Bell Telephone System was in need of reexamination.

The brilliant answer which Alfred P. Sloan, as the new president of General Motors, gave in the early 1920s to the question "What is GM's business?" also held good for an amazingly long time, right through World War II and the postwar recovery. But by 1960 or so, while Sloan, though retired, was himself still alive, the answer had become inadequate and inappropriate. That GM has not raised the question again and apparently has not seen the need to think it through again surely has a lot to do with the evident vulnerability of the company to consumer dissatisfaction, public pressures, and political attack, and with its inability to attain leadership position in the world automobile market.

Very few definitions of the purpose and mission of a business have anything like a life expectancy of thirty, let alone fifty, years. To be good for ten years is probably all one can normally expect.

In asking "What is our business?" management therefore also needs to add, "And what *will* it be? What changes in the environment are already discernible that are likely to have high impact on the characteristics, mission, and purpose of our business?" and "How do we *now* build these anticipations into our theory of the business, into its objectives, strategies, and work assignments?"

The method and approach needed to tackle this question—and the next question—"What *should* our business be?"—will be discussed in Chapter 10, "Strategic Planning." But what basic questions to ask belongs here.

Again the market, its potential and its trends, is the starting point. How large a market can we project for our business in five or ten years—assuming no basic changes in customers, in market structure, or in technology? And, what factors could validate or disprove these projections?

The most important of these trends is one to which few businesses pay much attention: changes in population structure and population dynamics. Traditionally businessmen, following the economists, have assumed that demographics are a constant. Historically this has been a sound assumption. Populations used to change very slowly except as a result of catastrophic events, such as major war or famine. This is no longer true, however. Populations nowadays can and do change drastically, in developed as well as in developing countries.

Every developed country (with the single exception of Great Britain perhaps) had at least a small baby boom in the decade following World War II. Young married women had many more babies than before, and had them in closer sequence. Ten years later this was followed by an equally spectacular "baby bust," in which the number of live births went down very sharply.

In the developing countries the birth rate did not increase, but the number of babies who survived infancy increased spectacularly, and is still increasing. In other words, in a short twenty-five years, the whole population structure changed drastically. In the United States, for instance, the largest single age group in 1950 were the thirty-eight- to forty-year-olds. Ten years later the largest age group were the seventeen-year-olds. But by 1980 the largest single age group in America will be the twenty-five-year-olds. Since 1945, also, there has been an educational explosion in every developed country. In the developing countries there has been rapid urbanization, as a result of which Latin America, for instance, has ceased to be rural in its population structure and has become predominantly urban.

The importance of demographics does not lie only in the impact population structure has on buying power and buying habits, and on the size and structure of the work force. Population shifts are the only events regarding the future for which true prediction is possible. People do not enter the labor force till they are at least in their teens—and in the developed countries, increasingly, not until they are twenty. They do not form households until then either, nor become primary customers in their own right. In other words, major trends in markets, buying power and buying behavior, customer needs, and employment can be predicted with near-certainty by analyzing what has already happened in population dynamics and population structure.

Any attempt to anticipate tomorrow—and this is, of course, what we are trying to do by asking "What will our business be?"—has to start with demographic analysis as the sturdiest and most reliable foundation.

The massive impact of even fairly minor demographic changes is illustrated by the sharp shift in the American magazine industry.

As late as 1950 the mass-circulation magazine was America's most successful and most profitable communications medium, and seemed impregnable. But the leaders of those days—*Collier's, The Saturday Evening Post, Look,* and *Life*—have disappeared. The survivors are fighting for their lives. The development is often blamed on television. But magazines as a whole have not suffered from television—just as they did not earlier suffer from radio. On the contrary, total magazine circulation as well as magazine advertising have gone up faster since television appeared than they did before, and they are still going up fast. What has happened is that population has changed—partly because of the change in age structure, but primarily because of the change in educational levels. The undifferentiated mass audience is gone. Its place has been taken by a large number of specialty mass markets, that is, groups of substantial but still limited size, of much higher education and purchasing power, and of sharply defined and specialized interests. These groups read magazines even more than the earlier generation—for the simple reason that they read more. They are a better market for magazine advertisers—for the simple reason that they buy more. Each of these better-educated and affluent audience segments is, in itself, a mass audience—but a specialized one.

This change in audience could easily have been anticipated in 1950—the demographic development had already happened. It was seen clearly by a number of publishers. On this understanding are based all the American magazine successes of the last twenty years, from *Business Week* to *Modern Bride,* from *Sports Illustrated* to *Playboy,* from *Scientific American* to *Psychology Today* or *TV Guide.* All these new magazines apply basic concepts which the mass-circulation magazines first developed, in editorial, in circulation, and in advertising. But they apply them in accordance with the new population structure, that is, to a demographic segment characterized by a common interest. All of them have circulations well above half a million, if not larger; but they deliberately do not appeal to a general audience. All of them represent a conscious and deliberate exploitation of demographic opportunities. They can obtain their audience at low—or at least at reasonable—circulation-acquisition costs. The old mass-audience magazines, however, have increasingly had to buy circulation, that is, to invest far more in subscription acquisition than they can possibly get back in subscription revenue. As a result the new specialty mass magazines soon also get the advertising.

Management needs to anticipate changes in market structure resulting from changes in the economy; from changes in fashion or taste; from moves by competition. And competition must always be defined according to the customer's concept of what product or service he buys and thus must include indirect as well as direct competition.

## The Unsatisfied Wants of the Customer

Finally, management has to ask which of the consumer's wants are not adequately satisfied by the products or services offered him today. The ability to ask this question and to answer it correctly usually makes the difference between a growth company and one that depends for its development on the rising tide of the economy or of the industry. But whoever contents himself to rise with the tide will also fall with it.

One example of a successful analysis of the customer's unsatisfied wants is Sears, Roebuck, of course. But the topic is so important as to warrant further illustration.

Sony asked the question "What are the customer's unsatisfied wants?" when it first decided to move into the American consumer market in the mid-fifties. Sony had been founded right after the end of World War II as a manufacturer of tape recorders and had achieved modest success with its products in its own domestic market. It had entered the U.S. as a small but reliable supplier of high-priced professional tape-recording equipment for broadcasting studios. Yet the product with which it first established itself in the American mass-consumer market was a product it had never made before—portable transistor radios. Young people, Sony's analysis of the market showed, were taking the existing heavy, clumsy, and expensive equipment—phonographs weighing many pounds, or battery-powered radios with audio tubes—on picnics, camping trips, and other excursions. Surely here was an unsatisfied want for a light, cheap, and yet dependable instrument. Sony did not develop the transistor—Bell Laboratories had done that, in America. The Bell Laboratories people, however, as well as all the electronic manufacturers in America, had decided that the customer was not yet ready for transistorized equipment. They looked at the wants of the customer that were satisfied by the existing equipment, wants for equipment that was meant to be kept in one place. Sony, by asking "What are the *un*satisfied wants?" identified a new growth market—and within an incredibly short period established itself worldwide as the leader and the pacesetter.

Of the world's leading businesses, Unilever has probably done the most work on "What *will* our business be?" The method Unilever has developed and the models it has built for each of its major product lines and each of its major national markets take into account a large number of factors, from national income to changes in retail distribution, and from eating habits to taxation. But the foundation and starting point are population figures and population trends. These one does not have to forecast; one can build on what has already happened.

### "What Should Our Business Be?"

"What *will* our business be?" aims at adaptation to anticipated changes. It aims at modifying, extending, developing the existing, ongoing business.

But there is need also to ask "What *should* our business be?" What opportunities are opening up or can be created to fulfill the purpose and mission of the business by making it into a *different* business?

IBM had long defined its business as data processing. Prior to 1950, this meant punch cards and equipment for sorting them. When the computer came, and with it a new technology in which IBM had not the slightest expertise, IBM, asking, "What *should* our business be?," realized that data processing henceforth would have to mean computers rather than punch cards.

Businesses that fail to ask this question are likely to miss their major opportunity. The American life insurance industry has long defined its business as providing basic investment and financial security to the American family. Right through World War II, the life insurance policy was indeed the best way to discharge this purpose and mission. Since World War II, however, the majority of the American people has attained incomes that enable it to accumulate savings beyond what is needed to buy adequate life insurance protection. At the same time, the whole population has become acutely conscious of inflation, that is, of the erosion of the value of the traditionally conservative and safe investments of fixed money value. The life insurance companies have the access to the market and the selling organization. In their own list of policyholders they have the largest inventory of financial customers in the country. Yet very few of them have asked the question "What *should* our business be?" As a result, life insurance has steadily been losing market standing. Before World War II life insurance was, next to the family's home, the leading investment of the middle class. It has now slipped to third or fourth place and is still going down. The new savings increasingly have not been going into life insurance but into mutual funds and pension funds.

What the life insurance companies lacked was not innovation. The needed financial instruments had all been developed much earlier. What they lacked was the willingness to ask "What *should* our business be?" and to take the question seriously.

Next to changes in society, economy, and market as factors demanding consideration in answering "What should our business be?" comes, of course, innovation, one's own and that of others.

Changes in the nature of the business arising out of innovation are too well known to require much documentation. All major enterprises in the engineering and chemical fields have largely grown by converting innovation into new business. The Eurodollar which these last ten years has financed a good deal of world trade was (as said earlier) not invented by the large American commercial banks. But they immediately saw its significance, and their success in making the Eurodollar into an international currency explains, in large measure, their rapid growth in multinational banking.

Finally—a special but important reason for changing what "our business is" to "what it should be"—then is the business of "the wrong size." (See Chapter 55, "On Being the Wrong Size.")

## The Need for Planned Abandonment

Just as important as the decision on what new and different things to do is planned, systematic abandonment of the old that no longer fits the purpose and mission of the business, no longer conveys satisfaction to the customer or customers, no longer makes a superior contribution.

An essential step in deciding what our business is, what it will be, and what it should be is, therefore, systematic analysis of all existing products, services, processes, markets, end uses, and distribution channels. Are they still viable? And are they likely to remain viable? Do they still give value to the customer? And are they likely to do so tomorrow? Do they still fit the realities of population and markets, of technology and economy? And if not, how can we best abandon them—or at least stop pouring in further resources and efforts? Unless these questions are being asked seriously and systematically, and unless managements are willing to act on the answers to them, the best definition of "What our business is, will be, and should be" will remain a pious platitude. Energy will be used up in defending yesterday. No one will have the time, resources, or will to work on exploiting today, let alone to work on making tomorrow.

Planned abandonment was first discussed and advocated in my book *Managing for Results*. It first was adopted as a systematic policy a few years later by the General Electric Company. Most long-range planning in large companies, like Unilever, focuses on the question "What *will* our business be?" GE's strategic business planning developed in the late sixties is an exception. Its aim is to answer "What *should* our business be?" Yet GE's planning does not start out with the question "What *new* things should we go into?" It starts out with "What existing product lines and businesses should we abandon?" and "Which ones should we cut back and deemphasize?"

Defining the purpose and mission of the business is difficult, painful, and risky. But it alone enables a business to set objectives, to develop strategies, to concentrate its resources and to go to work. It alone enables a business to be managed for performance.

# 8

## The Power and Purpose of Objectives: The Marks & Spencer Story and Its Lessons

*Social Revolution as Business Purpose and Mission—The Concentration Decision—The Objectives: Marketing; Innovation; Key Resources; Productivity; Social Responsibilities—Profit as Result Rather Than as Goal—Converting Objectives into Work Assignments—The Lessons—Specifications for Objectives—Objectives Needed in All Survival Areas—The Eight Areas of Objectives—The Basis for Work and Assignments—Objectives and Measurements—The Use of Objectives*

One company in the Western world can (as has been said earlier) be compared with Sears, Roebuck: Marks & Spencer. It might even be slightly ahead in growth of sales and profits over a long period of years.

Like Sears, Marks & Spencer is a chain retailer. It opened its first penny bazaar in 1884, or just about the time Richard Sears made his first mail-order offer of cheap but reliable watches to the Midwestern farmer. By 1915 the company was building variety stores. It has been growing fast ever since. Its most spectacular growth period, however, was the ten years between 1963 and 1972—a period in Britain's economic history which was characterized by "stagflation," i.e., inflationary stagnation, rather than growth. During this difficult period Marks & Spencer more than doubled its sales volume (from £184 million to £463 million, or in U.S. dollars, $460 million to $1,100 million). Profits went up just as fast, from £22 million to £54 million ($55 million to $135 million). Equally remarkable was the profit margin—almost 12 percent on sales before taxes—which is double what any other retail merchant (except Sears) would consider fully satisfactory.

## Social Revolution as Business Mission

By the mid-twenties the four brothers-in-law (Simon Marks, Israel Sieff, Harry Sacher, and Norman Laski) who had built the penny bazaars of 1915 into a major chain of variety stores owned a successful business. They might have been satisfied to rest on their laurels and to enjoy their considerable wealth. Instead they decided—following a trip to America by Simon Marks in 1924 in the course of which he carefully studied Sears, Roebuck—to rethink the purpose and mission of their business. The business of Marks & Spencer, they decided, was not retailing. It was social revolution.

Marks & Spencer redefined its business as the subversion of the class structure of nineteenth-century England by making available to the working and lower middle classes upper-class goods of better than upper-class quality, and yet at prices the working and lower-middle-class customer could well afford.

Marks & Spencer was by no means alone in the England of the twenties in seeing a major opportunity in the rapid social changes of the post-World War I period (another contemporary example was Montague Burton, the "Fifty Shilling Tailor"). What made Marks & Spencer unique and successful, however, was its conversion of the definition of "what our business is, and should be" into clear, specific, operationally effective and multiple *objectives.*

This required first a decision as to what to concentrate on, that is, a *basic strategy objective.*

Marks & Spencer had been a variety store chain like many others, offering a large assortment of products which had nothing in common except low price. Now the company decided to concentrate on wearing apparel (to which it soon added household textiles such as towels and draperies).

This was a rational decision. In the England of that time dress was still highly class-determined and the most visible of all class distinctions. Yet all of Europe, after World War I, had become fashion conscious. At the same time mass-production facilities for good-quality but inexpensive fabrics and clothes had come into being, in large part as a result of the huge demand for uniforms during World War I. New textile fibers, such as rayon and acetate, were coming on the market. There was still, however, no mass-distribution system in England for well-designed, up-to-date, and inexpensive clothing for the masses.

Within a few years the new Marks & Spencer had become the leading clothing and textile distributor in England, a position held ever since. By 1972 clothing sales accounted for a full three-quarters of total Marks & Spencer volume, i.e., for £327 million (roughly $800 million).

After World War II the same thinking was applied to a new major product category: food. During World War II the English people, formerly known for their dogged resistance to any innovation in eating, learned to accept new foods. Marks & Spencer's food business accounted, in 1972, for the remaining one-fourth of its sales.

From having been a successful variety chain in the early twenties, and even in the early thirties, Marks & Spencer purposefully changed itself into a highly distinct "specialty" marketer—maybe the largest in the world.

The concentration decision then enabled the company to set specific *marketing* objectives. The decision enabled it to decide who its customer was and should be; what kind of store it needed and when; what pricing policy to follow; and what market penetration to aim at.

The next area which Marks & Spencer tackled was that of *innovation objectives*. The clothing and textiles Marks & Spencer needed did not exist at the time. Marks & Spencer started out with quality control, like any other large retailer. But it rapidly built its quality-control laboratories into research, design, and development centers. It developed new fabrics, new dyestuffs, new processes, new blends, and so on. It developed designs and fashions. Finally, it went out and looked for the right manufacturer, whom it often had to help get started—for the existing old-line manufacturers were for obvious reasons none too eager to throw in their lot with the brash upstart who tried to tell them how to run their business. And when, after World War II, the company moved into prepared and processed foods, bakery goods, and dairy products, it applied the same innovative approach to a new industry.

Marks & Spencer set innovation goals in marketing. It pioneered, for instance, in consumer research in the early thirties, when such work was still so new* that Marks & Spencer had to develop the needed techniques.

Marks & Spencer set objectives for the supply and development of key resources. It early copied and adapted the Sears program for recruiting, training, and developing managers. It set objectives for the systematic development of financial resources, and measurements to control the utilization of these resources. And it set objectives for the development of its physical facilities, that is, for retail stores.

Hand in hand with these objectives for resources went objectives for their productivity. Marks & Spencer had originally taken its measurements and controls from America. In the twenties and early thirties it began to set its own objectives for continuously improving the productivity of key resources.

As a result, Marks & Spencer has a singularly high productivity of capital

---

*General Motors had a consumer research activity well before 1929. I doubt that this was known to Marks & Spencer, however; it was not generally known even within the American automobile industry.

—surely one of the keys to its success. Unnoticed, by and large—but fully as important—is the productivity of the Marks & Spencer retail store, which exceeds, to my knowledge, anything to be found anyplace else, including even Sears, Roebuck or Kresge, the acknowledged store-management virtuosi of the American retail scene.

Up till the late twenties the expansion of Marks & Spencer had been achieved primarily by opening new stores. Since the thirties Marks & Spencer's expansion has been achieved primarily by making each store more productive and by raising sales per square foot of selling space. Marks & Spencer, measured by the number of its stores, is still a small chain—there are only 250 stores. The stores themselves are not large, even by English standards; the average selling area is only 20,000 square feet per store. (The large American supermarket, by comparison, goes up to 100,000 square feet.) Yet these small stores sell something like $4 million apiece a year, which is many times what even highly successful retail stores of other companies do. The only explanation is continual upgrading of volume per store, that is, upgrading of merchandise, display, and sales per customer. Store selling space is the controlling resource of a retail merchant; Marks & Spencer's success in raising its utilization was central to its performance.

Marks & Spencer set objectives for its social responsibilities, and especially for areas of major impact: its own work force and its suppliers. It introduced "staff manageresses" into its stores to look after the employees, to take care of personal problems, and to make sure employees are treated with intelligence and compassion. Personnel management remains the job of the store manager. The staff manageress was set up to be the "people conscience" of the company.

Similarly Marks & Spencer developed objectives for its relations with its suppliers. The more successfully a supplier works with Marks & Spencer, the more dependent upon the company he will be. To safeguard the supplier against exploitation by the company became a concern of the company's management. It set out to develop a "putting out" system which, unlike its pre-industrial predecessor of early eighteenth-century England, would not impoverish the supplier and make him less secure but would, on the contrary, enrich the supplier and give him security.

But what about a profit objective? The answer is that there has never been one. Profit goals have been anathema at Marks & Spencer. Obviously the company is highly profitable and highly profit conscious. But it sees profit not as an objective but as a requirement of the business, that is, not as a goal but as a need. Profit, in the Marks & Spencer view, is the *result* of doing things right rather than the purpose of business activity. It is, above all, determined by what is necessary to attain company objectives. Profitability is a measurement of how well the business discharges its functions in serving market and customer. Above all, it is a restraint; unless profit is adequate to cover the risks, a company will not be able to attain its objectives.

I do not know how conscious Marks & Spencer's top management was in the early years, the late twenties and early thirties, of the full import of the decisions they then made. There was probably no master plan. But the young key executives who were brought into the firm in those years to take on new jobs such as innovation or the development of productivity objectives and standards were fully aware that their company had committed itself to a definition of what its business was—and they knew what the definition entailed. They were highly conscious of the company's social and business objectives. They knew what these objectives meant to each of them individually in terms of performance goals, performance standards, and demands for their own contribution.

Marks & Spencer from the start converted objectives into work assignments. It thought through what results and contributions were needed in each objectives area. It assigned responsibility for these results to someone and held him accountable. And it measured performance and contribution against the objectives.

## The Lessons

The Marks & Spencer story reaffirms the central importance of thinking through "what our business *is* and what it *should* be." But it also shows that this, by itself, is not enough. The basic definition of the business and of its purpose and mission have to be translated into objectives. Otherwise, they remain insight, good intentions, and brilliant epigrams which never become achievement.

The Marks & Spencer story brings out the specifications for objectives. Each of them will be discussed in some detail in the next chapter. But here is the list:

1. Objectives must be derived from "what our business is, what it will be, and what it should be." They are not abstractions. They are the action commitments through which the mission of a business is to be carried out, and the standards against which performance is to be measured. Objectives, in other words, are the *fundamental strategy of a business.*

2. Objectives must be *operational.* They must be capable of being converted into specific targets and specific assignments. They must be capable of becoming the basis, as well as the motivation, for work and achievement.

3. Objectives must make possible *concentration* of resources and efforts. They must winnow out the fundamentals among the goals of a business so that the key resources of men, money, and physical facilities can be concentrated. They must, therefore, be selective rather than encompass everything.

4. There must be *multiple objectives* rather than a single objective.

Much of today's lively discussion of management by objectives is concerned with the search for the "one right objective." This search is not only likely to be as unproductive as the quest for the philosopher's stone; it does harm and misdirects.

To manage a business is to balance a variety of needs and goals. And this requires multiple objectives.

5. Objectives are needed in all areas on which the *survival* of the business depends. The specific targets, the goals in any objective area, depend on the strategy of the individual business. But the areas in which objectives are needed are the same for all businesses, for all businesses depend on the same factors for their survival.

A business must first be able to create a customer. There is, therefore, need for a *marketing objective.* Businesses must be able to innovate or else their competitors will obsolesce them. There is need for an *innovation objective.* All businesses depend on the three factors of production of the economist, that is, on the *human resource,* the *capital resource,* and *physical resources.* There must be objectives for their supply, their employment, and their development. The resources must be employed productively and their productivity has to grow if the business is to survive. There is need, therefore, for *productivity objectives.* Business exists in society and community and, therefore, has to discharge social responsibilities, at least to the point where it takes responsibility for its impact upon the environment. Therefore objectives in respect to the *social dimensions* of business are needed.

Finally, there is need for *profit*—otherwise none of the objectives can be attained. They all require effort, that is, cost. And they can be financed only out of the profits of a business. They all entail risks; they all, therefore, require a profit to cover the risk of potential losses. Profit is not an objective but it is a requirement that has to be objectively determined in respect to the individual business, its strategy, its needs, and its risks.

Objectives, therefore, have to be set in these eight key areas:

—Marketing
—Innovation
—Human Organization
—Financial Resources
—Physical Resources
—Productivity
—Social Responsibility
—Profit Requirements

Objectives in these key areas enable us to do five things: to organize and explain the whole range of business phenomena in a small number of general statements; to test these statements in actual experience; to predict behavior; to appraise the soundness of decisions while they are still being made; and to let managers on all levels analyze their own experience and, as a result, improve their performance.

## The Basis for Work and Assignments

Objectives are the basis for work and assignments.

They determine the structure of the business, the key activities which must be discharged, and, above all, the allocation of people to tasks. Objectives are the foundation for designing both the structure of the business and the work of individual units and individual managers.

Objectives are always needed in all eight key areas. The area without specific objectives will be neglected. Unless we determine what shall be measured and what the yardstick of measurement in an area will be, the area itself will not be seen. (On this see Chapter 39.)

The measurements available for the key areas of a business enterprise are still haphazard by and large. We do not even have adequate concepts, let alone measurements, except for market standing. For something as central as profitability we have only a rubber yardstick; and we have no real tools at all to determine how much profitability is necessary. In respect to innovation and, even more, to productivity, we hardly know more than that something ought to be done. In the other areas—including physical and financial resources—we are reduced to statements of intentions; we do not possess goals and measurements for their attainment.

However, enough is known about each area to give a progress report at least. Enough is known for each business to go to work on objectives.

## How to Use Objectives

We know one more thing about objectives: how to use them.

If objectives are only good intentions they are worthless. They must degenerate into work. And work is always specific, always has—or should have—clear, unambiguous, measurable results, a deadline and a specific assignment of accountability.

But objectives that become a straitjacket do harm. Objectives are always based on expectations. And expectations are, at best, informed guesses. Objectives express an appraisal of factors that are largely outside the business and not under its control. The world does not stand still.

The proper way to use objectives is the way an airline uses schedules and flight plans. The schedule provides for the 9 A.M. flight from Los Angeles to get to Boston by 5 P.M. But if there is a blizzard in Boston that day, the plane will land in Pittsburgh instead and wait out the storm. The flight plan provides for flying at 30,000 feet and for flying over Denver and Chicago. But if the pilot encounters turbulence or strong headwinds he will ask flight control for permission to go up another 5,000 feet and to take the Minneapolis-Montreal route. Yet no flight is ever operated without schedule and flight plan. Any change is immediately fed back to produce a new schedule and flight plan. Unless 97 percent or so of its flights proceed on the original schedule and flight plan—or within a very limited range of deviation from either—a well-run airline gets another operations manager who knows his job.

Objectives are not fate; they are direction. They are not commands; they are commitments. They do not determine the future; they are means to mobilize the resources and energies of the business for the making of the future.

# 9

# Strategies, Objectives, Priorities, and Work Assignments

*The Foundation Areas: Marketing and Innovation—The Concentration Decision—The Market-Standing Decision—Innovation Objectives—Resources, Their Supply, Utilization, and Productivity—Marketing Objectives in the Resources Areas—The Bell System's Capital-Market Planning—Union Relations as an Objectives Area—Productivity: The First Test of Management Competence—The Danger of the Wrong Trade-Offs—Contributed Value as an Indicator of Productivity—The Social Dimension—Profit as a Need and a Limitation—Why Profit Maximization Leads to Inadequate Profitability—What Is the Minimum Profitability Needed?—The Japanese Example—Profitability and the Cost of Capital—How to Compute and Measure Profitability—Profitability as a Limitation—Balancing Objectives—The Time Span of Objectives—The Role of Budgeting—Managed and Capital Expenditures—Priorities—From Objectives to Doing—A Note on Inflation*

Marketing and innovation are the foundation areas in objective setting. It is in these two areas that a business obtains its results. It is performance and contribution in these areas for which a customer pays. All objectives must be performance objectives, aimed at doing rather than at good intentions. In all other objective areas the purpose of doing is to make possible the attainment of the objectives in the areas of marketing and innovation.

It is somewhat misleading to speak of a marketing objective. Marketing performance requires a number of objectives:

—for existing products and services in existing and present markets;
—for abandonment of "yesterday" in product, services, and markets;

—for new products and services for existing markets;
—for new markets;
—for the distributive organization;
—for service standards and service performance;
—for credit standards and credit performance, and so on.

Many books have been written on every one of these areas. But it is almost never stressed that objectives in these areas can be set only after two key decisions have been made: the decision on concentration, and the decision on market standing.

## The Concentration Decision

Whereas objectives are "strategy," the concentration decision is "policy." It is, so to speak, the decision in what theater to fight a war. Without such a policy decision, there can be rules of warfare but no strategy, that is, no purposeful action.

At about the same time at which Marks & Spencer chose concentration on wearing apparel and textiles, Sears, Roebuck faced up to the concentration decision. The area of concentration it decided on was household appliances. This was a very different decision from that of Marks & Spencer but it was the right decision considering both Sears's basically different theory of its business and the conditions prevailing in the American market in the late twenties. Sears did not drop textiles from its stores. But until World War II it paid little attention to them and did not aggressively compete in the apparel market. The Sears concentration decision led the company into different directions from those Marks & Spencer took, e.g., into very large stores; into heavy emphasis on a service organization, which eventually led into the automotive field as a second concentration area; and into heavy investment in the ownership of appliance makers.

Archimedes, one of the great scientists of antiquity, is reported to have said: "Give me a place to stand on, and I can lift the universe off its hinges." The place to stand on is the area of concentration. It is the area which gives a business the leverage that lifts the universe off its hinges. The concentration decision is, therefore, a crucial decision. It converts, in large measure, the definition of "what our business is" into meaningful operational commitment. It makes possible work on one's mission and purpose. It is the foundation for effective strategy.

Wherever we find a business that is outstandingly successful, we will find that it has thought through the concentration alternatives and has made a concentration decision.

During the first fifteen years of the computer, that is, until the mid-sixties, only two companies out of fifty or so who had entered the field worldwide managed to make any profit on computers and obtain any kind of market position: IBM and the much smaller Control Data Corporation. Both owed their success largely to facing up to the concentration decision. IBM, in the very infancy of computers, decided to concentrate on the business market and to offer the computer essentially as an accounting machine for large-scale, repetitive handling of conventional data such as accounting and payroll. Control Data, at almost the same time, made the radically opposite decision to concentrate on large-scale scientific applications. Both companies did very well. The other computer companies all tried to "cover the market"; none succeeded.

This is big-company stuff, many might say. But neither IBM nor Control Data was a big company when it made its concentration decision (see Chapter 60)—nor, incidentally, was Marks & Spencer way back in the 1920s. Actually, a small company needs the concentration decision even more than a big one. Its resources are limited and will produce no results unless concentrated.

The concentration decision is highly risky. It is a genuine decision. It has to be tested again and again against the market, its dynamics, its trends, and its changes. Without concentration, marketing objectives—but also innovation objectives—are promises and good intentions rather than true goals. Without them, the resources of the business will not be allocated to performance.

## The Market-Standing Decision

The other major decision underlying marketing objectives is that on market standing. One common approach is to say, "We want to be the leader." The other one is to say, "We don't care what share of the market we have as long as sales go up." Both sound plausible, but both are wrong.

Obviously, not everybody can be the leader. One has to decide in which segment of the market, with what product, what services, what values, one should be the leader. It does not do much good for a company's sales to go up if it loses market share, that is, if the market expands much faster than the company's sales do.

A company with a small share of the market will eventually become marginal in the marketplace, and thereby exceedingly vulnerable. In the slightest economic setback its customers are likely to concentrate their buying—and then they will concentrate on suppliers that have a substantial share; distributors and retailers will try to cut inventory by eliminating the marginal supplier. The sales volume of the marginal supplier may become too small to give the needed service—one of the main reasons why marginal appliance manufacturers, no matter how good their product, or how well known their brand name, do not usually survive long.

Market standing, regardless of the sales curve, is therefore essential. The point at which the supplier becomes marginal varies from industry to industry. But to be a marginal producer is dangerous for long-term survival. And this is just as true for a department store, for a bank, for an airline, or for an insurance company as it is for a manufacturer. (On this, see Chapter 55, "On Being the Wrong Size.")

There is also a maximum market standing above which it may be unwise to go—even if there were no antitrust laws. Market domination tends to lull the leader to sleep; monopolists flounder on their own complacency rather than on public opposition. Market domination produces tremendous internal resistance against any innovation and thus makes adaptation to change dangerously difficult. Also, it usually means that the enterprise has too many of its eggs in one basket and is too vulnerable to economic fluctuations.

There is also well-founded resistance in the marketplace to dependence on one dominant supplier. Whether it is the purchasing agent of a manufacturing company, the procurement officer in the Air Force, or the housewife, no one likes to be at the mercy of the monopoly supplier.

Finally, the dominant supplier in a rapidly expanding, especially a new, market is likely to do less well than if he shared that market with one or two other major and competing suppliers. This may seem paradoxical—and most businessmen find it difficult to accept. But the fact is that a new market, especially a new major market, tends to expand much more rapidly when there are several suppliers rather than only one. It may be very flattering to a supplier's ego to have 80 percent of a market. But if as a result of domination by a single source, the market does not expand as it otherwise might, the supplier's revenues and profits are likely to be considerably lower than they would be if two suppliers shared a fast-expanding market. Eighty percent of 100 is considerably less than 50 percent of 250. A new market which has only one supplier is likely to become static at 100. It will be limited by the imagination of the one supplier who always knows what his product or service cannot or should not be used for. If there are several suppliers, they are likely to uncover and promote markets and end uses the single supplier never dreams of. And the market might grow rapidly to 250.

Du Pont seems to have grasped this. In its most successful innovations Du Pont retains a sole-supplier position only until the new product has paid for the original investment. Then Du Pont licenses the innovation and launches competitors deliberately. As a result, a number of aggressive companies start developing new markets and new uses for the product. Nylon would surely have grown much more slowly without Du Pont-sponsored competition. Its markets are still growing, but without competition it would probably have begun to decline in the early fifties, when newer synthetic fibers were brought on the market by Monsanto and Union Carbide in the U.S., Imperial Chemicals in Great Britain, and AKU in Holland.

The market standing to aim at is not the maximum but the *optimum*. This requires careful analysis of customers, of products or services, of market segments, and distribution channels. It requires a market strategy, and it requires a decision of high risk.

## Innovation Objective

The innovation objective is the objective through which a company makes operational its definition of "what our business should be."

There are essentially three kinds of innovation in every business: innovation in product or service; innovation in marketplace and consumer behavior and values; and innovation in the various skills and activities needed to make the products and services and to bring them to market. They might be called respectively product innovation, social innovation (e.g., installment credit), and managerial innovation.

Innovation may arise out of the needs of market and customer; necessity may be the mother of innovation. Or innovation may come out of the work on the advancement of skill and knowledge carried out in universities and laboratories and so on.

The problem in setting innovation objectives is the difficulty of measuring the relative impact and importance of various innovations. Technological leadership is clearly desirable, especially if the term technology is used in its rightful sense as applying to the art, craft, or science of any organized human activity. But how are we to determine what weighs more: a hundred minor but immediately applicable improvements in packaging a product, or one fundamental chemical discovery which after ten more years of hard work may change the character of the business altogether? A department store and a pharmaceutical company will answer this question differently; but so may two different pharmaceutical companies.

Innovating objectives can, therefore, never be as clear and as sharply focused as marketing objectives. To set them, management must first anticipate the innovations needed to reach marketing goals—according to product lines, existing markets, new markets, and, usually, also according to service requirements. Second, it must appraise developments arising or likely to arise out of technological advancement in all areas of the business and in all of its activities. These forecasts are best organized in two parts: one for the immediate future, and projecting fairly concrete developments which, in effect, only implement innovations that have already been made; another for the more distant future and aiming at what might be.

While innovating objectives will not be as unequivocal as marketing objectives, they need to be specific and quantified—usually they can be quantified, if only roughly.*

Deliberate emphasis on innovation may be needed most where technological changes are least spectacular. No one in a pharmaceutical company or in a company making synthetic organic chemicals needs to be told that survival depends on the ability to replace three-quarters of the company's products by entirely new ones every ten years. But how many people in an insurance company realize that the company's growth—perhaps even its survival—depends on the development of new forms of insurance, the modification of existing policies, and the constant search for new, better, and cheaper ways of selling policies and of settling claims? The less visible or prominent technological change is in a business, the greater is the danger that the whole organization will ossify; hence the emphasis on innovation is doubly important.

It may be argued once more that such goals are big-company stuff, suitable for General Electric or for General Motors but unnecessary for a small business. But the small company's need for innovation is as great as that of the large company. And, as the managements of several small companies I know assert, the comparative simplicity of planning for innovation may be one of the main advantages of small size. As the president of one of them puts it, "When you are small, you are sufficiently close to the market to know fairly fast which new products are needed. And your engineering staff is too small to become ingrown. They know they can't do everything themselves and, therefore, they keep their eyes and ears wide open for any new development on the outside that they could possibly use."

## Resources, Their Supply, Utilization, and Productivity

A group of objectives deals with the resources a business needs to be able to perform, with their supply, their utilization, and their productivity.

All economic activity, economists have told us for two hundred years, requires three kinds of resources: land, that is, products of nature; labor, that is, human resources; and capital, that is, the means to invest in tomorrow. The business must be able to attract all three and to put them to productive use. In these three areas, therefore, every business needs objectives: in addition, it needs an objective for the productivity of these resources. Again, each of these areas will require a plurality of objectives rather than a single one.

In respect to human resources, for instance, it is highly desirable to have

---

*For methods to do this, see my book *Managing for Results* and the very different but penetrating approach of Michael J. Kami, in "Business Planning as Business Opportunity" in *Preparing Tomorrow's Business Leaders Today,* edited by Peter F. Drucker. There is also a list of innovation goals in my book *The Practice of Management* (1954).

specific objectives for manager supply, development, and performance, but also specific objectives for major groups within the nonmanagerial work force, and for relations with labor unions. There is need for objectives on employee attitudes as well as on employee skills.

Similarly a business needs physical facilities, and if a manufacturer, raw-materials resources. Retail chains, such as Sears, Roebuck and Marks & Spencer, need an objective for the development of stores and the utilization of shelf space, but also for the development of sources of supply for the merchandise they plan to sell.

The capital area is equally crucial—and very few businesses have yet tackled it. Again, objectives are needed for the supply of capital, as well as for its utilization.

Each of these areas, but especially the areas of human resources, and of capital, are "marketing areas." A business markets its job opportunities, and a business markets its financial investment. The job and career markets and the capital market are genuine "outside" markets in which there are true "customers" who have expectations, values, and needs. A business that cannot attract the people and the capital it needs will not last long.

The first sign of decline of an industry is loss of appeal to qualified, able, and ambitious people. The American railroads, for instance, did not begin their decline after World War II—it only became obvious and irreversible then. The decline actually set in around the time of World War I. Before World War I, able graduates of American engineering schools looked for a railroad career. From the end of World War I on—for whatever reason —the railroads no longer appealed to young engineering graduates, or to any educated young people. As a result there was nobody in management capable and competent to cope with new problems when the railroads ran into heavy weather twenty years later, around the time of World War II.

In the two areas of people and capital supply, genuine marketing objectives are therefore required. "What do our jobs have to be to attract and hold the kind of people we need and want? What is the supply available on the job market? And, what do we have to do to attract it?" Similarly, "What does the investment in our business have to be, in the form of bank loans, long-term debts or equity, to attract and hold the capital we need?" (On the career market, see Chapter 33, "Developing Management and Managers.")

One American company that systematically and for many years has applied market planning to the supply of capital is AT&T, the Bell Telephone System. A telephone business is highly capital-intensive; it depends on continuing heavy investment. The customer is, in effect, prefinanced to the tune of three years of future revenues from him. As one of his last contributions—and one of his most important ones—Theodore Vail thought through the problem. He realized, at the end of World War I, that the American capital market was changing and that Bell no longer could expect to obtain its capital from the traditional sources, such as the estates of wealthy Bostonians. Instead, a mass-capital market was coming into being. As a result of his analysis, Vail designed a brand-new security, unknown up to this time, and unparalleled ever since: an AT&T common share with an almost-guaranteed dividend, which was both an equity investment with a promise of long-term capital gains and, in large measure, a fixed-income-producing investment. It thus appealed to a new middle class which could not afford to risk much, but still had some savings available for investment after paying for life insurance or home mortgage.

Forty years later, in the early 1960s, the Bell System's top management realized that this investment instrument had ceased to be appropriate. It drastically changed the nature of the AT&T common share to make it attractive to the new capitalists, the large investment institutions, such as pension funds and investment trusts.

Setting marketing objectives for careers and for investment requires also objectives for the structure, basic policies, jobs, and directions of the business itself. They are not selling objectives; they are genuine marketing objectives, and as such have to be built into the way the business itself is set up, directed, structured, and run.

Setting objectives also applies to objectives concerning union relations or workers' attitudes. Union relations, most executives will argue, are beyond their control. For short periods of time this is indeed true. Circumstances beyond any management's control, e.g., governmental policies or inflation, strongly mold union attitudes and demands, as well as union strength. But this is all the more reason for setting long-range objectives for the relationship with the labor union.

One may criticize the labor relations policies of General Motors and General Electric. But these two companies, alone perhaps among major American businesses, thought through their union relations, developed objectives for them, and based their policies on them. The policies, while basically different in strategy and in tactics, are both very "tough" ones. Both aim at maintenance of the company's initiative in labor relations and of the company's control of worker assignment and worker productivity. Both companies are willing to take a strike over matters of principle and refuse to buy short-term union concessions on money issues by yielding on long-term fundamentals. Both policies have been remarkably successful in maintaining productivity and competitive positions for the two companies. Though labor bitterly criticizes the two companies and has never ceased to attack their policies, their labor negotiators are among the few, in major companies, whom labor respects. Indeed, GM and GE lose fewer man-hours to strikes and slowdowns than companies enjoying a much "better" relationship but relying on short-run expediency.

Resource objectives have to be set in a double process. One starting point is the anticipated needs of the business, which then have to be projected on the outside, that is, on the market for land, labor, and capital. But the other starting points are these "markets" themselves, which then have to be projected onto the structure, the direction, the plans of the business. It is no longer adequate, as most managers still seem to think, to say, "This is what we need; how much do we have to pay for it?" One also has to say, "This is what is available; what do we have to be, how do we have to behave, to get the fullest benefit?"

## Productivity: The First Test of Management's Competence

Attracting resources and putting them to work is only the beginning. The task of a business is to make resources productive. Every business, therefore, needs productivity objectives with respect to each of the three major resources, land, labor, and capital; and with respect to overall productivity itself.

A productivity measurement is the best yardstick for comparing managements of different units within an enterprise, and for comparing managements of different enterprises. For productivity includes all the efforts the enterprise contributes; it excludes everything it does not control. Productivity is the first test of management's competence.

All businesses have access to pretty much the same resources. Except for the rare monopoly situation, the only thing that differentiates one business from another in any given field is the quality of its management on all levels. The first measurement of this crucial factor is productivity, that is, the degree to which resources are utilized and their yield.

The continuous improvement of productivity is one of management's most important jobs. It is also one of the most difficult; for productivity is a balance between a diversity of factors, few of which are easily definable or clearly measurable.

The goal is not to try to find the one perfect productivity measurement, but to use a number of measurements—at least one gains insights that way. Output per man-hour, for instance, is by itself almost meaningless, even though governmental statistics in most countries are based on it. It does not even measure labor productivity. It becomes meaningful only if the figures show output in dollars per man-hour, as well as in units, but also profit per man-hour. In addition, we need figures that show output in units, output in dollars, that is, sales, profits per dollar of wages, and so on.

Similarly, we need to measure productivity in other areas by a number of yardsticks to gain insight and judgment. Labor is only one of the three factors of production. And if productivity of labor is accomplished by making the other resources less productive, there is actually loss of productivity.

A telling example is the paper industry worldwide. Very few industries have enjoyed as much of a rise in demand and sales. Few industries can match the technical advances of the paper industry, for instance, the stepup in the speed of paper machines. Since World War II the industry has been enjoying a boom in sales and output. Yet it has been unable, in most years, to produce any but marginal profits—well below what money earns in a savings bank. The break-even point of most up-to-date paper mills is just barely below 100 percent of capacity operations. The explanation for this puzzling phenomenon is a long secular decline in the productivity of capital in the industry. Paper prices have risen faster than the prices for papermaking equipment. Yet, where it took 80 cents of capital investment to build productive capacity for a dollar of paper sales forty years ago, it takes today two to three dollars of capital investment to produce one dollar's worth of paper sales. Labor productivity in the paper industry has gone up much faster than in most other industries. The paper industry, in other words, has substituted capital for labor on a massive scale. But the trade-off was a thoroughly uneconomical one. In fact, the paper industry represents a massive triumph of engineering over economics and common sense.

A century ago, Karl Marx based his confident prediction of the imminent demise of capitalism on the premise that the productivity of capital is bound to go down. This decline was to Marx the basic "contradiction of capitalism." That the prophecy has not been fulfilled so far is the result of our ability to innovate, that is, to develop new processes and new industries with higher productivity of capital. But Marx was right in his basic premise: the key to the survival of a business, a company, or an economy is, in the last analysis, productivity of capital. Productivity of capital is the area most companies pay least attention to—if only because so many people mistakenly think that profitability by itself measures it.

But, as the Marks & Spencer example shows, the productivity of physical resources needs to be measured fully as much, and objectives for each category need to be set. For productivity includes all three factors of production. The wrong trade-off, that is, an increase in the productivity of one factor of production paid for by a disproportionate drop in another factor results, as the paper industry shows, in a loss of overall productivity.

We do not have one single yardstick. But at least we have a basic concept that enables us to define productivity for the whole business—the economist calls it "contributed value."

Contributed value is the difference between the gross revenue received by a company from the sale of its products or services and the amount paid out for the purchase of raw materials and for services rendered by outside suppliers. Contributed value, in other words, includes all the costs of all the efforts of the business and the entire reward received for these efforts. It accounts for all the resources the business itself contributes to the final product and the appraisal of their efforts by the market.

Contributed value can be used to analyze productivity only if the allocation of costs is economically meaningful. The movement in accounting during the last twenty years from financial accounting and tax accounting to management accounting, while still only in its early stages, is thus a major step toward making business manageable and managed.

Contributed value will not measure productivity resulting from qualitative, rather than quantitative, factors. Contributed value is strictly a quantitative tool. Yet qualitative factors have major impact on productivity. Organization structure, for instance, the utilization of knowledge in the business, or the quality of tomorrow's management are fundamental factors in productivity, over the short or the long range. However, they elude our existing measurements. Finally, contributed value can be used, by and large, only in businesses that make something, that is in manufacturing businesses.

Within these limitations contributed value makes possible the rational analysis of productivity and the setting of goals for its improvement. In particular, it makes it possible to apply such tools as Operations Research to the systematic study of productivity. For these tools aim at working out alternative courses of action and their predictable consequences. The productivity problem is always one of seeing the range of alternative combinations of the various resources, and of finding the combination that gives the optimal ratio of output to cost effort and risk. (On this point see Chapter 40, "The Manager and the Management Sciences.")

Productivity is a difficult concept, but it is central. Without productivity objectives, a business does not have direction. Without productivity measurements, it does not have control.

## The Social Dimension

Only a few years ago managers as well as economists considered the social dimension so intangible that performance objectives could not be set. We have now learned that the intangible can become very tangible indeed. Such lessons as consumerism, or the attacks on industry for the destruction of the environment, are expensive ways to learn that business needs to think through its impacts and its responsibilities and to set objectives for both.

The social dimension is a survival dimension. The enterprise exists in society and economy. Within an institution one always tends to assume that the institution exists by itself in a vacuum. And managers inevitably look at their business from the inside. But the business enterprise is a creature of society and economy. Society or the economy can put any business out of existence overnight. The enterprise exists on sufferance and exists only as long as society and economy believe that it does a job, and a necessary, useful, and productive one.

Again, many managers will say, "This is big-company stuff." But the small company is also an employer, also exists in a community, and also depends on support or at least on sufferance by community and society. It needs social objectives fully as much as the big business—though it may need very different ones.

What such objectives might be will be discussed further on (in the section titled "Social Impacts and Social Responsibilities" on p. 312). But that such objectives need to be built into the strategy of a business, rather than be statements of good intentions, needs to be stressed here. These are not objectives that are needed because the manager has a responsibility to society. They are needed because the manager has a responsibility to the enterprise.

## Profit as a Need and a Limitation

Only after the objectives in the above seven key areas have been thought through and established can a business tackle the question "How much profitability do we need?" To attain any of the objectives entails high risks. It requires effort, and that means cost. Profit is, therefore, needed to pay for attainment of the objectives of the business. Profit is a condition of survival. It is the cost of the future, the cost of staying in business.

A business that obtains enough profit to satisfy its objectives in the key areas is a business that has the means of survival. A business that falls short of the profitability demands made by its key objectives is a marginal and endangered business.

The profitability needed to support the objectives of the business in the seven key areas discussed so far is also the quantitative expression of the profitability needed to fulfill the social and economic function of profit:

—as the "risk premium" covering the costs of staying in business;
—as the source of capital to finance the jobs of tomorrow;
—as the source of capital for innovation and for growth of the economy.

Profit planning is necessary. But it is planning for a needed minimum profitability rather than for that meaningless shibboleth "profit maximization." The minimum needed may well turn out to be a good deal higher than the profit goals of many companies, let alone their actual profit results.

## The Japanese Example

By historical accident the only economy which understands that profit is a minimum rather than a maximum concept is the Japanese economy.

There has been heated discussion whether Japan has a lower cost of capital or a higher cost of capital than the West—the Westerners contending that Japan's cost of capital is lower, the Japanese that it is higher. Both are wrong. The cost of capital of a Japanese business is pretty much the same as that of a Western business. Only the method of computation differs. Japan finances its businesses mostly by bank loans. Legally these are short-term credits. Economically, they are permanent equity investments by the bank. The reason for this is that Japan in the nineteenth century did not have a capital market; the banks were created largely by the industrial groups to be their suppliers of capital. In the West the situation is the reverse, the result of the fact that a capital market existed in England and America when industry started to grow. (The continental European situation is somewhat in between, as discussed in Chapter 49, "Georg Siemens and the Deutsche Bank.")

A Japanese company typically carries 70 percent debt capital and 30 percent equity capital whereas the typical American company in the same industry has the reverse ratio. The costs of capital for the two are then as follows: on the 70 percent debt capital, the Japanese company has to pay at least 10 percent interest, or 7 percent on its total capital; on the 30 percent equity, it is expected to earn after taxes about 8 percent, or 2.4 percent on its total capital, making a 9.4 percent rate of return on total capital employed. The American company has to earn 7 percent (the average for interest rates in the twenty-five years after World War II) on its 30 percent debt, amounting to 2.1 percent on its total invested capital. It has to earn 10 percent after taxes on its equity capital, which, at a rate of equity capital of 70 percent of the total, amounts to 7 percent.

Both come out, in other words, at the same overall cost of capital. (The Japanese carry a much lower tax burden, since interest on loans in Japan is considered, as in the West, a deductible business expense. The tax burden is much higher in the West—but whether this is to be considered as being borne by the business, by the consumer, or by the investor is a moot point on which economists cannot agree.)

The profitability needed by a Japanese company is what the bank needs to attract deposits to pay its own operating expenses and to cover its risks. It is the margin between the cost of capital to the bank—maybe 6 percent —and the interest income the bank charges for what, in effect, are equity investments in the businesses it finances. For the Japanese business manager the central fact of life is that he has to earn at least enough to carry the interest on the money he owes to the banks with a margin adequate to maintain his credit standing.

The Japanese manager, therefore, starts out with the clear aim to *minimize* the capital he needs to operate. He sees profit as a need, rather than as something desirable and nice to have. He knows that he will go out of business if he does not produce the minimum profit needed to obtain the capital required. He is no less profit-conscious than the Westerner, but, by historical accident, he is in a position where he understands the function of profit, and where, therefore, he tends to plan more rationally and more purposefully to obtain the profitability on which the survival and growth of his business depend.

The Japanese illustration shows clearly that the *minimum* rate of profitability adequate to the needs of a business is the cost of capital.* The minimum rate is the capital market rate needed to obtain the financial resources the business needs to attain its objectives.

In the case of self-financing, which at certain times (e.g., in the U.S. in the fifties) plays an important part in the supply of capital to existing businesses, there must be enough profit both to yield the capital market rate of return on money already in the business and to produce the additional capital needed. Otherwise the minimum rate of profitability the business requires will not be produced. As Childs points out, the fact that the American chemical industry in the fifties and sixties, when its cash flow was high, reinvested retained earnings in ventures yielding less than the cost of capital on the market was a major reason for its sharp drop in growth in earnings and in ability to attract capital in the years after 1965.

The cost of capital is never higher than the minimum profitability needed —at least not when there is a capital market rather than government allocation of capital. But it might well be lower than the minimum. It is, however, the best starting point for profit planning.

Whether the business is large or small, complex or simple, profitability should be computed as an average of the profits of both good and bad years. Let us assume that a business needs a profitability of 20 percent before taxes on its invested capital. If the 20 percent is being earned in a good year, it is unlikely to be earned over the lifetime of the investment. We may need a 40 percent return in good years to average 20 percent over a dozen years. And we have to calculate how much we actually need to get the desired average.

### How to Measure Profitability

How to measure profitability is a much debated question. No one yardstick will do. Profit on sales, that is, the profit margin, is clearly not adequate by itself. For profit is profit margin multiplied by the rate of turnover of capital. Profit margin is a meaningful figure, if only because it shows where the opportunities for profit improvement lie. Return on invested capital makes sense; but in practice it is the worst of all yardsticks—rubber of almost infinite elasticity. What is "invested capital"? Is a dollar invested

*On this see the excellent though highly technical discussion in John F. Childs, *Earnings per Share and Management Decisions* (Prentice-Hall, 1971). It is perhaps the best treatment of financial structure and financial policy for the large business written so far.

in 1950 the same thing as a dollar invested in 1970? Is capital to be defined by the accountant as original cash put in less subsequent depreciation? Or is it to be defined by the economist as future wealth-producing capacity, discounted at capital-market interest rates to current cash value? The search for a perfect yardstick for measuring profitability is likely to be frustrating and futile. It is far sounder to use a number of yardsticks simultaneously and look at them for what they tell us about the business, particularly as no one has been able to make a convincing case for including depreciation in measuring capital investment or, for that matter, for excluding it.

## Profitability as a Limitation

Profitability is not only a need, it is also a limitation. The objectives of a business must not exceed the profitability with which it can expect to operate. The minimum profitability must not be so high that one cannot prudently expect to attain it. The profitability need, therefore, has to be projected back on the objectives. If profitability is inadequate to the objectives, the objectives have to be pruned. The company's eyes ought not be bigger than its stomach.

Almost any business, in setting objectives in key areas, will come up with greater efforts and higher risks than it is likely to be able to support in terms of profitability. Any business, therefore, will have to balance objectives.

## Balancing Objectives

There are three kinds of balance needed in setting objectives. Objectives have to be balanced against attainable profitability. Objectives have to be balanced as to the demands of the immediate and the distant future. They have to be balanced against each other, and trade-offs have to be established between desired performance in one area and desired performance in others.

In setting objectives, management always has to balance the immediate future against the long range. If it does not provide for the immediate future, there will be no long-range future. But if it sacrifices the long-range needs of "what our business *will* be" and "what our business *should* be" to immediate results, there will also be no business fairly soon.

Setting objectives always requires a decision on where to take the risks, a decision as to how much immediate results should be sacrificed for the sake of long-range growth, or how much long-range growth should be jeopardized for the sake of short-run performance. There is no formula for these decisions. They are risky, entrepreneurial, uncertain—but they must be made.

Management has to balance objectives. What is more important, an expansion in markets and sales volume, or a higher rate of return? How much time, effort, and energy should be expended on improving manufacturing productivity? Would the amount of effort or money bring greater returns if invested in new-product design?

The growth companies of the fifties and sixties promised both more sales and higher profits indefinitely. This alone was reason to distrust them. Every experienced manager should have known that these two objectives are not normally compatible. To produce more sales almost always means to sacrifice immediate profit. To produce higher profit almost always means to sacrifice long-range sales. In almost every case, this irrational promise and the resulting refusal to make balancing decisions between growth and profitability objectives was the direct cause of the large losses and the equally large write-offs of the growth companies in the late sixties and early seventies.

There are few things that distinguish competent from incompetent management quite as sharply as performance in balancing objectives. There is no formula for doing the job. Each business requires its own balance—and it may require a different balance at different times. Balancing is not a mechanical job. It is risk-taking decision. (For further discussion of these strategic decisions, see Chapter 10, "Strategic Planning.")

## The Role of Budgeting

Setting and balancing objectives does require a mechanical expression. The budget is the instrument, and especially the budget for managed and capital expenditures.

Budgeting is commonly conceived as a financial process. But only the notation is financial; the decisions are entrepreneurial. Today the so-called managed expenditures and the capital expenditures are usually considered quite separate. But the distinction is an accounting (and tax) fiction and misleading; both expenditures commit scarce resources to an uncertain future; both are, economically speaking, expenditures of capital that are investments in the future. To be viable, the expenditures have to express the same basic decisions on survival objectives. Finally, today most of our attention in budgets is given, as a rule, to other than the managed expenses, especially to the so-called variable expenses, e.g., wages; historically that is where the most money was being spent. But no matter how large or small the sums, decisions on the managed expenses determine the future of the enterprise.

We have little control over what the accountant calls variable expenses, those which relate directly to units of production and are fixed by a certain way of doing things. We can change them, but slowly. We can change a relationship between units of production and labor costs (which we, with a certain irony, still consider variable expenses despite the fringe benefits).

But within any time period these expenses can only be kept at a norm and cannot be changed. This is, of course, even more true for expenses with respect to past decisions, the fixed expenses. We cannot undo them at all, whether they are the cost of past capital investment, local taxes, or insurance premiums to protect assets. They are beyond management's control.

The expenses under management's control are the expenses for the future. The capital expenses and the managed expenses express management's risk-taking decisions. These include expenses on facilities and equipment, on research and merchandising, on product development and people development, on management and organization, on customer service, and on advertising. A managed expense budget is the area in which a business makes its real decisions on its objectives.*

## Setting Priorities

The two budgets regarding the future, capital expenditures and managed expenditures, also express the priorities which management sets.

No business can do everything. Even if it has the money, it will never have enough good people. It has to set priorities. The worst thing is to try to do a little bit of everything. This makes sure that nothing is being accomplished. It is better to pick the wrong priority than none at all.

Setting priorities is risky. For whatever does not receive priority is, in effect, abandoned.† There is no formula for making the decision, but it has to be made, and the mechanism for making it is the budgets for capital and managed expenditures.

## From Objectives to Doing

One final step remains: to convert objectives into doing. Action rather than knowledge is the purpose of asking, "What *is* our business, what *will* it be, what *should* it be?" and of thinking through objectives. The aim is to focus the energies and resources of the organization on the right results. The end product of business analysis, therefore, is a work program and specific and concrete work assignments with defined goals, with deadlines, and with clear accountability. Unless objectives are converted into action, they are not objectives; they are dreams.

*A Note on Inflation.* One additional aspect of profitability should be mentioned: the impact of inflation on profits. Traditionally it has been held

---

*The best work in this area, and in microeconomics, is still that of the German *Betriebswissenschaft,* to which far too little attention has been paid outside of Germany.
†For a discussion of priority setting, see my book, *The Effective Executive.*

that productive assets are a hedge against inflation; they are in a sense. A steel mill will still be standing, capable of producing steel, even when the currency has gone to rack and ruin. The original cost of the mill will have become zero or negligible so that a larger share of its revenue becomes available to the equity owners. Yet this is a simplistic view: inflation also destroys assets. It creates spurious profits, profits which in effect represent destruction of capital. In an inflation, even in very rapid inflations at the rate of 40 or 60 percent a year, such as many South American countries have been experiencing, asset values are, as a rule, not adjusted in the books. In fact, in most countries this is forbidden (no longer in Brazil, by the way). Depreciation charges are, therefore, based on yesterday's currency value; and, with a shrinking currency, depreciation rapidly becomes inadequate. Sooner or later, the asset will have to be replaced, and then the costs in depreciated currency will be many times greater than the book value. If this loss is not recognized—and few managements are even aware of it—profits will be shown which, in effect, are underdepreciation, and dividends will be paid out which are in effect distributions of capital. The Securities and Exchange Commission (SEC) in the United States long ago recognized this with respect to the investments of American companies overseas. It demands that the asset value of such investments—in a subsidiary in Brazil, for instance—be adjusted each year to reflect the hidden loss. (Paradoxically, the American tax authorities refuse to accept this adjustment and make a business pay taxes on a profit which the SEC has forced it to show as a loss in its published accounts.)

In an inflationary situation—and that means in most countries at the present time—inflation should be considered a genuine cost. There is good reason to adopt, at least for internal purposes, a method of accounting in "constant dollars" or "constant yen" or "constant marks." At least it forces management to realize that inflation rather than its own performance underlies a good profit showing.

If American companies had used accounting in constant dollars during the late sixties, most of them would have realized that they produced no profits, let alone the profit records of these inflation years. Few of them showed after-tax profits of more than 8 percent on their assets—yet the U.S. then had an annual 8 percent inflation rate. Had managers realized this, they would not have been so surprised at the collapse of the stock market price of the growth companies in 1969–70.

# 10

## Strategic Planning: The Entrepreneurial Skill

*The Surge in Long-Range Planning—The Time Spans of Planning—Strategic Decision-Making Rather Than Long-Range Planning—What Strategic Planning Is Not—Not a Bag of Tricks—Not Forecasting—The Importance of the Unique Event—The Futurity of Present Decisions—Planning Is Purposeful Risk-Taking—What Strategic Planning Is—Sloughing Off Yesterday—What New Things Do We Have to Do When?—Everything Degenerates into Work—People Assignments, the Test of Planning—The Need for Measurement and Feedback*

There has been a tremendous upsurge in long-range planning these last twenty years. The very idea was practically unknown a few decades ago. Now it is the rare large company (at least in the U.S. and in Japan) that does not have a long-range planning staff and elaborate long-range plans.

It is true that practically every basic management decision is a long-range decision—ten years is a rather short time span these days. Whether concerned with research or with building a new plant, designing a new marketing organization or a new product, every major management decision takes years before it is really effective. And it has to be productive for years thereafter to pay off the investment of men and money. Managers, therefore, need to be skilled in making decisions with long futurity on a systematic basis.

Management has no choice but to anticipate the future, to attempt to mold it, and to balance short-range and long-range goals. It is not given to mortals to do well any of these things. But lacking divine guidance, management must make sure that these difficult responsibilities are not overlooked or neglected but taken care of as well as is humanly possible.

121

The future will not just happen if one wishes hard enough. It requires decision—now. It imposes risk—now. It requires action—now. It demands allocation of resources, and above all, of human resources—now. It requires work—now.

The idea of long-range planning—and much of its reality—rests on a number of misunderstandings. The present and the immediate short range require strategic decisions fully as much as the long range. The long range is largely made by short-run decisions. Unless the long range is built into, and based on, short-range plans and decisions, the most elaborate long-range plan will be an exercise in futility. And conversely, unless the short-range plans, that is, the decisions on the here and now, are integrated into one unified plan of action, they will be expedient, guess, and misdirection.

"Short range" and "long range" are not determined by any given time span. A decision is not short range because it takes only a few months to carry it out. What matters is the time span over which it is effective. A decision is not long range because in the early seventies we resolve on making it in 1985; this is not a decision but an idle diversion. It has as much reality as the eight-year-old boy's plan to be a fireman when he grows up.

The idea behind long-range planning is that "What *should* our business be?" can and should be worked on and decided by itself, independent of the thinking on "What *is* our business?" and "What *will* it be?" There is some sense to this. It is necessary in strategic planning to *start* separately with all three questions. What *is* the business? What *will* it be? What *should* it be? These are, and should be, separate conceptual approaches. With respect to "What *should* the business be?" the first assumption must be that it will be different.

Long-range planning should prevent managers from uncritically extending present trends into the future, from assuming that today's products, services, markets, and technologies will be the products, services, markets, and technologies of tomorrow, and, above all, from dedicating their resources and energies to the defense of yesterday.

Planning what *is* our business, planning what *will* it be, and planning what *should* it be have to be integrated. What is short range and what is long range is then decided by the time span and futurity of the decision. Everything that is "planned" becomes immediate work and commitment.

The skill we need is not long-range planning. It is strategic decision-making, or perhaps strategic planning.

General Electric calls this work "strategic business planning." The ultimate objective of the activity is to identify the new and different businesses, technologies, and markets which the company should try to create long range. But the work starts with the question, "What *is* our present business?" Indeed, it starts with the questions "Which of our *present* businesses should we abandon? Which should we play down? Which should we push and supply new resources to?"

This may sound like semantic quibbling—and, to a point, it is. But the confused semantics have led to confused thinking. They have tended to paralyze strategic decision-making rather than to mobilize for it. They are largely to blame for the failure of many large companies so far to obtain results from elaborate planning efforts.

## What Strategic Planning Is Not

It is important for the manager to know what strategic planning is *not:*
1. *It is not a box of tricks, a bundle of techniques.* It is analytical thinking and commitment of resources to action.

Many techniques may be used in the process—but, then again, none may be needed. Strategic planning may require a computer, but the most important questions, e.g., "What *is* our business?" or "What *should* it be?" cannot be quantified and programmed for the computer. Model building or simulation may be helpful, but they are not strategic planning; they are tools for specific purposes and may or may not apply in a given case. (See Chapter 40, "The Manager and the Management Sciences.")

Quantification is not planning. To be sure, one uses rigorous logical methods as far as possible—if only to make sure that one does not deceive oneself. But some of the most important questions in strategic planning can be phrased only in terms such as "larger" or "smaller," "sooner" or "later." These terms while quantitative cannot easily be manipulated by quantitative techniques. And some equally important areas, e.g., those of political climate, social responsibilities, or human (including managerial) resources, cannot be quantified at all. They can be handled only as restraints, or parameters, but not as factors in the equation itself.

Strategic planning is *not* the "application of scientific methods to business decision" (as one well-known text on planning defines it). It is the application of thought, analysis, imagination, and judgment. It is responsibility, rather than technique.

2. *Strategy planning is not forecasting.* It is not masterminding the future. Any attempt to do so is foolish; the future is unpredictable. We can only discredit what we are doing by attempting it.

If anyone still suffers from the delusion that man is able to forecast beyond a very short time span, let him look at the headlines in yesterday's paper, and ask which of them he could possibly have predicted a decade or so ago. For example, could he, in 1960, in the waning days of the Eisenhower Administration, have forecast the almost explosive growth of the Black middle class in America, which by 1970, had raised two-thirds of

Black families above the poverty line and had given the American Negro family an average income well above the average family income of affluent Great Britain?

Could he have forecast ten years ago that the unprecedented economic advance of the American Negro—the fastest and most massive economic advance of any class or ethnic group in American history—would only have made the race problem more acute and riveted our attention on both the desperate plight of the remaining Negro poor, and on the remaining discrimination against the achieving Black?

Could he have predicted the chronic American balance-of-payments deficit of the 1960s and the world financial crisis of 1971? Could he have predicted that Britain would stay out of the Common Market until 1973? Could he have predicted the Eurodollar market, by means of which the European investor has financed the expansion of American-based businesses into Europe? Could he have forecast the rise of consumerism? Could he have forecast the development of multinational corporations?

We must start out with the premise that forecasting is not a respectable human activity and not worthwhile beyond the shortest of periods. *Strategic planning is necessary precisely because we cannot forecast.*

Another, even more compelling reason why forecasting is not strategic planning is that forecasting attempts to find the most probable course of events or, at best, a range of probabilities. But the entrepreneurial problem is the unique event that will change the possibilities; the entrepreneurial universe is not a physical but a social universe. Indeed, the central entrepreneurial contribution, which alone is rewarded with a profit, is to bring about the unique event or innovation that changes the economic, social, or political situation.

This was what Xerox Corporation did in the fifties when it developed and marketed photocopying machines. This is what the entrepreneurs in mobile housing did in the 1960s, when the trailer became the new, permanent, and immobile home and took over practically the entire U.S. low-cost housing market. The unique event of Rachel Carson's book *Silent Spring,* in the fifties, changed the attitude of a whole civilization toward the environment. On the social and political scene, this is what the leaders of the civil rights movement did in the 1960s, and possibly what the leaders in women's rights were doing at the start of the seventies.

Since the entrepreneur upsets the probabilities on which predictions are based, forecasting does not serve the purposes of planners who seek to direct their organizations to the future. It certainly is of little use to planners who would innovate and change the ways in which people work and live.

Forecasting is therefore not an adequate basis even for purely adaptive behavior, let alone for the entrepreneurial decisions of strategic planning.

3. *Strategic planning does not deal with future decisions. It deals with the futurity of present decisions.* Decisions exist only in the present. The question that faces the strategic decision-maker is not what his organization should do tomorrow. It is, "What do we have to do today to be ready for an uncertain tomorrow?" The question is not what will happen in the future. It is, "What futurity do we have to build into our present thinking and doing, what time spans do we have to consider, and how do we use this information to make a rational decision now?"

Decision-making is a time machine which synchronizes into one present a great number of divergent time spans. We are only learning this now. Our approach still tends toward making plans for something we will decide to do in the future, which may be entertaining but is futile. We can make decisions only in the present and yet we cannot make decisions *for* the present alone; the most expedient, most opportunistic decision—let alone the decision not to decide at all—may commit us for a long time, if not permanently and irrevocably.

4. *Strategic planning is not an attempt to eliminate risk.* It is not even an attempt to minimize risk. Such an attempt can lead only to irrational and unlimited risks and to certain disaster.

Economic activity, by definition, commits present resources to the future, i.e., to highly uncertain expectations. To take risks is the essence of economic activity. One of the most rigorous theorems of economics (Boehm-Bawerk's Law) proves that existing means of production will yield greater economic performance only through greater uncertainty, that is, through greater risk.

While it is futile to try to eliminate risk, and questionable to try to minimize it, it is essential that the risks taken be the right risks. The end result of successful strategic planning must be capacity to take a greater risk, for this is the only way to improve *entrepreneurial* performance. To extend this capacity, however, we must understand the risks we take. We must be able to choose rationally among risk-taking courses of action rather than plunge into uncertainty on the basis of hunch, hearsay, or experience, no matter how meticulously quantified.

## What Strategic Planning Is

We can now attempt to define what strategic planning is. It is the continuous process of making present entrepreneurial *(risk-taking) decisions* systematically and with the greatest knowledge of their futurity; organizing systematically the *efforts* needed to carry out these decisions; and measuring the results of these decisions against the expectations through organized, *systematic feedback*.

As such, planning, whether long range or short range, is nothing new. It is the organized performance of an old task. But we have learned that the task will rarely get done unless organized. Above all, it will rarely become achievement unless done purposefully.

## Sloughing Off Yesterday

Planning starts with the objectives of the business. In each area of objectives, the question needs to be asked, *"What do we have to do now* to attain our objectives *tomorrow?"* The first thing to do to attain tomorrow is always to be sloughing off yesterday. Most plans concern themselves only with the new and additional things that have to be done—new products, new processes, new markets, and so on. But the key to doing something different tomorrow is getting rid of the no-longer-productive, the obsolescent, the obsolete.

The first step in planning is to ask of any activity, any product, any process or market, "If we were not committed to this today, would we go into it?" If the answer is no, one says, "How can we get out—fast?"

Systematic sloughing off of yesterday is a plan by itself—and adequate in many businesses. It will force thinking and action. It will make available men and money for new things. It will create willingness to act.

Conversely, the plan that provides only for doing additional and new things without provision for sloughing off old and tired ones is unlikely to have results. It will remain plan and never become reality, yet getting rid of yesterday is the decision that most long-range plans in business (and even more in government) never tackle—maybe the main reason for their futility.

## What New Things Do We Have to Do—When?

The next step in the planning process is to ask, "What *new* and different things do we have to do, and when?"

In every plan there will be areas where all that is needed—or appears to be needed—is to do more of what we already do. It is prudent, however, to assume that what we already do is never adequate to the needs of the future.* But, "What do we need?" is only half the question. Equally important is "When do we need it?" for it fixes the time for beginning work on the new tasks.

There is indeed a "short" range and a "long" range to every decision. The time between the commitment to a course of action, e.g., to building a steel mill and the earliest possible moment for results, i.e., getting finished steel,

---

*On this see the brilliant essay "Business Planning as Business Opportunity" by Michael J. Kami, in *Preparing Tomorrow's Business Leaders Today.* Edited by Peter F. Drucker.

is the short range of a decision. And the twenty-plus years it takes before, at the earliest, we get back with compound interest the money invested in the steel mill is the long range. The long range is the time during which the initial decision must remain reasonably valid—as to markets, process, technology, plant location, etc.—to have been the right decision originally.

But it is meaningless to speak of short-range and long-range plans. There are plans that lead to *action today*—and they are true plans, true strategic decisions. And there are plans that talk about action tomorrow—they are dreams, if not pretexts for nonthinking, nonplanning, nondoing. The essence of planning is to make present decisions with knowledge of their futurity. It is the *futurity* that determines the time span, and not vice versa.

There are limitations on futurity. In business decisions, the most precise mathematical statement is often that of my eighth-grade teacher: Parallels are two lines which do not meet this side of the school yard. In the expectations and anticipations of a business, the old rule of statistics usually applies that anything beyond twenty years equals infinity; and since expectations more than twenty years hence have normally a present value of zero, they should receive only a minimal allocation of present efforts and resources.

However, results that require a long gestation period will be obtained only if initiated early enough. Hence, long-range planning requires knowledge of futurity: "What do we have to do today if we want to be in some particular place in the future? What will not get done at all if we do not commit resources to it today?"

To repeat an oft-used illustration: If we know that it takes ninety-nine years to grow Douglas firs in the Northwest to pulping size, planting seedlings today is the only way we can provide for pulp supply in ninety-nine years. Someone may well develop some speeding-up hormone; but we cannot bank on it if we are in the paper industry. It is quite conceivable—perhaps highly probable—that we will use wood primarily as a source of chemicals long before these trees grow to maturity. The paper supply thirty years hence may depend on less precious, less highly structured sources of cellulose than a tree, which is the most advanced chemical factory in the plant kingdom. This simply means, however, that forests may put their proprietors into the chemical industry sometime within the next thirty years and they had better learn now something about chemistry. If, however, paper plants depend on Douglas fir, planning cannot confine itself to twenty years, but must consider ninety-nine years.

For other decisions, even five years would be absurdly long. If our business is buying up distress merchandise and selling it at auction, next week's clearance sale is long-range future; anything beyond is largely irrelevant to us. Thus, the nature of the business and the nature of the decision determine the time spans of planning.

Time spans are neither static nor "given." The time decision itself is a risk-taking decision in the planning process. It largely determines the allocation of resources and efforts. It largely determines the risks taken. One cannot repeat too often that to postpone a decision is in itself a risk-taking and often irrevocable decision. The time decision largely determines the character and nature of the business.

To sum up: What is crucial in strategic planning is, first, that systematic and purposeful *work* on attaining objectives be done; second, that planning start out with sloughing off yesterday, and that abandonment be planned as part of the systematic attempt to attain tomorrow; third, that we look for new and different ways to attain objectives rather than believe that doing more of the same will suffice; and finally, that we think through the time dimensions and ask, "When do we have to start work to get results when we need them?"

## Everything Degenerates into Work

The best plan is *only* a plan, that is, good intentions, unless it *degenerates into work.* The distinction that marks a plan capable of producing results is the commitment of key people to work on specific tasks. The test of a plan is whether management actually commits resources to action which will bring results in the future. Unless such commitment is made, there are only promises and hopes, but no plan.

A plan needs to be tested by asking managers, "Which of your best people have you put on this work today?" The manager who comes back (as most of them do) and says, "But I can't spare my best men now. They have to finish what they are doing now before I can put them to work on tomorrow" —this manager simply admits that he does not have a plan. But he also proves that he needs a plan, for it is precisely the purpose of a plan to show where scarce resources—and the scarcest is good people—should be working.

Work implies not only that somebody is supposed to do the job, but also accountability, a deadline, and finally the measurement of results, that is, feedback from results on the work and on the planning process itself.

In strategic planning, measurements present very real problems, especially conceptual ones. Yet precisely because what we measure and how we measure determine what will be considered relevant, and determine thereby not just what we see, but what we—and others—do, measurements are all-important in the planning process. Above all, unless we build expectations into the planning decision in such a way that we can realize early whether they are actually fulfilled or not—including a fair understanding of what are significant deviations both in time and in scale—we cannot plan. We have no feedback, no way of self-control from events back to the planning process.

The manager cannot decide whether he wants to make risk-taking decisions with long futurity; he makes them by the definition of his role. All that is within his power is to decide whether he wants to make them responsibly or irresponsibly, with a rational chance of effectiveness and success, or as a blind gamble against all odds. And both because the decision-making process is essentially a rational process and because the effectiveness of the entrepreneurial decisions depends on the understanding and voluntary efforts of others, the approach will be more responsible and more likely to be effective if it is rational, organized, and based on knowledge, not prophecy. The end result, however, is not knowledge but strategy. *Its aim is action now.*

Strategic planning does not substitute facts for judgment, does not substitute science for the manager. It does not even lessen the importance and role of managerial ability, courage, experience, intuition, or even hunch—just as scientific biology and systematic medicine have not lessened the importance of these qualities in the individual physician. On the contrary, the systematic organization of the planning job and the supply of knowledge to it strengthen the manager's judgment, leadership, and vision.

# Performance in the Service Institution

The public-service institutions—government agency and hospital, school and university, armed service and professional associations—have been growing much faster than businesses in this century. They are the growth sector of a modern society. And within business, the service staffs have been growing much faster than the operating units. Yet performance has not kept up with growth or importance. What explains the lag in—or absence of—performance in the service institutions? What is needed to manage service institutions for performance?

# 11

# The Multi-Institutional Society

*Service Institutions Society's Growth Sector—Service Institutions within Business—Society, Including Business, Depends on the Performance of Service Institutions—Are Service Institutions Managed?—Are They Manageable?—Performance and Results the Exceptions in Service Institutions —The Importance of the Exceptions—Making the Service Institution Perform as a Central Managerial Challenge*

Business enterprise is only one of the institutions of modern society, and business managers are by no means our only managers. Service institutions —government agencies; armed services; schools and universities; research laboratories; hospitals and other health-care institutions; labor unions; professional practices such as the large law firm or the large (and often multinational) accounting firm; professional, industry, and trade associations, and many others—are equally institutions and, therefore, equally in need of management. They all have people who are designated to exercise the management function and who are paid for doing the management job, even though they may not be called managers, but administrators, commanders, directors, executives, or some such title.

These public-service institutions—to give them a generic name—are the real growth sector of a modern society.

It is not that business has become less powerful, less strong, or less successful; the others, the service institutions, have proportionately become more powerful, larger, and, above all, more important than they were.

We have a multi-institutional society rather than a business society. The traditional title of the American college course still tends to read "Business and Government." But this is an anachronism; it should read "Business, Government, and Many Others."

## Service Institutions within Business

Within business enterprises, the growth sector has also been "service institutions." In every larger business—and many fairly small businesses—there has been rapid increase in service groups and service functions, such as staffs, research departments, planning groups, coordinators, management information systems, and so on. All these are service institutions rather than operating units. They have no direct relationship to the economic performance and the results of the business. While they operate within an economic institution, none of them produces economic results directly or performs economically by itself.

These service institutions within business also have managers, of course. They also need to be managed for performance.

All service institutions are being paid for out of the economic surplus produced by economic activity. They are overhead—either social overhead or business overhead. The growth of the service institutions in this century is thus the best testimonial to the success of business in discharging its economic task, i.e., producing economic surplus.

Yet—unlike the early nineteenth-century university—the service institutions are not luxury or ornament. They are pillars of a modern society, load-bearing members of the main structure. They *have* to perform if society and business are to function. It is not only that these service institutions are the main expense of a modern society; as said earlier (Chapters 1 and 3) half of the gross national product of the U.S. (and of most of the other developed countries) is spent on public-service institutions. Every citizen in the developed, industrialized, urbanized societies depends for his survival on the performance of the public-service institutions. But these institutions also embody the values of developed societies. Education, health care, knowledge, and mobility—rather than primarily more food, clothing, and shelter—are the fruits of our society's increased economic capacities and productivity.

The service institutions within business too are—or should be—load-bearing members of the structure. It is not just their steadily increasing cost that makes it mandatory for them to be managed for contribution and performance. Business enterprise depends on the performance of its service staffs, its planners, researchers, information specialists, analysts, and accountants.

Yet the evidence for performance in the service institutions is not impressive, let alone overwhelming. Schools, hospitals, and universities are all big today beyond the imagination of an earlier generation. Their budgets have grown even faster. Yet everywhere they are in crisis. A generation or two ago their performance was taken for granted. Today they are being attacked on all sides for lack of performance. Services which the nineteenth century managed with aplomb and apparently with little effort—the postal service, for instance, or the railroads—are deeply in the red, require enormous and growing subsidies, and give poorer service everywhere. Government agencies, both in national and in local governments, are constantly being reorganized so as to be more efficient. Yet in every country the citizen complains ever more loudly of bureaucracy in government. What he means by this complaint is that the government agency is being run for the convenience of its employees rather than for contribution and performance. This is mismanagement.

The most persistent critics of bureaucracy in government and in the public-service institutions tend to be business executives. But it is by no means certain that business's own service institutions are any more effective than the public-service bureaucracies.

In the last twenty years, staff activities, planning departments, coordinators, and management information systems have snowballed in all large corporations. Judged by their ability to get their budgets funded, they have been tremendous successes. Many also have truly impressive functional knowledge, employ men of great ability and competence, and are producing a rapidly growing literature. However, it is by no means clear that many of them make a contribution. Worse still, I would not know in most cases how to judge their performance or how to measure their results—nor do they themselves.

As the service staffs have been growing, the whole staff concept has come under increasing attack. The concept certainly does not perform as its original designers fifty years ago expected it to work—any more than the American government agency performs as the liberal enthusiasts of government activism in the New Deal days of the thirties or the intellectuals of the Kennedy Administration in the sixties expected it to perform.

Research activities in business have grown perhaps even faster than service staffs. And so has government-sponsored research in the universities and in separate research institutes. With respect to research, too, disenchantment has set in. Far too many companies have little to show except beautiful buildings for all the research money they spent. Worse still, it is the rare research department that can answer the question, "And what have you *contributed*?"—and uncommon to find a research department that asks this question.

### Are Service Institutions Managed?

The service institutions themselves have become "management conscious." Service institutions increasingly turn to business to learn management. In all service institutions, manager development, management by objectives, and many other concepts and tools of business management are now common.

This is a healthy sign but it does not mean that the service institutions understand the problems of managing themselves. It only means that they begin to realize that at present they are not being managed.

### But Are They Manageable?

There is another and very different response to the performance crisis of the service institutions. A growing number of critics, especially among the disenchanted liberals of yesterday, have come to the conclusion that service institutions are inherently unmanageable and incapable of performance.

The most radical expression of this conclusion is the demand to deschool society, first voiced by the former priest Ivan Illich, and most clearly presented by the teacher and educational critic John Holt.* Schools, Illich and Holt agree, cannot perform and cannot be made to perform. If only schools were abolished, children would learn.

This is, of course, another "noble savage" fantasy. Society was "deschooled" not so long ago—not much more than a century ago. We have ample documents from this "preschool" era, e.g., the copious investigations into the life and development of children in early Victorian England, or in mid-nineteenth-century Germany. There is precious little support in these documents for the belief that children will become creative and learn by themselves if only they are not subjected to the mismanagement of the school. Schools at all levels do indeed need drastic changes. But what we need is not a "nonschool," but a properly functioning and properly managed learning institution.†

There is no possibility that we can or will do away with the service institutions. There is not the slightest evidence that today's society is willing to do without the contributions the service institutions are created to provide. The very people who preach deschooling society want more rather than less education. The people who most vocally attack the shortcomings

---

*John Holt, *Freedom and Beyond* (Dutton, 1972).

†On this see my article "What We Already Know About Tomorrow's School," in *Psychology Today*, June, 1972.

of the hospitals want more and better health care. The voters who are most bitter about government bureaucracy vote for more government programs. Similarly, business is not going to do without the contribution of knowledge, expertise, and systematic thinking which service staffs and research departments are intended to furnish.

We have no choice but to learn to manage the service institutions for performance.

*And they can be managed for performance.*

## The Importance of the Exceptions

Performance in the service institution—whether public service or service staff in business—is the exception rather than the rule. But there are exceptions, and they prove that service institutions can perform.

Several examples of performing service institutions will be discussed in Chapter 13, "The Exceptions and Their Lessons," but a few might be mentioned here. Among American government agencies of the last forty years, two performers stand out: the Tennessee Valley Authority (TVA), the big regional electric-power and irrigation project in the Southeastern United States (especially during its early years, in the thirties and forties, when it was headed by David Lilienthal), and in the sixties, the National Aeronautics and Space Agency (NASA), which managed the American space program. Among universities attempting mass higher education some of the new English "red brick" universities (e.g., the University of Bradford, especially in engineering and management education) have been notably effective. While a great many—perhaps most—schools in the inner-city, Black ghettos of America deserve all the strictures of the deschooling movement, a few schools in the very worst ghettos (e.g., in New York's South Bronx) have shown high capacity to make the most disadvantaged children acquire the basic skills of literacy.

What then is it that inhibits the typical service institution from performing? And what is it that the few performing service institutions do—or eschew—that makes them capable of performance? These are the questions to ask, and they are *management* questions.

Managing the service institutions for performance will increasingly be seen as the central managerial challenge of a developed society, and as its greatest managerial need.

The service institution does not differ much from a business enterprise in any area other than its specific mission. It faces very similar—if not the same—challenges to make work productive and the workers achieving. It does not differ significantly from a business in its social responsibility.

The term social responsibility used to be reserved for the relationship between business and its social environment. Indeed, the original term read "the social responsibilities of business." Recent events have shown that the service institutions face the same problems in their relationship with the environment and with society, whether they be university, government agency, school, or hospital. The worst polluters today are, after all, governments—local governments with inadequate sewer plants. What will be discussed later in this book (in the section titled "Social Impacts and Social Responsibilities" on p. 312) applies with little modification to all institutions, public or private.

Nor does the service institution differ very much from business enterprise with respect to the manager's work and job, organization design and structure, or even the job and structure of top management. Internally the differences tend to be differences in terminology rather than in substance.

But the service institution is different fundamentally from business in its "business." It is different in its purpose. It has different values. It needs different objectives, and it makes a different contribution to society. Performance and results are quite different in a service institution from what they are in a business. Managing for performance is the one area in which the service institution differs significantly from a business.

We have no coherent theory of institutions and their management that would encompass the service institution. Compared to the work done in business management over the last seventy years, little has been done on the management of the service institution. All we can attempt so far is a first sketch.

We do understand why the service institution has difficulty performing. And we can define what is needed to offset the built-in obstacles in the service institution to performance and results.

# 12

## Why Service Institutions Do Not Perform

*The Three Popular Explanations—They Are Not Businesslike—They Need Better Men—Results Are Intangible—All Three Are Alibis Rather Than Explanations—What Makes the Service Institution Different—Misdirection by Budget—What Performance and Results Mean in the Budget-Based Institution or Staff—Earning One's Way versus Deserving It*

There are three popular explanations for the common failure of service institutions to perform:

—their managers aren't businesslike;
—they need better men;
—their objectives and results are intangible.

All three are alibis rather than explanations.

1. The service institution will perform, it is said again and again, if only it is managed in a businesslike manner.

Colbert, the great minister of Louis XIV, first blamed the performance difficulties of the nonbusiness, the service institution, on this lack of businesslike management. Colbert, who created the first modern public service in the West, never ceased to exhort his officials to be businesslike. The cry is still repeated every day—by chambers of commerce, by presidential and royal commissions, by ministers in the communist countries, and so on. If only, they all say, their administrators were to behave like businessmen, service institutions would perform. This belief underlies today's management boom in the service institutions. It is the wrong diagnosis, and being businesslike is the wrong prescription for the ills of the service institution.

The service institution has performance trouble precisely because it is not a business. What businesslike means in a service institution is control of cost. What characterizes a business, however, is control by performance and results. It is *effectiveness and not efficiency which the service institution lacks.* Effectiveness cannot be obtained by businesslike behavior as the term is understood, that is, by greater efficiency.

To be sure, there is need for efficiency in all institutions. Because there is usually no competition in the service field, there is no outward and imposed cost control on service institutions as there is for business in a competitive (and even an oligopolistic) market. But the basic problem of service institutions is not high cost but lack of effectiveness. They may be very efficient—some are. But they tend not to do the right things.

The belief that the service institution will perform if only it is put on a businesslike basis underlies the many attempts to set up such services as separate public corporations—again an attempt that dates back to Colbert and his establishment of crown monopolies (the so-called *Régies*). There may be beneficial side effects such as freedom from petty civil-service regulation. But the intended main effect, performance, is seldom achieved. Costs may go down (though not always; setting up London Transport and the British Post Office as separate businesslike corporations, and thereby highly vulnerable to labor-union pressures, has, for instance, led to skyrocketing costs). Services essential to the fulfillment of the institution's purpose may be slighted or lopped off in the name of efficiency.

The best and worst example of the businesslike approach in the public-service institution may well be the Port of New York Authority, set up in the twenties to manage automobile and truck traffic throughout the two-state area (New York and New Jersey) of the Port of New York. The Port Authority has from the beginning been businesslike with a will. The engineering of its bridges, tunnels, docks, silos, and, later on, airports, has been outstanding. Its construction costs have been low and under control. Its financial standing is extremely high so that it could always borrow at most advantageous rates of interest. Being businesslike—as measured, above all, by its standing with the banks—is its goal and purpose. It did not concern itself with transportation policy in the New York metropolitan area even though its bridges, tunnels, and airports generate much of the traffic on New York's streets. It did not ask, "Who are our constituents?" Instead it resisted any such question as political and unbusinesslike. In the end it has come to be seen as the villain of the New York traffic and transportation problem. When the Port Authority needed help, e.g., in finding a place for New York's badly needed fourth airport, it found itself without a single supporter, except the bankers. Consequently, the Port Authority may well become politicized—denuded of its efficiency without gaining anything in effectiveness.

2. The cry for better people is probably even older than Colbert. It can be found in the earliest Chinese texts on government. It has been the constant demand of all American reformers, from Henry Adams, shortly after the Civil War, to Ralph Nader today. They all have believed that the one thing lacking in the government agency is better people.

Service institutions can no more than businesses depend on supermen or lion tamers to staff their managerial and executive positions. There are far too many institutions to be staffed. It is absurd to expect that the administrator of every hospital in the world be a genius or even a great man. If service institutions cannot be run and managed by men of normal and fairly low endowment; if, in other words, we cannot organize the task so that it will be done adequately by men who only try hard, it cannot be done at all.

There is no reason to believe that the people who staff the managerial and professional positions in our service institutions are any less qualified, any less competent or honest, or any less hard-working than the men who manage businesses. Conversely, there is no reason to believe that business managers, put in control of service institutions, would do better than the "bureaucrats." Indeed, we know that they immediately become bureaucrats themselves.

In World War II large numbers of American business executives who had performed very well in their own companies moved into government positions. Many rapidly became bureaucrats; the men did not change, but whereas they had been capable of obtaining performance and results in a business, in government they found themselves primarily producing procedures and red tape—and deeply frustrated.

An even better proof that there is little to the argument that what the service institutions need are better people is the French government service. No other government service can draw on a similar elite for its senior positions. Positions of influence and importance in the French government service are reserved for the brilliant graduates of France's most prestigious school, the École Polytechnique. Yet few government services are as ineffectual and as bureaucratic as the French, despite the brilliant *polytechniciens* who run them. The *fonctionnaire,* the government employee who runs his office to suit his convenience, is the butt of the most bitter French jokes— and deservedly so, as anyone who has ever tried to get a French government service to perform knows only too well. Yet the *polytechniciens* themselves do not become bureaucrats. Twenty years after they have entered government service, when they have risen to the top, most of them traditionally move over into the top positions in the major French companies and prove themselves, as a rule, capable of high performance.

The *polytechnicien* may not be to everybody's liking. He tends, in the manner of scholastic elites, to be intellectually arrogant, somewhat narrow, and rather smug. Yet, the problem of the French government service is surely not the lack of good men, nor is anything likely to happen by bringing in better men. The fault is in the system and not in the men.

3. The most sophisticated and, at first glance, the most plausible explanation for the nonperformance of service institutions is the last one: the objectives of service institutions are "intangible" and so are their results. This is at best a half-truth.

The definition of what "our business is" is always intangible, for a business as well as for a service institution. To say, as Sears, Roebuck does, "Our business is to be the informed buyer for the American family" is intangible. To say, as Marks & Spencer did, "Our business is to subvert the British class system" is surely not tangible. To say, as Vail did at Bell Telephone, "Our business is service to the customer" may sound like pious platitude. At first glance these statements would seem to defy any attempt at translation into operational, let alone into quantitative, terms. To say, "Our business is electronic information," as Sony of Japan does, is equally intangible, as is IBM's definition of its business as data processing. Yet as these businesses have shown, it is not too difficult to derive from such intangible definitions concrete and measurable goals and targets.

"Saving souls" as the definition of the objectives of a church is intangible. At least the bookkeeping is not of this world. But church attendance is measurable. And so is "getting the young people back into the church."

"The development of the whole personality" as the objective of the school is, indeed, intangible. But "teaching a child to read by the time he has finished third grade" is by no means intangible and can be measured easily and with considerable precision.

"To abolish racial discrimination" is equally difficult of clear operational definition, let alone of measurement. But to increase the number of Black apprentices in the building trades is a quantifiable goal, the attainment or nonattainment of which can be measured.

"Economic and social development of an underdeveloped nation" is intangible. But, "creating 100,000 jobs in five years" or "building 40,000 housing units a year" is tangible indeed.

Achievement is never possible except against specific, limited, clearly defined targets, in business as well as in a service institution. Only if targets are defined can resources be allocated to their attainment, priorities and deadlines set, and somebody be held accountable for results. But the starting point for effective work is a definition of the purpose and mission of the institution, which is almost always intangible.

"What is our business?" is as ambiguous and as controversial a question for a business as it is for a service institution. As has been said earlier, there has to be dissent and controversy before a viable definition is found. Service institutions have a great many constituents. The school is of vital concern not only to children and their parents, but to teachers, to taxpayers, to the community at large. Similarly the hospital has to satisfy the patient, but also the doctors, the nurses, the technicians, the patient's family—and again taxpayers or, as in the United States, employers and labor unions who together provide the bulk of the support of most hospitals through their insurance contributions. But business also has a plurality of constituencies. Every business, as said before, has at least two different customers, and often a good many more. And employees, investors, and the community at large—and management itself—are also constituencies.

## Misdirection by Budget

The one basic difference between a service institution and a business is the way the service institution is paid.

Businesses (other than monopolies) are paid for satisfying the customer. They are paid only when they produce what the customer wants and what he is willing to exchange his purchasing power for. Satisfaction of the customer is, therefore, the basis for assuring performance and results in a business.

Service institutions, by contrast, are typically paid out of a budget allocation. This means that they are not paid for what taxpayer and customer mean by results and performance. Their revenues are allocated from a general revenue stream which is not tied to what they are doing but obtained by tax, levy, or tribute.

This is as true for the service institution within a business as it is, for instance, for the public school. The typical staff department is not being paid for its results. It is, as a rule, not even paid according to the extent to which its customers, that is, the managers, use it. It is being paid—in many cases inevitably so—out of an overhead allocation, that is, out of a budget. The fact that the service institution within a business tends to exhibit the same characteristics and to indulge in the same behavior as service institutions in the public sector indicates that it is not business that makes the difference. It is the mode of payment.

The typical service institution—including most service staffs in business —are furthermore endowed with monopoly powers. The intended beneficiary has no choice. Most service institutions have power beyond what the most monopolistic business enjoys.

If I am dissatisfied with the service of the local power company or of the telephone company, I have no other place to go to for electric power or telephone service. But if I choose to do without either power or telephone, I do not have to pay for it; and one can still survive as an individual without either—though this freedom is increasingly theoretical rather than practical. This choice is not true, however, of most service institutions. There the customer pays whether he wants to use the service or not. Behind the service institution stands the police power of the state, which exacts payment, not for services rendered but for the support of a governmental agency.

Most service staffs in business have coercive monopoly power too. Operating managers know that they are largely being judged by how well they cooperate with the staff services; and only rarely are they permitted to go elsewhere than their own company's staff service for advice or expertise in the staff service's area.

The American household pays school taxes whether it has children of school age or not. Parents may choose to send their children to a private or a parochial school but they still pay taxes for the public school, even though they do not use it and consider it inappropriate or unsatisfactory for their own children.

Being paid out of a budget allocation changes what is meant by performance, or results. Results in the budget-based institution mean a larger budget. Performance is the ability to maintain or to increase one's budget. Results, as the term is commonly understood, that is, contributions to the market or achievement toward goal and objectives, are, in effect, secondary. The first test of a budget-based institution and the first requirement for its survival is to obtain the budget. And the budget is not, by definition, related to contribution but to good intentions.

## When Efficiency Is a Sin

Efficiency and cost control, however much they are being preached, are not really considered virtues in the budget-based institution. The importance of a budget-based institution is measured essentially by the size of its budget and the size of its staff. To achieve results with a smaller budget or a smaller staff is, therefore, not performance. It might actually endanger the institution. Not to spend the budget to the hilt will only convince the budget maker—whether legislature or the budget committee of a company—that the budget for the next fiscal period can safely be cut.

Thirty or forty years ago it was considered characteristic of Russian planning, and one of its major weaknesses, that Soviet managers, toward the end of the plan period, engaged in a frantic effort to spend all the money allocated to them, which usually resulted in total waste. Today the disease has become universal as budget-based institutions have become dominant everywhere. End-of-year pressure on the executive of a budget-based institution certainly accounts for a good deal of the waste in the American defense effort. And "buying-in," that is, getting approval for a new program or project by grossly underestimating its total cost, is also built into the budget-based institution.

"Parkinson's Law" lampooned the British Admiralty and the British Colonial Office for increasing their staffs and their budgets as fast as their work and role were shrinking, that is, as fast as the British Navy and the British Empire went down. Parkinson's Law attributed this to inborn human perversity. But it is perfectly natural behavior for someone on a budget. It is the budget, after all, that measures performance and importance.

It is not compatible with efficiency for the acid test of performance to be obtaining the budget; that as a consequence, administrators are subtly discouraged from trying to do the job cheaply and efficiently, and are, indeed, likely to be penalized for doing so; and that they are forever encouraged to "buy in." Yet these are the consequences of being budget-based.

But effectiveness is even more endangered by reliance on the budget allocation. It makes it dangerous to raise the question what the business of the institution should be. The question is always controversial; but controversy is likely to alienate support and will, therefore, be shunned by the budget-based institution. At best the institution will achieve effectiveness by deceiving the public and itself.

The U.S. Department of Agriculture, for instance, has never been willing to ask whether its goal should be farm productivity or support of the small family farm. It has known for decades that these two objectives are not identical as had originally been assumed, and that they are becoming increasingly incompatible. To admit this, however, would have created controversy that might have endangered the Department's budget. As a result, American farm policy has frittered away an enormous amount of money and human resources on what can only (and charitably) be called a public relations campaign, that is, on a show of support for the small family farmer. Its effective activities, however—and they have been very effective indeed—have been directed toward eliminating the small family farmer and replacing him by the far more productive "agrobusinesses," that is, large, highly capitalized and highly mechanized farms, run as businesses and not as a "way of life." This emphasis may have been right, but it was not what the Department was founded to do, nor what the legislators, in approving the Department's budget, expected it to do.

The farm policy of the Common Market today faces the same dilemma —and, again, tries to obscure it by substituting money for policy, and public relations for performance.

The American community hospital is not governmental but private, though nonprofit. Yet, like hospitals everywhere, it presents the same confusion of missions and objectives, with the resulting impairment of effectiveness and performance.

Should a hospital be, in effect, a physician's plant facility—as most older American physicians maintain? Should it be a community health center? Should it focus on the major health needs of a community or try to do everything and be abreast of every medical advance, no matter how costly and how rarely used the facility will be? Should it focus on preventive medicine and on health education for the community? Or should it concentrate on the repair of health damage that has already been done?

Every one of these definitions of the business of the hospital can be defended. Every one deserves a hearing. The effective hospital will certainly be a multipurpose institution and strike a balance between various objectives. What most hospitals do, however, is pretend that there are no basic questions to be decided. The result, predictably, is confusion and impairment of the capacity of the hospital to serve any function and to carry out any mission.

A service organization within a business has the same tendency to avoid controversy over function, mission, and objectives.

Is it the first function of the personnel department to obtain the most effective utilization of the company's human resources? Or is the personnel department a welfare department and babysitter? Is the purpose of the personnel department to make employees accept the policies, rules, and regulations of the company? Or is the purpose to help develop the organization structure and job structure that make sense for the employee and will enable him to develop and achieve? All these are legitimate definitions of the personnel job. Each could be the foundation for a truly effective personnel department. But practically no personnel department I know will face up to these questions. They are controversial. As a result, the personnel department says different things to different constituents. It is likely to end up ineffectual and frustrated.*

Being dependent on a budget allocation militates against setting priorities and concentrating efforts, yet nothing is ever accomplished unless scarce resources are concentrated on a small number of priorities.

A shoe manufacturer who has 22 percent of the market for work shoes may have a profitable business. If he succeeds in raising his market share to 30 percent, especially if the market for his kind of footwear is expanding, he is doing very well indeed. He need not concern himself too much with the 70 percent of the users of work shoes who buy from somebody else. And the customers for ladies' fashion shoes are of no concern to him at all.

Contrast this with the situation of an institution on a budget. To obtain its budget, it needs the approval, or at least the acquiescence, of practically everybody who remotely could be considered a constituent. Where a market share of 22 percent might be perfectly satisfactory to a business, a rejection by 78 percent of the constituents—or even a much smaller proportion—would be absolutely fatal to a budget-based institution. It might survive if 22 percent of its constituents do not actively support it. But it certainly

*On this see Chapter 23.

would consider itself in serious danger if it could not get a larger base of support, or at least of acquiescence. And this means that the service institution cannot concentrate; it must instead try to placate everyone.

An extreme case is the police department in the large American city. It knows what its priorities should be. In the residential neighborhood, for instance, the first priority might be safety on the streets. This is an attainable goal—what is needed primarily is an increase in the number of policemen on patrol. In the slums of the inner city, the first priority would probably be safety in the home, that is, protection against rape, burglary, and theft. This is a much more difficult objective to attain, especially in crowded tenements, with their large numbers of drug addicts desperate for money, though measurable progress toward the goal can be made. But there is the old lady who phones in that a cat is caught in a tree outside her home. There is the respectable householder who has locked himself out and wants the police to open his door for him. There is the householder who complains about the noisy party next door, and so on. Every desk sergeant who answers such calls knows that he should say, "We are public servants, not private servants," but this answer is never given. The old lady, after all, would immediately telephone her councilman and complain that she, a taxpayer, does not even receive courteous treatment from the police. As a result, every police force in the country, while it knows what the priorities should be and where it should concentrate its slender resources, splinters itself—indeed, it may have no choice. This means, however, that there is neither safety on the streets in the residential suburb nor safety in the home in the slums.

Finally, being budget-based makes it even more difficult to abandon the wrong things, the old, the obsolete. As a result, service institutions are even more encrusted than businesses with the barnacles of inherently unproductive efforts.

No institution likes to abandon anything it does. Business is no exception. In an institution that is being paid for its performance and results and that stands, therefore, under a performance test, the unproductive, the obsolete, will sooner or later be killed off by the customers. In a budget-based institution no such discipline is being enforced. On the contrary; what such an institution does is always virtuous and likely to be considered in the public interest.

The temptation is great, therefore, to respond to lack of results by redoubling efforts. The temptation is great to double the budget, precisely because there is no performance. The temptation, above all, is to blame the outside world for its stupidity or its reactionary resistance, and to consider lack of results a proof of one's own righteousness and a reason in itself for keeping on with the good work.

The tendency to perpetuate the unproductive is by no means confined to service institutions in the public sector. It is just as common in staff services within today's large business enterprise. The organization planner, the computer specialist, or the operations researcher all tend to argue that the resistance of operating managers to their wares is *prima facie* evidence of the need for their services and reason for doubling the "missionary effort." Sometimes this argument is, of course, valid. But more often than not it makes impossible concentration of efforts on the areas where performance and results are both needed and attainable.

All service institutions are threatened by the tendencies to cling to yesterday rather than to slough it off, and to put their best and ablest people on defending what no longer makes sense or serves a purpose. Government is particularly prone to this disease.*

Underlying traditional political theory is the axiom that the functions of government are eternal. There is an implicit belief, held almost with the strength of dogma, that whatever government does is for all times. Yet government is a human activity. Everything human beings do, except their biological and spiritual functions, obsoletes sooner or later. The proper rule for government today, as for all other institutions, is not, "Whatever we do we'll do forever"; the proper rule is, "Whatever we do today will in all likelihood be a candidate for abandonment within a fairly short period of years."

## Earned or Deserved Revenue

Human beings will behave as they are being rewarded—whether the reward is money and promotion, a medal, the autographed picture of the boss, or a pat on the back. This is the one lesson the behavioral psychologist has taught us during the last fifty years (not that it was unknown before). A business or any institution which is paid for its results and performance in such a way that the dissatisfied or disinterested customer need not pay has to earn its income. An institution which is financed by a budget—or which enjoys a monopoly which the customer cannot escape—is rewarded for what it deserves rather than for what it earns. It is paid for good intentions and for "programs." It is paid for not alienating important constituents rather than for satisfying any one group. It is misdirected by the way it is being paid into defining performance and results as what will produce the budget rather than as what will produce contribution.

This is an inherent characteristic of the budget-based institution. Amazingly enough, it has escaped the attention of the economists—perhaps

---

*See on this my book, *The Age of Discontinuity* (1969), especially Chapter 6, "The Sickness of Government."

because so few of them seem to be aware of the fact that upwards of 50 percent of the gross national product these days does not go to businesses, that is, to institutions paid for performance and results, but rather to service institutions paid for promises or, at best, for efforts.

Being based on a budget is not necessarily bad or even undesirable. Self-supporting armies, for instance, such as the armies of the fifteenth century or the traditional armies of the Chinese warlords, had forever to engage in warfare, terrorize the citizens of their own nation, and depend on looting and raping for their support. Such armies can never be instruments of policy. Civilian control and defense budgets paid out of taxes were instituted precisely to stop free enterprise in warfare.

Similarly, most service staffs in business will have to be on a budget allocation. It is the only desirable basis for a research laboratory. To pay a research laboratory for results, for instance, in the form of a royalty on the sales of the new products and processes it produces (as has been tried in several businesses) is almost certain to misdirect the research laboratory even more than the budget allocation does. It is likely to deflect resources from research into gadgetry. But there is also no question that budget allocation induces research directors to inflate the research staff, to come up with an impossible list of projects, and to hang on to projects which are unlikely to produce results or which have proven unproductive.

However necessary or even desirable, being paid out of a budget allocation misdirects. (So does being paid for efforts—as are hospitals or universities—that is, for costs rather than for results.) In many, perhaps in most cases, this cannot be eliminated. But it can be limited, counteracted, and, in large measure, even offset.

# 13

# The Exceptions and Their Lessons

*The Exceptions: Bell Telephone; the Nineteenth-Century American University; TVA; Meiji Japan—The Market Approach and "Socialist Competition"—The Limits of the Market—"Public Policy" Is Not Enough—The Special Problem of the Old, Obsolete, and Unproductive—The Danger of Yesterday's Success*

The exception, the comparatively rare service institution that achieves effectiveness, matters as much as the great majority which achieve only procedures. For the exception provides the lessons. It shows that effectiveness in the service institution is achievable—though by no means easy. It shows what different kinds of service institutions can do and need to do. It shows limitations and pitfalls. But it also shows that the service-institution manager can do unpopular and highly controversial things only if he himself faces up to the risk-taking decision as to what the business of his institution is, will be, and should be.

## Bell Telephone

The first and perhaps simplest example is that of the Bell Telephone System. A telephone system is a natural monopoly. Within a given area, one supplier of telephone service must have exclusive rights. The one thing any subscriber to a public telephone service requires is access to all other subscribers, which means territorial exclusivity for one monopolistic service. As a whole country or continent becomes in effect one telephone system, this monopoly has to be extended over larger and larger areas.

An individual may be able to do without a telephone—though in today's society only at prohibitive inconvenience. But a professional man, a tradesman, an office, or a business must have a telephone. Residential phone service may still be an option. Business phone service is compulsory.

Theodore Vail, as has been said earlier, saw this in the early years of this century. He also saw that the American Telephone Company, like the telephone systems in all other industrially developed nations, could easily be taken over by government. To prevent this, Vail thought through what the telephone company's business was and should be, and came up with his famous definition: "Our business is service."

This statement of the Telephone Company's business then enabled Vail to set specific goals and objectives and to develop measurements of performance and results in terms of his definition of what the business was and should be. His customer-satisfaction standards and service-satisfaction standards created, in effect, nationwide competition between telephone managers in various areas. The standards became the measurements by which the managers were judged and rewarded. As a result, the Telephone Company's managers were directed, despite the monopolistic nature of their company, toward performance and results.

Vail's solution worked for more than half a century. Until the inflationary squeeze of the sixties, the Bell System steadily improved service while lowering rates.

Vail did something even more heretical for his day (and, by and large, even for this day). He identified Bell's constituencies. The regulatory agencies, i.e., the public utility commissions of the various states, had been considered "pernicious socialism" and the "enemy" by any right-thinking businessman of his day. Vail, however, decided that the public was, indeed, a legitimate constituency, so that it was the job of the telephone company to make the regulatory agencies function. He tried to think through what their objectives were and should be. There is little doubt that the Bell System would have been nationalized long ago if the American public did not feel that the regulatory agencies had been doing their job, albeit fitfully. There is also little doubt that but for Vail and his recognition of the regulatory agencies as a distinct constituency, the American public utility commissions would never have acquired the capacity to function and the ability to understand their own work.*

*What the "Regulatory Commission" is may need a word of explanation even for American readers: outside the U.S. the institution is largely unknown. First devised in the 1880s to regulate railroads and grain terminals, the function of the regulatory agency is to make private enterprise function in the public interest under conditions of "natural" monopoly where competition cannot effectively do the job. These agencies, by and large, have three functions: to maintain as far as feasible competition in a service area; to protect the public against

## The American University

The building of the modern American university from 1860 to World War I also illustrates how service institutions are made to perform. The American university as it emerged during that period is primarily the work of a small number of men: Andrew W. White (president of Cornell, 1868–1885); Charles W. Eliot (president of Harvard, 1869–1909); Daniel Coit Gilman (president of Johns Hopkins, 1876–1901); David Starr Jordan (president of Stanford, 1891–1913); William Rainey Harper (president of Chicago, 1892–1904); and Nicholas Murray Butler (president of Columbia, 1902–1945).

These men all had in common one basic insight: the traditional college —essentially an eighteenth-century seminary to train preachers—had become totally obsolete, sterile, and unproductive. It was dying fast; America in 1860 had far fewer college students than it had had forty years earlier for a much smaller population. The men who built the new universities shared a common objective: to create a new institution, a true university. They all realized that while European examples, especially Oxford and Cambridge and the German universities, had much to offer, these new universities had to be *American* institutions.

Beyond these shared beliefs, however, they differed sharply on what a university should be and what its purpose and mission were.

Eliot, at Harvard, saw the purpose of the university in educating a leadership group with a distinct style. His Harvard was to be a national institution rather than the parochial preserve of the "proper Bostonian," for whom Harvard College had been founded. But it also was to restore to Boston—and to New England—the dominance of a moral elite, such as had been held by the "Elect," the Puritan divines, and their successors, the Federalist leaders in the early days of the Republic. Butler at Columbia— and to a lesser degree Harper at Chicago—saw the function of the university as the systematic application of rational thought and analysis to the basic problems of a modern society—education, economics, government, foreign affairs. Gilman at Johns Hopkins saw the university as the producer of advanced knowledge; originally Johns Hopkins was to confine itself to

exploitation by "natural" monopolies through control of prices and service standards; and to limit the earnings of "natural" monopolies, whether railroads, airlines, power companies, or broadcasters, to a "fair return" geared to the cost of capital. The "regulatory agency" thus presents an attempt to find a "third way" between the uncontrolled private monopoly and— equally uncontrolled—government monopoly. Regulatory commissions exist both at the federal level and in the various states; the commissioners are either government-appointed (as on all federal commissions) or elected, as in many states.

advanced research and was to give no undergraduate instruction. White at Cornell aimed at producing an educated public, and so on.

Each of these men knew that he had to make compromises. Each knew that he had to satisfy a number of constituencies and publics, each of whom looked at the university quite differently. Both Eliot and Butler, for instance, had to build their new universities on existing, old foundations (the others could build from the ground up) and had to satisfy—or at least to placate—existing alumni and existing faculty. They all had to be exceedingly conscious of the need to attract and hold financial support.

It was Eliot with all his insistence on "moral leadership" who invented the first placement office and set out to find for the Harvard graduates well-paid jobs, especially in business. It was Butler, conscious that Columbia was a latecomer and that the millionaire philanthropists of his day had already been snared by his competitors (e.g., Rockefeller by Chicago), who invented the first public relations office in a university, designed—and most successfully—to reach the merely well-to-do and get their money.

Each of these men gave priority to his definition of the university's purpose and mission. These definitions did not outlive the founders. Even during the lifetime of Eliot and Butler, for instance, their institutions escaped their control, began to diffuse objectives and to confuse priorities. In this century all these universities—and many others, e.g., California and other major state universities—have converged toward a common type.

Today it is hard to tell one "multiversity" from another. Yet the imprint of the founders has still not been totally erased. It is hardly an accident that the New Deal picked primarily faculty members from Columbia and Chicago to be high-level advisers and policy-makers; for the New Deal was, of course, committed to the application of rational thought and analysis to public policies and problems. Thirty years later when the Kennedy Administration came in with an underlying belief in the "style" of an elite, it naturally turned to Harvard.

In 1860 higher education in America hardly existed; and what existed was discredited and unsupported by the public. By 1900 the American university had become established as a leader, a major power center, and as an intellectual, social, and political authority. In 1860 America had a smaller proportion of its young people in college than any other leading country; by 1900 it already had a larger proportion in its colleges and the foundations for mass higher education were being laid. In 1860 America depended for scholarship, research, and science on Europe; Americans who distinguished themselves in such pursuits (e.g., Francis Parkman as a historian, Emerson as a philosopher, or Joseph Henry as a physicist) had no university connection. And America's pride was the self-taught inventors. By 1900 America had attained both achievement and self-confidence in scholarship, research, and science. Men of intellectual or scientific distinction (e.g., William James in philosophy, John Dewey in education, Charles Beard and Frederick J. Turner in history, Albert Michelson in physics) were all members of a university. At the same time the American university of 1900 was a distinctly American institution, no matter how many of its professors had done their graduate work in Germany, or how many could be heard to sigh for the Oxford amenities of high table and port.

What underlay this example of high effectiveness and high achievement was, above all, a clear commitment to one specific definition of purpose and mission.

## Lilienthal and the TVA

A different but equally instructive example is that of the Tennessee Valley Authority (TVA, the public utility and public works complex in the south-central United States). Built mainly in New Deal days, the TVA today is no longer controversial. It is just another large power company except for being owned by the government rather than by private investors. This was not the case in its early days, forty years ago. Then the TVA was a slogan, a battle cry, a symbol. Some, friends and enemies alike, saw in it the opening wedge of the nationalization of electric energy in the United States. Others saw in it the vehicle for a return to Jeffersonian agrarianism based on cheap power, government paternalism, and free fertilizer. Others still were primarily interested in flood control and navigation. There was such a wealth of conflicting expectations that TVA's first head, Arthur Morgan, a distinguished engineer and economist, floundered completely. Unable to think through what the business of the TVA should be and how varying objectives might be balanced, Morgan accomplished nothing. Finally, President Roosevelt replaced him with an almost totally unknown young lawyer with little previous experience as an administrator, David Lilienthal.

Lilienthal faced up to the need to define TVA's business. He concluded that the first objective was to build truly efficient electric plants and to supply an energy-starved region with plentiful and cheap power. All the rest, he decided, hinged on the attainment of this first need, which then became his operational priority. Today TVA has accomplished many other objectives as well, flood control, navigable waterways, fertilizer production, and even balanced community development. But it was Lilienthal's insistence on a clear definition of TVA's business and on setting priorities that explains why TVA is now taken for granted, even by those who, forty years ago, were its implacable enemies.

## The Lesson of Meiji

The most important example of service-institution performance may be the development of Japan in the second half of the nineteenth century, after the so-called Meiji Restoration of 1868. Thirty years later Japan, previously an exceedingly poor and largely rural country, encased in a rigid straitjacket of class and caste, had become a modern nation, a major military power capable of defeating Imperial Russia, and a major factor in world trade. At the same time it had become the first country in which illiteracy was virtually unknown.

The Meiji statesmen, patriots, and business leaders who brought about this transformation included no more than a handful of truly remarkable men. But, of course, these were still a tiny minority even within the leadership group. The job was done by ordinary, competent, hard-working men. What explains their success was the willingness of the Meiji generation to think through objectives, to set a few priorities, and to concentrate on them.

The purpose of the Meiji Restoration was defined as the preservation of Japanese independence and of Japanese culture and tradition in a world dominated by Western imperialism. These objectives were summarized in the slogan "a wealthy country, a strong army," which required general literacy and uniform local administration and justice throughout the country. The five goals of economic growth, modern army and navy, literacy, uniform local government, and a strong professional judiciary became the priorities on which the men of Meiji concentrated.

One can quarrel with these priorities—a great many Japanese and foreign critics have done so. Little was done, for instance, to improve the peasant's lot or to cushion the poor against the upheavals of forced-draft industrialization. Little was done to make the highly literate new Japanese middle class capable of self-government. The men of Meiji were conscious of these omissions but they decided deliberately that there had to be priorities, thought through what they should be, and then concentrated on them the energies of a gifted, hard-working, and patriotic people.

There are other examples. To illustrate effectiveness in a university, for instance, Wilhelm von Humboldt's founding of the University of Berlin in the darkest days of German defeat by Napoleon might be mentioned. Another example, as said before, is some of the new English "red brick" universities, founded since World War II as a result, largely, of the thinking on objectives and priorities done by a distinguished economist, Lionel Robbins. The few New York ghetto schools in which the kids learn have also been mentioned earlier. Another example from education would be the Folk High School, which the Danish Bishop Nikolaj Grundtvig conceived almost

150 years ago, and which became the foundation both for the evolution of the Scandinavian countries into model democracies and for all continuing education today. I might have taken a few examples of service effectiveness from other areas, e.g., health care or research labs.

Each of these effective public-service institutions can be said to be *sui generis.* Each is certainly completely different. But these examples demonstrate that service institutions can be managed for performance.

## Market Approach and "Socialist Competition"

Our examples illustrate, first, that the task cannot be accomplished on the basis of either one of the traditional and prevailing approaches. Neither the approach that says "Let the market do the job" nor the one that says "Let public interest prevail and drive the money-changers out" can work for the budget-based service institution.

The market approach is commonly considered "capitalist." But this is a misunderstanding. The market approach can equally be "socialist." Whether ownership is in capitalist hands or not is no longer primary. What matters is managerial autonomy and accountability. What matters is whether resources are being allocated to produce results and on the basis of results.

The prevailing idea that the U.S. economy is capitalistic because ownership is private is a misunderstanding. Decisive ownership of American big business is in the hands of the people—that is, in the hands of the mutual funds and pension funds who are the fiduciaries for the middle class and workers. Big business in the U.S. has not been nationalized, but it has largely been socialized. In terms of the classical definition, the U.S. is, at best, a mixed and may steadily be approaching a socialist economy in which the public owns the means of production. But the U.S. manages largely on the basis of local autonomy of the enterprise and allocates resources on the basis of results. It is still a market economy.

Japan conforms even less to the traditional identification of ownership as the determinant. If anyone in Japan can be said to own the big companies, it would be their employees and especially their managers. Since they cannot be dismissed but have lifetime employment, they are what the law calls the beneficial owners even though they have no legal title. Yet, Japan is clearly not a socialist economy.

The most searching discussion of market economics in the last fifty years has not been conducted in the free-enterprise countries or in the free-enterprise camp. It has been the discussion of what is known as socialist competition, that is, competition in an economy in which the means of production are not owned by private capitalists.

This discussion goes back to the years immediately following World War I when the Social Democrats, newly in power, expected to nationalize German business. They set up a powerful Socialization Commission to work out the transition from a capitalist to a socialist economy. The economists on the Socialization Commission were themselves mostly committed socialists. But they had also experienced first-hand the inefficiency, ineffectiveness, and wastefulness of Germany's planned economy during World War I. Instead of a blueprint of a socialist economy, they produced what can only be called a "capitalist manifesto."*

The German Socialization Commission did advocate strong direction by government, but for the economy itself it recommended a basically oligopolistic market economy, in which large privately owned and privately managed companies would compete with each other in each major market.†

This, of course, was totally unacceptable to orthodox Marxists, but the logic was unassailable. Government monopolies, the Germans had shown conclusively, would not produce and would not build a strong economy.

The Russian planning approach, developed a few years later, was designed to answer and to confute this heresy. Another answer, however—and one of greater subtlety and importance—was given by a Polish Marxist, Oscar Lange (who for many years taught at the University of Chicago, before returning after World War II to die in his native country), who called his alternative "socialist competition." Lange's model provides for public ownership of the means of production, thus eliminating the capitalist. But it also provides for autonomous businesses, under their own managements, competing in a market economy and getting paid for results. What Lange said, in other words, is that socialist doctrine demands that ownership be socialized. But the allocation of resources has to be done by performance and results, that is, on the basis of the market test, if an economy is to allocate its resources rationally and be capable of performance.

The one basic weakness of Lange's approach is that it completely omits the market for capital, that is, the allocation of resources to the future. Yet it does introduce accountability and a focus on results. Lange's socialist competition underlies all proposals for liberalization in the Soviet bloc, such

---

*A striking parallel is the impact of World War II on American economists. Most of the economists who joined the World War II economic-control agencies were inclined toward planning and controls when they went in. Their formative experiences and background were, after all, the Depression years. But most came out of the World War II agencies as confirmed enemies of controls and believers in the market, at least as the lesser evil.

†This blueprint, by the way, bears a striking resemblance both to what Adenauer's Germany after World War II adopted as "social market economy" and to the way today's Japan actually runs its "free economy."

as the abortive economic reforms of the Czechs in 1967 and 1968 which provoked Russian military invasion.*

The Russian opposition to the attempts at socialist competition was, of course, not based on arguments of economic rationality and economic performance. It was based on the perfectly valid argument that making business management autonomous will weaken, perhaps fatally, the total political control of the Communist party. Lange, as all economists should do, put performance before power. The rulers of a police state always put power before performance.

Lange's ideas were being converted into reality in Yugoslavia in the late sixties. There major businesses, while nominally owned by the government, are managed autonomously and have to prove themselves in a market in which there is a good deal of competition. Yugoslav businesses are no longer financed directly by allocation on the basis of a national plan. Instead they have to compete for capital on the basis of the expected return on the investment, that is, on a "capitalist" and profit-making basis.

All attempts in the Soviet Union to inject performance into the economy are essentially attempts to introduce Lange's socialist competition, that is, managerial autonomy and accountability based on market performance and market result (though both Lange's name and the term "socialist competition" are still *verboten*). There is little resistance anymore to the argument of the reformers that socialist competition would yield vastly superior economic results; the resistance is to the risk of losing political control.

In other words, the debate over the market and the morality of private ownership for profit is largely becoming irrelevant. The debate should be conducted over the performance capacity of a system under which business is being paid for results and performance as against a system in which it is being financed out of budget allocations. On that score there is essentially no debate. *Wherever a market test is truly possible, it will result in performance and results*—not because of the greater "virtue" of free enterprise or of autonomous managers but because being paid for performance and results directs toward performance and results.

### The Limits of the Market

But it is equally clear that the market is not capable of organizing all institutions.

Service institutions are a most diverse lot. They include natural monopo-

---

*On this see Ota Sik, *Czechoslovakia: The Bureaucratic Economy* (International Arts and Sciences Press, 1972); Sik was the economic architect of the Czech reforms until ousted by the Russians.

lies, which are obviously economic institutions—the telephone service, the postal service, but also the electricity supply in a given area. Service institutions also include the administration of justice and defense, which, equally obviously, are not and should not be economic institutions. The one and only thing they all have in common is that, for one reason or another, they cannot be organized under a competitive market test.*

## The Limits of Public Policy

The traditional conclusion of capitalists and socialists alike has been that where the market cannot provide a performance test, "public policy" will provide guidance and control; but, as our discussion of the impact of the budget basis shows, this is not an adequate answer. To be sure, service institutions, including those within a business, must be controlled by policy. But they need more than programs, promises, good intentions, and hard work, the whole underwritten by a budget. They need a system and structure that directs them toward performance—wherever possible. As our examples show, service institutions also need the discipline of planned obsolescence and planned abandonment of their policies. In every one of our cases, effectiveness was obtained for a time—but not forever.

Vail's solution worked for a half-century—but, as said earlier, it is by no means sure that it works any longer. The American university has outgrown the structure its founders built a century ago. It needs now new thinking about its mission and function, its objective and governance, its priorities and the criteria by which it should measure its accomplishments and results. The TVA has performed so well as to make itself irrelevant. What it pioneered forty years ago is now commonplace; no one any longer expects salvation by electrification.

Japan ultimately became a prisoner of the success of Meiji. The men of Meiji were very conscious that they had chosen priorities and had postponed or subordinated important areas. Their successors refused to consider any other priorities. As a result, military strength, which to the men of Meiji was a means to the end of Japanese independence, became an end in itself and ultimately brought catastrophe on Japan, almost wrecking the great achievement of the Meiji generation.

---

*This may no longer be necessarily true for the postal service; at least an independent postal company in the U.S. is trying to organize a business in competition to the government's postal monopoly. Should this work out, it would do more to restore performance to the mails than setting up a postal monopoly as a separate "public corporation" that is on a "businesslike" basis.

# 14

## Managing Service Institutions for Performance

*Principles of Effectiveness in Service Institutions—How to Apply the Principles—The Three Kinds of Service Institutions and Their Specific Needs—Auditing Objectives and Activities for Organized Abandonment—Managing Service Institutions for Performance*

Different classes of service institutions need different structures. But all of them, we may conclude, need first to impose on themselves such discipline as did the managers and leaders of the institutions in the examples in Chapter 13.

1. They need to define "what is our business and what should it be." They need to bring alternatives of definition into the open, and to think them through carefully, perhaps even to work out (as did the presidents of the emerging American universities) the balance of different and perhaps even conflicting definitions of "what our business is and what it should be."

2. They need to derive *clear objectives and goals* from their definition of function and mission.

3. They then have to think through *priorities* of concentration which enable them to select targets, to set standards of accomplishment and performance, that is, to define the minimum acceptable results; to set deadlines; to go to work on results, and to make someone accountable for results.

4. They need to define *measurements of performance*—the customer-satisfaction measurements of the Telephone Company, or the literacy figures by which the men of Meiji measured their progress.

5. They need to use these measurements to *feed back* on their efforts, that is, to build *self-control from results* into their system.

6. Finally, they need an organized audit of *objectives and results*, so as

to identify those objectives that no longer serve a purpose or have proven unattainable. They need to identify unsatisfactory performance, and activities which are obsolete or unproductive, or both. And, they need a mechanism for *sloughing off* such activities rather than wasting their money and their energies where the results are unsatisfactory.

The last requirement may be the most important one. The absence of a market test removes from the service institution the discipline that forces a business eventually to abandon yesterday—or else go bankrupt. Assessing and abandoning low-performance activities in service institutions, outside and inside business, would be the most painful but also the most salutary innovation.

To test objectives and their appropriateness, priorities, and, above all, results against expectations, is perhaps needed most for yesterday's successes.

No success, as our examples show, is "forever." Yet it is far more difficult to abandon yesterday's success than it is to reappraise failure. Success breeds its own hubris. It creates emotional attachment, habits of mind and action, and, above all, false self-confidence. A success that has outlived its usefulness may, in the end, be more damaging than failure.

In a service institution particularly, yesterday's success becomes "policy," "virtue," "conviction," if not holy writ, unless the institution imposes on itself the discipline of thinking through its mission, its objectives, and its priorities, and of building in feedback control from results and performance on policies, priorities, and action. We are in such a "welfare mess" today in the United States, largely because the welfare program of the New Deal had been such a success in the thirties that we could not abandon it and, instead, misapplied it to the radically different problem of the Black immigrants in the cities in the fifties and sixties.

To make service institutions perform, it should by now be clear, does not require great men. It requires instead a system. The essentials of this system are not too different from the essentials of performance in a business enterprise, but the application will be quite different. The service institutions are not businesses; performance means something quite different in them.

The applications of the essentials will and should differ greatly for different service institutions. As our examples showed—and were meant to show—there are at least *three* different kinds of service institutions—institutions that are not paid for performance and results, but for efforts and programs.

## The Three Kinds of Service Institutions

1. There is first the natural monopoly. It does produce economic goods and services, or at least it is supposed to; yet it cannot be paid for out of results and performance precisely because it is a monopoly.

The economist defines as natural monopoly those businesses which have to have exclusive rights in a given area—the telephone service or the electric power service. But the research laboratory within a business is also a natural monopoly within its business.

2. The next group of service institutions are those that have to be *paid for out of a budget allocation.* While they share a common character, their individual purpose and the specific way in which they try to accomplish it need not be uniform; and the priorities can—and indeed often should—be quite diverse.

The American university is one example. Each of the six university presidents in our case history was concerned with higher education. Each was out to build a university on the ruins of the old, decayed eighteenth-century denominational academy. They all saw alternative missions and functions. Each tried to structure his university so as to give different emphasis among these alternatives of "what our business is or should be," and each set different priorities. They knowingly and deliberately built competing institutions though all were universities and had the same structure: trustees, an administration, faculty and students, and similar courses leading to the same degrees.

3. Finally, there are those service institutions in which means are as important as ends, and in which, therefore, uniformity is of the essence. Here belongs the administration of justice or defense and most of the areas which, in traditional political philosophy, were considered policy areas.

## The Institutions' Specific Needs

What does each of these institutions need?

The natural monopoly needs the least structure. It is closest to results even though not directly being paid for them. All it needs, in other words, is to do what any business should be doing anyhow, but to do it far more systematically.

This, incidentally, is a strong argument in favor of keeping natural monopolies under public regulation rather than under public ownership. An unregulated natural monopoly, as economists and political scientists learned long ago, will inevitably exploit, in addition to being ineffective and inefficient. A government-owned monopoly may not exploit, but the customer has no redress against inefficiency, poor service, high rates, and general disregard of his needs. An independently managed monopoly under public regulation is likely to be far more responsive to customer dissatisfactions and consumer needs than either the unregulated private or the government-owned monopoly. The regulated but independently managed monopoly depends on public opinion, expressed to and through a political agency, the regulatory body, for its rates and, therefore, for its revenues and profits.

The French telephone customer knows perfectly well that he gets the worst telephone service in any developed country (excepting only the Soviet Union). Because telephone service is a government-owned monopoly, he has no power and can only grumble. In the late sixties, the operating efficiency of the American telephone system declined in some areas, notably New York City, and waiting periods for service or for repair became longer (a result, largely, of inattention to demographics in the Telephone Company's plans); customers could and did take effective action. They began immediately to oppose requests from the telephone company for rate increases—and a more effective means of disciplining a monopoly is hard to imagine.

The American customers, however, are like the French in respect to the postal service, where rates have been rising steeply for forty years, and services have been deteriorating even faster. Since the postal service is government-owned, we have no redress.

In addition, the regulatory agency through which a government body deals with a private company on an arm's-length basis can provide the means for building into the structure of regulated monopolies the systematic performance of the job Theodore Vail built in sixty years ago for the American Telephone Company. Both the Federal Communications Commission in its study of the long-lines (that is, long-distance) service of the Bell System and the Federal Power Commission in its study of electric-power supply in the mid-Atlantic states have moved toward demanding such self-discipline from the various companies.

With respect to the monopoly which the research laboratory represents within a business, top management can and should demand the discipline of thinking through objectives, setting goals and priorities, measuring performance, and sloughing off the unproductive. This is the only way to make the research laboratory productive, responsive to the company's needs, opportunities, and responsibilities.

Management should also demand that goals of contribution be spelled out and results be appraised against them. This need not be quantitative—indeed, it often cannot be quantified. Still, the goals should be specific and the appraisal rigorous.

One of the most effective research managers—himself a scientist of world renown—makes it his practice to ask, "What have you in this research lab contributed to the company's vision, knowledge, and results during the last three to five years?" And then he asks, "And what do you expect to contribute to the company's vision, knowledge, and results during the next five years?" He reports that he never gets an answer the first time he asks the question. All he gets are speeches on the "intangibility" of research and its beatitudes. After asking the question for a few years more, he begins to get answers; and a few years later he even gets research results.

## "Socialist Competition" in the Service Sector

The second kind of service institution is exemplified by school and university, and also by the hospital. Most of the service staffs within business organizations belong here too. What they need is Lange's socialist competition.

The "customer" of this kind of service institution is not really a customer; he is a tributary. He pays for the service institution whether he wants to or not, out of taxes, levies such as compulsory insurance, or overhead allocations. The products of these institutions are not meant to supply a want. They are meant to supply a need. School and hospital, but also the typical service staff in business, supply what everybody should have, ought to have, must have, because it is "good for him," or good for society.

This kind of service institution is normative, to use the logician's term. It aims at making its "customers" be something, do something, behave in a certain way, know certain things, or believe in certain things. Most of the service institutions of this second kind also provide a public good which could not be furnished—often not even at the most prohibitive cost—except on a collective basis. Both because they are normative and because they supply a public good, they can be financed only out of taxes, overhead allocation, or other compulsory levies.

The service institutions of this second kind are the typical service institutions of a developed society and are its institutional hallmark. Monopolies and institutions of government—the service institutions of the first and third categories—dominate undeveloped societies. But the service institution of the second category becomes central in the process of economic and social development. Its performance is crucial to modern developed society. And in developed societies—or developed businesses—it is this service institution that most closely touches the daily life of the citizen—or of the manager.

Our rhetoric talks of the "right of every child to an education." The young people, however, complain about the compulsion to go to school— they are more nearly right than the traditional rhetoric. We talk of the "right of every citizen to *decent* health care." In the United States this is still, in part, an unfulfilled promise. Yet we are already well on the way toward *compulsory* health care. In many companies, for instance, executives are required to have an annual physical checkup or else they lose their vacation or are not paid. If and when the focus shifts to preventive medicine for large numbers of people, as is likely to happen within a fairly short period, we will soon demand of everybody that he avail himself of health-care facilities. In other words, we will make health care compulsory.

Compulsory utilization of the service staff is prescribed in a good many businesses. The marketing managers in the divisions of a decentralized company are not asked, as a rule, whether they want to attend the marketing seminars put on by the central marketing staff. They are told to come.

The objective—the overall mission—must be general for this kind of service institution. There should be minimum standards of performance and results. But for the sake of performance, it is highly desirable, particularly for public-owned institutions, that they should have managerial autonomy and not be run by government even if they are supervised and regulated by it.* Also, there should be a fair amount of consumer choice between different ways of accomplishing the basic mission, between different priorities and different methods. There should be enough competition for these institutions to hold themselves to performance standards.

We talk today in the U.S. about a voucher system for elementary and high school education under which the government would pay to whatever accredited school the child attends an amount equal to the cost of teaching a child in the public schools. No matter how much latitude schools would be given under such a voucher plan, surely none will, however, be considered qualified under it unless it promises to give its pupils a modicum of proficiency in basic skills such as reading, writing, and figuring. We may leave it up to the school what method it uses—there is room for experimentation, from the strictest traditional school discipline to the behavioral manipulation of the English "open school" or to "free-form" methods of education. But, fundamental goals and minimum standards will, and should be, insisted upon. Similarly, schools teaching, say, urban guerrilla warfare in Black neighborhoods are unlikely to stay long on the approved list—and should not. And there will be no choice as to whether a child of school age goes to school or not—he goes, whether he and his parents like it or not.

In health care, too, we may well move to a system that establishes the principle that everyone is entitled to prepaid health care—paid for either out of employees' insurance or by government for the aged and the poor. Yet we may well encourage considerable differentiation among different plans, and considerable competition between different kinds of health-care institutions with different plans and different priorities. This is the approach of the oldest national health-care plan, that of Germany.

Here is an example of the application of the same approach to the service

---

*In an earlier book, *The Age of Discontinuity*, I called this "re-privatization" for want of a better term. This, however, has been widely misunderstood as meaning return to private ownership, which is not at all what I had in mind (though I would not exclude it either). What is important is the autonomy of the institution, its subjection to performance tests and to some form of competition, albeit in many cases "socialist competition."

staff in a major business. One large multinational company, primarily producing and selling branded consumer goods, defines its business as "marketing." With such a definition, one would expect to find a large marketing services staff in the company. But the staff is remarkably small. There is a marketing vice-president in top management—he is, in effect, the number two man in the company. But marketing services do not report to him but to a director of marketing services. The marketing services staff has a small budget that pays for such activities as training the marketing services personnel, research in the marketing field, the library, and so on, but not for marketing services to the company's businesses. Every one of the forty-five to fifty decentralized and autonomously managed businesses of the company located in more than thirty countries is held responsible for its marketing performance and marketing results. To help his business reach these results, the local general manager may use the marketing services staff but is under no compulsion to do so. He is entitled to use outside consultants of his choice, or, if he so desires, he need not use any marketing staff but be his own marketing consultant. Only if he does use the marketing services staff does he pay for marketing services. The marketing staff, however, audits the marketing standards and marketing performance of every unit. When last heard of, eighteen or twenty of the divisional and territorial managers of the company used the marketing services staff. Eleven or twelve used outside consultants. Another dozen did not use any service staff, whether inside or outside the company. The marketing results of these men show no correlation to their methods. Among the best and among the poorest performers are divisions which use the company's marketing staff, divisions which use outside consultants, and divisions which do not use any marketing staff at all. Even the poor performers in this company have remarkably high standards and good marketing results. And the marketing services staff is among the best I know, in its effectiveness, in its performance, and in its spirit and enthusiasm.

## The Institutions of Governance

The third category of service institutions is, by and large, the traditional government activities—the administration of justice and defense and all the activities concerned with policy-making as the term used to be understood. These institutions do not provide public goods in the economist's sense of the term; they provide governance.

Here managerial autonomy is not possible. Competition, if possible at all, would be most undesirable. These institutions have to be under direct government control and directly government-operated, yet their activities require the discipline of objectives, priorities, and measurement of results.

Such institutions require, therefore, an organized, independent audit of their promises, the assumptions on which they base themselves, and their performance. There is no way of building any feedback from results into these institutions. The only disciplines, therefore, to which they can be subjected are analysis and audit.

The institution of the auditor-general became accepted in government during the nineteenth century (though it goes back to the France of Louis XIV, that is, the late seventeenth century, and was established pretty much in its present form as early as 1760 or so by Frederick the Great in Prussia). By now it is commonplace for government to establish a separate agency, independent of executive and legislative branches, which audits expenditures and exposes to public notice dishonesty, irregularity, and gross inefficiency.

Now that service institutions have become so central, so important, and so costly, we need an auditor-general of objectives and performance. We need to force ourselves to look at proposed government policies, laws, and programs—but also at the policies, programs, and activities of service staffs —and ask, "Are the objectives realistic? Are they attainable or pure rhetoric? Do they relate appropriately to the needs they are supposed to satisfy? Have the right targets been set? Have priorities been thought through? And, do results relate to promises and expectations?"

The American government may have begun to realize the need. This explains the recent change of name from Bureau of the Budget to Office of Management and Budget. But this new organ is still an agency of the president and located in his executive office. To produce results it will have to be independent. It will also need the right and the duty to monitor proposed legislation, that is, audit the legislature, as it is now supposed to monitor the execution of programs that have already been adopted. So far the Office of Management and Budget is mostly promise, but at least it has now been recognized that making the service institutions of the federal government perform requires organized review of objectives and performance and organized abandonment of yesterday.

We need to go further and accept as a basic premise that every governmental agency and every act of the legislature be conceived as impermanent. A new activity, a new agency, a new program should be enacted for a limited time, to be extended only when results prove the soundness of the objective and of the means chosen. This may sound utopian—and in government it may still be. Outside of government, in other service institutions— including those that should be autonomous even though public (e.g., school or hospital)—this will have to come to pass. Society is becoming too dissatisfied with the lack of performance and results of service institutions to tolerate the traditional system forever.

Failure to abolish nonperforming programs accounts for many of our worst problems. It underlies the failure of the U.S. and the Common Market farm programs; it underlies the "welfare mess" that threatens to destroy our cities; it underlies the failure of our international development programs which threatens to bring about worldwide race war of poor nonwhites against rich whites.

Failure to feed back from results may well, tomorrow, endanger the environment and our efforts to save it. Results are badly needed. But so far we have neither faced up to the need to think through what we are after nor set priorities; nor have we organized a feedback from results on the direction, the priorities, and the efforts of the environmental crusade. Predictably, this can only mean no results, and rapid disenchantment.

What the service institutions need is not to be more businesslike. They need to be subjected to performance tests—if only to that of "socialist competition"—as much as possible. But they need to be more hospital-like, university-like, government-like, and so on. In other words, they need to think through their own specific functions, purposes, and missions.

What the service institutions need is not better people. They need people who do the management job systematically and who focus themselves and their institution purposefully on performance and results. They do need efficiency, that is, control of costs, but above all they need effectiveness, that is, emphasis on the right results.

Few service institutions today suffer from having too few administrators; most of them are overadministered, and suffer from a surplus of procedures, organization charts, and management techniques. What now has to be learned is to manage service institutions for performance. This may well be the biggest and most important management task in this century.

## Productive Work
## and Achieving Worker

Making work productive and the worker achieving is the second major dimension of the management task. We know little about it. Folklore and old wives' tales abound, but solid, tested knowledge is scarce. We do know that work and the work force are undergoing greater changes today than at any time since the beginning of the industrial revolution two centuries ago. We do know that, at least in the developed countries, radically new approaches are needed—to the analysis, synthesis, and control of work and production; to job structure, work relationships, and the structure of economic rewards and power relations; to making workers responsible. We do know that we have to move from "managing personnel" as a "cost center" and a "problem" to the leadership of people.

# 15

# The New Realities

Few words in the language are as ambivalent as "work," and as emotion-laden. There are "work and rest"; and "rest" is clearly "good." But whether "retirement" is better than "work" is already questionable. There is no doubt that work is preferable to "idleness." And being "out of work" is far from "good"—is, indeed, a catastrophe.

There are "work and play." "Play" carries a favorable connotation. But "playing at being a surgeon" is not good at all. Work can be high achievement, as in the phrase "an artist's life work." Or it can be sheer drudgery, backbreaking, and utter boredom.

Language thus makes it abundantly clear that work is complex and that it is embedded in man's life, in his emotions, in his existence in society and community, and in his relationship to himself.

Work is both noun and verb. There are "work" and "working." They are totally dependent on each other. Unless someone is working, no work gets done. But unless there is work, there is also no working.

Yet work and working are quite different. Work is impersonal, and objective. It is a "something." Not all work can be weighed or measured.

Even the most intangible piece of work is outside the worker and independent of him.

What distinguishes work from play is an old question that has never been answered satisfactorily. The activity itself is often the same, down to the smallest detail. Yet psychologically and socially, the two are quite different. The true distinction may well be that work, unlike play, is impersonal and objective. Work has a result that is outside of the worker. The purpose of play lies in the player; the purpose of work lies with the user of the end product. Where the end product is not determined by the player but by others, we do not speak of play, we speak of work. We say that someone is playing chess—but we say also that someone is working on a chess problem.

Even the work of the artist is impersonal and a "thing." To have artistic validity, a work of art must indeed be an extension of the artist's personality. Otherwise it is sterile, academic, without power to move. But even the most subjective painter, when looking at a picture he has just finished, will not ask, "Is this me?" He will ask, "Is it right?" And, as has often been remarked, no listener could possibly guess at the turmoil and despair in which Beethoven lived when he wrote his most joyful and happiest symphony, the Seventh. Indeed, knowing the conditions under which the work was produced adds nothing to the listener's enjoyment, to his appreciation of the music, or to its power to move.

But working is done by a human being, a worker. It is a uniquely human activity. Working, therefore, is physiology and psychology, society and community, personality, economics, and power. As the old human relations tag has it, "One cannot hire a hand; the whole man always comes with it."

Work and working, therefore, follow different rules. Work belongs to the realm of objects. It has its own impersonal logic. But working belongs to the realm of man. It has dynamics. Yet the manager always has to manage both work and working. He has to make work productive and the worker achieving. He has to integrate work and worker.

Both work and worker are in a period of rapid change. The changes that will dominate the rest of this century—and probably most of the next century as well—are the most radical changes since the beginning of the industrial revolution more than two hundred years ago.

Most of the working population, certainly in the developed countries, now work as employees. They work in organizations rather than by themselves. They work outside of and away from their families. Society has become an employee society. Only a century ago the great majority of people—especially, of course, farmers—worked either by themselves or in very small groups. Work still centered around the home.

At the same time the center of gravity of the work force is shifting from the manual worker to the knowledge worker. A larger and larger proportion of the labor force in all developed countries does not work with its hands, whether as skilled or as unskilled workers, but with ideas, concepts, theories. In the Marxist—or Russian—usage of the term, they are "intelligentsia." Their output is not a physical object, but knowledge and ideas. Again, only half a century ago, knowledge work was primarily performed by independent professionals working either alone or in very small groups. The bulk of the labor force was manual workers.

Knowledge work need not be highly skilled or highly schooled. Filing, after all, requires neither high mental capacity nor advanced schooling. But the tool of the file clerk is not hammer or sickle, but the alphabet, that is, a high-level abstraction and a symbol rather than a thing. One does not learn the alphabet through experience but through formal education.

## The Crisis of the Manual Worker

These changes mean, first, a crisis with respect to the manual worker and to his specific organization, the labor union.

For two hundred years the manual worker in industry, the child of the Industrial Revolution, has been struggling to gain economic security, status, and power in industrial society. During the last fifty years, since the end of World War I, his progress was dazzling. In most developed countries the manual worker, only yesterday a "proletarian" scratching a bare living at the margin of subsistence, has acquired substantial economic security, an income level higher than that of the well-to-do middle class of yesterday, and increasing political power.

With the rise of the knowledge worker, he is endangered again. His economic security is not threatened—on the contrary, it is likely to become even more firmly established. But his social position and status are rapidly diminishing. In the developed countries, the industrial worker sees himself severely deprived. He is defeated, a loser, before he even starts—especially the younger one. This is not a result of managerial actions, but of social developments and of the pressures they generate.

Increasingly in all developed societies the able, intelligent, and ambitious members of the working class stay in school beyond the point at which they are eligible for manual work. All the pressures of society, family and neighbors, community and school, push the youngster toward more schooling. The one who leaves school at the age at which he once would have graduated into the manual work force—fifteen or so—is a dropout, a failure, a reject.

The young manual worker of today therefore starts out with a feeling of rejection, a feeling of failure, a conviction of being a second-class citizen.

In most developed countries (Britain and France are perhaps the only exceptions so far, though things are changing there rapidly too) close members of his own family, a brother, a sister, or a cousin, stay on in school and graduate into knowledge work and into a superior social class. Indeed, the young blue-collar workers themselves tend to be highly schooled, at least in the U.S. Most of them have finished secondary school; and more than half have gone on to some kind of college at least for a year—and then dropped out. But this only adds to the sense of defeat and rejection for the younger manual worker. Seventy-five or one hundred years ago there was a self-respecting working class, that is, a working class that knew itself to be the equal of its "betters," except in income and economic position.

But the manual worker of today in the developed countries does not respect himself. This inevitably makes him bitter, suspicious, distrustful of himself as well as of organization and management, and resentful. He is not a revolutionary, as his parents and grandparents were. For it is obvious to him that revolution cannot alter the fundamental conditions—apart from the fact that, in sharp contrast to the Marxian prophecy of fifty years ago, knowledge workers are rapidly becoming the majority instead of the proletarians. But the manual worker of today is a militant and likely to become more militant as the center of social gravity keeps on shifting toward knowledge work and knowledge worker.

The rhetoric of workers' parties and movements still talks of the wicked capitalists and lambasts the profit system. But the true class war is increasingly being fought between the hard hats—manual workers—and the liberals—the employed, middle-class knowledge workers. It was their coalition everywhere—in America's New Deal as well as in the social democratic and labor parties of Europe (beginning with the "Lib-Lab" coalition that put into power the first "modern" government, Lloyd George's 1907 cabinet in Britain)—which created the progressive Left and dominated politics in all developed countries during most of this century so far. The major political event for the remainder of this century may well be a growing split between these two groups.

In the U.S.—and to a lesser extent in Great Britain and Western Europe—the years since World War II have brought a massive shift in opportunities, power, and status from the worker to the middle-class professional, that is, to teachers, social workers, and administrators of government programs. The relative shares of national income from wages and salaries and from income on property changed little in these years, nor did the income distribution between high and low incomes change much. But the middle group gained greatly, especially relative to workers. Whatever the social programs of the last twenty-five years in the developed countries were meant to achieve, they all had as their first—and often as their main—result a growth in numbers, income, and power of the employed, middle-class knowledge worker.

Considerable doubt has been cast on the old assumption that higher school expenditures per child necessarily mean better education and better schools. But they certainly mean higher incomes for more teachers. Whether the programs of America's war on poverty helped many of the poor is questionable, but they created untold well-paying jobs for social workers, accountants, and administrators. While the environment may, one hopes, benefit more from the environmental crusade than the poor did from the war on poverty, the first beneficiaries are, of course, biologists, engineers, chemists, and so on. All these programs are paid for out of taxes on the middle-income groups—there is no other large tax base in a developed country; and "middle-income group" is the economist's euphemism for "workers," who, inescapably, pay the cost for most of these programs that directly benefit better paid and more educated "knowledge people." That these exactions are levied in the name of progress and for liberal or "left-wing" causes adds insult to the injury—at least in the eyes of the hard hat.

## The Crisis of the Labor Union

The changes in the status of the manual worker that attend the shift in emphasis to knowledge work and knowledge worker not only create a new class cleavage—more divisive, potentially, than the one that set proletarian against bourgeoisie in the opening decades of the nineteenth century—but also create severe difficulties for the manual worker's own institution, the labor union. Perhaps the most visible sign of this is the sharp drop in the quality of trade-union leadership—in large measure as a result of the "educational explosion." Labor-union leadership was the career opportunity for the able and ambitious young worker of yesterday whom lack of means forced out of school early and thus deprived of the opportunity to move out of the working class into the middle class, if not into the ranks of the bosses.

The late Walter Reuther of the United Automobile Workers' Union for twenty-five years was the best known, the most respected, and perhaps the most powerful American labor leader. Reuther started, in the 1920s, to go to college. If he had been able to stay on and to get his degree, he might well have been, twenty years later, one of the top men in the automobile industry. He had drive, ambition, intelligence, and an intuitive grasp of economic and business problems. He was a skillful organization politician who knew how to build an internal political machine. But he was also a loyal organization man. That he started out with deep socialist convictions might have made little difference. After all, Henry Ford was widely considered at one time to be an "anarchist." Many of the men who ran the automobile industry in the forties and early fifties—including Charles Wilson, who succeeded Alfred P. Sloan as chief executive at GM—had the same background and, like Reuther, grew up in working-class homes, in which Eugene Debs, the American socialist leader of pre-World War I days, was the chief deity.

But when the early Depression years forced Reuther to drop out of college, he became instead a machinist on the assembly line. From then on all the energies of an able and ambitious man were channeled into the one career opportunity available to him, union leadership.

In the developed countries today the able and ambitious youngster stays in school—and may go on to a graduate degree. As a result, he moves into the professional and managerial ranks. His convictions may still be "left." But his leadership qualities are lost to the working class. The leaders who are moving into the vacuum this creates are likely to be men driven by resentment rather than by ambition, of far lower ability, and above all, men without self-confidence. They are weak leaders—and the worst situation for an industry to be in is to have to deal with weak union leadership.

At the same time, the fact that the young worker sees himself a "loser" makes him resist and resent the very union leaders he selects and puts into office. The moment a man holds an important leadership position in the trade union, he automatically becomes "establishment." He has to consort with the mighty, whether in government or in business. He has to exercise power. He has to have the trappings of power—the big office, the retinue of aides and assistants, the four telephones on the desk, and so on. In order to be effective, he has to become one of "them" and ceases to be one of "us." Yesterday's worker looked upon union power as representing him. He was proud of the fact that the union leader had become a person of authority. Today's young worker, feeling keenly that he is a loser and a reject, resists, understandably, the union leader's authority even more than he resists the rest of the bosses. As a result, union leaders are increasingly losing control over their own members, are repudiated by them, resisted by them, disavowed by them. This, in turn, makes the union increasingly weak. For a union is impotent if it cannot deliver the union member's vote and behavior, cannot guarantee observance of a contract agreement, and cannot count on the members' support for the leader's position and actions.

The future of the trade union and its role in industrial society, especially in developed countries, is beyond the scope of this book. There is very little doubt that collective bargaining, whether between an individual company and a trade union, or—as in Western Europe and Japan—between an industry and an industry-wide union, is in trouble. Whether the "civilized industrial warfare" of collective bargaining—a major achievement of the early years of the twentieth century—can even survive is questionable. What could take its place is altogether obscure.

All attempts to replace collective bargaining by some other arrangement, such as the Swedish and Dutch approaches to tripartite settlements worked out in the national interest by representatives of public, management, and labor together, have been short-lived. They work in an emergency—such as the period in which Holland rebuilt its economy after World War II. But they have proven unable to survive major pressures, such as inflation. They are increasingly rejected by the new breed of workers.

No economy—and indeed, no society—can tolerate either unbridled industrial warfare, and especially unbridled industrial guerrilla warfare, or the constant escalation of labor costs and constant heavy inflation. Government control is no answer either. Wage-price policies have so far worked fitfully at best and for limited periods only.

But an organ for the representation of the worker against management, or at least to management, is needed—by the workers, but also by society.*

Management, no matter how selected or constituted, is, and has to be, a power. Any power needs restraint and control—or else it becomes tyranny. The union is a very peculiar, an almost unprecedented, organ of restraint on the political power of management. It is an opposition which can never become the government. Yet within its limited scope it serves an essential function in industrial society. But it is increasingly becoming incapable of discharging this function.

The opposition function of the labor union will be needed more in the future than ever in the past. The manual worker is beginning to feel—rightly—that he can no longer depend on a political party and its appeal to a majority. That is the consequence of the gradual dissolution of the New Deal, Labor, or social democratic marriage between worker and liberal. Increasingly, also, the power which needs restraining is not that of the bosses or the capitalists but of the educated middle class of knowledge workers. They are not greatly interested in profits, but all the more in power. The most bitter power conflicts are not those that erupt in private enterprise or in business; they are conflicts between janitors and school boards, medical orderlies and hospital administrators, teaching assistants and graduate faculties, or, as in the Swedish steel industry, between workers and their staunchly socialist bosses in a nationalized industry. They are conflicts between workers and the public interest (at least as defined by the liberals). In such conflicts political parties which aim at mass support and at attracting a majority of the voters are almost bound to be on the side of the bosses, if only because no amount of rhetoric can conceal that the price for a settlement will not be paid out of profits but surely out of prices or taxes.

Public-service institutions may face a much more difficult industrial rela-

*On this see my book, *The New Society* (New York and London, 1950).

tions problem than business and are much less prepared for it. Hospitals, schools, government agencies, and so on have all become increasingly unionized. In these institutions the manual worker—or the lower ranking clerical worker—feels even more "dispossessed," and even more confined to second-class citizenship than the manual worker does in manufacturing or service industries.

The unions themselves are incapable of thinking through their own future role and developing new approaches to their own structure and function. One reason is that the new leaders who replace the dying or retiring pioneers are so often men of lesser ability, lesser maturity, and lesser competence. But as important is the fact that the new leaders can keep their slender grip on the membership only by being "against" everything. The new leaders dare not even ask questions, let alone come up with answers. They dare not lead but are forced to make violent motions to stay in place. The pitiful failure of the British trade unions to tackle the problems of union reform to which every new General Secretary of the Trades Union Congress commits himself in ringing tones when he assumes office is one example of many.

The politician too is unlikely to ask these questions, let alone answer them. He is paralyzed by the split between workers and liberals. If he himself is a liberal, he is caught in the crossfire between the two constituencies whose support he needs to get elected and to stay in office. If he is not a liberal, he must increasingly be attracted by the hope to gain for himself the support of one of the embittered partners in the former marriage. Every conservative leader of recent years—Nixon in the U.S., Heath in England, De Gaulle and Pompidou in France—has, therefore, ducked the issue fully as much as the liberals. They can, under the pressures of a public opinion that is increasingly tired of industrial warfare and especially of strikes "against the public interest" (or, more bitterly resented, "against the public convenience"), clamp down on union power. They may even within the foreseeable future be pushed into action against union monopolies—with respect to craft jurisdiction and restraint of access to a trade, for instance. But they are highly unlikely to be willing or able to tackle new basic policy.

We need new policy in industrial relations. In all developed countries—but in developing ones as well—managers in business and in public-service institutions will, therefore, have to think through the future of the union, its role, its function, and its position, both within the institution and in society. This is a major social responsibility of management. But it is also a business responsibility of management. The future of business and of the economy, as well as that of society, will be influenced greatly by the way we solve or fail to solve the growing and deepening crisis of the labor unions. To think through the role and function of the labor union is also self-interest for management. To believe that labor-union weakness means management strength is sheer self-delusion. One may deplore unionization (I myself have rarely been considered pro-union by anyone in the labor movement). But once there is a union—and unionization is a fact in all developed noncommunist countries—a weak union, that is, one without established role, function, and authority and without strong, secure, and effective leadership, means strife, demagoguery, irresponsible demands, and increasing bitterness and tension. It does not mean management strength; it means management frustration.

## Managing the Knowledge Worker; the New Challenge

Managing the manual worker and labor-union relations, while crucial to society, are essentially rearguard actions for the manager. All he can hope to do is to contain damage which two hundred years of industrial history have left behind. Even this limited objective will require very drastic changes in policies and practices. It will certainly require even more drastic changes in managerial assumptions and managerial attitudes. But the aim will have to be fairly modest. Not to lose ground will be difficult enough —whether in productivity, in motivation, or in relationships. To regain ground lost in two hundred years of what can only be called industrial mismanagement is badly needed, but it must today be considered a hope rather than a rational expectation.

Managing knowledge work and knowledge worker is "today and tomorrow" rather than "yesterday." Because it is essentially a new task, we know even less about it than we know about the management (or mismanagement) of the manual worker. It is, therefore, going to be the more difficult task. But there is no long legacy of bitterness, of mutual suspicion, of resentment masquerading as scientific theories, and of folklore that has set into the hard concrete of restrictions, rules, and regulations. Managing knowledge work and knowledge worker therefore can focus on developing the right policies and practices. It can focus on the future rather than on undoing the past, on the opportunities rather than on "problems."

Managing knowledge work and knowledge worker will require exceptional imagination, exceptional courage, and leadership of a high order. In some ways it will be a far more demanding task than managing the manual worker was until very recently. For the weapon of fear—fear of economic suffering, fear of job security, physical fear of company guards or of the state's police power—which for so long substituted for managing manual work and the manual worker, is simply not operative at all in the context of knowledge work and knowledge worker. The knowledge worker, except on the very lowest levels of knowledge work, is not productive under the spur of fear; only self-motivation and self-direction can make him productive. He has to be achieving in order to produce at all.

The productivity, indeed the social cohesion, of every developed society rests increasingly on the ability to make knowledge work productive and the knowledge worker achieving. This may be the central social problem of the new, the knowledge society. There are no precedents for the management of knowledge work. Knowledge work traditionally has been carried out by individuals working by themselves in small groups.* Now knowledge work is carried out in large, complex, managed institutions. The knowledge worker is not even the successor to yesterday's "knowledge professional." He is the successor to yesterday's skilled worker. His status, his function, his contribution, his position in the organization, therefore, still have to be defined.

Worse, we cannot truly define, let alone measure, productivity for most knowledge work. One can define and measure it for the file clerk or the salesgirl in the variety store. But productivity is already a murky term with respect to the field salesman of a manufacturing business. Is it total sales? Or is it the profit contribution from sales, which might vary tremendously with the product mix individual salesmen might sell? Or is it sales (or profit contribution) related to the potential of a sales territory? Perhaps a salesman's ability to hold old customers should be considered central to his productivity. Or perhaps it should be his ability to generate new accounts. These problems are far more complex than the definition and measurement of the productivity of even the highly skilled manual worker. There one can almost always define and measure productivity in terms of the quantity of output—e.g., the number of pairs of shoes produced per hour, per day, or per week above a minimum quality standard.

Far more difficult even is a definition of productivity for the design engineer or the service engineer; for the quality control man or the sales forecaster; for the teacher (almost hopeless) or the research scientist; finally, for the manager.

Achievement for the knowledge worker is even harder to define. No one but the knowledge worker himself can come to grips with the question of what in work, job performance, social status, and pride constitutes the personal satisfaction that makes a knowledge worker feel that he contributes, that he performs, that he serves his values, and that he fulfills himself.

## The Segmentation of the Work Force

Manual workers and knowledge workers are not the only work-force segments, however. The clerical worker who is a production worker without being a machine worker is probably a distinct and important group. Equally

*On this see my book, *The Age of Discontinuity.*

important is the fact that the work force in all developed countries is segmenting itself according to sex.

Till fairly recently, women employees were essentially either temporary, working in the interlude between school and marriage, or distinctly lower class. Wives of "respectable" workers did not accept employment and work outside the home. Such upper-class women as worked were largely independent professionals, e.g., the few women doctors, women lawyers, and women university professors. The exceptions were schoolteachers and hospital nurses; and they either stayed unmarried or had to quit.

In all developed countries—the one exception so far being Japan—this is changing drastically. It might well be the sign of a developed country that a very large proportion of its women work as employees. The married middle-class woman is increasingly becoming the typical woman employee. With family size limited and with housework greatly reduced—both because of simpler housekeeping and because of mechanical appliances— more and more middle- and upper-class women are joining the work force. The trend is likely to continue. The driving forces are economic, social, and psychological, rather than "women's lib." But the working woman requires a different job structure appropriate to her realities and conditions. She requires different treatment from the male worker with respect to job, economic rewards, and social status in the plant community. Women with children, for example, often need part-time work or flexible hours. And for married women retirement pensions are often of little interest compared with higher cash incomes.

Various segments of the work force also have different needs with respect to benefits. When it comes to cash wages they may all consider the same rewards "value." But when it comes to retirement pay, housing or educational allowances, health and other benefits, their needs and expectations vary greatly with sex, age, and family responsibilities, with the stage in the life cycle and that of their families, and so on.

Traditionally an employer, whether a business or any other institution, has had one personnel policy. In the future there will be need for as many personnel policies as there are segments of the work force. Increasingly the segmentation of the work force will require differentiated approaches to the task of making work productive, and especially to the task of making the worker achieving.

There are additional shifts: the shift from manual work to automation, and the shift within manual work to high mechanization; rapid changes in technology which make skills, whether manual or mental, obsolescent within a few short years and, therefore, threaten established crafts and established knowledges; the steady lengthening of the human life span, which makes working life increasingly a preparation for long years of nonwork, that is, of retirement; and many others.

But the three main challenges to managing work and worker are *the arrival of the employee society;* the changed psychological and social *position of the manual worker:* better educated and better paid, he still sees himself moving down from yesterday's self-respecting working class into second-class citizenship; and the *emergence of knowledge work and the knowledge worker* as the economic and social center of what some people now call post-industrial society.

## The New Breed

It is these changes that explain the arrival of the new breed of workers, that is, the young people, and especially the highly educated young people, who in the developed countries are challenging the traditional management of work and workers, traditional organization, and traditional economic and power relationships as well.

This is often attributed to affluence, as the result of which, we are being told, the old Protestant ethic is crumbling.* This is far too glib and superficial an explanation. To be sure, affluence is something new under the sun. Throughout all of man's history the great majority of people has always lived at the margin of subsistence. The great majority never knew where its next meal was going to come from. Now, in the developed countries, the great majority is economically secure, at least in traditional terms. But there is no sign that the great majority—or any but the tiniest of minorities—has lost its appetite for economic rewards, whether material or immaterial. On the contrary, the great majority, now that they have tasted some of the fruits of productivity, are clearly eager for more—much more than the economy can produce so far, if not more than the limited resources of our planet could produce.

The shift in the structure and character of work has created a demand that work produce more than purely economic benefits. To make a living is no longer enough. Work also has to make a life.

The rising level of expectations rather than affluence is the central phenomenon. This means that it will be more important than ever to make work productive. At the same time, both the manual worker with his deep psychological insecurity and the knowledge worker with his new and ill-defined status expect work to provide nonmaterial psychological and social satisfactions. They do not necessarily expect work to be enjoyable but they expect it to be achieving.

*It does not seem to have occurred to Western sociologists that the strongest practitioners of the Protestant ethic have for long periods of time been such notorious non-Calvinists as the Japanese and the Chinese.

# 16

## What We Know (and Don't Know) About Work, Working, and Worker

*The Primitive State of Our Knowledge—The Three Requirements of Productive Work—Taylor's Analysis, Its Contribution, and Its Limitations—Synthesis and Control of Work—The Five Dimensions of Working: Physiology; Psychology; Community; Economics; Power—Machine Design and "Human Design"—Work as Curse and Blessing—Work as Social and Community Bond—"Wage Fund" and "Capital Fund"—Work as Living and Work as Cost—The Mirage of Worker Ownership—The Power Dimension of Working—Organization Is Alienation—The Sixth Dimension: Power in the Economic Sphere—Organization as a Redistributive System—The Fallacy of the Dominant Dimension—Wants as Hierarchy and as Configuration—Wants Change in the Process of Being Satisfied—What Can the Manager Do?*

Work has been central to man's consciousness for untold ages. Man is not truly defined as the toolmaker, but making tools, the systematic, purposeful, and organized approach to work, is specific and unique human activity. Work has, therefore, been a profound concern for millennia.

Concern with work stands at the very beginning of what we call the Western tradition. In the Bible work is both man's punishment for original sin and God's gift to make man's fallen estate bearable. At the dawn of Greek civilization, there is Hesiod's great narrative poem, *Work and Days* —and "work" stands before "days" in defining man's estate and man's life. Life, Hesiod said, is "work over time."

What was always a profound concern became central with the industrial revolution. The economic and social theories of the last two hundred years center on work. This is true not only of Marxism, with its oversimplification of history according to which society is always organized according to the way the means of production, that is, the tools for work, are being controlled; it is equally true of the orthodox economists, of the philosophical sociologists of early nineteenth-century France, or of most other "isms" of the last two hundred years.

However central work has been to man all along, organized study of work did not begin until the closing decades of the nineteenth century. Frederick W. Taylor was the first man in recorded history who deemed work deserving of systematic observation and study. On Taylor's "scientific management" rests, above all, the tremendous surge of affluence in the last seventy-five years which has lifted the working masses in the developed countries well above any level recorded before, even for the well-to-do. Taylor, though the Isaac Newton (or perhaps the Archimedes) of the science of work, laid only first foundations, however. Not much has been added to them since—even though he has been dead all of sixty years.

The worker has been given even less attention—and the knowledge worker has received so far almost none. Rhetoric there is aplenty, but serious, systematic study has been confined to a few aspects of working.

There is *industrial physiology,* dealing with the relationship of such things as lighting, tool and machine speeds, design of the work place, and so on, to the human being who is the worker; the fundamental work here was done in the early years of this century, e.g., in the fatigue and vision studies of the German-born Harvard psychologist Hugo Muensterberg. Cyril Burt, an Englishman, might be called the father of *industrial psychology.* During World War I he studied aptitudes, that is, the relationship between the demands of specific manual work and the physical skill, motor coordination, and reactions of individual workers. Finally, in the early nineteenth century, Australian-born Elton Mayo, working primarily at Harvard, developed *human relations,* that is, the study of the relationship between people working together—though in human relations work itself, that is, the task to be done, received almost no attention.

The totality of "worker" and "working," the totality of task and job, perception and personality, work community, rewards and power relations, has received practically no attention. It may be far too complex ever to be truly understood.

The manager cannot wait till the scientists and scholars have done their work. Nor can the worker. The manager has to manage today. He has to put to work the little we know, inadequate though it is. He has to try to make work productive and the worker achieving. It might, therefore, be appropriate to put down what we know about work and working.

The most important thing we know is that work and working are fundamentally different phenomena. The worker does, indeed, do work; and work is always done by a worker who is working. But what is needed to make work productive is quite different from what is needed to make the worker achieving. The worker must, therefore, be managed according to both the logic of the work and the dynamics of working. Personal satisfaction of the worker without productive work is failure; but so is productive work that destroys the worker's achievement. Neither is, in effect, tenable for very long.

Work, as has been said in the preceding chapter, is impersonal and objective. Work is a task. It is a "something." To work, therefore, applies the rule that applies to objects. Work has a logic. It requires analysis, synthesis, and control.

As with every phenomenon of the objective universe, the first step toward understanding work is to *analyze it*. This, as Taylor realized a century ago, means identifying the basic operations, analyzing each of them, and arranging them in logical, balanced, and rational sequence.

Taylor worked, of course, on manual operations. But Taylor's analysis applies just as well to mental and even to totally intangible work. The "outline" which the budding writer is being told to work out, before he starts to write, is in effect scientific management. And the most advanced, most perfect example of scientific management was not developed by industrial engineers during the last hundred years. It is the alphabet, which enables all words in a language to be written with a very small number of repetitive and simple symbols.

But then—and Taylor did not realize this—work has to be synthesized again. It has to be put together into a process. This is true for the individual job. It is, above all, true for the work of a group, that is, for a work process. We need *principles of production* which enable us to know how to put together individual operations into individual jobs, and individual jobs into "production."

Some of Taylor's fellow pioneers, especially Gantt, saw this clearly. The Gantt Chart, in which the steps necessary to obtain a final work result are worked out by projecting backward, step by step from end result to actions, their timing and their sequence, though developed during World War I, is still the one tool we have to identify the process needed to accomplish a task, whether making a pair of shoes, landing a man on the moon, or producing an opera. Such recent innovations as PERT chart, critical path analysis, and network analysis are elaborations and extensions of Gantt's work.

But the Gantt Chart tells us very little about the logic that is appropriate to given kinds of processes. It is, so to speak, the multiplication table of work design. It does not even tell us when to multiply, let alone what the purpose of the calculation is.

Finally, work, precisely because it is a process rather than an individual operation, needs a built-in control. It needs a feedback mechanism which both senses unexpected deviations and with them the need to change the process, and maintains the process at the level needed to obtain the desired results.

Those three elements, analysis, synthesis into a process of production, and feedback control, are particularly important in knowledge work. For knowledge work by definition does not result in a product. It results in a contribution of knowledge to somebody else. The output of the knowledge worker always becomes somebody else's input. It is, therefore, not self-evident in knowledge work, as it is in making a pair of shoes, whether the work has results or not. This can be seen only by projecting backward from the needed end results. At the same time, knowledge work, being intangible, is not controlled by its own progress. We do not know the sequence of knowledge work in the way we know—at least since Taylor and Gantt—the sequence of manual operations. Knowledge work, therefore, needs far better design, precisely because it cannot be designed *for* the worker. It can be designed only *by* the worker.

## The Five Dimensions of Working

Working is the activity of the worker; it is a human being's activity and an essential part of his humanity. It does not have a logic. It has dynamics and dimensions.

Working has at least *five dimensions*. In all of them the worker has to be achieving in order to be productive.

## Machine Design and Human Design

1. There is, first, a *physiological* dimension. The human being is not a machine and does not work like a machine.

Machines work best if they do only one task, if they do it repetitively, and if they do the simplest possible task. Complex tasks are done best as a step-by-step series of simple tasks in which the work shifts from machine to machine, either by moving the work itself physically, as on the assembly line, or, as in modern computer-controlled machine tools, by bringing machines and tools in prearranged sequence to the work, with the tool changing with each step of the process. Machines work best if run at the same speed, the same rhythm, and with a minimum of moving parts.

The human being is engineered quite differently. For any one task and any one operation the human being is ill-suited. He lacks strength. He lacks stamina. He gets fatigued. Altogether he is a very poorly designed machine tool. The human being excels, however, in coordination. He excels in relating perception to action. He works best if the entire human being, muscles, senses, and mind, is engaged by the work.

If confined to an individual motion or operation, the human being tires fast. This fatigue is not just boredom, which is psychological; it is genuine physiological fatigue as well. Lactic acid builds up in the muscles, visual acuity goes down, reaction speed slows and becomes erratic.

The human being works best at a configuration of operations rather than at a single operation. But also—and this may be even more important—the human being is singularly ill-equipped to work at an unvarying speed and a standard rhythm. He works best if capable of varying both speed and rhythm fairly frequently.

There is no "one right" speed and no "one right" rhythm for human beings. Speed, rhythm, and attention span vary greatly among individuals. Studies of infants strongly indicate that patterns of speed, rhythm, and attention span are as individual as are fingerprints, and vary fully as much. Each individual, in other words, has his own pattern of speeds and his own need to vary speeds. He has his own pattern of rhythms, and he has his own pattern of attention spans. Nothing, we now know, creates as much fatigue, as much resistance, as much anger, and as much resentment, as the imposition of an alien speed, an alien rhythm, and an alien attention span, and above all, the imposition of one unvarying and uniform pattern of speed, rhythm, and attention span. That is alien and physiologically offensive to every human being. It results speedily in a buildup of toxic wastes in muscle, brain, and bloodstream, in the release of stress hormones, and in changes in electrical tension throughout the nervous system. To be productive the individual has to have control, to a substantial extent, over the speed, rhythm, and attention spans with which he is working—just as an infant, learning to speak or to walk, has to have substantial control over learning speed, learning rhythm, and learning attention span.

While *work* is, therefore, best laid out as uniform, *working* is best organized with a considerable degree of diversity. Working requires latitude to change speed, rhythm, and attention span fairly often. It requires fairly frequent changes in operating routines as well. What is good industrial engineering for work is exceedingly poor human engineering for the worker.

## Work as Curse and Blessing

2. The next dimension of man at work is *psychological.* Work, we know, is both a burden and a need, both a curse and a blessing. Whether this is genetic or culturally conditioned, we do not know—and it does not greatly matter. By the time a human being has reached the age of four or five, he

has been conditioned to work. To be sure, child labor is outlawed in most countries, but learning the fundamentals of being a person, especially learning to talk, is work and creates the habit of work. Unemployment we long ago learned* creates severe psychological disturbances, not because of economic deprivation, but primarily because it undermines self-respect. Work is an extension of personality. It is achievement. It is one of the ways in which a person defines himself or herself, measures his worth, and his humanity.

"Loafing" is easy, but "leisure" is difficult. For younger people especially, it is likely to mean frantic activity—or the hard work of bucking traffic on overcrowded highways—rather than *otium cum dignitate,* i.e., philosophical repose. "To be an aristocrat one has to start learning dignified idleness in early childhood," was a common saying in that most snobbish of all Western societies, the Whig society of late eighteenth- and early nineteenth-century England. And, "The devil finds work for idle hands," says an even older proverb.

The peculiar characteristic of the work ethic of the West—which goes back all the way to Saint Benedict of Nursia in the sixth century rather than to Calvin in the sixteenth—is not that it glorified and sanctified work. That was neither new nor particularly Western. It sanctified the "calling"; it preached that *all* work was service and contribution and equally deserving of respect. The Benedictine monks made *manual* work in field and workshop equal to the work of praying and teaching. This was a deliberate break with the earlier beliefs of antiquity which held that the "gentleman" or the "free man" had to be freed from manual chores to have time for higher work, for learning, for statecraft, for civic duties, and for military service. As a result, antiquity—but also most non-Western civilizations—ordered different kinds of work in a hierarchy of personalities, with manual work pertaining to the ignoble, whether slave, peasant, or artisan, and soldiers' and knowledge work pertaining to the full personality. Neither Socrates nor Cicero believed in idleness; on the contrary, their full personality was working harder than the ignoble or obscure—and did more demanding, more responsible work. When the Chinese Mandarin retired to his ancestral estate after a successful government career, he was not supposed to lead a life of leisure. He was supposed instead to take up other but even more productive work, calligraphy and painting, music and writing. And the justification of these activities was above all their social contribution; in the Confucian social ethic, these pursuits are necessary to maintain the social harmony on which all else depends.

*First in the studies which Paul F. Lazarsfeld and Maria Jahoda conducted in the twenties among chronically unemployed textile workers in Austria.

There is little doubt, however, that the commercial and industrial revolutions of the eighteenth and nineteenth centuries brought a sharp stepup in the hours man worked—farmers, machine tenders, merchants, and industrialists alike.

In large measure this reflected a sizable improvement in living conditions and, above all, in nutrition, which greatly increased the physical energy available for work (just as the eighteenth-century English draft animal, whether horse or ox, could do far more work in the course of a year than its grandsire a hundred years earlier had been able to do, because the invention of the silo provided adequate food during the winter months). No matter how horrible living conditions were in the nineteenth-century slums of the industrial towns—or today in the slums and shanty towns that ring Latin America's cities—they were better with respect to food than the living conditions under which the landless laborer or the weavers and spinners in the cottage industries had subsisted. If anyone doubts this he need only note the food on which seamen in the sailing vessels were supposed to live and work; there are abundant records in such literary classics as Dana's *Two Years Before the Mast,* Melville's *Typee* and *Moby Dick,* or in the once widely popular naval stories of Captain Marryat. Yet sailors, by all reports, were the best-fed workers, both because the work was hard and made great physical demands and because of the ever-present danger of mutiny.

The great increase in working in these centuries also represented a shift in values. Economic rewards became more meaningful—mostly, perhaps, because economic satisfactions became more generally available. The proletarian in the slums of Liverpool or Manchester could not buy much; he lacked purchasing power. But purchasing power would not have helped his grandfather, the landless laborer; there wasn't anything much around to buy.

The rejection of the work ethic—if there is such a phenomenon outside of the headlines—therefore does not represent hedonism. In part it represents a reaction against long decades of overworking, and a righting of the balance. In larger part it may, however, represent a return to earlier elitist work concepts which relate certain kinds of work to nobility or to baseness of the person. What lends support to this hypothesis is the strong, positive value which the educated young people who supposedly repudiate the work ethic give to the work of teacher and artist. Teaching and art, however, are far more demanding taskmasters than tending machines or selling soap.

The workless society of the futurist utopia may, indeed, be ahead. Should it come, it would, however, produce a major personality crisis for most people. It is perhaps fortunate that so far there is not the slightest fact to support the prediction of the imminent demise of work. So far the task is still to make work serve the psychological need of man.

## Work as Social and Community Bond

3. Work is *social bond* and *community bond*. In the employee society it becomes primary access to society and community. It largely determines status. For a man to say, "I am a doctor" or "I am a plumber" is a meaningful statement about himself, his position in society, and his role in the community.

Perhaps more important, work, since time immemorial, has been the means to satisfy man's need for belonging to a group and for a meaningful relationship to others of his kind. When Aristotle said that man is a *zoon politikon,* i.e., a social animal, he said in effect that man needs work to satisfy his need for community.

To be sure, few people are determined in their social and community functions solely by and through the work group to which they belong. Most people have other societies and communities. It is by no means unusual to find a man who ranks low socially in his work group but who is a "big shot" elsewhere; the inconspicuous engineer who is a big man in the Boy Scouts or in his church, for instance. But even for this man, work will provide much of his companionship, group identification, and social bond.

Work is for most people the *one* bond outside of their own narrow family —and often more important than the family, especially for the young not-yet married and for older people whose children have grown up. This is exemplified strongly by the experience of companies who hire mature women for part-time work. They make the most loyal employees. The work place becomes their community, their social club, their means of escaping loneliness, with their own man at his job and the children gone.

The Bell Telephone Company, for instance, has many women employees who leave the job to raise a family but a dozen years later become available for part-time work. They are hired to handle clerical peak loads, especially in such large-scale financial work as new stock or bond issues, mailing dividends or annual reports, and so on. The work, when available, is usually rushed and high-pressure, the hours long, and the pay far from exceptional. Yet the competition for a place on the roster is intense, and the morale of the group exceptionally high. When, for whatever reasons, a few months go by without such work, the "old girls" will start to call in and ask, "How soon can I come in again? I want to see my friends; I want to know what they are doing; I miss their company."

Similarly every company that has polled its retired employees has found the same reaction. "What we miss isn't the work; it's our colleagues and friends." "What we want to know isn't how the company is doing but what the people do with whom we worked, where they are, how they are coming along." "Don't, please, send me the annual report," a retired senior vice-president of a big company once said in a burst of candor, "I'm no longer interested in sales. Send me the gossip. I miss even the people I couldn't stand."

This last comment puts the finger on the greatest strength of the work bond and its singular advantage compared to all other bonds of community. It is not predicated on personal likes or dislikes. It can function without making emotional demands. A man can work very well with somebody whom he never sees away from the job, and for whom he feels neither friendship nor warmth nor liking. He can even function well in a work relationship with somebody whom he cordially dislikes—if only he respects the other man's workmanship. But the fellow worker can also be a close friend with whom one spends as many hours away from work as possible, with whom one goes hunting or fishing, spends one's vacation, spends one's evenings, and shares much of one's life. The work relationship has an objective, outside focus, the work itself. It does make possible strong social and community bonds that are as personal or as impersonal as one desires.

This may explain why, throughout man's history, and above all, among primitive peoples, work groups have always been sexually differentiated. Men work together and women work together. But we rarely hear, either in history or in cultural anthropology, of work groups of mixed sex. Men hunt and women tend the village. Men build boats and women grow yams. In Europe women have traditionally milked the cows, in America men; but on neither side of the Atlantic has milking been done by sexually mixed groups.

## The Economic Dimension

4. Work is a *"living."* It has an economic component the moment a society adopts even the most rudimentary division of labor. The moment people cease to be self-sufficient and begin to exchange the fruits of their labor, work creates an economic nexus, but also an economic conflict.

There is no resolution to this conflict. One has to live with it.

Work is a living for the worker. It is the foundation of his economic existence. But work also produces the capital for the economy. It produces the means by which an economy perpetuates itself, provides for the risks of economic activity and the resources of tomorrow, especially the resources needed to create tomorrow's jobs and with them the livelihood for tomorrow's workers. There is need in any economy for a wage fund and for a capital fund.

But the capital fund is in direct competition with the workers' need for a livelihood here and now. Marx tried to deny the need for a capital fund.

The great appeal of Marxism to the working man was precisely that it presented capital accumulation as exploitation and as unnecessary. The great appeal of Marxism was its prophecy that the capital fund would disappear once the workers owned the means of production. This very soon was seen as a total misunderstanding. No matter how bitterly Lenin attacked the German "revisionist socialists" who pointed out in the early years of this century that the capital fund was an objective necessity and not founded in social or power structure, every communist regime, most of all the Soviet Union, has put the capital fund into the center of its economic planning. In other words, they all have realized that profit is not a result of power, let alone exploitation, but objective necessity.*

Still, it does little good to argue, as the classical economists did, that there is no conflict between the demands of the capital fund, that is, the demands for a surplus, and the demands of the wage fund. The classical economists argued that, in the long run, these two harmonize. The worker needs the capital fund fully as much as he needs the wage fund. He needs, more than anyone else, to be protected against the risks of uncertainty. He, more than anyone else, needs the jobs of tomorrow.

The rapid improvement in wages and living standards of the American worker has in large measure been the result of steadily increasing capital investment, that is, the capital fund. The researches of Simon Kuznets (first at the University of Pennsylvania and later at Harvard), e.g., into capital formation in the United States, have demonstrated this. But "the worker" is an abstraction. The beneficiary of the capital fund is rarely the same worker who has made the contribution to the fund. The capital accumulated in one industry, e.g., the American textile industry in the 1890s, went to finance a new industry such as the chemical industry, rather than to create new jobs in the textile industry. Also, the capital fund creates jobs and incomes tomorrow, whereas the contribution to it has to be made today.

There is, in addition, the tremendous problem of comparative gains and sacrifices among different kinds of workers. It is probably true, as labor economists have argued (especially Paul Douglas, originally an economist at the University of Chicago, and later for many years a prominent U.S. senator), in their studies of real wages, that trade-union activities do not—and cannot—much influence the total level of real wages in an economy. It is still true, however, that one group of workers, e.g., workers in the building trades, can and do obtain sizable wage advantages at the cost of other groups of workers.

In other words, it is true that there is no ultimate conflict between wage

*For a cogent restatement of the dilemma by a contemporary, orthodox Marxist, see Michael Harrington, *Socialism* (Saturday Review Press, 1972).

fund and capital fund but this is largely irrelevant for the individual. For him there is a real and immediate conflict.

## Work as Living and Work as Wage

There is an even more fundamental conflict between wage as living and wage as cost. As "living," wage needs to be predictable, continuous, and adequate to the expenditures of a family, its aspirations, and its position in society and community. As "cost," wage needs to be appropriate to the productivity of a given employment or industry. It needs to be flexible and to adjust easily to even minor changes in supply and demand in the market. It needs to make a product or service competitive. It is determined, in the last result, by the consumer, that is, without regard to the needs or expectations of the worker. Again, here is conflict which cannot easily be resolved and can at best be assuaged.

No society, no matter how designed, has been able to eliminate these conflicts. Expropriating the capitalist, the traditional Marxist formula, does not change the situation. All it might do is to make possible a larger capital fund because the state has absolute control. But even this Russia could achieve only by outlawing labor unions. Japan has traditionally been able to minimize the conflict between wage as living and wage as cost (see Chapter 20), but rising living standards threaten the Japanese accommodation. The conflict between wage fund and capital fund rages as fiercely in Japan as any place else. The Yugoslavs, by vesting ownership of a plant in the worker's plant community, rather than in the state, hoped to abolish the conflict. Under the Yugoslav system, the needs of the capital fund should be more clearly apparent to the plant community than under any other system known so far, but they are being resisted just as much. The Yugoslav experiment is in danger of collapsing because of the inflationary pressures generated by workers' demands for more wages than the enterprise can afford to pay either under the aspect of wages as cost or in consideration of its own and the economy's need for the capital fund.

Worker ownership has been the alternative to both capitalism, that is, ownership by the providers of capital, and nationalization, that is, owner-ship by the government. It has a long—though not a very distinguished—history. Today it is again being proposed seriously, especially by such men as Ota Sik, the architect of the economic liberalization in Czechoslovakia which the Russians crushed.

It may be highly desirable that workers have a financial stake in the business. But wherever tried—and we have been trying worker ownership for well over a century—it has worked only as long as the enterprise is doing well. It works only in highly profitable businesses. And so do all the variants of workers' participation in profits, such as the American Scanlon Plan of profit and productivity bonuses. As soon as business profits drop, worker ownership no longer resolves the conflict between wage as living and wage as cost, or that between the wage fund and the capital fund.

A financial stake in the business must always remain a secondary interest to the worker compared to his job. Even in the most prosperous business, profit, that is, the contribution to the capital fund, is never more than a small fraction of wages. In manufacturing industries, wage costs typically are 40 percent or so of gross sales. Profits after taxes are rarely more than 5 or 6 percent, that is, one-eighth of wage costs. In the total economy the wage and salary bill runs around 65 percent of gross national product, profits fluctuate from zero to 7 percent or so—they are at most one-tenth of the wage bill (most of the remainder is income of small proprietors, farmers, shopkeepers, professionals, that is, in effect, another compensation for labor rather than contribution to the capital fund, i.e., profits).

Profits, at their lushest, can, therefore, rarely contribute more than a very small additional bonus—welcome but not fundamental.

It is also highly debatable whether worker ownership is in the worker's own *financial* interest. No enterprise will be profitable forever. And if the worker then, as in the typical worker-ownership plan, is dependent for his future, e.g., for his retirement benefits, on investment in the company he works for, he is exceedingly vulnerable. The worker should no more than any other investor have all his financial eggs in one basket. In that respect, the approach to pensions adopted in the United States in the last twenty-five years—development of a pension fund which invests broadly, and typically does not invest at all in the business that employs the future beneficiaries —is financially far sounder and far more in the worker's own financial interest than worker ownership in the enterprise he works for.

From a theoretical point of view, the developments in the United States during the last twenty or thirty years would seem to represent the optimal approach to the resolution of these conflicts. The employees of American business are gradually becoming the true "owners" through their pension funds and mutual funds, which have become the dominant investors in the American economy. By now these institutional investors, i.e., the trustees for the employee and his savings, control, in effect, the large publicly owned American corporations. America, in other words, has socialized ownership without nationalizing it. Yet this has by no means resolved—or even lessened—the conflict between wage fund and capital fund and between wage as living and wage as cost.

It would help if we learned to think and speak of the costs of capital and of the costs of the future rather than of profit. (It would also, as was said in Chapter 6, result in raising profitability requirements). But it would only help; it would not make the conflicts go away. They are built into this situation, whether business operates in a market economy or in a government-run one, whether it is privately owned, government-owned, or plant community-owned.

## The Power Dimension of Working

5. There is always a *power relationship* implicit in working within a group, and especially in working within an organization.

The farmer of old who tilled his own stony acres had to impose on himself a very strict discipline. What he *wanted* to do was not very relevant, if haying had to be done. But the forces to which he was subordinated were impersonal. They were wind and weather, season and frost, or the impersonal forces of a market. But in any organization, no matter how small, there has to be a personal authority. The organization member's will is subordinated to an alien will.

The imposition of the clock on a man's life which forces him to come to work at a given hour might appear a trivial exercise of power, and one that affects everybody equally. But it came as a tremendous shock to pre-industrial people, whether peasants in developing countries, the former craftsmen in the mills of England in the early years of the industrial revolution, or Blacks from the ghettos of the American city today. In an organization jobs have to be designed, structured, and assigned. Work has to be done on schedule and in a prearranged sequence. People are promoted or not promoted. In short, authority has to be exercised by someone.

Anarchists are right in their assertion that "organization is alienation." Modern organization theorists such as Yale University's Chris Argyris who hope for organization without alienation are romantics (though many of their concrete proposals for "participation" are highly constructive, and needed). Modern society is an employee society and will remain one. This means power relationships that affect everybody directly and in his capacity as a worker. Authority is an essential dimension of work. It has little or nothing to do with ownership of the means of production, democracy at the work place, worker representation at the board of directors, or any other way of structuring the "system." It is inherent in the fact of organization.

## The Sixth Dimension: The Power Dimension of Economics

6. In all modern organization there is what might be called a sixth dimension of working: a need for authority with respect to *economic shares*.

Power and economics are inextricably tied together in the modern organization, whether business enterprise, government agency, university, or hospital. Apportioning the economic rewards of the members of the institution demands a central organ of authority with power of decision. The reason is not capitalism or any other "ism." It is the fundamental fact that the modern institution is an organ of society, existing to provide satisfactions outside of itself. It, therefore, must obtain its revenue from the outside—either from a customer in the marketplace, from the taxpayers through a budget-making authority, or from preset fees paid by users such as patients in a hospital, patrons of the post office, or students in a college. At the same time, the contribution of the individual member of the institution cannot be directly related to the revenue. It is impossible to say, even approximately, how much of the sales of a business an individual employee contributes, whether chief executive or lowliest sweeper. The same is true of hospital or university. Does the great scholar in ancient Chinese with his six graduate students contribute more or less than the graduate assistant teaching English composition to a freshman class of 150? And what about the dean? All one can say is that everybody's contribution is, in theory, indispensable, although not everybody's contribution enters into every single product or performance, nor is everybody's contribution in any way equal in importance, skill, or difficulty.

An authority is, therefore, needed which divides the revenue available among the members. The institution itself, whether business enterprise or hospital, is necessarily a *redistributive system.*

Where the contributions are simple, similar, and few in number, redistribution on the basis of complete equality is possible. This is, for instance, the case in the Israeli kibbutz, where everybody works on the farm, producing a very few products, most of them for internal consumption, that is, for basic self-sufficiency. But the moment the kibbutz went into industrial production, as a good many did, it had to abandon the principle of primitive socialism on which it had been founded and under which everybody receives exactly the same. It had to become an employer. In Israel the Trade Union Federation owns most of industry and is the country's leading employer. Most of Israel's industry is, in effect, "socialized," but that has not in any way changed the power position of the "employer" nor eliminated the problems of labor relations. While the kibbutz has had enormous psychological and political impact on Zionism, its economic role in Israel is almost negligible and is shrinking. Kibbutzim now contain less than 5 percent of Israel's population; and the young are leaving them for the fleshpots of the consumer society of the cities.

The simple fact that the results of a modern institution always lie outside of itself and that, therefore, the economic rewards for its members always come from the outside and are not determined internally, inescapably leads to power and authority. In fact, it creates two power relationships. There is a power relationship between management and labor. But the various groups within the work force, while in a common power relationship to management, also stand in sharp and intense competition to each other with respect to their relative shares in the total "product" available for internal distribution.

Marx might have been excused, a century ago, for believing that the transfer of the title of ownership would resolve this problem—though his predecessors, the utopian socialists, especially the French such as Fourier, saw, long before Marx, that the problem lay in the nature of modern institutions rather than in "exploitation," ownership, or any other legal, political, or social structure. Fourier in particular saw that true industrial democracy required a completely self-contained and self-sufficient economic unit, that is, something like an Israeli kibbutz.

If the last hundred years have taught us anything, however, it is that the distribution problem is generic rather than historical. It cannot be manipulated away. There has to be a decision how to divide the revenue available from the outside among the members inside the enterprise. The moment the institution, business, hospital, or other, produces more than a very few simple commodities, meant mostly for consumption within the group, the relationship between the individual input and the institution's output can no longer be determined "impersonally" or "scientifically." At this moment also, equality of reward becomes at once impossible—as the Russians learned in the thirties, and as all other socialist experimenters, e.g., the Yugoslavs and the Chinese, have learned since.

There has then to be a redistribution and an authority to make the redistribution decisions. Redistribution, however, is, in effect, a political rather than an economic decision. It is influenced and restrained by a great number of forces: supply and demand, social convention, traditions, and so on. But in the last analysis, a decision by authority and a decision based on power structure and power relationships has to be made somehow by somebody. And this decision, no modern institution—and least of all, the business enterprise—can escape.

## The Fallacy of the Dominant Dimension

These dimensions of working—the physiological, the psychological, the social, the economic, and the power dimension—are separate. Each can—and, indeed, should—be analyzed separately and independently. But they always exist together in the worker's situation and in his relationship to work and job, fellow workers and management. They have to be managed together. Yet they do not pull in the same direction. The demands of one dimension are quite different from those of another.

The basic fallacy of our traditional approaches to working has been to proclaim one of these dimensions to be *the* dimension.

Marx—and most other economists—saw the economic dimension as dominating everything else. If only economic relationships could be changed, there would be no more alienation. Marxism became bankrupt when it became apparent that the "expropriation" of the "exploiters" did not fundamentally change the worker's situation and his alienation because it did not change in any way any of the other dimensions (and did not indeed even change the economic problem).

This explains, by the way, the vogue of the "young Marx" among Marxists today. This—largely fictitious—personage is said to have seen alienation as the existential evil of the social system and as moral rather than as purely economic. But it did not take the mature Marx long to realize that neither program nor action could be based on such general and vague *Weltschmerz*.

Elton Mayo, to give another and radically different example, saw the dominant dimension as the interpersonal relations within the work group, that is, in psychological and social aspects. And yet it is not only true that one cannot "hire a hand; the whole man always comes with it"; the work itself matters and affects group relations. And neither the economic nor the power dimension were seen by Mayo and his associates.

These dimensions stand in highly complex relationship to each other. They are a true "configuration" but one that changes rapidly as the worker's circumstances change.

The late Abraham H. Maslow, the father of humanist psychology,* showed that human wants form a hierarchy. As a want of a lower order is being satisfied, it becomes less and less important, with a want of the next-highest order becoming more and more important. Maslow applied to human wants what might be called "marginal utility"—and his was a profound and lasting insight. Maslow put economic want at the bottom and the need for self-fulfillment at the top. But the order is not of first importance. What matters is the insight that wants are not absolute; the more one want is being satisfied, the less its satisfaction matters.

But what Maslow did not see is that a want changes in the act of being satisfied. As the economic want becomes satisfied, that is, as people no longer have to subordinate every other human need and human value to getting the next meal, it becomes less and less satisfying to obtain more economic rewards. This does not mean that economic rewards become less important. On the contrary, while the ability of the economic reward to provide a positive incentive diminishes, its capacity to create dissatisfaction,

*Especially in his book, *Motivation and Personality* (Harper & Row, 1954).

if disappointed, rapidly increases.* In Herzberg's words, economic rewards cease to be "incentives" and become "hygiene factors." If not properly taken care of—that is, if there is dissatisfaction with the economic rewards —they become deterrents.

This is, we now know, to be true of every one of Maslow's wants. As a want approaches satiety, its capacity to reward and with it its power as an incentive diminishes fast. But its capacity to deter, to create dissatisfaction, and to act as a disincentive rapidly increases.

Two vice-presidents in the same company whose salaries are only a few hundred dollars apart are equals economically. At that salary level, the income tax is so high as to make the pay differential meaningless. Yet the vice-president with the lower salary may be eaten up by frustration and envy. No matter how good his income, it will be a thorn in his side. The same applies all the way down the organization. Every trade-union leader knows that his biggest problem today is not absolute pay scales. It is the pay differentials among various kinds of workers within his union. There is no way of satisfying either the skilled worker who insists on receiving 20 percent more than the semiskilled man, or the semiskilled man. They are equally dissatisfied. If the pay differential is being narrowed, the skilled worker will feel that he has been deprived. And if the differential is not being narrowed, the semiskilled worker will feel deprived.

But also, contrary to what Maslow seemed to imply, the various dimensions of man at work change their character as they approach being satisfied. Pay, as we have just seen, becomes part of the social or psychological dimension rather than the economic one.

The opposite can also happen; power and status can become the basis for economic demands. In Yugoslav industry, for instance, the worker representatives on the workers' council, who hold positions of great social prestige and considerable power, almost immediately want more money as well. At the least, they want perquisites—housing, an office, a secretary, preferential prices at the company store, and so on—which are, as they see it, economic rewards befitting their new rank.

We need to know much more than we now know about the dimensions of working and about their relationships. We are dealing with a configuration likely to defy analysis.

Nevertheless, the manager has to manage now. He has to find solutions

*This was first noted in my book, *The New Society*. Since then Frederick Herzberg has provided ample documentation in his two books, *The Motivation to Work* (Wiley, 1959) and *Work and the Nature of Man* (World, 1966).

—or at least accommodations—which will enable him to make work productive and the worker achieving. He has to understand what the demands are. He cannot expect to succeed by continuing the practices of the last two hundred years. He will have to develop new approaches, new principles, and new methods—and fast.

# 17

## Making Work Productive: Work and Process

*Work Is Generic—Skill and Knowledge Are in the "Working," Not in the Work—The Four Steps Toward Productive Work—The Analysis of Work —Taylor and His Disciples—What Industrial Engineering Is and Is Not— Focus on the End Product—Laying out "Jobs" Not Part of Work Analysis —Work Analysis Only the First Step—The Principles of Production— Unique Product Production—Rigid and Flexible Mass Production—Process Production—What Each Principle Demands*

We speak of unskilled work, skilled work, and knowledge work, but this is misleading. It is not the work that is unskilled, skilled, or knowledgeable, it is the worker. Skill and knowledge are aspects of working. The work itself is the same whether it requires no skill or high skill, a lot of knowledge or very little.

To make a pair of shoes one used to have to be "highly skilled." For almost a century now, we have been able to make shoes practically without skill. It would be no great trick (though probably uneconomical) to automate shoemaking fully so that it requires no manual work. Yet the shoe itself has hardly changed. Nor has the process. It requires the same steps, from preparing leather, to cutting, forming, stitching, and gluing. The steps are being carried out in the same sequence, to the same requirements and standards, and result in the same finished product. The work of shoemaking remains the same, even though tools and skill requirements have changed drastically. Only an expert could tell whether a shoe had been made entirely by hand and with great craft skill or in an entirely automated process.

This may seem to be quibbling. Yet the realization that work is general and generic and that skill and knowledge are in the working rather than in the work is the key to making work productive. The generic nature of work —certainly as far as manual or any other production work is concerned— implies that work can be worked on systematically, if not scientifically.

The first step toward making the worker achieving is to make work productive. The more we understand what the work itself demands, the more can we then integrate the work into the human activity we call working. The more we understand work itself, the more freedom we can give the worker. There is no contradiction between scientific management, that is, the rational and impersonal approach to work, and the achieving worker. The two complement each other, though they are quite different.

Whatever study of work has been done so far has confined itself to manual work—for the simple reason that, until quite recently, this was the main work around. In describing what is known about making work productive, this book, therefore, of necessity, focuses on manual work. But the same principles and approaches also apply to any other production work, e.g., to most service work. They apply to the processing of information, that is, to most clerical work. They even apply to most knowledge work. Only the applications and the tools vary. Precisely because work is general and generic, there is essentially no difference among work the end product of which is a thing, work the end product of which is information, and work the end product of which is knowledge.

Making work productive requires four separate activities, each having its own characteristics and demands.

First, it requires *analysis.* We have to know the specific *operations* needed for work, their sequence, and their requirements.

But we also need *synthesis.* The individual operations have to be brought together into a *process* of production.

Third, we need to build into the process the *control* of direction, of quality and quantity, of standards, and of exceptions.

Fourth, the appropriate *tools* have to be provided.

One more basic point needs to be made. Because work is objective and impersonal and a "something"—even if it is intangible, like information or knowledge—making work productive has to start out with the end product, the output of work. It cannot start with the input, whether craft skill or formal knowledge. Skills, information, knowledge, are tools; and what tool is to be applied when, and for what purpose, must always be determined by the desired end product. The end product determines what work is needed. It also determines the synthesis into a process, the design of the appropriate controls, and the specifications for the tools needed.

## The Analysis of Work

The analysis of work—known by such names as work study, scientific management, and industrial engineering—is by now almost a century old. As said earlier, it goes back to Frederick W. Taylor's work in the 1880s on individual manual operations, such as his famous study of shoveling sand in a steel mill. It was essentially completed in its present form shortly after Taylor died during World War I. In those war years and in the period immediately following, Taylor's most productive disciples, Frank Gilbreth and Henry Gantt, added to Taylor's scientific management what might be called the script and the syntax for the analysis of work.

Gilbreth studied, identified, and classified all the motions involved in manual work, such as "lifting," "moving," and "putting down." His Therbligs (Gilbreth spelled backwards), which list the entire range of manual operations, specify how each can best be done, what motion it requires, and how much time it needs, are not, as sometimes has been said, an alphabet. They are more like Chinese ideographs, that is, symbols of a fundamental unit which in themselves contain all the information needed to engineer them.

Gantt, at the same time, addressed himself to the configuration of operations in work. His Gantt Chart, which starts out with the desired end product and then outlines every step needed to attain it, with its place in the sequence and the time needed, created, in effect, a syntax for work.

Not only has the discipline of work analysis been with us for a long time; the practice has become general too. The industrial engineer is a common feature of production work, in the factory, in transportation, and increasingly in clerical work. Industrial engineering is a recognized academic discipline with a tremendous literature of its own. And the impact, as has been said earlier, has been almost overwhelming.

Managers, therefore, tend to believe that they know all they need to know about industrial engineering. They may be excused for believing that the analysis of work is as useful, but also as well known a tool as cost accounting, for instance, and requires very little managing on their part. They are convinced they know the essentials. The analysis of work, they would tell a questioner, consists essentially of the following:

1. Identification of all operations necessary to produce a known end product, a known piece of work.

2. Rational organization of the sequence of operations so as to make possible the easiest, smoothest, and most economical flow of work.

3. Analysis of each individual operation and its redesign so as to make possible its most efficient performance—including the provision of the ap-

propriate tools, the needed information, and the required materials where and when needed.

4. Integration of these operations into individual jobs.

And this is actually what, in essence, the books on industrial engineering say and what the courses on this subject teach. It is, however, not—or at least not truly—what the analysis of work has to be to be effective.

In the first place, the standard answer omits the first crucial step in work analysis. Work analysis does not begin with identifying operations. It begins with defining the desired end product. As Gantt showed sixty years ago— and as far too few people have learned since—the analysis of the work has to start with the question "What do we want to produce? What is the work itself? How can the end product be designed so as to make possible the easiest, the most productive, the most effective work?"

Taylor—and this is perhaps the only valid criticism of a great man's work —may have been responsible for the common failure to see something so obvious, for Taylor always took the end product for granted. His focus was the individual task rather than the joint result.

To start out with the task rather than with the end product may result, however, in beautiful engineering of work that should not be done at all. One cannot, as Taylor did, assume that the end product is rational, systematic, consistent. In most processes it represents little but untested assumptions, a lot of history, traditions and customs, and geological strata of human errors. Anyone who starts out with an analysis of the final product, the work itself, will soon find himself asking the question "Why do we do this and why do we do that?" Usually there is no answer other than, "We have always done it." What proportion of inefficiency, that is, of lost productivity, can be contributed to the unquestioning acceptance of the final product as given, no one knows, but I have heard experienced industrial engineers put it as high as 30 percent of total cost and total effort—and I would not consider this estimate improbably high.

The manager, therefore, needs to know that his work analysts have to participate in the design of product and process. Obviously the finished product cannot be engineered primarily to make work easier. Its basic specifications are set by the needs and values of the user and not by those of the producer. But within the restraints set by these basic specifications, there is usually considerable leeway to design a product or service so as to be produced efficiently or inefficiently, simply or with unnecessary complications, with economy of work or wastefully.

The next—and much better known—weakness of the traditional definition of work analysis is that it includes something which does not belong in it. The fourth, and last, step which most managers—and most industrial engineers, at least in the West—would include in their definition of industrial engineering is not truly part of the job. Laying out jobs is no longer analysis. Or rather, the analysis that is required is not that of work, but that of working. And while the industrial engineer has a role to play in this process, it is a totally different role from the one he plays in the analysis of the work (as will be discussed in Chapter 21).

The inclusion of job design in work analysis is responsible in large measure for the traditional resistance to industrial engineering on the part of workers. It is largely responsible for the hostility of the intellectual to modern technology, and to modern industry and organization altogether.

But what is resisted and criticized is a misapplication of work analysis rather than work analysis itself. Taylor is usually blamed for the resulting "dehumanization" of the worker, especially by today's psychologists, but this is unfair and unjust.*

Taylor did not invent the assembly line—he had, in fact, nothing to do with it. Taylor's aim from the beginning was strictly in accord with the most humanist approach to working. Taylor, as his writings show, knew that making the work productive was but the first step. But he also knew that neither an empty stomach nor a spent and broken body is a good foundation for the full life. Taylor addressed himself to the priority task of creating the economic and physical base for the worker's welfare. It was not an accident that Taylor's most ardent supporter was the greatest American humanist of the early years of this century, Louis D. Brandeis, later to become the great liberal Supreme Court justice and the strongest fighter on the Court for human rights and human dignity. It was Brandeis, for instance, who, as Taylor's self-appointed public relations man, coined the term "scientific management" to get attention for Taylor's work.

The fact remains, however, that scientific management or industrial engineering has been content to stop where Taylor stopped. Few of its scholars and practitioners have concerned themselves with working, i.e., with the synthesis of operations into a job.†

The manager needs to know that the logic of work analysis and the analysis of job structure are two different logics. The one is the logic of work; the other the logic of working.

The last and most common misunderstanding of the industrial engineer is the belief that work analysis is the whole job. It is only the first step in

*To belittle Taylor because in 1880 he did not know post-Freudian psychology is, as I said at another occasion (when I received in 1967 the Taylor Key of the Association for Advancement of Management), somewhat like belittling Isaac Newton for not knowing quantum mechanics or non-Euclidian geometry in 1690.

†An important exception was one of Taylor's disciples, Allen Mogensen, who, in the 1920s, pioneered what he called "work simplification"—startlingly similar to what is now being rediscovered as "job enrichment," if not way ahead of it.

making work productive. Analysis identifies individual specific operations, their sequence, and their interrelationships. It deals with pieces. It is not concerned with the process of production as a whole, with its structures, its economy, or its performance.

## The Principles of Production

Production is not the application of tools to materials. It is the application of logic to work. The more clearly, the more consistently, the more rationally the right logic is applied, the less of a limitation and the more of an opportunity production becomes.

This definition implies that there must be principles of production. There must be a small number of basic models, each with its own constraints, its own requirements, its own characteristics. The definition further implies that the more closely a process of production can be designed according to one of these principles, the smoother, the more effective, and the more productive it will be.

Each system of production makes its own demands on management—in all areas and on all levels. Each requires different competence, skill, and performance. One set of demands is not necessarily "higher" than another, any more than non-Euclidian geometry is "higher" than Euclidian geometry, but each is different. Unless management understands the demands of its system of production, it cannot truly make work productive.

Such understanding is particularly important today when many processes —in manufacturing as well as in information work—are moving from one system of production into another. If this move is considered a mere matter of machines, techniques, and gadgets, the enterprise will reap inevitably only the difficulties of the new system. To reap its benefits management must realize that the new system involves new principles, and must understand what these are.

There are four such principles of production known to us so far. Each has been worked out for industrial production, that is, largely for traditional manual work. But each is equally applicable to producing and handling information, that is, to most clerical work. The principles are applicable also to knowledge work, at least to knowledge work concerned with the learning of known knowledge (i.e., already available and learnable) and its application.

The four systems are: (1) unique-product production; (2) rigid mass production; (3) flexible mass production; and (4) process or "flow" production. Each of these four has its own specifications; each makes specific demands on management.

There are two general rules for advancing production performance and pushing back limitations: (1) The limitations on production are pushed back further and faster the more consistently and thoroughly the principles pertaining to the system in use are being applied. (2) The systems themselves represent a distinct order of advance, with unique-product production the least advanced, process production the most advanced. They represent different stages of control over physical limitations. This does not mean that opportunities for advance lie everywhere in moving from the unique-product system to the process-production system. Each system has its specific applications, requirements, and limitations. But we advance to the extent to which we can organize parts of production on the principles of a more advanced system and learn, at the same time, how to harmonize different systems within the same process.

There are also two general rules concerning the demands on management competence made by each system. (1) The systems differ not just in the difficulty of their demands, but in the variety of competence and the order of performance. Management, in moving from one system to another, has to learn how to do new things rather than learn to do old things better. (2) The more we succeed in applying consistently the principles of each system, the easier it becomes for management to satisfy its demands.

Each management has to meet the demands of the system it ought to have according to the nature of its products and process, rather than those of the system it actually uses. Being unable or unwilling to apply what would be the most appropriate system results only in lack of performance; it does not result in lower demands on management, but inevitably increases the difficulties of managing the business.

One case in point is basic steelmaking, which has, in the batch process, primarily a unique-product system. There is probably no industry that has worked harder or more successfully on perfecting a unique-product system. Yet the problems the managements of basic-steel companies face are process-production problems: high fixed capital requirements and the need for continuous production, resulting together in high break-even points; the need for a high and constant level of business; the need to make basic investment decisions for a long time ahead, etc. As a result the cost structure of the steel industry is that of capital-intensive process production. At the same time the basic-steel industry enjoys few of the economic benefits of process production. The steel industry is thus caught in a perpetual squeeze between the cost characteristics of process production and the revenue characteristics of unique-product production. In periods of very rapid growth and extremely high demand, i.e., in the early stage of industrialization by and large, it can be very profitable for a few years. But over any extended period of time, steel industry profitability will always be marginal and inadequate to the industry's own needs—until such time as the basic steelmaking process shifts from mechanical unique-product production to what would in effect be a chemical flow-process.

It is, in summary, of major importance in managing a business to know which system applies; to carry its principles through as far as possible; to find out which parts of production can be organized in a more advanced system and to organize them accordingly; and to know what demands each system makes on management.

Where historical and technological obstacles have barred the organization of production in the appropriate system, as in the basic-steel industry, it is a major challenge to management to work systematically on overcoming these obstacles. Emphasis should not be on working a little more effectively what is basically the wrong system.

Because it acted counter to these rules, the steel industry has misdirected a great deal of its tremendous technological efforts. Focused on improving the traditional process, the efforts will turn out to have been wasted when steelmaking will finally become process production—and that point is not very far off.

A business using the wrong system has to satisfy all the demands that the appropriate and more advanced system would make on management. Yet it does not have the wherewithal to pay for them, for this can come only out of the increased ability to produce which the more advanced system provides.

All four principles of production provide the foundation for both production work *and* achieving worker. All are compatible with the dynamics of working or can be made compatible. When they fail to do so, it is not the principle that is at fault; it is its misapplication.

Specifically, the failure of mass production to give the worker achievement is essentially poor engineering. It is either failure to understand the meaning of mechanization (see the next chapter) or it is failure to understand the difference between work and working (as will be discussed in Chapter 21).

## Unique-Product Production

What, then, are these four systems of production and their principles?

In the first, the production of a unique product, each product is distinct. Of course, strictly speaking, there is no such thing as manufacturing unique products—they are produced only by the artist. But building a battleship, a big turbine, or a skyscraper comes close to turning out a unique product. So does the traditional way of building houses, one at a time, and, in most cases, batch production in a job shop.

What is unique in unique-product production is the product. In fact, unique-product production is always organized around standardized tools, and it typically works with standardized materials.

Goldsmiths and silversmiths use the same tools and they produce very similar final products. Yet the two crafts have traditionally been organized separately because they use different materials. This may be an extreme case, and overspecialization; but it illustrates the fundamental characteristics of unique-product production.

In unique-product production the basic organization is by homogeneous stages. In the building of the traditional single-family house—one of the oldest examples of unique-product production—we can distinguish four such stages. First, digging the foundation and pouring concrete for the foundation walls and the basement floor. Second, erecting frame and roof. Third, installing plumbing and wiring equipment in the walls. Finally, interior finishing. What makes each of these a distinct stage is that work on the house can stop after each is completed, without any damage—even for a fairly long time. On the other hand, within each stage, work has to be carried right through; or else what has been done already will be damaged and may even have to be done again. Each stage can be varied from house to house without too much trouble or adjustment and without delaying the next stage. Each of these stages by the inner logic of the product, that is, the house, is an entity in itself.

Unique-product production, with its organization of the work by homogeneous stages, is radically different from craft organization, in which a carpenter does all the carpentry, a plumber all the plumbing, etc. Properly organized, unique-product production does not go by craft skills but by stage skills.

The model is the telephone installation man who, without being a skilled electrician, carpenter, plumber, or roofer, installs electric wiring, saws through boards, makes a ground connection, and can take up a roof shingle and replace it. In other words, either every man engaged in the work of a particular stage must be able to do everything needed within that stage; or, as in the building of a big turbine, there must be an integrated team for each stage which contains within itself all the stage skills needed. No skill is needed by individual or team that goes beyond the requirement of that particular stage.

This is largely how the U.S. succeeded in building ships at such a tremendous rate during World War II. It was not mass production that resulted in the unprecedented output of ships. It was the division of the work into homogeneous stages; the systematic organization of the work group for the specific requirements of each stage; and the systematic training of a large number of people to do all the work required within one stage. This in turn made possible the progressive scheduling of the work flow, which was the greatest timesaver.

## Rigid and Flexible Mass Production

Most people when they hear the term "mass production" think immediately of the assembly line. But this is misunderstanding. Very little mass production work is assembly line work. The assembly line is the rare exception even in true mass production of the most rigid kind.

A good example is the assembly of electronic appliances such as radios, TV sets, and telephones. It is true mass production, but one worker does the entire operation from start to finish. The operations are indeed in sequence. In that sense there is a line which goes from putting in the first rivet to soldering all wiring connections, and then to final inspection. But there is no line in the traditional sense. The work itself never moves but stays at the individual work place.

Altogether the assembly line, despite its prominence in popular imagination and in the sociological literature of "alienation," is quite rare in reality. Only one out of every fifty workers in America in 1970 worked on an assembly line. Even in manufacturing employment assembly lines are rare —with fewer than 6 percent of American manufacturing workers doing assembly-line work. Assembly-line work is even the exception in the automobile industry; of General Motors's 550,000 employees, only one-third do assembly-line work.

The traditional picture of the assembly line assumes, moreover, that there is only rigid mass production. The principle of production that is clearly in the ascendant is "flexible" mass production.

What both principles have in common is that the final product is assembled out of *standardized parts*. In unique-product production, tools and materials are standardized. In mass production, the parts are also standardized. And they, in turn, are, as a rule, built of standardized parts as well. Mass production, in other words, assembles rather than makes.

Modern mass production goes back to the making of rifles for the American infantryman in the War of 1812. By 1880, long before Henry Ford, mass-production methods were actually in wide use throughout American industry, and also in such plants as the German Zeiss Optical Works and the Ericsson telephone plant in Sweden.

It may be the origin in gun manufacture which explains why for long years "rigid" mass production was considered to be the only available mass-production technology. In making guns for soldiers it is obviously highly desirable to have a completely uniform end product. It is highly desirable that each rifle be like any other, use exactly the same ammunition, require exactly the same cleaning, and be repaired easily with parts taken from any rifle.

In rigid mass production, therefore, the end product—in addition to tools, materials, and parts—is also standardized and uniform. Flexible mass production, however, uses standardization of parts to make possible diversity of end products.

Historically, flexible mass production antedates rigid mass production by many hundreds of years. It was developed long before industrialization. We know far too little about the building methods of the ancients to know what production processes they applied, though it is highly likely that the profusion of Greek and Roman temples in Europe and the Near East could have been built only on the basis of flexible mass production. For the Gothic cathedral, and for all the thousands of Gothic churches built in Northern and Western Europe between 1100 and 1300, the evidence is fully available. There is not the slightest doubt that these were the product of flexible mass production. The basic parts, building blocks, roofing, and so on, were fully standardized. But their assembly varied with the architect's plan. Only windows, ornaments, doors, i.e., the features that make one church look different, were produced by unique-product production methods. But—and this is vitally important—all these are features that are added on to the basically finished building. Diversity of product, in other words, in the Gothic cathedrals, and even more in the small Gothic parish church, was provided at the very end of the process. The basic process itself was standardized, though it resulted in a very large diversity of finished products.

Similarly, the enormous number of Japanese Buddhist temples built between A.D. 700 and 1600 were also built by flexible mass-production methods. Each of these temples looks quite different. And yet each is put together out of essentially standardized parts, such as beams standardized as to width and length; standardized roofing and roof tiles; standardized intervals between the various levels of a pagoda, and so on. The individually distinctive features, e.g., doors or iron grilles or the ornamentation of the tiles on the roof's edge, were added only at the very end, thus creating brilliant diversity based, however, on true mass production, that is, on standardized parts assembled according to prearranged patterns. Japanese temples, built of wood, burned down again and again. But they could always be rebuilt exactly from drawings showing only exterior appearance. Everything structural was so standardized that any skilled craftsman knew exactly what it had to be.

Without mass-production methods, neither the Gothic cathedrals and churches nor the Japanese temples could have been built. They had to be built essentially by semiskilled, if not unskilled, workers. Skilled men in the numbers that would have been needed to erect such major structures in such enormous quantities were simply not available in what were then poor, largely illiterate, and thinly populated areas. Mass-production methods alone made it possible for ordinary farm folk, drafted for a few months of work in the summer, or volunteering for the spiritual rewards of participation in such holy work, to do the great bulk of the work, with skilled artisans needed only to supervise and to execute the distinctive finishing touches.

When the principle of mass production was rediscovered, however, in the nineteenth century, uniform standardized end products were taken for granted. Henry Ford illustrates this perfectly.

When Henry Ford said, "The customer can have a car in any color as long as it's black," he was not joking. He meant to express the essence of mass production as the manufacture of uniform products in large quantity. Of course, he knew that it would be easy enough to give his customer a choice of color; all that was needed was to give the painter at the end of the assembly line three or four spray guns instead of one. But Ford also realized, rightly, that the uniformity of the product would soon be gone altogether once he made any concession to diversity. To him the uniformity of the product was the key to mass production.

However, from the beginning, the alternative, flexible mass production, was actually being used—though rarely understood. Otto Doering, who built the first mail-order plant for Sears, Roebuck, designed a genuine mass-production plant to handle an enormous diversity of individual orders. The individual items in the mail-order catalog were the "standardized parts." Every order went through the same process in being filled. But what was finally assembled was not a "standard order," it was whatever the customer had ordered, on one shipping pallet, with one invoice, and yet with a range of diversity almost beyond belief. Very early in Sears, Roebuck's history the catalog came to contain many thousands of items, which meant theoretically—and to a large extent practically—that the end product had to be assembled in millions of different combinations, with the probability of any two orders being identical practically nil.

Even earlier, Ernst Abbé (as discussed in Chapter 20) had organized lens-making in the Zeiss Optical Works in Jena, Germany, as flexible mass production.

Another example, this one from the 1930s and 1940s, was the farm-equipment manufacturer in Southern California who designed and made specialized cultivating machines for large-scale farming on irrigated land. Every one of his designs was unique. He made, for instance, a machine that performs, with various attachments, all operations needed in large-scale cucumber growing—from preparing the hills in the spring, to harvesting cucumbers at the right stage of their growth, to pickling them. He rarely made more than one of each machine at a time. Yet every one of his more than seven hundred different machines was made up entirely of mass-produced, uniform, standardized parts, which someone in the American economy turned out by the thousands. His biggest job was not to design a machine that identified cucumbers of the right ripeness for pickling, but to find a mass producer of a part that, though originally designed for an entirely different purpose, would, when put on the cucumber cultivator, do whatever was needed.

The specific technique for applying the principle of flexible mass production is the systematic analysis of products to find the pattern that underlies their apparent diversity. Then this pattern can be organized so that the minimum number of standardized parts will make possible the assembly of the maximum number of products. The burden of diversity, in other words, is taken out of manufacturing and shifted to assembly.

There are obviously processes in which standardization of the end product is desirable. Rifles for the infantryman are but one example. There are other processes in which enough diversity of appearance can be engineered into a rigid mass-production process to satisfy the market need.

General Motors often points out that there are so many options on its cars—colors, body styles, seat fabrics, accessories, and so on—that the customer can actually choose from millions of different final-product combinations. More important—though not often advertised by General Motors—is the fact that all makes of General Motors (Chevrolet, Pontiac, Oldsmobile, Buick, Cadillac) use the same frames, the same bodies, and very substantially the same engine, let alone the same brakes, the same lighting system, and so on. Yet the cars look different, have different characteristics, and represent a great variety of combinations of basic standardized elements. All these cars (excepting only Cadillac) are put together on the same assembly line. All of them are, in effect, products of rigid mass production and are turned out in a process that has remained almost unchanged since Henry Ford's early days.

To obtain the appearance of diversity from rigid mass production requires, however, a volume of production for every one of the parts to be assembled on which few industries, other than the automobile industry, can count. Unless the volume for any one constituent type is very large, rigid mass production can, as Ford saw, turn out only a truly standardized product.

American Motors, for instance, is at a very real disadvantage because it has to turn out a fair diversity of end products—at least in looks and styling —without the General Motors volume. And yet it produces 300,000 to 400,000 cars a year—a very large volume by any measure other than that of the American automobile industry.

For most mass-production processes the preferred principle should be flexible mass production. Until recently, however, mechanization and flexible mass production were hard to combine. The tools appropriate to mass production were inherently inflexible.

The advent of the computer is rapidly changing this, for the computer, and especially the small process computer, which is, so to speak, a part of the machine or machine tool, eliminates the inflexibility of the tool and with it the main obstacle to flexible mass production. In traditional mass production—and in traditional machine production altogether—any change in product or process requires stopping the process. Change requires altering the machine setup, cleaning tools, changing the position of work and of materials, changing speeds, and so on. As long as this had to be done by hand, it required far too much time. Worse still, changing one tool meant stopping the entire process. Computer control, e.g., numerical control on a machine tool, eliminates the time need. The computer can make the change instantly on the basis of a preset command. Instead of taking hours, changes take seconds, or at most minutes.

This is not automation. (On mechanization and automation, see the next chapter.) This is a radical improvement in mechanization. Two examples are the shipbuilders of Japan and Sweden. That these two countries were able in the sixties to gain a dominant position in world shipbuilding and all but crowd out such old and experienced producers as the Scots at the Clydeside and the Germans in Hamburg is not the result of lower wages. Swedish wages are, if anything, higher than wages in Germany and Scotland. It is the result of the application of computer control to convert shipbuilding, traditionally a unique-product process, to flexible mass production. As a result, Swedish and Japanese shipyards can build ships from standardized parts and yet turn out final products of great diversity, not only in appearance but also in size, structure, speed, and so on. The job is still, as in the traditional unique-product process, organized by stages. But within each stage the process is a mass-production process in which the parts are standardized but in which the configuration of parts has almost infinite flexibility. The process results both in much lower cost and in much greater speed—and above all, in almost complete predictability of the building cycle and in such tight control of scheduling that—almost for the first time in the history of shipbuilding—a reliable and dependable delivery date for the finished product can be set far in advance.

Computerized control of process changes has also been applied—and with similar results—to other products, e.g., to the making of glass bottles.

Computerized control requires redesign of the process. It is difficult, expensive, and requires hard, time-consuming analysis of product and process. But wherever it has been used to convert a rigid process to flexible mass production, there has been major cost reduction—sometimes reaching 50 to 60 percent. Production speeds have been substantially increased. Scheduling has become as reliable as in rigid plant production. At the same time, true marketing has become possible.

The architects of the Gothic cathedrals and churches could design a church to fit the needs of the individual customer, the bishop, cathedral chapter, or parish, and yet have what, in effect, was a standardized production process using standardized parts and with semiskilled, if not totally unskilled, labor.

Similarly, flexible mass production can turn out a very large variety of truly different products and yet have a totally standardized process of production. For this reason one can predict that it is flexible mass production that will increasingly become the mass-production system of tomorrow, with rigid mass production increasingly confined to the very small number of end products where basic uniformity is in itself a fundamental customer need and customer specification.

## Process Production

The fourth system is process production. Here process and product become one.

The classic example of a process industry is the oil refinery. The end products that a refinery will obtain out of crude oil are determined by the process it uses. It can produce only the oil distillates for which it is built and only in definite proportions. If new distillates have to be added or if the proportion of the various distillates is to be changed significantly, the refinery has to be rebuilt. Process production is the rule in the chemical industries. It is, with minor variations, the basic system of a milk-processing or a plate-glass plant.

Process production is an integrated system. There are no stages in it, there are no parts. There is only one process. Typically, process production starts with one basic material. But by the logic of that material, e.g., crude oil, it ends up with a multitude of very different end products for very different end uses. The process itself has high rigidity—more rigidity even than rigid mass production. The end product typically has far more diversity than even unique-product production.

Because process production is a system, it has tremendous economies and tremendous productivity where it is appropriate. But where it is misapplied, or where it is not truly developed into process production—as in the example of basic steelmaking given above—its rigidity and cost tend to outweigh its benefits.

Process production is, or should be, the model for a great many production processes which historically have been organized as unique-product production or as rigid mass production. The basic difference in performance between a well-run telephone system and most post offices is that telephone service is organized as process production and as a true system. Post offices everywhere are organized at best on mass-production principles—and, in effect, by and large, still on unique-product principles with "stages" of the process and with totally different processes for different "products," that is, different kinds of mail, or letters versus parcels. To be sure, it is easier to move electronic impulses than it is to move paper, let alone heavy parcels. But wherever a mail service has been able to improve its performance significantly, it has done so by trying to approximate its system to a model of process production.

All transportation, whether of mail, freight, or people, should be considered process production. The means of transportation always have to be a system, have to have great rigidity, have to be scheduled and have to be integrated with one another. But each letter, each parcel, let alone each passenger, has a separate destination. There is, therefore, almost infinite diversity of "end products." And this only a system, that is, essentially, process production, can organize and can perform effectively, productively, and with high satisfaction to the customer.

## What Each Principle Demands

Each of the four principles has different characteristics and makes different demands. Each has its own costs. Each has its own vulnerabilities. Each has its own strengths.

*Unique-product* production is labor-intensive. Even when highly mechanized—and it does not lend itself to automation—capital investment will be comparatively low compared to labor cost. But it has great flexibility. Costs for the individual product are high, but break-even points are low. Unique-product production can operate at a low volume of output or with considerable fluctuation in output. It makes high demands on skill, but little or no demands on judgment.

*Rigid mass production* is also labor-intensive rather than capital-intensive. But it requires high volume—indeed, very high volume. Even minor fluctuations in output adversely affect the economies of the system. It needs high skill in the design of the process, as well as in its maintenance, and low or no skill in actual operations. It requires a high degree of judgment in design, but practically no judgment in operations.

*Flexible mass production* tends to become increasingly capital-intensive. It still, however, requires a substantial amount of labor. It requires high volume of total output but has great flexibility with respect to the composition of the output, the product mix. It requires high skill in designing the system and maintaining it. Operating it, as a rule, requires little skill. But it requires a good deal of judgment.

*Process production* requires very high capital investment. The only princi-

ple of production appropriate to industries with very high capital investment is process production. It should, therefore, not also be labor-intensive.

Any industry that is both highly capital-intensive and highly labor-intensive is likely to use the wrong principle of production. It has not learned
how to apply process-production principles. Steelmaking is the obvious
example, but so is papermaking. The airlines are another example, but so
is the hospital. These are inherently highly vulnerable industries or services
which combine the worst of both worlds, such as high break-even points and
inflexibility of product mix. We usually do not know how to put such
industries on true process-production, but the more closely such industries
or services can attain genuine process production in part of their activities,
the better will they perform, both in quality and in economic terms.

Process production requires continuing high volume. The typical process
plant in the chemical industry or in the plate-glass industry can operate only
at or near peak capacity. Otherwise it has to be shut down. It has great
diversity of product mix, but it has little or no flexibility. It can produce
only the products for which the system has been designed. It requires
extreme skill in design. It may require very high skill in operation, e.g., on
the part of schedulers, pilots, and maintenance people of an airline. But it
may also require very little skill, as in the typical oil refinery. But it requires
a very high degree of judgment by practically every employee.

Since product and process have, so to speak, become one in process
production, new products will be created by changes in the process, even
if there is no demand for them in the existing market. This is a common
occurrence in the chemical industry, but also typical of the airlines industry.
When a new, bigger plane comes in, a new market has to be created. It is
characteristic of process production that the volume of production cannot
be increased gradually. The minimum unit of production—whether a new
chemical plant or a new jumbo jet—is so large that it requires a quantum
jump in production, and with it new markets.

In *unique-product production,* management's first job is to get an order.
In both kinds of *mass production,* the job is to build an effective distributive
organization and to educate the customer to adapt his wants to the available
range of product variety. In *process production,* the first task is to create,
maintain, and expand a market and to create new markets. To distribute
kerosene lamps free to the Chinese peasants to create a market for kerosene
—the famous Standard Oil story of eighty years ago—is a good example of
what this means.

In the *unique-product* system the time span of decisions is short. Under
both types of *mass production* it becomes longer: a distributive organization,
for instance, may take ten years to build. But under a *process system,*
decisions are made for an even longer future. Once built, the productive

facilities are relatively inflexible and can be changed only at major expense; the total investment is likely to be large; and the development of a market is long range. The marketing systems of the big oil companies are good examples.

The more advanced the production organization, the more important are decisions for the future.

Each system requires different management skills and organization. *Unique-product production* requires people good at technical functions. *Mass production*, rigid and flexible, requires management trained in analytical thinking, in scheduling, and in planning. *Flexible mass production* as well as *process production* require management trained in seeing a business as a whole, in conceptual synthesis, and in decision-making.

There are significant differences with respect to the work force and its management. Unique-product production can usually adjust its work force to economic fluctuations, keeping in bad times only foremen and a nucleus of the most highly skilled. It can, as a rule, find what other skills it needs on the labor market. Precisely because they have limited skill, the workers in mass production must increasingly demand employment stability from the enterprise. The work force in process production represents such an investment in judgment that the business must try to maintain employment stability. It is neither accident nor philanthropy that the oil companies—typical process businesses—have tried so hard to keep employment steady even in bad depression years.

These four principles of production are "pure" types. But there are many businesses—and equally many nonbusinesses (the hospital would be an example)—where different parts of the work are best organized on different principles. How then can these principles be combined?

The hospital needs unique-product production. Patient care can be given only on that basis, even though the great majority of patients in any hospital fall into a very small number of highly predictable and highly repetitive categories, such as childbirth, minor orthopedic surgery, cardiac cases, and so on. At the same time, the medical services, from X-ray to medical laboratory to physical therapy, have to be organized in what is essentially flexible mass production. The same applies to the "hotel" services, i.e., the feeding of patients, the housekeeping, and so on. Other parts of the hospital require a genuine system design, i.e., process production. Yet all this has to be integrated into one hospital, one management, and one process and has to be delivered to the same patient at his bedside.

Few industrial processes are as complicated as the hospital; but an airline also has a variety of "production principles" which inform different parts of its work, and even different parts of its transportation operation.

The rule for the use of different principles in one organization is simple

—though by no means easy of application. Different principles of production can work well in the same organization; but they must not be mixed.

It is fairly easy to organize, for instance, the bulk of the production process as mass production, either rigid or flexible, with unique-product production both at the end and at the beginning of the process, which was what the builders of the Gothic cathedrals or the Japanese temples did. This is what today's mass builder of houses does who designs three or four basic models from the same standardized parts, then adapts these models to a fairly large variety of different end products with different floor plans, different lighting and decorating schemes, and different exterior trim.

But where different principles of production have to be mixed together, there is confusion, there is friction, there is inefficiency. This is a basic problem of the hospital, where no one so far has found a way to separate what are, in effect, quite different principles of production in the delivery of patient care.

Managers, therefore, need to understand what principles of production are truly appropriate to the different stages of the production process they have to manage. They have to analyze the logic of each stage. And if they find that they require different principles to be organized, they have then to try to separate these stages so that they do not interfere with each other. This organization, however, cannot be done by imitating what others are doing. It requires that management—whether of a business or of a public-service institution—analyze its own work and its own production processes. It also requires that management understand the basic principles of production, their characteristics, their limitations, and their requirements.

# 18

# Making Work Productive: Controls and Tools

*Control of Work and Process—Control Must Be a Tool of the Worker—Control a Principle of Economy, Not of Morality—Inspection Is Not Control—Routines and Exceptions—The Patterns of Routines—Work and Tools—Bigger Is Not Better—Modernization and Automation—Tools as the Bridge Between Work and Working—Men Are Poor Machine Parts—The Principles of Automation—Beyond Manual Work—Processing Information—Application and Learning of Known Knowledge—What about the Generation of New Knowledge?—The Challenge*

Work is a process, and any process needs to be controlled. To make work productive, therefore, requires building the appropriate controls into the process of work.

Specifically the process of production needs built-in controls in respect to:

—its direction;

—its quality;

—the quantity it turns out in a given unit of time and with a given input of working;

—its standards, such as machine maintenance or safety;

—its economy, that is, the efficiency with which it uses resources.

Each work process needs its own controls. There is no "standard" control, but all control systems have to satisfy the same basic demands and have to live up to the same overall specifications.

The first thing to know is that controlling the work process means control

217

of the work, and not control of the worker. Control is a tool of the worker and must never be his master. It must also never become an impediment to working.

The most extreme cases of controls impeding work are not to be found in manufacturing but in retailing and in the hospital. There controls have been permitted to become an end in themselves to the point where they encroach upon the work and seriously harm it.

In the department store a great many controls are undoubtedly required. Each sale has to be recorded. There is need for information for inventory control, billing, credit, delivery, and so on. But in far too many department stores the salesperson is supposed to provide all the control information. As a result, he or she has less and less time to do what he is paid for, that is, selling. In some large American retail stores, two-thirds of the salesperson's time is devoted to paperwork with only one-third left for selling. The remedy is a simple one and works wherever tried. Once the salesperson has done his or her job, which is to serve the customer, the entire paperwork is turned over to a separate clerk who services a number of sales people and does the paperwork for them. The impact both on the ability of salespeople to sell and on their morale is astonishing.

In the hospital, controls are needed in tremendous number, from medical records to billing to the handling of insurance claims for reimbursement, for the patient's personal physician, and so on. Yet to have the nurse handle this paper flood—as is the practice in the typical hospital—is gross miscontrol. It makes the nurse deskbound so that she has less and less time for the patient. Again the remedy is simple: a floor clerk, usually a young management trainee in hospital administration, who takes on the information load including providing the nurse with what she needs herself to do her own job. This is not only economical, since management trainees are paid much less than nurses (and should, of course, be paid less), it is, above all, the proper use of scarce skills.

It should always be remembered that control is a principle of economy and not of morality (on this see Chapter 39, "Controls, Control, and Management"). The purpose of control is to make the process go smoothly, properly, and according to high standards. The first question to ask of the control system is whether it maintains the process within a permissible range of deviation with the *minimum effort*. To spend a dollar to protect 99 cents is not control. It is waste. "What is the minimum of control that will maintain the process?" is the right question to ask.

Seventy years ago this was clearly understood by the men who built Sears, Roebuck. In the early days of the mail-order business, the money in incoming orders was not counted. The orders were weighed, unopened. (These were, of course, the days when currency was still metallic.) Sears, Roebuck had run enough tests to know what average weights corresponded to overall amounts of money—and this was sufficient control.

Many years later, in the 1950s, Marks & Spencer similarly developed a system of minimum controls. The late Lord Marks, it is said, was appalled at the paperwork he found when he visited one of the stores. He forthwith ordered *all* paperwork to be stopped. Control instead is exercised by frequent small samples—and this greatly increased the ability of the people in the store to sell and with it the profitability of the business. It also increased the morale of the people at work. They were finally able to do their work rather than to waste time and effort on controls which impeded them.

The second thing to know about controls is their basic characteristics. Controls have to be preset. There has to be a decision as to the desired performance and as to the permissible deviation from the norm. Control has to be essentially by "exception": only significant deviation from the norm triggers the control. As long as the process operates within the preset standards, it is under control and does not require any action.

Third, control has to be by feedback from the work done. The work itself has to provide the information. If it has to be checked all the time, there is no control.

One implication of this—and a very important one—is that inspection is not control. Inspection, especially final inspection, is, of course, needed for both goods and services. But if used as control, it fast becomes excessively cumbersome, excessively expensive, and a drag on the process itself. Above all, it does not really control, even if there is 100 percent inspection, that is, if every product is tested and analyzed. The end result would still be poor quality, excessive defects, and malfunction.

Inspection, in other words, is the control of the control system rather than the control system itself. And it too, to be effective, has to satisfy the specifications of control, above all, the principle of economy.

The control itself has to be exercised where the malfunction is likely to occur. The control action may then be performed by the machinery itself. The classical example is the governor on Watts's steam engine. Another one is the thermostat that runs the central heating unit of the modern home.

Or the worker may be alerted to take the proper remedial action—and this is also feedback control. What is important is not who takes the action but what action to take. Equally important is that the action be taken as a result of the working of the process itself and at the place where the action is appropriate, that is, the place where correction of the process, or a change in its direction (such as shutting off or turning on the heating unit), is to be performed.

This implies that a control system has to designate the *key point* at which contol is to be built in. This is not primarily a technical decision but a managerial one. At what point in the system is there sufficient information to know whether control action is needed? At what point in the system is there scope for effective action? Control at any other point is undesirable. But so is control when it is too late, or very late, to prevent damage. What part of the process requires continuous control? What part requires control only at specific stages? Where is preventive control needed, or at least control at a very early stage? And, where is control essentially remedial? These are questions that are rarely being asked in designing a control system. Yet unless they are being asked—and answered—a control system that truly satisfies the needs of the work process cannot be designed.

## Routines and Exceptions

A control system can control only the regular process. It must identify genuine exceptions, but it cannot handle them. It can only make sure that they do not clog the process itself.

Any process is an attempt to make order out of the chaos of the universe so that the great majority of phenomena, of actions, of problems, of situations, can be routinized and do not require individual and specific decision. A control system is a tool to enable men of average competence to do things which if tackled as unique events could be done only by exceptional skill, if not by genius. A control system that violates this rule and tries to provide for handling the exceptions will, therefore, defeat the process. It will sacrifice the 97 percent we understand to the 3 percent we do not understand.

Exceptions can never be prevented but they can be eliminated from the work process. They then can be handled separately and as exceptions. To make a control system take care of exceptions misdirects and undermines both the work process and the control system.

The examples that best illustrate this are not to be found in manufacturing industry but in the processing of information in the life insurance business. Every life insurance company handles every day a veritable avalanche of death claims. Every life insurance company has learned that death claims have to be handled fast or else the company rapidly loses its standing in the market. Hence, every life insurance company long ago adopted the rule that routine death claims are to be paid within twenty-four hours.

The great majority—well over 90 percent—of all the claims are routine and need only to be checked off. Are all the needed forms provided? Is all the required information in hand? If the answer is yes—and it should not take more than a few seconds to find this out—payment is authorized.

In a small number of cases, the information is not complete. The death certificate is missing or it has not been signed by a physician or it does not state a cause of death; the name on the death certificate is different from the name on the policy; or the age is significantly different, and other such, usually petty, clerical shortcomings.

Death claims are sorted alphabetically (or sometimes by area) when they are received and then handed to a claims clerk to work up. In the typical American company, until very recently, the claims clerk was expected to handle all the claims in his or her area as they came in. This usually meant that the claims clerk worked up a dozen claims and then came to one where routine checking was not adequate control. The claims clerk then began to work on it. Sometimes he could settle the problem in a few seconds, e.g., by sending it back to the agent in the field with the appropriate form letter asking for whatever information was lacking. But sometimes he had to spend half an hour or even an hour on handling one claim. As a result, routine claims backed up. And by twelve o'clock, the clerk was usually way behind, and routine claims that should have been authorized for payment had not been processed.

The typical British insurance company handles this differently. There the claims clerk inspects each claim to see whether it is routine or not. Any claim that is not so simple that it can be cleared for payment immediately is handed over to a special small group of "experts," usually older and highly experienced claims clerks, who then begin to work on it. In the meantime, the flow of routine claims continues unimpeded.

There is yet another way of handling this, used in some European and Japanese life insurance companies. The claims clerk puts aside, on a separate table, every claim which he cannot immediately clear for payment. So do three or four other claims clerks working within the same claims unit. When the pile of routine claims has dwindled and the pile of nonroutine claims has grown, say, around 10:30 or 11 in the morning, the claims clerks then divide the unusual claims among them according to their workload at the moment. As a result, they usually manage to work up all claims, routine and nonroutine, by noon in the morning and by closing time in the afternoon.

The traditional American system is misapplication of control. It subordinates the routine to the exceptions. The traditional British system is effective control. It eliminates the exceptions from the process, which keeps flowing. But it stultifies the worker; it is a good control system for a machine process rather than for human work. The German or Japanese system satisfies both the demands of work and those of working.

The best control system, however, is not found in business. It is the differential diagnosis of the physician as it was developed in the early nineteenth century. The differential diagnosis proceeds from the ascertainable systems in a preset order. It eliminates step by step all the inapplicable diagnoses, that is, all the exceptions. It makes the process of discovery into a routine.

To design a control system, one has to think through what is routine and what is exception.

## The Patterns of Routines

There are three patterns of routines. First is the pattern in which both input and output are highly standardized. This is the case in rigid mass production—but in flexible mass production as well.

Life insurance claims belong in this pattern. The input is totally standardized—a claim for payment because of one event, death of the policyholder. The output is equally standardized. It is a check in payment of the claim. Only the amount of the check varies. And the amount, of course, is determined in advance by the policy itself. The handling of life insurance death claims is a perfect example of rigid mass production—perhaps a better one than the automobile assembly line. In this pattern, control consists of organizing the routine flow and eliminating the exceptions to be handled separately.

In the second pattern, the apparent diversity of events actually represents a configuration of subpatterns, each of which is highly routinized. One example is casualty insurance, such as insurance against fire, burglary, losses at sea, and so on. Here there seems to be bewildering variety both of risks and of claims. Actually, there are no more than half a dozen patterns.

Another example is the hospital. The first impression is one of total unpredictability. Each "process," i.e., each patient, seems to require a unique control system of his own; this is the way most physicians see the hospital. Actually, there are no more subpatterns in a hospital than there are in a casualty insurance business, let alone in many manufacturing businesses. A dozen or so common illnesses account for 90 percent or more of all patient days in the hospital. Each of these illnesses requires medical care within a known and fairly narrow range of procedures, makes predictable demands on hospital facilities such as operating theaters, X-ray, medical laboratories, and physical therapy, and has a predictable prognosis within a narrow range. For each there is an average to which the great majority of events closely conforms. A hospital can, therefore, be controlled by controlling a fairly small number of preset patterns. The exceptions are important—indeed, they are often the most difficult medical challenges. But they are being controlled by being taken out of the system and treated as genuine exceptions, that is, as truly unique events.

Wherever a process seems unpredictable the most probable assumption is that it actually consists of a number of highly predictable subpatterns. They appear unpredictable only because they interfere with each other. The key to designing a control system is to identify these subpatterns. Each can then be routinized, standards can be set, and a control system established that makes sure that the process operates within a preset range of norms.

Finally, there are processes where unique events prevail. They are rare in manufacturing; even unique-product production usually consists of a fairly small number of highly predictable, repetitive subpatterns. But unique-event processes are found, fairly frequently, in some service work.

Workmen's compensation insurance, which provides for the payment of lost income and damages to people injured while working and as a result of their work—but also for the medical costs and the rehabilitation of men contracting occupation-related diseases—is such a process. No two claims are basically alike. Each has to be treated as a separate claim, with respect not only to the payment due, but to the medical, surgical, or rehabilitation action required. Each frequently also calls for changes in work methods or in the tools used in order to eliminate or lessen the hazard for the future. Yet the claims adjuster of workmen's compensation insurers has to have almost complete authority to settle claims. The great majority of claims is settled speedily, to the satisfaction of both the employer and the injured worker, and with a high success in cure or rehabilitation. Workmen's compensation plans have a better record of medical performance than most medical practice has.

The way to handle this pattern of unique events is to think through and define the standards. What are the minimum standards which every single piece of work, e.g., a settled workmen's compensation claim, has to satisfy in respect to the investigation of the claim, to the management of the medical or surgical work needed, to the time it takes for settlement, and so on? What, in other words, are the measurements by which a claims adjuster can measure and direct himself? To be sure, even in such a situation of unique events, there are patterns. But there are too many, and each of them embraces too small a proportion of the total phenomenon, to devise a control system for each pattern. The only control—but a very effective one —is standards which enable the individual worker to develop his own routine and his own control.

This last pattern is of particular importance because it is the typical pattern for such knowledge work as teaching, medical practice, and any other professional work. The professional, by definition, works by himself. By definition he also deals with unique events—unique at least within the small universe to which an individual professional is exposed. And then control has to be by standards. The dissatisfaction with the professional that is so widespread today—whether teacher, lawyer, or doctor—is largely based on the lack of such standards, that is, on the lack of a control system appropriate to a unique-events process.

## Work and Tools

The final step in making work productive is to fit the right tools to the work.

Different kinds of work require different tools. There are far too many tools, from very simple to very complex, and from very small to giant, to be analyzed and presented even in the biggest book. And tool design, tool organization, and tool application are technical subjects rather than managerial ones.

Yet the manager, whether he manages industrial production, the processing of information, or knowledge work, needs to understand the basic *managerial* requirements of tool usage.

A tool is not necessarily better because it is bigger. A tool is best if it does the job required with a minimum of effort, with a minimum of complexity, and with a minimum of power.

Contrary to popular belief, most assembly-line work, while fully mechanized, is done with small hand tools. They are modified to serve the particular job to be done. But they are still hammers, screwdrivers, mallets, pliers, and so on. Good assembly-line tooling provides the worker with the simplest tool he needs for a given job, when he needs it, and wherever he needs it.

This needs to be stressed. For it is one of the weaknesses of technology —or rather of technologists—that bigger is considered better.

The worst offender throughout history has been the military. It has always been hypnotized by bigness and complexity. Some of the worst military disasters of history have been the result. It was the worship of bigness that defeated the Persians when they attacked Greece. The Mongols in the thirteenth century overran Europe because the knights of chivalry were hypnotized by "advanced technology." They became the victims of their own and their horses' heavy armor and heavy weapons while the Mongols, on small and light ponies, with a minimum of weaponry, could ride rings around them. Similarly, Hitler lost in Russia to a large extent because he put his trust in heavy tanks and in heavy artillery which could not maneuver, let alone be supplied, on the soft and roadless plains of Russia. And Vietnam taught a similar lesson.

The right question for the manager is not "Isn't there a bigger tool for the job?" It is always "What is the simplest, the smallest, the lightest, the easiest tool that will do the job?"

The second simple rule is that the tool has to serve the work. The work does not exist for the sake of the tool; the tool exists for the sake of production. This rule is constantly violated by today's computer users. They become fascinated by the capacity, the speed, the memory, the computational ability of a new generation of computers. As a result, when the new computer arrives, a frantic search begins to find things for it to do. In the end, it is being used to turn out endless reams of information which nobody wants, nobody needs, and nobody can use. Keeping the tool going becomes an end. As a result, nobody has any information.

The argument for making the work serve the tool rather than the tool serve the work is usually, "The capital investment is so high that the tool can be justified only if it is being used all the time." It is true that it is wasteful to keep idle a substantial capital investment. Capital costs keep on running whether the tool works or not. Yet it is still infinitely more economical to absorb these costs than to have the expensive tool produce garbage. To produce expensive garbage is far more wasteful than not to produce at all.

## Mechanization and Automation

The most important thing for a manager to know about tools and work is, however, that tools are the *bridge* between work and working. Tools serve the work. They also serve the worker. They must, therefore, be engineered for making both work productive and the worker achieve. This requires that the manager understand what mechanization is and what constitutes proper mechanization.

Mechanization is a fairly recent word. Most people believe that it pertains only to modern tools, that is, to the tools of an advanced technology. But all tools are "mechanization." Over the millennia we have changed the energy source for tools—from human and animal muscle to wind and water and to fossil fuels and nuclear power. But tools have changed very little. Tools from the beginning were a uniquely human phenomenon. All tools are an extension of man. They either extend his body, as does the hammer, or they extend his mind, as do multiplication table and computer. Or they provide man with capacities for which his own body is not engineered—such as the wheel or the ax. But all tools are tools of man and must, therefore, serve him in his double need of making work productive and worker achieving.

There is a great deal of fear today that modern technology is becoming man's master rather than his servant. The definitive comment on this was given to me many years ago by a student who was one of the early computer engineers. "I am being asked all the time," said the young man, "whether I am not afraid of becoming the computer's servant. I do not understand the question. All I have to do is pull the plug."

While the fear of technology becoming the master and enslaving man is unfounded—and professed mostly by people who know nothing about technology and understand even less (and who, in addition, tend to believe that technology is an invention of the industrial revolution)—there is real danger that mechanization will be misapplied. Mechanization to be properly applied must always extend the sphere of human capacity, must always add to man's capacity to achieve. If it does not do this, it is poor engineering. It will not even make work more productive. It will, in effect, cut down output.

Specifically, there are two dangers to watch out for. The first is the danger of making man a part of the machine. Men are very poor machine parts. If the human effort is misengineered into the system so that it does machine work, the system works poorly. The second danger is to misuse the tool as a divisive element in the work group, thus frustrating man's basic need to establish a community bond through working.

The modern assembly line, as Henry Ford set it up, does both. Man on the traditional automobile assembly line is, in effect, a part of the machinery. He does very poorly, very slowly, and very sloppily what a machine should be doing. This is the essence of doing one repetitive motion at the same unvarying speed and rhythm over and over and over again. Worse still, the automobile assembly line makes each man a threat rather than a resource to his fellow worker. If one man on the line works a little faster, he threatens his neighbor. Working at his most productive, that is, with varying speeds and rhythms, becomes a threat to everybody else. And he cannot, by working better, help his neighbor. He is confined to his operation.

This, it should be said again, is not inherent in the assembly line. It is poor engineering of the assembly line. We shall see (in Chapter 21) that these defects can be overcome—even on the traditional automobile assembly line. They are, indeed, in the process of being overcome. But they are symptomatic of what happens if managers—or engineers—forget that tools are the bridge between work and working, and engineer the tools so as to serve the work alone.

What is to be done when mechanization becomes inimical to working, that is, when the organization of the tool that is most conducive to making work productive threatens to do harm to working and worker? One answer —the one that is available in most cases—is to re-engineer mechanization, as will be discussed in Chapter 21. The other answer is to transcend mechanization and move to automation.

The term automation is a fairly new one. It was coined in the late 1940s by a Ford Motor Company executive. The concept, however, is much older.

The best illustration of what automation means antedates the term—let alone public concern with the phenomenon—by many decades. It is the telephone system. The telephone system does not work "untouched by human hands," nor does it operate without human work. The user, in dialing the number he wants to reach, programs the system. And this is "work." But given these instructions, the system runs itself, switches to the appropriate channels, returns a signal that tells the dialer whether his call goes through or not, and disconnects at the end of the conversation. It also does the ancillary work, such as recording the calls for billing purposes. If need be, it could easily perform additional chores such as signaling a repair center that a line is out of order.

The telephone exchange exhibits the *four principles of automation*. First, the entire process is seen as a system. There is, so to speak, no beginning and no end. Everything is integrated. Second, the system is based on the assumption that phenomena of the natural universe fall into discernible patterns and can be routinized on the basis of a probability distribution. Third, the system controls itself through feedback.

Finally, the human worker does not work. He programs. He makes decisions based on judgment within the range of patterns the system is designed to handle. He may be almost totally unskilled—as is the user of the telephone. Or he may be exceedingly highly skilled, e.g., the people who design microcircuits on automated equipment such as computers, to be produced by totally automated equipment. But whether skilled or unskilled, the worker is discriminating. His tool is judgment rather than manual or even conceptual skill.

Whenever mechanization reaches the point where the worker is engineered to be a machine part, we can automate. We can design a machine to do machine's work. This may not, in a given case, be desirable or economical. We may not even have the technology as yet to do it, but it is always possible. It is not necessarily the best alternative to re-engineering mechanization to make it serve working as well as work, but it is always an alternative that should be taken seriously.

Automation is not an arrangement of machines. It is not the ultimate in mechanization. It is a basically different concept. It can work perfectly without any machines. The abacus, which Japanese and Chinese ten-year-olds use with high speed and accuracy, is, in effect, automation and data processing, fully as advanced and as sophisticated as anything the computer does. It does not require machinery and advanced technology, but it embodies the basic concept of automation.

Any work needs its tools. Any work, therefore, needs to be mechanized. "The workman is only as good as his tools"; but it is also true that the tools work only as well as the workman. In designing tools for work, therefore, the manager has to be conscious of both dimensions, that is, of work and working.

## Beyond Manual Work

Work analysis, principles of production, controls, and tools have primarily been worked out, at least in systematic fashion with respect to manual work. Up till very recently the bulk of all people did manual work. Manual work, in turn, produced the overwhelming preponderance of whatever was being produced.

In a modern economy and society, however, manual work is increasingly of less importance—thanks primarily to our advances in understanding and organizing work and our resulting ability to make work productive. Hence, the question arises whether the same approaches, the same concepts, and the same principles apply to other than manual work.

There is no question of the applicability of the same approaches and the same principles to manual work which is not technically production, that is, to manual work on the railroad, in construction, and other kinds of physical work which the economist does not consider to be agriculture, mining, or manufacturing, but "services." This is a distinction of great importance to economics but of none to management.

It is also clear that the same approaches, principles, and methods apply, almost without change, to the processing of information, that is, to most clerical work.

Turning out insurance policies, handling orders, billing, key punch operations, and most accounting work are essentially production work. Indeed, most clerical work is mass production—some rigid, some flexible. It requires the same industrial engineering, that is, the same analysis of work, as manual work, the same process of production, the same kinds of control.

Processing information is easier to organize than most physical production. Information always comes coded in fairly simple form, electric impulses, figures, words, or, at its most complex, graphic information composed of a few parts, i.e., light, shadows, and at most a few colors.

Processing information, therefore, can always be done by standardizing the parts and assembling the final product, that is, by mass production.

Most true services work is not fundamentally different from producing things insofar as the principles of work are concerned. Selling in a retail store is basically flexible mass production. The individual sale varies greatly. The process varies hardly at all. And it can be organized in standardized parts. It is best organized so as to give the retail clerk a predesigned routine with the appropriate tools but with wide latitude of judgment. Unless, however, the routine has been designed and the tools supplied, even the best judgment on the part of an experienced retail clerk will not produce sales.

What may surprise most people, however, is that we know that the same approaches, principles, and methods also apply to the work of applying and learning known knowledge. Indeed in the application and learning of knowledge, work had been made productive systematically for a long time, though no one understood this.

One important example, already mentioned, is the differential diagnosis which the nineteenth-century physician worked out. Even older is the systematizing of the work of the surgeon—both the basic analysis and the integration of steps into a process were done during the eighteenth century, especially by the great English surgeon John Hunter (1728–1793).

The blueprint also antedates modern work study—it is a product of the mid-nineteenth century. It also is a systematic and purposeful application of the same basic work concepts to the application of knowledge.

The most important example of the application of the approaches and principles of work study and work organization to a knowledge area is, however, acquisition of existing knowledge, that is, *learning*.

For thousands of years people have been talking about improving teaching—to no avail. It was not until the early years of this century, however, that an educator asked, "What is the end product?" Then the answer was obvious. It is not teaching. It is, of course, learning. And then the same educator, the great Italian doctor and teacher Maria Montessori (1870–1952), began to apply systematic analysis of the work and systematic integration of the parts into a process—without, of course, any awareness that this was what she was doing. Montessori's own system is surely not the "final answer." But her approaches have provided the foundation for all subsequent work, e.g., that of the Swiss psychologist Jean Piaget, who has studied how children learn, and of the American behaviorists who have studied learning as a dynamic process of continuous work with its own logic and its own controls. The English open classroom in which the work of these people has been embodied in a real learning environment may be the first major change in education and the first systematic learning work. Its methodology is specifically the analysis of the work, the integration of the work into a process—a cross between flexible mass production and true process production—the design of the appropriate control system and the provision of the appropriate tools.

These examples show that the application and learning of knowledge are fundamentally no different from any other work. To be sure, the product is entirely different and so are the materials and the tools. But the process is basically the same. In its application lies one of the greatest managerial opportunities for making work productive.

The most conspicuous area in which we need to organize as systematic work the application and acquisition of already existing knowledge is perhaps the development work in industry, i.e., the work of converting new knowledge into marketable products or marketable services. The knowledge is already there as a result of research or invention. What is needed now is to apply what we already know. This, by and large, is not yet done systematically. Where, however, development work has been organized on the methodology of work (and again, primarily as flexible mass production), as in some pharmaceutical companies, the results have been impressive, in the speed of the work, in its productivity, and in the economic success of the developed product or service.

The one area in which it is not yet proven that the systematic methodology of work applies is the generation of new knowledge, whether invention or research. There is, however, considerable reason to believe that the same methodology should apply at least to substantial parts of the activity.

Edison, perhaps the most productive inventor of the nineteenth century, applied a systematic method to make inventing work productive. He always started out with a clear definition of the product desired. He then broke down the process into constituent parts and worked out their relationship and sequence. He set specific controls for key points. He laid down the standards, and so on. To be sure, Edison did not take out the "creative spark." But he tried, and successfully, to give creativity a solid foundation in system and method. One indication that he may have been on the right path is the large number of his assistants who became successful inventors in their own right, though clearly devoid of outstanding creativity—e.g., Frank J. Sprague (1857–1934), who was by all accounts a mere plodder but whose inventions were largely responsible for the electric streetcar.

But so far, we have only a few isolated examples—enough to indicate potential but not enough for proof. Clearly, there are limits to methodology —the artist's vision lies well outside its scope (though the artist's work does not). But research, that is, the organized search for new scientific or industrial knowledge, falls in all probability well within these limitations.

# 19

# Worker and Working: Theories and Reality

*McGregor's Theory X and Theory Y—The Evidence for "Theory Y"—And Its Weaknesses—Maslow's Criticism—What Is the Manager's Reality?— Why "the Stick" No Longer Works—"Big Fear" and "Little Fears"—The Overly Potent "Carrot"—The Myth of Antimaterialism—The Demand for "Much More"—And Its Toxic Side Effects—From Master to Manager— Can We Replace Carrot and Stick?—Enlightened Psychological Despotism —Why It Will Not Work—What Then Can Work?*

---

Since the writings of the human-relations school first came to the notice of managers around World War II, there has been a proliferation of books, papers, and studies on motivation and achievement, on industrial psychology and industrial sociology, on interpersonal relations at work and on worker satisfaction. Indeed, the literature on managing worker and working, in quantity at least, exceeds the literature in any other management field, including even the management sciences and the computer.

The most widely read and most often quoted of these books is probably Douglas McGregor's *The Human Side of Enterprise,** with its Theory X and Theory Y. McGregor conducted no original research. He acknowledged freely in his book that he had developed no new ideas but had formulated the ideas of others (and especially those I had put forth in three earlier books†). But his book fully deserves the wide attention it has received. McGregor powerfully presented fundamental choices for managing worker and working. His Theory X—the traditional approach to worker

*McGraw-Hill, 1960.
†*Concept of the Corporation; The New Society;* and *The Practice of Management.*

and working—assumes that people are lazy, dislike and shun work, have to be driven and need both carrot and stick. It assumes that most people are incapable of taking responsibility for themselves and have to be looked after. By contrast, Theory Y assumes that people have a psychological need to work and want achievement and responsibility. Theory X assumes immaturity. Theory Y assumes fundamentally that people want to be adults.

McGregor presented these two theories as alternatives and pretended to impartiality. Yet no reader ever doubted—or was meant to doubt—that McGregor himself believed wholeheartedly in Theory Y.

There is impressive evidence for Theory Y. On most jobs most workers, even those hostile to boss and organization, want to like their work and look for achievement. In most jobs even the most alienated workers manage to find something that gives them satisfaction.

This was first brought out in the late 1940s, when General Motors conducted a large-scale contest on "My Job and Why I Like It" (of which unfortunately few results have been published). Almost 190,000 workers wrote in and discussed their jobs—by far the largest sample of worker attitudes we have ever obtained. Very few were uncritical. But even fewer did not find something that made them like the job, did not mention some challenge in it, some achievement and satisfaction, some true motivation.

Equally convincing are the extensive studies of Frederick Herzberg on knowledge workers (already mentioned in Chapter 16). Herzberg produced example after example that knowledge workers want achievement and will indeed *work* only if there is achievement in their job. Otherwise they will at best go through the motions.

The most moving statement of Theory Y antedates behavioral science by thousands of years. It is the funeral oration for the fallen Athenians which Thucydides has Pericles deliver in his great history of the Peloponnesian War. What Pericles said, in effect, was that Athens was a Theory Y society as against the Spartans, who were probably the world's most consistent practitioners of Theory X.

Yet things are far less simple than McGregor's followers would make us —and themselves—believe. In the first place, we have learned that Theory Y is not by itself adequate. When I first propounded what McGregor later formulated and popularized as Theory Y, I laid great stress on the fact that this was not "permissive." On the contrary, I said that to manage worker and working by putting responsibility on the worker and by aiming at achievement made exceedingly high demands on both worker and manager. McGregor also saw this, though he did not stress it.*

---

*An oversight repaired in his posthumous *The Professional Manager* (McGraw-Hill, 1967).

## Maslow's Criticism

An ardent enthusiast for Theory Y, the late Abraham H. Maslow, pointed out that the demands are actually much higher than even I had seen. Maslow spent one year working closely with a small company in Southern California which at the time tried to practice Theory Y. In the book he wrote on his experience,* Maslow pointed out that the demand for responsibility and achievement may well go far beyond what any but the strong and healthy can take. He sharply criticized me and McGregor for "inhumanity" to the weak, the vulnerable, the damaged, who are unable to take on the responsibility and self-discipline which Theory Y demands. Even the strong and healthy, Maslow concluded, need the security of order and direction; and the weak need protection against the burden of responsibility. The world is not, Maslow concluded, peopled by adults. It has its full share of the permanently immature.

Of course, Maslow only paraphrased Dostoyevsky's famous legend of the Grand Inquisitor in *The Brothers Karamazov.* Unlike Dostoyevsky's Grand Inquisitor, Maslow, however, did not conclude that paternalist oppression is the only way to manage and, in fact, the only kindness to man. His conclusion was far more important and far more valid. Maslow—who, until his death a few years later, remained a strong advocate of Theory Y— concluded that it is not enough to remove restraints. One has to *replace* the security of Theory X and the certainty it gives by another but different structure of security and certainty. There is need to provide by different means what commands and penalties do under Theory X. Theory Y, in other words, has to go far beyond Theory X. It cannot simply be substituted for it.

This is an important insight. And it is clearly proven by all our experience with Theory Y.

In fact, while Maslow wrote *Eupsychian Management,* one of McGregor's closest friends and disciples proved Maslow's point. Warren Bennis, himself a distinguished industrial psychologist (and the editor of McGregor's posthumous book, *The Professional Manager,* mentioned above), attempted in the late sixties to convert the University of Buffalo, in upstate New York, from an old, tired, and rundown school into a major, first-rate university. His approach and that of his colleagues was clearly based on Theory Y—but without giving structure, direction, and security. The result was tremendous excitement but also total failure. Instead of achievement, there was lack of direction, lack of objectives, lack of controls,

*Eupsychian Management* (Irwin, 1965).

and frustration—as Bennis (who later became president of the University of Cincinnati) himself recounts.

One conclusion from Maslow's work is that Theory Y is not permissive, as so many of its advocates believe. It is not freedom from restraint. It is not, as its critics contend, indulging the worker, let alone coddling him. It is a stern taskmaster, sterner in many ways than the Theory X which it replaces. It has to achieve what Theory X achieved, and then do a good deal more—or else it will prove too great a burden and will make demands human beings cannot meet.

It has now become clear that Theory X and Theory Y are not, as McGregor maintained, *theories about human nature* (a position never shared by me, by the way). Whether we will ever know enough about human nature to have any theories about it remains to be seen. But so far, the evidence is not at all conclusive.

Everybody knows that there are undoubtedly lazy people as there are undoubtedly energetic ones. Far more important, however, is that ordinary, everyday experience teaches us that the same people react quite differently to different circumstances. They may be lazy and resist work to the point of sabotaging it in one situation. They may be motivated to achievement in another one. It is clearly not human nature nor personality structure that is at issue. Or at the very least, there are different human natures which behave differently under different conditions.

Modern American slang talks of being "turned on" or "turned off" by an assignment, a teacher, a job, or a boss. These terms have been criticized as dehumanizing. They refer to people, it is being said, as if they were electrical appliances. But everyday experience shows that this is exactly how a great many people behave. They react rather than act. The motivation, the drive, the impulse lie outside of them.

But this is not compatible with either Theory X or Theory Y. It implies that it is not human nature but the structure of job and work that, in effect, determines how people will act and what management they will require.

We also now know that individuals can acquire the habit of achievement but can also acquire the habit of defeat. This again is not compatible with either the Theory X or the Theory Y of human nature.

The best-known work in this area has been done by David C. McClelland at Harvard.* McClelland has taken the position that the desire to achieve is conditioned largely by culture and by experiences, both of which can be changed even in a nonachieving culture such as that of the Indian caste system. The most extensive study of actual worker behavior in large-scale industry, the work which the Canadian-born English psychiatrist Elliott

---

*See his book, *Motivating Economic Achievement* (Free Press, 1969).

Jaques* conducted for many years at the Glacier Metal Company in London (together with the company's chief executive, Wilfred Brown), supports the same conclusion.

## What Is the Manager's Reality?

The debate over the scientific validity of Theory X versus Theory Y is, therefore, largely a sham battle. The question the manager needs to ask is not "Which theory of human nature is right?" The question is "What is the reality of *my* situation and how can I discharge *my* task of managing worker and working in today's situation?"

The basic fact—unpalatable but inescapable—is that the traditional Theory X approach to managing, that is, the carrot-and-stick way, no longer works. In developed countries, it does not even work for manual workers, and nowhere can it work for knowledge workers. The stick is no longer available to the manager, and the carrot is today becoming less and less of an incentive.

The stick of the traditional approach to managing worker and working was hunger and fear. Traditionally, all but a handful of men in every society lived at the very margin of subsistence and in imminent threat of starvation. One bad harvest was enough to force an Indian or Chinese peasant to sell his daughters into prostitution. One bad harvest was enough for him to lose the tiny plot of land which was all that stood between him and beggary. Now, even in only moderately affluent countries, there is an economic floor well above subsistence level, even for the very poor. The worker knows today, in every developed country, that he and his family will not starve if he loses his job. He may have to do without a lot of things he would like to have, but he can survive.

Marx's *Lumpenproletariat,* that is, the unemployables, still exist even in some very rich countries. But Marx's proletariat has disappeared—and with it the stick of Theory X.

Even where fear exists, it has largely ceased to motivate. Instead of motivation, fear is becoming a demotivator. One reason for this is the spread of education, the other reason is the emergence of the society of organization. The spread of education makes people employable. It gives them a wider horizon. Even poorly educated people in today's society now know of opportunities. In a society of organizations it is possible to gain access to a new job. In a society of organizations there is lateral mobility. Losing one's job is still unpleasant. But it is no longer catastrophe.

*See his books, *Changing Culture of the Factory* (Dryden Press, 1952), and *Equitable Payment; a General Theory of Work; Differential Payment and Individual Progress* (Wiley, 1961).

The English tenant farmer, no matter how accomplished or industrious, who was evicted by his landlord became a "sturdy beggar." There was no other employment for him, except an occasional day of work as a casual laborer helping out with the harvest. Losing one's job was more than a life sentence; it usually condemned a man's children and his grandchildren. It made a man an outcast. Now the man who loses his job registers with the employment exchange for another one. Even at the depth of a serious recession today—e.g., the American recession of 1970–1971—there were hardly any long-term unemployed adult male workers.

In addition, there is rising employment security which protects a man in his job. It takes many forms. In Sweden a three-partite board guarantees a man another job and provides for his training and support between jobs (see Chapter 22). In most European (and Latin American) countries, there are legal restrictions on firing. There are seniority provisions which make job security into a right. In the United States, increasingly, income, if not employment, is maintained for long periods through such contractual provisions as supplemental unemployment compensation.

All developed countries are moving toward the system of the modern university, where a faculty member after a few years of service acquires tenure, which all but completely commits his employer to a job for him. At the same time, the faculty member has almost unlimited mobility and can freely move from one university position to another.

Japan has lifetime employment, which binds both employer and worker. Fear of being fired, therefore, does not exist in Japan, at least not in the "modern" sector. This (as the next chapter will discuss) is a major factor in Japan's economic achievement.

The Japanese example also shows that the more fear disappears as a stick, the more counterproductive remnants of fear become. The Japanese worker knows that he is tied to an employer and is unlikely to find other employment if he loses his present job. This makes him dedicated to the welfare of the organization that employs him. But it also makes him resent bitterly any structural change in the economy that might threaten the industry or occupation that employs him—the reason, for instance, for the extremely bad labor relations on the Japanese National Railroads. The Japanese worker's inability to move also makes him defenseless against the pressure to conform exerted by the organization. This is increasingly unacceptable to the young educated people. Indeed, while still expecting the security of lifetime employment, they increasingly demand for themselves the right to move to another employer. Rousseau pointed out two hundred years ago that the "right to emigrate" is the ultimate safeguard of personal liberty.

Japan, it is reasonable to predict, will move toward a system under which the worker has guarantees of income and job, but also mobility.

Modern behavioral psychology has demonstrated that great fear coerces, while remnants of fear cause only resentment and resistance. Fear in all developed countries has lost its coercive power. The lesser fears that still remain do not motivate. They destroy motivation—precisely because they lack full power and full credibility.

## "Big Fear" and "Little Fears"

The "big fear" still motivates where it is truly credible, as is shown by the quite unexpected success which a new approach to "curing" alcoholism has had. Everybody has "known" that the true alcoholic cannot stop drinking until he is completely down and out, if then. But a good many employers are now finding that a very large percentage of alcoholic workers do indeed stop drinking—permanently—if told in unequivocal language that they will otherwise be fired and that potential new employers will be told of their problem, so that they are unlikely to find another job.

But, save in such exceptional cases as the alcoholic who knows that he is rapidly becoming unemployable, the big stick, the horrible fear which drove workers yesterday, is no longer available to today's manager in the developed countries, whether the manager likes it or not. It is extremely foolish to try to depend on "little sticks," that is, whatever remnants of fear are still available. To be sure, any organization needs disciplinary devices, but their role and purpose is to take care of marginal friction. They cannot provide the drive. If misused to drive, disciplinary devices can cause only resentment and resistance. They can only demotivate.

## The Overly Potent Carrot

The carrot of material rewards has not, like the stick of fear, lost its potency. On the contrary, it has become so potent that it must be used with great caution. It has become too potent to be a dependable tool.

The Sunday issue of every newspaper these days contains an article by a learned sociologist or philosopher reporting that people are turning away from material satisfactions. On the front page of the same paper, Sundays *and* weekdays, there is then always a story that this or that group of workers —teachers or electricians, newspaper reporters or firemen, salesclerks or stevedores—have presented the biggest wage demand ever or have obtained the biggest wage raise ever.

When the youthful rebels against material civilization half a century ago went back to nature, all they needed was a tent or a sleeping bag. These days, turning one's back on material civilization seems to require an $8,000 camper-truck. The youthful rebels of the 1920s played their back-to-nature songs on a ukulele; today we need an electronic guitar to express our rejection of technology. The same European intellectuals who so vocally inveigh against American materialism use the fees they get for their lectures and articles for such nonmaterial satisfactions as a sports car, an airplane trip to a plush resort, or the purchase of a villa on a Mediterranean beach.

There is not one shred of evidence for the alleged turning away from material rewards. On the contrary, affluence means that everybody believes that material rewards are and should be within his easy reach. Samuel Gompers, the long-time head of the American labor movement, used to define the aims of a labor union in one word: "more." He would surely have to change this today to "much more." Antimaterialism is a myth, no matter how much it is extolled. So far, at least, the reality is tremendous and steadily rising material expectations, i.e., expectations for more goods and services.

This is not confined to the capitalist world. It has become the massive reality of communist societies as well. In the thirties Stalin did not hesitate to cut back drastically on the people's diet when Russia had a bad harvest. His successors, in 1972, faced by a much less poor harvest, instead dipped deeply into Russia's strategic gold reserves to buy grain from the archenemy, the United States. Mao, in the years of the Great Cultural Revolution in the sixties, thundered against "economism," i.e., against material incentives and rewards. By the early seventies the emphasis in China had shifted to heavy stress on such capitalist incentives as bicycles and sewing machines as rewards for performance.

The demand for much more is obviously going to run ultimately into the finite limitations of the earth's resources and the need to preserve the environment. What we experience today may therefore indeed be the final frenzied agony of the "material civilization." But, at least for the foreseeable future, this will mean above all an even faster shift from goods to services as carriers of satisfaction, and with it, from material-intensive to labor-intensive (and especially knowledge-labor-intensive) wants and purchases. It is most unlikely, for the foreseeable future, to alter the basic characteristics. On the contrary; that rising raw-material prices and ecology costs will push up the cost of goods is almost certain to add fuel to the fire of demands for more, much more, monetary rewards.

It is precisely the rising level of material expectations that makes the carrot of material rewards less and less effective as a motivating force and as a managerial tool.

The increment of material rewards capable of motivating people to work has to become larger. As people get more they do not become satisfied with a little more, let alone with less. They expect much more. This is, of course, one of the major causes of the relentless inflationary pressures that besiege every major economy today. Whereas a 5 percent wage boost was, a short few years ago, a major satisfaction, the teamsters—or the teachers or the physicians—now demand 40 percent and expect 20 percent.

This may be a manifestation of Maslow's rule that the closer a need comes to being satisfied, the larger an increment of additional gratification will be required to produce the same satisfaction. But the demand for more and much more of material satisfactions has also been accompanied by a change in values that does not fit Maslow's scheme at all. Economic incentives are becoming rights rather than rewards. Merit raises are always introduced as rewards for exceptional performance. In no time at all they become a right. To deny a merit raise or to grant only a small one becomes punishment. The same is true of Japan's semiannual bonus.

But whatever the explanation, the result of the increasing demand for material rewards is rapidly destroying their usefulness as incentives and managerial tools. The manager must try to deemphasize the role of material rewards rather than use them as a carrot. If only very large—and steadily larger—increments have an incentive effect, then using material incentives becomes self-defeating. The expected result in terms of motivation will be obtained, but the cost will be so high as to exceed the benefits. The cost will eat up the additional productivity. This is, of course, what has been happening with respect to material incentives for managers (e.g., stock option or extra compensation plans) as well as with respect to material incentives for all other classes of workers.

That inflation has become the central problem of the developed economies is, in terms of traditional or Keynesian economic theory, pure paradox. Inflation should not occur under conditions of high productive capacity and high productivity. Instead it is the norm. The reason is the totally unexpected size of economic appetites, the totally unexpected potency of material rewards. The result, however, is that to enable economy, society, and enterprise to survive, managers must try to curb and to contain economic incentives rather than rely on them. The economic incentive that has a true carrot effect is "too much." Only economic rewards that fall well below the threshold of motivational effectiveness are likely to be defensible economically and in terms of productivity and contribution.

This also means that the social side effects of the carrot are reaching toxic proportions. A potent medicine always has side effects; and the larger the dosage, the greater the side effects. Material incentives and rewards is a very strong medicine indeed, and becoming more potent. It therefore is bound to have potent side effects, which become more pronounced and more dangerous as the dosage required for effectiveness increases. In particular (as said before in Chapter 16) the more total income goes up, the more powerful does dissatisfaction over relative compensation become. As all our studies show—beginning with the GM contest "My Job" in the late forties

—there is no more powerful disincentive, no more effective bar to motivation, than dissatisfaction over one's own pay compared to that of one's peers. Once people's incomes rise above the subsistence level, dissatisfaction with relative incomes is a far more powerful sentiment than dissatisfaction with one's absolute income. The "sense of injustice," as Edmond Cahn, the American legal philosopher, convincingly argued, is deeply ingrained in man. Nothing is as likely to offend the sense of injustice as dissatisfaction with relative economic rewards in an organization. An organization is a redistributive economy (see Chapter 16); relative economic rewards are therefore power and status decisions on the *worth* of a person or a group.

Reliance on the carrot of economic rewards therefore runs the risk of alienating both the recipient and all others. It runs the risk of dividing the group against itself while uniting it against the system, i.e., against the employing institution and its management.

Clearly no deemphasis of material rewards is likely. Managers face instead the tremendous challenge of finding some means to relate the growing emphasis on "much more" to economic reality, i.e., to productivity and profitability. Material rewards are too potent to be relied on as the main positive motivator. This can only mean growing inflationary pressures— and growing dissatisfaction.

This applies to managers as well as to blue-collar workers. There is little doubt that managerial carrots have grown into seven-course Victorian meals, e.g., from small bonuses to massive stock option plans. (This also raises serious problems of social responsibility, which will be discussed in Chapter 28.) With respect to managerial incentives, we are moving from more to much more. At the same time there is growing evidence that inequalities in managerial incentives—real or fancied—are more demotivating than the rewards themselves satisfy and motivate.

The limitations of the effectiveness of carrot and stick apply with particular force to two groups in the work force: the new breed of manual workers and knowledge workers.

In managing manual workers, the manager in the developed country more and more has to deal with men (and to a lesser extent with women) who (as said in Chapter 15) start out as "losers," feel rejected, feel already defeated. These are people who have been driven all their lives and yet have not achieved. But losers always learn one thing, and that to perfection: resistance against being driven. They may not be able to achieve, but they know how to sabotage.

The best text on this is not a learned study by a professor of psychology but a best-selling humorous novel of the twenties, *The Good Soldier Schweik,* by the Czech writer Jaroslav Hasek. Schweik, one of the world's defeated, the archetypal dropout, single-handedly stultifies and frustrates the whole Theory X apparatus of the mighty army of a great power, pre-World War I Austria-Hungary. He does nothing overt. He knows how to sabotage.

To drive the new breed of manual workers therefore will not be successful. Hunger and fear no longer dominate them as they did their grandparents. But their very failure has made them impervious to pressures.

The knowledge worker will not produce if managed under Theory X. Knowledge has to be self-directed and has to take responsibility.

Fear is altogether incompatible with the production of knowledge. It may produce efforts and anxieties. It will not produce results. And fear inhibits learning, a basic finding of modern behavioral psychology. Rewards and reaffirmation will produce learning. In anything that has to do with knowledge, fear will produce only resistance.

Theory X assumes a "master." But in a society of organizations there are no masters. The manager is not a master. He is a superior, but he is a fellow employee. For the first time in history there is a society which lacks masters.

This is not the case in communist societies, which have assiduously worked at replacing the old masters with new masters. The role of the Communist party in a communist state is to be a master. It is in crisis precisely because even under communism a modern society becomes a society of organizations and as such requires managers and cannot tolerate masters.

The manager, not being a master, lacks both the master's authority and the master's credibility. The master's power is independent of the support he receives, either from his servants or from society around him. One can kill a master, but one cannot oust him. But, as the sixties amply showed, e.g., in the case of countless university presidents, even the chief executive of an organization can be ousted, precisely because he is a fellow employee. The authority he exercises is not his own, and cannot survive a challenge.

In terms of the ancient law of master and servant, the chief executive officer of the largest corporation is a fellow servant. Others may be subordinate in rank, but they are equal in law. They are not the chief executive's servants, they are his fellow workers.

This is much more than a semantic shift. It means that neither stick nor carrot will actually work if used by a manager, no matter how well they used to work for the master of old.

## Can We Replace Carrot and Stick?

Can we replace the carrot of monetary rewards and the stick of fear with a new carrot and a new stick appropriate to the new managerial reality? After all, carrot and stick have worked for an amazingly long time. One does not lightly toss out the tradition of the ages. Over the millennia during which working and worker have been managed, society has changed fundamentally. Yet managing worker and working has shown amazing continuity. The same Theory X principles that were applied to managing worker and working in the building of the great pyramids of Egypt still inform the organization of worker and working in the modern mass-production plant. Henry Ford's best-known epigram is "History is bunk." Ford was a bold innovator in organizing work, in marketing, and in economics, but when it came to managing worker and working he was completely the prisoner of history and a traditionalist.

The traditional way of managing working and worker cuts across all of man's cultures. There is no great difference between West and East, between pagan antiquity and Christendom, between China and the Occident, between Inca Peru and Mogul India. Nor does the organization of society itself seem to make much difference.

In that respect the Marxist analysis has altogether failed. The factory and office in Soviet Russia or in the Soviet satellites in Europe are organized no differently from the wicked capitalist West. Nor, all evidence clearly shows, is the worker any more achieving or the bosses any less the bosses. The same applies to the far more imaginative Yugoslav experiment of direct worker control of individual businesses, to direct worker ownership, to ownership by a cooperative, and so on.

We therefore know Theory X management. What to put in its place is —or so it seems—largely guesswork and speculation. Surely it would be the better part of wisdom to try to maintain the essence of Theory X by substituting "modern" drives for the old driving force of fear and money. What we need, one might argue, is to find the organizational equivalent to the gasoline engine which replaced the horse—but to keep the wheeled vehicle.

Not only managers ask this question. The labor unions are perhaps even more eager to keep the Theory X structure. The unions, after all, have a stake in the coercive relationship between master and servant of Theory X; if there were no master, what, indeed, would the union's role be? Also labor leaders derive their pride and sense of mission from opposition to Theory X, know how to behave under it, and have its rhetoric down pat.

When the younger workers in some General Motors plants began to talk about humanizing the assembly line, the greatest resistance did not come from General Motors management. It came from the United Automobile Workers' leadership, which insisted on talking about money, pensions, hours off, coffee breaks—and so on. The UAW leaders, in other words, insisted, against their own members, on maintaining and even strengthening a Theory X management on the part of the company.

To look for a new set of drives to take the place of the old carrot and stick seems not only rational but tempting. Such replacement drives are indeed being offered managers in the form of a new "enlightened psychological despotism."

Most, if not all, of the recent writers on industrial psychology profess allegiance to Theory Y. They use terms like "self-fulfillment," "creativity," and "the whole man." But what they talk and write about is control through psychological manipulation. They are led to this by their basic assumptions, which are precisely the Theory X assumptions: man is weak, sick, and incapable of looking after himself. He is full of fears, anxieties, neuroses, inhibitions. Essentially he does not want to achieve but wants to fail. He therefore wants to be controlled. Indeed, for his own good he needs to be controlled—not by fear of hunger and incentive of material rewards but through his fear of psychological alienation and the incentive of "psychological security."

I know that I am oversimplifying. I know that I am lumping under one heading half a dozen different approaches. But they all share the same basic assumptions, those of Theory X, and they all lead to the same conclusions. Psychological control by the superior, the manager, is possible; and psychological control by the superior, the manager, is "unselfish" and in the worker's own interest. By becoming his workers' psychological servant, however, the manager retains control as their "boss."

This is "enlightened" whereas the old carrot-and-stick approach may be condemned as crassly coercive (and is condemned as such by the psychologists). But it is despotism nonetheless. Under this new psychological dispensation, persuasion replaces command. Those unconvinced by persuasion would presumably be deemed sick, immature, or in need of psychotherapy to become adjusted. Psychological manipulation replaces the carrot of financial rewards; and empathy, i.e., the exploitation of individual fears, anxieties, and personality needs, replaces the old fear of being punished or of losing one's job.

This is strikingly similar to the eighteenth-century philosopher's theory of the enlightened despot. As in modern organization today, affluence and education—in this case, the affluence and rising education of the middle class—threatened to deprive the sovereign of his carrot and stick. The philosopher's enlightened despot was going to maintain absolutism by replacing the old means with persuasion, reason, and enlightenment—all in the interest of the subjects, of course.

Psychological despotism, whether enlightened or not, is gross misuse of psychology. The main purpose of psychology is to acquire insight into, and mastery of, oneself. Not for nothing were what we now call the behavioral sciences originally called the moral sciences and "Know thyself" their main precept. To use psychology to control, dominate, and manipulate others is self-destructive abuse of knowledge. It is also a particularly repugnant form of tyranny. The master of old was content to control the slave's body.

We are concerned, however, here neither with the proper use of psychology nor with morality. But can the Theory X structure be maintained through psychological despotism? Can psychological despotism work?

Psychological despotism should have tremendous attraction for managers. It promises them that they can continue to behave as they have always done. All they need is to acquire a new vocabulary. It flatters them. And yet managers, while avidly reading the psychology books and attending psychological workshops, are shying away from trying the new psychological Theory X.

Managers show sound instincts in being leery. Psychological despotism cannot work any more than enlightened despotism worked in the political sphere two hundred years ago—and for the same reason. *It requires universal genius on the part of the ruler.* The manager, if one listens to the psychologists, will have to have insight into all kinds of people. He will have to be in command of all kinds of psychological techniques. He will have to have empathy for all his subordinates. He will have to understand an infinity of individual personality structures, individual psychological needs, and individual psychological problems. He will, in other words, have to be omniscient. But most managers find it hard enough to know all they need to know about their own immediate area of expertise, be it heat-treating or cost accounting or scheduling.

And to expect any large number of people to have "charisma"—whatever the term might mean—is an absurdity. This particular quality is reserved for the very few.

Managers should indeed know more about human beings. They should at least know that human beings behave like human beings, and what that implies. Above all, like most of us, managers need to know much more about themselves than they do; for most managers are action-focused rather than introspective. And yet, any manager, no matter how many psychology seminars he has attended, who attempts to put psychological despotism into practice will very rapidly become its first casualty. He will immediately blunder. He will impair performance.

The work relationship has to be based on mutual respect. Psychological despotism is basically contemptuous—far more contemptuous than the traditional Theory X. It does not assume that people are lazy and resist work, but it assumes that the manager is healthy while everybody else is sick. It assumes that the manager is strong while everybody else is weak. It assumes that the manager knows while everybody else is ignorant. It assumes that the manager is right, whereas everybody else is stupid. These are the assumptions of foolish arrogance.

Above all, the manager-psychologist will undermine his own authority. There is, to be sure, need for psychological insight, help, counsel. There is need for the healer of souls and the comforter of the afflicted. But the relationship of healer and patient and that of superior to subordinate are different relationships and mutually exclusive. They both have their own integrity. The integrity of the healer is his subordination to the patient's welfare. The integrity of the manager is his subordination to the requirements of the common task. In both relationships there is need for authority; but each has a different ground of authority. A manager who pretends that the personal needs of the subordinate for, e.g., affection, rather than the objective needs of the task, determine what should be done, would not only be a poor manager; no one would—or should—believe him. All he does is to destroy the integrity of the relationship and with it the respect for his person and his function.

Enlightened psychological despotism with its call for an unlimited supply of universal geniuses for managerial positions and its confusion between the healer's and the manager's authority and role is not going to deliver what it promises: to maintain Theory X while pretending to replace it.

But what then *can* work?

It is not simply McGregor's Theory Y. The manager must indeed assume with Theory Y that there are at least a substantial number of people in the work force who want to achieve. Otherwise there is little hope. Fortunately the evidence strongly supports this assumption. The manager must further accept it as his job to make worker and working achieving. He must be willing, as a result, to accept high demands on himself, his seriousness, and his competence. But the manager cannot assume, as Theory Y does, that people will work to achieve if only they are given the opportunity to do so. More is needed—much more—to make even the strong and healthy accept the burden of responsibility. The structure we need cannot depend on driving the worker; neither carrot nor stick is dependable any more. But the structure must also provide substitutes to the weak—and not only to them —for Theory X's security of command and of being looked after.

What would such an organization look like? And how would it work? Fortunately we do not have to speculate. Some such organizations—though certainly not examples of Theory Y—exist and can be examined.

# 20

## Success Stories: Japan, Zeiss, IBM

*Industrial Engineering in Japan—Continuous Training; Zen versus Confucius—Lifetime Employment—But Flexible Labor Costs—To Each According to His Needs; the Benefit System—The Godfather System—Upward Responsibility—Ernst Abbé and the Zeiss Optical Works—The IBM Story —The Lessons—Not Permissive Management but Organized Responsibility*

In general, the history of working and worker is not a particularly happy one. But there are significant exceptions. Again and again, we find either a period or a particular organization in which working is achievement and fulfillment. The usual case is a great national emergency, in which the worker sees himself contributing to a cause. This happened, for instance, in Great Britain in the months after Dunkirk. On a smaller scale it occurred in the United States during World War II. Jobs did not change. Bosses did not become more intelligent or more humane. But the basic satisfaction of working changed completely, if only for a limited period.

This can also be achieved, examples show, without great national emergency, indeed, without any outside spur. Robert Owen made his workers achieve in his Lanark textile mills in Scotland 150 years ago—and he did not do anything revolutionary.

There are similar exceptions to be found in modern industry. The most important—if only because of its success in worldwide economic competition—is Japan's organization of working and worker.

At first sight, nothing looks more like the extreme of Theory X than a Japanese factory or office. Japan is not a permissive country but a very rigid one. Its way of managing working and worker is anything but flexible. But it differs significantly from any other way we know, whether rigid or flexible, autocratic or democratic. At the same time its way is not hoary tradition. The most important features of the Japanese system were developed in the twenties and thirties of this century and for use in modern large-scale organization. The main impetus was the importation of Taylor's scientific management, which began around 1920.

The industrial engineers in Japanese industry use the same methods, tools, and techniques as the Westerner to study and to analyze work. But the Japanese industrial engineer does not *organize* the worker's job. When he has reached the point at which he understands the work, he turns over the actual design of jobs to the work group itself. Actually, the industrial engineer begins to work with the people who have to do the job long before he finishes his analysis. He will study the work the same way his Western counterpart does. But he will, in his study, constantly use the work force itself as his "resource." When he has finished his analysis, the synthesis will essentially be done by the work group itself. The industrial engineer continues his activities, but he does so as "assistant" to the work group rather than as outside analyst.

The Japanese worker very largely also takes responsibility for improving his tools. Machines in modern industry are, of course, designed by the engineer, but when a new machine or a new process is being introduced, the workers are expected to take an active part in the final adjustment, the final arrangement, the specific application of machine and tools. In many businesses the work force actually participates in machine design and acts as a resource to machine or process designer.

### Zen versus Confucius

The mechanism for making the worker take responsibility for job and tools is what the Japanese call "continuous training." Every employee, often up to and including top managers, keeps on training as a regular part of his job until he retires. The weekly training session is a regular and scheduled part of a man's work. It is not run, as a rule, by a trainer but by the men themselves and their supervisors. The technical people, e.g., the industrial engineers, may attend but do not lead; they are there to help, to inform, to advise—and to learn themselves.

The training session does not focus on any one skill. It is attended by all men on a given job level and focuses on all the jobs within the unit. The training session which the plant electrician attends will be attended also by the machine operator in the same plant, by the man who sets up and maintains the machines, and by the sweeper who pushes a broom—and by all their supervisors. Its focus will be the working of the plant rather than the job of this or that man.

Similarly, the accountant is expected to be trained—or to familiarize himself in the training sessions of his office group, and through correspondence courses, seminars, or continuation schools—in every single one of the professional jobs needed in his company, such as personnel, training, and purchasing.

The president of a fairly large company once told me casually that he could not see me on a certain afternoon because he was attending his company's training session in welding—and as a student, rather than as an observer or teacher. This is unusual. But the company president who takes a correspondence course in computer programming is fairly common. The young personnel man does so as a matter of course.

Underlying this is a very different concept of the purpose and nature of learning from that prevailing in the West—but also in the China of the Confucian tradition. The Confucian concept, which the West shares, assumes that the purpose of learning is to qualify oneself for a new, different, and bigger job. The nature of learning is expressed in a learning curve. Within a certain period of time this student reaches a plateau of proficiency, where he then stays forever.

The Japanese concept may be called the "Zen approach." The purpose of learning is self-improvement. It qualifies a man to do his present task with continually wider vision, continually increasing competence, and continually rising demands on himself. While there is a learning curve, there is no fixed and final plateau. Continued learning leads to a break-out, that is, to a new learning curve, which peaks at a new and higher plateau, and then to a new break-out.

All we have learned about learning in this century indicates that the Zen concept is the correct one, and the Confucian (and Western) concept actually a bar to true learning.

Continuous training gives every worker a knowledge of his own performance, of his own standards, and at the same time of the activity of his fellow workers on his level. It creates a habit of looking at "our work." It creates a community of working and workers.

Japanese institutions are far more rigidly departmentalized and sectionalized than most Western institutions—though probably less rigidly than the highly bureaucratic Soviet organization. Departments in Japan fight fiercely for their territorial integrity. They have utmost expertise in "empire building." The individual member of a department is expected to be completely loyal to it, yet the individual employee tends to see beyond the boundaries of his own specialty and his own department. He knows what goes on. He knows the work of others, even though he himself has never performed it. He sees a genuine whole, and he is expected to be concerned with the performance of every single job in this genuine whole. He, therefore, can see his own place in the structure and his own contribution.

Finally, continuous training creates receptivity for the new, the different, the innovative, the more productive. The focus in the training sessions is always on doing the job better, doing it differently, doing it in new ways. The training sessions actually generate pressure on the industrial engineers. In the West, the industrial engineer starts out with the assumption of resistance to his approach by the employee, whether in manual or in clerical work. In Japan the industrial engineer tends to complain that the employees expect and demand too much from him.

The commitment to continuous training makes the entire work force in a Japanese institution receptive to change and innovation rather than resistant to it. At the same time, training mobilizes the experience and knowledge of the employee for constructive improvement.

One basic problem in studies of employee satisfaction in the West has always been that there are two kinds of dissatisfaction. There are negative and positive dissatisfaction. There is the complaint about frustration, arbitrariness, speed-up, poor pay, poor working conditions—the negative dissatisfactions. There is also impatience with poor working methods, desire to do a better job, demand for better, more intelligent, more systematic management. The Japanese continuous training mobilizes positive dissatisfaction and makes it productive.

## Lifetime Employment

The Japanese system, as everybody knows, is different in its approach to economics. Everyone has heard that there is "lifetime employment" in Japan. The majority of Japanese workers, at least in the modern Japanese economy (i.e., the economic institutions that were started after 1867 and in all other modern institutions such as government agencies), are guaranteed a job once they have joined an employer. At the same time, they cannot, as a rule, leave and go to work for somebody else. Both employee and employer are tied to each other. This is becoming less true. The labor shortage, especially among younger industrial workers, has led to a good deal of raiding. Highly trained technical people—engineers, physicists, and chemists—have acquired considerable mobility. But it is still true that the typical Japanese large employer cannot usually dismiss or lay off an employee, except in extreme emergency.

As a result, the fear of losing one's job for the ordinary economic reasons, because of technological changes, or because of arbitrary management action, is largely absent in Japan. There is a haunting fear in the Japanese system, the fear of losing one's membership in the employing institution. In the Japanese tradition there is no place for *ronin,* the masterless man. Nor, if only because of the seniority system of wages, is it possible, as a rule, for a man to find a job except on the entrance level, so that anyone who is unemployed past age thirty is practically unemployable. This creates tremendous fear of the consequences of personal misbehavior, i.e., tremendous pressure for conformity. It also creates genuine fear lest the enterprise itself may go under—which, in turn, then makes the Japanese willing to go to very great lengths to maintain the competitive position of their employer, whether the competitive position of a business in the market, or the competitive position of a government agency in the continuous infighting of Japanese politics.

The fear of dismissal or of being out of work are minimized in the Japanese system. It has to operate without the stick of Theory X. It also has to do without the carrot of economic rewards. Pay, except for a tiny group of top managers—and then only after age forty-five or so—has been tied to length of service for the last half century (and again, mainly in modern institutions). In each of the three categories in which Japanese tradition divides the work force, if not all humanity—manual worker, clerical worker, and manager—entrance pay is the same for everybody in the company, and so is the entrance age—respectively fifteen, eighteen, and twenty-two. Progression in pay, as well as progression in title, are then automatic—for manual and clerical worker until retirement, for managers until age forty-five. Pay and title depend on length of service.

## But Flexible Labor Costs

The Japanese system, most Westerners would say, can work only as long as pay levels are very low. The system, so it would appear to any Westerner, must lead to totally inflexible and rigid labor costs. But Japan actually has remarkable flexibility in labor costs.

One minor explanation of this is the existence of a temporary work force, which can be laid off without any notice. Women are, almost by definition, always considered temporary workers; very few married women work in Japan, except on the farm and in small retail shops, i.e., in "premodern" work. In Japanese traditional businesses, such as the old workshop industries producing lacquer, pottery, or silk, workers are almost never permanent, but almost always temporary and paid often by the hour. But the temporary work force is shrinking fast. In most modern industries it is by now almost nonexistent except for women workers. Yet labor costs are far from rigid. Only the flexibility of labor costs is structured so as to be a minimum threat to the worker's job and income security.

Actually, most Japanese companies, especially the larger ones, can and do lay off a larger proportion of their work force, when business falls off, than most Western companies are likely or able to do. Yet they do so in such a fashion that the employees who need incomes the most are fully protected. The burden of adjustment is taken by those who can afford it and who have alternate incomes to fall back on.

What makes labor costs more flexible than they are in most countries and industries of the West is the retirement system (or perhaps it should be called the nonretirement system). This system harmonizes in a highly ingenious fashion the worker's need for job and income guarantees with the economy's need for flexible labor costs.

Official retirement in Japan is at age fifty-five—for everyone except a few who at forty-five become members of top management and are not expected to retire at any fixed age. At fifty-five, it is said, the employee, whether he is a floor sweeper or a department head, retires. Traditionally, he gets a severance bonus equal to about two years of full pay. (Many companies, strongly backed by the government, are now installing supplementary pension payments, but by Western standards these payments are still exceedingly low.)

Considering that life expectancy in Japan is now fully up to Western standards, so that most employees can expect to live to seventy or more, this bonus seems wholly inadequate. Yet one hears few complaints about the dire fate of the pensioners. More amazing still, one encounters in every Japanese factory, office, and bank, people who cheerfully admit to being quite a bit older than fifty-five and who quite obviously are still working. What is the explanation?

The rank-and-file blue-collar or white-collar employee ceases to be a permanent employee at age fifty-five and becomes a temporary worker. This means that he can be laid off if there is not enough work. If there is enough work—and, of course, there has been from 1950 on—he stays on, very often doing the same work as before, side by side with the permanent employee with whom he has been working for many years; but for this work he now gets at least one-third less than he got when he was a permanent employee.

The rationale is simple. As the Japanese see it, the man has something to fall back on when he retires—the two-year pension. This, they freely admit, is not enough to keep a man alive for fifteen years or so. But it is usually enough to tide him over a bad spell. And since he no longer has, as a rule, dependent children or parents whom he has to support, his needs should be considerably lower than they were when he was, say, forty and probably had both children and parents to look after.

If my intent were to describe the Japanese employment system, I would now have to go into a great many rather complicated details, such as the role of the semiannual bonus. But I am concerned only with what we in the West might learn from the Japanese. For us, the main interest of the Japanese system, I submit, is the way in which it satisfies two apparently mutually contradictory needs: (1) job and income security; and (2) flexible, adaptable labor forces and labor costs.

In the West, during the last twenty-five years, more and more employees have attained income maintenance that may often exceed what the Japanese worker gets under life employment. There is, for instance, the supplementary unemployment benefit of the U.S. mass-production industries which, in effect, guarantees the unionized worker most of his income even during fairly lengthy layoffs. Indeed, it may well be argued that labor costs in U.S. mass-production industries are more rigid than they are in Japan, even though American managements can rapidly adjust the number of men at work to the order flow, in contrast to the Japanese practice of maintaining employment for permanent employees almost regardless of business conditions. Increasingly, also, we find in the heavily unionized mass-production industries provisions for early retirement, such as were written in the fall of 1970 into the contract of the U.S. automobile industry.

Still, unionized employees in the West are laid off according to seniority, with the ones with the least seniority going first. As a result, we offer the least security of jobs and incomes to the men who need predictable incomes the most—the fathers of young families (who also may have older parents to support). Where there is early retirement, it means, as a rule, that the worker has to make a decision to retire permanently. Once he has opted for early retirement, he is out of the work force and unlikely to be hired back by any employer. In short, the U.S. labor force (and its counterparts in Europe) lacks the feeling of economic and job security which is so pronounced a feature of Japanese society.

The West pays for a high degree of income maintenance. We have imposed on ourselves high rigidity with respect to labor costs, but we get very few tangible benefits from these practices. Also, we do not get the psychological security which is so prominent in Japanese society—i.e., the deep conviction of a man of working age that he need not worry about his job and his income. Instead we have fear. The younger men fear that they will be laid off first, just when the economic needs of their families are at their peak; the older men fear that they will lose their jobs in their fifties, when they are too old to be hired elsewhere.

In the Japanese system there is confidence in both age groups. The younger men feel they can look forward to a secure job and steadily rising income while their children are growing up; the older men feel they are still wanted, still useful, and not a burden on society.

In practice, of course, the Japanese system is no more perfect than any other system. There are plenty of inequities in it. The young, especially the young highly trained knowledge people, are grossly underpaid—to the point where they have to postpone marriage and the start of a family until they have eight to ten years of seniority. The young are, indeed, in rebellion against the enforced subsidy to the older worker, which the Japanese pay system exacts from them. Despite the outward deference paid to age, the treatment of older people over fifty-five leaves much to be desired. They are often ruthlessly exploited, especially in the small workshop industries of "preindustrial" Japan and in the multitude of small service businesses. But the basic principle which the Japanese have evolved—not by planning rationally, but by applying traditional Japanese concepts of mutual obligation to employment and labor economics—seems to make more sense and works better than the expensive patchwork solutions we in the West have developed, which do not come to grips with the problem itself. Economically, it might be said, we have greater security in our system—we certainly pay more for it. Yet, we have not obtained what the Japanese system produces, the psychological conviction of job and income security.

## To Each According to His Needs; the Benefit System

Western analysis of Japan focuses on money wages, if only because in the West they have traditionally been the main, if not the sole, element of labor cost. But in Japan, nonwage labor costs have, for many years, if not for centuries, been at least as important as wages. The importance of the fringes is rapidly diminishing in Japan as wage incomes have been rising. Still, they are a larger part of the total labor-cost bill than in Western or communist countries. In many industries they still almost equal cash wages.

At first sight the Japanese benefit system is incomprehensible to an outsider. There is no system. In one company there are housing allowances; a second company builds workers' housing; a third one does nothing about housing. There are educational allowances in one company. The next company runs a company school for women employees which teaches the traditional accomplishments of the Japanese "lady," i.e., flower arrangement, the tea ceremony, dressmaking (and a little English conversation). One company seems to take care of the widow and orphaned children of a deceased employee, another company seems to pay no attention to them.

Actually, there is a system: to shape benefits according to the need of specific groups within the work force. If the company employs a large number of young women, the great majority of whom will get married very soon, pension benefits—or even a first-rate medical plan—are of little value. But learning the accomplishments of the married woman is of very great value. If an employee dies and leaves a destitute widow with small children, the company is expected to take responsibility. If the widow is well off, or has a well-to-do brother, there is no need for the company to concern itself, and accordingly, no obligation.

The paternalism of the Japanese benefits system would not be acceptable in the West nor would the absence of legally grounded rights and obligations. In fact, it is questionable how long this will be acceptable even in Japan. There is tremendous pressure, from public opinion, from workers, from the government (but amazingly enough, not from labor unions) to systematize the benefits system and to give the employee predictable rights.

The basic concept, however, that benefits should be structured to the needs of the employee, particularly to the needs of specific groups within the employees—e.g., young women workers or old male workers, people with large families or unmarried or older couples whose children have grown up—is fundamental to the Japanese approach to managing worker and working.

## The Godfather System

The house of Mitsui is the oldest of the world's big businesses. It dates back to 1637, half a century before the Bank of England was founded. It also was the largest of the world's big businesses until the American occupation split it into individual companies. (As these companies come back together into a fairly close confederation, Mitsui may well again become the world's biggest business.)

In the more than three hundred years of its business life, Mitsui has never had a chief executive (the Japanese term is "chief banto"—literally, chief clerk) who was not an outstanding man and a powerful leader. This accomplishment is not matched by any other institution, whether the Catholic Church, any government, army, navy, university, or corporation.

What explains this amazing achievement? In Japan one always gets the same answer: until recently, the chief banto—himself never a member of the Mitsui family but a hired hand—had one main job: manager development, manager selection, and manager placement. He spent a great deal of time with the young people who came in as junior managers or professionals. He knew them. He listened to them. As a result, he knew, by the time they had reached thirty or so, which ones were likely to reach top management, what experiences and development they needed, and in what job they should be tried and tested.

At first sight nothing would seem less likely to develop strong executives than the Japanese system. It would seem, rather, to be the ideal prescription for developing timid men selected for proven mediocrity and trained not to rock the boat.

The young men who enter a Japanese company's employ directly from the university—and, by and large, this is the only way to get into a company's management, since hiring from the outside and into upper-level positions is the rare exception—know that they will have a job until they retire, no matter how poorly they perform. Until they reach age forty-five, they will be promoted and paid by seniority and by seniority alone.

There seems to be no performance appraisal, nor would there be much point to it, when a man can be neither rewarded for performance nor penalized for nonperformance. Superiors do not choose their subordinates: the personnel people make personnel decisions as a rule, often without consulting the manager to whom a subordinate is being assigned. It seems to be unthinkable for a young manager or professional to ask for a transfer, and equally unthinkable for him to quit and go elsewhere.

This process goes on for twenty to twenty-five years, during which all the emphasis seems to be on conforming, on doing what one is being asked to do, and on showing proper respect and deference.

Then suddenly, when a man reaches forty-five, the day of reckoning arrives, when the goats are separated from the sheep. A very small group is picked to become company directors—that is, top management. They can stay in management well past any retirement age known in the West, with active top-management people in their eighties by no means a rarity. The rest of the group, from department director on down, generally stay in management until they are fifty-five, usually with at best one more promotion. Then they are retired—and, unlike the rank-and-file employees, their retirement is compulsory.

Limited but important exceptions to this rule are made in the case of outstanding men who, while too specialized to move into the top management of the parent company, are assigned to the top management of subsidiaries or affiliates. In such positions they can also stay in office for an indefinite period of time.

To an outsider who believes what the Japanese tell him—namely, that this is really the way the system works—it is hard to understand on what basis the crucial decision at age forty-five is made. It is even harder to believe that this system produces independent and aggressive top managers who have marketed Japanese exports successfully all over the world and who have, in the space of twenty years, made into the second-ranking economic power in the world a nation that, at the eve of World War II, was not even among the first dozen or so in industrial production or capital.

It is precisely *because* Japanese managers have lifetime employment and can, as a rule, be neither fired nor moved, and *because* advancement for the first twenty-five years of a man's working life is through seniority alone that the Japanese have made the care and feeding of their young people the first responsibility of top management.

The practice goes back almost four hundred years, when the samurai, the retainers of a military clan, were organized into tight hereditary castes with advancement from one to the other officially not permitted. At the same time, the government of the clan had to find able people who could run the clan's affairs at a very early age and take their opportunities without offending higher ranking but less gifted clan members.

Today, of course, it is no longer possible for the chief banto of Mitsui to know personally the young managerial people, as his predecessor did a few generations ago. Even much smaller companies are too large and have far too many young managerial and professional employees in their ranks. Yet top management is still vitally concerned with the young. It discharges this concern through an informal network of senior middle-management people who act as "godfathers" to the young men during the first ten years of their careers in the company.

The Japanese take this system for granted. Every young manager knows who his godfather is, and so does his boss and the boss's boss.

The godfather is rarely a young man's direct superior; he may not even be in the direct line of authority over the young man or his department. He is rarely a member of top management and rarely a man who will get into top management. He tends to be picked from members of upper-middle management who will, when they reach fifty-five, be transferred to the top management of a subsidiary or affiliate. In other words, godfathers are people who know, having been passed over at age forty-five for the top management spots, that they are not going to make it in their own organization. Therefore, they are not likely to build factions of their own or to play internal politics. At the same time, they are the most highly respected members of the middle-management group.

During the first ten years or so of a young man's career, the godfather is expected to be in close touch with his godchild, even though in a large company he may have a hundred of them at any one time. He is expected to know the young man, see him fairly regularly, be available to him for advice and counsel, and, in general, look after him.

If a young man gets stuck under an incompetent manager and needs to be transferred, the godfather knows where to go and how to do what officially cannot be done and, according to the Japanese, is never done. Yet nobody will ever know about it. If the young man is naughty and needs to be disciplined, the godfather will spank him in private. By the time a young man is thirty, the godfather knows a great deal about him, and so does top management.

The great weakness of all Japanese organizations is their tendency toward the formation of cliques—the Japanese word is *habatsu*. Personal loyalty to a clique leader becomes the first duty of a man. In turn, belonging to the right clique becomes the one requirement of success. The incompetent but loyal *habatsu* man finds himself rewarded, while the most competent man who does not belong to the victorious *habatsu* may find himself out in the cold. The godfather system can clearly become the worst kind of clique—and sometimes does. Equally, it can easily degenerate into the worst kind of paternalism and into tremendous pressure for conformity.

Still, the young knowledge worker in the Japanese organization is not left orphaned. Nor is he being neglected. He has somebody to go to with his questions, his doubts, whether about himself or about his organization, with his aspirations and expectations. In turn, there is somebody in the company who cares for him, somebody who knows how the machinery works and who can smooth the young man's path, who can guide the young man's steps, but who can also administer, in complete privacy, very effective discipline.

The manual worker and the clerical worker also have their godfathers. For the manual worker, the role is being played by one of the supervisors. He is, indeed, far less a supervisor than he is a counselor if only because he has no weapons of enforcement. He cannot dismiss a man. He cannot prevent his getting more pay when he acquires the proper seniority. He cannot block a promotion.

By Western standards there is little courtesy and less warmth to the relationship between supervisor and man in the Japanese organization. There is not even much civility. Terms of personal abuse which would bring about an immediate work stoppage in any unionized Western plant—and would be unthinkable in most Western offices—are common. In this respect, Japan still follows the old tradition in which the teacher of the young warrior or the great Zen master showed his concern for the pupil by beating him. At the same time, the superior in Japan is expected to concern himself with the needs, the expectations, the aspirations, the questions of the younger man. And the seniority system makes sure that the subordinate is always a younger man.

### Upward Responsibility

The Japanese organization is infinitely more autocratic than anything that can be found in the West, outside of the military. The deference accorded the superior, beginning with the language used toward him, goes far beyond the most deferential of Western traditions. And yet authority from the top down is always matched by responsibility from the bottom up.

This is the real meaning of the phrase "consensus decision." It is not true that the Japanese make decisions by consensus. This would clearly result in the wrong decisions. Above all, it would inevitably lead to compromise. If there is one thing that is typical of Japanese decisions, it is that they are not compromises. The typical Japanese decision is a radical departure—the system is so complex and cumbersome that small decisions cannot be taken. (On this see Chapter 37.)

At every level of the organization, subordinates are expected to participate in the responsibility for the decision. They are expected to think through what the decision is all about. They are expected to do so by taking responsibility for the performance of the whole, for the good of the organization, rather than for their own narrow parochial point of view (though every Japanese will admit that this is hope rather than reality).

There are limitations. The participants in the decision-making process must always be members of one's own group. In other words, manual workers are not expected to concern themselves with a managerial decision. Similarly, top management would not normally concern itself with the organization of work and jobs. This is for the workers, for the supervisors, for the engineers in the plant.

Participation, however, is not in decision-making. It is in "decision-thinking." It is not in terms of Western constitutional theory participation in authority. It is, however, genuine participation in responsibility.

Though these Japanese practices are not "old Japan" but of very recent origin and developed since the 1920s, if not since the end of World War II, they do, of course, reflect basic Japanese beliefs and basic Japanese values. They cannot be transplanted into the cultural soil of the West. But that the underlying approaches are not specifically "Japanese" is proven by Western examples where similar approaches have been used, and with equal effectiveness.

## Ernst Abbé and the Zeiss Optical Works

In the economic rise of nineteenth-century Germany, the optical industry played a key part. By 1890 Germany had a virtual world monopoly on precision optics. While this monopoly was broken by World War I, Germany retained a dominant position until World War II. Precision optics were principally the achievement of one firm, the Carl Zeiss Works in Jena. Carl Zeiss (1816–1888), whose name the company still bears, was himself a major innovator and inventor, but his greatest contribution was his early realization that modern industry has to be based on modern science. Himself a craftsman and descended from a long line of lens makers, he early established a partnership with a university-trained physicist, Ernst Abbé (1840–1905). After Zeiss's death in 1888, it was Abbé who took over the management of the company.

Abbé was one of the first of the great scientist-inventors—and an exceedingly productive one. He revolutionized both the making of optical glass and the making of precision lenses. But his greatest achievement was not in science nor in business but in managing working and worker.

Independently of Taylor, Abbé applied what can only be called scientific management, that is, the systematic study of work. He analyzed the constituent operations needed to make optical glass and then to convert optical glass into precision lenses. He then synthesized both processes. The solution he came up with, around 1880 or 1885, can only be described as flexible mass production. But Abbé did not, as Henry Ford was to do twenty years later, proceed to organize working on the basis of these operations. Instead he turned over responsibility for working out the jobs to the work force itself. He called in the masters and journeymen from the plant, explained to them the new techniques and disciplines, and asked them to organize the jobs and to do the work.

To make optical glass in the quality and quantity needed—let alone at a cost that would allow its use in such everyday instruments as microscopes, cameras, or spectacles—required entirely new machinery and new tools. From the beginning, Abbé insisted that the skilled worker himself, with the assistance of the university-educated scientist and engineer, develop the machinery. The world monopoly which Zeiss held for so many years rested, above all, on equipment designed, or at least improved, by the workers themselves.

Abbé also introduced continuous training. By 1880 German industry had largely systematized apprentice training by combining work under a master with schoolwork in apprentice classes. Abbé added systematic training classes for fully trained and highly skilled craftsmen which they were expected to attend throughout their entire working life. There were frequent refresher sessions. The most highly skilled men were expected to join with the engineers, chemists, lens designers, and instrument designers in working on better methods, on new products, and on improvements in process and technology. The focus, as in Japan, was not on training for promotion, but on training for improvement of skill, tool, process, and product.

In one respect, Abbé went far beyond the Japanese. He insisted on feedback information to the worker regarding his output and performance. "A craftsman is in control of his work" was a slogan he constantly repeated.

There was no formal guarantee of employment security at Zeiss. Abbé, as well as his German craftsmen, would have rejected as immoral the Japanese custom of keeping an incompetent or lazy man on the payroll as long as he is "loyal." But if a man had learned to perform and showed himself willing to work hard, he was assured of his job at Zeiss regardless of economic fluctuations.

In his will, Abbé turned over the controlling ownership of Zeiss to a foundation to which all profits were to go and of which the Zeiss workers were to be the sole beneficiaries. This did not mean worker control. The Ernst Abbé Foundation is, in effect, run by Zeiss management and its appointed trustees. It did not make "capitalists" out of the workers, nor was it intended to do so. Indeed, the Zeiss workers were proud social democrats from early days. Nor did it mean more money to the workers. With owner-ship vested in the foundation, the Zeiss firm had to depend on internally generated funds for its expansion, which, in all likelihood, meant that dividends had to be kept very low. But the Abbé Foundation could finance benefits for the workers, and from Abbé's own days on, these benefits were tailored to the needs of major groups within the work force, whether schol-arships for workers' children, health benefits, or housing allowances. This made a little money go very far toward protecting Zeiss workers against major risks and toward providing truly meaningful benefits.

## The IBM Story

The final success story to be presented here is that of IBM.*

Long before IBM became the world's leading computer manufacturer, it was a producer of fairly sophisticated technical products—at least for that time. Today, of course, IBM's computers and the software that goes with them are among the most complex, most highly engineered, most precise industrial products made anywhere. At the same time, they must be capable of operation by mechanically unskilled personnel and must stand up under rough usage and under a great variety of conditions.

This equipment is not produced by highly skilled individual craftsmen. The equipment could be turned out neither in large quantities nor at a price the customer could afford to pay were its production dependent on craft skills. IBM uses semiskilled machine operators. It is prime evidence that scientific management and flexible mass-production principles can be ap-plied to the production of the most complex precision instruments in great diversity and in small numbers. Of a particular model, an advanced elec-tronic computer, for instance, only one piece may ever be made. Yet by dividing into homogeneous stages the job of building this unique product, IBM is able to use semiskilled labor for all but a small part of the work. But each job is designed so as always to contain a challenge to judgment, and control of the speed and rhythm of his work by the worker. The story goes that Thomas J. Watson, Sr., the company's founder and for many years its president, once saw a woman operator sitting idly at her machine. Asked

*I am indebted to the study of IBM—written just before IBM's meteoric rise as the leading computer manufacturer—by Charles R. Walker and F. L. W. Richardson, *Human Relations in an Expanding Company* (Yale University Press, 1948).

why she did not work, the woman replied, "I have to wait for the setup man to change the tool setting for a new run." "Couldn't you do it yourself?" Watson asked. "Of course," said the woman, "but I am not supposed to." Watson thereupon found out that each worker spent several hours each week waiting for the setup man. It would, however, take only a few additional days of training for the worker to learn how to set up his own machine. Thus, machine setup was added to the worker's job. Shortly thereafter, inspection of the finished part was included too; again little additional training equipped the worker to do the inspecting.

Enlarging the job in this way produced such unexpected improvements in output and quality of production that IBM decided to make jobs big systematically. The operations themselves are engineered to be as simple as possible, but each worker is trained to be able to do as many of these operations as possible. At least one of the tasks the worker is to perform —machine setting, for instance—is always designed so as to require some skill or some judgment, and a range of different operations permits variations in the rhythm with which the worker works.

This approach has resulted in a constant increase in productivity at IBM. It has also significantly affected the attitudes of workers. In fact, many observers both inside and outside the company think that the increase in the worker's pride in the job he is doing is the most important gain.

IBM then redefined the supervisor's job. There is no supervisor in the traditional sense. Where other companies speak of supervisor or foreman, IBM speaks of an "assistant." This is exactly the role the supervisor is supposed to discharge. He is to be the "assistant" to his workers. His job is to be sure that they know their work and have the tools. He is not their boss.

The policy of maximizing jobs has also enabled IBM to create significant opportunities for semiskilled workers. In each foreman's department there are one or more job instructors. They are senior workers who do their own work but who also help the other, less experienced workers learn higher technical skills and solve problems requiring experience or judgment. These positions are greatly coveted and carry high prestige. They have proven to be an excellent preparation for manager. They both train and test men so well that IBM has little difficulty in finding candidates for promotion. Nor is it plagued by the failure of newly promoted foremen to perform or to command their subordinates' respect. In most other industrial plants these are real problems. In some companies less than half of all promotions to foreman really "take."

The second IBM innovation also seems to have developed half by accident. When one of the first electronic computers was being developed in the late forties, demand for it was so great (or maybe engineering design had taken so much longer than expected) that production had to begin before the engineering work was fully completed. The final details were worked out on the production floor with the engineers collaborating with foremen and workers. The result was a superior design; the production engineering was significantly better, cheaper, faster; and each worker, as a result of participating in engineering the product and his work, did a significantly better and more productive job.

The lesson of this experience is being applied whenever IBM introduces a new product or a major change in existing products. Before design engineering is completed, the project is assigned to one of the work crews. The "assistant" becomes manager of the project. He works on the final details of design with the engineers and with the workers who will produce the machines. He and his workers—with whatever expert technical help is needed—plan the actual production layout and set up the individual jobs. The worker, in other words, gets in on the planning of the product, of the production process, and of his own job. This method, wherever used, has given the same benefits in design, production costs, speed, and worker satisfaction as were obtained the first time.

IBM has been equally unorthodox in its rewards and incentives for workers. Originally it used the standard approach; output norms set by the industrial engineer for each operation, a base wage for production according to the norm, and incentive premium pay for production above the norm. Then, in 1936, it did away with the traditional norms and with pay incentives. Instead of wages per unit produced, IBM pays each worker a straight salary (plus, of course, overtime payments, vacation pay, etc.). Instead of output norms imposed from above, each worker develops with his own foreman his own rates of production. Of course, both know pretty well how much output can normally be expected. But even for new operations or for major changes in process or job, the determination of output norms is left to the men themselves. IBM maintains that there is no such thing as a norm, but that each man works out for himself, with his assistant's help, the speed and flow of work that will give him the most production.

One important result of this has been increasing emphasis by foremen and workers alike on training and, especially, on placement. It is obvious to everybody at IBM that there are tremendous differences in the ability of men to do even unskilled work. Consequently, each foreman tries hard to put each man on the job for which he is best fitted. And the man himself tries to find the job he can do best—or to acquire the skills to do his own job better.

When worker output went up right after the new salary plan had been installed, many people critical of the whole idea (including a good many in IBM) explained this away as owing to the worker's fear of losing his job;

1936, after all, was a Depression year. But worker output kept on climbing right through the war years, when even large wage incentives could not prevent its slipping in most other industries. And it has continued to go up. Worker output, however, would hardly have stayed up, let alone risen steadily, but for the company's policy of stable employment. This, the most radical of IBM's innovations, was adopted early in the Great Depression. IBM is a capital-goods producer. Its products are used primarily by business. By definition, employment in such an enterprise is extremely sensitive to economic fluctuations. At IBM's main competitors, employment was cut back sharply during the Depression years. IBM management decided, however, that it was its job to maintain employment. There was obviously only one way to do this: to develop new markets. IBM was so successful in finding and developing these markets that employment was actually fully maintained right through the thirties.

## The Lessons

None of these cases deals with a miracle. None of these, more importantly, presents a panacea.

This is certainly true of Japan. Indeed, the Japanese approaches, policies, and practices are rapidly becoming inappropriate to Japanese social reality. They are being undermined by the same forces which undermine the organization of working and work everywhere: the education explosion, and affluence. The education explosion is rapidly creating a labor shortage in the group from which manual workers in Japan have always been recruited. There are no longer many youngsters, and especially not very many young males, who leave school at age fifteen. As a result the neat and tidy wage structure of traditional Japan is under increasing inflationary pressure which threatens to explode the entire system of low entrance wages, guaranteed wage increases by seniority, the benefits structure, and so on. At the same time the young knowledge worker, the engineer or accountant, increasingly chafes under a system that denies him mobility and opportunity to rise by performance rather than by length of service. Altogether Japan probably needs as much innovation in managing working and worker in the next twenty years as it did when it first became a major industrial society, around 1920.

Ernst Abbé's foundation still owns and runs the Zeiss companies in West Germany. And Zeiss is still one of the most honored names in world optics. But long ago, well before World War II, Zeiss began to lose the momentum which Abbé had given it. And a main reason for Zeiss's relative stagnation has, paradoxically, been Ernst Abbé himself. By providing for exclusive ownership of the Zeiss companies in the interest of the worker Abbé's will bars outside financing and makes it impossible for Zeiss to raise the capital it needs to grow and to move into new fields.

At IBM one of the crucial principles of the founder can hardly be maintained any longer: employment security. With 260,000 employees, IBM cannot guarantee every job, as it did forty years ago when employment was in the hundreds or so. IBM has already had to lay off people—though so far it has confined layoffs to managerial and professional personnel and has been able to maintain the employment guarantee for manual workers, for whom it was, of course, originally designed.

Still, while these policies are neither panaceas nor likely to endure for eternity, they have surely been highly successful.

The spirit of its labor force has been one of the central factors in the emergence of Japan as the world's second-ranking industrial power. Zeiss owed its rapid rise and its long leadership position to the strength of its work community, the enthusiasm of its workers, and the creative impact they had on product, process, and tools. IBM has had the most rapid expansion of work force any one company in industrial history has ever reported—from a few thousand as late as 1950 to 260,000 or so twenty years later. Yet IBM has had no labor troubles anywhere—even in the one major plant that is located in the worst industrial "earthquake zone," in the "Red suburbs" of Paris. It has not had major production problems, even though the labor force more than doubled each year. The only explanation is that the IBM workers were ready to accept responsibility for, and to train the newcomers. While no computer manufacturer is likely to have particularly high labor efficiency so far—efficiency rarely goes together with constant upheaval—IBM, by common consent in its industry, is about as far ahead in efficiency compared to its competitors as General Motors is ahead in the automobile industry.

What then is the essence of these success stories? What do the Japanese, Zeiss, and IBM do that the rest of us do not do, and what do they not do that the rest of us do?

Neither the Japanese, nor Zeiss, nor IBM practice "permissive management." Management in Japan is notoriously autocratic. No one has ever mistaken an order by a Japanese company president for a polite request. Abbé, according to all reports, was not permissive either. While a kind man by all accounts, he was very much the German "Herr Professor" and was used to unquestioned authority. Thomas Watson, Sr., was a tyrant. Abbé and Watson demanded excellence in performance and did not accept good intentions as a substitute.

These are not examples of "democratic management," let alone of "participatory democracy." There is no doubt in a Japanese company who is boss. Neither Abbé nor Thomas Watson, Sr., was in the least reluctant to make decisions by fiat.

Neither the Japanese, nor Zeiss, nor IBM have much use for "free-form" organization. The typical Japanese company is tightly structured, with formal lines of command clearly drawn and meticulously observed. So was Abbé's Zeiss and Watson's IBM.

These success stories in managing working and worker exemplify something far more important than any current ism. Most theories of managing working and worker—including such present cure-alls as "permissiveness" or "participatory democracy"—are concerned with organizing authority. The Japanese, Abbé at Zeiss, and Thomas Watson, Sr., at IBM based managing working and work on *organizing responsibility.*

# 21

# The Responsible Worker

*Focus on the Job—The Prerequisites of Responsibility—The Fallacy of "Creativity"—Feedback Information for Self-Control—Continuous Learning—Planning and Doing—The Worker as a "Resource" in "Planning"—The Need for Clear Authority—Responsibility for Job and Work Group—Assembly Line and Job Enrichment—Worker Responsibility and the "New Breeds"—The "Rejected"—The "Pre-Industrials"—The Knowledge Workers—Saving the Supervisor—Plant and Office as Communities—And as Power Structures—The Needs and Limits of Governance—The Need for Leadership Opportunities—Work-Community Activities—The Self-Governing Work Community—From "My Workers" to "Fellow Employees" to "Fellow Managers"*

What does the worker—unskilled or skilled, manual, clerical, or knowledge worker—*need* to be able to take the burden of responsibility? What tools does he require? What incentives? What security? And what do manager and enterprise have to do to be able to ask the worker to take responsibility and to expect him to respond to this demand?

The focus has to be on the job. The job has to make achievement possible. The job is not everything; but it comes first. If other aspects of working are unsatisfactory, they can spoil even the most achieving job—just as a poor sauce can spoil the taste even of the best meat. But if the job itself is not achieving, nothing else will provide achievement.

This may be childishly obvious, but the major approaches to managing the worker, throughout history, have focused on elements external to the job.

Marxists, for example, focus on ownership but have, by and large, left unchanged the structure of jobs and the traditional practices of managing workers. Paternalism focuses on welfare, i.e., on things like housing and health care—very important, to be sure, but not substitutes for job achievement. More recent solutions such as the "co-determination" which the German labor unions are pushing put union representatives on the board of directors and into top management but do not concern themselves with the worker's job itself.

The fundamental reality for every worker, from sweeper to executive vice president, is the eight hours or so he spends on the job. In our society of organizations, it is the job through which the great majority has access to achievement, to fulfillment, and to community.

To enable the worker to achieve, he must therefore first be able to take responsibility for his job.

This requires: (1) productive work; (2) feedback information; and (3) continuous learning.

It is folly to ask workers to take responsibility for their job when the work has not been studied, the process has not been synthesized, the standards and controls have not been thought through, and the physical information tools have not been designed. It is also managerial incompetence.

## The Fallacy of Creativity

This goes counter to the old—and continually revived—slogan of the individual's creativity. "Free people from restraint and they will come up with far better, far more advanced, far more productive answers than the experts," is an old belief. It was popular long before the eighteenth century, though it was then given its classical formulation by Rousseau. But there is no evidence to support it. Everything we know indicates that creativity can become effective only if the basic tools are given. Everything we know also indicates that the proper structure of work—of any work—is not intuitively obvious.

People have shoveled sand for untold centuries. Most of the time, one can assume, nobody told them how to do it. If making work productive depended on the creativity of people, they would undoubtedly have found the best way of doing the job before the dawn of history. Yet when Taylor first looked at the job in 1885, he found everything wrong. The size and shape of the shovel were unsuited to the job. The length of the handle was wrong. The amount of sand the shoveler lifted in one operation was the wrong amount, was indeed the amount most calculated to tire him and do him physical harm. The containers were the wrong shape, the wrong size, and in the wrong position, and so on.

The same thing held for the work of the physician through the ages. The nineteenth-century differential diagnosis, i.e., the systematic analysis of the work of the physician, organized the work differently from the way in which countless practitioners of high intelligence, high skill, and considerable education had done it "intuitively" through the ages.

The best proof that creativity is no substitute for analysis and knowledge are the experiences of those enterprises which were expropriated by governments with the professionals either expelled or leaving. Among them is the Mexican takeover of the petroleum industry in the 1930s, the Iranian takeover of the big oil refinery in Abadan under Premier Mossadegh, the expropriation of the Bolivian tin mines, and the expropriation of the Chilean copper mines and copper smelters. Every one of these moves was wildly popular among the workers of these enterprises. Every one released a flood tide of enthusiasm. But as soon as the managers, professionals, and technicians departed or were thrown out, productivity collapsed and was not restored until managers and professionals returned.

## Feedback Information for Self-Control

The second prerequisite for worker responsibility is feedback information on his own performance. Responsibility requires self-control. That in turn requires continuous information on performance against standards.

There has been a great deal of interest lately in the application of "behavior modification" to work. In particular there has been great interest in the approach worked out by a major air freight forwarder, Emery Air Freight, which found out that workers on all levels will manage their own performance if only they are being informed immediately what their performance actually is. Actually we have known this for many years.

Zeiss, as has been said before, built in feedback information almost a hundred years ago. IBM did so forty years ago. The Japanese continuous-learning session is a way to provide feedback information. Modern medical practice was founded 150 years ago designing a feedback from autopsy results to diagnosis.

We also know that people can control and correct performance if given the information, even if neither they nor the supplier of information truly understand what has to be done or how. This applies even to processes that are, by definition, "uncontrollable," such as a great many processes in the human body, e.g., heartbeat, brain waves, or asthma attacks. Visual feedback which enables an asthmatic child to see on a control panel information on the constriction of blood vessels and muscles in his throat does not tell the child what to do. Indeed, no one knows. Yet if the child knows that the needle which depicts graphically the state of the blood vessels and muscles should stay in the center of the panel, he can, in many cases, abort an asthma attack.

Few work processes are as inaccessible to analysis as brain waves or asthma attacks, yet in a good many we still cannot exactly know the process. The worker himself, given the information, can control his own work and output.

Emery Air Freight had conducted industrial engineering studies for many years. Yet management did not really know what an individual truck driver would have to do to make the largest possible number of calls on his route. The drivers, however, without analyzing driving time or length of a call, could in practically every case control their own schedule and raise the number of calls significantly once they knew how many calls they actually made as against the numbers they had planned to make.

This approach applies even to such advanced knowledge work as research. Feedback in research does not mean a daily report as in the case of truck drivers. Rather it means sitting down with the research scientists several times a year and saying, "Here are the things of significance this research group has contributed to the company during the last six and twelve months. And here are the impacts earlier research work has had on the company's performance during the last six and twelve months."

The information the worker needs must satisfy the requirements of effective information (see Chapter 18). It must be timely. It must be relevant. It must be operational. It must focus on his job. Above all, it must be *his* tool. Its purpose must be self-control rather than control of others, let alone manipulation.

The real strength of feedback information—and the major reinforcer—is clearly that the information is the tool of the worker for measuring and directing himself. The worker does not need praise or reproach to *know* how he is doing. He knows.

## Continuous Learning

The third requirement for achievement in work and for a responsible worker is continuous learning.

There is need for workers, whether unskilled, skilled, or knowledge worker, to be trained for new skills. Continuous learning does not replace training. It has different aims and satisfies different needs. Above all, it satisfies the need of the employee to contribute what he himself has learned to the improvement of his own performance, to the improvement of his fellow worker's performance, and to a better, more effective, but also more rational way of working.

It is also the one way to come to grips with two basic problems: the resistance of workers to innovation, and the danger that workers will become "obsolete."

"Engineers become obsolete within ten years," we are now being told. If indeed true, it is a severe indictment of the employer. An engineer who starts with the proper foundation of knowledge for his work has no business becoming obsolete. The continuing improvement of his own skill and knowledge at his own job should be built into his daily work.

Continuous learning need not be organized as a formal session the way it is traditionally done in Japan. But it always needs to be organized. There is need for the continuing challenge to the worker: "What have you learned that can make your job and the job of all of us more productive, more performing, and more achieving? What do you need by way of knowledge, by way of tools, by way of information? And how do we best prepare ourselves for new needs, new methods, new performance capacities?"

Continuous training is as appropriate to clerical work as it is in manual work. It is of particular importance in knowledge work. The very fact that knowledge work, to be effective, has to be specialized creates a need for continuous exposure to the experiences, the problems, the needs of others, and in turn, for continuous contribution of knowledge and information to others. Whether the knowledge work be accounting or market research, planning or chemical engineering, the work group has to be seen and has to see itself as a learning group.

## Planning and Doing

These three prerequisites, (1) productive work, (2) feedback information, and (3) continuous learning, are, so to speak, the planning for worker responsibility for job, work group, and output. They are therefore management responsibilities and management tasks. But they are not "management prerogatives," i.e., things management does alone, by itself, and unilaterally. Management does indeed have to do the work and make the decisions. But in all these areas the worker himself, from the beginning, needs to be integrated as a "resource" into the planning process. From the beginning he has to share in thinking through work and process, tools and information. His knowledge, his experience, his needs are resource to the planning process. The worker needs to be a partner in it. Every attempt should be made to make accessible to the worker the necessary knowledge. He need not become an industrial engineer or a process designer, but the fundamentals of industrial engineering and their application to a man's own job and work can be grasped by almost anyone without great difficulty.

One of the first attempts—and one of the most successful ones—to make workers a resource in making work productive was (as mentioned earlier) "work simplification." One of Taylor's disciples, Allan Mogensen, ran this program for many years, from the twenties to the forties, at Lake Placid, New York. Mogensen's thesis was that scientific management would be successful if supervisors understood its principles, could apply them themselves, and could teach them to their own workers. What was needed, Mogensen argued, was for scientific management to become a simple, everyday, comfortable tool of the working group itself. He showed that unschooled people who, however, knew what working was, could obtain results as good as those of the most highly trained industrial engineer.

There is no reason why work simplification has to be taught at a special institute and away from the work place. In Japanese industry, beginning with the first application of scientific management in the 1920s by such companies as Sumitomo Electric and Mitsubishi Electric, supervisors and workers have learned the principles of industrial engineering as a matter of course in the continuous-training sessions.

Worker *responsibility* for job, work groups, and output cannot be expected, let alone demanded, until the foundations of productive work, feedback information, and continuous learning have been established. Worker *participation* in designing these foundations should be brought into play from the very beginning.

Creativity, if by that is meant undirected, unstructured, untutored, and uncontrolled guessing, is not likely to produce results. But a system which does not tap and put to use the knowledge, experience, resources, and imagination of the people who have to live with the system and make it work is as unlikely to be effective.

This is not seen generally, largely because of a confusion of planning and doing with planner and doer. It was Taylor who first enunciated as a principle that planning and doing are different. Taylor saw that planning won't get done if it is mixed in with doing. Long before Taylor, however, the designers of the German General Staff in the early nineteenth century had set up planning as a separate task.

The two are separate activities, like reading and writing, and require different methods and different approaches. But planner and doer, like reader and writer, need to be united in the same person. They cannot be divorced—or else the planning will cease to be effective and will indeed become a threat to performance.

The planner is needed to supply the doer with direction and measurements, with the tools of analysis and synthesis, with methodology, and with standards. He is needed also to make sure that the planning of one group is compatible with the planning of the others. But in turn, the planner needs the doer as his resource and as his feedback control. And unless the planner knows what the doer does and needs, his planning, while theoretically perfect, may never become execution. Conversely, unless the doer understands what the planner tries to accomplish, the doer will not perform or will try to resist performance specifications that to him seem unreasonable, arbitrary, or just plain silly.

And the less capable the planner is of analyzing the work and its individual operations, the more does he depend on the doer. In knowledge work, above all, the doer has to take a responsible part in the planning process for it to be effective at all.

But still, the foundations for worker responsibility are planning and are therefore managerial responsibilities.

## The Need for Clear Authority

One more thing is needed to make responsibility acceptable to the worker: he needs to have the security of a clear authority structure. He has to know what areas and decisions are beyond his power and beyond his purview and therefore reserved for a different or a higher authority. Management has to work out what the task is, what the objectives are, what the standards are. Again, the doers should be used as a source of information. But the job is management's.

Also, organization stands under the threat of the "common peril." There is always the chance of an emergency situation which has not been anticipated and for which there are no rules. The common peril may be physical—in business it will more often be economic. Whatever its nature, *one man* has to make the decision in such a situation, and fast, or everybody is endangered. Who this man is has to be known in advance, or there is chaos. And this man has to be able to say, "This needs to be done; you do it; this way." The survival of the group depends on his unquestioned authority. Without it no one in the work group can feel secure.

## Responsibility for Job and Work Groups

The layout of individual jobs to do the work and to meet its standards, and the design, structure, and relationship of the work group in which these jobs are integrated into a community, are and should be the responsibility of workers and work group. They need professional help. They need knowledge, experience, and teaching from their supervisor. They need advice and service from the industrial engineer and from many other technicians and professionals. Management must retain a veto power, and will often exercise it. But the responsibility for job design and work-group design belongs to those who are responsible for output and performance. And that is the worker and the work group.

Worker responsibility for job and group will vary greatly with the kind of work to be done, with the educational, skill, and knowledge level of the work force, and with cultures and traditions. It will certainly look very different when the workers are research scientists rather than hard-core unemployables from the black ghetto or guest workers in German industry from the hill farms of eastern Anatolia.

But the principles are the same: the worker and his group are responsible for their own jobs and for the relationships between individual jobs. They are responsible for thinking through *how* the work is to be done. They are responsible for meeting performance goals and for quality as well as for quantity. And they are responsible for improving work, job, tools and processes, and their own skills.

These are exacting demands. Yet whenever we have made them, they have been met—provided that the planning had been done. Indeed in most cases—IBM is the typical example—workers will set higher performance goals than the industrial engineer and will tend to outdo their own goals.

The reason is not that work has become fun—nor should it. It is not just motivation, though psychological factors undoubtedly play an important part. In large measure, worker responsibility for job design and work-group design are effective because they make use of the worker's knowledge and experience in the one area where he *is* the expert.

To expect worker creativity in making work productive is, as said earlier, sentimental twaddle. But it is realistic to expect knowledge and expertise with respect to the worker's own job, that is, in putting conceptual and physical tools into use and performance. Here the worker is the only expert. For a job is a configuration. It defies analysis. But it is easily accessible to perception. Particularly if feedback information is provided, the individual can normally work out his own optimal job design fairly fast and fairly effectively.

For the design of the work group, responsibility on the part of the members is even more important. We now know* that the work itself, whether heat-treating, selling furniture, or probing the molecular structure of a hormone, is a vital factor in job design and work-group structure. But we do not know what job design and work-group structure correspond to this or that task and work.

In retrospect, the way every one of the groups studied by Joan Woodward

*E.g., through the work of Joan Woodward and her group in England; see especially her book, *Industrial Organization: Theory and Practice* (Oxford University Press, 1965). The intensive studies of work, work group, and worker which Charles R. Walker of Yale University made in the forties and fifties reported, for instance, in Charles R. Walker and Robert H. Guest, *The Man on the Assembly Line* (Harvard University Press, 1952), had reached and documented the same conclusions earlier.

organizes itself is obvious and right. But nothing can be deduced from one such solution for the optimal structure and organization of the next job. There are general rules. But they are so general, e.g., "Work-group structure and organization will be appropriate to the task to be performed, the personalities, skills and values of the workers, the physical environment and the tools," that no "how-to-do-it" conclusions emerge.

Work-group structure is a configuration of great complexity even though it is composed of a fairly small number of fairly simple elements. It resembles a kaleidoscope. Fairly small shifts drastically change the pattern. And the number of combinations and permutations is so large as to approach infinity.

In such a situation the only way to arrive at the right, the optimal solution is trial. The outsider, e.g., the industrial engineer, can help. But he cannot analytically arrive at the answer. The group itself, however, usually arrives at a right answer fairly fast and without much trouble. It works things out.

### Assembly Line and Job Enrichment

The pressure for changes in the traditional ways of managing worker and working has been building up these last decades as the "new breed" has come into the work force and as the old motivating drives of hunger and fear have rapidly lost their power. The pressure has been greatest on the traditional assembly line of manufacturing industry. The conventional view has always been that the assembly line is, by its very nature, incapable of being run any other way than from the top and by command.

IBM and Zeiss, as mentioned before, disproved this long ago. So did our World War II experience in defense production. Nothing that is now being proposed, for instance, goes quite as far in demanding responsibility from the worker as some of the U.S. defense plants of World War II. There the worker had to take responsibility because of the shortage of industrial engineers, supervisors, and managers.

An example* was one of the largest aircraft engine plants with a product which, by the standards of the times, was exceedingly complex and required high skill. Yet each team assembled one entire engine—a product considerably more complex than any automobile. Each team organized the job slightly differently, with different men doing different operations at different times. Each, however, started out with a foundation in work study and was supplied with full information. And each engaged in continuous learning. It met several times a week with its foreman and with the engineering staff

---

*Other examples are discussed in both my books, *Concept of the Corporation* and *The New Society*.

to discuss improvements in work and jobs. Each team exceeded, by substantial margins, the output standards which the engineers had suggested.

These World War II experiences—and they could be matched by similar experiences in all major industrial countries—were forgotten again. They seemed to reflect a temporary emergency rather than fundamentals. Now we are rediscovering the same principles again. And wherever tried, the results are the same.

Among the most significant changes are those of the most rigid and most highly engineered line, the automobile assembly line.

In the United States, Chrysler is experimenting with responsibility on the part of the workers for assembly line operations. In a Chrysler plant in Detroit, employees were actually asked to reevaluate the entire manufacturing operation as a result of which the whole plant was reorganized, resulting in higher output with fewer men.

The most systematic approaches to worker responsibility to automobile assembly line jobs are those taken by the two Swedish automobile makers, Saab and Volvo, both acting under the pressure of severe labor shortages.*

In one Swedish plant, one work group will take responsibility for the assembly of the total car. The output standard, that is, the number of cars per hour, and the quality standard will be set by the plant. The process will have been worked out. But the structure of jobs, their scope, their relationship, and the organization of the work group are worked out by the men themselves with their supervisors and the industrial engineer.

Other features of the Swedish experiment include the formation of development groups which include production workers and which discuss such matters as new tool and machine design before they are approved for construction; temporary assignment of workers to a team of production engineers to work on specific production problems, and the shifting of responsibility for process inspection from a separate quality inspection unit to the production worker. The quality inspection unit now concentrates exclusively on the completed product (in line with the principle stated in Chapter 18 that inspection is not quality control of the product but is the quality control of the quality control process itself). Finally, workers' tasks have been expanded by the workers themselves to include maintenance of the equipment, which was previously the responsibility of special mechanics —thus applying to the automobile assembly line what Ernst Abbé did for the production of precision optics in the 1890s and Thomas Watson for the

---

*For these experiments, see Jan-Peter Norstedt, *Work Organization and Job Design of Saab-Scandia in Södertalje* (Stockholm, Swedish Employers Federation, 1970) and "How to Counter Alienation in the Plant," by Richard E. Walton (*Harvard Business Review*, November/December, 1972). This article gives several more examples from other industries, mainly in the United States.

production of electronic equipment in the 1940s and 1950s. These examples could be multiplied ad infinitum.

In a major American department-store chain responsibility for job design was turned over to the salespeople. Salespeople in these stores are on commission and competition among individuals is high. Yet the salespeople immediately tackled job design as a group problem—with the clear goal of optimizing every salesperson's opportunity to earn the maximum commission. They focused on the question "What changes in the way the work is being done would help all of us?" They came up with a demand for continuous training—in merchandising, in selling methods, in paper handling, and so on. What they wanted—and got—was a little time each week to sit down together with an experienced expert from store operations or sales training to discuss their experiences and to suggest to each other whatever methods would work the best. But they also came up with suggestions for changes in the way the selling floor was organized. The idea of having a clerk who handles the paperwork for all the salespeople in the department (mentioned in Chapter 18 above) was one of their ideas, for instance, and first tried by them.

But outside of the assembly line there is also growing demand for "job enrichment."* In job enrichment the expert, e.g., the industrial engineer, defines the "modules" of the work, the individual operations that have to be performed. He establishes the standards and analyzes the information the worker needs. But then the worker himself designs his or her job, that is, the number of modules that constitute "my" job, their sequence, speed, rhythm. The result is higher output, better quality, and a sharp drop in employee turnover.

Job enrichment has so far been tried primarily in clerical operations. It would seem, however, to be particularly applicable to knowledge work.

Zeiss, IBM, and a good many Japanese companies have been practicing job enrichment for decades. And the way claims settlement has been done for decades in some German and Japanese insurance companies (see Chapter 18) is job enrichment pure and simple. Even the American automobile industry practiced it—way beyond anything job enrichment now tries to do —during World War II.† We have *known* what to do for a very long time. That it is now being heralded as a discovery is somewhat ironic—but harmless as long as it is being done.

But what is not so harmless is the belief that job enrichment is *the* answer. It is only a first step. IBM, the Japanese, and Zeiss mobilized the energies

*The best short description containing a wealth of examples is the article, "Job Enrichment Lessons from AT&T" by Robert N. Ford, in the January/February 1973 issue of the *Harvard Business Review.*

†See, for instance, the example of totally unskilled Negro women workers producing high-precision parts and assembling them, in Chapter 22 of my *Practice of Management.*

of the work *group*. Job enrichment confines the worker's responsibility to his own individual job. But he also should be expected to assume responsibility for the work group, its relationship in and through the work process, its structure and its cohesion.

## Worker Responsibility and the "New Breeds"

Worker responsibility for job and work group is important for all kinds of workers in today's organizations. It is fundamental to a civilization in which three out of every four people at work are employees in organizations.

But worker responsibility is particularly important for the three groups one might call "the new breeds"—though for different reasons.

The first of these groups is the new breed of young manual workers. These men and women (as said in Chapter 15) arrive at work already rejected, already losers. Yet, though they are the rejects of the educational system, they have had long years of schooling and have, by any historical standard, a high degree of education. They are not the wretched illiterates of the industrial slums of 1850. Their formal knowledge may be limited. But their horizon is wide—if only because of TV. And they are, by and large, not motivated by carrot and stick. They are resentful—in many cases with good reason—because the lack of scholastic success which has condemned them to inferior status does not appear to them a genuine, a true, a valid criterion. At the same time, they have doubts about their own ability to perform and to achieve, about their own manhood, about their own dignity. These men (and women) need achievement to overcome their habit of defeat. Otherwise, they will forever be in a state of smoldering resentment and rebellion. They need responsibility to overcome their feelings of inferiority. They need a challenge in which they can succeed. They are suspicious—every earlier contact with authority has conditioned them to be suspicious. Yet they need self-assurance and security, more than any other group in the work force.

This is, above all, the lesson of the widely publicized revolt of General Motors workers at the new Lordstown assembly plant in Ohio. That these young men resented the imposition of the rigid General Motors assembly line discipline is not surprising and is nothing new. At every major assembly plant General Motors had built during the last thirty years, the workers reacted the same way. The newspaper account of Lordstown read exactly like the interviews with, and reports on, workers of the big assembly plant in New England which General Motors built in the late forties.*

The real difference—and it is an important one—is that the young white

*See Charles R. Walker and Robert H. Guest, *The Man on the Assembly Line* (Harvard University Press, 1952).

and Black workers at Lordstown felt almost to a man that they could have done a better job designing their own work and the assembly line than the General Motors industrial engineers did.

Lordstown got all the publicity. But not too far away, in the same Midwestern industrial area, another company opened a major new plant at about the same time GM opened Lordstown. It employs the same kind of labor—perhaps an even larger proportion of Blacks than Lordstown—pays the same wages, and has very similar assembly line work. It too is fully unionized. Yet this plant had apparently very little trouble. And its productivity from the beginning was at least as high as the standards the Lordstown workers decried as "speed-up" and rejected. The one difference is that this other new plant studied and applied IBM's policies. It engineered the work thoroughly. It worked out the worker's and the foreman's information needs, by bringing worker and foreman into the planning process as participants and a resource. And then it demanded from the work group responsibility for job design and work-group design—and obtained it.

## The "Pre-Industrials"

The second group, an entirely different one whatever its outward similarity, is the large number of recent immigrants from pre-industrial civilizations into modern city and modern organization: the Turks and other guest workers in Germany, the Sicilians in Torino, the Blacks in the United States, the sharecroppers from the drought-ridden sugar plantations of Brazil's Northeast in São Paulo, and Indians from the *pueblo* in Mexico City.

In many ways these workers need paternalism. They need to be looked after. They are not at home in modern society; they are frightened by it, lost in it. But at the same time, they need to be integrated into modern society for their own sake as well as for that of the society to which they move. Otherwise they will become a disturbing, an unsettled, a pathological influence. Again, what is needed is to inculcate in these workers the habit of responsibility and the taste of achievement.

While Fiat in Torino has been largely unable to integrate Sicilian immigrants and has at times been all but paralyzed by their despair, anger, and resistance, Olivetti, in nearby Ivrea, has apparently had little trouble with the same Sicilian immigrants. Olivetti went through pretty rough times in the sixties after the death of its founder, when the very survival of the company was in jeopardy; Fiat had a boom with steadily rising wages and high employment security. Both companies are highly paternalistic. But at Olivetti there is a long tradition—somewhat reminiscent of Zeiss—of worker responsibility for job and work group.

The most dramatic demonstration I know of the need of this pre-industrial group and of its willingness to assume responsibility is the experience of a large textile mill on South America's west coast. The mill is almost entirely manned by Indians from the High Andes who have only recently migrated to the coastal city and are strangers to modern society and even to the Spanish spoken in the city. For years management had depended on fear. Production and performance at the mill, however, had been going down steadily. By the early 1950s the mill was near collapse. Quality had become so bad that the output was almost unsalable. Machines were antiquated and had not been maintained for years. A new general manager brought in from Europe submitted to the owners a comprehensive plan to rebuild the plant, buy new machinery, train supervision, and so on. But the needed capital could not be raised. Yet the mill could not be closed for political and legal reasons. The new general manager thereupon decided to do the only thing left: to lay out work as productively as could be done on the obsolete machines; to set specific standards for department and section; to supply the men in each department and section with feedback on their own performance; and to impose on them responsibility for the design of jobs, the arrangement of tools and machines, and the structure of work groups. Productivity, within a year or so, almost tripled and in some areas, such as the dye shed, almost quadrupled. Where production up to minimum quality standards had been the exception, it became the rule. And for the first time in many years, it became possible to introduce new materials, new patterns, and new techniques.

## The Knowledge Worker

Finally there is the knowledge worker, and especially the advanced knowledge worker. He has to be a "knowledge professional" (on this see Chapter 30, "What Makes a Manager?"). This means that no one can motivate him. He has to motivate himself. No one can direct him. He has to direct himself. Above all, no one can supervise him. He is the guardian of his own standards, of his own performance, and of his own objectives. He can be productive only if he is responsible for his own job.

## Saving the Supervisor

To make the worker responsible for his job and for that of the work group is also the best—and may be the only—way to restore the supervisor to health and function.

For a half century or more the first-line supervisor, especially in manufacturing and clerical work, has seen his role shrinking in status, in importance, and in esteem. Where a supervisor was "management" to the employee only half a century ago, he has now, by and large, become a buffer between management, union, and workers. And like all buffers, his main function is to take the blows.

Indeed, in the modern industrial plant the supervisor is increasingly becoming the "enemy." He is separated from the men he supervises by an ever-higher wall of resentment, suspicion, and hostility. At the same time, he is separated from management by his lack of technical and managerial knowledge. Similarly ambivalent is the role of the supervisor of knowledge workers. His subordinates consider him their spokesman and expect him to protect them and their knowledge area against managerial demands and managerial ignorance. Management, on the other hand, expects him to integrate the knowledge and expertise of the people in his area with the mission, purpose, and objectives of the institution. Increasingly he finds himself disavowed by both, by his subordinates because he is no longer truly a scientist or an expert but has "sold out" to management, and by management because he is parochial, departmentalized, and one-sided.

Frederick Taylor seventy-five years ago saw clearly that the traditional supervisor was losing function. His proposed solution was to split the job into a number of functions, and to have different supervisors for scheduling and training, for tool maintenance, and for discipline, all of them acting together as a "planning committee" but each with direct authority in his field over the men.

This did not prove to be feasible; there has to be one focal point for the work group. But the functional competences for which Taylor wanted to have separate supervisors have nonetheless been taken over by an array of specialists: personnel people and quality control men; maintenance people and schedulers, coordinators and planners. As a result, the supervisor has been left with the sole function of maintaining discipline, that is, with the function of being feared.

The crisis of the supervisor has been studied the most in the United States. But it is worldwide. It may have gone even further in Great Britain, for instance, where the supervisor has been rendered impotent by union militants who can and do negotiate directly with plant and company management. The respected *Meister* of the German tradition is fast becoming a thing of the past, as countless articles and speeches in Germany assert. And when the Swedes went into the radical redesign of the automobile assembly line, one of the main reasons given was the plight of the supervisor and the difficulty of getting good men to accept supervisory positions.

No organization can function well if its supervisory force does not function. Supervisors are, so to speak, the ligaments, the tendons and sinews, of an organization. They provide the articulation. Without them, no joint can move. It is the supervisor's job to be in the middle. Hence he must have responsibility, function, and respect in both his relationships, upward to management and downward to the work group.

The crisis of the supervisor would by itself be reason enough to think seriously about the organization of the worker and working. For making the worker achieving, making him responsible, is the one way of making the supervisor function again. In organizations—again, Zeiss and IBM are the examples—where worker responsibility has been the guiding concept for managing worker and working, the supervisor is effective. Only he is effective differently. He becomes resource for the worker and the work group.

Worker and work group, in order to take responsibility, have to have an organized source of knowledge, of information, of direction, of arbitration, and a channel for contact and information flow to and from the various experts. Worker and work group also need discipline—though correctional discipline, which in today's manufacturing plant tends to be the supervisor's main job, should rarely have to be exercised. But the proper role of the supervisor is not supervision. It is knowledge, information, placing, training, teaching, standard-setting and guiding. It is not an easy role—old supervisors find it difficult—but it is a tenable role. It no longer imposes a conflict of loyalties—between the supervisor's work group and management; between the demands of personality and the demands of work; between human relations and discipline. As the resource to the achieving worker and his work group, the supervisor can again become whole. He can serve, in one and the same act and in one and the same role, both the objective needs of the enterprise for performance and the personal needs of workers for achievement.

## Plant and Office as Communities

Plant and office are more than just geographic locations. They are communities. We speak meaningfully of the prevailing atmosphere of an office or of a mill. We study their "culture." We speak of "patterns" of "formal" or "informal" organization, of prevailing "values," of "career ladders." And though there are great differences in degree between the most paternalistic and the most impersonal plant and office, all are expected to discharge community functions. There is, in other words, a work community.

To make workers achieving they must also take substantial responsibility for the work community.

Plant and office need governance. The power dimension is an inherent and inescapable dimension of organization.

But not all decisions within an organization are inherent in its purpose and mission or directly related to its performance. There are decisions which, while necessary, have their origin in the needs and realities of the work community rather than in the mission, purpose, and performance capacity of the organization itself. They are incidental to the purpose of the organization rather than integral to it.

It is a law of governance that it restrict itself to the *necessary* decisions. Any governing body will be the more effective, and more powerful, the more it eschews decisions it does not have to make.

An incidental decision which does not materially add to the performance capacity of the institution takes just as much time as a basic and necessary one. Incidental decisions clog the governing machinery, load down the governing and decision-making group, and detract it from the important things. At the same time, authority over such decisions is not in effect legitimate. Such decisions are not grounded in the "purposes for which government was instituted among men," to use the old and elegant phrase. To be sure, they have to be made. But the governing body of the institution is the wrong authority for making them.

Work-community decisions are decisions that should be decentralized. They are not, however, business decisions, i.e., the decisions which federal decentralization of business enterprise lodges in lower, operating decentralized managements (see Chapter 46). They are social decisions, decisions regarding the affairs of the work community. They therefore need to be lodged in the work community—and the principle behind this is not too different from the principle behind decentralization of business decision-making.

If management makes work-community decisions, it loads itself down with matters which appear petty to management, though they are of great importance to the plant community itself. There are decisions on the cafeteria, on vacation schedules, on running recreational activities, and so on. In the typical enterprise management people deal with these things. This is costly, inefficient, and a constant cause of friction and dissatisfaction. These activities are run poorly and the decisions are made badly because for management the areas are not important, do not deserve a high priority and are not accorded respect.

These are, however, important matters of "hygiene" to the work community and its members. If these things are run badly, they impede morale. But running them superbly well adds little, if they are run from above. The responsibility for these activities and decisions needs to be placed squarely on the work community.

## The Need for Leadership Opportunities

At the same time, these areas offer major opportunities for leadership, for responsibility, for recognition, and for learning. The men who head these activities are important people in the work community. The people making the decisions in these areas are also forced to learn what managing is and what managerial responsibility means. They learn that choices have to be made, priorities have to be set, and that the infinite number of things it would be nice to have must be fitted to the available resources.

In the absence of such opportunities for leadership in the work community, the abilities, energies, and ambitions within the work force may be directed against management and against the work community. They will be negative, destructive, demagogic. The one who can make the most trouble for the bosses will be the leader rather than the one who can perform the best for the plant community.

The shop steward who, as so many do in English and American plants, defines his role as "harassment" and who is elected for revolutionary rhetoric rather than for capacity and performance is the alternative to leaders chosen to be responsible and to perform.

Responsibility is not by itself a guarantee of performance. But lack of responsibility breeds the demagogue.

## Work-Community Activities

The list of activities for which a work community might be asked to take responsibility is almost endless.*

Richard E. Walton (in the *Harvard Business Review* article mentioned earlier) describes a plant built by a large food manufacturer in 1958 which systematically imposes responsibility for work-community decisions on the work force. Among them are such tasks as the control of manning assignments to cover for temporarily absent employees; selecting men from the plant to serve on plant committees or task forces; screening and selecting employees to fill vacancies; counseling workers who do not meet standards with respect to absences or punctuality. Members of the plant community also were put on the plant safety committee. Safety is, after all, a concern of the people in the plant—and they also know more about it than anybody else, as a rule, or at least know more about where the safety problems are.

Another example of self-government in a work community is the nuclear submarine. Obviously, a submarine cannot be a permissive place. The captain has to be the final authority whose word nobody dares dispute. Yet the crew, regardless of rank, acts and works as one unit. No one can join the crew unless he is accepted by it. And while the captain decides what should be done, each man on his own station then has to decide how to do a specific job and do it as if the life of everybody depended on him, as indeed it does.

*Many of them are mentioned in my earlier books; especially *Concept of the Corporation* and *The New Society*.

## The Self-Governing Work Community

A self-governing work community is not "participatory democracy."
Neither at Zeiss nor in the food company mentioned earlier, nor in a
submarine, are there elections or mass meetings. The working teams are
organized by management for specific operations and specific jobs.

Work-community self-government may not be—and maybe should not
be—"democracy" altogether. Authority and assignments may go by seniority—as they do in Japanese plants, but as they also largely did at Zeiss.
What matters is that self-government of plant-community tasks be *local*
self-government and that it put responsibility where the consequences of the
decisions have to be lived with.

We do not have all the answers to managing worker and working. The
society of organizations is new—only seventy years ago employees were a
small minority in every society. The attenuation of carrot and stick as
driving forces is new. The emergence of a highly schooled work force is new.
The new breed of manual workers is new. And the emergence of the
knowledge worker is also new.

But we know what the questions are. We know the approaches. And we
know the goals—though we may never attain them.

The attenuation of carrot and stick was heralded around 1900 by a
semantic change. In the old days the "boss" issued a proclamation or order
"to my workers." After 1900 he increasingly addressed himself "to our
fellow employees." At about the same time the German *Unternehmer* began
to talk of *Mitarbeiter* (literally "fellow employee")—a term that had first
been coined by the civil service a century earlier. Often enough, of course,
the new term was only a semantic mask for tyranny. But it reflected the
passing of the "master" and the arrival of modern organization in which
even the top man is another hired hand, another employee who derives
whatever authority he has from responsibility and performance rather than
from birth, rank, title, or wealth.

No one yet addresses workers as "fellow managers"—I hope no one ever
will. Yet this is the goal. There will be—and there has to be—the reality
of management power and authority, of command and of decision-making,
of higher and lower incomes, of superior and subordinate. But there also
is the task of building and leading organizations in which every man sees
himself as a "manager" and accepts for himself the full burden of what is
basically *managerial* responsibility: responsibility for his own job and work
group, for his contribution to the performance and results of the entire
organization, and for the social tasks of the work community.

# 22

## Employment, Incomes, and Benefits

*Job Security and Income Stability—Resistance to Change and Job Insecurity—American Job Mobility: Myths and Reality—The Shortcomings —The Rehn Plan—Needed: Organized Placement—Profits, Productivity, and Benefits—Making "Benefits" Benefit—What Benefits Should Be— Benefits and the Work Community*

---

Living in fear of loss of job and income is incompatible with taking responsibility for job and work group, for output and performance. That the fear is becoming less pervasive—to the point where it no longer acts as a spur —makes it all the more destructive. It contrasts so sharply with the standard of living and the standard of security to which most workers in a developed society have become accustomed.

To accept the burden of responsibility, the worker—the unskilled as well as the skilled worker, and the manual as well as the knowledge worker— needs a fair measure of security of job and income.

At the same time, however, the worker needs also mobility. Every worker needs to be able to escape the wrong job. Every worker needs to be able to move from a dying company or industry into one that grows or at least into one that has a chance for survival. And the knowledge worker, especially the highly educated one, needs to be able to move where his skill and knowledge can make the greatest contribution. To leave knowledge skill underutilized is impoverishment of society and individual alike.

The economy also needs a fair degree of labor-cost flexibility, and so does every business. The widespread belief that wages take the main brunt of economic fluctuation is, of course, nonsense. The main burden is carried by the capital fund—as it should be. In a bad year profits go down sharply or disappear. But the share of wage incomes in total revenue—whether of the economy or of a business—actually goes up sharply in recession years. Capital costs, in other words, are the least "fixed" costs of an economy—despite the accountant's contrary terminology. And labor costs are the most nearly fixed costs of an economy or of a business. But there is still need for flexibility, still need for relating wage costs to the level of economic activity, to the other costs of an economy, to the profit requirements of the capital fund, and to productivity.

Finally there is need to assuage the conflict between wage fund and capital fund. It cannot be eliminated. But there is need for some mechanism that establishes a tie between the two, both to make visible the worker's long-term stake in the capital fund and to enable him to understand the function of profit and profitability.

There is nothing very new to these requirements. In different ways different economies and different businesses have been struggling with them all along. But managements have, by and large, not managed employment, incomes, and benefits. They have reacted and adapted. These are, however, areas of genuine managerial responsibility. These are management tasks.

## Job Security and Income Stability

That workers resist higher productivity and innovative changes is a very old theme. The cloth workers of Florence in the days of the Renaissance rioted against new technology as a threat to their jobs.

But the resistance of workers on all levels against higher productivity and against innovation is not based solely on the fear of working oneself out of one's own job. Equally important is the fear that the achieving worker will work other workers out of their jobs. As a result, group pressure is brought into play against the worker who, by wanting to achieve, becomes a threat to the security of his fellow workers.

Resistance to change and resistance to innovation are not inherent in human nature. The Japanese experience proves this. And wherever a Western business has provided comparable job and income security, resistance to change or to innovation has disappeared.

This was the experience of Zeiss in the last century, as it has been the experience of IBM in the twenty-five years after World War II.

Another example is Krupp in Germany, where workers were, until recently, assured of lifetime employment and where resistance to change and innovation were virtually unknown. This in large measure explains the ability of Krupp, for long periods of time, to hold a leadership position in the steel fabricating industry on the European continent.

Similarly, Marks & Spencer in England, while having no formal job guarantees, does, in effect, provide stable and practically guaranteed employment—and again there is no resistance to change or to innovation. That resistance to change has its origin in fear of loss of job is proved by a Japanese example. For not all Japanese industry is receptive to change. A significant exception is the Japanese National Railways. Workers on the railways have guaranteed employment security, and yet they are haunted by the fear of job loss. For everybody in Japan, and especially the railway employee himself, knows that the railways are grossly overstaffed. Any change in work rules, in procedures, in regulations, threatens to expose the basic redundancy and excess manpower of the system. Every such change is, therefore, bitterly resisted and, in fact, prevented by the employees. And Japanese railway workers, while probably the best-paid workers in Japan, have the worst and most bitter industrial relations with their employer, the government.

It is not, in other words, just legal or contractual guarantees of job and income that are needed. To give the worker the security he needs to take responsibility, there must be reality to the promise. To keep people on the payroll for whom there is no job may create insecurity as great as actual loss of job. What is needed is not just the guarantee of income, but a system which actively and systematically provides work, that is, productive membership in society.

In the West a *formal* guarantee of jobs and incomes is the exception rather than the rule—though I have, I believe, given enough examples to show that the exceptions are far more numerous than most people (and practically all union leaders) believe. But job security and income assurance have increasingly been built into this system.

The first step was unemployment compensation. But on top of this individual companies and individual industries, with or without union contracts, have developed a multitude of provisions: supplemental unemployment compensation; severance pay; and seniority rules in layoffs which, in effect, give older employees practical job security.

As a result, labor costs in the West have, in effect, become more and more inflexible. They may today, at least in basic industries, be less flexible than the labor costs of Japan. A U.S. employer in mass-production industry can lay off employees fairly easily—certainly far more easily than a Japanese, or even a European employer could. But he is then committed to severance pay, to high supplementary unemployment compensation payments, and to other burdens which, in effect, mean that he still keeps on paying something like three-quarters or more of the laid-off worker's wages for something like from six to nine months.

At the same time, Western labor forces, at least compared to the Japanese, have fairly high mobility. Knowledge workers, in particular, can and do move easily from one employer to another.

There is, even in the U.S., a belief that American workers, and especially knowledge people, change jobs all the time. But with respect to managers and professionals this is largely myth.

In the large—and in most small—American companies actual turnover is quite low among managers and professionals. There is considerable turnover in the entrance jobs, that is, in the first three to five years of a man's employment. There is considerable turnover—considerably more than used to be common in Europe, let alone Japan—in top management jobs. In between, though—among older workers, lower and middle management, and among professional and technical knowledge workers—job change is the exception rather than the rule. In every large American company the great majority of the middle ranks are filled with people who have at most changed jobs once, and that within a few years after their graduation from college. Their first job change, made when they were still quite young, is usually their last one. After that they may move geographically from one location of the company to another, but they very rarely change employers. There is almost no difference in length of service and in career patterns between managerial, professional, and technical people in an American large company and in a European company, say, between General Electric and Siemens. There is not even tremendous difference in the middle ranks and in the age group between the late twenties and the late fifties, between the typical large American company and the Japanese company.

Job stability is also the rule rather than the exception for blue-collar workers in the U.S. A good measure of this is the experience of the private pension plans in American industry which cover virtually all large- and medium-sized enterprises (and probably a majority of small businesses as well). These plans are under sharp attack these days because "only 70 percent of the employees actually receive a pension." This is indeed a serious shortcoming and needs to be remedied—by earlier "vesting" of pension rights, for instance, and by making them "portable," that is, transferable from one employer to another. But the problem arises because in most U.S. pension plans eligibility is conditional upon working for the same employer twenty-five to thirty years. Two-thirds of the work force, in other words, have what is in effect lifetime employment—a far larger proportion, by the way, than in Japan. The "average" job mobility of the U.S. worker is indeed high. But again the great bulk of the turnover, as in the case of managers and professionals, is in the very early years, when many young people change jobs two or even three times a year. After they have worked for five or six years, have married, and have begun to raise a family, they tend to stop moving—and soon acquire enough seniority to have substantial job security.

## The Shortcomings

Economically (in terms of total labor costs and incomes) the developed countries have arrived at a high degree of employment security and income stability. And yet both "models," the American-European and the Japanese, have serious shortcomings.

The American-European system may actually, as said before, have less flexibility of labor costs than the Japanese. But *psychologically* the fear persists. Income stability is least assured when the worker needs it the most, that is, when his children are small and when he may have old parents to support. For then he has comparatively low seniority. There is also no true "system" but rather a confused mess of ad hoc improvisations. As a result, the individual case is almost unpredictable. One man may actually have all but complete income security even for prolonged periods of unemployment or sickness. Another man may have little or none.

Mobility is available in the West (though by no means unrestricted—there are very real obstacles, especially in the form of union restrictions and demarcations that close access to crafts and jobs to newcomers). But information on job opportunities, except in a few areas of knowledge work, is scarce. Statistically, the danger of long-term unemployment is very small (except in a genuine depression in an economy, industry, or isolated geographic region). But the individual sees no pattern. The fear of being out of a job therefore remains.

One of the most beneficial social innovations of recent years may have been the "headhunter," that is, the professional executive-recruitment firm. It provides an information system for job opportunities for managerial and professional people. It has greatly diminished uncertainty and with it fear. But nothing comparable exists in most countries for rank-and-file workers and clerks.

The Japanese system gives to employees in Japan's "modern" organizations a high degree of psychological security. But its lack of mobility is a weakness, and one that will become increasingly serious. It commits Japan to maintenance of employment in yesterday's industries while it starves tomorrow's industries, especially in a period—such as the 1970s and 1980s —when the supply of new workers will shrink because of population changes. The restriction on mobility is becoming increasingly irksome to young, highly qualified knowledge people. They also increasingly become economic waste as highly qualified people—e.g., engineers, computer experts, and accountants—cannot move where their knowledge would make the greatest contribution but are forced to stay put even if there is little real work for them. And with the center of gravity of the work force shifting to knowledge workers even faster in Japan than in the West as a result of the education explosion, this threatens to become an increasing impairment.

## The Rehn Plan

The Swedish experience shows that these shortcomings are not preordained either by economic or by social "laws." The Swedish system was devised by a union leader, Goesta Rehn, in the early fifties. Rehn realized that Sweden had to change industrial and economic structure and had to shrink traditional low-technology and low-productivity industry. At the same time, he realized that the worker had to be given security. Under the Swedish system—in sharp contrast to that favored in most other Western countries—industries and companies are not being encouraged to maintain employment. On the contrary, they are being encouraged to anticipate any redundancy in employment that might result from technological development or economic change. At the same time businesses and industries are expected to anticipate future needs for additional workers and their skills. This information is fed to the Rehn Board, a semigovernmental, semiprivate organization in which government, employers, and labor unions work together. The Board then underwrites the income of the redundant employee. It trains him. It finds a new job for him and places him in it. If necessary it moves him to a new location and pays for the move.

The Rehn Plan explains in large measure the economic transformation of Sweden. As late as 1950 Sweden was still almost an underdeveloped country for most of her population. The bulk of the labor force was employed in low-productivity and low-income activity. Twenty years later Sweden had become one of the technological leaders of the world with a living standard second only to that of the United States. A larger proportion of the work force than in any other country, including Japan, has moved from one kind of employment to another, with a minimum of disruption, with almost no resistance to change, and with extraordinary willingness to acquire new skills and to learn new things.

The Swedish example shows that, even in a major economic shift, insecurity of jobs and income is not a very big problem. The fear is real and paralyzing. But the problem itself, in statistical terms, is marginal.

A Swedish trade union leader who at first opposed the Rehn Plan (as he told me) found the perfect analogy: "Remember," he said, "when every mother was scared stiff of polio every summer? Yet, statistically polio was a very minor risk, far less than that of any other illness around. All of us were as afraid of unemployment and job loss as mothers used to be of polio. The fear paralyzed us. And the reason was exactly the same as that which made mothers panic at the very thought of polio. Every case, however rare, was unpredictable, mysterious, and catastrophe."

Sweden, under the Rehn Plan, took responsibility for the worker way beyond what even the Japanese do. Yet the expense was marginal. In fact, Sweden—despite very high unemployment compensation—pays probably less for the maintenance of jobs and incomes than does American industry under its various supplementary compensation and severance plans.

## Needed: Organized Placement

We need to make explicit the actuality of high job security and (in the West) even higher income stability. In the West we need also to build in the Japanese relationship between income assurance and the need for income security of different groups, especially with respect to stages in a family's life cycle. The Japanese, in turn, will surely have to develop mobility, especially for the knowledge worker.

But in addition, job security and employment stability require organized placement activity. The cost is almost insignificant. But lacking systematic placement, the employer will be "frozen in." He will not be able to reduce employment—or at least labor costs. Yet there will still be fear and insecurity unless the employer takes active responsibility, one way or another, for placing employees who have to be let go. Wherever an employer has accepted the commitment to finding a job for redundant workers, the result has been psychological security. Examples abound: Zeiss again led the way. While Zeiss had employment security through periods of minor economic fluctuations, it did experience occasional truly poor years. And there was a fair amount of technological redundancy despite continuous learning. Then Zeiss tried to place the men whose jobs were being abolished—and rarely had any difficulty finding for them at least as good a job as they had had at Zeiss.

A more recent example is a major American manufacturer of glass and plastic containers which, for many years, and without any formal announcement, has considered it the employer's duty to find jobs for people who because of technological or economic change become redundant— whether they are rank-and-file manual workers, clerical workers, professionals, or managers. The number of people who have to be placed is reasonably small in any one year. In most cases the manager of the unit, with the help of people in the personnel department, can place the handful of "problem cases" easily and within his own locality. Once in a while it becomes necessary to retrain a man at company expense. And once in a while it becomes necessary to give a man early retirement with a fairly substantial pension. Over the years the program has cost almost nothing. In that company workers are willing to take a very high degree of responsibility for their own jobs and their own achievement. And resistance to technological change and to higher productivity is minimal.

A very different example is that of a major worldwide management consulting firm. Professional employees have no employment security the first three to five years. They are on probation, and turnover is fairly high. Men who last beyond this probationary period and become consultants will, it is clearly understood, not be kept on the payroll past age thirty-eight or forty unless they are accepted by the group as full partners. Only one out of every six or seven therefore stays on past forty. Yet there is no fear in the group, no demand for job or income security. For the firm, without legal commitment, undertakes to place everyone who has passed the probationary period but then does not qualify within the ensuing ten years for full partnership. The senior partners themselves do most of the placement through their personal acquaintances throughout world business. Every junior knows that he will be asked in all probability to leave the firm just when he needs job and income the most, that is, at a time when his family needs are greatest. Yet he is not very much concerned. He knows that the firm will take responsibility for placing him and, with it, for maintaining, if not improving, his income.

The Swedish system would clearly not work in a major economic depression. Nor would any other, including the Japanese system. But a major economic depression is a rare event, and people know then that there is no protection and do not expect miracles.

The basic problem in job and income security is not general catastrophe. It is the impact on the individual of minor changes, technological advances which obsolete one company, one industry, or one craft; improvements in productivity which lead to a cutting back of the labor force required; minor shifts in economic demands; in transportation economics, in product line, or in process. Statistically these are marginal events. For the individual they are "polio."

This is no longer a problem of money. The money is being spent to provide job security and income stability. The need now is, first—in the West, in particular—to make explicit, overt, and visible the security that exists. And second, as the Swedes have shown, the mobility which economy, enterprise, and worker require needs to be organized. What is needed, in other words, is a little intelligence and some hard work.

## Profits, Productivity, and Benefits

The job as a living is the worker's first concern with respect to the economic dimension of working. But there is also the apparent conflict between wage fund and capital fund, that is, between the worker's economic interest in wage and salary and the need of economy and enterprise (and ultimately of workers) for profits and productivity.

In the United States, at least, this conflict should by now be moot and a thing of the past. For increasingly in the American economy, the worker is the beneficiary of both the wage fund and the capital fund.

Increasingly American industry—at least the large and middle-sized American business—is being "owned" for the employees' benefit by the trustees of the employees. By 1990—or at the latest by the year 2000—the pension funds and the mutual funds (and most shareholders in mutual funds are low- and middle-income employees) will own between two-thirds and three-quarters or more of the large and medium-sized businesses of America. Already by now, that is, in the early 1970s, these trustees of the workers have become the largest single group of shareholders and owners in the American economy. They are the only true "capitalists" around.

Yet the fact that worker and shareowner are becoming one and the same person seems to have very little impact, if any, on the hostility to profit. Even total worker ownership and the elimination of all outside owners does not have much impact, it seems.

One large American company that is totally employee-owned is United Parcel Service (which has, in effect, replaced the U.S. Post Office as the main provider of parcel post services throughout the country). Yet, United Parcel has for years been plagued by labor troubles. The employees clearly do not identify themselves with the "bosses" against whom they strike.

On a much larger scale, Yugoslavia teaches the same lesson. All larger businesses in Yugoslavia are owned by their workers, with an elected workers' council the enterprise's governing organ. Yet, no Yugoslav management has reported any pressure from the owners for higher profits. On the contrary, managements have to fight for adequate profits against worker resistance. The constant demand is for lower profits and higher wages, to the point where the Yugoslav experiment of worker-ownership of industry is seriously being endangered by wage inflation.

The most curious case is probably Japan. The employees of the company, especially of the large, modern one, are the only true owners. Since an employee, whether rank-and-file worker or executive vice-president, cannot be fired, as a rule, the enterprise is actually run for the employees. They are the "beneficial owners," in legal (or economic) terms. And since they cannot find a job elsewhere as a rule, the employees have an overriding self-interest in the survival and prosperity of the company that employs them. In the West, it used to be said that "all the worker owns is his capacity to work." In Japan he does not even own that; his only real property is the welfare of his company. Yet in no other country is resistance to profits so great. Indeed one is told again and again that for "us Japanese" profit is a dirty word and synonymous with exploitation.

The worker-owner who resists profits and rejects the needs of the capital fund is, however, not altogether irrational. And to explain his resistance as the result of "socialist agitation," as conservatives have done for a hundred years, is fatuous.

The main reason is simply that profit is too small in relation to wage and salary to tilt the balance for the worker-owner. This is particularly true in the society of organizations where most working people are employees on a wage or a salary. Wage and salary income of employees in such a society is about two-thirds of a country's total personal income, after-tax profits a scant 5 or 6 percent. The real property of the employee, in other words, and the income on which he depends, is his job. Profit—even if he gets all of it—is a fringe benefit, and not a very big one. Rational behavior for the employee is clearly to maximize wage and salary income, even at the expense of his own share in profits.

A second—but not secondary—explanation is that plans which pay out profit shares or productivity shares as *income*, are, of necessity, fair-weather plans. They work well as long as profits and productivity go up. They create resentment and frustration the moment profit shares and productivity bonuses no longer go up but go down. And, in any given year, two-fifths of the businesses in any economy do not have a profit but operate at a loss.

It is basic fallacy to treat profit as income. Profit is capital fund, that is, savings. Only if used to build a capital fund for the worker can it have meaning. Only then can the function of profit even be understood.

Wherever profit as capital fund has been structured as an employee benefit, the impact has been great. In some cases the resistance to profit has almost completely disappeared.

One example—admittedly an atypical one—is the Sears, Roebuck profit-sharing pension fund. There is a clear relationship between company profits and a major need of the employee, namely, retirement pensions. There is a clear link between the profitability of the company and the size of the pension which a retiring employee will receive. To be sure, Sears has been a singularly profitable company so that its plan has been a bonanza for long-serving employees. But it is also reasonable to assume that the employee's knowledge that the company's profitability meant a larger retirement pension for him may have had something to do with the company's profitability. Employees on all levels, from the very lowest on up, and including members of militant unions, have been willing to contribute to profits and willing to accept increased company profitability as objective for themselves.

The Sears example, as also the Zeiss example, would indicate that *benefits* are the area in which a meaningful link between company profitability and worker needs can be attempted. In the benefit areas the individual employee builds up his capital fund. He needs certainty with respect to his expectations and provision against risk. At the same time, individual certainty can be provided in many benefit areas on the basis of a probability distribution, that is, at a fairly low cost per individual.

One of these areas is the risk of survival, that is, the need for some retirement provision. With present life expectancy, survival to retirement has become the great probability. If spread over enough years and over a large enough group, the certainty of adequate retirement income can be financed by a fairly low annual payment per individual covered. Another such area where there is need for certainty of benefits is health care. The individual economic risk goes beyond anything even the rich can carry. But there is a probability distribution which makes collective coverage reasonably cheap. Finally, there is job and income security, again a risk of catastrophe for the individual, but, on a probability basis, a fairly low group risk.

These are benefits which can be provided for out of fluctuating profits. In any one year the contribution to a retirement fund, a health plan, or a job and income maintenance fund can fluctuate. What matters is that the provision be adequate over a three- to ten-year period, that is, that low contributions in one year be compensated for by higher contributions in another, more profitable year.

## Making "Benefits" Benefit

But to be effective, benefit plans, however generous, will have to be restructured.

There is no lack of fringe benefits in developed countries. They have grown like weeds. They began to develop around 1920. Since then two systems have come into being.

One is the Japanese system where benefits are highly selective. They are focused on the needs of individual groups and individuals. There is no systematic plan, as a rule. The individual has no rights. Employer contributions to benefits are not made according to actuarial projections, generally, but according to the needs of the moment.

In the West, benefits have developed into highly structured rights with rigid plans. By and large, there is flexibility neither in contribution nor in beneficiary. The employer pays a certain fixed amount per employee. And all employees, regardless of age, sex, skill, and so on, receive exactly the same benefits, absolutely or in proportion to salary, whether they fit their major needs or not.

Both systems have made the worker, in effect, the major recipient of profits, that is, the major recipient of, and conduit for, the capital fund. For provisions for workers' retirement or for workers' education are capital investments rather than wages, at least in economic terms. Yet neither system is adequate to either the needs of the worker or the needs of enterprise and economy.

One basic weakness of the Western system is that it lacks selectivity. Every group in the work force gets the same benefits whether they truly benefit the group or not. As a result, no group gets in full the benefits that would mean the most for it. And every group gets benefits which it does not truly need and therefore does not greatly value, but for which it pays, of course, one way or another.

A reason for this is the pervasive belief of employees—on all levels—that there are "free benefits." If the employer pays for them, many employees believe they do not cost anything. The labor unions are among the foremost victims of this particular delusion. Needless to say, there are no free benefits. All benefits are part of the cost of enterprise and economy. Since some two-thirds of personal income in every developed society is wages and salaries (which does not include the incomes oᶠ farmers, small shopkeepers, and independent professionals) there is no one but the recipients of wages and salaries who could possibly pay for benefits.

Another reason why benefits in the West are not structured to give the most benefit to the recipient is the belief of the labor unions that what costs the enterprise the most is thereby of most benefit for the employee. The labor union measures the value of benefits by how much they "hurt" the enterprise.

In addition, most benefits in the West are not related to the performance of the enterprise—or at least, not in visible form. They are fixed. What is needed, however, are plans that have a "floor" with contributions actually determined though fluctuating from year to year according to the company's profits and productivity. But there needs to be no "ceiling." Extraordinary profitability or productivity might, as at Sears, Roebuck, make possible sizable increases in benefit levels without creating a permanent burden.

The Japanese system provides probably greater worker satisfaction with a lower burden on enterprise and economy. This is a result of its selectivity, that is, of its ability to tailor the benefits of one group or one employee to specific needs. But at the same time, the Japanese system is arbitrary. Management decides what is good for the employee. There is no plan and little predictability. As a result, there is increasing pressure in Japan for clear, agreed-upon contractual plans, that is, for the Western approach.

In addition, the Japanese system does even less than the Western system to relate benefits to profitability and productivity. In Japan, far more than in the West, employee benefits are capital investment: a small dowry for the woman worker upon her marriage; housing built by the employer or low-interest mortgage loans to enable the employee to build his own home; the two-year salary that still serves as retirement payment for most workers. Yet this capital fund for the worker is rarely related to the enterprise's or the economy's capital fund, that is, to profitability or rising productivity. In the West most employees know—if only vaguely—that a declining business will cut back on benefits. Whenever that happens in Japan, it seems to come as a tremendous shock and surprise.

## What Benefits Should Be

It is not surprising that benefits yield so little of their potential benefit. Almost no benefit plan anywhere in the world was planned, designed, thought through. Practically all of them just grew. Indeed, Americans still call them "fringes"—even though benefits are a little more than a quarter of the *total* labor cost of American business, which is somewhat wide for a fringe. And in Europe, let alone in Japan, this fringe is even wider.

In most businesses, Western or Japanese, benefits are the third largest cost next to wages and materials. Yet while individual benefit programs, e.g., the retirement plan or the health-care plan, are managed, the benefit system is essentially unmanaged. To leave so large a cost center unmanaged is poor management. And far more is at stake in benefits than cost. It is high time that management assume true managerial responsibility for benefits.

We can specify what benefits should be and should do.

1. Benefits need to be structured so as to give the beneficiary, the worker, the most for the money.

A good example of what not to do is America's most widely used health insurance plan, the nonprofit Blue Cross Plan which is particularly popular with labor unions. Blue Cross health coverage has become increasingly expensive. Yet it does not provide for payment of medical and hospital bills when the worker needs it the most, that is, when he is out of work. But it pays full expenses for the minor illnesses of his family while he is employed —which is a major reason for the high premium. Yet an employed worker in the United States earns more than enough to pay for minor illnesses of his nonworking family members. A $100 "deductible" for medical costs of nonworking dependents would pay for substantial medical cost coverage for up to two years of unemployment. This would be of far greater benefit to the insured than reimbursement for sums which he can easily pay when employed and working.

2. The floor of benefits needs to be fixed. But it should be financed on a fluctuating basis with a clear relationship to profitability and perhaps to productivity, and higher benefits (especially retirement benefits) in the event of extraordinary profitability and productivity gains. There needs to be a *minimum* contribution on the part of the employer. And any deficiency

in the benefit fund must be made up on a regular periodic basis. But the more flexibility the employer has, the greater his contribution can be. At the same time, the closer and more visible the relationship is between benefits and a company's profits, the more will benefits help to attenuate the conflict between wage fund and capital fund.

3. Instead of individual benefits programs, each with its own contribution, it might be well to decide first the total size of the benefit package and then work out options to give to each group the combination of benefits that best serves its needs.

There need to be safeguards, of course. I would imagine that no worker would be allowed to opt out of health insurance. But a worker might be given the option between a health insurance plan that reimburses him in full for all medical and hospital expenses for himself and his family, and one in which he pays for the first few hundred dollars of medical expenses each year out of his own pocket. That would enable him to increase the contribution to his pension plan or to get low-interest loans for the college expenses of his children or for building a house.

I, personally, would go much further. I would strongly favor plans under which workers are entitled to cut their cash wage, up to a substantial percentage, to improve their benefits. In the West, where younger workers (unlike Japan) are paid essentially the same as older men doing similar work, a younger worker who does not yet have substantial family obligations or mortgage payments on a house might be encouraged, for instance, to withhold a share of his cash earnings to be put into his retirement annuity. After all, a dollar paid into an annuity account at age twenty-five buys a great deal more than a dollar paid into the same account twenty years later.

Wherever plans of this kind have been offered, they have met with tremendous response, both on the part of younger workers in general and especially on the part of knowledge workers of all ages. Examples are some stock purchase plans and savings plans of American companies. The Internal Revenue Service has encouraged such a plan for some employees of nonprofit institutions such as college professors who can withhold a substantial part of their salary to be invested in their retirement pension, with the income taxable only when received, that is, after retirement and presumably at a much lower rate. This plan has been chosen by a very large proportion of the men eligible under it—proving that it makes sense to a great many workers to manage cash incomes and benefits as one income stream.

At the same time we might give workers at certain stages of their family life the option to take down part of the benefit money as additional cash wage. This would be bitterly fought by the labor unions, since it would create what labor unions fear the most: unequal cash wages for equal work (though total actual income, i.e., cash wages plus benefits, would of course remain the same). But it would make sense, especially if the same worker has earlier, that is, before the time of heavy family obligations, withheld part of his cash income and put the money into benefits.

4. The administration of benefits should as much as possible be made a responsibility of the work community.

Investing pension-fund money requires high professional skill. And so does running a mortgage bank for employee housing. But the work community needs to participate, if only to learn. And it should be primarily responsible for the design of benefit programs and benefit options for various groups in the work force. No one else knows what the true needs are. No one else can convince the work force that choices have to be made and that the available options represent the best balance of choices.

Workers the world over have shown two strong preferences as incomes went up.

One is the preference for leisure over more cash income. What part of the added productivity of a modern economy is taken in the form of leisure rather than in the form of cash income is hard to compute. But at all levels (except the top) workers clearly consider leisure a major employee benefit.

The second preference has been for benefits. This is a rational preference. Retirement pensions and life insurance protection; medical and health care; housing and education, are all values which are best procured on a collective basis, that is, on the basis of certainty for the recipient and probability distribution of risk and cost. And these are the values which loom the larger the more basic economic needs are satisfied.

Benefits, one can predict, are likely to continue to be a major worker demand and a major worker need. Benefits are, therefore, likely to become a larger rather than a smaller part of the labor costs of an economy. At the same time, they become increasingly the channel through which the capital fund is being fed. It is, therefore, incumbent on management to assume responsibility for employee benefits. It is no longer adequate to consider them fringes, as managements do in the West, or benevolence, as managements do in Japan.

# 23

## "People Are Our Greatest Asset"

*The Confusion of Authority with Power—The Lesson of Decentralization—
The Demands on Management—Leadership of People—The Traditional
Approaches—Welfare Paternalism—The Krupp Example—Personnel
Management—People as a Cost and as a Threat—"Our Greatest Resource
Is People"—The Practices of People Management—Treating People as a
Resource—Placement—the Leadership of People*

Everything discussed in the preceding chapters of this section has been
known for years. Everything has actually been practiced in a good many
companies, if only in bits and pieces rather than systematically. Wherever
tried, these approaches have worked and have made for stronger and more
prosperous institutions, and for stronger management.

Managements everywhere have nodded with approval when learning or
reading about these approaches. Yet few managements have acted. Only
now when major shifts in work, work group, and working threaten to make
ineffectual both carrot and stick are managements willing to pay more than
lip service.

What explains this resistance, this unwillingness to learn from such eminently respectable and successful examples as, for instance, Zeiss and IBM?

The first, and in many ways the main, reason for the reluctance of
managers to face up to the problem of making the worker achieving is a
confusion of power with authority in managerial minds. Managers resist as
abdication of authority the demand for worker responsibility, whether on
the part of the manual worker on the shop floor or of the knowledge
professional. They see their authority undermined by "giving up power."

Japanese managements can hardly be accused of having abdicated. They have more authority than managements in the West. Nor can IBM be accused of having abdicated. Indeed, the main criticism of IBM by "liberals" for many years has been that IBM is in effect a tyranny. And Zeiss was anything but permissive and operated under strict discipline.

Power and authority are two different things. Management has no power. Management has only responsibility. And it needs and must have the authority to discharge its responsibilities—but not one whit more.

American managements still sometimes invoke "management prerogatives," especially to resist union demands. This is a singularly unfortunate phrase. A prerogative is a privilege of rank. Management has no claim to any such privilege. It exists to discharge a function. Its job is to make productive the resources in its trust. A prerogative is never based on responsibility or contribution—originally the word was used to denote "divine right." And even the most autocratic management is unlikely to claim divine right. Management has authority only as long as it performs.

To invoke management prerogatives undermines managerial authority. Managements who refuse to demand responsibility from the members of the organization are actually losing necessary authority, especially to the labor union and to government.

Managers of business are by no means alone in their confusion of power with authority. Indeed, managers of business, by and large, have been more willing to work on building an achieving work force than managers of public-service institutions. The government agency and the hospital have been even more reluctant to make their workers responsible, have even more depended on prerogatives rather than on the authority appropriate to their responsibilities. As a result, they have actually lost true and needed authority, are even more hedged in by restraints and restrictions, and have even greater difficulty mobilizing the human resources of their organizations.

## The Lesson of Decentralization

This is not the first time that managements have suffered from this confusion of authority with power, to their detriment and that of their organizations. A similar confusion was common a few decades ago, with respect to organization structure.

There was considerable resistance to decentralization in the forties and fifties. It was widely feared that it would weaken top management and would indeed lead to "top management abdication."

By now managers everywhere have learned that decentralization strengthens top management. It makes it more effective and more capable of doing its own tasks. It results in greater authority for top management (on this see Chapter 46).

Similarly, the Japanese managers, IBM, or, much earlier even, Zeiss, learned that to make the worker achieving strengthens management's authority. It makes management more effective by enabling it to focus on the tasks which mangement needs to perform and to relieve itself of those tasks which management need not perform, does poorly, and spends far too much time on if loaded down with them.*

Responsible worker, responsible work group, and self-governing work community are decentralization. What is being decentralized is not business management, it is work management. But the principle is similar. And just as decentralization was the main thrust in the years of the management boom, so the responsible worker should be central to the years of management performance ahead.

Responsibility built into the work force from top to bottom is needed, above all, to reverse the erosion of management authority which is a threat to the functioning of management and of our institutions altogether. Carrot and stick no longer suffice. But nothing has truly taken their place. As a result there is an authority vacuum. It is most noticeable among the knowledge workers in business, in the government agency, and in the other service institutions. Its symptom is cynicism—a more dangerous disease than rebellion against authority. The only way to counteract it and to restore management's authority is to *demand* responsibility of each member of the work force.

## The Demands on Management

There was a second reason why top managements twenty years ago resisted decentralization. They feared the high demands it makes on top management. And a similar fear also explains the resistance of managers to worker and work-community responsibility.

A responsible work force does indeed make very high demands on managers. It demands that they be truly competent—and competent as managers rather than as psychologists or psychotherapists. It demands that they take their own work seriously. It demands that they themselves take responsibility for their jobs and their performances.

Responsibility is a harsh taskmaster. To demand it of others without demanding it of oneself is futile and irresponsible. The worker cannot

---

*This is brought out clearly in the book by Shigeru Kobayashi of Sony Corp., *Creative Management* (American Management Association, 1971).

assume the burden of responsibility for his own job, work group, and work-community affairs unless he can be confident of the seriousness, responsibility, and competence of his company. He must be able to have confidence that the boss knows his own job and work. He must take it for granted that the boss provides the tools the worker himself needs to be able to do productive work and the information the worker needs to direct and control himself.

Nothing quenches motivation as quickly as a slovenly boss. People expect and demand that managers enable them to do a good job and work productively and intelligently. People have indeed a right to expect a serious and competent superior.

In Japanese companies industrial engineers, as has been said before, do not complain about workers' resistance. Rather they tend to complain that workers demand too much of them. The Japanese work force, which holds itself responsible for production, rightly expects the people on whom it depends for its "tools," that is, for the understanding of work and process, to perform to exacting standards.

People do not expect perfection. They know that the boss is also a human being. But people who take responsibility for their own work demand that managers do what they are being paid for: that they plan; that they set objectives and think through priorities; that they think through assignments and set standards. Above all, they expect that the manager take responsibility for his own work and performance.

Napoleon has been called many things, but "likable" is not one of them. The "great leader" is rarely "warm"; a good many have been icy. He is not often "outgoing" or "affable"; he tends to be austere and aloof. He has little "empathy"; he makes demands. A good many have had not a trace of charisma. But a leader always inspires confidence, always commands respect.

It has been said, and only half in jest, that a tough, professionally led union is a great force for improving management performance. It forces the manager to think through what he is doing and to be able to explain his actions and behavior.

A responsible work force is an even more stringent discipline. It brings into the open the positive dissatisfactions within the group, all the desires to do a better job, all the impatience with bumbling, laziness, petty restraints, and lame excuses. But unlike a union, an achieving work force does not exert its pressure as an adversary. It exerts it in cooperation. It "plays on the same team." But for this reason it expects team captains and team leaders, that is, managers, to hold themselves to high standards and to take their own jobs seriously.

## The Leadership of People

Finally, to make the worker "achieve" demands that managers look upon labor as a resource rather than as a problem, a cost, or an enemy to be cowed. It demands that managers accept responsibility for making human strengths effective. And this means a drastic shift from personnel management to the leadership of people.

There are three traditional approaches to managing people. There is the welfare approach, which sees people as problems which need help. There is the personnel management approach, which sees activities and chores to be performed whenever large numbers of people have to work together. Third is the approach which sees labor as a cost and as a threat and sees the job in controlling cost and in fighting "crises."

People are indeed "problems." And people do need help. The welfare approach can be highly effective, especially in managing people who truly are helpless.

The best example, at least in the West, is the House of Krupp. Alfred Krupp, who built the firm in the middle of the nineteenth century, was not a brilliant engineer. Nor did Krupp's rise rest on major innovations in product or process. It rested squarely on the tremendous support Alfred Krupp built into his work force. Having grown up in extremes of poverty and near-destitution, he, perhaps alone of the major business builders of the mid-nineteenth-century Europe, had compassion for the large masses of unskilled, unlettered, helpless peasants who were being driven out of their wretched tenant farms in East Prussia by the new "scientific agriculture" of the Junkers and who fled helter-skelter into the newly industrializing Ruhr. Long before his firm became profitable and prosperous, he provided housing, schooling, health care, training, small loans at low interest, and so on. Indeed, Krupp at Essen might be called the first welfare state.

It was a state ruled by an autocrat. Yet the "Kruppianers," the descendants of Alfred Krupp's original workers, never forgot the compassion of the original founder. They gave their loyalty to firm and family even though Alfred Krupp was succeeded by three generations of incompetents. It was largely their dedication to the memory of Alfred Krupp which enabled the firm to come back twice—after World War I and after the almost total destruction of World War II.

But the Krupp example also shows the danger of welfare paternalism. It eventually destroys itself. For it creates expectations which, in the long run, no business enterprise—and no institution—can live up to.

Krupp's paternalism was a major reason, and perhaps *the* reason for the ultimate collapse of the Krupp family. Krupp's overexpansion after World

War II was in large measure motivated by the need to live up to the Krupp promise that every Kruppianer would forever have a job. This in turn meant that the very parts of the Krupp concern that had the least potential for growth in the post-World War II economy, e.g., coal mines and steel mills located far inland, had to be expanded the most. This ultimately brought the company to the verge of collapse. The family was ousted from management and, in effect, expropriated by the banks as their price of rescuing the business. Large numbers of old, loyal Kruppianers had to be laid off in the middle of a serious recession in the German coal and steel industry when no other jobs were available.

Even more serious is the aftermath of a welfare paternalism which the "children" ultimately outgrow and reject. It leaves behind a legacy of bitterness and of mutual contempt that goes beyond anything the most bitter industrial warfare could have produced.

Two of the nastiest and most bruising of recent labor conflicts were rebellions against a paternalism that had outlived itself. One was the strike at the Pilkington Brothers Glass Company at St. Helen's, England, in 1971 —after almost a century of successful paternalism. Twenty years earlier the employer with the greatest welfare concern for employees in the United States—the Hershey Chocolate Company in Hershey, Pennsylvania—had similarly come to the end of the paternalist road in a strike that was made all the more bitter by the fact that the company is not owned by "capitalists" but by a foundation for the benefit of the employees.

The more successful welfare paternalism is—and the more needed—the more should management prepare for its self-liquidation. And the way to do this is, of course, to develop the fullest possible responsibility for job, work group, and work-community affairs or worker and work force.

The Marks & Spencer staff manageress (see Chapter 8) was a welfare worker in the 1920s, when there was need for a highly paternalist approach. The shopgirl who sold in the Marks & Spencer store in those days came straight out of the worst slums of the old industrial cities. She was, as a rule, ignorant, illiterate, helpless, frightened, if not indeed, brutalized. But as the work force changed with the changes in British society the staff manageress ceased to be a welfare worker and became teacher, coach, and a kind of ombudswoman. Her primary job is no longer welfare. It is to be the conscience of the company in its management of people. She serves, above all, as a communications channel from the employees to management.

For knowledge workers welfare paternalism is altogether inappropriate. But it also makes less and less sense for manual workers who are well paid, have middle-class standards of living, and have substantial education.

This probably applies even to Japan with her strong tradition of group belonging and of group responsibility for the individual. And indeed, while

Japanese companies are maintaining the traditional welfare paternalism for their young women workers recruited largely from rural areas, and for manual workers in general, a good many of them are shifting slowly but steadily away from the traditional "family" concept for their knowledge workers—and for good reasons. Japanese business, now, when the need for paternalism is rapidly disappearing, might well turn over the welfare functions to the work community. Otherwise Japan may soon face a crisis of welfare paternalism, as damaging to the economy as Krupp's overcommitment, and as destructive to industrial cohesion as the Pilkington and Hershey strikes.

Even at its most successful, the welfare approach is not an approach for *managing* people. It is an approach for *helping* people. It assumes that people are defined by their weakness. It does not try to find and make productive their strengths. It is a complement to the managing of people rather than its substance.

The welfare approach is a temporary expedient. It is a crutch. As such it may be very effective, may indeed be crucial to survival. But if taken for permanent and seen as the final answer, it will eventually cripple management and workers, company, economy, and society.

## Personnel Management

The second approach to the management of people is personnel management. It arose during and after World War I as an organized and systematic management function.*

Personnel management is methodical and systematic discharge of all the activities that have to be done where people are employed, especially in large numbers: their selection and employment; training; medical services, the cafeteria, and safety; the administration of wages, salaries, and benefits, and many others.

Personnel management has to be done. Otherwise there is serious malfunction. But personnel management activities bear the same relationship to managing people as vacuuming the living room and washing the dishes bear to a happy marriage and the bringing up of children. If too many dirty dishes pile up in the sink, the marriage may come apart. But spotless dishes do not by themselves contribute a great deal to wedded bliss or to close and happy relationships with one's children. These are hygiene factors. If neglected, they cause trouble. They should be taken for granted.

Personnel management concerns itself largely with matters of great con-

---

*The pioneer was an American, Thomas Spates, who, after World War I, worked first in the International Labor Office and then for many years as personnel vice-president for a major American corporation, General Foods.

cern to the work community. They should not be considered management functions. They should be work-community functions and organized as such. To regard personnel management as managing people at work, as has been the tendency, is nonmanagement. It is substituting procedures for policies and forms for substance.*

Personnel management departments have grown at an astronomical rate since World War II in all countries and in all industries. They have grown even faster in the public-service sector. Yet personnel managers everywhere complain that they are "not listened to," "not supported," "have not been truly accepted" by their management colleagues. There is substance to these complaints. But in the main they reflect a feeling on the part of the personnel people that there is something wrong with what they are doing and that they are not addressing themselves to what they profess to deal with, namely the management of people.

There is need in any organization for a "conscience" with regard to people (see Chapter 42); and conscience functions are top-management work. But personnel management cannot discharge the conscience job; it is too busy with activities. Its usual work is "support" (again see Chapter 42). But it is primarily support to the work community—and this is where it should be lodged.

Last among traditional approaches to managing people is to see in them a cost and a threat.

There is need for the control of labor costs. There is need for the control of labor productivity. There is need for "fire fighting." There is need for the organized guerrilla warfare of union relations—or at least we have let this need develop. To take care of these things is necessary and may, at times, be crucial. But it is not managing people. It is dealing with problems that result from the failure to manage people. In anything as complex as a modern organization, there will be such failures. But preventing them, or even curing them, does not make the system work and produce.

Managing means making the strengths of people effective. Neither the welfare approach, nor the personnel management approach, nor the control and fire-fighting approach address themselves to strength, however.

People are weak; and most of us are pitifully weak. People cause problems, require procedures, create chores. And people are a cost and a potential "threat." But these are not the reason why people are employed. The reason is their strength and their capacity to perform. And, to say what will be said many times in this book, the purpose of an organization is to make the strengths of people productive and their weaknesses irrelevant.

*On this see the chapter "Is Personnel Management Bankrupt?" in my book, *The Practice of Management.*

### "People Are Our Greatest Asset"

Managers are fond of saying, "Our greatest asset is people." They are fond of repeating the truism that the only real difference between one organization and another is the performance of people. All other resources one organization commands to exactly the same extent as does any other. And most managers know perfectly well that of all the resources, people are the least utilized and that little of the human potential of any organization is tapped and put to work.

But while managers proclaim that people are their major resource, the traditional approaches to the managing of people do not focus on people as a resource, but as problems, procedures, and costs.

Realization of this underlies recent proposals to put people into a company's financial accounts as "assets." One such proposal—made by Michael Schiff, a distinguished accounting scholar at New York University—is to show sales and marketing forces as "investment," as they indeed are.

It is perfectly true that the accounting treatment of people shows them as "costs." And human beings are always directed by the information and measurements they receive, even if they know them to be one-sided, biased, or deficient (on this see Chapter 39, "Controls, Control, and Management"). An accounting system which would show people as "capital investments" would therefore make a major difference.

But it is not easy to see how one could show people as assets on the books. An asset is by definition something one can sell and something that has a value when a company goes into liquidation. But a company does not own people. And an asset which can give notice and leave is not an asset in any sense of the word. There are equally serious practical objections. How does one, for instance, measure the return on training?

Still, the idea has merit. It clearly would be highly desirable for managers to be led by their own measurements and their own controls to acting on their profession that "people are our greatest asset." We clearly need something more powerful than meetings, seminars, "sensitivity training," sermons, or proclamations.

Above all, however, we need *practices*. And they are easier to obtain than changes in vision or attitude.

First, of course, is the practice of building responsibility and achievement into job and work force. There need to be objectives for every job, set by the man who is to attain the objectives, together with his manager. The work itself has to be made productive so that the worker can work at making himself achieving. And the worker needs the demand, the discipline, and the incentive of responsibility.

Second, the manager must treat the people with whom he works as *resource* to himself. He has to look to them for guidance regarding his own job. He has to demand of them that they accept it as their responsibility to enable their manager to do a better and more effective job himself. The manager needs to build upward responsibility and upward contribution into the job of each of his subordinates.

One way to do this is to ask each subordinate to think through and answer a few simple questions: "What do I do as your manager, and what does your company do that helps you the most in *your* job?"; "What do I do as your manager, and what does the company do, that hinders you the most in *your* job?"; and "What can you do that will help me, as *your* manager, do the best job for the company?"

These may seem obvious questions. But they are rarely asked. Whenever they are being asked, the answers turn out to be far from obvious.

In every case I have come across it turned out that things the manager did in order to help his people perform their jobs did not help them at all and indeed hampered them. And it turned out that very few, if any, of his subordinates had even given thought to the question of what they might have to do to enable their manager to perform better.

Such questions force both manager and subordinate to focus on common performance. They both focus on the purpose of their relationship. And they are likely to induce in the manager a new perspective on the people who work for him. He will make himself look to them as his resource, but will also guide them to looking to him as their resource.

## Placement

The final but perhaps the most important element in managing people is to place them where their strengths can become productive.

Personnel management stresses selection for employment. It is debatable whether the results justify the tremendous effort and the elaborate and ingenious methods of tests, interviews, and selection procedures that have been developed. In particular it is doubtful that the complex selection procedures for knowledge people really "select" anyone.

We know how to identify specific physical traits which render an individual less likely to perform a specific manual activity, e.g., laying bricks. We know nothing, however, about configurations of character, personality, and talent such as come into play in knowledge work and especially in work as a manager. Most American large companies have been building large staffs of college recruiters who try to find "potential" among college and professional school graduates. Insofar as it is the job of these people to attract graduates to their employer, their activity makes sense. But with respect to their ability to "spot" the "comers," their record is dismal. Otherwise, three out of every five of their "recruits" would not quit their first employer within the first two or three years. Random selection, e.g., of every third one who applies, is likely to produce better results. The reason is not lack of skill of the college recruiter. The reason is that we do not know what we look for in management potential, and have no way of testing it except in performance.

And neither the elaborate, ritualistic game of the English house party nor the grueling but purely formalistic entrance tests of the large Japanese companies make more sense. Their only refinement over the American practice is greater mental cruelty.

Placement, however, is left largely to chance. Yet no two people have the same configuration of strengths and weaknesses. And no one has only strengths; there are no "universal geniuses."* It is the manager's job to optimize resources. And placement is the way to optimize the most expensive resource of them all: the human being.

The Japanese, precisely because they cannot fire a man and are stuck with him, often do a better job in placement than managers in the West. Indeed (as said in Chapter 20), placing the young knowledge professional and manager is one of the tasks the "godfather" is expected to discharge systematically albeit behind the scenes.

In the West, we should be able, however, to do a much better job of placement than the Japanese do. For the Western manager can take responsibility for placing people both inside and outside his organization. The "nonperformer" should not be permitted to stay in the organization—excepting only the "conscience cases" of old, deserving, employees who have given long years of performance and have *earned* an organization's loyalty. For the nonperformer damages the entire organization. He imposes a load on his fellow employees, who have to "carry" him. He undermines morale, the organization's standards, and its self-respect.

However, the nonperformer is often—and perhaps in most cases—not a "dud." He is only in the wrong place—the proverbial square peg in the round hole. He belongs elsewhere, where what he can do is needed and contributes. It is the manager's job, especially with the young knowledge worker, to think through where a nonperformer might be productive and effective, and to say to him, "You are in the wrong business—you belong *there*."

Such practices will not satisfy the many critics of traditional people management who call for new convictions and for a fundamental change

---

*On placement see also the chapter "Making Strength Effective" in my book, *The Effective Executive.*

in attitudes. To be sure, treating people as a resource to the manager and emphasis on placement where their strengths can be effective are only "practices." But they are a good deal more than rhetoric and pious platitude. They are hard, demanding work. They will not create utopia-in-organization. But they will point organizations toward performance rather than conformance. These practices will not make dull jobs and dull people interesting. But they will go a long way toward preventing interesting jobs and interesting people from being dulled. They will not eliminate the basic functions and tensions of organization and make its problems of economies and power go away. But they might release countervailing forces of trust and achievement. These practices will not make unnecessary the traditional approaches to people as problems, as chores, as cost, and as threat.

But, though only the first steps, they move manager and management beyond personnel management and toward the leadership of people.

## Social Impacts
## and Social Responsibilities

The quality of life is the third major task area for management. Managements of all institutions are responsibile for their by-products, that is, the impacts of their legitimate activities on people and on the physical and social environment. They are increasingly expected to anticipate and to resolve social problems. They need to think through and develop new policies for the relationship of business and government, which is rapidly outgrowing traditional theories and habits. What are the tasks? What are the opportunities? What are the limitations? And what are the ethics of leadership for the manager who is a leader but not a master?

# 24

## Management and the Quality of Life

*The Changed Meaning of "Social Responsibility"—What Explains It? —
The Price of Success—The Disenchantment with Government—The New
Leadership Groups—Why Public Relations Are Inadequate—Three Cautionary Tales—Union Carbide and Vienna, West Viginia—Swift do Argentina and Deltec—Civil Rights and the Quaker Conscience—Social Responsibilities Have to Be Managed*

The "social responsibilities of business" have been discussed for a century.
Indeed, a chapter or two on social responsibility—or some similar heading
—can be found in almost any text on general management.

But since the early sixties the meaning of the words "social responsibility
of business" has changed radically.

Earlier discussions of social responsibilities of business centered in three
areas. One was the perennial question of the relationship between private
ethics and public ethics. To what extent is a manager in charge of an
organization beholden to the ethics of the individual and to what extent
does his responsibility to the organization permit him—or perhaps even
compel him—to resort to privately unethical behavior for the good of his
organization? The text for this discussion, consciously or not, is an old
epigram of the politicians: "What scoundrels we would be if we did in our
private lives what we do in our public capacity for our countries."

The second major topic was the social responsibility which the employer
bears toward his employees by virtue of his power and wealth. The classic
discussion is to be found in a book by the English Quaker industrialist and
philanthropist B. Seebohm Rowntree, *The Human Needs of Labor* (1918).

Finally, social responsibility was the term used to assert—or assign—leadership responsibility of the businessman with respect to the "culture" of the community: support of the arts, the museums, the opera, and the symphony orchestra; service as a trustee on the boards of educational and religious institutions, and also giving money to philanthropic and other community causes. And in the United States in particular, willingness to serve in governmental or quasi-governmental positions has become in this century an important social responsibility of the executive.

By and large the traditional approach was not concerned, as it claimed to be, with the social responsibility of business but with the social responsibility of businessmen. And the greatest emphasis was put on what businessmen should or might contribute outside of business hours and outside their businesses.

After World War II there was increasing emphasis on the contribution of business. But this was a result of tax laws which, on the one hand, slowed down the accumulation of large fortunes by individuals, and on the other hand, encouraged and made highly attractive charitable contributions on the part of a company. The emphasis otherwise remained unchanged. Where an earlier generation had looked to the "rich businessman" to endow a hospital, post-World War II big business was expected to support worthy causes. Emphasis was still on outside "causes" rather than on the behavior and actions of business itself.

Some earlier writers took a broader view. Eiichi Shibusawa in the Japan of early and mid-Meiji, that is, before 1900, and Walter Rathenau in Germany in the years before World War I wrote extensively on the relationship between business, especially large business, and the society around it. But even Shibusawa and Rathenau were mainly concerned with setting limits to business and with making business and businessmen fit themselves to social and community values.

When social responsibilities are being discussed these days, however, the emphasis is quite different. It is on what business should or might *do* to tackle and solve problems of society. The emphasis is on the contribution business can make to such social problems as racial discrimination and racial integration in the United States, or on the maintenance and restoration of the physical environment. One of the best examples of the new attitude comes from Sweden.

Several large Swedish companies, especially ASEA, the big electrical-apparatus company, were harshly attacked in the late sixties in the Swedish press for participating in a major electric-power project in Africa. The project was sponsored by the UN and financed by the World Bank; it also had been endorsed by the socialist government of Sweden. Its purpose was to raise the living standards of a desperately poor region of Black Africa.

But it was located in a Portuguese colony. Hence, it was vehemently argued, the Swedish companies participating in it "supported colonialism" by helping to raise the standards of living of the native population. It was their duty, so the argument ran, to work for the "downfall of colonialism," which would best be achieved by keeping the natives desperately poor rather than have them prosper under an "imperialist exploiter."

The most extreme assertion of social responsibilities of business is perhaps a statement made during the sixties by the Mayor of New York City, John Lindsay.

The Mayor called on the big corporations of New York City to "adopt" a Black ghetto neighborhood and to make sure that the people in that neighborhood would have the necessities of life, would get education, and would get jobs. He then added that he hoped that these major corporations would also make sure that each Black family had a man in the house who would be husband to the wife and father to the children.

Only ten years earlier one could not have imagined anyone, not even the most extreme "leftist" of "progressive," berating business for its refusal to nullify the foreign policy of its own government (and a socialist one to boot) or for shunning paternalistic control over the sex life of citizens who were not even employees.

This new concept of social responsibility no longer asks what the limitations on business are, or what business should be doing for those under its immediate authority. It demands that business take responsibility for social problems, social issues, social and political goals, and that it become the keeper of society's conscience and the solver of society's problems.

But increasingly such social responsibility is also being demanded of nonbusiness institutions in society. Universities, hospitals, and government agencies, but also learned societies, whether of physicists, historians, or linguists, are all increasingly being confronted with similar demands and attacked for not assuming responsibility for society's ills and problems.

In the early sixties student riots against the university arose out of student grievances. But the student riots of 1968 that almost destroyed Columbia University in New York City were sparked by complaints that the university had failed to take full social responsibility for the neighboring Black community of Harlem and had failed to subordinate its own educational goals to the alleged needs of Harlem's hard-core unemployables.

## What Explains It?

The most popular and most obvious explanation is the wrong one. It is not hostility to business that explains the surge of demands for social responsibility. On the contrary, it is the success of the business system which leads to new and, in many cases, exaggerated expectations. The demand for social responsiblity is, in large measure, the price of success.

In developed countries we now take economic performance for granted. This has led to the belief that there is, or should be, universal capacity for economic performance. It has led us to believe that the same efforts which, within a century, lifted one-third of humanity from poverty into affluence can in much less time raise the remaining two-thirds of mankind into affluence, or can at least bring them into rapid economic development.

Less than two generations ago, in the years around World War I, poverty was still taken for granted as the universal condition of mankind. No one then assumed economic development to be the rule. It was considered an exception. What was considered surprising in 1900, or even in 1950, was not that India remained poor. Indeed anyone who would then have talked about the economic development of India would have been considered inane. What was exceptional, and truly surprising, was that Japan had managed to break out of the all but universal poverty of mankind and to start on the road to development. Today lack of development is considered the exception and the "problem." And no matter how rapid development is—e.g., in Brazil since World War II—it is considered inadequate because it does not transform an entire country, within one generation, from extreme misery to comfortable affluence.

No one, only two generations ago, expected poverty to disappear, even in the developed and wealthy countries at that time. Few people today would believe the descriptions and illustrations in the first systematic survey of the poor in what was then the world's richest city, London, which Charles Booth published just before the turn of the century.* Only the horror stories that come out of Calcutta equal them today. Yet, to contemporaries, the London poor of the 1890s seemed so affluent by comparison with the conditions described and illustrated twenty years earlier,† that Marx's partner, Friedrich Engels, in reissuing in 1896 his earlier *The Conditions of the Working Classes in England*, was forced to admit that his and Marx's earlier prophecy of the increasing "pauperisation" of the "proletariat" could no longer be maintained.

In particular, the poverty that is most offensive to us today, that is, poverty in the midst of affluence, was then taken for granted. No one in the nineteenth or early twentieth centuries expected pre-industrial immigrants into the industrial cities to be other than poor, destitute, incompetent, and wretched. No one expected a rapid transformation of the slums of industrial

---

*Charles Booth, *Life and Labour of the People in London*, published between 1892 and 1897.
†For instance, by Charles Dickens the Younger, in his famous *Dictionary of London*, first published in 1879 and intended as a guide to "enjoyment" for the tourist visiting the city.

Lancashire or of the industrializing Vienna in Austria around 1900. All anyone expected was a little humanity to assuage the worst of the suffering, and a little charity. At best there were attempts to help a few of unusual endowment and personal ambition to raise themselves out of the slough of despond. To the orthodox Marxist even this was sentimental romanticism. Following his master he considered these people *Lumpenproletariat* and incapable of improving themselves either individually or collectively.

Nothing in earlier social and economic history equals the recent economic and social development of the American Negro. Within twenty years, from 1950 to 1970, two-thirds of one of the least prepared and most disadvantaged of pre-industrial immigrants into modern civilization have risen from extreme poverty into middle-class status. They have acquired competence and jobs. A larger proportion of their children acquire higher education than of the children of older immigrant groups in the city, such as Italians or Poles who encounter no "racial" barrier.

Admittedly the American Negro is a very special problem. But still, the difference between what was considered success only a half century ago and what is now considered grim failure illustrates the extent to which success has changed expectations. Even rather well-to-do "middle-class" people yesterday had only little of the qualities of life we now expect routinely.

The apartment buildings of the late nineteenth century still stand in most European cities. They are hardly "good housing"—airless and dark, with mean little flats, five floors high without elevator, heating—a coal or wood stove—only in the "parlor," and with one tiny, grimy bathroom for a family of seven. Yet they were built for the new middle classes. Health care was almost nonexistent, education beyond the elementary level a privilege of the few, the newspaper a luxury. And no matter how serious an environmental problem the automobile poses in today's big city, the horse was dirtier, smelled worse, killed and maimed more people, and congested the streets just as much.

And life on the farm, that is, life for the great majority, was, if anything, poorer, dirtier, more dangerous to life and limb, and more brutish.

As late as 1900 or 1914 quality of life was a concern only of the few rich. To all the others it was "escapism" that could be permitted in the syrupy romances that sold by the millions and were devoured alike by servant girls and their "ladies." Reality, however, was the numbing daily struggle for a little food, a dreary job and enough money to pay the premium on burial insurance.

That we can worry about the qualities of life is thus very great success. And it is only right and natural that the same leadership groups which were responsible for the success in providing the quantities of life are expected to assume responsibility now for providing the quality of life.

The same reason explains the demand for social responsibility on the part of the university. For the university too is a success story of the twentieth century.

"If science can tell us how to put a man on the moon," the student activists of the sixties said again and again, "it surely can tell us how to create a decent environment, save our cities from drugs, make marriages happy and children enjoy school. If it doesn't, the only explanation must be 'wrong value priorities' or malicious conspiracy."

To be sure, these arguments are naïve. But they are not irrational. The clamor for social responsibility expects too much. But it expects the right things. Its root is not hostility to authority, but overconfidence in managers and management.

## The Disenchantment with Government

On top of this comes the growing disenchantment with government, the growing disbelief in government's ability to solve major social problems.*

Only a generation ago the people who now demand social responsibility from business (or the university) expected government to be able to take care of every problem of society, if not of every problem of the individual as well. There is still, in all countries, pressure for more and more government programs—though there is also growing resistance to more and more expenditures and taxes. But even the most fervent advocate of an activist government no longer truly expects results, even in countries where respect for and belief in government are still high, such as in Japan, Sweden, and Germany. Even the most fervent advocate of a strong government no longer believes that a problem has been solved the moment it has been turned over to government. As a result, the people most concerned with these problems, the liberals and progressives who, a generation ago, rallied under the banner of "more government," now increasingly look to other leadership groups, other institutions, and, above all, to business, to take on the problems which government should but is not able to solve.

Robert Kennedy, rather than the National Association of Manufacturers, proposed that the rehabilitation of the slums in the big American cities be taken on by business. And one of the staunchest and most respected advocates of government activism, and America's leading labor union theoretician, the late Frank Tannenbaum of Columbia University, at the very end of his life, in the spring of 1968, proclaimed (in the *Journal of World*

*On this see also Chapter 10, "The Sickness of Government," in my book, *The Age of Discontinuity.*

*Business,* published by Columbia University) that the multinational corporation was "the last best hope" and the only foundation of a peaceful world.

## The New Leadership Groups

Altogether it is the succession of management to the leadership position in society that underlies the demands for social responsibility.

In this century the managers of our major institutions have become the leaders in every developed country, and in most developing countries as well. The old leadership groups, whether the aristocracy or the priesthood, have either disappeared entirely or have become insignificant. Even the scientists, the priesthood of the post-World War II period, have lost much of their prestige. The only new leadership groups to emerge are managers, managers of business enterprise and of universities, of government agencies and of hospitals. They command the resources of society. But they also command the competence. It is, therefore, only logical that they are expected to take the leadership role and take responsibility for major social problems and major social issues.

As a result of these shifts—the emergence of managers as the major leadership group; the growing disenchantment with government, and the shift in focus from the quantities of life to the quality of life—the demand has arisen that managers, and especially business managers, make concern for society central to the conduct of business itself. It is a demand that the quality of life become the business of business. The traditional approach asks, "How can we arrange the making of cars (or of shoes) so as not to impinge on social values and beliefs, on individuals and their freedom, and on the good society altogether?" The new demand is for business to *make* social values and beliefs, create freedom for the individual, and produce the good society.

This demand requires new thinking and new action on the part of the managers. It cannot be handled in the traditional manner. It cannot be handled by public relations.

Public relations asks whether a business or an industry is "liked" or "understood." Public relations would therefore be worried that Black Power advocates blame the profit motive for the ghetto, and that they presumably like business just as little as they like any other part of the white establishment. But what really matters is that the Black Power leaders expect business to perform miracles with respect to ghetto employment, ghetto education, ghetto housing; and they expect these miracles virtually overnight. The relevant questions are: "Can business tackle these huge problems? How? Should business tackle them?" These are not questions which public relations is equipped to handle.

## Three Cautionary Tales

Books and magazines these days are full of horror stories of "business irresponsibility," of "greed," and "incompetence." There is no doubt that there are irresponsible, greedy, and incompetent managers and businesses. Mangers, after all, are members of the human race. But the real problems of social responsibility are not irresponsibility, greed, and incompetence. If they were, the problem would be easy. One could then set forth standards of conduct and hold business to them. Unfortunately the basic problems of social responsibility are different. They are problems of good intentions, honorable conduct, and high responsibility—gone wrong.

This can be illustrated by three "cautionary tales."

## Union Carbide and Vienna, West Virginia

West Virginia, never one of the more prosperous areas of the United States, went into rapid economic decline in the late twenties as the coal industry, long the state's mainstay, began to shrink. The decline of the coal industry was hastened by rising concern with mine accidents and miners' diseases. For many of the coal mines of West Virginia were small and marginal and could not afford modern safety precautions or adequate health protection.

By the late 1940s the leading industrial company in the state became alarmed over the steady economic shrinkage of the region. Union Carbide, one of America's major chemical companies, had its headquarters in New York. But the original plants of the company had been based on West Virginia coal, and the company was still the largest employer in the state, other than a few large coal mines. Accordingly, the company's top management asked a group of young engineers and economists in its employ to prepare a plan for the creation of employment opportunities in West Virginia, and especially for the location of the company's new plant facilities in areas of major unemployment in the state. For the worst afflicted area, however, the westernmost corner of the state on the border of Ohio, the planners could not come up with an attractive project. Yet this area needed jobs the most. In and around the little town of Vienna, West Virginia, there was total unemployment, and no prospects for new industries. The only plant that could possibly be put in the Vienna area was a ferroalloy plant using a process that had already become obsolete and had heavy cost disadvantages compared to more modern processes such as Union Carbide's competitors were already using.

Even for the old process, Vienna was basically an uneconomical location.

The process required very large amounts of coal of fair quality. But the only coal available within the area was coal of such high sulfur content that it could not be used without expensive treatment and scrubbing. Even then —that is, after heavy capital investment—the process was inherently noisy and dirty, releasing large amounts of fly ash and of noxious gases.

In addition, the only transportation facilities, both rail and road, were not in West Virignia but across the river, on the Ohio side. Putting the plant there, however, meant that the prevailing westerly winds would blow the soot from the smokestacks and the sulfur released by the power plants directly into the town of Vienna, on the other bank of the river.

Yet the Vienna plant would provide 1,500 jobs in Vienna itself and another 500 to 1,000 jobs in a new coal field not too far distant. In addition, the new coal field would be capable of being strip-mined, so the new mining jobs would be free from the accident and health hazards that had become increasingly serious in the old and worked-out coal mines of the area. Union Carbide top management came to the conclusion that social responsibility demanded building the new plant, despite its marginal economics.

The plant was built with the most up-to-date antipollution equipment known at the time. Whereas even big-city power stations were then content to trap half the fly ash escaping their smokestacks, the Vienna plant installed scrubbers to catch 75 percent—though there was little anyone could do about the sulfur dioxide fumes emitted by the high-sulfur coal.

When the plant was opened in 1951, Union Carbide was the hero. Politicians, public figures, educators, all praised the company for its social responsibility. But ten years later the former savior was fast becoming the public enemy. As the nation became pollution-conscious, the citizens of Vienna began to complain more and more bitterly about the ash, the soot, and the fumes that floated across the river into their town and homes. About 1961 a new mayor was elected on the platform "fight pollution," which meant "fight Union Carbide." Ten years later the plant had become a "national scandal." Even *Business Week*—hardly a publication hostile to business—chastised Union Carbide (in February, 1971) in an article entitled "A Corporate Polluter Learns the Hard Way."

There is little doubt that Union Carbide's management did not behave very intelligently. They should have realized in the early sixties that they were in trouble, rather than delay and procrastinate, make and then break promises—until the citizens, the state government, the press, the environmentalists, and the federal government all were aiming their biggest guns at the company. It was not very smart to protest for years that there was nothing wrong with the plant and then, when governmental authorities began to get nasty, announce that the plant would have to be closed as it could not be brought up to environmental standards.

Yet this is not the basic lesson of this cautionary tale. Once the decision had been made to employ an obsolescent process and to build an economically marginal plant in order to alleviate unemployment in a bitterly depressed area, the rest followed more or less automatically. This decision meant that the plant did not generate the revenues needed to be rebuilt. There is very little doubt that on economic reasoning alone the plant would never have been built. Public opinion forced Union Carbide to invest substantial sums in that plant to remedy the worst pollution problems—though it is questionable whether the technology exists to do more than a patch-up job. Publicity also forced Union Carbide to keep the plant open. But, once the spotlight shifts elsewhere, most of the jobs in the Vienna, West Virginia, plant are likely to disappear again, if indeed the plant remains open at all.

## Swift do Argentina and Deltec

The Swift meat-packing plant in the Buenos Aires port district has been the largest meat-packing plant in Argentina for many years. It has also been a major employer in a poor area of Buenos Aires. Originally a subsidiary of Swift of Chicago, the company became independent, though still under American ownership, shortly after World War II.

But the Argentinian meat-packing industry fell on evil days after World War II—in part because of government measures that have been driving up the price of Argentinian cattle, while cutting down the supply, thus making Argentinian beef increasingly noncompetitive in the world market and depriving meat-packers of their source of raw materials. Swift became increasingly unprofitable. The owners finally sold out in 1968 to a Canadian-based "multinational," Deltec, a company that is active in many parts of Latin America, primiarily in financial service businesses. Deltec promptly started to modernize the Swift plant to make it competitive again. But the Argentinian meat-packing industry continued on its decline.

Swift's two major competitors, both foreign-owned, decided in the late sixties to close down. They paid off the workers according to Argentinian law and went out of business. Deltec, however, decided that it could not afford to do this in view of its many other interests in Latin America. It had to maintain employment in an area where unemployment was far too high anyhow. Deltec worked out an agreement with the labor unions under which employment was substantially cut and productivity greatly improved. The company poured substantial amounts of money into the plant and used its financial connections to obtain foreign bank loans for it. Still the meat business in Argentina did not improve.

By 1971 Swift had used up all the capital Deltec could make available to it and was still not back on a profitable and competitive basis. Thereupon

Swift worked out a voluntary agreement with the creditors, including the company's workers, for full repayment of all debts over an extended period —with Deltec being the last creditor to receive any payment. Eighty-six percent of the creditors, far more than required by law, accepted this agreement. But to everyone's surprise the Argentinian judge, whose approval had been expected as a mere formality, turned the agreement down. He decided that Deltec had obtained it improperly, declared Swift do Argentina bankrupt, ordered its liquidation, and asked the Argentinian government to appoint a liquidator. In effect he expropriated the company and its property. He not only refused to recognize any rights of Deltec as a creditor but decided that all Deltec holdings in other Argentinian companies be impounded as security for Swift's debts to Argentinian creditors.

There was no public pressure for such an action—and no legal pressure either. The Swift workers, although members of the most militant of Argentinian unions, fully supported Deltec. Yet the decision found tremendous approval in Argentina, even among people who by no stretch of the imagination could be considered antibusiness or even anti-American. "The other foreign-owned meat-packers," a good many people said, "did the right thing in closing down their plants and paying off their workers when they could no longer operate economically. Deltec, by trying to keep going, raised expectations which it then cruelly had to disappoint."

## Civil Rights and the Quaker Conscience

In the late 1940s a major American steel company appointed a new general manager for its large southern division, located in one of the most strongly "white supremacy" areas in the South. Traditionally, all top-management positions in that division had been held by Southerners. The new appointee was a Northerner. Moreover, he was a scion of one of the old Philadelphia Quaker families and had been active in several civil rights organizations.

Upon his appointment top management called him in and said, "We know what we are doing and why we are appointing you. To be sure, your performance has earned this promotion. But you are also a Northerner and committed to employment equality for the Black man. And this, of course, is what both the laws of the United States and our union contract demand of us. Yet, as we all know, our southern division has never given employment opportunities to Blacks. No Black, however skilled, no matter what his job, has ever been paid more than 'helper's' wages. We have never been able to make a dent in this down south. But we know that we will not be able much longer to defend and to keep up these practices. We expect you, therefore, to move as fast as you can for civil rights for our Negro employees, as the laws of the country and our union contract demand. Try to get the support and cooperation of the top people in the union which represents our workers. We know that you have been working with them in several civil rights organizations."

The new general manager spent about a year getting accepted by his new associates, getting known in the local community, and establishing friendly relations with the union leaders in the mill. Then he saw his opportunity. A new major extension to the mill was about to be opened, and a number of new furnaces had to manned. The new general manager strictly applied the hiring provisions of the union contract. As a result, a small but still substantial number of Black workers with high job skills and considerable seniority got positions on the new crews. In no case was a white worker deprived of his seniority rights or put under a Black man as his supervisor.

The morning after the new manning tables had been posted, as required by the union contract, a delegation of local union leaders called on the general manager. "You know that there are several hundred grievances," they said, "which have been pending for far too long a time without a settlement. The patience of our men is exhausted. We are going out on strike in thirty-six hours. But we don't want to be unreasonable. If the company makes even a token gesture of goodwill, we will postpone this strike. All you have to do is to suspend those manning tables you just posted, and let us, together with the supervisors, work out the composition of the crews for the new furnaces. In the meantime, here is the official strike notice as required by our contract."

The general manager first tried to reach the president and the general counsel of the union. Unaccountably, neither could be found, nor did their secretaries know where they could be reached or when they would return. Then the general manager bethought himself of an old friend, one of the "sages" of the Quakers and a "radical" on race relations, and especially on employment opportunities for Blacks. But to the general manager's immense surprise, the "sage" was not one bit sympathetic with his plight. "I fully agree with you, as you know, in considering employment discrimination against the Negro to be illegal, immoral, and sinful," the sage said. "But what you have done, while legal, is just as immoral. You have used the economic muscle of a big company to impose your mores and values on the community in which you operate. Yours are the right mores and the right values. But, still, you are using the economic power of a business, the power of the employer, and the authority of your office to dictate to the community. This is 'economic imperialism' and it cannot be condoned, no matter how good the cause."

The general manager resigned and took another job up north. The company quietly dropped the manning tables. The mills remained open. And a few years later, needless to say, the company came under bitter attack—in which the union's general counsel joined loudly—for its failure to take leadership in race matters. As the biggest employer in the community, the critics charged, the company had a social responsibility not to condone practices which it must have known to be both illegal and immoral.

Clearly, the demand for social responsibility is not as simple as most books, articles, and speeches on the subject make it out to be. But it is not possible to disregard it, as such distinguished economists as Milton Friedman of Chicago have urged. To be sure, Friedman's argument that business is an economic institution and should stick to its economic task is well taken. There is danger that social responsibility will undermine economic performance and with it society altogether. There is surely an even greater danger that social responsibility will mean usurpation of power by business managers in areas in which they have no legitimate authority.*

But it is also clear that social responsibility cannot be evaded. It is not only that the public demands it. It is not only that society needs it. The fact remains that in modern society there is no other leadership group but managers. If the managers of our major institutions, and especially of business, do not take responsibility for the common good, no one else can or will. Government is no longer capable, as political theories still have it, of being the "sovereign" and the "guardian of the common good" in a pluralist society of organizations. The leadership groups in this society, and this means the managers of the key institutions, whether they like it or not —indeed whether they are competent or not—have to think through what responsibilities they can and should assume, in what areas, and for what objectives.

If there is one moral to these cautionary tales, it is not that social responsibility is both ambiguous and dangerous. It is that social impacts and social responsibilities are areas in which business—and not only big business—has to think through its role, has to set objectives, has to perform. *Social impacts and social responsibilities have to be managed.*

*On this see Chapter 26 and also the Epilogue to the new (1972) edition of my book, *Concept of the Corporation*.

# 25

## Social Impacts and Social Problems

*Responsibility for Impacts—The High Price of Neglect—Anticipating Impacts—"Technology Assessment" or "Technology Monitoring"—How to Deal with Impacts—Their Elimination as a Business Opportunity—When Regulation Is Needed—The Trade-Offs—Impacts as Business Responsibility—Social Problems as Business Opportunities—Solving a Social Problem —Sears, Ford, IBM—Second Careers for the Middle-Aged Knowledge Worker—The "Degenerative Diseases" of Society—Are There Limits to Social Responsibility?*

Social responsibilities—whether of a business, a hospital, or a university—may arise in two areas. They may emerge out of the social impacts of the institution. Or they arise as problems of the society itself. Both are of concern to management because the institution which managers manage lives of necessity in society and community. But otherwise the two areas are different. The first deals with what an institution does *to* society. The second is concerned with what an institution can do *for* society.

The modern organization exists to provide a specific service to society. It therefore has to be in society. It has to be in a community, has to be a neighbor, has to do its work within a social setting. But also it has to employ people to do its work. Its *social impacts* inevitably go beyond the specific contribution it exists to make.

The purpose of the hospital is not to employ nurses and cooks. It is patient care. But to accomplish this purpose, nurses and cooks are needed. And in no time at all they form a work community with its own community tasks and community problems.

The purpose of a ferroalloy plant is not to make noise or to release noxious fumes. It is to make high-performance metals that serve the customer. But in order to do this, it produces noise, creates heat, and releases fumes.

Nobody in his right senses wants to create a traffic jam. But if a lot of people are employed in one place and have to enter and leave at the same time, a traffic jam will be a totally unintended and yet inescapable by-product.

These impacts are incidental to the purpose of the organization. But in large measure they are inescapable by-products.

Social problems, by contrast, are dysfunctions of society rather than impacts of the organization and its activities.

The steel company discussed in the preceding chapter did, of course, practice racial discrimination. But racial discrimination was not caused by its activities; it was not an impact. On the contrary, the racial problem of the old South has all along been considered by business a major obstacle to industrialization and economic development. It has been an external condition to which any institution operating in southern society had to conform. Similarly, Swift do Argentina—or the Argentinian meat-packers as a whole—did not cause the long-time secular decline of the Argentinian livestock industry and the resulting unemployment in the Port of Buenos Aires. On the contrary, they fought the government policies responsible for the decline.

Still, both the U. S. steel company operating in the South and Swift do Argentina could not escape concern. Such problems are the degenerative diseases or the toxic wastes of the society and community in which a business exists. Since the institution can exist only within the social environment, is indeed an organ of society, such social problems affect the institution. They are of concern to it even if, as in the steel company's case, the community itself sees no problem and resists any attempt to tackle it.

A healthy business, a healthy university, a healthy hospital cannot exist in a sick society. Management has a self-interest in a healthy society, even though the cause of society's sickness is none of management's making.

## Responsibility for Impacts

One is responsible for one's impacts, whether they are intended or not. This is the first rule. There is no doubt regarding management's responsibility for the social impacts of its organization. They are management's business.

In the Union Carbide story in the preceding chapter, the main reason why the community became so incensed against the company was probably not the pollution it caused. The community knew as well as Union Carbide that the pollution was incidental to production, and thereby to the jobs on which the community depended. But what the community bitterly resented, and with reason, was Union Carbide's refusal for long years to accept responsibility. This is indeed irresponsible.

Because one is responsible for one's impacts, one minimizes them. The fewer impacts an institution has outside of its own specific purpose and mission, the better does it conduct itself, the more responsibly does it act, and the more acceptable a citizen, neighbor, and contributor it is. Impacts which are not essential, and which are not part of the discharge of one's own specific purpose and mission, should be kept to the absolute minimum. Even if they appear to be beneficial, they are outside the proper boundaries of one's function and will, therefore, sooner or later be resented, be resisted, and be considered impositions.

One of the main reasons why management should, in its own self-interest, foster self-government of the work community (see Chapter 21) is precisely that the community functions of the plant are incidental to the purpose of the business. They are not essential to it. The business exists to produce shoes or candy, or to turn out insurance policies. Any control that goes beyond what is strictly necessary to get the work done is incidental to the main function. It is an impact. And it should, therefore, be minimized, if it cannot be eliminated.

Impacts are at best a nuisance. At worst they are deleterious. They are never beneficial. Indeed they always carry within themselves a cost and a threat. Impacts use up resources, burn up or waste raw materials, or at the least, tie up management efforts. Yet they add nothing to the value of the product or to the customer's satisfaction. They are "friction," that is, non-productive cost.

But even minor impacts are likely to become "crises" and "scandal" and to result in serious damage to business—or to any other institution that disregards its impacts. What only yesterday seemed harmless—and indeed even popular—suddenly becomes an offense, a public outcry, a major issue. Unless management has taken responsibility for the impact, thought it through, and worked out the optimal resolution, the result will be punitive or restrictive legislation and an outcry against the "greed of business" or the "irresponsibility of the university."

It is not enough to say, "But the public doesn't object." It is, above all, not enough to say that any action to come to grips with such a problem is going to be "unpopular," is going to be "resented" by one's colleagues and one's associates, and is not required. Sooner or later society will come to regard any such impact as an attack on its integrity and will exact a high price from those who have not responsibly worked on eliminating the impact or on finding a solution to the problem.

Here are some examples.

In the late forties and early fifties, one American automobile company tried to make the American public safety-conscious. Ford introduced cars with seat belts. But sales dropped catastrophically. The company had to withdraw the cars with seat belts and abandoned the whole idea. When, fifteen years later, the American driving public became safety-conscious, the car manufacturers were sharply attacked for their "total lack of concern with safety" and for being "merchants of death." And the resulting regulations were written as much to punish the companies as to protect the public.

Several large electric-power companies had tried for years to get the various state utility commissions to approve low-sulfur fuels and cleaning devices in smokestacks. The commissions discouraged them again and again, with the argument that the public was entitled to power at the lowest possible cost. They pointed out that neither a more expensive fuel nor capital investment to clean the smoke could be permitted in the rate base as a legitimate cost under the state laws. Yet when eventually air pollution became a matter of public concern, the same power companies were roundly berated for "befouling the environment."

Public-service institutions similarly pay the price of neglecting impacts or of dismissing them as trivial. Columbia University was almost destroyed because it did not take responsibility for an impact but had comforted itself with the notion that the impact was trivial. The explosion which rocked Columbia to its foundations in 1968 came over a perfectly harmless and minor matter: a plan to build a new university gymnasium which would be available equally to university students and to the residents of the Black ghetto which abuts Columbia. But the causes for the explosion lay much deeper. They were the conviction on the part of Columbia and of its faculty that a liberal educational institution does not have to concern itself with its relations with its Black ghetto neighborhood.

Another example of impact is the business that is "too big" for its own good and that of the community. (On this see Chapter 55, "On Being the Wrong Size.") The business that is too big, especially the business that is too big for the local community, is a threat to its community but, above all, to itself. It is incumbent on management to correct the situation in the interest of the business (or of the university or hospital). To ignore the problem is to put ego, desire for power, and vanity ahead of the good of the institution and of the community. And this is irresponsible.

## Identifying Impacts

The first job of management is, therefore, to identify and to anticipate impacts—coldly and realistically. The question is not "Is what we do right?" It is "Is what we do what society and the customer pay us for?" And if an activity is not integral to the institution's purpose and mission, it is to be considered as a social impact and as undesirable.

This sounds easy. It is actually very difficult. The best illustration is the problem of "technology assessment," that is, the identification of social and economic impacts of new technology at the time of its introduction.

There is, these days, great interest in technology assessment, that is in anticipating impact and side effects of new technology *before* going ahead with it. The U.S. Congress has actually set up an Office of Technology Assessment. This new agency is expected to be able to predict what new technologies are likely to become important, and what long-range effects they are likely to have. It is then expected to advise government what new technologies to encourage and what new technologies to discourage, if not to forbid altogether.

This attempt can end only in fiasco. Technology assessment of this kind is likely to lead to the encouragement of the wrong technologies and the discouragement of the technologies we need. For *future* impacts of *new* technology are almost always beyond anybody's imagination.

DDT is an example. It was synthesized during World War II to protect American soldiers against disease-carrying insects, especially in the tropics. Some of the scientists then envisaged the use of the new chemical to protect civilian populations as well. But not one of the many men who worked on DDT thought of applying the new pesticide to control insect pests infesting crops, forests, or livestock. If DDT had been restricted to the use for which it was developed, that is, to the protection of humans, it would never have become an environmental hazard; use for this purpose accounted for no more than 5 or 10 percent of the total at DDT's peak, in the mid-sixties. Farmers and foresters, without much help from the scientists, saw that what killed lice on men would also kill lice on plants and made DDT into a massive assault on the environment.

Another example is the population explosion in the developing countries. DDT and other pesticides were a factor in it. So were the new antibiotics. Yet the two were developed quite independently of each other; and no one "assessing" either technology could have foreseen their convergence—indeed no one did. But more important as causative factors in the sharp drop in infant mortality which set off the population explosion were two very old "technologies" to which no one paid any attention. One was the elementary public-health measure of keeping latrine and well apart—known to the Macedonians before Alexander the Great. The other one was the wire-mesh screen for doors and windows invented by an unknown American around 1860. Both were suddenly adopted even by backward tropical villages after World War II. Together they were probably the main causes of the population explosion.

At the same time, the technology impacts which the experts predict almost never occur. One example is the "private flying boom," which the experts predicted during and shortly after World War II. The private plane, owner-piloted, would become as common, we were told, as the Model T automobile had become after World War I. Indeed, experts among city planners, engineers, and architects advised New York City not to go ahead with the second tube of the Lincoln Tunnel, or with the second deck on the George Washington Bridge, and instead to build a number of small airports along the west bank of the Hudson River. It would have taken fairly elementary mathematics to disprove this particular technology assessment —there just is not enough airspace for commuter traffic by air. But this did not occur to any of the experts; no one then realized how finite airspace is. At the same time, almost no experts foresaw the expansion of commercial air traffic and anticipated, at the time the jet plane was first developed, that it would lead to mass transportation by air, with as many people crossing the Atlantic in jumbo jets in one day as used to go in a week in the big passenger liners. To be sure, transatlantic travel was expected to grow fast —but of course it would be by ship. These were the years in which all the governments along the North Atlantic heavily subsidized the building of new super-luxury liners, just when the passengers deserted the liner and switched to the new jet plane.

A few years later, we were told by everybody that automation would have tremendous economic and social impacts—it has had practically none. The computer offers an even odder story. In the late forties nobody predicted that the computer would be used by business and governments. While the computer was a "major scientific revolution," everybody "knew" that its main use would be in science and warfare. As a result, the most extensive market research study undertaken at that time reached the conclusion that the world computer market would, at most, be able to absorb 1,000 computers by the year 2000. Now, only twenty-five years later, there are some 150,000 computers installed in the world, most of them doing the most mundane bookkeeping work. Then a few years later, when it became apparent that business was buying computers for payroll and billing, the experts predicted that the computer would displace middle management, so that there would be nobody left between the chief executive officer and the foreman. *"Is middle management obsolete?"* asked a widely quoted *Harvard Business Review* article in the early fifties; and it answered this rhetorical question with a resounding "Yes." At exactly that moment, the tremendous expansion of middle-management jobs began. In every developed country middle-management jobs, in business as well as in government, have grown about three times as fast as total employment in the last twenty years; and their growth has been parallel to the growth of computer usage.

Anyone depending on technology assessment in the early 1950s would have abolished the graduate business schools as likely to produce graduates who could not possibly find jobs. Fortunately, the young people did not listen and flocked in record numbers to the graduate business schools so as to get the good jobs which the computer helped create. (For the middle-management boom, see Chapter 35.)

But while no one foresaw the computer impact on middle-management jobs, every expert predicted a tremendous computer impact on business strategy, business policy, planning, and top management—on none of which the computer has, however, had the slightest impact at all. At the same time, no one predicted the real revolution in business policy and strategy in the fifties and sixties, the merger wave and the conglomerates.

It is not only that man has the gift of prophecy no more with respect to technology than with respect to anything else. The impacts of technology are actually more difficult to predict than most other developments. In the first place, as the example of the population explosion shows, social and economic impact are almost always the result of the convergence of a substantial number of factors, not all of them technological. And each of these factors has its own origin, its own development, its own dynamics, and its own experts. The expert in one field—e.g. the expert on epidemiology —never thinks of plant pests. The expert on antibiotics is concerned with the treatment of disease, whereas the actual explosion of the birthrate resulted largely from elementary and long-known public health measures.

But equally important, what technology is likely to become important and have an impact, and what technology either will fizzle out—like the "flying Model T"—or will have minimal social or economic impacts—like automation—is impossible to predict. And which technology will have social impacts and which will remain just technology is even harder to predict. The most successful prophet of technology, Jules Verne, predicted a great deal of twentieth-century technology a hundred years ago (though few scientists or technologists of that time took him seriously). But he anticipated absolutely no social or economic impacts, only an unchanged mid-Victorian society and economy. Economic and social prophets, in turn, have the most dismal record as predictors of technology.

The one and only effect an Office of Technology Assessment is therefore likely to have would be to guarantee full employment to a lot of fifth-rate science-fiction writers.

## The Need for Technology Monitoring

The major danger is, however, that the delusion that we can foresee the impacts of new technology will lead us to slight the really important task.

For technology does have impacts and serious ones, beneficial as well as detrimental. These do not require prophecy. They require careful monitoring of the actual impact of a technology once it has become effective. In 1948, practically no one correctly saw the impacts of the computer. Five or six years later, one could and did know. Then one could say, "Whatever the technological impact, *socially* and *economically* this is not a major threat." In 1943, no one could predict the impact of DDT. Ten years later, DDT had become worldwide a tool of farmer, forester, and livestock breeder, and as such, a major ecological factor. Then thinking as to what action to take should have begun, work should have been started on the development of pesticides without the major environmental impact of DDT, and the difficult trade-offs should have been faced between food production and environmental damage—which neither the unlimited use nor the present complete ban on DDT sufficiently considers.

Technology monitoring is a serious, an important, indeed a vital task. But it is not prophecy. The only thing possible with respect to *new* technology is *speculation* with about one chance out of a hundred of being right—and a much better chance of doing harm by encouraging the wrong, or discouraging the most beneficial new technology. What needs to be watched is "developing" technology, that is, technology which has already had substantial impacts, enough to be judged, to be measured, to be evaluated.

And monitoring a developing technology for its social impacts is, above all, a managerial responsibility.

But equally important—and totally overlooked by the advocates of technology assessment—are the impacts of nontechnological, that is social and economic innovations and developments. They are just as hard to predict until they have emerged and can be identified, evaluated, and measured. They too, therefore, need being monitored. And that too is a management responsibility.

### How to Deal with Impacts

Identifying incidental impacts of an institution is the first step. But how does management deal with them? The objective is clear: impacts on society and economy, community, and individual that are not in themselves the purpose and mission of the institution should be kept to the minimum and should preferably be eliminated altogether. The fewer such impacts the better, whether the impact is within the institution, on the social environment, or on the physical environment.

Wherever an impact can be eliminated by dropping the activity that causes it, this is therefore the best—indeed the only truly good—solution. Managerial authority over, and control of, work-community affairs is perhaps the one area where this can be done—and with direct benefit to institution and management themselves.

In most cases the activity cannot, however, be eliminated. Hence there is need for systematic work at eliminating the impact—or at least at minimizing it—while maintaining the underlying activity itself.

The ideal approach is to make the elimination of impacts into a profitable business opportunity. One example is the way Dow Chemical, one of the leading U. S. chemical companies, has for almost twenty years tackled air and water pollution. Dow decided, shortly after World War II, that air and water pollution was an undesirable impact that had to be eliminated. Long before the public outcry about the environment, Dow adopted a zero-pollution policy for its plants. It then set about systematically to develop the polluting substances it removes from smokestack gases and watery effluents into salable products and to create uses and markets for them.

A variant is the Du Pont Industrial Toxicity Laboratory. Du Pont, in the 1920s, became aware of the toxic side effects of many of its industrial products, set up a laboratory to test for toxicity and to develop processes to eliminate the poisons. Du Pont started out to eliminate an impact which at that time every other chemical manufacturer took for granted. But then Du Pont decided to develop toxicity control of industrial products into a separate business. The Industrial Toxicity Laboratory works not only for Du Pont but for a wide variety of customers for whom it develops nonpoisonous compounds, whose products it tests for toxicity, and so on. Again, an impact has been eliminated by making it into a business opportunity.

## When Regulation Is Needed

To make elimination of an impact into a business opportunity should always be attempted. But it cannot be done in many cases. More often eliminating an impact means increasing the costs. What was an "externality" for which the general public paid becomes business cost. It therefore becomes a competitive disadvantage unless everybody in the industry accepts the same rule. And this, in most cases, can be done only by regulation —that means by some form of public action.

Whenever an impact cannot be eliminated without an increase in cost, it becomes incumbent upon management to think ahead and work out the regulation which is most likely to solve the problem at the minimum cost and with the greatest benefit to public and business alike. And it is then management's job to work at getting the right regulation enacted.

Management—and not only business management—has shunned this responsibility. The traditional attitude has always been that "no regulation is the best regulation." But this applies only when an impact can be made into a business opportunity. Where elimination of an impact requires a restriction, regulation is in the interest of business, and especially in the interest of responsible business. Otherwise it will be penalized as "irresponsible," while the unscrupulous, the greedy, the stupid, and the chiseler cash in.

And to expect that there will be no regulation is willful blindness.

Whenever there has been the kind of crisis which the automobile industry ran into with respect to automotive safety or the public utilities with respect to air pollution, the penalty imposed on business in the end has been high. Such a crisis always leads to a scandal. It leads to governmental inquisition, to angry editorials, and eventually to loss of confidence in an entire industry, its management, and its products by broad sectors of the public. Finally, there is punitive legislation.

The fact that the public today sees no issue is not relevant. Indeed it is not even relevant that the public today—as it did in every single one of the examples above—resists actively any attempts on the part of farsighted business leaders to prevent a crisis. In the end, there is the scandal.

One example is the failure of the international petroleum companies to think ahead and develop the successor to the "petroleum concession," the impacts of which could clearly be anticipated at the end of World War II. Another example is the failure of U.S. industry to think through the regulation of foreign investment which Canada might adopt to preserve both political identity and access to capital (for both examples, see Chapter 59).

The American pharmaceutical industry knew, as early as 1955, that the existing rules and procedures to test new drugs were not working. They had been written long before the arrival of the modern potent wonder drugs and their—equally potent—side effects. Yet any pharmaceutical company that tried to get the industry to face up to the problem was shushed by the other members of the club. "Don't rock the boat," the prospective innovator was told. One company, it is reported, actually worked up a comprehensive new approach and new regulatory procedures. It was prevailed upon to bury them in its archives.

And then came the Thalidomide scandal. It actually *proved* the effectiveness of the American control system; for while Thalidomide was approved for medical practice in the European countries, the U. S. regulatory authorities became concerned very early about the drug's toxic side effects and withheld approval. As a result there are no deformed Thalidomide babies in the U. S. as there are in Germany, Sweden, and England. Still, the scandal released an enormous tidal wave of anxiety about drug testing and drug safety in the U. S. And because industry had not faced up to the problem and had not thought through and agitated for the right solution, Congress panicked into passing legislation that threatens seriously to impair the development and market introduction of new medicines—and yet, paradoxically, would probably not prevent another Thalidomide.

Yet business does not seem to learn the lesson. Business will only have itself to blame if legislation impairs or undermines the private pension system in the U. S. Since the 1940s, when pension plans first came into wide use in American business, managements have known that most pension plans have two major undesirable impacts. First they penalize an employee who moves to another employer, even if the move is involuntary and the result of being laid off. Second, they do not protect the employee in the event of bankruptcy and liquidation of his employer, or at least not in the majority of private pension plans. It would have been relatively easy and cheap to take care of these two side effects. But it would have been unpopular to raise the issues, especially in the unionized company. Management therefore evaded the problem. As a result, the pension system of American business is in danger of being restricted, if not legislated out of existence. And the costs of pensions to the employing business will, in all likelihood, go up sharply, way beyond what would have been needed to give the employees the protection they need.

## The Trade-Offs

Any solution to an impact problem requires trade-offs. Beyond a certain level elimination of an impact costs more in money or in energy, in resources or in lives, than the attainable benefit. A decision has to be made on the optimal balance between costs and benefits. This is something people in an industry understand, as a rule. But no one outside does—and so the outsider's solution tends to ignore the trade-off problem altogether.

Where is the trade-off between the overdue concern for a natural environment threatened by the strip-mining of coal and the lives saved in switching from underground mining to strip-mining? Underground mining can never be truly safe. It will also always remain a health hazard because of the coal dust and the contaminated air in which underground work has to be performed. Strip-mining, on the other hand, should be a fairly safe occupation and has few health hazards. But where is the trade-off between lives and natural beauty and clean, unpolluted streams?

But there is, in the strip-mining issue, also a trade-off between the costs of environmental damage and the cost in jobs, living standards, and in the health hazard of cold homes and the safety hazards of dark streets implicit in dear and scarce energy.

What happens if management fails to face up to an impact and to think through the trade-off is illustrated by the American experience with the control of automotive emissions.

That such controls would be needed has been known since the end of

World War II when smog first became a household word in Los Angeles. The automobile industry, however, relied on public relations, which told it that the public was not concerned about smog. Then, suddenly, in the sixties, the public panicked and forced through drastic emission-control legislation. Whether the new controls will actually cut pollution is quite doubtful. They control emissions in new cars, but are unlikely to control emissions in the great majority of cars on the road, which are more than two to three years old. One thing is, however, certain. These emission controls will themselves cause substantial new pollution. They greatly increase the energy needed to drive the car and will therefore have to use more gasoline. This will require more petroleum refining—one of the most polluting of industrial activities. At the same time, they will add very substantially to the cost of the car and of automotive service. What the right trade-offs would have been we do not know—for industry did not do its work. But both industry and public will pay and suffer.

The public welcomes an intelligent solution for such a problem if management presses for one before the scandal. This has been the experience of the Committee for Economic Development (CED) in its twenty years of existence, and of any other business or industry group which took responsibility for an impact and brought to bear on it the knowledge, competence, and seriousness of its best people.

Most managers know this. And yet they hope against hope that the problem will go away. They postpone thinking about it, let alone taking action. At the most they make speeches. And they fight a rearguard action after they have lost.

Responsibility for social impacts is a management responsibility—not because it is a social responsibility, but because it is a business responsibility. The ideal is to make elimination of such an impact into a business opportunity. But wherever that cannot be done, the design of the appropriate regulation with the optimal trade-off balance—and public discussion of the problem and promotion of the best regulatory solution—is management's job.

## Social Problems as Business Opportunities

Social problems are dysfunctions of society and—at least potentially—degenerative diseases of the body politic. They are ills. But for the management of institutions, and, above all, for business management they represent challenges. They are major sources of opportunity. For it is the function of business—and to a lesser degree of the other main institutions—to satisfy a social need and at the same time serve their institution, by making resolution of a social problem into a business opportunity.

It is the job of business to convert change into innovation, that is, into new business. And it is a poor businessman who thinks that innovation refers to technology alone. Social change and social innovation have throughout business history been at least as important as technology. After all, the major industries of the nineteenth century were, to a very large extent, the result of converting the new social environment—the industrial city—into a business opportunity and into a business market. This underlay the rise of lighting, first by gas and then by electricity, of the streetcar and the interurban trolley, of telephone, newspaper, and department store—to name only a few.

The most significant opportunities for converting social problems into business opportunities may therefore not lie in new technologies, new products, and new services. They may lie in *solving* the social problem, that is, in social innovation which then directly and indirectly benefits and strengthens the company or the industry.

The success of some of the most successful businesses is largely the result of such social innovation. Here are some American examples:

Julius Rosenwald, the "city slicker" who built Sears, Roebuck, invented and for many years financed the County Farm Agent. The social problem he identified was the poverty, ignorance, and isolation of the American farmer who still, in the early years of this century, constituted half the U. S. population. Knowledge to enable the farmer to produce more, to produce the right things, and to get more for his efforts was available. But it was inaccessible to the farmer. The County Farm Agent—rather than new technology, new machines, or new seeds—became a main force behind the "productivity explosion" on the American farm. Rosenwald saw a genuine social problem. But he also saw a genuine business opportunity. For the farmer's poverty, ignorance, and isolation were major obstacles to Sears. As the farmer's position and income grew, so did the Sears market. And Sears came to be identified by the farmers as the "farmer's friend."

Tackling a social problem as a business opportunity also played a substantial part in the meteoric rise of Ford in its early days.

The years immediately prior to World War I were years of great labor unrest in the United States, growing labor bitterness, and high unemployment. Hourly wages for skilled men ran as low as 15 cents in many cases. It was against this background that the Ford Motor Company, in the closing days of 1913, announced that it would pay a guaranteed $5-a-day wage to every one of its workers—two to three times what was then standard. James Couzens, the company's general manager, who had forced this decision on his reluctant partner, Henry Ford, knew perfectly well that his company's wage bill would almost triple overnight. But he became convinced that the workmen's sufferings were so great that only radical and highly visible action could have an effect. Couzens also expected that Ford's actual labor cost, despite the tripling of the wage rate, would go down—and events soon proved him right. Before Ford changed the whole labor economy of the United States with one announcement, labor turnover at the Ford Motor Company had been so high that, in 1912, 60,000 men had to be hired to retain 10,000 workers. With the new wage, turnover almost disappeared. The resulting savings were so great that despite sharply rising costs for all materials in the next few years, Ford could produce and sell its Model T at a lower price and yet make a larger profit per car. It was the saving in labor cost produced by a drastically higher wage that gave Ford market domination. At the same time Ford's action transformed American industrial society. It established the American workingman as fundamentally middle class.

IBM also owes its rise largely to a frontal attack on a social problem. During the years of the Great Depression IBM was a very small company and had little visibility. Hence its action had none of the impact of Ford's $5-a-day wage twenty years earlier. Yet in giving workers employment security and then putting them on a salary instead of an hourly wage (as related in Chapter 20) IBM was as bold and innovative as Ford had been. IBM's action too was aimed at a major social problem of the time, the fear, insecurity, and loss of dignity that the Depression inflicted on workers in America. It too turned a social disease into a business opportunity. It was this action, above all, which created the human potential for IBM's rapid growth and, then, a decade later, for its aggressive move into the totally new computer technology.

And here is a European example.

The growth of Olivetti into one of the world's leading producers of office equipment rests on two insights of the late Adriano Olivetti, who, in the 1920s, inherited a small, unknown, and barely viable family company in the small town of Ivrea in northern Italy. Adriano Olivetti saw the opportunity to give his company and his products distinction through good design. Olivetti's design gave him market recognition within a decade. He also saw in Italy's corrosive class hatred an opportunity. The community in which he tried to fuse management and worker in Ivrea gave him exceptional labor productivity, high-quality production, and a work force willing to accept new technology and changes—and with it competitive strength and profitability.

In present-day society one area where a serious social problem might be solved by making it into an opportunity could well be the fatigue, frustration, and "burning-out" of the middle-aged knowledge worker and his need for a second career.* The hidden cost of the middle-aged knowledge work-

*On this see my book, *The Age of Discontinuity*, especially Chapter 13.

ers—managers and knowledge professionals—who have "retired on the job," have lost interest, and just go through the motions, may well be larger than that of Ford's labor turnover in 1913. At the same time, the frustration and silent despair of these men and women may pose as great a social danger to society as the misery, bitterness, and despair of the suffering manual worker of yesterday. Nothing is as corrosive as success turned into frustration. The first company which tackles this problem as both a social problem and an opportunity might well reap benefits fully as great as those reaped by Ford sixty years ago and Olivetti and IBM forty years ago.

To cure social ills by making them into opportunities for contribution and performance is by no means a challenge to business enterprise alone. It is the responsibility as well of all the other institutions of our society of organizations.

There is a great deal of talk today about the crisis of the university; and the crisis is real. In some places, however, it has been seized as an opportunity. In Great Britain there is the Open University, which uses television to make university education available to anyone who is willing to do the work. In California the medium-sized and little-known University of the Pacific, in Stockton, is building a new kind of university. It utilizes the desire of young people to learn but also to be responsible participants in their learning.

Rosenwald, Ford, IBM's Watson, and Olivetti were all initially ridiculed as visionaries. No one could solve the problems they tackled, they were told. Ten or fifteen years later, their solutions were dismissed as "obvious." The right solution is always obvious in retrospect. What matters is that these men and their companies identified a major social problem and asked, "How can it be solved as a business opportunity?"

Any business, and indeed any institution, needs to organize innovative efforts to convert social problems into opportunities for performance and contribution.

In the last quarter century organized technological research has become commonplace. Social innovation is still largely left to chance and to the individual entrepreneur who stumbles upon an opportunity. This is no longer adequate. In the society of organizations, every institution needs to organize its R & D for society and community fully as much as it had been organizing it for technology. Management has to organize to identify the issues, the crises, the problems in society and community, and to work at the innovations that will make their solution into a profitable opportunity.

## The "Degenerative Diseases" of Society

Social problems that management action converts into opportunities soon cease to be problems. The others, however, are likely to become "chronic complaints," if not "degenerative diseases."

Not every social problem can be resolved by making it into an opportunity for contribution and performance. Indeed, the most serious of such problems tend to defy this approach.

No business could, for instance, have done much about America's most serious degenerative disease throughout our history—the racial problem. It could not even be tackled until the whole society had changed awareness and convictions—by which time it was very late, if not altogether too late. And even if one management solves such a problem, the rest may not follow. There may be a solution; but while known and visible, it is not being used. The problem stays acute and unresolved.

American business had to follow Ford's lead between 1914 and 1920—though the labor shortage of World War I had as much to do with this as Ford's example. But few American companies imitated IBM and even fewer Italian companies imitated Olivetti, despite their visible success.

What then is the social responsibility of management for these social problems that become chronic or degenerative diseases?

They are management's problems. The health of the enterprise is management's responsibility. A healthy business and a sick society are hardly compatible. Healthy businesses require a healthy, or at least a functioning, society. The health of the community is a prerequisite for successful and growing business.

And it is foolish to hope that these problems will disappear if only one looks the other way. Problems go away because someone does something about them.

With any such problem, management had better find out whether someone has, in fact, done something that works. That few, if any, U. S. businesses have followed IBM, few Italian businesses have followed Olivetti, and few German businesses have followed Zeiss is management failure. It is basically not too different from the management failure to keep technology and products competitive. And the reasons are not too different either; they are shortsightedness, indolence, and incompetence.

Yet there remain the big, tough, dangerous dysfunctions of society, the social problems for which no one has worked out a solution, and which cannot, it seems, be resolved, or perhaps not even assuaged, by being made performance opportunities.

To what extent should business—or any other of the special-purpose institutions of our society—be expected to tackle such a problem which did not arise out of an impact of theirs and which cannot be converted into an opportunity for performance of the institution's purpose and mission? To what extent should these institutions, business, university, or hospital, even be permitted to take responsibility?

Today's rhetoric tends to ignore that question. "Here is," Mayor Lindsay of New York says, "the Black ghetto. No one knows what to do with it. Whatever government, social workers, or community action try, things seem only to get worse. *Therefore* big business better take responsibility."

That Mayor Lindsay frantically looks for someone to take over is understandable; and the problem that is defeating him is indeed desperate and a major threat to his city, to American society, and to the Western world altogether. But is it enough to make the problem of the Black ghetto the social responsibility of management? Or are there limits to social responsibility? And what are they?

# 26

## The Limits of Social Responsibility

*Management's First Responsibility: Its Own Institution—The Need to Know Minimum Profitability Requirements—To "Do Good" and to "Do Well" —The Limits of Competence—The Limitations of One's Value System— The Areas of Incompetence—The Limits of Authority—No Responsibility without Authority—When to Say No—The Commitment to Working Out Alternatives—The Limits of Social Responsibility as a Central Problem to Management and to the Society of Organizations*

The manager is a servant. His master is the institution he manages and his first responsibility must therefore be to it. His first task is to make the institution, whether business, hospital, school, or university, perform the function and make the contribution for the sake of which it exists. The man who uses his position at the head of a major institution to become a public figure and to take leadership with respect to social problems, while his company or his university erodes through neglect, is not a statesman. He is irresponsible and false to his trust.

The institution's performance of its specific mission is also society's first need and interest. Society does not stand to gain but to lose if the performance capacity of the institution in its own specific task is diminished or impaired. Performance of its function is the institution's first social responsibility. Unless it discharges its performance responsibly, it cannot discharge anything else. A bankrupt business is not a desirable employer and is unlikely to be a good neighbor in a community. Nor will it create the capital for tomorrow's jobs and the opportunities for tomorrow's workers. A university which fails to prepare tomorrow's leaders and professionals is not socially responsible, no matter how many "good works" it engages in.

The first "limitation" on social responsibility is, therefore, the higher responsibility for the specific performance of the institution which is the manager's master. This needs particular stress with respect to the business enterprise, the economic institution of society. Any solution of a social impact or of a social problem except to make it into an opportunity for performance and results creates social overhead costs. These costs cannot be borne out of profits, no matter what popular rhetoric may say. They are paid for either out of current costs—that is, by consumer or taxpayer—or they are paid for out of capital—that is, by fewer and poorer jobs tomorrow and impaired standards of living. The only way to cover costs and to accumulate capital is through economic performance. All other satisfactions of society are being paid for, one way or another, out of the surplus between current production and current consumption, that is, out of the surplus of the economy.

This again underscores the responsibility of managers to anticipate problems and to think through the trade-offs involved in their solutions. At what point does a solution become prohibitively expensive for society because it impairs the performance capacity of existing and needed institutions, whether of the economy, of health care, of education, or of the military? What is the optimal balance between the need to take care of a social problem and the need to preserve the performance capacity of the existing social institutions? And at what point does one risk losing social performance—and thereby creating new and bigger problems—by overloading the existing institutions? At what point do we achieve the best balance between the old costs and the new benefits?

Managers need to be able to think through the limits on social responsibility set by their duty to the performance capacity of the enterprises in their charge.

In the case of the business enterprise this requires knowing the objectives in the key areas (see Chapters 8 and 9). For these objectives set the *minimum* performance goals for the attainment of the enterprise's mission. As long as they can be attained, the enterprise can perform. If the objective in any one area is seriously jeopardized, the performance capacity of the entire business is endangered.

Above all, management needs to know the *minimum profitability* required by the risks of the business and by its commitments to the future. It needs this knowledge for its own decisions. But it needs it just as much to explain its decisions to others—the politicians, the press, the public. As long as managements remain the prisoners of their own ignorance of the objective need for, and function of, profit—i.e. as long as they think and argue in terms of the "profit motive"—they will be able neither to make rational decisions with respect to social responsibilities, nor to explain these decisions to others inside and outside the business.

A popular pun these days says, "It is not enough for business to do well; it must also do good." But in order to "do good," a business must first "do well" (and indeed "do very well").

Whenever a business has disregarded the limitation of economic performance and has assumed social responsibilities which it could not support economically it has soon gotten into trouble.

Union Carbide was not socially responsible when it put its plant into Vienna, West Virginia, to alleviate unemployment there. It was, in fact, irresponsible. The plant was marginal to begin with. The process was obsolescent. At best the plant could barely keep its head above water. And this, inevitably, meant a plant unable to take on social responsibility, even for its own impacts. Because the plant was uneconomical to begin with, Union Carbide resisted so long all demands to clean it up. This particular demand could not have been foreseen in the late 1940s when concern with jobs far outweighed any concern for the environment. But demands of some kind can always be expected. To do something out of social responsibility which is economically irrational and untenable is therefore never responsible. It is sentimental. The result is always greater damage.

Similarly, Deltec in Buenos Aires may be vulnerable to the charge that to keep a plant open when every other major meat-packer had reached the conclusion that the business could not survive was sentimentality rather than social responsibility. It was an assumption of responsibility beyond tenable limits. The intentions were good and honorable—as in Union Carbide's case. It may be argued that Deltec took a calculated risk. Also, the outcome was far more the result of internal Argentinian politics than of anything Deltec did or omitted to do. Yet Deltec management took a greater risk than might be compatible with true social responsibility.

The same limitation on social responsibility applies to noneconomic institutions. There, too, the manager is duty-bound to preserve the performance capacity of the institution in his care. To jeopardize it, no matter how noble the motive, is irresponsibility. These institutions too are capital assets of society on the performance of which society depends.

This, to be sure, is a very unpopular position to take. It is much more popular to be "progressive." But managers, and especially managers of key institutions of society, are not being paid to be heroes to the popular press. They are being paid for performance and responsibility.

## The Limits of Competence

To take on tasks for which one lacks competence is irresponsible behavior. It is also cruel. It raises expectations which will then be disappointed.

An institution, and especially a business enterprise, has to acquire whatever competence is needed to take responsibility for its impacts. But in areas of social responsibility other than impacts, right and duty to act are limited by competence.

In particular an institution better refrain from tackling tasks which do not fit into its value system (on this see also Chapter 58, "Managing Diversity"). Skills and knowledge are fairly easily acquired. But one cannot easily change personality. No one is likely to do well in areas which he does not respect. If a business or any other institution tackles such an area because there is a social need, it is unlikely to put its good people on the task and to support them adequately. It is unlikely to understand what the task involves. It is almost certain to do the wrong things. As a result, it will do damage rather than good.

What not to do was demonstrated when the American universities in the sixties rushed into taking social responsibility for the problems of the big city. These problems are real enough. And within the university were to be found able scholars in a variety of areas with relevance to the problems. Yet the tasks were primarily political tasks. The values involved were those of the politician rather than the scholar. The skills needed were those of compromise, of mobilizing energies, and above all, of setting priorities. And these are not skills which the academician admires and respects, let alone excels in. They are almost the opposite of the objectivity and the "finding of truth" which constitute excellence in academia. These tasks exceeded the competence of the university and were incompatible with its value system.

The result of the universities' eager acceptance of these tasks was therefore, inevitably, lack of performance and results. It was also damage to the prestige and standing of the university, and to its credibility. The universities did not help the problems of the city; but they seriously impaired their own performance capacity in their own area.

The major corporations in New York City would have acted totally irresponsibly had they responded to Mayor Lindsay's call to "adopt the Black ghetto." All they could have done (as they apparently realized) was damage—to the ghetto and to themselves.

What the limits of competence are depends in part on circumstances. If a member of a climbing team develops acute appendicitis in the high Himalayas and is almost certain to die unless operated on, any medical man in the group will operate, even though he may be a dermatologist who has never done a single operation in his life. The dermatologist, though a qualified physician, will be considered irresponsible and vulnerable to both a malpractice suit and a conviction for manslaughter, should he operate on an appendix in a place where a qualified surgeon, or even a general practitioner, are within reach.

Management therefore needs to know at the very least what it and its institution are truly *incompetent* for. Business, as a rule, will be in this position of absolute incompetence in an "intangible" area. The strength of business is accountability and measurability. It is the discipline of market test, productivity measurements, and profitability requirement. Where these are lacking businesses are essentially out of their depth. They are also out of fundamental sympathy, that is, outside their own value systems. Where the criteria of performance are intangible, such as "political" opinions and emotions, community approval or disapproval, mobilization of community energies and structuring of power relations, business is unlikely to feel comfortable. It is unlikely to have respect for the values that matter. It is, therefore, most unlikely to have competence.

In such areas it is, however, often possible to define goals clearly and measurably for *specific partial tasks*. It is often possible to convert parts of a problem that by itself lies outside the competence of business into work that fits the competence and value system of the business enterprise.

No one in America has done very well in training hard-core unemployable Black teenagers for work and jobs. But business has done far less badly than any other institution: schools, government programs, community agencies. This task can be identified. It can be defined. Goals can be set. And performance can be measured. And then business can perform.

Before acceding to the demand that it take on this or that social responsibility, and go to work on this or that problem, management better think through what, if any, part of the task can be made to fit the competence of its institution. Is there any area which can be defined in terms of tangible goals and measurable performance—as business managers understand these slippery terms? If the answer is yes, one is justified in thinking seriously about one's social responsibility. But when the answer is no—and this will be the answer in a good many areas—business enterprise better resist, no matter how important the problem and how urgent the demand for business to take it over. It can only do harm to society and to itself. It cannot perform and therefore cannot be responsible.

## The Limits of Authority

The most important limitation on social responsibility is the limitation of authority. The constitutional lawyer knows that there is no such word as "responsibility" in the political dictionary. The term is "responsibility *and* authority." Whoever claims authority thereby assumes responsibility. But whoever assumes responsibility thereby claims authority. The two are but different sides of the same coin. To assume social responsibility therefore always means to claim authority.

Again, the question of authority as a limit on social responsibility does not arise in connection with the impacts of an institution. For the impact is the result of an exercise of authority, even though purely incidental and unintended. And then responsibility follows.

But where business or any other institution of our society of organizations is asked to assume social responsibility for one of the problems or ills of society and community, management needs to think through whether the authority implied in the responsibility is legitimate. Otherwise it is usurpation and irresponsible.

Every time the demand is made that business take responsibility for this or that, one should ask, "Does business have the authority and should it have it?" If business does not have and should not have authority—and in a great many areas it should not have it—then responsibility on the part of business should be treated with grave suspicion. It is not responsibility; it is lust for power.

Milton Friedman's position (see Chapter 24) that business should stick to its business, that is, to the economic sphere, is not a denial of responsibility. It is indeed the only consistent position in a free society. It can be argued with great force that any other position can only undermine and compromise a free society. Any other position can only mean that business will take over power, authority, and decision-making in areas outside of the economic sphere, in areas which are or should be reserved to government or to the individual or to other institutions. For, to repeat, whoever assumes responsibility will soon have to be given the authority. History amply proves this.

From this point of view the present "critics" of big business can rightly be accused of pushing big business into becoming our master.

Ralph Nader, the American consumerist, sincerely considers himself a foe of big business and is accepted as such by business and by the general public. Insofar as Nader demands that business take responsibility for product quality and product safety, he is surely concerned with legitimate business responsibility, i.e., with responsibility for performance and contribution. The only question—apart from the accuracy of his facts and the style of his campaign—would be whether Nader's demand for perfection is not going to cost the consumer far more than the shortcomings and deficiencies which Nader assails. The only questions are the trade-offs.

But Ralph Nader demands, above all, that big business assume responsibility in a multitude of areas beyond products and services. This, if acceded to, can lead only to the emergence of the managements of the big corporations as the ultimate power in a vast number of areas that are properly some other institution's field.

And this is, indeed, the position to which Nader—and other advocates of unlimited social responsibility—are moving rapidly. One of the Nader task forces published in 1972 a critique of the Du Pont Company and its role in the small state of Delaware, where Du Pont has its headquarters and is a major employer. The report did not even discuss economic performance; it dismissed as irrelevant that Du Pont, in a period of general inflation, consistently lowered the prices for its products, which are, in many cases, basic materials for the American economy. Instead it sharply criticized Du Pont for not using its economic power to force the citizens of the state to attack a number of social problems, from racial discrimination to health care to public schools. Du Pont, for not taking responsibility for Delaware society, Delaware politics, and Delaware law, was called grossly remiss in its social responsibility.

One of the ironies of this story is that the traditional liberal or left-wing criticism of the Du Pont Company for many years has been the exact opposite, i.e., that Du Pont, by its very prominence in a small state, "interferes in and dominates" Delaware and exercises "illegitimate authority."

The Nader line is only the best-publicized of the positions which, under the cover of antibusiness rhetoric, actually plead for a society in which big business is the most powerful, the dominant, the ultimate institution. Of course such an outcome is the opposite of what Nader intends. But it would not be the first time that a demand for social responsibility has had results opposite from those intended.

The most likely result of the Nader line neither he nor management would want. It is either a destruction of all authority, that is, complete irresponsibility. (A parallel would be the way in which the demand that the barons of early feudal society take social responsibility led around the year 1000 to the complete destruction of the crown's authority on the European continent and to the uncontrolled despotism of the feudal grandees.) Or it is totalitarianism—another form of irresponsibility.

Yet Milton Friedman's "pure" position—to eschew all social responsibility—is not tenable either. There are big, urgent, desperate problems. Above all, there is the "sickness of government" which is creating a vacuum of responsibility and performance—a vacuum that becomes stronger the bigger government becomes. Business and the other institutions of our society of organizations cannot be pure, however desirable that may be. Their own self-interest alone forces them to be concerned with society and community and to be prepared to shoulder responsibility beyond their own main areas of task and responsibility.

But in doing this they have to be conscious of the danger—to themselves and to society. They have to be conscious of the risk. No pluralist society such as ours has become, has ever worked unless its key institutions take responsibility for the common good. But at the same time, the perennial threat to a pluralist society is the all-too-easy confusion between the common good and one's own lust for power.

In a few areas guidelines can be developed. It is not the task of business (or of the university) to substitute its authority for that of the duly constituted political sovereign, the government, in areas that are clearly national policy. In a free society a business is, of course, entitled not to engage in activities, even though they are sanctioned and even encouraged by governmental policy. It can stay out. But it is surely not entitled to put itself in the place of government. And it is not entitled to use its economic power to impose its values on the community.

By these criteria, the Quaker sage who chided his friend the steel-mill manager (see Chapter 24) for using the economic power of a big company to impose a little racial justice on a southern U.S. city in the 1940s was right. That the end was surely right and moral does not sanction the means, that is, the exercise of an authority which a business does not possess. This is as much "imperialism" as any which the most fervent believer in racial equality denounces. The steel company can be faulted—deservedly so, I would say—for having done nothing for long years to work toward the racial justice in which it professed to believe. It can be faulted, and with cause, for not finding whatever possibilities for racial justice could have been put into practice. But two wrongs do not make a right, two examples of irresponsibility do not add up to responsibility.

By these criteria also the demand that a Swedish company such as ASEA stay out of a power project in a Portuguese colony in Africa which its own Swedish socialist government supports is dubious in logic and in ethics. A short time ago the "Old Left" used to criticize business as immoral and irresponsible for sabotaging national policies the Old Left approved of. It is just as immoral and irresponsible for business to sabotage national policies of Old Left governments of which the New Left does not approve.

## When to Say No

Demands for social responsibility which in effect ask of business—or any other institution—that it usurp authority are to be resisted. They are to be resisted in business's own self-interest; the usurper's power is always shaky. They are to be resisted on grounds of true social responsibility. For they are, in effect, demands for irresponsibility. Whether they are made sincerely and out of honest anguish, or whether they are rhetoric to cloak the lust for power, is irrelevant. Whenever business, or any other of our institutions, is being asked to take social responsibility beyond its own area of performance and its own impact, it better ask itself, "Do we possess authority in the area and should we have it?" And if the answer is no, then the socially responsible thing is not to accede to the demand.

Yet in many cases it may not be enough to say no. Management must resist responsibility for a social problem that would compromise or impair the performance capacity of its business (or its university or its hospital). It must resist when the demand goes beyond the institution's competence. It must resist when responsibility would, in fact, be illegitimate authority. But then, if the problem is a real one, it better think through and offer an alternative approach. If the problem is serious, something will ultimately have to be done about it. And if management then has been purely obstructionist and has blocked any approach—even though its objection to any one proposed course of action was legitimate and indeed responsible—the ultimate solution is likely to do even more damage.

In a pluralist society responsibility for the common good is a central problem that is never solved. The only way concern for social responsibility could disappear would be for society to become totalitarian. For it is the definition of a totalitarian government that it has authority over everything and responsibility for nothing.

For this reason managements of all major institutions, including business enterprise, need too to concern themselves with serious ills of society. If at all possible they convert solution of these problems into an opportunity for performance and contribution. At the least they think through what the problem is and how it might be tackled. They cannot escape concern; for this society of organizations has no one else to be concerned about real problems. In this society managers of institutions are the leadership group.

But we also know that a developed society needs performing institutions with their own autonomous management. It cannot function as a totalitarian society. Indeed, what characterizes a developed society—and indeed makes it a developed one—is that most of its social tasks are carried out in and through organized institutions, each with its own autonomous management. These organizations, including most of the agencies of our government, are special-purpose institutions. They are organs of our society for specific performance in a specific area. The greatest contribution they can make, their greatest social responsibility, is performance of their function. The greatest social irresponsibility is to impair the performance capacity of these institutions by tackling tasks beyond their competence or by usurpation of authority in the name of social responsibility.

# 27

## Business and Government

A crucial social responsibility for the manager, and especially for the business manager, is the relationship of business and government. Yet it is rarely even mentioned when the social responsibilities of management are being discussed.

Few relationships are as critical to the business enterprise itself as the relationship to government. The manager has responsibility for this relationship as part of his responsibility to the enterprise itself. It is an area of social impact of the business. To a large extent the relationship to government results from what businesses do or fail to do.

The business-government relationship is also a social problem, for the relationship between business and government in every major country is in disrepair. It urgently needs rethinking, reappraisal, and restructuring. In every developed country—and in most developing ones—there are no clear rules, little common understanding, and at best a confused patchwork of laws and prejudices, regulations, traditions, and ad hoc improvisation, ranging from guerrilla warfare to the closest partnership. At the same time, there are new major problems which cannot be fitted into the existing relationships. The environment is one. And so is the multinational corporation.

The increasing confusion threatens government even more than business.

It undermines its capacity for making policy and giving direction, that is, its basic institutional integrity. It tempts governments to tackle far more than they are competent to do. But it also makes them hesitant and timid in areas where political leadership is needed (e.g., in the international economy). Yet a competent, clearly defined, and functioning government is a first need for our complex and interdependent society.

Ultimately we will need new political theories appropriate to the realities and needs of the society of organizations. In the meantime, business and government will have to go on with their respective jobs. They will have to know which of these jobs have to be tackled together and which have to be kept apart. It is far too early to think of solutions. But approaches and specifications will have to be designed, if only on a case-by-case basis. And great care will have to be taken lest these interim solutions commit us to the wrong long-term pattern, foreclose valuable options, and commit society by default to patently undesirable relationships.

To work out these interim solutions and to watch over them will be primarily the job of the manager. He cannot wait for the political philosopher. Too much is at stake, for his enterprise, for the economy, and for society.

To discharge this responsibility the manager needs, above all, to understand the *historical background* to the government-business relationship. Political and administrative traditions with respect to this relationship differ greatly in different countries. They largely determine what is considered "right" and "appropriate" in individual countries—by politicians, civil servants, political scientists, but also by the public and by the businessman himself. These traditions also explain in large part why the government-business relationship is in disarray and crisis these days. Yet, few books—whether on government or on business—have paid much attention to the historical setting and to the administrative and political theories that underlie the government-business relationship in the developed countries.

## The Historical Models

The textbooks still talk of laissez-faire as the model for the business-government relationship in capitalist (i.e., "market") economies. But in the first place laissez-faire was a model of economic theory rather than of political theory and governmental practice. Except for Bentham and the young John Stuart Mill, no political writer of any importance or influence in the last two hundred years paid even lip service to it. Second, even as an economic theory laissez-faire was being practiced in only one country, Great Britain, and only for a fairly short period in the mid-nineteenth century.

The two political models that have set the norm for the business-government relationship were very different ones. They might be called, respectively, mercantilism (or, with the French, dirigisme) and constitutionalism.

Of the two, the mercantilist (or "dirigiste") model is the older. It goes back to the seventeenth and, especially, the eighteenth century. It is essentially still the prevailing model for most of continental Europe, and especially for France. It is the model for the Japanese relationship between business and government. It has set the pattern in India, both under the British and since independence. And the business-government relationship of Communist Russia is dirigisme—far more a continuation of Czarist bureaucratic administration than revolutionary, and far closer to mercantilism than to Marx.

In the mercantilist model the economy is seen as the foundation of political sovereignty and especially of the military strength of the nation. National economy and national sovereignty are seen as co-extensive. Both essentially are organized *against* an outside world. It is the main function of the economy to provide the means of survival to the nation-state against the threats from the outside. Within the nation-state there may be friction, conflict, competition, dispute. But, as in a beleaguered fortress, all disputes and disagreements stop at the wall.

In the original crude concept of mercantilism, as it was developed in the late seventeenth century, business was seen as the provider of specie, i.e., gold and silver, with which to pay the soldiers, who in turn protected national independence and survival. Adam Smith demolished the respectability of this line of reasoning. But still, the mercantilist model sees the economic foundation of political sovereignty in competitive performance abroad. Exports are the objective—and the test.

It has become fashionable these last few years to speak of "Japan, Inc." —that is, of a Japanese system in which government and business are one in promoting Japanese exports throughout the world. One could have spoken thus of a "Germany, Inc." in 1880 or 1900, or of a "France, Inc." under De Gaulle.

In the mercantilist model the businessman is considered socially inferior to the civil servant in government administration. This was as true in the France of Louis XIV as in Bismarck's Germany or in Japan before World War II. Still, the task of the government administrator is to support, to strengthen, to encourage business, and especially to support and encourage exports. As the inferiority of businessmen attenuated—especially with the rise of technology and of the professional manager—business became, so to speak, a part of the national establishment. But it is still junior to, though a partner and in symbiosis with, government.

Symptomatic of this is the position which associations and organizations of business have in a mercantilist system. In France—and to a considerable extent, in Germany—membership in the trade or industry association is compulsory. In Japan these associations are quasi-governmental bodies. The trade association official, the executive secretary for instance, is often a former civil servant of high rank. He often enjoys more status and power than any but the very biggest and strongest members of the industry themselves. Labor union agreements are typically negotiated by the industry association and are then binding on member companies. But the government also handles its relations with industry and business through trade and industry associations, as it did, for instance, in the planning process of De Gaulle's France.

The constitutionalist model developed in the nineteenth century—above all, in the United States—sees government as standing, essentially, in an adversary relationship to business. The relationship is governed by laws rather than administered. It is conducted at arm's length.

Constitutionalism no more than mercantilism believes in laissez-faire. It accepts that government cannot stay out of economy and business. "Business," both concepts say, "is too important to be left to the businessmen." But where the mercantilist guides and directs and pays subsidies, the constitutionalist says "thou shalt not" and uses antitrust laws, regulatory agencies, and criminal indictments. The mercantilist tries to encourage business, provided it moves in the direction he deems conducive to national political and military strength. The constitutionalist is determined to keep business out of government; it taints. And he sets limits of political morality to business activity.

While continental Europe is the birthplace of mercantilism, the U.S. developed constitutionalism. Jefferson may be said to have been the first constitutionalist—deeply suspicious of business and convinced that the business interest had to be kept out of government. But it was not until Andrew Jackson, twenty years later, i.e., around 1830, that constitutionalism became the prevailing intellectual model for business-government relationship in the U.S.

It was also during the Jackson Administration that constitutionalism fixed the social position of the businessman in American life. Since then businessmen have been socially equal to any group in American society.

Indeed, in the late nineteenth and early twentieth centuries in the United States, the businessman was perhaps the socially dominant figure. His competitors for social rank were not, as in mercantilist countries, the civil servants, but the clergy and, later on, the university professor. In the constitutionalist model, since Jackson's days, the businessman is also supposed to be a patriot and available, especially in times of crisis, to serve the nation and to assume political leadership positions. And yet, when Franklin D. Roosevelt, a hundred years after Jackson, called businessmen "malefactors of great wealth," he spoke in the purest constitutionalist vein.

Symptomatic for the constitutionalist approach is, again, the treatment and position of trade and industry associations. In the constitutionalist tradition they are looked upon with great suspicion and are rarely used as a conduit for the relations between government and the business community. They are not compulsory and have no coercive powers or official standing, no matter how influential they might be behind the scenes, e.g., as lobbying groups in Congress.

Symptomatic also is the fact that in the country where constitutionalism has been most influential, that is the U.S., the Department of Commerce, i.e., the ministry supposed to represent business in government and to watch out for the interests of business, was not set up as a cabinet office until 1913 —a hundred to a hundred and fifty years later than the ministries of commerce in continental Europe.

Equally symptomatic is the fact that until World War II, the United States refused to have a defense industry. It relied, instead, on government-owned arsenals. To build a contractual partnership with outside independent businesses would have run counter to the constitutionalist tradition. Since the work had to be performed, however, it had to be performed by government itself.

## Models and Reality

Both dirigisme and constitutionalism are intellectual models of political —or administrative—theory. They are norms of what ought to be. And reality always falls far short of such an ideal.

This applies particularly to constitutionalism. Even in the United States the doctrine of adversary, arm's-length relationship between business and government had, from the beginning, to contend with a powerful American version of mercantilism. It began with Jefferson's great adversary, Alexander Hamilton (1757–1804). A generation later Henry Clay (1777–1852) in his "American System" adapted mercantilism to American conditions. The "enemy" was not outside. It was the trackless wilderness beyond the frontier. Instead of exports, Clay advocated "internal improvements," that is, canals, railroads, farming, and industries for the domestic market. And from the beginning the adversary relationship to business went hand in hand with subsidies, especially to canals and railways. And few countries have been as consistently protectionist with respect to trade as the U.S.

Indeed, many critics, American and especially European, have called the official U.S. constitutionalist policy position mere hypocrisy and a complete sham. But this misses the powerful impact constitutionalism has actually had and still has. It largely informs America's traditional opposition to the "system," the Populist Crusade. It explains why the American radical traditionally has opposed business as such whereas the European Leftist has traditionally been "for" business and wants only to replace the "wicked capitalist" with his own "good guys"—that is, government administrators. (In this respect, the recent surge of a New Left in Europe with a demand for "changing the system" actually represents ideological Americanization of a particularly ironic kind. It is no accident that its main enemy is the traditional, that is, mercantilist Left of the European tradition such as the old-line communists.) Constitutionalism also explains the peculiar forms of U.S. economic and business legislation and regulation. But there is considerable substance to the old remark that, in her attitude to business and economy, the U.S. has been Jeffersonian (i.e., constitutionalist) in theory and Hamiltonian (i.e., mercantilist) in practice.

Mercantilism has been undoubtedly far more widely practiced. And when the one country that had actually done what economic theory advocated and had kept government out of the economy—that is, Great Britain—shifted, in the late 1800s, to a political approach to business and economy, it shifted toward dirigisme (of the German rather than the French model) rather than toward constitutionalism.

But even the mercantilist model was never fully realized in practice. From the beginning there were tensions in it. Business again and again slipped out of administrative control. Even in Japan, government and the business community see themselves as adversaries as much as partners.

And constitutionalism made substantial inroads. The most influential school of political economy on the continent of Europe in the late nineteenth and early twentieth centuries, that is, in the days when the government-business alliance on the continent was at its peak, were the German academic socialists *(Katheder-Socialisten)*. These powerful and influential professors wanted to separate business and government and to replace the mercantilist alliance with something much closer to the constitutionalist model. After World War II the Germans actually committed themselves to constitutionalism. The "social market economy," which both major German parties adopted in the Adenauer years, was not laissez-faire, it was constitutionalism.

Yet these two models have, for well over a century, been the guides and set the norms. They told governments and politicians what should be. They established the criteria for right and wrong in the public mind. They did not perhaps determine the business-government relationship, but they set the limits within which specific relationship problems could be worked out on a case-by-case, issue-by-issue, "scandal-by-scandal" basis.

## The New Problems

By now, however, both models are obsolescent. Neither model offers much guidance anymore, either to government or to business. Neither model can cope with the new relationship problems which, however, demand solutions. The most important—or at least the most visible—of these new problems have been caused by:

1. the "mixed economy";
2. the multinational corporation;
3. government's loss of its position as *the* institution; and
4. the emergence of the professional manager.

1. The first of these realities is today's "mixed economy."

Both of the models were developed for a capitalist economy. Both could also function in a socialist economy (for the adaptation of constitutionalism to socialist competition see Chapter 14). But neither model can handle a mixed economy in which government activities and business activities intertwine and compete at the same time.

Every developed economy is a complex mixture of regulations, governmental controls, subsidies and penalties, business autonomy in areas formerly considered government (e.g., autonomous postal services), and direct government operations of business. There are institutions that, while incorporated as private companies, are publicly owned and discharge public functions. There are also institutions which while government owned operate in fairly competitive markets and discharge "private-sector" functions. And there is a welter of the most complex partnerships. Defense procurement is but one example; for in every noncommunist country today defense procurement is done in a contractual relationship, half partnership, half duel, between government and autonomously managed and largely privately owned contractors.

Defense procurement may be considered a special case. In the U.S., for instance, the mixed economy in defense is still being explained away as a "temporary emergency" almost thirty years after the end of World War II, which first created it. Everyone concerned knows that there is nothing temporary about it and that the fiction of "temporary emergency" is a major cause of the serious problems in defense procurement. Yet everyone concerned also knows that any attempt to think through and restructure the relationship would immediately run head on into philosophical contradictions, fundamental political convictions and traditions, and irreconcilable differences between "what ought to be" and what is needed. As one high Defense Department official once put it, "We know it's chaos; but that's still better than paralysis."

But even in areas other than defense, what is "public" and what is "private," what is "government" and what is "business" can no longer be separated.

NASA, the National Aeronautics and Space Administration, which put a man on the moon in the 1960s, is an even "fuzzier" area than defense procurement. (On NASA and its structure see Chapter 47.) NASA is a government agency. And yet the American space effort was a cooperative enterprise in which a large number of independent and autonomous organizations—government agencies, universities, individuals and, above all, business—worked together on a common task. The legal structure for this was a contractual relationship. The actual work was done in a partnership in which at many times private businesses took the leadership, made public policy, and set goals and standards. "In defense procurement," a NASA executive explained, "it's always the government that has an inspector in the contractor's plant to control his work. In NASA it is not at all uncommon for a contractor who is a private business to have an inspector in a government installation who controls the work the government is doing."

There are going to be more and more *joint tasks* in which government and business will have to be in a team, with leadership taken by one or the other as the situation demands. There are the tasks of the environment. There is the enormous task of husbanding the resources of the world. There are the problems of the big city. There is research—technological as well as social—and many others. Quality-of-life tasks are perhaps by definition joint tasks in which nongovernmental institutions have to take social responsibility for doing while governments may have to provide the money.

This is difficult enough to fit in with dirigisme. The civil servant no longer guides and shapes a separate business community. In some relationships he will have to be a partner, and not necessarily the senior partner. In some relationships, e.g., in many areas of banking and insurance, he has to become the spokesman for business—some of it private, some, especially in Europe, government-owned—against public policy. In others, especially in relations with "multinationals," private businesses represent the "public policy" of their own government, for instance in European unification or in developing underdeveloped economies while the civil servant defends "private interests" of domestic industry. But, dirigisme can still accept this —though the strain is great.

But the mixed economy is quite incompatible with the constitutionalist model, which explains the extreme difficulty American political parties, American political rhetoric, and American political commentators have in explaining the way government and economy actually work.

2. The second factor which cannot be made to jibe with the traditional models is the multinational corporation. As will be explained later (in Chapter 59) the multinational corporation is a response to the divorce—or at least estrangement—of economy and sovereignty after three hundred years of marriage. The economy can no longer be defined as a national economy even in the biggest and most powerful countries such as the United States. Yet sovereignty is still exclusively national. There is no sign of

anything to take the place of the nation-state as the political sovereign. Yet there is a genuine world economy which carries the economic dynamics and actually determines economic developments worldwide, with direct impact on economic behavior, activity, and results within the national economies, and yet is largely impervious to political sovereignty.

The mercantilist model is most directly challenged by the development of which the multinational corporation is both carrier and effect. To mercantilism this divorce is unthinkable; yet it is happening. This was clearly understood by General De Gaulle. His decision not to permit French businesses to go multinational was completely rational. It was also completely futile.

The constitutionalist model, too, can hardly cope with the multinational corporation.

It is no accident that latter-day U.S. populism is attacking the multinational corporation. For the mercantilist tradition the crime of the multinational corporation is that it is not an instrument of political sovereignty and cannot be one. For the populist of the American constitutionalist tradition the crime of the multinational corporation is that it is not an instrument of American morality and cannot be one. On the contrary, it must fit itself in every country to the prevailing legal and moral beliefs of the political sovereignty in the country where it operates.

And neither model could cope with the logical corollary to an autonomous world economy, separate from, and outside of, the political sovereignty of any and all nation-states: a supranational currency and credit mechanism with its own autonomous nonnational "central bank." Yet this is clearly the direction ahead; indeed, the acceptance of International Drawing Rights (IDR) issued by the International Monetary Fund, as a "supercurrency" in the Smithsonian Agreement in December 1971, was a decisive step. If development continues along this line, neither the mercantilist nor the constitutionalist model could be maintained, even as intellectual abstractions.

3. In the society of organizations government becomes one special-purpose institution rather than *the* institution. Such a society creates social responsibility for the nongovernment leadership groups, and especially for the business manager. It thereby undermines the uniqueness of government's position and role. The other institutions can no longer be seen, as they were in the mercantilist model, as "handmaidens" of the Grand Design of national policy.

What made De Gaulle so impressive a figure was his refusal to accept this. De Gaulle instead insisted on the unchallenged primacy of *La Grande Politique*—not only over the economy but equally over arts and education.

This made De Gaulle consistent and clear. But it also made his policy appear old-fashioned and in the end almost absurd, even to fervent admirers of a great man.

But the constitutionalist too has difficulty with a society in which business is expected to assume social responsibility. His position all along, and the basis for his insistence on an adversary relationship to business, has been that business has to be restrained, policed, regulated, limited—and if need be, punished—lest it behave irresponsibly and antisocially. Hence the ambivalence approaching schizophrenia, of the traditional American liberal who demands in the same breath that GM or IBM be split up and that they mobilize their resources to solve major social problems.

4. Finally, there is the emergence of the professional manager as against the owner-entrepreneur. The traditional models speak of the businessman. But the reality of today is the manager. This means that the managers of business have emerged as a group which in origin, education, background, and values closely resembles the civil servant. (The one exception to this—changing fast though—is still Great Britain.) At the same time the civil servant (as well as the leadership groups in other institutions) are in the process of becoming managers.

This development creates a danger of making business bureaucratic. But it also abolishes the old demarcation lines. It thereby undermines the distinction on which both the mercantilist model and the constitutionalist model have been built.

The emergence of the manager as a leading group is particularly incompatible with the mercantilist model. But equally incompatible for the constitutionalist tradition is the growing trend toward considering business management as the model for public administration.

It may be argued that these are problems for government rather than for business. But too much is at stake for business and management to disregard the fact that the traditional, inherited relationship models cannot adequately organize and structure relationship realities any more.

Solutions, as said before, are not within sight.

The orthodox Marxist would dispute that. But the reality in communist countries is fully as much one of patchwork, increasing strain, ineffectual compromise, and malperformance. The struggle in the communist countries between the "conservatives," who want to maintain complete dirigisme, and the "realists" or "liberals," who argue for "autonomy" of enterprise and markets, is the result of the growing gap between the dirigiste model and reality. And the Russian fear of any deviation from the model, whether in Yugoslavia, in Czechoslovakia, or in China, is a fear of political rather than of economic consequences.

## Guidelines

Specific problems will have to be dealt with even though there are no known solutions, no new political theory, no new and more adequate model. What is needed are "specifications." What is needed are criteria by which specific answers to specific problems—ad hoc, pragmatic, temporary—can be tested and judged. What is needed—and is attainable—are guidelines that strengthen, or at least protect, in the ad hoc treatment of specific problems fundamental long-range needs and requirements of the body-politic, of government, and of economy and business enterprise.

1. The first such specification is that the economic organizations of society, i.e., business and their managers, require autonomy and accountability:

—in the interest of the economy;
—for the sake of strong and effective government; and
—in the interest of society.

"Accountable Enterprise" might be a better slogan than the by now hackneyed "Free Enterprise."*

To be accountable for performance, economic institutions and their managers have to have autonomy. One cannot be accountable for what one has no authority over and cannot control. Business enterprises and managements have to be under the performance test or they cease to perform. They have to be able to allocate society's and economy's resources in a rational manner and against objective criteria. Or resources will at once be misallocated.†

This is not a matter of ownership. It requires market test and market decision, in the three economic dimensions—the market for goods and services, the market for capital and investment, and the market for jobs and careers.

Of the three, the capital market may be most crucial. It is in the capital market that resources for the future are allocated on the basis of performance expectation. And it is the capital market which, therefore, while in need of regulation, also needs self-determination.

---

*If only because the word "free" has a different connotation in most other languages and is read as implying license rather than responsibility.

†On this, Ota Sik, the Czech communist theoretician and architect of the economic liberalization of Czechoslovakia in 1967 and 1968—now living in exile in Basel, Switzerland—has some profound things to say in his little book, *Czechoslovakia: The Bureaucratic Economy* (International Arts and Sciences Press, 1972). The book, containing lectures he gave to his compatriots in the critical weeks before the Russian invasion, is a graphic description of the self-destruction of a once highly productive economy resulting from the loss of business and managerial autonomy.

But there is need also for an open-ended economy, an economy in which businesses can be born, but one in which businesses can also die. It is a basic weakness of a state-owned or state-controlled economic system that businesses are not allowed to go bankrupt and can only rarely be liquidated. Yet clearly the welfare of society and economy demands a healthy business metabolism.

This will be particularly true in the decades ahead. They are going to be decades of change. Unless businesses, even big and apparently important businesses, are allowed to go out of existence, the body-economic will increasingly age, become sclerotic, ossify. This will not prevent change. It will rather make change into a catastrophic threat instead of a gradual adjustment.

There is need for a cushioning of the social impact of such changes. How this might be done has been discussed earlier (in Chapter 22 in connection with Sweden's Rehn Plan.) But the strength of the Rehn Plan is precisely that it converts what otherwise might be individual catastrophe into an "insurable risk" through full use of the market mechanism.

The performance capacity of government also rests on autonomy for business and management. A political process at best makes allocation decisions poorly and painfully. They clog government and overload it to the point where it cannot move at all, cannot make decisions, cannot devote itself to the governmental tasks properly.*

Society too requires management autonomy. Managers of the major organizations are collectively the leadership groups of the society of organizations. But a healthy society requires a pluralism of leadership groups with different values, different priorities, different "styles." It requires alternatives—in careers and career ladders, in points of view, in life-styles. Otherwise it degenerates into conformity, and loses its capacity for change. If the need for change arises—and it always does—no one can even imagine a behavior different from what everyone in the leadership group is accustomed to and considers "right" if not unmutable "law of nature." At the same time, those among the able and ambitious who do not fit easily into the one norm of the one leadership group are alienated.

A healthy society is a complex of "countercultures." They need not be in conflict—indeed, in a healthy society they mutually respect each other. But they must exist in competitive coexistence. In a society in which the cultures and life-styles are increasingly those of the key organizations, social health requires autonomy for major leadership groups. It requires autonomous business with autonomous managements.

2. But society also needs a healthy and functioning government, especially in as complex and interdependent a society as ours has become.

*On this too, Sik (op. cit.) is most instructive.

Government is needed as the political decision-maker, more than ever before perhaps. And at the same time, the capacity of government to be the political decision maker is increasingly jeopardized by its weight, size, and bureaucratization. It is increasingly jeopardized by government tendency to take on too many things, to promise too much, and to "do" too much. The fatter government becomes, the flabbier and weaker it actually is.*

Business and business management cannot restore government to health. This is a political job. But they can at least be conscious of the need and avoid, in working out the business-government relationship, whatever might weaken the performance capacity of government as the central political decision-maker. In this area their responsibility is *"Primum non nocere"*—"not knowingly to do damage." (See the next chapter.)

## The Multinational Corporation

3. The twin needs, for economic autonomy and effective government, come together in one major problem of the business-government relationship.

The multinational corporation (again see Chapter 59) is a central economic achievement of the period since World War II and perhaps the most fruitful social innovation of the century. It is also a hard problem. What is needed is to work out a relationship which safeguards both a true world economy and the political sovereignty of national governments in peaceful coexistence. Otherwise we will impair or destroy altogether that most promising development, the multinational business, and undermine the capacity for political vision and action and for political community.

4. The need to think through the business-government relationship is not, in the main, the result of a crisis of business. It is the result of a serious crisis of government. Yet business managers will have to look upon the relationship to government and society as their task. They cannot wait for the political scientist or the theoretical economist. A purely negative attitude which fights every "encroachment of government" is not going to be effective. All it can do is delay. Positive, affirmative action is needed.

We do not need more laws. No country suffers from a shortage of laws these days. We need a new model. Yet all we can expect are temporary ad hoc answers to specific problems. These answers should, however, be compatible with minimum specifications: they should preserve the autonomy

*On this see my book, *The Age of Discontinuity,* especially Chapter 10, "The Sickness of Government."

and accountability of business enterprise and business management; they should safeguard a free and flexible society capable of change; they should harmonize the world economy of the multinational and the sovereignty of the nation-states; and they should encourage strong and performing government.

# 28

## *Primum Non Nocere:* The Ethics of Responsibility

*The Ethics of Businessmen: The Wrong Question?—Leadership Groups but Not Leaders—What Being a Professional Means—An Ethic of Responsibility—Primum non nocere—Social Responsibility vs. "Club Membership"— Executive Compensation and Income Inequality—The "Golden Fetters"— The Rhetoric of the Profit Motive—Private Function and Public Character*

Countless sermons have been preached and printed on the ethics of business or the ethics of the businessman. Most have nothing to do with business and little to do with ethics.

One main topic is plain, everyday honesty. Businessmen, we are told solemnly, should not cheat, steal, lie, bribe, or take bribes. But nor should anyone else. Men and women do not acquire exemption from ordinary rules of personal behavior because of their work or job. Nor, however, do they cease to be human beings when appointed vice-president, city manager, or college dean. And there has always been a number of people who cheat, steal, lie, bribe, or take bribes. The problem is one of moral values and moral education, of the individual, of the family, of the school. But there neither is a separate ethics of business, nor is one needed.

All that is needed is to mete out stiff punishments to those—whether business executives or others—who yield to temptation. In England a magistrate still tends to hand down a harsher punishment in a drunken-driving case if the accused has gone to one of the well-known public schools or to Oxford or Cambridge. And the conviction still rates a headline in the evening paper: "Eton graduate convicted of drunken driving." No one expects an Eton education to produce temperance leaders. But it is still a badge of distinction, if not of privilege. And not to treat a wearer of such a badge more harshly than an ordinary workingman who has had one too many would offend the community's sense of justice. But no one considers this a problem of the "ethics of the Eton graduate."

The other common theme in the discussion of ethics in business has nothing to do with ethics.

Such things as the employment of call girls to entertain customers are not matters of ethics but matters of esthetics. "Do I want to see a pimp when I look at myself in the mirror while shaving?" is the real question.

It would indeed be nice to have fastidious leaders. Alas, fastidiousness has never been prevalent among leadership groups, whether kings and counts, priests or generals, or even "intellectuals" such as the painters and humanists of the Renaissance, or the "literati" of the Chinese tradition. All a fastidious man can do is withdraw personally from activities that violate his self-respect and his sense of taste.

Lately these old sermon topics have been joined, especially in the U.S., by a third one: managers, we are being told, have an "ethical responsibility" to take an active and constructive role in their community, to serve community causes, give of their time to community activities, and so on.

There are many countries where such community activity does not fit the traditional mores; Japan and France would be examples. But where the community has a tradition of "voluntarism"—that is, especially in the U.S. —managers should indeed be encouraged to participate and to take responsible leadership in community affairs and community organizations. Such activities should, however, never be forced on them nor should they be appraised, rewarded, or promoted according to their participation in voluntary activities. Ordering or pressuring managers into such work is abuse of organizational power and illegitimate.

An exception might be made for managers in businesses where the community activities are really part of their obligation to the business. The local manager of the telephone company, for instance, who takes part in community activities, does so as part of his managerial duties and as the local public-relations representative of his company. The same is true of the manager of a local Sears, Roebuck store. And the local real estate man who belongs to a dozen different community activities and eats lunch every day with a different "service club" knows perfectly well that he is not serving the community but promoting his business and hunting for prospective customers.

But, while desirable, community participation of managers has nothing to do with ethics, and not much to do with responsibility. It is the contribution of an individual in his capacity as a neighbor and citizen. And it is something that lies outside his job and outside his managerial responsibility.

## Leadership Groups but Not Leaders

A problem of ethics that is peculiar to the manager arises from the fact that the managers of institutions are *collectively* the leadership groups of the society of organizations. But *individually* a manager is just another fellow employee.

This is clearly recognized by the public. Even the most powerful head of the largest corporation is unknown to the public. Indeed most of the company's employees barely know his name and would not recognize his face. He may owe his position entirely to personal merit and proven performance. But he owes his authority and standing entirely to his institution. Everybody knows GE, the Telephone Company, Mitsubishi, Siemens, and Unilever. But who heads these great corporations—or for that matter, the University of California, the École Polytechnique or Guy's Hospital in London—is of direct interest and concern primarily to the management group within these institutions.

It is therefore inappropriate to speak of managers as leaders. They are "members of the leadership group." The group, however, does occupy a position of visibility, of prominence, and of authority. It therefore has responsibility—and it is with this responsibility that the preceding chapters of this section are concerned.

But what are the responsibilities, what are the ethics of the individual manager, as a member of the leadership group?

Essentially being a member of a leadership group is what traditionally has been meant by the term "professional." Membership in such a group confers status, position, prominence, and authority. It also confers duties. To expect every manager to be a leader is futile. There are, in a developed society, thousands, if not millions, of managers—and leadership is always the rare exception and confined to a very few individuals. But as a member of a leadership group a manager stands under the demands of professional ethics—the demands of an ethic of responsibility.

## Primum Non Nocere

The first responsibility of a professional was spelled out clearly, 2,500 years ago, in the Hipprocratic oath of the Greek physician: *primum non nocere*—"Above all, not knowingly to do harm."

No professional, be he doctor, lawyer, or manager, can promise that he will indeed do good for his client. All he can do is try. But he can promise that he will not knowingly do harm. And the client, in turn, must be able to trust the professional not knowingly to do him harm. Otherwise he cannot trust him at all. The professional has to have autonomy. He cannot be controlled, supervised, or directed by the client. He has to be private in that his knowledge and his judgment have to be entrusted with the decision. But it is the foundation of his autonomy, and indeed its rationale, that he see himself as "affected with the public interest." A professional, in other words, is private in the sense that he is autonomous and not subject to political or ideological control. But he is public in the sense that the welfare of his client sets limits to his deeds and words. And *Primum non nocere,* "not knowingly to do harm," is the basic rule of professional ethics, the basic rule of an ethics of public responsibility.

There are important areas where managers, and especially business managers, still do not realize that in order to be permitted to remain autonomous and private they have to impose on themselves the responsibility of the professional ethic. They still have to learn that it is their job to scrutinize their deeds, words, and behavior to make sure that they do not knowingly do harm.

One, perhaps the most important one, of these areas has already been discussed (in Chapter 25). The manager who fails to think through and work for the appropriate solution to an impact of his business because it makes him "unpopular in the club" knowingly does harm. He knowingly abets a cancerous growth. That this is stupid has been said. That this always in the end hurts the business or the industry more than a little temporary "unpleasantness" would have hurt has been said too. But it is also gross violation of professional ethics.

But there are other areas as well. American managers, in particular, tend to violate the rule not knowingly to do harm with respect to:

—executive compensation;
—the use of benefit plans to impose "golden fetters" on people in the company's employ; and
—in their profit rhetoric.

Their actions and their words in these areas tend to cause social disruption. They tend to conceal healthy reality and to create disease, or at least social hypochondria. They tend to misdirect and to prevent understanding. And this is grievous social harm.

## Executive Compensation and Economic Inequality

Contrary to widespread belief, incomes have become far more equal in all developed countries than in any society of which we have a record. And they have tended to become steadily more equal as national and personal incomes increase. And, equally contrary to popular rhetoric, income equality is greatest in the United States.

The most reliable measure of income equality is the so-called Gini coefficient in which an index of zero stands for complete equality of income and an index of 1 for total inequality in which one person in the population receives all the income. The lower the Gini co-efficient, the closer a society is to income equality. In the U.S. the Gini in the early 1970s stood around 0.35—with about the same figure in Canada, Australia, and Great Britain, and probably also in Japan. West Germany and the Netherlands are about 0.40. France and Sweden are around 0.50*

Specifically, in the typical American business the inequality of income between the lowest-paid people and the people in charge—that is, between the machine operator and the manager of a large plant—is at most one to four, if taxes are taken into account. The take-home pay of the machine operator after taxes in 1970 was around $7,500 a year; the after-tax income of very few plant managers was larger than $25,000, all bonuses included. If fringes are taken into account, the ratio is even lower, i.e., one to three (or $12,000 to $35,000 maximum). And similar ratios prevail in other developed countries, e.g., in Japan. This, it should be said, is far greater income equality than in any communist country for the simple reason that the economic level of a communist country is lower.

In Soviet Russia, where there are practically no income taxes, the income differential between industrial worker and plant manager runs around 1 to 7, without taking into account the noncash benefits of the Russian manager. And Russian managers operate at an extreme of profit maximization; their profit-based bonus system of compensation so directs them. In China, the differential between workers and plant managers seems to run around 1 to 6 or so.

Whether the degree of inequality of incomes that actually prevails in the U.S. economy is "too high" or "too low" is a matter of opinion. But clearly it is much lower than the great majority of the American public accepts or even considers desirable. Every survey shows that an "income ratio of 1 to 10 or 12" between the blue-collar in the factory and the "big boss" would be considered "about right." That would make the "after-tax take-home pay" of the "big boss" somewhere around $75,000 to $100,000 a year, which would be equal to a pre-tax salary of at least $200,000. And only a mere handful of executives earn that much, bonuses included. If the comparison is made—as it should be—between total incomes including fringes, deferred compensation, stock options, and all other forms of extra compensation, a 1 to 12 ratio would work out to an after-tax top figure of $150,000. And no more than a dozen or so top men in the very largest companies have pre-tax "total compensation package" of $300,000 and up, which is needed

*On this see the article by Sanford Rose, "The Truth about Income and Equality in the U.S." in *Fortune,* December, 1972.

to produce an after-tax value of $150,000. The "extremely rich" are not employed executives—the tax system takes care of those (as it should); they are either a few heirs of the millionaires of pre-tax days or owners of small businesses.

And relative to the incomes of manual and clerical workers, after-tax executive compensation, and especially the income of the men at the very top, has been going down steadily for fifty years or more.

The facts of increasing income equality in U.S. society are quite clear. Yet the popular impression is one of rapidly increasing inequality. This is illusion; but it is a dangerous illusion. It corrodes. It destroys mutual trust between groups that have to live together and work together. It can only lead to political measures which, while doing no one any good, can seriously harm society, economy, and the manager as well.

In some considerable measure, the belief in growing income inequality in the U.S. reflects, of course, America's racial problem. The emergence into visibility, that is, into the big cities, of a disenfranchised nonworking population of Blacks has created a marginal but highly visible group suffering from extreme inequality of incomes. That the income of the employed Negro has been going up rapidly and is likely, within a decade or so, to be equal to that of the employed white doing the same kind of work—and that four-fifths of the American Negroes are employed and working—tends to be obscured by the dire poverty of the much smaller but highly concentrated groups of unemployed or unemployables in the Black ghettos of the core cities.

Another reason for the widespread belief in growing inequality is inflation. Inflation is a corrosive social poison precisely because it makes people look for a villain. The economists' explanation that no one benefits by inflation, that is, that no one gets the purchasing power that inflation takes away from the income recipients, simply makes no sense to ordinary experience. Somebody must have benefited, somebody "must have stolen what is rightfully mine." Every inflation in history has therefore created class hatred, mutual distrust, and beliefs that, somehow, "the other fellow" gains illicitly at "my" expense. It is always the middle class which becomes paranoid in an inflationary period and turns against the "system." The inflations of the sixties in the developed countries were no exceptions.

But the main cause of the dangerous delusion of increasing inequality of income is the widely publicized enormous *pre-tax* incomes of a few men at the top of a few giant corporations, and the—equally widely publicized— "extras" of executive compensation, e.g., stock options.

The $500,000 a year which the chief executive of one of the giant corporations is being paid is largely "make-believe money." Its function is status rather than income. Most of it, whatever tax loopholes the lawyers might find, is immediately taxed away. And the "extras" are simply attempts to put a part of the executive's income into a somewhat lower tax bracket. Economically, in other words, neither serves much purpose. But socially and psychologically they "knowingly do harm." They cannot be defended.

One way to eliminate the offense is for companies to commit themselves to a maximum range of *after-tax* compensation. The 1 to 10 ratio that the great majority of Americans would consider perfectly acceptable, would, in fact, be wider than the actual range of most companies. (There should, I would argue, be room, however, for an occasional exception: the rare, "once-in-a-lifetime," very big, "special bonus" to someone, a research scientist, a manager, or a salesman, who has made an extraordinary contribution.)

But equally important is acceptance of social responsibility on the part of managers to work for a rational system of taxation,* which eliminates the temptation of "tax gimmicks" and the need for them.

There is a strong case for adequate incentives for performing executives. And compensation in money is far preferable to hidden compensation such as perquisites. If he gets money the recipient can choose what to spend it on rather than, as in the case of "perks," taking whatever the company provides, be it a chauffeur-driven car, a big house, or (as in the case of some Swedish companies) a governess for the children. Indeed it may well be that real incomes in American business are not sufficiently unequal and that the compression of income differentials in the years since 1950 has been socially and economically detrimental.

What is pernicious, however, is the delusion of inequality. The basic cause is the tax laws. But the managers' willingness to accept, and indeed to play along with, an antisocial tax structure is a major contributory cause. And unless managers realize that this violates the rule "not knowingly to do damage," they will, in the end, be the main sufferers.

## The Danger of "Golden Fetters"

A second area in which the manager of today does not live up to the commitment of *Primum non nocere* is closely connected with compensation.

Since World War II compensation and benefits have been increasingly misused to create "golden fetters."

Retirement benefits, extra compensation, bonuses, and stock options are

---

*We know the specifications of such a system—and they are simple: *no* preferential tax rates for *any* personal income, whether from salaries or from capital gains, and a limit on the maximum tax—say 50 percent of total income received.

all forms of compensation. From the point of view of the enterprise—but also from the point of view of the economy—these are "labor costs" no matter how they are labeled. They are treated as such by managements when they sit down to negotiate with the labor union. But increasingly, if only because of the bias of the tax laws, these benefits are being used to tie an employee to his employer. They are being made dependent on staying with the same employer, often for many years. And they are structured in such a way that leaving a company's employ entails drastic penalties and actual loss of benefits that have already been earned and that, in effect, constitute wages relating to past employment.

This may be proper in a society which, like that of Japan, is built on lifetime employment and excludes mobility. Even in Japan, however, "golden fetters" are no longer acceptable to professional and technical employees who increasingly should have mobility in their own interest, in that of the Japanese economy, and even in that of the Japanese company. In the West, and especially in the United States, such golden fetters are clearly antisocial.

Golden fetters do not strengthen the company. They lead to "negative selection." People who know that they are not performing in their present employment—that is, people who are clearly in the wrong place—will often not move but stay where they know they do not properly belong. But if they stay because the penalty for leaving is too great, they resist and resent it. They know that they have been bribed and were too weak to say no. They are likely to be sullen, resentful, and bitter the rest of their working lives.

The fact that the employees themselves eagerly seek these benefits is no excuse. After all, medieval serfdom also began as an eagerly sought "employee benefit."*

It is incumbent, therefore, on the managers to think through which of these benefits should properly—by their own rationale—be tied to continued employment. Stock options might, for instance, belong here. But pension rights, performance bonuses, participation in profits, and so on, have been "earned" and should be available to the employee without restricting his rights as a citizen, an individual, and a person. And, again, managers will have to work to get the tax law changes that are needed.

## The Rhetoric of the Profit Motive

Managers, finally, through their rhetoric, make it impossible for the public to understand economic reality. This violates the requirement that managers, being leaders, not knowingly do harm. This is particularly true

---

*On the "golden fetters" see also Chapter 11 of my book, *The Age of Discontinuity.*

of the United States but also of Western Europe. For in the West, managers still talk constantly of the profit motive. And they still define the goal of their business as profit maximization. They do not stress the objective function of profit. They do not talk of risks—or very rarely. They do not stress the need for capital. They almost never even mention the cost of capital, let alone that a business has to produce enough profit to obtain the capital it needs at minimum cost.

Managers constantly complain about the hostility to profit. They rarely realize that their own rhetoric is one of the main reasons for this hostility. For indeed in the terms management uses when it talks to the public, there is no possible justification for profit, no explanation for its existence, no function it performs. There is only the profit motive, that is, the desire of some anonymous capitalists—and why that desire should be indulged in by society any more than bigamy, for instance, is never explained. But profitability is a crucial *need* of economy and society.

Managerial practice in most large American companies is perfectly rational. It is the rhetoric which obscures, and thereby threatens to damage both business and society. To be sure, few American companies work out profitability as a *minimum* requirement. As a result, most probably underestimate the profitability the company truly requires (let alone, as said in Chapter 9, the inflationary erosion of capital). But they, consciously or not, base their profit planning on the twin objectives of ensuring access to capital needed and minimizing the cost of capital. In the American context, if only because of the structure of the U.S. capital market, a high "price/earnings ratio" is indeed a key to the minimization of the cost of capital; and "optimization of profits" is therefore a perfectly rational strategy which tends to lower, in the long run, the actual cost of capital.

But this makes it even less justifiable to keep on using the rhetoric of the profit motive. It serves no purpose except to confuse and to embitter.

These examples of areas in which managers do not hold themselves to the rule "not knowingly to do harm" are primarily American examples. They apply to some extent to Western Europe. But they hardly apply to Japan. The principle, however, applies in all countries, and in the developing countries as much as in developed ones. These cases are taken from business management. The principle, however, applies to managers of all institutions in the society of organizations.

In any pluralist society responsibility for the public good has been the central problem and issue. The pluralist society of organizations will be no exception. Its leaders represent "special interests," that is, institutions designed to fulfill a specific and partial need of society. Indeed the leaders of this pluralist society of organizations are the servants of such institutions. At the same time, they are the major leadership group such a society knows or is likely to produce. They have to serve both their own institution and the common good. If the society is to function, let alone if it is to remain a free society, the men we call managers will remain "private" in their institutions. No matter who owns them and how, they will maintain autonomy. But they will also have to be "public" in their ethics.

In this tension between the private functioning of the manager: the necessary autonomy of his institution and its accountability to its own mission and purpose, and the public character of the manager, lies the specific ethical problem of the society of organizations. *Primum non nocere* may seem tame compared to the rousing calls for "statesmanship" that abound in today's manifestos on social responsibility. But, as the physicians found out long ago, it is not an easy rule to live up to. Its very modesty and self-constraint make it the right rule for the ethics managers need, the ethics of responsibility.

# PART TWO

# THE MANAGER: WORK, JOBS, SKILLS, AND ORGANIZATION

———

*Managers do not hold their jobs by "delegation." They are thus autonomous and grounded in the needs and realities of enterprise. There are thus managerial jobs: there is managerial work; there are managerial skills; and there is distinct managerial organization.*

# 29

## Why Managers?

*Managers, the Basic Resource of a Business, the Scarcest, Most Expensive, and Most Perishable—The Ford Story: A Controlled Experiment in Mismanagement—Siemens and Mitsubishi as Examples—Ford and Lenin— The Lesson of the Ford Story—Management Precedes Ownership—The "Management Lag" of British Industry—Management. "Change of Phase" Rather Than Adaptation—Management an Autonomous Function, Not a Delegated One*

Managers are the basic resource of the business enterprise. In a fully automatic factory there may be almost no rank-and-file employees at all. But there will be managers—in fact, there will be many more then there used to be in the factory of yesterday.

Managers are the most expensive resource in most businesses—and the one that depreciates the fastest and needs the most constant replenishment. It takes years to build a management team; but it can be depleted in a short period of misrule. The number of managers as well as the capital investment each manager represents are bound to increase steadily—as they have increased in the past half century. Parallel with this will go an increase in the demands of the enterprise on the ability of its managers. These demands have doubled in every generation; there is no reason to expect a slowing down of the trend during the next decades.

How well managers manage and are managed determines whether business goals will be reached. It also largely determines how well the enterprise manages worker and work. For the worker's attitude reflects, above all, the attitude of his management. It directly mirrors management's competence and structure. The worker's effectiveness is determined largely by the way he is being managed.

During the last quarter century managers everywhere have subjected themselves to a steady barrage of exhortations, speeches, and programs in which they tell each other that their job is to manage the people under them, urge each other to give top priority to that responsibility, and furnish each other with copious advice and expensive gadgets for "downward communications." But I have yet to sit down with a manager, whatever his level or job, who was not primarily concerned with his upward relations and upward communications.* Every vice-president feels that relations with the president are the real problem. And so on down to the first-line supervisor, the production foreman, or chief clerk, who is quite certain that he could get along with his men if only the "boss" and the personnel department left him alone.

This is not, as personnel people seem inclined to think, a sign of the perversity of human nature. Upward relations are properly a manager's first concern. To be a manager means sharing in the responsibility for the performance of the enterprise. A man who is not expected to take this responsibility is not a manager.

These problems of upward relations that worry the manager—the relationship to his own boss; his doubts as to what is expected of him; his difficulty in getting his point across, his program accepted, his activity given full weight; the relations with other departments and with staff people, and so forth—are all problems of managing managers.

## The Rise, Decline and Rebirth of Ford

The story of Henry Ford, his rise and decline, and of the revival of his company under his grandson, Henry Ford II, has been told so many times that it has passed into folklore. Everybody has heard

—that Henry Ford, starting with nothing in 1905, had built fifteen years later the world's largest and most profitable manufacturing enterprise;

—that the Ford Motor Company, in the early twenties, dominated and almost monopolized the American automobile market and held a leadership position in most of the other important automobile markets of the world;

—that, in addition, it had amassed, out of profits, cash reserves of a billion dollars or so;

*This will be treated further in Chapter 38, "Managerial Communications."

—that, only a few years later, by 1927, this seemingly impregnable business empire was in shambles. Having lost its leadership position and barely able to stay a poor third in the market, it lost money almost every year for twenty years or so, and remained unable to compete vigorously right through World War II; and

—that in 1944 the founder's grandson, Henry Ford II, then only twenty-six years old and without training or experience, took over, ousted two years later his grandfather's cronies in a palace coup, brought in a totally new management team and saved the company.

But it is not commonly realized that this dramatic story is far more than a story of personal success and failure. It is, above all, what one might call a controlled experiment in mismanagement.

The first Ford failed because of his firm conviction that a business did not need managers and management. All it needed, he believed, was the owner-entrepreneur with his "helpers." The only difference between Ford and most of his contemporaries in business, in the U.S. as well as abroad, was that, as in everything he did,* Henry Ford stuck uncompromisingly to his convictions. The way he applied them—e.g., by firing or sidelining any one of his "helpers," no matter how able, who dared act as a "manager," make a decision, or take action without orders from Ford—can only be described as a test of a hypothesis that ended up by fully disproving it.

In fact, what makes the Ford story unique—but also important—is that Ford could test the hypothesis, in part because he lived so long, and in part because he had a billion dollars to back his convictions. Ford's failure was not the result of personality or temperament but first and foremost a result of his refusal to accept managers and management as necessary and as grounded in task and function rather than in "delegation" from the "boss."

But Ford was by no means alone in his belief that managers are unnecessary. This is shown by the experience of two other major growth businesses of the period before World War I: Siemens in Germany and Mitsubishi in Japan.

Werner von Siemens (1816–1892) was as different a personality from Henry Ford as can be imagined. One of the nineteenth century's greatest inventors, he was a man of utmost concern and consideration for people, whether workers or fellow scientists. To this day the company he founded is characterized by a rare sense of mutual loyalty and of responsibility for people. But Siemens did not have "managers." He had "helpers" and "assistants." Growing spectacularly until the late 1870s, the company began to slow down, gradually slipped out of control, and became "unmanage-

*On Henry Ford, see my essay "Henry Ford" in my book, *Men, Ideas and Politics* (Harper & Row, 1971); English edition is called *The New Markets* (Heinemann, 1971).

able" and practically unmanaged. The English Siemens company, originally the most prosperous business of the Siemens group, was destroyed by mismanagement and had to be abandoned. When competition appeared in the late eighties—especially from the German General Electric Company (AEG) founded by Emil Rathenau in close cooperation with the American General Electric Company—Siemens, despite its long lead, rapidly lost ground in the very markets it had formerly dominated. Unlike Ford though, Siemens did not have practically unlimited financial resources. When, in 1897, five years after the founder's death, the company had to take recourse to the capital market, a banker—Georg Siemens, a cousin of Werner and by that time head of the Deutsche Bank (see Chapter 49)—used the need for money to force the founder's reluctant sons and heirs to accept a management structure and managers.

Descendants of the founder remained powerful in the company until World War II and still sit on the company's board today, but the reorganization of 1897 created managerial jobs that were grounded in task and function, and independent of the whims—and even the wishes—of the family members. Within a few years the company, which had been floundering, had regained its vigor; in the early years of the century, when the German electrical industry went through a period of shake-outs and consolidations, it was around Siemens that the new industry structure was being built. The new, professional management, brought in ten years earlier under Georg Siemens's pressure, and largely from within the company, worked out these mergers and integrated the newly acquired companies into the Siemens structure, thus ensuring for the company another forty years of leadership in Europe's electrical industry.

Yataro Iwasaki (1834–1885), the founder of Mitsubishi, was also a personality totally different from Henry Ford, and from Werner von Siemens as well. He had, to the highest degree, the faculty of attracting, developing, and using first-rate men. But, like the other two men, he did not believe in managers. In a sharp and conscious break with the Japanese tradition of the *Ie*—the "household community" in which power goes by seniority rather than ownership and in which work is done by teams*—Iwasaki insisted on the sole authority and responsibility of the owner-entrepreneur. This, to him, was "progressive" and "Western." Like Ford he was forced to incorporate his company. Like Ford he considered this a mere formality—an irksome one, to boot—and decreed that all ownership should forever be vested in one man: the head of the family. This man, and this man alone, should make all the decisions; the others should be his "assistants" and carry out his orders. Iwasaki started in 1867—right after the Meiji Restora-

---

*On this see Chie Nakane, *Japanese Society* (University of California Press, 1970), a "must" for anyone who wants to understand how Japanese organizations work.

tion —as a penniless samurai (hereditary warrior). Fifteen years later his concern was the leading industry in Japan, having outstripped the much older business powers, Mitsui and Sumitomo, whose roots went back to the seventeenth century. But by that time—comparable to Ford's situation in 1920—Mitsubishi began to slow down, to drift, and to show clear signs of incipient decay. Fortunately for the company, Iwasaki died, barely fifty years old, in 1885. His trusted associates, though sworn to uphold the constitution he had laid down and to vest full authority in the head of the family, immediately restructured and built the strongest, most truly professional and most autonomous management group in Japan, from which the family, while treated with the greatest deference, was completely excluded. And it was then that the rise and growth of Mitsubishi truly began.

But it was not only the nineteenth-century *business* leader who refused to accept managers and management. Lenin also did not accept management; and his refusal underlies basic problems and difficulties of communism.

It can be argued that Ford's personal misrule, his estrangement from reality and his increasing dependence on a secret police chief who ruled through espionage and terror were not so much traits of his personality as consequences of his doctrine. Similarly, it may well be that Stalinism, with its terror, purges, paranoid suspicions, and dependence on police informers and toadies, reflects the—inevitable—consequences of the belief that managers and management are superfluous and that the "great man" can govern big and complex organizations and structures with his assistants and helpers—that is, his courtiers.

## GM—The Countertest

In the early twenties, when Ford set out to prove that managers are not needed, Alfred P. Sloan, Jr., the newly appointed president of General Motors, put the opposite thesis to the test. GM at that time was almost crushed by the towering colossus of the Ford Motor Company and barely able to survive as a weak number two. Little more than a jerry-built financial speculation, stitched together out of small automobile companies that had been for sale because they could not stand up to Ford's competition, GM did not have one winning car in its line, no dealer organization, and no financial strength. Each of the former owners was allowed autonomy, which in effect meant that he was allowed to mismanage his former business his own way and as his own personal fief. But Sloan thought through what the business and structure of GM should be* and converted his undisci-

*On Alfred P. Sloan, Jr., see my book, *Managing for Results* and Sloan's own book, *My Years with General Motors* (Doubleday, 1964).

plined barons into a management team. Within five years GM had become
the leader in the American automobile industry and has remained the leader
ever since.

Then, twenty years later, Henry Ford's grandson put Sloan's hypothesis
to the test again. The Ford Motor Company by then was nearly bankrupt;
the entire billion dollars of cash assets it had held in the early twenties had
been poured into paying for the deficits since. As soon as young Henry Ford
II took over in 1946, he set out to do for his company what Sloan had done
for GM two decades earlier. He created a management structure and a
management team. Within five years the Ford Motor Company regained its
potential for growth and profit, both at home and abroad. It became the
main competitor to General Motors and even outstripped GM in the fast-
growing European automobile market.

## The Lesson of the Ford Story

The lesson of the Ford story is that managers and management are the
specific need of the business enterprise, its specific organ, and its basic
structure. We can say dogmatically that enterprise cannot do without
managers. One cannot argue that management does the owner's job by
delegation. Management is needed not only because the job is too big for
any one man to do himself, but because managing an enterprise is something
essentially different from managing one's own property.

Henry Ford—and Siemens and Iwasaki—failed to see the need to change
to managers and management because they believed (as the textbooks still
tell us) that a large and complex business enterprise "evolves" organically
from the small one-man shop. Of course, Ford, Siemens, and Iwasaki
started small. But the growth brought more than a change in size. At one
point quantity turned into quality. At one point they no longer ran "their
own business" but moved over into a *business enterprise*, that is, into an
organization requiring different structure and different principles—an organization requiring managers and management.

Legally, management is still seen as delegation from ownership, even in
the Soviet system. But the actual doctrine that is slowly evolving is that
management precedes and indeed outranks ownership, at least in the large
enterprise. Even total ownership of such an enterprise is dependent on
proper management. If the owner does not subordinate himself to the
enterprise's need for management his ownership—while legally unrestricted
—will in fact be curtailed, if not taken away from him.

This was, one assumes, in Georg Siemens's mind when he confronted his
young cousins with the choice between accepting management or being
ousted from control. As legal doctrine—though a nascent rather than a

clearly formulated one—it probably was first laid down by the U.S. Air Force in the early fifties in dealing with Howard Hughes and the Hughes Aircraft Company. Hughes owned the company lock, stock, and barrel. He refused to let professional managers run it and insisted on running it himself the way Ford, thirty years earlier, had run the Ford Motor Company. Thereupon the Air Force, the company's main customer, gave Hughes an ultimatum: either you put your shares into a trust and let professional management take over, or we put the company into bankruptcy and force you out altogether. Hughes retained ownership title through one of his foundations but relinquished control entirely.

The next case also concerns Howard Hughes. As all but complete owner of one of America's major airlines, TWA, he, it is alleged, subordinated TWA's interests to those of other companies of his. For an owner this is perfectly legitimate behavior; he is supposed to do with his property as he pleases. But TWA management sued Hughes for $150 million in damages. It lost the suit only in 1973 in the Supreme Court—having won it in two lower courts—on a technicality; the Supreme Court ruled that this was a matter for the Civil Aeronautics Board over which the ordinary courts had no jurisdiction. But the principle that even the owner has to act as a manager, at least in a large company, was not disputed.

The same principle also underlies the treatment of the Krupp family when the German banks came to their company's rescue in the late sixties. The company was wholly owned by the family. But the banks clearly felt that Krupp's treatment of the company as property was improper. Whereas Siemens, seventy years earlier, had still tried to maintain family ownership, the German banks in the Krupp settlement forced the family to divest themselves completely of both ownership and control.

Genetically, so to speak, management did not evolve out of the small owner-managed firm and as a result of its growth. It was designed *ab initio* for enterprises that were large and complex to begin with.

The large American railroad which covered vast distances—and which wrestled with the complex interplay between the engineering task of building a railbed, the financial task of raising very large sums of capital, and the political-relations tasks of obtaining charters, land grants, and subsidies—was the first enterprise that can be called "managed." Indeed, the management structure designed shortly after the Civil War for the first long-distance and transcontinental American railroads has essentially remained unchanged to this day. In continental Europe, at about the same time, management was designed for the first banks founded expressly to be national rather than local banks.* And in faraway Japan, the builders of the

*On this see the story of Georg Siemens and the Deutsche Bank, in Chapter 49.

Zaibatsu of the Meiji Period—Mitsui, Sumitomo, and Iwasaki's successors at Mitsubishi—using traditional Japanese approaches in a new manner, also fashioned a management system for the large and complex enterprise.

It was not until thirty or forty years later that the concept of management was transferred from the enterprise that started out large to the enterprise that had grown large. How George Siemens forced his reluctant cousins at the Siemens Electrical Company to do so in 1897 by using their need for capital as a lever has already been recounted. At about the same time Andrew Carnegie and John D. Rockefeller, Jr., introduced management into the steel and petroleum industries respectively. A little later still Pierre S. du Pont restructured the family company (E.I. du Pont de Nemours & Co.) and gave it a management, both to make it capable of growth and to preserve family control.* The management structure Pierre du Pont built in his family company between 1915 and 1920 became, a few years later, the starting point for the General Motors structure of "professional management" after the Du Ponts had acquired control of the near-bankrupt and floundering automotive conglomerate and had put Alfred P. Sloan, Jr., in as president.

It cannot be proven, but there is a high probability that the decline of Great Britain in the late nineteenth century from her position of economic world leadership was not primarily caused by technological lag but by management lag, that is, by the failure to restructure what had become large and complex enterprises on a genuine managerial foundation.

Rather than restructure their companies the British compromised. The "board" became neither a supervisory organ nor genuine management but a mixture of the two. As a result the role, function, and authority of managers was not clearly established. To see the difference one need only compare the account of the development of the British chemical industry† —the world leader in 1870, the "also ran" twenty years later—with Chandler's account of the Du Ponts. As late as 1926, when Imperial Chemical Industries (ICI) was formed by merging all large British chemical companies into one, the first "board" was both the top management organ and a mélange of wealthy amateurs representing former founder-families—without clear structure within the board or below it. The German I. G. Farben was formed in a similar fashion a few months earlier. But from the beginning the Germans took financial, family, and prestige problems out of the management structure and dumped them on a nonmanaging board of

---

*On Pierre du Pont see Alfred D. Chandler, Jr., and Stephen Salisbury, *Pierre S. du Pont and the Making of the Modern Corporation* (Harper & Row, 1971); also Alfred J. Chandler, Jr., *Strategy and Structure* (M.I.T. Press, 1962).

†W. J. Reader, *Imperial Chemical Industries: A History, vol. one 1870–1926* (Oxford University Press, 1970).

supervisors. A few members of the founding families were taken on the board of management. But they served as professional managers, that is, had a specific job, function, and authority, and were equals on a team dominated by professionals without family or ownership background.

## Management as a "Change of Phase"

The change from a business which the owner-entrepreneur can run with "helpers" to a business that requires a management is what the physicists call a "change of phase" such as the change from fluid to solid. It is a leap from one state of matter, from one fundamental structure, to another. Sloan's example shows that it can be made within one and the same organization. But Sloan's restructuring of GM also shows that the job can be done only if basic concepts, basic principles, and individual vision are changed radically.

One can compare the business which the older Ford tried to run and the business which Sloan designed to two different kinds of organisms—the insect, which is held together by a tough, hard skin, and the vertebrate animal, which has a skeleton. The English biologist D'Arcy Thompson showed that animals supported by a hard skin can reach only a certain size and complexity. Beyond this, a land animal has to have a skeleton. Yet the skeleton has not genetically evolved out of the hard skin of the insect; it is a different organ with different antecedents. Similarly, management becomes necessary when a business reaches a certain size and complexity. But management, while it replaces the "hard-skin" structure of the owner-entrepreneur, is not its successor. It is, rather, its replacement.

When does a business reach the stage at which it has to shift from "hard skin" to "skeleton"?* The line lies somewhere between 300 and 1,000 employees in size. More important, perhaps, is the increase in complexity; when a variety of tasks have all to be performed in cooperation, synchronation, and communication a business needs managers and a management. Otherwise, things go out of control; plans fail to turn into action; or, worse, different parts of the plans get going at different speeds, different times, and with different objectives and goals, and the favor of the "boss" becomes more important than performance. At this point the product may be excellent, the people able and dedicated. The boss may be—indeed often is—a man of great ability and personal power. But the business will begin to flounder, stagnate, and soon go downhill unless it shifts to the "skeleton" of managers and management structure.

Henry Ford—like the young Siemenses, Iwasaki, and Lenin—wanted no

---

*On this see also Chapters 53 and 54.

managers. But the only result was that he misdirected managers, set up their jobs improperly, created a spirit of suspicion and frustration, misorganized his company and stunted or broke management people. The only choice management has in these areas is therefore whether it will do the jobs well or badly. But the jobs themselves cannot be evaded. And whether they are being done right or not will determine largely whether the enterprise will survive and prosper or decline and ultimately fall.

# The Manager's Work and Jobs

What makes a manager is responsibility for contribution to the results of the enterprise rather than "responsibility for the work of others." It is responsibility for his own work; and there is a distinct "work of the manager," there are distinct "managerial jobs." There is a distinct way to manage managers: by objectives and self-control. There are also new requirements as we move from "middle management" to the "knowledge organization." Finally, managers have to be managed so as to engender in them a spirit of performance.

# 30

## What Makes a Manager?

*The Traditional Definition—Its Inadequacy—Manager and Member of Management—The Career Professional—Defining a Manager by Function Rather Than Power—Title, Function, and Pay of the Career Professional*

What characterizes a manager? And what defines him?

The words "manager" and "management" are slippery, to say the least. They are untranslatable into any other language. In British English they do not have the meaning they have in the United States. And even in American usage, their meaning is far from clear.

The word "manager" has no exact counterpart in German, French, Spanish, Italian, or Russian; yet the words used in these languages are as imprecise and elusive as "manager" is in American. Most people, when asked what they mean by "manager," will reply "a boss." But when the sign over the shoeshine stand in an airport reads "John Smith, Manager," everybody (at least in America) knows that this means that Mr. Smith is not the boss, i.e., not the proprietor, but a hired hand with a minimum of authority and a salary just above that of the workers who shine the shoes.

Early in the history of management a manager was defined as someone who "is responsible for the work of other people." This served a useful purpose at the time. It distinguished the manager's function from that of the "owner." It made clear that managing was a specific kind of work which could be analyzed, studied, and improved systematically. The definition focused on the essentially new, large and permanent organization emerging to perform the economic tasks of society.

Yet, the definition is not at all satisfactory. In fact, it never was. From the beginning, there were people in the enterprise, often in responsible positions, who were clearly management and yet did not manage, that is, who were not responsible for the work of other people. The treasurer of a company, the man responsible for the supply and use of money in the business, may have subordinates and in that sense be a manager in terms of the traditional definition. But clearly, the treasurer himself does most of the treasurer's job. He works with the company's underwriters, with the financial community, and so on. He is an "individual contributor," rather than a manager. But he is a member of top management.

Also, the definition focuses on the tools for a task rather than on the task itself. The man in charge of market research in a company may have a large number of people reporting to him and is thus a manager in the traditional sense. But it really makes no difference to his function and contribution whether he has a large staff, a small staff, or no staff at all. The same contribution in terms of market research and market analysis can well be made by a man to whom no one reports. He may even make a greater contribution when he is not forced to spend a great deal of his time with subordinates and on their work. He thus may make market research more effective in the business, better understood by his associates in management, and more firmly built into the company's basic business decisions and into its definition of what "our business is and should be."

In line with the traditional definition of a manager as a man who "is responsible for the work of others" we should talk of a "manager of market researchers." Instead, we always talk of a "manager of market research." This common usage is right in its intuitive understanding of what the responsibility of the managerial position is and should be, and how the incumbent should be measured.

The traditional definition has become increasingly inappropriate and a bar to effective management, effective organization, and true performance.

The most rapidly growing group in any organization, especially in today's business enterprise, are people who are management, in the sense of being responsible for contribution to and results of the enterprise.* However, they are clearly not managers in that they are not, as a rule, the bosses and responsible for the work of other people. The most rapidly growing group in business enterprise today are individual professional contributors of all kinds who work by themselves (perhaps with an assistant and a secretary) and yet have impact on the company's wealth-producing capacity, the direction of its business, and its performance.

Such people are not to be found only in technical research work, though it was here that they first emerged as a distinct group. The senior chemist

*On this see especially Chapter 35.

in the laboratory has major responsibility and makes major decisions, many of them irreversible in their impact. But so also does the man who works out and thinks through the company's organization and designs managerial jobs, whether his title be organization planner or director of management development. Here also belongs the senior cost accountant who determines the definition and allocation of costs. By defining the measurements for management, he, in effect, largely decides whether a certain product will be kept or will be abandoned. Other people in the same category are the man charged with the development and maintenance of quality standards for a company's products, the man working on the distributive system through which the company's products are being brought to the market, and the advertising director, who may be responsible for the basic promotion policy of a company, its advertising message, the media it uses, and the measurements of advertising effectiveness.

The traditional definition is responsible, in large measure, for the fact that the individual professional contributor presents a problem within the structure and a problem to himself. His title, his pay, his function, and his career opportunities are confused, ambiguous, and a cause of dissatisfaction and friction. Yet the number of these career professionals is increasing fast.

There needs to be greater flexibility in assigning people within the management group—to task forces, teams, and other organizational units which do not fit the traditional concept of a "line organization," that is, an organization in which one member is the boss, while the others are subordinates.*

Managers in the traditional sense will have to be able to move into situations where they are not superiors, indeed, into situations where they are the "juniors" to nonmanagers on a team or a task force. Conversely, career professionals without managerial function or title in the traditional sense will have to be able to be team leaders or task force leaders. The traditional separation between managers and nonmanagers will increasingly become a hindrance and inappropriate.

## The New Definition of a Manager

It is necessary and urgent, that we think through what really defines a manager and who should be considered management.

The first attempt at solving the problem, made in the early 1950s, supplemented the definition of the manager with a new definition of an "individual professional contributor"† with "parallel paths of opportunity" for both.

---

*On the team as organizational design see Chapter 45.

†The pioneer in this effort was the General Electric Company, especially its former vice-president—management services, Harold F. Smiddy, who realized the central importance of this problem and made the first attempts at solving it.

This made it possible to pay a man properly for "professional" work rather than make higher pay dependent upon promotion into a "manager's" job, that is, into a position of responsibility for the work of others.

Yet this formula has not fully solved the problem. The companies that have adopted it report that the individual professional contributor is only slightly less dissatisfied than he was before. He remains convinced that true opportunities for advancement still exist only, or at least primarily, within the administrative structure, and that one has to become a "boss" to "get ahead." Above all, the separation of the managerial world into two groups serves to emphasize the inferiority of those who do their own work as compared with those responsible for the work of others. The emphasis is still on power and authority rather than on responsibility and contribution.

Outside of the U.S. the problem may be even worse. In Japan there are no career opportunities at all for the individual contributor. Seniority forces a Japanese to become an administrator—as a result of which, for instance, the ablest newspapermen are forced to stop writing and the ablest scientists in the research labs to become "research managers" and to stop researching.

Any analysis which does not start out from the traditional definition but looks at the work itself will come to the conclusion that the traditional definition of a manager as one responsible for the work of others emphasizes a secondary, rather than a primary, characteristic.

As we will see (in the next chapter), one can define the work of a manager as planning, organizing, integrating, and measuring. The career professional—e.g., a market researcher who works by himself, or a senior cost accountant—also has to plan, to organize, and to measure his results against his objectives and expectations. He also has to integrate his work with the work of other people in the organization. He has to integrate his work into that of the unit of which he is a part. Above all, if he is to have results, he has to integrate "sideways," that is, with the people in other areas and functions who have to put his work to use.

Similarly, the "manager" has to integrate "downwards," that is, with the work of the people who report to him—which is what the traditional definition stresses. The most important relation areas in which he has to integrate the work of his unit, if it is to have any results, cut again sideways —that is, with people over whom he has no managerial control.

The essence of the first-line supervisor's job in the plant or office is the management of the people who report to him. Upward or sideways relations are secondary on that level. Yet common usage does not consider the first-line supervisor a manager. We speak of the supervisor as a "member of management," implying that he should be a manager but really is not, or only marginally so. The reason is, of course, that the first-line supervisor, whether in the factory or in the office, is not commonly expected to take much responsibility for his contribution and results. He is expected to deliver according to objectives set for him by others—in the typical mass-production plant this is all he possibly can or should do. This makes the supervisor's job ambiguous and difficult.* But the fact that we are reluctant to call the supervisor a manager, even though his job fits the traditional definition better than the jobs of people who hold higher and much more important positions in the executive hierarchy, only demonstrates that the definition accentuates the secondary, rather than the primary.

It would, therefore, seem appropriate to stress that the first criterion in identifying those people within an organization who have management responsibility is not command over people. *It is responsibility for contribution. Function rather than power has to be the distinctive criterion and the organizing principle.*

But what should these people be called? Many organizations have experimented with new definitions or have tried to give old terms a new meaning.† Perhaps the best thing is not to coin a new term, but to follow popular usage which speaks of the "management group." Within the management group, there will be people whose function includes the traditional managerial function, responsibility for the work of others. There will be others who do not carry this responsibility within their specific assignment. And there will be a third group which is somewhat ambiguous and in-between, people whose job is that of team leader or task force captain, or people who combine both the function of advisor to top management and the "conscience" of a business in a certain area, with supervisory and administrative responsibility over a staff in a given area. This is not a neat, let alone a perfect, solution. In every organization there are people who are true specialists and who, while anything but rank-and-file workers, do not see themselves as part of management either. They want to remain specialists and are not, fundamentally, much concerned with the whole of which they are a part. Their allegiance is to their technical or professional skill, rather than to their organization. The psychologist within a personnel department sees himself as a professional—that is, a member of the world of his academic specialty—rather than as an executive of this or that company (or even as a faculty member of this or that university). And so does the computer specialist.

Conversely, in many traditions other than the American, there are people

*See Chapter 21.
†In my book, *The Effective Executive*, I proposed to call these people "executives," the term to embrace both the traditional "managers" and the nonmanaging professionals with responsibility for determining the objectives of contribution and results of their work, who are expected to make decisions that affect the performance and wealth-producing potential of the entire business.

who fully accept the responsibility for their contribution but are not deemed managers, or part of management, even though they may be responsible for the work of others. An example is the German *Meister,* the highly skilled worker who has risen to leadership within his craft, who is in most cases the true "boss" within his craft area, and who yet considers himself a skilled worker rather than a manager. He corresponds, in many ways, to the noncommissioned officer in the military, the long-serving master sergeant, for instance, who within his own area, e.g., supply, is the real "boss," but who will never become an officer and does not expect to be one.

Yet though fuzzy, to define the management group by function and responsibility enables us to work out the relationship between the manager and the career professional.

## The Career Professional

The career professional—and particularly the specialist—needs a manager. His major problem is the relation of his area of knowledge and expertise to the performance and results of the entire organization. The career professional therefore has a major problem of communication. He cannot be effective unless his output becomes the input of other people. But his output is ideas and information. This requires that the users of his output understand what he is trying to say and to do. But, by the nature of his task, he will be tempted to use his own specialized jargon. Indeed, in many cases, this is the only language in which he is fluent. It is the job of the manager to make the specialist realize that he cannot become effective unless he is understood, and that he cannot be understood unless he tries to find out the needs, the assumptions, and the limitations of his "customers," the other people (also, often, specialists in their own areas) within the organization. It is the manager who has to translate the objectives of the organization into the language of the specialist, and the output of the specialist into the language of the intended user. It is the manager, in other words, on whom the specialist depends for the integration of his output into the work of others.

Yet, while the career professional needs a manager to be effective, the manager is not his boss. The manager is his "guide," his "tool," and his "marketing arm." The manager is the channel through which the career professional, and especially the true specialist, can direct his knowledge, his work, and his capacities toward joint results, and through which in turn, he finds out the needs, the capacities, and the opportunities of the enterprise of which he is a member.

In one way, indeed, the true career professional will and should be the "superior" of his manager. He must be the "teacher" and the "educator."

It is the career professional's job to teach management, to raise its vision, to show new opportunities, new horizons, new and more demanding standards. In that sense, every career professional should be expected to be the senior in his relationship to his manager and, indeed, to managers within the organization. If he does not take the responsibility for leadership within his area of expertise and knowledge he is not a true career professional. He is instead a subordinate "technician."

### Title, Function, and Pay of the Career Professional

The thorny problems of title, function, and pay of managers and career professionals cannot be completely solved. But they can be deprived, in substantial measure, of their capacity to disturb and to misdirect.

Traditionally, there has been only one line of advancement in organizations; a man could acquire higher pay and status by becoming a manager. As a result, a good many people who deserved recognition and reward did not receive them. Or, in order to give recognition and reward, people who neither wanted to manage nor were competent in doing so were put into management positions.

This system is inappropriate to the reality of today's organization, and especially of today's business enterprise. Men should be able to move freely from one kind of work to the other as they advance. We should therefore have a system of rank and title that differentiates clearly between a man's function and his standing within the organization.

In the military services the separation between rank and function has long been routine. A man is a Major and this establishes his rank. But it does not tell us whether he is in command of a battalion—that is, a manager —or whether he works in the Pentagon as a researcher—that is, as an individual professional contributor. His rank is Major; but his functional title, Battalion Commander or Communications Specialist, describes his assignment.

It might make sense to call all members of the management group executives and to have only four ranks within an organization: junior executive; executive; senior executive; and corporate executive. Then one could have a system of rank which cuts across the distinction between managerial and nonmanagerial positions. One could, then, describe a man's position, whether it be Senior Engineer—Heat Treating or Manager—Cost Control, and separate thereby rank and function. Such a system is more likely to succeed than a system which tries to build "parallel ladders."

The traditional definition of a manager also implies that he, being the superior, must get more money than the men who report to him and who are considered his "inferiors." This makes sense on the assembly line and in clerical work. It is also appropriate for the junior knowledge worker who is not yet a career professional and who is not expected to take full responsibility for his objectives and contribution. But it makes little sense for the true professional, that is, for the man who is considered to be the leader in his field within an enterprise and the pacesetter within his area. For him, the right rules are those that apply to "performers," whether in the arts or in sports.

No one finds it strange that the star baseball player gets more money than his coach or even the team's manager. Nobody is surprised that the prima donna gets more for one appearance than the opera manager may earn in the entire year. It is clearly understood by everybody that the top-flight athlete or the outstanding singer needs a manager—and yet their contributions are different and justify differential payment as a result of which, the organizationally "subordinate" receives more money than the "superior," that is, the manager.

There is even an instructive business precedent for this. When Pierre S. du Pont and Alfred P. Sloan, Jr., first attempted, in 1920, to bring order into the chaos of the General Motors Company, they set the same salary for the heads of the operating divisions as for the president, Pierre du Pont. But, at his own request, Sloan received substantially less as the operating vice-president to whom the division heads reported. The manager of a unit composed of career professionals or specialists will, of course, receive more money than most of the men in the unit, but it should not be considered unusual, let alone undesirable, for one or two "stars" of the group to receive more money than the manager. This can apply just as well to salesmen; a star salesman should be expected to make more money than the regional sales manager. It should apply in the research laboratory, and in all other areas where performance depends on individual skill, effort, and knowledge.

There should be no distinction between members of the management group who are managers and those who are career professionals in the demands made on them. The managers differ from the other professionals only in having one extra dimension in their responsibility and performance. The difference between the market research manager with a staff of fifty people and the market researcher who does the same job without any staff is in means rather than in contribution, let alone in function. Both should be held to the same demand. Both are "management" and "managers."

# 31

## The Manager and His Work

*How Does the Manager Do His Work?—The Work of the Manager—*
*Information: The Tool of the Manager—Using His Own Time—The Mana-*
*ger's Resource: Man—The One Requirement: Character*

To be a manager requires more than a title, a big office, and other outward
symbols of rank. It requires competence and performance of a high order.
But does the job demand genius? Is it done by intuition or by method? How
does the manager do his work?

A manager has two specific tasks. The first is creation of a true whole that
is larger than the sum of its parts, a productive entity that turns out more
than the sum of the resources put into it. One analogy is the conductor of
a symphony orchestra, through whose effort, vision, and leadership individual instrumental parts become the living whole of a musical performance.
But the conductor has the composer's score; he is only interpreter. The
manager is both composer and conductor.

This task requires the manager to make effective whatever strength there
is in his resources—above all, in the human resources—and neutralize
whatever there is of weakness. This is the only way in which a genuine
whole can be created.

It requires the manager to balance and harmonize major functions of the
business enterprise: managing a business; managing worker and work; and
managing the enterprise in community and society. A decision or action
that satisfies a need in one of these functions by weakening performance in
another weakens the whole enterprise. A decision or action must always be
sound in all three areas.

The task of creating a genuine whole also requires that the manager in every one of his acts consider simultaneously the performance and results of the enterprise as a whole and the diverse activities needed to achieve synchronized performance. It is here, perhaps, that the comparison with the orchestra conductor fits best. A conductor must always hear both the whole orchestra and, say, the second oboe. Similarly, a manager must always consider both the overall performance of the enterprise and, say, the market research activity needed. By raising the performance of the whole, he creates scope and challenge for market research. By improving the performance of market research, he makes possible better overall business results. The manager must simultaneously ask two double-barreled questions: What better business performance is needed and what does this require of what activities? And: What better performances are the activities capable of and what improvement in business results will they make possible?

The second specific task of the manager is to harmonize in every decision and action the requirements of immediate and long-range future. He cannot sacrifice either without endangering the enterprise.* He must, so to speak, keep his nose to the grindstone while lifting his eyes to the hills—which is quite an acrobatic feat. Or, to vary the metaphor, he can afford to say neither "We will cross this bridge when we come to it," nor "It's the next hundred years that count." He not only has to prepare for crossing distant bridges—he has to build them long before he gets there. And if he does not take care of the next hundred days, there will be no next hundred years—there may not even be a next five years. Whatever the manager does should be sound in expediency as well as in basic long-range objective and principle. And where he cannot harmonize the two time dimensions, he must at least balance them. He must calculate the sacrifice he imposes on the long-range future of the enterprise to protect its immediate interests, or the sacrifice he makes today for the sake of tomorrow. He must limit either sacrifice as much as possible. And he must repair as soon as possible the damage it inflicts. He lives and acts in two time dimensions, and he is responsible for the performance of the whole enterprise and of his own component in it.

## The Work of the Manager

Most managers spend most of their time on things that are not "managing." A sales manager makes a statistical analysis or placates an important customer. A foreman repairs a tool or fills out a production report. A manufacturing manager designs a new plant layout or tests new materials.

*On this see also Chapters 4 and 10.

A company president works through the details of a bank loan or negotiates a big contract—or spends hours presiding at a dinner in honor of long-service employees. All these things pertain to a particular function. All are necessary and have to be done well.

But they are apart from the work which every manager does whatever his function or activity, whatever his rank and position, work which is common to all managers and peculiar to them. We can apply to the job of the manager the systematic analysis of scientific management. We can isolate that which a man does because he is a manager. We can divide it into its constituent operations. And a man can improve his performance as a manager by improving his performance of these constituent activities.

There are five basic operations in the work of the manager. Together they result in the integration of resources into a viable growing organism.

A manager, in the first place, sets objectives. He determines what the objectives should be. He determines what the goals in each area of objectives should be. He decides what has to be done to reach these objectives. He makes the objectives effective by communicating them to the people whose performance is needed to attain them.

Second, a manager organizes. He analyzes the activities, decisions, and relations needed. He classifies the work. He divides it into manageable activities and further divides the activities into manageable jobs. He groups these units and jobs into an organization structure. He selects people for the management of these units and for the jobs to be done.

Next, a manager motivates and communicates. He makes a team out of the people that are responsible for various jobs. He does that through the practices with which he works. He does it in his own relations to the men with whom he works. He does it through his "people decisions" on pay, placement, and promotion. And he does it through constant communication, to and from his subordinates, and to and from his superior, and to and from his colleagues.

The fourth basic element in the work of the manager is measurement. The manager establishes yardsticks—and few factors are as important to the performance of the organization and of every man in it. He sees to it that each man has measurements available to him which are focused on the performance of the whole organization and which, at the same time, focus on the work of the individual and help him do it. He analyzes, appraises, and interprets performance. As in all other areas of his work, he communicates the meaning of the measurements and their findings to his subordinates, to his superiors, and to colleagues.

Finally, a manager develops people, including himself.

Every one of these categories can be divided further into subcategories, and each of the subcategories could be discussed in a book of its own. Moreover, every category requires different qualities and qualifications.

Setting objectives, for instance, is a problem of balances: a balance between business results and the realization of the principles one believes in; a balance between the immediate needs of the business and those of the future; a balance between desirable ends and available means. Setting objectives clearly requires analytical and synthesizing ability.

Organizing, too, requires analytical ability. For it demands the most economical use of scarce resources. But it deals with human beings, and therefore stands under the principle of justice and requires integrity. Analytical ability and integrity are similarly required for the development of people.

The skill needed for motivating and communicating is primarily social. Instead of analysis, integration and synthesis are needed. Justice dominates as the principle, economy is secondary. And integrity is of much greater importance than analytical ability.

Measuring requires, first and foremost, analytical ability. But it also demands that measurement be used to make self-control possible rather than abused to control people from the outside and above—that is, to dominate them. It is the common violation of this principle that largely explains why measurement is the weakest area in the work of the manager today. As long as measurements are abused as a tool of control (for instance, as when measurements are used as a weapon of an internal secret police that supplies audits and critical appraisals of a manager's performance to the boss without even sending a carbon copy to the manager himself) measuring will remain the weakest area in the manager's performance.*

Setting objectives, organizing, motivating and communicating, measuring, and developing people are formal, classifying categories. Only a manager's experience can bring them to life, concrete and meaningful. But because they are formal, they apply to every manager and to everything he does as a manager. They can therefore be used by every manager to appraise his own skill and performance and to work systematically on improving himself and his performance as a manager.

Being able to set objectives does not make a man a manager, any more than the ability to tie a small knot in a confined space makes a man a surgeon. But without ability to set objectives a man cannot be an adequate manager, just as a man cannot do good surgery without tying small knots. And as a surgeon becomes a better surgeon by improving his knot-tying skill, so a manager becomes a better manager by improving his skill and performance in all categories of his work.

*On this see also Chapter 39.

### The Manager's Resource: Man

The manager works with a specific resource: man. And the human being is a unique resource requiring peculiar qualities in whoever attempts to work with it.

"Working" the human being always means developing him. The direction which this development takes decides whether the human being—both as a man and as a resource—will become more productive or cease, ultimately, to be productive at all. This applies, as cannot be emphasized too strongly, not alone to the man who is being managed but also to the manager. Whether he develops his subordinates in the right direction, helps them to grow and become bigger and richer persons, will directly determine whether he himself will develop, will grow or wither, become richer or become impoverished, improve or deteriorate.

One can learn certain skills in managing people—for instance, the skill to lead a conference or to conduct an interview. One can set down practices that are conducive to development—in the structure of the relationship between manager and subordinate, in a promotion system, in the rewards and incentives of an organization. But when all is said and done, developing men still requires a basic quality in the manager which cannot be created by supplying skills or by emphasizing the importance of the task. It requires integrity of character.

There is tremendous stress these days on liking people, helping people, getting along with people, as qualifications for a manager. These alone are never enough. In every successful organization there is one boss who does not like people, who does not help them, and who does not get along with them. Cold, unpleasant, demanding, he often teaches and develops more men than anyone else. He commands more respect than the most likable man ever could. He demands exacting workmanship of himself as well as of his men. He sets high standards and expects that they will be lived up to. He considers only what is right and never who is right. And though often himself a man of brilliance, he never rates intellectual brilliance above integrity in others. The manager who lacks these qualities of character—no matter how likable, helpful, or amiable, no matter even how competent or brilliant—is a menace and should be adjudged "unfit to be a manager and a gentleman."

What a manager does can be analyzed systematically. What a manager has to be able to do can be learned (though perhaps not always taught). But one quality cannot be learned, one qualification that the manager cannot acquire but must bring with him. It is not genius; it is character.

# 32

# Design and Content of Managerial Jobs

*The Indian Civil Service—Managers Must Manage—The Common Mistakes—The Job That Is Too Small to Grow In—Satisfaction through Promotion Rather Than Performance—The Importance of Age Balance—The Nonjob of the "Assistant to"—The Busy Nonjobs of "Meeting" and "Traveling"—Titles in Lieu of Function—The "Widow-Maker" Job—Should a Job Fit the Person or the Person Fit the Job?—"Style" and Substance—The Span of Managerial Relationships—The Fourfold Definition of a Manager's Job—The Manager's Authority—The Manager, His Superior, His Subordinates, and the Enterprise*

Politically, the history of the British rule of India is a history of muddle, indecision, lack of direction and, in the last analysis, failure. What kept the British in control and power for two hundred years was, in part, India's weakness and disunity. But above all, the British stayed in power because of a supreme administrative accomplishment: the Indian Civil Service. In its greatest period, the second half of the nineteenth century, it never numbered more than a thousand men. Most were very young, mere lads in their early twenties, for life expectancy was brutally short for the white man in India's hostile climate, in which malaria and dysentery were endemic and cholera an annual visitor.

Most of these young men of the alien race who administered the huge subcontinent were stationed in total isolation in small villages or on dusty crossroads in which they did not see for months on end anyone who spoke their language and shared their concerns. Only a few survived long enough to retire, with modest pensions, to the England whence they had come and of which they always dreamed.

These young men who administered British India were rather dull and uninteresting. After a short apprenticeship, they were put into an assignment of their own to sink or swim.* These men were younger sons of poor country parsons, with no prospects at home and little standing in English society. Their pay was low; and such opportunities for loot or gain as their predecessors had enjoyed in the swashbuckling days of the East India Company a hundred years earlier had, by 1860, been completely eliminated by both law and custom.

These untrained, not very bright, and totally inexperienced youngsters ran districts comparable in size and population to small European countries. And they ran them practically all by themselves with a minimum of direction and supervision from the top. Some, of course, became casualties and broke under the strain, falling victim to alcohol, to native women or —the greatest danger of them all—to sloth. But most of them did what they were expected to do, and did it reasonably well. They gave India, for the first time in its long and tragic history, peace, a measure of freedom from famine, and a little security of life, worship, and property. They administered justice impartially and, at least as far as they themselves were concerned, honestly and without corruption. They collected taxes, by and large, impartially and equitably. They did not make policy; and in the end they foundered because they had none. But they administered, and administered well.†

This remarkable administrative achievement, the achievement of a middle management which, for two hundred long years, could in large measure offset the top-management failure of the system—or rather, the fact that there was no top management—rested on exceedingly simple foundations.

The jobs the young men were assigned were big and challenging. There was enough scope in each of them to keep even a good man interested and occupied for many years. The job was the young man's own job, and not a job as an "assistant to" anybody. He was accountable. He was responsible. And it was up to him to organize the job as he saw fit. Performance standards were high and uncompromising. A young, basically untrained and unprepared amateur was expected to give perfect justice; to be totally impartial; to maintain public order, safety on the roads and in the villages, and religious and civil peace. And he had to do this by persuasion, by the

---

*Leonard Woolf, who served as a young district commissioner in Ceylon in the early years of this century, has given the best picture—both of the isolation and of the challenges of the life—in one volume of his autobiography, *Growing* (Harcourt, Brace, 1962).

†The most perceptive book I know on the British in India, Philip Woodruff's *The Men Who Ruled India* (two volumes, St. Martin's Press, 1954), makes the point that the basic failure of the British was their belief in the "philosopher king," that is, their belief that administration could suffice and could take the place of policy, decision, and direction.

authority of his own person and by his mere presence; to have to invoke force, for instance to call in the military, was considered failure. And while the individual job was anonymous, the Service had high pride in itself and a deep commitment to standards and mission. It was imbued with the highest spirit.

A manager's job should be based on a task that has to be done to attain the company's objectives. It should always be a real job—one that makes a visible and, if possible, measurable contribution to the success of the enterprise. It should have the broadest rather than the narrowest scope and authority. The manager should be directed and controlled by the objectives of performance rather than by his boss.

The activities that have to be performed and the contributions that have to be made to attain the company's objectives should always determine what managerial jobs are needed. A manager's job exists because the task facing the enterprise demands its existence—and for no other reason. The job has to have its own authority and its own responsibility. *For managers must manage.*

The job should always have managerial scope and proportions. Since a manager is someone who takes responsibility for, and contributes to, the final results of the enterprise, the job should always embody the maximum challenge, carry the maximum responsibility, and make the maximum contribution.

## Common Mistakes in Designing Managerial Jobs

There is no formula that will guarantee the right job design for a managerial job. Yet six common mistakes that impair the effectiveness of manager and managerial organization can be avoided.

1. The most common mistake is to design the job so small that a good man cannot grow. Any managerial job is, in all likelihood, a terminal job —that is, a job on which the incumbent will stay until he retires. Even in rapidly growing organizations this is the rule rather than the exception.

The number of jobs at the top is inevitably far smaller than the number of jobs at the bottom. Out of every ten men on a given organizational level, no more than two or three can normally expect even one promotion. The rest are likely to stay where they are. They may get a bigger title and, as a rule, more money. But what they do is unlikely to change a great deal.

If a job is designed so small that the incumbent can learn everything about it in a few years, the majority of managers will be frustrated, bored, and no longer really working. They will, so to speak, "retire on the job." They will resist any change, any innovation, any new idea, for change can only be a change for the worse for them and threaten their security. Knowing very well that they are not actually contributing any more, they are fundamentally insecure.

Managerial jobs should, therefore, be designed so as to enable a man to grow, to learn, and to develop for many years to come. There is little harm, as a rule, in a job that is designed too big. This mistake shows up soon and can easily be corrected. A job that is too small, however, is an insidious, slow poison which paralyzes both the man and the organization.

All managerial jobs should be designed to provide satisfaction through performance. They should in themselves challenge and reward. If the main satisfaction of the job is promotion, the job itself has lost significance and meaning. And since the majority of men in managerial positions are bound to be disappointed in their hopes for promotion—by arithmetic rather than by organization politics—it is unwise to focus on promotion whether in compensation structure, in recognition, or in manager development. The emphasis should always be on the job itself rather than on the next job.

In fact, there are few things quite as dangerous as an organization in which promotions are so rapid as to become the accepted reward for doing a decent job. When this boom comes to an end, as all booms do sooner or later, entire groups are bound to become disgruntled. The men who rose fast but did not quite make it to the top will find themselves boxed in behind men not much older than they are, who got to the top by the sheer accident of having started in the organization a little earlier. The men who entered the organization just before the boom peaked will have expectations based on the careers of their seniors, which are bound to be disappointed.

An extreme example is the situation of some of the large New York commercial banks. Very few young people were hired in the banking industry in the thirties and forties when commercial banks in New York were shrinking rather than expanding. When the banking business expanded again after World War II, a series of mergers (such as the one between the Chase Bank and the Bank of the Manhattan Company, which created the Chase Manhattan; or that between the National City Bank and the First National Bank of New York, which created the First National City) actually created a surplus of managers. By the early fifties, however, large numbers of the men, who had started before 1929, reached retirement age, and the banks began to hire large numbers of youngsters, fresh out of college or graduate business school. Within seven or eight years many of them rose to positions of substantial pay and exalted title such as vice-president and senior vice-president. Before they were thirty large numbers of these "young comers" reached, in other words, what must be their terminal position. Yet —in large part because these young men did not have much experience— these jobs, whatever the big title and the good salary, are quite limited in scope and authority. By the time they reach forty, these men are going to be bored, cynical, frustrated, and no longer excited about the job and its challenge.

A company that is expanding rapidly is well-advised to bring into important positions a few seasoned and older outsiders, who have made a career elsewhere. Otherwise it is bound to create expectations among its own young managers, which, a few years later, it must frustrate.

## The Importance of Age Balance

Another important reason why jobs and a job structure focused on rapid promotion are to be avoided is that they result in an unbalanced age structure. Both an age structure that is overbalanced on the side of youth and one overbalanced on the side of age create serious organizational turbulence.

The management structure needs continuity and self-renewal. There must be continuity so that the organization does not have to replace all of a sudden a large number of experienced but old managers with new and untried men. And there has to be enough "managerial metabolism" so that new ideas and new faces can assert themselves. A management group that is of the same age is a management group headed for crisis. Yet the management group that is uniformly old may be preferable to the one that is uniformly too young. At least, the crisis comes sooner and is over faster.

2. Worse even than the job that is too small is the job that is not really a job, the job of the typical "assistant to."

The managerial job must have specific objectives and a specific purpose and function. A manager must be able to make a contribution which can be identified. He must be accountable.

But the typical assistant does not have a job that can make a contribution. He cannot be held accountable and his function, purpose, and objectives cannot be identified. He is a "helper" who does whatever the boss thinks he needs done or whatever the assistant can "sell" to the boss. Such a job corrupts. The holder becomes either a wire-puller who abuses his intimacy with an important executive or a toady who tries to make his career by licking his boss's boots. The assistant position also corrupts the organization. No one ever knows what the role, authority, and actual power of the assistant are. As a rule, other managers will flatter him, use him, and exploit his insecurity of tenure.

This does not mean that the title "assistant" has to be eschewed—the reality should be avoided.

Also, a specific, detailed assignment for a young manager may be excellent training. But, preferably, it should be limited in time; after finishing one such special assignment a man should normally go back to a regular managerial job.

3. Managing is work. But it is not, by itself, full-time work. The way to design a managerial job is to combine "managing" with "working," that is, responsibility for a specific function or job of one's own. As a rule, the manager should be both a manager and an individual career professional.

A manager should have enough to do—otherwise he is likely to try to do his subordinates' work for them. The common complaint that managers do not "delegate" usually means that managers do not have enough to do and therefore take on the job the subordinate should be doing. But also, it is rather frustrating not to have work of one's own—especially for people who have grown up in the habit of work. And it is not particularly desirable for a man not to have a job of his own. He soon loses the sense of workmanship and the respect for hard work without which, however, a manager is likely to do more harm than good. A manager should be a "working boss" rather than a "coordinator."

4. As far as possible, a manager's job should be designed so that it can be done by one man working by himself and with the people in the unit which he manages. It is a mistake to design a job so that it requires continuous meetings, continuous "cooperation" and "coordination." There is no need, especially not in managerial jobs, to provide for more "human relations." The job by its very nature requires far more human relations than most people are capable of. And one can either work or meet. One cannot do both at the same time.

Another mistake that is fairly common—and usually unnecessary—is to design a job in which the incumbent has to spend a great deal of time traveling. Just as one cannot meet and work at the same time, one cannot travel and work at the same time. Person-to-person and face-to-face meetings with colleagues, associates, subordinates, customers, and superiors are absolutely essential. There is no substitute. But it is far better to spend a substantial amount of time once every two years with the managers and the main customers of a subsidiary company than to "commute"—that is, leave New York on Tuesday, spend Wednesday in Paris, and be back on the job in New York on Thursday. This means only that no work gets done for four days: one needs, after all, at least one day to recover from this futile attempt to be in two places at once.

5. Titles should never be used as rewards, let alone to cover up lack of function. Titles "in lieu of a raise" are not nearly as bad, nor as common, as titles "in lieu of a job."

An example is the large commercial bank, both in the United States and in Germany. In the United States everybody has to be a vice-president or at least an officer. In Germany everybody has to be a Herr Direktor. There are reasons for this. The customer of a bank, say, the head of a small business, will not discuss his financial problems with anybody but an officer. But this also deforms. It makes those who do not get the title, for instance because their job does not entail close customer contact, exceedingly dissatisfied. It adds greatly to the dissatisfaction of people who reach the exalted title of vice-president at an early age and then find that they are locked into the same humdrum routine for the rest of their working lives.

One reason for the misuse of title has been discussed in Chapter 30: the tradition in business (but also in government) to use the identification of function (e.g., manager of market research) as indicator of rank. Another common reason is the narrowness of salary ranges under many wage and salary plans; in order to give a man the raise he has earned by performance it is necessary under these plans to pretend that he has been promoted to a different and bigger job. Finally, the traditional limitation of career opportunities in business to managerial positions often leads to inventing a fancy and managerial-sounding title (e.g., Coordinator of Materials Planning for a senior purchasing clerk) for an experienced and accomplished specialist, who continues, of course, to do precisely what he has been doing all along.

The rule should be: for first-rate work we pay—and pay well. But we change title only when a man's function, position, and responsibility change.*

Titles do create expectations. They do imply rank and responsibility. To use them as empty gestures—that is, as substitutes for rank and responsibility—is asking for trouble.

6. Finally, jobs that are "widow-makers" should be rethought and restructured. In the heyday of the great sailing ships, around 1850, just before the coming of steam, every shipping company had a "widow-maker" on its hands once in a while. This was a ship which, for reasons nobody could figure out, tended to get out of control and kill people. After it had done this a few times a prudent shipowner pulled the ship out of service and broke it up, no matter how much money he had invested in it. Otherwise, he soon found himself without captains or mates.

In many companies there are jobs which manage to defeat one good man after the other—without any clear reason why. These jobs seem to be logical, seem to be well constructed, seem to be do-able—yet nobody seems to be able to do them. If a job has defeated, in a row, two men who in their previous assignments have done well, it should be restructured. It then

---

*I would exempt from the rule "honorifics" that primarily bespeak seniority such as "junior" and "senior," especially for individual career professionals but would then strongly insist that such titles be used *only* to denote seniority—more or less in the fashion in which the title monsignor in the Catholic Church (at least in the U.S.) is almost automatically bestowed on any man who has served twenty-five years in the priesthood and stayed out of trouble.

usually becomes clear, though only by hindsight, what was wrong with the job in the first place.

A typical "widow-maker" has been the job of international vice-president in a large American company. Nobody seems to know why the job should not work, but in the great majority of cases one good man after the other fails in it. The reason is usually that the company has outgrown the volume of business which justifies treating "international" as a stepchild. (On this, see Chapter 59, "The Multinational Corporation.") But this becomes clear only in retrospect, after one has restructured the job and has found the man —or men—who can do the work.

In a good many consumer-goods companies—Procter & Gamble is an example—there is a top marketing manager and a top promotion and advertising manager, both members of the company's top management. Logically this should be one position since promotion and advertising are part of marketing. These companies have learned, however, that combining these two functions into one job usually means frustrating and defeating a good man. The reason, as one consumer-goods executive once put it, is that "marketing aims at moving goods, promotion aims at moving people." These two aims require men of different temperament who look at their work differently and apply different measurements of performance to themselves and to their units.

The "widow-maker" job is usually the result of accident. One man who somehow combined in himself temperamental characteristics which are not usually found in one person, created the job and acquitted himself well. In other words, what looked like a logical job was an accident of personality rather than the result of a genuine function. But one cannot replace personality.

## Job Structure and Personality

The abuse of titles and the "widow-maker" job relate closely to one of the most hotly debated issues with respect to managerial jobs and managerial structure: Should the organization be structured so that jobs fit people? Or should the organization be "functional," with people fitted to jobs?

As commonly propounded, this is a pseudoproblem. Quite obviously, people have to fill the jobs, and therefore jobs have to fit people. We will indeed have to design jobs that really fit people, answer their needs, and fulfill their expectations. We will, increasingly, see "organization planning" in large companies, that is, attempts to make jobs fit people and serve them.

There is also no doubt that organization structure has to be impersonal and task-focused. Otherwise it is impossible to have continuity and to have people succeed each other. If the job is designed for an individual rather than for a task, it has to be restructured every time there is a change in the incumbent. And, as experienced managers know, one cannot restructure *one* job. There is a true "domino effect," a true chain reaction. Restructuring a job usually means restructuring a score of jobs, moving people around, and upsetting everybody.

There is one exception: the exceedingly rare, truly exceptional man for whose sake the rule should be broken.

Alfred P. Sloan, Jr., the architect of General Motors, was adamant that jobs had to be impersonal and task-focused.* But he made one exception to accommodate one of the great inventors of our century, Charles F. Kettering. Kettering was an exceedingly difficult man, and also a man who disregarded every single organizational rule. Yet his inventions, from the self-starter to the redesign of the diesel engine, were of major importance. Sloan offered to set up Kettering as an independent researcher. But Kettering wanted to be vice-president and a "big businessman." Sloan gave in, but the moment Kettering retired, the job was redesigned—from "resident genius" to manager of a large research laboratory.

The design of a job has to start out with the task, but it also has to be a design that can accommodate people with different temperaments, habits, and behavior patterns. This is a major reason why managerial jobs ought to be designed big rather than small. A job has to be big enough so that a good man can find within it his own satisfaction and achievement, his own way and method of working.

The Catholic Church offers an instructive lesson. The basic manager within the Catholic Church is the bishop. It has long been the custom to rotate temperaments in filling a bishop's See. If the incumbent is a pastor, concerned primarily with the care of souls, he may be succeeded by a theologian or by an administrator. In turn, a first-rate administrator is likely to be succeeded by a man whose main emphasis is on his priestly function, and so on. The Catholic Church learned long ago that the three qualifications—those of pastor, theologian, and administrator—are unlikely to be found in one person. Yet all three are needed to keep a diocese alive. Hence the bishop's job is designed very big indeed—big enough for a good man to make of it what suits him. And the standard of accomplishment is set by rotating the temperaments that occupy the See in succession.

"A job should be small enough so that a good man can get his arms around it" is a common saying. It is the wrong rule. "A job should be specific enough so that a good man can go to work on it, but so big that he can't get his arms around it" is the right rule.

*See Sloan's book, *My Years with General Motors.*

"Style" should never be a consideration, either in designing a managerial job or in filling it. The only requirement of a managerial job, and the only test of the incumbent, is performance. Every organization needs a clear understanding of the kind of behavior that is not acceptable. There must be a clear definition of the nonpermissible action, especially toward people, whether inside the business, i.e., employees, or outside, i.e., suppliers and customers. But within these limits a man should have the fullest freedom to do the job the way it best suits his temperament and personality.

"Style" is packaging. The only substance is performance.

## The Span of Managerial Relationships

In discussing how big a manager's job should be, the textbooks often start out with the observation that one man can supervise only a very small number of people—the so-called span of control. This in turn leads to that deformation of management: levels upon levels which impede cooperation and communication, stifle the development of tomorrow's managers, and erode the meaning of the management job.

In the first place, the principle of the span of control is rarely cited properly. It is not how many people report to a manager that matters. It is how many people *who have to work with each other* report to a manager. What counts are the number of relationships rather than the number of men.

The president of a company who has reporting to him a number of senior executives, each concerned with a major function, should indeed keep the number of direct subordinates to a fairly low number—between eight and twelve is probably the limit. For these men—the chief financial officer, the head of manufacturing, the head of marketing, and so on—have to work every day with each other and with the company's president. If they do not work together, they do not work at all. Therefore, the president is engaged in a great many relationships even though the number of direct subordinates may be quite small.

By contrast, a regional vice-president of Sears, Roebuck can—and does—have several hundred store managers report to him. Each store is discrete and autonomous. There is no need whatever for interaction between two different stores. All the stores do the same kind of work and have the same job. They can all be appraised and measured by the same yardsticks. Theoretically, there is no limit to the number of store managers a regional vice-president of Sears can manage and supervise. The limit is set by geography rather than by the span of control.

The second shortcoming of the span of control argument is that it assumes that a manager's main relationship is downward. But this is only one dimension. The manager, in the traditional definition as the man responsible for the work of other people, has a downward relationship, to be sure. But every manager and every career professional also has a superior. Indeed many managers, no matter what the organization chart says, have more than one boss. And the upward relationship to the superior is at least equal in importance to the downward relationship to the subordinates. Most important, however, managers and career professionals always have sideways relations, relationships with people who are neither their subordinates nor their superiors and, indeed, stand in no relationship of authority and responsibility to them. Yet these relationships are crucial both for the manager's own ability to do his work, and for the effectiveness of his work.

For example, the most important relationships for managers and career professionals in accounting are not the relationships to the company controller or to the junior accountants. They are their relationships to operating managers. The accounting manager's contribution depends on the ability and willingness of the operating managers to use as information and input what accounting produces. Conversely, the accounting manager's ability to perform depends on the willingness and ability of the operating managers to furnish him the information he needs. Yet accounting people, as a rule, slight this relationship no matter how much lip service they may pay to it.

Similarly, the basic weakness of a good many research managers and scientists is the neglect of their sideways relationships, especially their relationships with the marketing people. As a result, research quite often is uninformed regarding the needs and opportunities of the company and, conversely, valuable results of research remain unused because the marketing people simply do not understand what research is trying to accomplish.

What is needed, therefore, is to replace the concept of the span of control with another and more relevant concept: the span of managerial relationships.

We do not know how wide this span can be—though, assuredly, there are limits. But we do know that the span of managerial relationships is crucial in the design of a managerial job.

In the first place, these relationships define the place of the manager within the managerial structure. Second, they very largely define what his job is—for these relationships are a crucial and essential part of the job content. Finally, they do set limits—since a job that is only "relationships" and no "work" is not a job at all. In designing managerial jobs it is as important to think through the managerial relationships and to make sure that they do not exceed an individual's grasp as it is to think through the specific function.

Again it is better to make the span of managerial responsibilities too wide than too narrow. This goes for the number of subordinates with whom a manager works and who constitute his unit and his team. It goes also for his upward relationships. The only area in which I would strongly counsel to keep rather tight limits on the span of managerial relationships are the sideways relationships. A managerial job, ideally, should have a small number of sideways relationships—every one of them of prime importance, both for the functioning of the entire organization and for the achievement of the manager's own function and objectives. It is not only that these are time-consuming relationships. If there are too many, they will be treated superficially, will not be thought through, and will not be worked at. And the common weakness of many organizations is, by and large, the lack of adequate concern for, and adequate work on, sideways relationships.

## Defining a Manager's Job

A manager's job is defined in several ways.

1. There is first the specific function, the job itself. This should always be a permanent, continuing job, one that is considered, in the light of the best available knowledge at the time, to be needed for a good long time to come. An example would be manager of market research or manufacturing manager. Both obviously are jobs which will have to be done for the foreseeable future.

2. But the functional definition of the job, which is what is expressed in the typical job description or position guide, does not define the specific contribution which a specific manager is expected to make. While the function is, at least in intent, permanent, there are assignments "here and now" which are what the enterprise and the manager's boss should hold the man accountable for. They contribute the second definition of a managerial position and job.

As I have said elsewhere, every manager should ask himself the question at least once a year, and always when taking on a new job: "What specific contribution can I and my unit make which, if done really well, would make a substantial difference to the performance and results of my company?"*

The position guide and job description are, so to speak, the mission statement of a managerial job. They correspond to the definition of "what is our business and what should it be" for the enterprise as a whole. The assignments are the objectives and goals and therefore need specific targets, a deadline, a clear statement of who is accountable, and a built-in measurement by feedback from results.

It is the mark of a performing manager that these assignments always exceed the scope of the job as outlined in the job description. One can only codify what has already been done; and a job description is codification.

*In my book, *The Effective Executive.*

What needs to be done to make the future always exceeds and goes beyond what has been done in the past.

3. A managerial job is defined by relationships—upward, downward, and sideways.

4. It is finally defined by the information needed for the job and by a manager's place in the information flow.

Every manager should ask himself: "What information do I need to do my job and where do I get it?" He should make sure that whoever has to provide that information understands the manager's needs—not only in terms of what is needed but also how it is needed.

This is particularly important today, when "management information" means increasingly "computer." The basic problem with the computer in business is not that computer technicians do not understand the managers' needs. It is that the managers do not take the time and trouble to think through their needs and to communicate them to the computer people.* How the computer people satisfy the needs of the manager is their business. What the needs are is the manager's business. To expect the computer people to define the information needs of the managers is abdication.

Managers need to think through the question "And who depends on information from me, and in what form, upward, downward, and sideways?"

Each of these four definitions of the managerial job is only a partial definition. All four are needed to define the manager's job—just as one triangulates a position on a map.

These four definitions which "triangulate" a manager's job are the manager's own responsibility. He should be expected to write his own job description; to work out his own proposal for the results and contributions for which he and his unit should be accountable; to work out and think through his relationships; and finally to define both his information needs and his information contribution. Indeed, responsibility for thinking through the four dimensions of his job is a manager's first responsibility, of which he should never be relieved. His superior has both the duty and the responsibility to approve or to disapprove what the individual manager proposes. But the responsibility for thinking and proposing is the manager's. There is no difference between a "managing" job, i.e., one with direct responsibility for the work of other people, and a job as a career professional.

## The Manager's Authority

That each manager's job be given the broadest possible scope and authority is nothing but a rephrasing of the rule that decisions be pushed down

*On this see also Chapters 38 and 40.

the line as far as possible and be taken as close as possible to the action to which they apply. In its effects, however, this requirement leads to sharp deviations from the traditional concept of delegation from above.

What activities and tasks the enterprise requires is worked out at the top. The analysis begins with the desired end product: the objectives of business performance and business results. From these the analysis determines step by step what work has to be performed.

But in organizing the manager's job we have to work from the bottom up. We have to begin with the activities on the "firing line"—the jobs responsible for the actual output of goods and services, for the final sale to the customer, for the production of blueprints and engineering drawings.

The managers on the firing line have the basic management jobs—the ones on whose performance everything else ultimately rests. Seen this way, the jobs of higher management are derivative, are, in the last analysis, aimed at helping the firing-line manager do his job. Viewed structurally and organically, it is the firing-line manager in whom all authority and responsibility center; only what he cannot do himself passes up to higher management. He is, so to speak, the gene of organization in which all higher organs are prefigured and out of which they are developed.

Quite obviously there are real limits to the decisions the firing-line manager can or should make, and to the authority and responsibility he should have.

He is limited as to the extent of his authority. A production foreman has no business changing a salesman's compensation. A regional sales manager has no authority in somebody else's region, etc. A manager is also limited with respect to the kind of decision he can make. Clearly, he should not make decisions that affect other managers. He should not alone make decisions that affect the whole business and its spirit. It is only elementary prudence, for instance, not to allow any manager to make by himself and without review a decision on the career and future of one of his subordinates.

The firing-line manager should not be expected to make decisions which he cannot make. A man responsible for immediate performance does not have the time, for instance, to make long-range decisions. A production man lacks the knowledge and competence to work out a pension plan or a medical program. These decisions certainly affect him and his operations; he should know them, understand them, indeed participate as much as is humanly possible in their preparation and formulation. But he cannot make them. Hence he cannot have the authority and responsibility for them; for authority and responsibility should always be task-focused. This applies all through the management hierarchy up to the chief executive himself.

There is one simple rule for setting limitations on the decisions a manager is authorized to make. The management charter of General Electric's Lamp Division, in paraphrasing the U.S. Constitution, expresses it by saying: "All authority not expressly and in writing reserved to higher management is granted to lower management." This is the opposite of the old Prussian idea of a citizen's rights: "Everything that is not expressly ordered is forbidden." In other words, the decisions which a manager is not entitled to make within the extent of his task should always be spelled out; for all others he should be supposed to have authority and responsibility.

## The Manager, His Superiors, His Subordinates, and the Enterprise

The manager's relationship to his superior and his relationship to his subordinate are two-way relationships. Both are formal and informal relationships of authority as well as of information. Both are relationships of mutual dependence.*

Every manager has the task of contributing what his superior's unit needs to attain its objectives. Every manager should think through what he and his unit need to do—and in what manner—to make his superior perform and achieve.

The manager has responsibilities downward, to his subordinates. He has first to make sure that they know and understand what is demanded of them. He has to help them set their own objectives. Then he has to help them to reach these objectives. He is responsible for their getting the tools, the staff, the information they need. He has to help them with advice and counsel, and, if need be, to teach them how to do better. If a one-word definition of this downward relationship be desired, "assistance" would come closest.

The objectives of a managerial unit should always consist of the performance that it has to contribute to the success of the enterprise. Objectives should always and exclusively focus upward.

But the objectives of the manager who heads the units include what he himself has to do to help his subordinates attain their objectives. The vision of a manager should always be upward—toward the enterprise as a whole. But his responsibility runs downward as well—to the men on his team. That his relationship toward them be clearly understood as duty toward them and as responsibility for making them perform and achieve rather than as "supervision" is a central requirement for organizing the manager's unit effectively.

---

*This Japan understands much better than the West does, if only because Japan did not take its concepts of organization from the military, as we did in the West. On this see Chie Nakarne, *op. cit.*

The final duty of the manager is toward the enterprise. For his job and function are grounded in the objective needs of the enterprise rather than in title or delegation of power.

Each manager, therefore, has to derive from the objectives of the enterprise the definition of his own objectives and those of the unit he heads.

The discussion in this chapter has focused on the manager in business enterprise. But everything said here applies just as much to the manager in the public-service institution, and especially to the manager in the government agency. He needs a job big enough for a good man to grow in. He needs satisfaction through performance rather than through promotion or title. His job needs to be designed around job and position; assignments; relationships; and information needs. He needs authority to do his task. And he has to derive his own objectives from those of the institution he serves.

Indeed, as has been said before (in Chapters 11 through 14), the manager in the public-service institution needs proper job design, proper job content, and proper job structure even more than the manager in a business. Yet, few public-service institutions seem to pay much attention to managerial jobs; their emphasis tends to be on title rather than on function, on procedure rather than on performance. The design of truly managerial jobs is the first—but may also be the biggest—step toward improving both performance and morale in public-service institutions.

# 33

## Developing Management and Managers

*The Management Development Boom—Why Management Development and Manager Development are Needed—What They Are Not—The Two Dimensions of Development—Designing the Jobs and Skills for Tomorrow—Self-Development of the Individual—The Role of Company and Superior in Self-Development*

The years since 1950 have seen a veritable management development boom within the wider management boom. In the mid-forties, when I first became interested in this subject, I could find only two companies that had given serious thought to the development of managers: Sears, Roebuck in America and Marks & Spencer in England. At that time there were only three university programs in America for the continuing advanced education of managers: the Sloan Program at the Massachusetts Institute of Technology; the programs at New York University Graduate Business School for the continuing education of managers and young professionals in banking and finance; and then, brand-new, the Advanced Management Program at the Harvard Business School.

Ten years later, in the mid-fifties, when an attempt was made to catalog the companies with specific management development programs, the number already ran to some three thousand. And a great many universities in the United States had gone into all kinds of advanced management programs.

Today, it is no longer possible to count the number of companies that, one way or another, work on the development of management and managers. The large company that does not make specific provision for such work and does not have a management development staff of its own is the exception. And so is the business school at university level without some form of management development program. In addition, an untold number of outside organizations: trade associations, consulting firms, and so on, have gone into the management development business.

This interest is by no means confined to the United States. It has spread to Europe and to Japan. Within the last few years it has broken through the Iron Curtain. Some of the Soviet satellites, such as Czechoslovakia, have started advanced management work and in 1970, the Soviet Union itself set up two major advanced management schools for industrial executives.

## Why Management Development?

Basic business decisions require an increasingly long time span for their fruition. Since no one can foresee the future, management cannot make rational and responsible decisions unless it selects, develops, and tests the men who will have to follow them through and bail them out—the managers of tomorrow.

Management is becoming increasingly complex. In addition to a rapidly changing technology, management today has to be able to handle many new "relations" problems—relations with the government, relations with suppliers and customers, relations with employees and with labor unions. On top of this are demands for entrepreneurship and innovation; for managing knowledge and the knowledge worker; for multinational and, often, multicultural management; or for managerial responsibility for the environment and for the quality of life. All these increase the standards against which managers are measured.

The numerical demand for executives is steadily growing. A developed society increasingly replaces manual skill with theoretical knowledge and the ability to organize and to lead—in short with managerial ability. In fact, ours is the first society in which the basic question is not "How many educated people can society spare from the task of providing subsistence?" It is "How many uneducated people can we afford to support?"

But management development is also necessary to discharge an elementary responsibility which a business enterprise owes to society; if business does not discharge this obligation by its own actions, society will impose it. For continuity, especially of the big business enterprise, is vital. Our society will not tolerate—and cannot afford—to see such wealth-producing resources jeopardized through lack of competent successors to today's management.

The member of a modern society looks to his work for more than a livelihood. He looks to it also for satisfactions that go beyond the economic, that is, for pride, self-respect, and achievement. Management development is only another name for making work and industry more than a way of making a living. By offering challenges and opportunities for the individual development of each manager to his fullest ability, the enterprise discharges, in part, the obligation to make a job in industry a "good life."

And if we know one thing today, it is that managers are made and not born. There has to be systematic work on the supply, the development, and the skills of tomorrow's management. It cannot be left to luck or chance.

## Why Manager Development?

The individual manager needs development just as much as company and society do. He should, first, keep himself alert and mentally alive. He needs to keep himself challenged. He must acquire today the skills which will make him effective tomorrow. He also needs an opportunity to reflect on the meaning of his own experience and—above all—he needs an opportunity to reflect on himself and to learn to make his strengths count.

And then he needs development as a person even more than he needs development as a manager.

One of the strengths, but also one of the weaknesses of a knowledge worker, i.e., manager and career professional, is to expect satisfaction and stimulation from one's work. In that respect, the knowledge worker is badly spoiled during his early formative years. The manual worker, whether skilled or unskilled, does not expect the work to challenge him, to stimulate him, to develop him. He expects a living from the work. The knowledge worker expects a life out of it.

Thus, the knowledge worker, and especially the highly accomplished knowledge worker, is likely to find himself in a spiritual crisis in his early or mid-forties. By that time the great majority will have reached, inevitably, their terminal positions. Perhaps they will also have reached what, within their business, is their terminal function—whether this be market research, personnel training, or metallurgy. Suddenly their work will not satisfy them any more. After fifteen or twenty years in market research in their industry, they know all there is to know about it. What, in his early thirties, when the job was new, was tremendous excitement to a man, is boring and humdrum fifteen years later.

A manager has to be able, in other words, to develop a life of his own, and outside the organization, before he is in his mid-forties.

He needs this for himself, but he needs it also for the organization. For the manager who, at age forty-five, "retires on the job" because he has no more interest in life, is not likely to make any further contribution to the business. He owes it to himself—and to the business—to develop himself as a person, so that he can build his own life and not depend entirely upon the organization, additional promotion, or on new and different work. He needs to focus on his own personality, on his own strengths, and on his own interests.

We will (as I have discussed in another book)* have to learn to develop *second careers* for accomplished professional and managerial people when they reach their late forties or so. We will have to learn to make it possible for the good accountant in a bank to become comptroller of a hospital or business manager of a college. We will have to make it possible for people who have worked for twenty years or so in a business and in a function— that is, for the great majority of managers—to find new challenge, new opportunity, and new contributions in doing something different, or at least in being effective in different surroundings and in a different institution.

No manager today can be considered as discharging his duty toward himself, toward his family, and also toward his employer, the enterprise, unless he makes himself ready for such new opportunity.

There are, thus, good reasons why the development of management and managers has become a central concern.

But what do we really mean by the terms "management development" and "manager development"? Any boom such as we have experienced these last two decades is suspect. Undoubtedly there have been as many fads and follies as there have been sound ventures. There must be—and there are— quite a few charlatans, and many more who preach management development only because it is the fashionable thing to do.

## What Management Development Is Not

For these reasons, it is best to start by spelling out what management and manager development are not.

1. It is not taking courses. Courses are a tool of management development. But they are not management development.

Any course—whether it is a three-day seminar in a special skill or a two-year "advanced" program three evenings a week—has to fit the development needs of a management group or the development needs of an individual manager. But the job, the superior, and the development planning of both company and individual are far more important developmental tools than any course or courses.

Indeed, some of the most popular courses are of questionable value. I have come to doubt, e.g., the wisdom of courses which take a manager away from his job for long periods of time. The most effective courses, in my

* *The Age of Discontinuity.*

experience, are those which are done on the manager's own time and after hours, e.g., the evening programs offered by a good many metropolitan universities in the United States, or, for instance, by the Polytechnic Colleges in Great Britain. And the most effective full-time courses alternate periods at school with periods of work; a man spends a week or two off the job in an intensive learning experience, after which he gets back to his job and applies what he has learned.

Managers are action-focused; they are not philosophers and should not be. Unless they can put into action right away the things they have learned, the things they have considered and reconsidered, the course will not "take." It will remain "information" and never become "knowledge." Pedagogically it is not sound not to have the reaffirmation of action to strengthen learning, that is, not to be able to put into practice on Monday what one has learned the preceding Friday. Finally, the manager who has been away 13 weeks on an advanced course may well find himself a "displaced person" and homeless when he gets back to his organization after such a long absence.

Similarly, I have learned to be wary of courses for top management. Not that top-management people do not have a good deal to learn; they do. But most of the courses I have seen (including some famous ones) are not courses for top-management people but for youngsters without experience and without responsibility. Only the fee is "top-management." Such a course is a waste of top-management time.

2. Manager development and management development are not promotion planning, replacement planning, or finding potential. These are useless exercises. They may even do harm.

The worst thing a company can do is to try to develop the "comers" and leave out the others. Ten years hence, 80 percent of the work will have to be done by those left out. If they have not developed themselves to the point where they can understand, accept, and put into action the vision of the few "comers," nothing will happen. The eight men out of every ten who were not included in the program will, understandably, feel slighted. They may end up by becoming less effective, less productive, less willing to do new things than they were before.

The attempt to find "potential" is altogether futile. It is less likely to succeed than random selection, e.g., taking every fifth man. Potential is elusive. By itself it is worthless. Performance counts. And the correlation between promise and performance is not a particularly high one. Five out of every ten "high potential" young men turn out to be nothing but good talkers by the time they reach forty. Conversely, five out of every ten young men who do not look "brilliant" and do not talk a good game will have proven their capacity to perform by the time they are in their early forties.

Also, the idea that the purpose of management development is to find "replacements" negates the entire reason for the activity. We need management development and manager development precisely because tomorrow's jobs and tomorrow's organization can be assumed, with high probability, to be different from today's jobs and today's organization. If all we had to do were to replace yesterday's and today's jobs, we would not need any such activity. We would be training people as apprentices under their present bosses and hope that they learn what their present bosses know and do.

I used to be in favor of replacement planning such as Joe Hyman preached and practiced when he tried to convert moribund English textile companies into new, vital enterprises through his Viyella mergers. Hyman asked each executive of the companies acquired to name the man he would like to see as his successor, should he be promoted, become disabled, or die tomorrow. I am no longer advocating this practice. It is taken by the organization itself as a promise that the job of an executive, as it exists today, will be continued in perpetuity. Second, it freezes future selection. In a few years the man named today as the most qualified successor may have proven his incompetence. Or another man may have come from nowhere to overtake him. Yet once a man has been named, there is a commitment that tends to become binding.

The worst kind of replacement planning is the search for a "crown prince." A crown prince either has a legal right to succeed; or else nomination is likely to destroy him. No matter how carefully concealed, picking a crown prince is an overt act which the whole organization very rapidly perceives. And then all the other possible contenders unite against the crown prince and work to bring him down—and they usually succeed.

The Catholic Church long ago recognized this. It will not single out anyone as a successor to a bishop or archbishop except in rare cases when the incumbent is obviously old or very ill. Then, however, it will appoint an auxiliary bishop with the *right* to succession who automatically takes over when the See becomes vacant. This auxiliary *cum inre successionis* has a legal title and is in control—and the other contenders have to accept that fact and work with him.

3. Finally, management development and manager development are not means to "make a man over" by changing his personality. Their aim is to make a man effective. Their aim is to enable a man to use his strengths fully, and to make him perform the way he is, rather than the way somebody thinks he ought to be.

An employer has no business with a man's personality. Employment is a specific contract calling for specific performance, and for nothing else. Any attempt of an employer to go beyond this is usurpation. It is immoral as well as illegal intrusion of privacy. It is abuse of power. An employee owes no "loyalty," he owes no "love" and no "attitudes"—he owes performance and nothing else.

We have altogether not the slightest idea how to change the personality of adults. We do know to some extent how to make them more effective—and this is what we should focus on.

Management and manager development deal with the skills people need. They deal with the structure of jobs and of management relations. They deal with what an employee needs to learn to make his skills effective. They should concern themselves with changes in behavior likely to make a man more effective. They do not deal with who a man is—that is, with his personality or his emotional dynamics. The tendency to psychological manipulation is no more defensible than any other manipulative paternalism—in fact, it is considerably more reprehensible.

Attempts to change a mature man's personality are bound to fail in any event. By the time a man comes to work his personality is set. The task is not to change his personality, but to enable him to achieve and to perform through what he is and with what he has.

## The Two Dimensions of Development

Development is not one, but two related tasks which mutually affect each other. One task is that of *developing management.* Its purpose is the health, survival, and growth of the enterprise. The other task is *manager* development. Its purpose is the health, growth, and achievement of the individual, both in his capacity as a member of the organization and as a person. *Management* development is a function and activity of the organization—no matter how it is being discharged. *Manager* development is the responsibility of the individual, though company and superior have an important part to play.

Management development starts out with the question "What kind of managers and career professionals will this business need tomorrow in order to achieve its objectives and to perform in a different market, a different economy, a different technology, a different society?"

Management development concerns itself with questions such as the age structure of the management group or the skills that managers need to acquire today in order to qualify for tomorrow. It also focuses on the organizational structure and the design of managerial jobs to satisfy the needs, expectations, and aspirations of tomorrow's "career customer," that is, tomorrow's young manager or young career professional. For the market for jobs and careers has become a genuine mass market. Every organization, therefore, needs to design a "career product" that will attract and satisfy the career customer of tomorrow.

The career customer will increasingly be a demanding customer. Like the customer who, in a healthy economy, always wants more and different goods and services for his money, the career customer, in a healthy society, always wants something better and different from the job. Where only a few short decades ago he expected a living, he now looks for a career and for an opportunity to make a contribution. At the same time, he looks increasingly for a chance to put knowledge to work.

Whether management development requires a separate staff depends on the size and complexity of the business. It is certainly not an activity that should require a great many people and run a great many programs. But it does need power and prestige, for its object is to change the basic planning of the company, the structure of its organization, and the design of managerial jobs.

Management development is outside-focused rather than inside-focused. It is, essentially, a form of lesson planning rather than a personnel activity. At the core of the task are planning the market, designing the product, and obsoleting existing jobs and existing organizational structures. Management development, seen this way, is an innovator, a disorganizer, a critic. It's function is to ask with respect to the company's human organization, "What is our business and what should it be ?"

The *development of a manager* focuses on the person. Its aim is to enable a man to develop his abilities and strengths to the fullest extent and to find individual achievement. The aim is excellence.

No one can motivate a man toward self-development. Motivation must come from within. But a man's superior and the company can do a good deal to discourage even the most highly motivated man and to misdirect his development efforts. The active participation, the encouragement, the guidance from both superior and company are needed for manager-development efforts to be fully productive.

The starting point for any manager-development effort is a performance appraisal focused on what a man does well, what he can do well, and what limitations to his performance capacity he needs to overcome to get the most out of his strengths. Such an appraisal, however, should always be a joint effort. It requires work on the part of the man himself; it has to be self-appraisal. But it also requires active leadership by a man's manager.

In appraising themselves people tend either to be too critical or not critical enough. They are likely to see their strengths in the wrong places and to pride themselves on nonabilities rather than on abilities.

There is, typically, the first-class engineer who judges himself to be a good manager because he is "analytical" and "objective." Yet, to be a manager requires equally empathy, ability to understand how others do their work, and a keen sense of such "nonrational" factors as personality. There is the sales manager who considers his strengths to lie in "strategy"—in reality he is a shrewd negotiator; and what he means by strategy is "next week's bargain sale." Only too frequently there is the good analyst and adviser who does not realize that he lacks the emotional courage to make hard and lonely decisions.

An appraisal should be based on the performance objectives which a man has set for himself in cooperation with his superior. It should start with his performance against these objectives. It should never start out with "potential." It should ask "What has this man done well—not once, but consistently?" This should lead to a recognition of the strengths of a man and of the factors which inhibit him from making these strengths fully effective. But a self-development appraisal should also ask, "What do I want out of life? What are my values, my aspirations, my directions? And what do I have to do, to learn, to change, to make myself capable of living up to my demands on myself and my expectations of life?" This question, too, is much better asked by an outsider, by someone who knows the man, respects him, but at the same time can have the insight which most of us do not possess about ourselves.

Self-development may require learning new skills, new knowledge, and new manners. But above all, it requires new experience. The most important factors in self-development, apart from insight into one's own strengths, are experience on the job and the example of the superior. Self-appraisal, therefore, should always lead to conclusions regarding the needs and opportunities of a man, both with respect to what he himself has to contribute and with respect to the experiences he needs. The question should always be asked, "What are the right job experiences for this man so that his strengths can develop the fastest and the furthest?"

A superior who works on his own development sets an almost irresistible example. His example encourages people to develop their strengths and helps them gain the experiences they need. The boss who discourages, who always knows what people cannot do, and who hangs on to them, rather than helping them get the job experiences most conducive to their growth, stunts self-development.

Development is always self-development. For the enterprise to assume responsibility for the development of a man is idle boast. The responsibility rests with the individual, his abilities, his efforts. No business enterprise is competent, let alone obligated, to substitute its efforts for the self-development efforts of the individual. To do this would not only be unwarranted paternalism, it would be foolish pretension.

But every manager in a business has the opportunity to encourage individual self-development or to stifle it, to direct it or to misdirect it. He should be specifically assigned the responsibility for helping all men working with him to focus, direct, and apply self-development efforts. And every company can make available to its managers development challenges and development experiences.

It is no longer necessary to debate whether management development and manager development are luxuries in which only big companies can indulge in boom times. Most large—and many small—companies know that the development of management and managers is no more of a luxury than is a research laboratory. It is not even necessary any longer to combat the old fear that a company may develop too many good people. Managements should have learned by now that the demand for good people is increasing faster than the capacity of even a successful development program to supply them. (The smart ones have, of course, always known that it has never done a company harm to be known as "the mother of presidents." On the contrary, the power of a company to attract good men is directly proportionate to its reputation as a developer of successful men for itself as well as for other companies.) The development of management and managers has become a necessity because the modern business enterprise has become a basic institution of our society. In any major institution—the Church, for instance, or the Army—finding, developing and proving out the leaders of tomorrow is an essential job to which the best men give fully of their time and attention.

It is a necessity for the spirit, the vision, and the performance of today's managers that they be expected to develop those who will manage tomorrow. Just as no one learns as much about a subject as the man who is forced to teach it, no one develops as much as the man who is trying to help others to develop themselves. Indeed, no one can develop himself unless he works on the development of others. It is in and through efforts to develop others that managers raise their demands on themselves. The best performers in any profession always look upon the men they have trained and developed as the proudest monument they can leave behind.

And again, developing both management and managers is as needed—and requires the same approaches—in the public-service institution as in business enterprise.

But above all, today's manager and career professional has a responsibility to develop himself. It is a responsibility he has toward his institution, as well as toward himself.

We hear a great deal today about the organization man and about alienation of people in organizations. I doubt whether there is more conformity in today's organization than there was in yesterday's small village with its tremendous pressures of class and kin, of caste and custom. I doubt seriously whether there is more alienation today than in earlier societies. The classic diagnosis of alienation, after all, was not derived from a study of the modern corporation but was made in a thoroughly agrarian pre-industrial society, the Denmark in which Kierkegaard lived and wrote in the early nineteenth century. But whether conformity and spiritual despair are greater or lesser today than they used to be, the one effective counterforce to both is the individual's commitment to self-development, the individual's commitment to excellence.

# 34

## Management by Objectives and Self-Control

*The Forces of Misdirection—Workmanship: A Necessity and a Danger— Misdirection by the Boss—Misdirection by Compensation—What Should the Objectives Be?—Management by Drives—How Should Managers' Objectives Be Set and by Whom?— Self-Control Through Measurements— Does It Demand Too Much of the Individual?—A Philosophy of Management*

———

Each member of the enterprise contributes something different, but all must contribute toward a common goal. Their efforts must all pull in the same direction, and their contributions must fit together to produce a whole— without gaps, without friction, without unnecessary duplication of effort.

Performance requires that each job be directed toward the objectives of the whole organization. In particular, each manager's job must be focused on the success of the whole. The performance that is expected of the manager must be directed toward the performance goals of the business. His results are measured by the contribution they make to the success of the enterprise. The manager must know and understand what the business goals demand of him in terms of performance, and his superior must know what contribution to demand and expect. If these requirements are not met managers are misdirected and their efforts are wasted.

Management by objectives requires major effort and special instruments. For in a business enterprise managers are not automatically directed toward a common goal. On the contrary, organization, by its very nature, contains four powerful factors of misdirection: the specialized work of most managers: the hierarchical structure of management; the differences in vision and work and the resultant insulation of various levels of management; and finally, the compensation structure of the management group. To overcome these obstacles requires more than good intentions, sermons, and exhortations. It requires policy and structure. It requires that management by objectives be purposefully organized and be made the living law of the entire management group.

An old story tells of three stonecutters who were asked what they were doing. The first replied, "I am making a living." The second kept on hammering while he said, "I am doing the best job of stonecutting in the entire country." The third one looked up with a visionary gleam in his eyes and said, "I am building a cathedral."

The third man is, of course, the true manager. The first man knows what he wants to get out of the work and manages to do so. He is likely to give a "fair day's work for a fair day's pay." But he is not a manager and will never be one. It is the second man who is a problem. Workmanship is essential: in fact, an organization demoralizes if it does not demand of its members the highest workmanship they are capable of. But there is always a danger that the true workman, the true professional, will believe that he is accomplishing something when in effect he is just polishing stones or collecting footnotes. Workmanship must be encouraged in the business enterprise. But it must always be related to the needs of the whole.

The majority of managers and of career professionals in any business enterprise are, like the second man, concerned with specialized work. True, the number of functional managers should always be kept at a minimum, and there should be the largest possible number of "general" managers who manage an integrated business and are directly responsible for its performance and results. Even with the utmost application of this principle the great bulk of managers will work in functional jobs, however.

A man's habits as a manager, his vision and his values, are usually formed while he does functional and specialized work. It is essential that the functional specialist develop high standards of workmanship, that he strive to be "the best stonecutter in the country." For work without high standards is dishonest; it corrupts the man himself and those around him. Emphasis on, and drive for, workmanship produces innovations and advances in every area of management. That managers strive to do "professional personnel management," to run "the most up-to-date plant," to do "truly scientific market research," to "put in the most modern accounting system," or to do "perfect engineering" must be encouraged.

But this striving for professional workmanship in functional and specialized work is also a danger. It tends to divert a man's vision and efforts from the goals of the business. The functional work becomes an end in itself. In far too many instances the functional manager no longer measures his performance by its contribution to the enterprise but only by his own professional criteria of workmanship. He tends to appraise his subordinates by their craftsmanship and to reward and to promote them accordingly. He resents demands made on him for the sake of business performance as interference with "good engineering," "smooth production," or "hard-hitting selling." The functional manager's legitimate desire for workmanship becomes, unless counterbalanced, a centrifugal force which tears the enterprise apart and converts it into a loose confederation of functional empires, each concerned only with its own craft, each jealously guarding its own "secrets," each bent on enlarging its own domain rather than on building the business.

This danger is being greatly intensified by the technological and social changes now under way. The number of highly educated specialists working in the business enterprise is increasing tremendously. And so will the level of workmanship demanded of these specialists. Our work force is increasingly becoming an "educated" work force in which the majority make their contribution in the form of specialized knowledge. The tendency to make the craft or function an end in itself will therefore become even more marked than it is today. But at the same time the new technology will demand much closer coordination between specialists. It will demand that functional men, even at the lowest management level, see the business as a whole and understand what it requires of them. The new technology will need both the drive for excellence in workmanship and the consistent direction of managers at all levels toward the common goal.

That university teachers no longer see the university as their "home" but rather give allegiance to their specialization is considered an important reason for the crisis of the university. But exactly the same tendency exists in all other institutions, business enterprise included.

## Misdirection by the Boss

The hierarchical structure of management aggravates the danger. What the boss does and says, his most casual remarks, his habits, even his mannerisms, tend to appear to his subordinates as calculated, planned, and meaningful. "All you ever hear around the place is human-relations talk; but when the boss calls you on the carpet it is always because overtime is too high; and when it comes to promoting a guy, the plums always go to those who do the best job filling out accounting-department forms." This is one of the most common tunes, sung with infinite variations on every level of management. It leads to poor performance—even in cutting overtime. It also expresses loss of confidence in, and absence of respect for, the company and its management.

Yet the manager who so misdirects his subordinates does not intend to do so. He genuinely considers human relations to be the most important task of his plant managers. But he talks about overtime because he feels that he has to establish himself with his men as a "practical man," or because he thinks that he shows familiarity with their problems by talking "shop" with them. He stresses the accounting-department forms only because they annoy him as much as they do his men—or he may just not want to have any more trouble with the comptroller than he can help. But to his subordinates these reasons are hidden; all they see and hear is the question about overtime, the emphasis on forms.

The solution to this problem requires a structure of management which focuses both the manager's and his boss's eyes on what the job—rather than the boss—demands. To stress styles and manners—as does a good deal of current management literature—is likely instead to aggravate the problem. Indeed, everyone familiar with business today has seen situations in which a manager's attempt to avoid misdirection through changing his manners has converted a fairly satisfactory relationship into a nightmare of embarrassment and misunderstanding. The manager himself becomes so self-conscious as to lose all easy relationship with his men. And the men in turn react with: "So help us, the old man has read a book; we used to know what he wanted of us, now we have to guess."

## Differences in Levels of Management

Misdirection can result from difference in concern and function between various levels of management. This problem, too, cannot be solved by attitudes and good intentions; for it is rooted in the structure of any enterprise. Nor can it be solved by "better communications," for communications presuppose common understanding and a common language, and it is precisely that which is usually lacking.

It is no accident that the old story of the blind men meeting up with an elephant on the road is so popular among management people. Each level of management sees the same "elephant"—the business—from a different angle of vision. The production foreman, like the blind man who felt the elephant's leg and decided that a tree was in his way, tends to see only the immediate production problems. Top management—the blind man touching the trunk and deciding a snake bars his way—tends to see only the enterprise as a whole; it sees stockholders, financial problems, altogether a host of highly abstract relations and figures. Operating management—the blind man feeling the elephant's belly and thinking himself up against a landslide—tends to see things functionally. Each level needs its particular vision; it could not do its job without it. Yet, these visions are so different that people on different levels talking about the same thing often do not realize it—or, as frequently happens, believe that they are talking about the same thing when in reality they are poles apart.

## Misdirection by Compensation

The most serious force for misdirection within the management group may be the compensation structure. At the same time, it is the most refractory one. Somehow management people have to be paid, but every compensation system is liable to misdirect.

Compensation is cost to the enterprise, and income to the recipient. But it also always expresses status, both within the enterprise and in society. It entails judgments on a man's worth as much as on his performances. It is emotionally tied to all our ideas of fairness, justice, and equity. Money is, of course, quantitative. But the money in any compensation system expresses the most intangible, but also the most sensitive, values and qualities. For this reason, there can be no truly simple or truly rational compensation system.

In Japan compensation, at least up to the time a manager reaches age forty-five, is based on one factor alone: seniority. But this too tends to misdirect, especially the younger men, into pleasing their superiors rather than toward achieving results. The fact that immediate compensation is not affected by performance only makes more important the deferred judgment, that is, the decision whether a given executive, at age forty-five, should be promoted into top management or should be kept a middle manager and retired ten years later. This, of course, does not affect the man who, early in his career, decides that he is not going to make it anyhow or that it is not worth the effort. But the ambitious, high performer—the very man who should be motivated properly—is bound to be seriously misdirected by the Japanese system. Acceptance by a clique rather than performance is likely to be his objective.

Any compensation system determines a man's place within the group. How his pay relates to the pay of others, and especially to the pay of the men he considers his peers, is always more important than the absolute amount of his salary. (On this see Chapters 16 and 18.) Compensation must always try to balance recognition of the individual with stability and maintenance of the group. No attempt at a "scientific formula" for compensation can therefore be completely successful. The best possible compensation plan is of necessity a compromise among the various functions and meanings of compensation, for the individual as well as for the groups. Even the best plan will still disorganize as well as organize, misdirect as well as direct, and encourage the wrong as well as the right behavior.

Yet, there is hardly a more powerful signal for managers than compensation and compensation structure. Its importance to them goes far beyond the economic meaning of money. It conveys to them the values of their top management and their own worth within the management group. It expresses in clear and tangible form a man's position, rank, and recognition within the group. At today's high tax rates a little more money means, as a rule, very little to senior men. It is, in effect, only so much more income tax to pay. But the status symbol of a little more money and its emotional impacts are incalculable.

The most damaging misdirection may result from those apparently eminently "fair" compensation systems for the heads of decentralized divisions and businesses which relate a manager's pay directly to performance, usually to performance measured by return on investment during the calendar year. If we want to *measure* performance, there is no other way. The man himself and his associates, that is, the people in charge of a decentralized business within a company, measure themselves by their annual profit or loss. In fact, to have them do so is one of the major reasons for decentralization. Yet, if return on investment or current profits are overemphasized, the managers of decentralized business will be misdirected toward slighting the future.

An able management team heading one of the major divisions of a chemical company failed for years to develop a badly needed new product. Year after year they reported to their top management that the new product was not yet quite ready. Finally, when the division manager was asked bluntly why he stalled on a project that was clearly vital to the success of his business, he answered: "Have you looked at our compensation plan? I myself have a guaranteed salary. But my entire management group gets its main income from a bonus geared to return on investment. The new product is the future of this business. But for five or eight years there will be only investment and no return. I know we are three years late. But do you really expect me to take the bread out of the mouths of my closest associates?" This story had a happy ending. The compensation plan was changed—somewhat in line with the plan Du Pont has had for years with respect to new developments. Du Pont does not put the cost of a development into the investment base of a division or a subsidiary until the new product has been introduced on the market. And within a year or two the new product was out and selling.

The danger is beginning to be widely recognized. General Electric Company, for instance, several years ago scrapped its compensation system, based on the return on investment of a division, and replaced it by one in which return on investment is only one factor in the compensation of divisional executives. Other factors that reflect provisions for the future are also included in determining divisional bonuses. This works quite a bit better. Still, nobody at GE considers the new system to be perfect, if only because of its complexity.

The preference should be for simple compensation systems rather than for complex ones. It should be for compensation systems that allow judgment to be used and that enable pay to be fitted to the job of the individual rather than impose one formula on everybody. But I would be the last person to claim that a "fair" let alone a "scientific" system can be devised. All one can do, to repeat, is to watch lest the compensation system reward the wrong behavior, emphasize the wrong results, and direct people away from performance for the common good.

## What Should the Objectives of a Manager Be?

Constant effort alone can counteract the inherent tendencies toward diffusion and misdirection. The superior needs to understand what he expects of his subordinate managers. The subordinate, in turn, needs to be able to know what in the way of results he should hold himself accountable for. Without special efforts, superior or subordinate will not know and understand this and their ideas will not be compatible, let alone identical.

Each manager, from the "big boss" down to the production foreman or the chief clerk, needs clearly spelled-out objectives. Otherwise confusion can be guaranteed. These objectives should lay out what performance the man's own managerial unit is supposed to achieve. They should lay out what contribution he and his unit are expected to make to help other units obtain their objectives. Finally, they should spell out what contribution the manager can expect from other units toward the attainment of his own objectives. Right from the start, in other words, emphasis should be on teamwork and team results.

These objectives should always derive from the goals of the business enterprise. A statement of his own objectives based on those of the company and of the manufacturing department should be demanded even of the foreman on the assembly line. The company may be so large as to make the distance between the individual foreman's production and the company's total output all but astronomical. Yet the foreman must focus on the objectives and goals of the company and needs to define his results in terms of his unit's contribution to the whole of which it is a part.

The objectives of every manager should spell out his contribution to the attainment of company goals in all areas of the business. Obviously, not every manager has a direct contribution to make in every area. The contribution which marketing makes to productivity, for example, may be indirect and hard to define. But if a manager and his unit are not expected to contribute toward any one of the areas that significantly affect prosperity and survival of the business, this fact should be clearly brought out. For managers must understand that business results depend on a balance of efforts and results in a number of areas. This is necessary both to give full scope to the craftsmanship of each function and specialty, and to prevent the empire-building and clannish jealousies of the various functions and specialties. It is necessary also to avoid overemphasis on any one key area.

This is particularly important for service staffs and for such highly specialized groups as the computer people. They may not always be able to relate their work directly to business objectives and business results. But unless they make the effort, they are likely to direct their work away from business objectives and business results.

To obtain balanced efforts the objectives of all managers on all levels and in all areas should also be keyed to both short-range and long-range considerations. And, of course, all objectives should always contain both the tangible business objectives and such "intangible" objectives as manager organization and development, worker performance and attitude, and public responsibility. Anything else is shortsighted and impractical.

## Management by Drives

Proper management requires balanced stress on objectives, especially by top management. It avoids the all-too-common business malpractice: management by crisis and drives.

That things always collapse into the *status quo ante* three weeks after a drive is over, everybody knows and apparently expects. The only result of an economy drive is likely to be that messengers and typists get fired, and that $25,000 executives are forced to do $150-a-week work typing their own letters—and doing it badly. And yet many managements fail to draw the obvious conclusion that drives are, after all, not the way to get things done.

Over and above its ineffectiveness, management by drive misdirects. It puts all emphasis on one phase of the job to the detriment of everything else. "For four weeks we cut inventories," a case-hardened veteran of management by crisis once summed it up. "Then we have four weeks of cost-cutting, followed by four weeks of human relations. We just have time to push customer service and courtesy for a month. And then the inventory is back where it was when we started. We don't even try to do our job. All top management talks about, thinks about, preaches about, is last week's inventory figure or this week's customer complaints. How we do the rest of the job they don't even want to know."

In an organization which manages by drives people either neglect their job to get on with the current drive, or silently organize for collective sabotage of the drive in order to get their work done. In either event they become deaf to the cry of "wolf." And when the real crisis comes, when all hands should drop everything and pitch in, they treat it as just another case of management-created hysteria. Management by drive is a sure sign of confusion. It is an admission of incompetence. It is a sign that management does not think. But, above all, it is a sign that the company does not know what to expect of its managers and that, not knowing how to direct them, it misdirects them.

## How Should Managers' Objectives Be Set and by Whom?

The goals of each manager's job must be defined by the contribution he has to make to the success of the larger unit of which he is a part. The objectives of the district sales manager's job should be defined by the contribution he and his district sales force have to make to the sales department, the objectives of the project engineer's job by the contribution he, his engineers, and draftsmen make to the engineering department. The objectives of the general manager of a decentralized division should be defined by the contribution his division has to make to the objectives of the parent company.

Higher management must, of course, reserve the power to approve or disapprove these objectives. But their development is part of a manager's responsibility; indeed, it is his first responsibility. It means, too, that every manager should responsibly participate in the development of the objectives of the higher unit of which his is a part. To "give him a *sense* of participation" (to use a pet phrase of human relations jargon) is not enough. It is the wrong thing. Being a manager means *having* responsibility. Precisely because his aims should reflect the objective needs of the business, rather than merely what the boss—or he himself—wants, he must commit himself to them with a positive act of assent. He must know and understand the ultimate business goals, what is expected of him and why, what he will be measured against and how. There must be a meeting of minds within the entire management of each unit. This can be achieved only when each of the contributing managers is expected to think through what the unit objectives are and is led to participate actively and responsibly in the work of defining them. And only if his lower managers participate in this way can the higher manager know what to expect of them and can make exacting demands.

This is so important that some of the most effective managers I know go one step further. They have each of their subordinates write a "manager's letter" twice a year. In this letter to his superior, each manager first defines the objectives of his superior's job and of his own job as he sees them. He then sets down the performance standards which he believes are being

applied to him. Next, he lists the things he must do to attain these goals
—and the things within his own unit he considers the major obstacles. He
lists the things his superior and the company do that help him and the
things that hamper him. Finally, he outlines what he proposes to do during
the next year to reach his goals. If his superior accepts this statement, the
"manager's letter" becomes the charter under which the manager operates.

This device, like no other I have seen, brings out how easily the unconsid-
ered and casual remarks of even the best boss can confuse and misdirect.
One large company has used the manager's letter for ten years. Yet almost
every letter still lists as objectives and standards things which baffle the
superior to whom the letter is addressed. And whenever he asks, "What is
this?" he gets the answer, "Don't you remember what you said last spring
going down with me in the elevator?"

The manager's letter also brings out whatever inconsistencies there are
in the demands made on a man by his superior and by the company. Does
the superior demand both speed and high quality when he can get only one
or the other? And what compromise is needed in the interest of the company? Does he demand initiative and judgment of his men but also that they
check back with him before they do anything? Does he ask for their ideas
and suggestions but never use them or discuss them? Does the company
expect of a small engineering force that it be available immediately whenever something goes wrong in the plant and yet bend all its efforts to the
completion of new designs? Does it expect a manager to maintain high
standards of performance but forbid him to remove poor performers? Does
it create the conditions under which people say, "I can get the work done
as long as I can keep the boss from knowing what I am doing"?

These are common situations. They undermine spirit and performance.
The manager's letter may not prevent them, but at least it brings them out
in the open, shows where compromises have to be made, objectives have to
be thought through, priorities have to be established, behavior has to be
changed.

As this device illustrates, managing managers requires special efforts not
only to establish common direction, but to eliminate misdirection. Mutual
understanding can never be attained by "communications down," can never
be created by talking. It can result only from "communications up." It
requires both the superior's willingness to listen and a tool especially designed to make lower managers heard.

## Self-Control through Measurements

The greatest advantage of management by objectives is perhaps that it
makes it possible for a manager to control his own performance. Self-
control means stronger motivation: a desire to do the best rather than do

just enough to get by. It means higher performance goals and broader vision. Even if management by objectives were not necessary to give the enterprise the unity of direction and effort of a management team, it would be necessary to make possible management by self-control.

So far in this book I have rarely talked of control; I have talked of measurement. This was intentional. For control is an ambiguous word. It means the ability to direct oneself and one's work. It can also mean domination of one person by another. Objectives are the basis of control in the first sense; but they must never become the basis of control in the second, for this would defeat their purpose. Indeed, one of the major contributions of management by objectives is that it enables us to substitute management by self-control for management by domination.

To be able to control his own performance a manager needs to know more than what his goals are. He must be able to measure his performance and results against the goal. It should be an invariable practice to supply managers with clear and common measurements in all key areas of a business. These measurements need not be rigidly quantitative; nor need they be exact. But they have to be clear, simple, and rational. They have to be relevant and direct attention and efforts where they should go. They have to be reliable—at least to the point where their margin of error is acknowledged and understood. And they have to be, so to speak, self-explanatory, understandable without complicated interpretation or philosophical discussion.

Each manager should have the information he needs to measure his own performance and should receive it soon enough to make any changes necessary for the desired results. And this information should go to the manager himself, and not to his superior. It should be the means of self-control, not a tool of control from above.

This needs particular stress today, when the ability to obtain such information is growing rapidly as a result of technological progress in information gathering, analysis, and synthesis. In the past, information on important facts was either not obtainable at all or could be assembled only so late as to be of little but historical interest. This was not an unmixed curse. It made effective self-control difficult; but it also made difficult domination of a manager from above; in the absence of information with which to control him, the manager had to be allowed to work as he saw fit.

The new ability to produce measuring information will make possible effective self-control; and if so used, it will lead to a tremendous advance in the effectiveness and performance of management. But if this new ability is abused to impose control on managers from above, the new technology will inflict incalculable harm by demoralizing management and by seriously lowering the effectiveness of managers.

## Self-Control and Performance Standards

Management by objectives and self-control asks for self-discipline. It forces the manager to make high demands on himself. It is anything but permissive. It may well lead to demanding too much rather than too little. This has indeed been the main criticism leveled against the concept. (See Chapter 19, especially the discussion of Maslow's criticism of Theory Y.)

Management by objectives and self-control assumes that people want to be responsible, want to contribute, want to achieve, and that is a bold assumption. Yet we know that people largely act as they are expected to act.

A manager who starts out with the assumption that people are weak, irresponsible, and lazy will get weakness, irresponsibility, and laziness. He corrupts. A manager who assumes strength, responsibility, and desire to contribute may experience a few disappointments. But the manager's first task is to make effective the strengths of people, and this he can do only if he starts out with the assumption that people—and especially managers and professional contributors—want to achieve.

Above all, he must make this assumption with regard to the young educated people of today who will be tomorrow's managers. They may not know what they mean when they demand to be allowed to "make a contribution." But their demand is the right demand. And they are right also that management, as it has been practiced so far in all institutions including business, does not act on the assumption that the young educated people want to make a contribution. They need to be subjected—and to subject themselves—to the discipline and the demands of management by objectives and self-control.

In the years since I first coined the term,* "management by objectives" has become a widely used slogan. There is a whole literature, and any number of management courses, seminars, and even movies, on the subject. Hundreds of companies have adopted a policy of management by objectives —though only a few have followed through with true self-control. But management by objectives and self-control is more than a slogan, more than a technique, more than a policy even. It is, so to speak, a constitutional principle.

## A Philosophy of Management

What the business enterprise needs is a principle of management that will give full scope to individual strength and responsibility, as well as common

*In *Practice of Management*.

direction to vision and effort, establish team work, and harmonize the goals of the individual with the commonweal. Management by objectives and self-control makes the commonweal the aim of every manager. It substitutes for control from outside the stricter, more exacting, and more effective control from inside. It motivates the manager to action, not because somebody tells him to do something or talks him into doing it, but because the objective task demands it. He acts not because somebody wants him to but because he himself decides that he has to—he acts, in other words, as a free man.

I do not use the word "philosophy" lightly; indeed I prefer not to use it at all; it's much too big a word. But management by objectives and self-control may properly be called a philosophy of management. It rests on a concept of the job of management. It rests on an analysis of the specific needs of the management group and the obstacles it faces. It rests on a concept of human action, behavior, and motivation. Finally, it applies to every manager, whatever his level and function, and to any organization whether large or small. It insures performance by converting objective needs into personal goals. And this is genuine freedom.

# 35

## From Middle Management to Knowledge Organization

*Middle Management's Predicted Demise—And the Middle Management Boom—The Needed Correction—The Danger of Overstaffing—The Need for "Weight Control"—Sloughing Off the Old—Where the Growth Occurred—The Emergence of the Knowledge Professional—The Social Structure of Traditional Middle Management—The European Tradition—The New Middle Manager: Middle Rank but Top-Management "Impacts"—The Knowledge Organization—Middle-Management Job Design—The Need for Clear Decision Authority—Top Management's Role in the Knowledge Organization—Middle Managers: "Juniors" and "Colleagues" Rather Than "Subordinates"*

In the early fifties when computer and automation were the headline makers, the imminent demise of middle management was widely predicted. By 1980, we were told by a number of experts, middle management would have disappeared. All decisions would be made by the computer or by top management on the basis of a "total information system."

Very few predictions have been disproven so fast and so completely. At the very time the predictions were being widely publicized, the middle-management boom began. And it kept going for twenty years. Indeed, the fifties and the sixties might have been called the era of middle management. No other group in the work force, in all developed countries, has been growing as fast.

There was, indeed, during this period, a powerful force at work reducing the number of middle-management jobs. It was not, however, the computer, automation, or any other new technology. It was the press of mergers, takeovers, and acquisitions, especially in the U.S. and in Great Britain. It resulted in consolidating or closing countless sales and accounting offices —and with it the abolition of middle-management positions by the score. Yet despite this force—which reached hurricane strength in the late sixties in the English-speaking world—the demand for middle-rank managerial people grew steadily except in periods of economic recession as in Great Britain in the late sixties and in the U.S. in 1970–71. And in companies not directly affected by mergers or acquisitions, or in public-service institutions, the demand grew spectacularly.

Here are some examples from manufacturing, that is, from the economic sector where automation has been most widely applied and where computers have become as commonplace, at least in big companies, as smokestacks were a few generations ago. One of the large American automobile companies recently built a major manufacturing plant to turn out the entire production of a new model. It was the company's first major automotive plant since 1949, when a similar plant, designed for a similar production volume, was opened. The number of rank-and-file employees, both blue-collar and clerical, is almost one-third less than that of the earlier plant— the result, however, of normal increases in productivity rather than of a shift of the process to automation. The top-management group in the new plant is about the same size. But the middle-management group, that is, the group that is paid more than a general foreman and less than the plant's general manager, is almost five times the size of the middle-management group in the 1949 plant.

Another manufacturing company—a producer of a wide range of industrial components—grew between 1950 and 1970 from a sales volume of $10 million to one of $100 million. In terms of units the growth was fivefold. During this period of rapid expansion, the top-management group grew from three men to five. Rank-and-file employment grew from 1,000 to 4,000. The middle-management ranks, again defined by salary, grew from 14 men to 235—that is, almost seventeen times—and this does not include salesmen.

Here is an example from England: One of the large materials companies —a worldwide leader in its industry—grew by 45 percent between 1950 and 1970, measured in volume of output and discounting for inflation and price increases. The top-management group at the end of the period was actually somewhat smaller as the result of two reorganizations in which older members of the founding families were being replaced by professional managers. The rank and file, both in the factories and in the office, grew by about a fifth. But the middle group tripled.

The same rapid expansion in the middle ranks has occurred in Japan. Middle management in Japan is synonymous with "university graduates on the payroll." And that number in Japan—and especially the number of university graduates working for business—has increased even faster than the Japanese economy. Indeed, the words "salary man," the Japanese term for the middle group, has become a slogan.

These examples actually understate the growth rate of middle management. During the period in which middle management was expected to disappear, the center of economic gravity and growth shifted to industries that have a much higher ratio of middle managers in their employ than have the industries which dominated the business scene in 1950. The symbol of economic dynamism in the United States economy of 1970 was no longer General Motors. It was IBM. And at IBM, or at any other computer manufacturer, the middle group is far bigger than in traditional manufacturing industries such as automobile or steel. The same is true of the pharmaceutical companies which grew so rapidly in the twenty years between 1950 and 1970.

Outside of manufacturing industries the growth has been even more rapid. It has been particularly pronounced in the nonbusiness service institutions. The prototype is the hospital.

Top management in the hospital—however one defines it—has not grown. There is still the hospital administrator, perhaps with an assistant in the larger hospital. There are in the community hospitals, the trustees, and there is a medical director. Rank-and-file employment in terms of number of employees per patient day has gone down rather than up. It is in the kitchen, in maintenance, and in the other rank-and-file areas that hospitals have become somewhat less labor-intensive. But the middle ranks —technicians, engineers, accountants, psychologists and social workers— have exploded. They have grown at least fourfold—in some big teaching hospitals even faster.

## The Needed Correction

Growth at such rates always overshoots the target. It is bound to be disorderly and wasteful. There is overstaffing because it is the fashion to go in for this or that activity whether needed or not. There is overstaffing because times are good and it is easier to accede to a demand for more people than to fight it. And in such a period of explosive growth no one pays much attention to the organization of the work. Yet expansion of such magnitude is always qualitative change rather than mere additional quantity. If the work and its organization are not studied and changed, waste, duplication of effort, and organizational obesity follow.

Examples of wasteful overstaffing in the middle ranks abound. The worst are some American defense projects. To design the Mirage fighter, the best military plane of the 1950–1970 period, the French employed some seventy engineers and designers who did the job in record time. A comparable American development might have been staffed with three thousand engineers and designers and have taken four times as long and, in the end, might have come out with an inferior design at infinitely greater cost.

But there are examples of blatant overstaffing in private industry too. It is quite unlikely that IBM, in its rapid expansion, could have put to productive work all the masses of middle-management people it hired, on the basis of their college diplomas as a rule rather than for proven performance or because the need for their services had been clearly established.

The middle-management boom therefore had to lead, like any other boom, to a "middle-management depression." At the first significant economic setback there had to be a sharp correction. This came first in Great Britain, where the fairly sharp recession of the late sixties coincided with a peak in mergers and takeovers, resulting in layoffs of middle-rank executives and professionals. In the United States, in the 1970/71 recession, the reaction was far milder: it consisted of a sharp two-year curtailment of college recruiting for management and professional positions, with very few layoffs of middle-management people already on the payroll (except in the particularly distressed aerospace and defense industries). And Japan, when scared by President Nixon's trade and economic offensive in 1971, also reacted by curtailing temporarily new hiring.

Such a reaction, however painful, is fundamentally healthy. It always goes too far, of course. But at least it forces management to think through what the work is and what it needs. Such thinking is particularly important with respect to middle-management work. There are few areas where overstaffing does as much damage as in the middle-management group. It costs a great deal more than money. It costs performance and motivation.

## The Danger of Overstaffing

Knowledge work—that is, the specific work of middle managers—should always be demanding. It should be lean, and err, if at all, on the side of understaffing. An overstaffed middle-management organization destroys motivation. It destroys accomplishment, achievement, and satisfaction. In the end, it destroys performance.*

The middle-management boom and the resulting overstaffing, especially in larger companies, did indeed undermine morale and motivation. Overstaffing is a main reason for the dissatisfaction and disenchantment of so many of the young middle-rank people, managers and career professionals,

---

*On this see especially the two books by Frederick Herzberg: *Work and the Nature of Man* (World Publishing Co., 1966) and *The Motivation to Work* (Wiley, 1959).

whom business, governments, school systems, and hospitals recruited in such large numbers during the fifties and sixties. They are well paid and well treated; but there is not enough for them to do, not enough challenge, not enough contribution, not enough accomplishment, and too much sheer busyness. There are too many bodies busily "interacting" with each other rather than doing their own work. When the able young educated people, e.g., the brightest graduates of the leading American business schools, are asked to explain their growing preference for a job in a small company or in the medium-sized city administration, they always say, "At least I'll have something to do."

The first lesson is to keep the middle ranks lean. "What really needs to be done?" is the first question. And the second and equally important one is "What no longer needs to be done and should be cut back or cut out?" The first lesson is the *need for weight control.*

In particular this means that a new middle-management activity should, as a rule, be sanctioned only if an old one is sloughed off or, at least, pruned back. The middle-management budget is predominately an "administered expense" (see Chapter 9) and needs to be constantly watched to make sure that good, performing people are allocated to opportunities, to results, and to making the future rather than wasted on problems, busyness, and on defending the past.

What needs even more thought and attention is, however, the work of middle management and its organization. The expansion of the middle ranks not only produced a qualitative change—it was itself produced by a change in the nature of the middle-management function.

Middle management will, it is safe to predict, continue to expand. But future growth will have to be directed, controlled, managed. It will have to be based on an understanding of the changing nature of middle management and of the resulting need for change in function, relationship, and structure.

## Where the Growth Occurred

The middle management of forty years ago has not disappeared. Rather it has grown, and quite substantially. There are today proportionately more plant managers around, more district sales managers, and more branch managers in banks than there were before World War II.

But the real growth of middle-rank people in management jobs has been in manufacturing engineers and process specialists; in tax accountants and market analysts; in product and market managers; in advertising and promotion specialists. It has been in a host of functions which, a generation ago, were hardly known. The new middle managers are the knowledge professionals (see Chapter 30).

The traditional middle manager is essentially a commander of men. The new middle manager is essentially a supplier of knowledge. The traditional middle manager has authority downward, over the people who report to him. The new middle manager essentially has responsibility sideways and upward, that is, to people over whom he exercises no command authority.

Above all, the traditional middle manager's job is largely routine. He did not make decisions. He carried them out. At the most, he implemented them and adapted them to local conditions. His job was to keep running a system that he had neither designed nor was expected to alter.

This underlay, of course, the traditional definition of a manager as someone who is responsible for the work of others rather than responsible for his own work. It also underlay the traditional social structure of management outside the U.S. and Japan, especially in Europe.

In the United States and Japan top management has traditionally been recruited from middle management, that is, from people who worked their way up in the business. In European countries this was not the pattern. In England there was—and to some extent still is—a tremendous gulf between managers and "the board," that is, top management. Even in large companies the board was until recently recruited from people who had never discharged operating management functions, if not from people who had never worked in a business, such as distinguished former public servants. In Holland top management, even in the large and professionally managed companies, rarely comes out of operations. In the large French company all positions in top and senior management are typically held by graduates of the Grandes Écoles. Most of them, especially top-management people, make their careers in government and then move directly into senior management jobs in business. Operating managers who come up in the business are normally considered unfit for top jobs, even if they are university graduates. The Germans tend to draw a sharp line between *Führung,* i.e., top management, and *Leitung,* operating management.*

Georg Siemens, the founder of the Deutsche Bank (see Chapter 29 and especially Chapter 49), became the head of a major financial institution as a young government lawyer barely thirty, without experience in the banking business. His youth was exceptional; his lack of business preparation and operating knowledge was not.

That this social structure could work—and work very well in many cases

---

*The semantic hurdle the word "management" has faced outside of the United States is a result. In most European languages—and thirty years ago even in British English—there is no one term comprising the totality of the management group. There are separate terms for the people at the top and for the people in the middle. And since "management" is usually being translated into these languages with the word that connotes the operating, middle-management people, the people at the top, such as the German *Unternehmer,* tended to conclude that management was concerned with routine operations rather than with crucial decisions and that, therefore, management was for "them" and not for "us."

—shows that the European view of the traditional middle manager as being concerned with routines rather than with decisions, and with maintenance of going operations rather than with direction, had a good deal of substance.

## The Decision Impact of the New Middle Manager

But as the new middle people are knowledge professionals, their actions and decisions are intended to have direct and major impact on the business, its ability to perform, and its direction.

Here are some fairly typical examples.

The product manager in companies such as Procter & Gamble's soap and detergent business, in Unilever's food business, or in the radio and TV business of Philips of Holland, is definitely middle management by rank and compensation. He has no command authority. The work is being carried out by people who report to their respective functional bosses, the manufacturing manager, the sales manager, the head of the chemical and development laboratories, and so on. But he is held responsible for the development, the introduction, and the performance of a product in the marketplace. He decides very largely whether a new product should indeed be developed. He decides what its specifications should be. He determines its price. He decides where and how to test-market it. And he decides the sales goals. He does not have any direct command authority and cannot issue an order. But he controls directly a major determinant of performance and success for a branded consumer product, the advertising and promotion budget.

The quality control engineer in a machine tool company also has no command authority and has no one, except junior quality engineers, reporting to him. But he decides the design and structure of the manufacturing process. His quality control standards largely decide the costs of the manufacturing process and the performance of the manufacturing plant. The manufacturing manager or the plant manager does indeed make the decisions. But the quality control man can veto them.

The tax accountant also has no command, can give no orders, and often has no one reporting to him except his secretary. Yet, in effect, he has a veto power over even top-management decisions. His opinion on the tax consequences of a course of action often determines both what a company can do and how it must do it.

The industry specialist in a large commercial bank, e.g., the man who is the expert on retail trade, is not supposed to make loans on his own authority. But the lending officers, in turn, are not supposed to make loans to a retail chain without his approval. And when a retail store customer of the bank gets into difficulties, it is the retail specialist who takes over. The retail specialist in the bank is also expected to determine on his own responsibility and based on his own knowledge whether the bank should, at any given time, expand or contract its lending to retail stores. He is expected to determine what the criteria for loans to retail stores should be. And if he sees a loan to a retail chain which, to him, seems dubious, he is not expected to go "upstairs." He picks up the telephone and calls the lending officer in charge of the account. He cannot "order" the lending officer to call the loan or to cut it back. Still, the lending officer, who may well outrank the retail-trade specialist will not say, "I was *advised* by the specialist to cut back this loan." He will say, "I was *told* by the specialist."

The product manager at Procter & Gamble, the quality engineer, and the tax accountant are not "line" managers. But neither are they "staff." Their function is not advice and teaching. They do "operating" work. Yet they have top-management impacts even though they are not top management in rank, compensation, or function.

To be sure, they cannot make some of the key decisions—what our business is and what it should be; what its objectives are; what the priorities are and should be; where to allocate key resources of capital and people. But even with respect to these decisions they contribute the essential knowledge without which the key decision cannot be made, at least not effectively. And the key decisions cannot become effective unless these new middle managers build them into their own knowledge and work on their own responsibility and on their own authority. In an earlier chapter (Chapter 30) it was argued that the knowledge professional is a manager even though no one reports to him. Now we see that in his impacts and responsibilities he is top management even though he may be five or six organizational levels down.

## The Knowledge Organization

Middle management has not disappeared, as was predicted. Indeed not even the traditional middle manager has disappeared. But yesterday's middle management is being transformed into tomorrow's *knowledge organization*.

This requires restructuring individual jobs, but also restructuring the organization and its design. In the knowledge organization the job, all the way down to the lowest professional or managerial level, has to focus on the company's objectives. It has to focus on contribution, which means that it has to have its own objectives. It has to be organized according to assignment. It has to be thought through and structured according to the flow of information both to and from the individual position. And it has to be placed into the decision structure. It can no longer be designed, as was the traditional middle-management job, in terms of downward authority alone. It has to be recognized instead as multidimensional.

Traditionally, middle-management jobs have been designed narrowly. The first concern has been with the limits on a middle manager's authority. In the knowledge organization we will instead have to ask, "What is the greatest possible contribution this job can make?" The focus will have to shift from concern with authority to stress on responsibility.

## The Need for Clear Decision Authority

The knowledge organization demands clear decision authority. It demands clear thinking through what decision belongs where (see Chapter 42). The knowledge organization is far more complex than the simple "line" organization it is replacing. Unless decision authority is clearly spelled out, it will tend to become confused.

The knowledge organization is also designed to take greater risks. Operating no longer is a "routine" in which the norms are clear. It is a decision-making organization rather than one that has no other function than to keep the machinery running at a preset speed and for already known results. Things, therefore, will go wrong, and in unexpected ways. And unless authority to change the decision is built into the decision itself, malfunction is bound to result.

A major pharmaceutical company decided to introduce seven new products in one year—twice as many as the company had ever introduced before in a single year. An elaborate multinational strategy was worked out in year-long sessions of task forces assembled from all functions, all levels, and all major territories. Some products were to be introduced first into European markets, some into the American market, some first with general practitioners of medicine, others with specialists or in hospitals. When the products were brought out, however, the two which had been considered the weakest unexpectedly developed into best sellers. But the two supposedly strongest products ran into unforeseen troubles which sharply slowed down their growth. In working out the strategy, no one had asked, "If things do not work out as planned, who is going to be responsible for changing the plan?" As a result, there were endless reports, endless studies, endless meetings—and no action. In the end, the company lost much of the benefit of its accomplishments. The two products that had shown unexpected success did not receive the support needed to exploit their acceptance by the medical profession. Competitors who moved in with near-imitations were therefore able to reap most of the harvest. Clinical testing and marketing efforts on the two products that had run into unexpected difficulties should either have been cut back sharply or should have been raised sharply. Everyone saw that; but no one had the authority to make the decision.

In the knowledge organization of the new middle management any program, any project, and any plan will have to ask and answer the question "Who has the authority to change the plan?" And this will lead to far greater devolution of authority to middle people than even the American middle management tradition ever envisaged. Even line managers will need more rather than less authority in the knowledge organization.

In the pharmaceutical company case the field sales manager of the relatively small French subsidiary was the only man who could have prevented the worst damage: the loss to competitors of the market for the one product which unexpectedly turned into a potential best seller. But he had neither the information to understand the significance of his sales results nor the authority to alter his sales goals and his sales plan. And yet nobody had "made a mistake." The French field sales manager was just being treated the way middle management has traditionally been treated, that is, as somebody who carries out orders. But in the knowledge organization the line manager must also be a part of the decision and understand what it implies. He must be given authority commensurate to his responsibility—and this is not knowledge authority, but command authority. Or, if in any area he cannot be given the command authority which his task—and his people—require, it must be perfectly clear, above all to him, where the command authority lies. (On the implications of this for organization structure see discussion of "task force team" and "functional" organization in Chapter 45.)

## Top Management's Role in the Knowledge Organization

In the knowledge organization, top management can no longer assume that the "operating people" do as they are being told. It has to accept that the middle ranks make genuine decisions. But the operating organization can also no longer assume that it can do its job in isolation from top management. It must understand the top-management decisions. Indeed middle management in the knowledge organization must take responsibility for "educating" top management. Top management must understand what the knowledge organization tries to do, what it is capable of doing, and where it sees the major opportunities, the major needs, the major challenges to the enterprise. Finally, middle management must insist that top management make decisions on what the business is and what it should be, on objectives, strategies, and priorities. Otherwise the middle ranks cannot do their own job.

Top management needs to know the knowledge organization and to understand it. It needs to establish communication with it. The traditional American assumption that the people in top management know the middle manager's job because they have been through it is no longer going to be valid. Even the men who have risen into top management through the middle-management organization can no longer expect to have been exposed directly to more than a small sample of the functional work of the knowledge organization. And some of the most important areas of middle management will no longer prepare and test a man for top-management positions.

Indeed the most capable men in such areas will not even want to get into top-management work but will prefer to stay in their specialty. The computer specialist wants, as a rule, to stay within his specialization and work on information and information technology. Equally, most researchers want to stay in research, whether in physical and technical fields, in research on people, or in economic research.

But the assumption that underlies the traditional European approach is also becoming invalid. Middle managers in knowledge organizations can no longer be taken for granted and be treated with condescension as people who, after all, do only routine tasks and only carry out and implement top-management decisions and orders. If it wants to be effective, top management therefore needs to establish team work with, and communications from and to, the knowledge organization.

The most important "public" in the knowledge organization for top management—and the one that most needs a relationship to top management—are the younger and highly specialized knowledge workers. They most need a "godfather" (see Chapter 20). They are least likely to understand what top management is trying to do, least likely to see the business whole, least likely to focus themselves on company objectives and performance. Yet they are likely, because of their knowledge, to have impact early in their careers. In any business of any size or complexity the top-management group needs to organize its relationship to these younger knowledge professionals.

Each member of the top-management team might sit down a few times a year with a group of younger knowledge people and say to them, "I have no agenda. I have nothing I want to tell you. I am here to listen. It is your job to tell me what you think we in top management need to know about your work and how you think we can make it most productive. It is your job to tell me where you see the problems and opportunities for this company and to tell me what we in top management do to help you in your job and what we do that hampers you. I shall insist on only one thing: that *you* have done *your* homework and that you take seriously your responsibility to inform and to educate."

But altogether in the knowledge organization it becomes a top-management job to mobilize, to organize, to place, and to direct knowledge. Knowledge people—and that means managers and career professionals in today's

organization—cannot be seen and treated as inferiors. They are
rank, pay, authority. But they are juniors and colleagues rather tl
dinates.

"Management" means, in the last analysis, the substitution of thought for brawn and muscle, of knowledge for folkways and superstition, and of cooperation for force. It means the substitution of responsibility for obedience to rank, and of authority of performance for authority of power. The knowledge organization, therefore, is what management theory, management thinking, management aspirations have been about, all along. But now the knowledge organization is becoming accomplished fact. The tremendous expansion of managerial employment since World War II converted the middle ranks into knowledge professionals—that is, people paid for putting knowledge to work and to make decisions based on their knowledge which have impact on performance capacity, results, and future directions of the whole enterprise. The task of making these new knowledge people in the middle ranks truly effective and achieving has barely begun. It is a central task in managing managers.

# 36

## The Spirit of Performance

*To Make Common Men Do Uncommon Things—The Test Is Performance, Not Good Feelings—Focus on Strength—Practices, Not Preachments—The Danger of Safe Mediocrity—What "Performance" Means—What to Do with the Nonperformer—"Conscience" Decisions—Focus on Opportunity— "People" Decisions: The Control of an Organization—Integrity, the Touchstone*

The purpose of an organization is to enable common men to do uncommon things.

No organization can depend on genius; the supply is always scarce and unreliable. It is the test of an organization to make ordinary human beings perform better than they seem capable of, to bring out whatever strength there is in its members, and to use each man's strength to help all the other members perform. It is the task of organization at the same time to neutralize the individual weaknesses of its members. The test of an organization is the spirit of performance.

The spirit of performance requires that there be full scope for individual excellence. The focus must be on the strengths of a man—on what he can do rather than on what he cannot do.

"Morale" in an organization does not mean that "people get along together"; the test is performance, not conformance. Human relations that are not grounded in the satisfaction of good performance in work are actually poor human relations and result in a mean spirit. And there is no greater indictment of an organization than that the strength and ability of the outstanding man become a threat to the group and his performance a source of difficulty, frustration, and discouragement for the others.

Spirit of performance in a human organization means that its energy output is larger than the sum of the efforts put in. It means the creation of energy. This cannot be accomplished by mechanical means. A mechanical contrivance can, at its theoretical best, conserve energy, but it cannot create it. To get out more than is being put in is possible only in the moral sphere.

Morality does not mean preachments. Morality, to have any meaning at all, must be a principle of action. It must not be exhortation, sermon, or good intentions. *It must be practices.* Specifically:

1. The focus of the organization must be on *performance.* The first requirement of the spirit of organization is high performance standards, for the group as well as for each individual. The organization must inculcate in itself the habit of achievement.

But performance does not mean "success every time." Performance is rather a "batting average." It will, indeed it must, have room for mistakes and even for failures. What performance has no room for is complacency and low standards.

2. The focus of the organization must be on *opportunities* rather than on problems.

3. The decisions that affect people: their placement and their pay, promotion, demotion and severance, must express the values and beliefs of the organization. They are the true controls of an organization.

4. Finally, in its people decisions, management must demonstrate that it realizes that *integrity* is one absolute requirement of a manager, the one quality that he has to bring with him and cannot be expected to acquire later on. And management must demonstrate that it requires the same integrity of itself.

## The Danger of Safe Mediocrity

The constant temptation of every organization is safe mediocrity. The first requirement of organizational health is a high demand on performance. Indeed, one of the major reasons for demanding that management be by objectives and that it focus on the objective requirements of the task is the need to have managers set high standards of performance for themselves.

This requires that performance be understood properly. Performance is not hitting the bull's-eye with every shot—that is a circus act that can be maintained only over a few minutes. Performance is rather the consistent ability to produce results over prolonged periods of time and in a variety of assignments. A performance record must include mistakes. It must include failures. It must reveal a man's limitations as well as his strengths. And there are as many different kinds of performance as there are different human beings. One man will consistently do well, rarely falling far below a respectable standard, but also rarely excel through brilliance or virtuosity. Another man will perform only adequately under normal circumstances but will rise to the demands of a crisis or a major challenge and then perform like a true "star." Both are "performers." Both need to be recognized. But their performances will look quite different.

The one man to distrust, however, is the man who never makes a mistake, never commits a blunder, never fails in what he tries to do. He is either a phony, or he stays with the safe, the tried, and the trivial.

A management which does not define performance as a batting average is a management that mistakes conformity for achievement, and absence of weaknesses for strengths. It is a management that discourages and demoralizes its organization. The better a man is, the more mistakes he will make —for the more new things he will try.

The man who consistently renders poor or mediocre performance should be removed from his job for his own good. People who find themselves in a job that exceeds their capacities are frustrated, harassed, anxiety-ridden people. One does not do a man a service by leaving him in a job he is not equal to. Not to face up to man's failure in a job is cowardice rather than compassion.

One also owes it to the man's subordinates who have a right to be managed with competence, dedication, and achievement. Subordinates have a right to a boss who performs, for otherwise they themselves cannot perform.

One owes it finally to all the people in the organization not to put up with a manager who fails to perform. The entire organization is diminished by the manager or career professional who performs poorly or not at all. It is enriched by the man who performs superbly.

At first sight the Japanese seem to violate this rule. For few, if any, people ever get fired for nonperformance in the Japanese organization. In actuality the Japanese organization may be as demanding and even as competitive as any in the West. The poor or mediocre performer is not fired; but he is quickly sidetracked and assigned to activities which are in effect "made work." And both he and the organization know it. Moreover, while everyone advances in pay and title according to seniority, there is a day of reckoning at or around age forty-five when the very few who will become company directors, that is, top management, are chosen from the many others who will, ten years later, retire as section managers or department directors.

The only thing that is proven by a man's not performing in a given assignment is that management has made a mistake by putting him in. It is a mistake that no manager can avoid, no matter how carefully he works on the placement of people. The fact that a man who has performed in earlier assignments does not perform in a new one proves nothing except that he should not have been put in the job in the first place.

"Failure" in such a case may mean only that a first-rate career professional has been miscast as a manager. It may mean that a man excellent at running an existing operation has been miscast as an innovator and entrepreneur. Or it may mean the opposite: that a man whose strength lies in doing new and different things has been miscast to head a continuing, well-established, and highly routinized operation.

Failure to perform on the part of a man who has a record of proven performance is a signal to think hard about the man and the job. And sometimes, of course (see the discussion of the "widow-maker" job in Chapter 32) it is the job rather than the man that is at fault.

George C. Marshall, Chief of Staff of the U.S. Army in World War II, was an uncompromising and exacting boss who refused to tolerate mediocrity, let alone failure. "I have a duty to the soldiers, their parents, and the country, to remove immediately any commander who does not satisfy the highest performance demands," Marshall said again and again. But he always asserted, "It was my mistake to have put this or that man in a command that was not the right command for him. It is therefore *my* job to think through where he belongs." Many of the men who emerged in World War II as highly successful commanders in the U.S. Army were once in the course of their careers removed by Marshall from an early assignment. But then Marshall thought through the mistake *he* had made—and tried to figure out where that man belonged. And this explains, in large measure, why the American Army, which had gone into World War II without a single one of its future general officers yet in a command position (these were all held by men past retirement age who had to be moved out), produced an outstanding group of leaders in a few short years.

## "Conscience" Decisions

The toughest cases, but also the most important ones, are those of people who have given long and loyal service to the company but who have outlived their capacity to contribute.

There is, for instance, the bookkeeper who started when the company was in its infancy and grew with it until, at age fifty or so, he finds himself controller of a large company and totally out of his depth. The man has not changed—the demands of the job have. He has given faithful service. And where loyalty has been received, loyalty is due. But still, he must not be allowed to remain as controller. Not only does his inability to perform endanger the company, his inadequacy demoralizes the entire management group and discredits management altogether.

These cases—fortunately not too numerous—challenge the conscience of an organization. To keep the man in his job would be betrayal of the enterprise and of all its people. But to fire a man who has given thirty years of faithful service is also betraying a trust. And to say, "We should have taken care of this twenty-five years ago," while true, is not much help.

The decision in such cases must be objective, that is, focused on the good of the company: the man must be removed from his job. Yet the decision is also a human decision which requires utmost consideration, true compassion, and an acceptance of obligations. That Henry Ford II could revive the moribund Ford Motor Company after World War II was in large measure the result of his understanding the crucial importance of these "conscience cases."

At that time, none of the nine management people in one key division was found to be competent to take on the new jobs created in the course of reorganization. Not one was appointed to these new jobs. Yet, for these nine men, jobs as technicians and experts were found within the organization, jobs which they could be expected to perform. It would have been easy to fire them. Their incompetence as managers was undisputed. But they had also served loyally through very trying years. Henry Ford II took the line that no one should be allowed to hold a job without giving superior performance but also laid down that no one should be penalized for the mistakes of the previous regime. And to the strict observance of this rule the company owes to a considerable extent its rapid revival. (Incidentally, seven of these men did indeed perform in their new jobs—one so well that he was later promoted into a bigger job than the one he originally held. Two men failed; the older one was pensioned off, the younger one discharged.)

The frequent excuse in a conscience case, "We can't move him; he has been here too long to be fired," is bad logic and rarely more than a weak-kneed alibi. It does harm to the performance of management people, to their spirit, and to their respect for the company.

But to fire such a man is equally bad. It violates the organization's sense of justice and decency. It shakes its faith in the integrity of management. "Here, but for the grace of God, go I," is what everybody will say—even though he would be the first to criticize if management left an incompetent in a position of importance.

A management that is concerned with the spirit of the organization therefore takes these cases exceedingly seriously. They are not too common, as a rule—or at least, they should not be. But they have impact on the spirit of the organization way beyond their numbers. How they are handled will tell the organization both whether management takes itself and its job seriously, and whether it takes the human being seriously.

### Focus on Opportunity

An organization will have a high spirit of performance if it is consistently directed toward opportunity rather than toward problems. It will have the thrill of excitement, the sense of challenge, and the satisfaction of achievement if its energies are put where the results are, and that means on the opportunities.*

Of course, problems cannot be neglected. But the problem-focused organization is an organization on the defensive. It is an organization that forever considers yesterday to have been the golden age. It is an organization that feels that it has performed well if things do not get worse.

A management that wants to create and maintain the spirit of achievement in its company therefore stresses opportunity. But it will also demand that opportunities be converted into results.

A management that wants to make its organization focus on opportunity demands that opportunity be given pride of place in the objectives and goals of each manager and career professional. "What are the opportunities which, if realized, will have the greatest impact on performance and results of the company and of my unit?" should be the first topic to which each manager and career professional should address himself in his performance and work plan.

### "People" Decisions—The Control of an Organization

An organization that wants to build a high spirit of performance recognizes that "people" decisions—on placement and on pay, on promotion, demotion, and firing—are the true "control" of an organization. They, far more than the accountant's figures and reports, model and mold behavior. For the people decision signals to every member of the organization what it is that management really wants, really values, really rewards.

The company which preaches "our first-line supervisors are expected to practice human relations" and which then, every time, promotes the supervisor who gets his paperwork in on time and neatly done, will not get "human relations." Even the dumbest foreman will learn very soon that what the company really wants is neat paperwork.

Indeed an organization tends to overreact to the people decisions of management. What to top management may look like an innocuous compromise to remove an obstacle or to solve a political impasse may well be

*On the opportunity focus, see also my book, *Managing for Results.*

a clear signal to the organization that management wants one kind of behavior while preaching another.

Placement and promotion are the most crucial people decisions. They, above all, require careful thinking and clear policy and procedures which live up to high standards of fairness and equity. They should never be made on the basis of opinions and on a man's "potential." They should always be based on a factual record of performance against explicit goals and objectives.

But the best placement and promotion procedures do not insure by themselves that these crucial decisions fortify and build the spirit of the organization rather than impair it. For this, top management must build itself into the promotion process. Above all, it must make sure that it participates in the key decisions on promotion, the decisions which, in effect, spell out to the organization what management's values and beliefs really are and at the same time determine—often irrevocably—the top management of tomorrow.

All top managements take an active role in the decisions on promotion to the jobs directly below or in the top-management group: the promotion into position of general manager of major divisions or into position as the head of major functional areas, such as manufacturing or marketing. But few top managements, especially in larger businesses, take much interest in the promotion decisions just below the top group, that is, into such jobs as head of market research, plant manager, head of pharmacology in the research lab, or even marketing manager of a division. They leave these decisions to the top people in the respective functions or divisions. Yet these upper-middle-management jobs are truly *the* management to the organization. People further down, and especially the younger managers and career professionals, know very well that their own careers depend on these upper-middle people rather than on the big boss. And it is the decision whom to put into one of these upper-middle spots which in effect decides who, a few years hence, will be eligible for a top-management assignment.

Above all, these promotional decisions have the highest symbolical value. They are highly "visible" and signal to the entire organization, "This is what this company wants, rewards, recognizes." For this reason, old and experienced organizations, such as the Army and the Catholic Church, put their main concern with promotion on upper-middle management—in the Army on promotion to the colonelcy, and in the Catholic Church on selecting an auxiliary bishop.

It would be wise for top management to learn from these examples. It is well worth top management's time to take an active part in the promotions to the levels which for the organization mean management.

## Integrity, the Touchstone

The final proof of the sincerity and seriousness of a management is uncompromising emphasis on integrity of character. This, above all, has to be symbolized in management's "people" decisions. For it is character through which leadership is exercised; it is character that sets the example and is imitated. Character is not something a man can acquire; if he does not bring it to the job, he will never have it. It is not something one can fool people about. The men with whom a man works, and especially his subordinates, know in a few weeks whether he has integrity or not. They may forgive a man a great deal: incompetence, ignorance, insecurity, or bad manners. But they will not forgive his lack of integrity. Nor will they forgive higher management for choosing him.

Integrity may be difficult to define, but what constitutes lack of integrity of such seriousness as to disqualify a man for a managerial position is not. A man should never be appointed to a managerial position if his vision focuses on people's weaknesses rather than on their strengths. The man who always knows exactly what people cannot do, but never sees anything they can do, will undermine the spirit of his organization. Of course, a manager should have a clear grasp of the limitations of his people, but he should see these as limitations on what they can do, and as challenges to them to do better. He should be a realist; and no one is less realistic than the cynic.

A man should not be appointed if he is more interested in the question "Who is right?" than in the question "What is right?" To put personality above the requirements of the work is corruption and corrupts. To ask "Who is right?" encourages one's subordinates to play safe, if not to play politics. Above all, it encourages them to "cover up" rather than to take corrective action as soon as they find out that they have made a mistake.

Management should not appoint a man who considers intelligence more important than integrity. This is immaturity—and usually incurable. It should never promote a man who has shown that he is afraid of strong subordinates. This is weakness. It should never put into a management job a man who does not set high standards for his own work. For that breeds contempt for the work and for management's competence.

A man might himself know too little, perform poorly, lack judgment and ability, and yet not do too much damage as a manager. But if he lacks in character and integrity—no matter how knowledgeable, how brilliant, how successful—he destroys. He destroys people, the most valuable resource of the enterprise. He destroys spirit. And he destroys performance.

This is particularly true of the people at the head of an enterprise. For the spirit of an organization is created from the top. If an organization is great in spirit, it is because the spirit of its top people is great. If it decays, it does so because the top rots; as the proverb has it, "Trees die from the top." No one should ever be appointed to a senior position unless top management is willing to have his character serve as the model for his subordinates.

This chapter has talked of "practices." It has not talked of "leadership." This was intentional. There is no substitute for leadership. But management cannot create leaders. It can only create the conditions under which potential leadership qualities become effective; or it can stifle potential leadership. The supply of leadership is much too uncertain to be depended upon for the creation of the spirit the enterprise needs to be productive and to hold together.

But practices, though seemingly humdrum, can always be practiced whatever a man's aptitudes, personality, or attitudes. They require no genius—only application. They are things to do rather than to talk about.

And the right practices should go a long way toward bringing out, recognizing, and using whatever potential for leadership there is in the management group. They should also lay the foundation for the right kind of leadership. For leadership is not magnetic personality—that can just as well be demagoguery. It is not "making friends and influencing people"— that is flattery. Leadership is the lifting of a man's vision to higher sights, the raising of a man's performance to a higher standard, the building of a man's personality beyond its normal limitations. Nothing better prepares the ground for such leadership than a spirit of management that confirms in the day-to-day practices of the organization strict principles of conduct and responsibility, high standards of performance, and respect for the individual and his work.

## Managerial Skills

Managing is specific work. As such it requires specific skills. Among them are:

—making effective decisions;
—communications within and without the organization;
—the proper use of controls and measurements;
—the proper use of analytical tools, that is, of the management sciences.

No manager is likely to master all these skills. But every manager needs to understand what they are, what they can do for him, and what, in turn, they require of him. Every manager needs basic literacy with respect to essential managerial skills.

# 37

## The Effective Decision*

Executives do many things in addition to making decisions. But only executives make decisions. The first managerial skill is, therefore, the making of effective decisions.

There are countless books on the techniques of decision-making. Complex logical and mathematical tools have been developed for the decision-making process. But there is little concern with the essential process itself. What is a "decision"? What are the important elements in it?

The only people who have developed a systematic and standardized approach to decision-making are the Japanese. Their decisions are highly effective. Yet their approach violates every rule in the books on decision-making. Indeed, according to the books, the Japanese should never be able to arrive at a decision, let alone an effective one. It might, therefore, be fruitful to take a look at the Japanese way of decision-making in order to find out what the elements of the process are.

---

*This chapter draws heavily on my earlier book, *The Effective Executive*.

### How the Japanese Make Decisions

If there is one point on which all authorities on Japan are in agreement, it is that Japanese institutions, whether business or government agencies, make decisions by consensus. The Japanese, we are told, debate a proposed decision throughout the organization until there is agreement on it. And only then do they make the decision.

This, every experienced Western manager will say with a shudder, is not for us, however well it might work for the Japanese. This approach can lead only to indecision or politicking, or at best to an innocuous compromise which offends no one but also solves nothing. And if proof of this were needed, the American might add, the history of President Lyndon B. Johnson's attempt to obtain a consensus would supply it.

But what stands out in Japanese history, as well as in today's Japanese management behavior, is the capacity for making 180-degree turns—that is, for reaching radical and highly controversial decisions. Let me illustrate:

No country was more receptive to Christianity than sixteenth-century Japan. Indeed, the hope of the Portuguese missionaries that Japan would become the first Christian country outside of Europe was by no means just wishful thinking. Yet the same Japan made a 180-degree turn in the early seventeenth century. Within a few years it completely suppressed Christianity and shut itself off from all foreign influences—indeed, from all contact with the outside world—and stayed that way for 250 years. Then, in the Meiji Restoration of 1867, Japan executed another 180-degree turn and opened itself to the West—something no other non-European country managed to do.

Toyo Rayon (Toray), the largest Japanese manufacturer of man-made fibers, made nothing but rayon as late as the mid-1950s. Then it decided to switch to synthetic fibers. But it did not phase out rayon making, as every Western company in a similar situation has done. Instead, it closed its rayon mills overnight, even though, under the Japanese system of employment, it could not lay off a single man.

As late as 1966, when I discussed this matter with its officials, the Ministry of International Trade and Industry was adamantly opposed to any Japanese companies going multinational and making investments in manufacturing affiliates abroad. But three years later, the same ministry officials, working for the same conservative government, had turned around completely and were pushing Japanese manufacturing investments abroad.

The key to this apparent contradiction is that the Westerner and the Japanese mean something different when they talk of "making a decision." In the West, all the emphasis is on the *answer* to the question. Indeed, our books on decision-making try to develop systematic approaches to giving an answer. To the Japanese, however, the important element in decision-making is *defining the question.* The important and crucial steps are to decide whether there is a need for a decision and what the decision is about. And it is in this step that the Japanese aim at attaining consensus. Indeed, it is this step that, to the Japanese, is the essence of the decision. The answer to the question (what the West considers *the* decision) follows from its definition.

During the process that precedes the decision, no mention is made of what the answer might be. This is done so that people will not be forced to take sides; once they have taken sides, a decision would be a victory for one side and a defeat for the other. Thus the whole process is focused on finding out what the decision is really about, not what the decision should be. Its result is a meeting of the minds that there is (or is not) a need for a change in behavior.

All of this takes a long time, of course. The Westerner dealing with the Japanese is thoroughly frustrated during the process. He does not understand what is going on. He has the feeling that he is being given the runaround.

To take a specific example, it is very hard for a U.S. executive to understand why the Japanese with whom he is negotiating on, say, a license agreement, keep on sending new groups of people every few months who start what the Westerner thinks are "negotiations" as if they had never heard of the subject. One delegation takes copious notes and goes back home, only to be succeeded six weeks later by another team of people from different areas of the company who again act as if they had never heard of the matter under discussion, take copious notes, and go home.

Actually—though few of my Western friends believe it—this is a sign that the Japanese take the matter seriously. They are trying to involve the people who will have to carry out an eventual agreement in the process of obtaining consensus that a license is indeed needed. Only when all of the people who will have to carry out the agreement have come together on the need to make a decision will the decision be made to go ahead. Only then do negotiations really start—and then the Japanese usually move with great speed.

There is a complete account of this process at work—though it does not concern a business decision. The account deals with the decision to go to war against the United States in 1941.*

When the Japanese reach the point we call a decision, they say they are

---

*See *Japan's Decision for War, Records of the 1941 Policy Conferences,* translated and edited by Nobutaka Ike (Stanford University Press, 1967).

in the *action stage*. Now top management refers the decision to what the Japanese call the "appropriate people." Determination of who these people are is a top-management decision. On that decision depends the specific answer to the problem that is to be worked out. For, during the course of the discussions leading up to the consensus, it has become quite clear what basic approaches certain people or certain groups would take to the problem. Top management, by referring the question to one group or the other, in effect picks the answer—but an answer which by now will surprise no one.

This referral to the appropriate people is as crucial as the parallel decision in the U. S. political process which baffles any foreign observer of American government—the decision to which committee or subcommittee of the Congress a certain bill is to be assigned. This decision is not to be found in any of the books on U. S. government and politics. Yet, as every American politician knows, it is the crucial step which decides whether the bill is to become law and what form it will take. For each committee—the one on Agriculture, for instance, or the one on Banking and Finance—has its own well-known point of view, its own "constituents" to whom it is willing to listen, and its own preferences, taboos, and sacred cows.

What are the advantages of this process? And what can we learn from it?

In the first place, it makes for very effective decisions. While it takes much longer in Japan to reach a decision than it takes in the West, from that point on they do better than we do. After making a decision, we in the West spend much time "selling" it and getting people to act on it. Only too often either the decision is sabotaged by the organization or, what may be worse, it takes so long to make the decision truly effective that it becomes obsolete, if not outright wrong, by the time the people in the organization actually make it operational.

The Japanese, by contrast, need to spend absolutely no time on selling a decision. Everybody has been presold. Also, their process makes it clear where in the organization a certain answer to a question will be welcomed and where it will be resisted. Therefore, there is plenty of time to work on persuading the dissenters, or on making small concessions to them which will win them over without destroying the integrity of the decision.

Every Westerner who has done business with the Japanese has learned that the apparent inertia of the negotiating stage, with its endless delays and endless discussion of the same points, is followed by a speed of action that leaves him hanging on the ropes.

It may take three years before a licensing agreement can be reached, during which time there is no discussion of terms, no discussion of what products the Japanese plan to make, no discussion of what knowledge and help they might need. And then, within four weeks, the Japanese are ready to go into production and make demands on their Western partner for information and people which he is totally unprepared to meet. Now it is the Japanese who complain, and bitterly, about the "endless delay and procrastination" of the Westerner. For they understand our way of making a decision and acting on it no better than we understand their way of considering a decision and acting on it.

The Japanese process is focused on understanding the problem. The desired end result is action and behavior on the part of people. This almost guarantees that all the alternatives will be considered. It rivets management attention to essentials. It does not permit commitment until management has decided what the decision is all about. Japanese managers may come up with the wrong answer to the problem (as was the decision to go to war against the United States in 1941), but they rarely come up with the right answer to the wrong problem. And that, as all decision-makers learn, is the most dangerous course, the irretrievably wrong decision.

Above all, their system forces the Japanese to make big decisions. It is much too cumbersome to be put to work on minor matters. It takes far too many people far too long to be wasted on anything but truly important matters leading to real changes in policies and behavior. Small decisions, even when obviously needed, are very often not being made at all in Japan for that reason.

With us it is the small decisions which are easy to make—decisions about things that do not greatly matter. Anyone who knows Western businesses, government agencies, or educational institutions knows that their managers make far too many small decisions as a rule. And nothing causes as much trouble in an organization as a lot of small decisions. Whether the decision concerns moving the water cooler from one end of the hall to the other or the phasing out of one's oldest business makes little emotional difference. One decision takes as much time and generates as much heat as the other.

To contrast the Japanese approach and the Western approach, let me illustrate: I once watched a Japanese company work through a proposal for a joint venture received from a well-known American company, with whom the Japanese had done business for many years. The Orientals did not even discuss the joint venture at the outset. They started out with the question "Do we have to change the basic directions of our business?" As a result, a consensus emerged that change was desirable; management decided to go out of a number of old businesses and start in a number of new technologies and markets; the joint venture was to be one element of a major new strategy. Until the Japanese understood that the decision was really about the *direction* of the business, and that there was need for a decision on that, they did not once, among themselves, discuss the desirability of the joint venture or the terms on which it might be set up.

In the West we are moving in the Japanese direction. At least, this is what the many task forces, long-range plans, strategies, and other approaches are trying to accomplish. But we do not build into the development of these projects the selling which the Japanese process achieves before the decision. This explains in large measure why so many brilliant reports of task forces and planners never get beyond the planning stage.

U. S. executives expect task forces and long-range planning groups to come up with recommendations—that is, to commit themselves to one alternative. The groups decide on an answer and then document it. To the Japanese, however, the most important step is understanding the alternatives available. They are as opinionated as we are. But they discipline themselves not to commit themselves to a recommendation until they have fully defined the question and used the process of obtaining consensus to bring out the full range of alternatives. As a result, they are far less likely to become prisoners of their preconceived answers than we are.

What are the essentials of the Japanese method of decision-making? First the focus is on deciding what the decision is all about. The Japanese do not focus on giving an answer; they focus on defining the question.

The Japanese, second, bring out dissenting opinions; because there is no discussion of the answer till there is consensus, a wide variety of opinions and approaches is being explored.

Third, the focus is on alternatives rather than on the "right solution." The process further brings out at what level and by whom a certain decision should be made. And finally, it eliminates selling a decision. It builds effective execution into the decision-making process.

The specific Japanese system is, indeed, *sui generis*. It could not be used elsewhere but presupposes the unique social organization of Japan and of Japanese institutions. But the principles which the Japanese put to work in their decision-making process are generally applicable. They are the essentials of effective decision-making.

### Facts or Opinions?

A decision is a judgment. It is a choice between alternatives. It is rarely a choice between right and wrong. It is at best a choice between "almost right" and "probably wrong"—but much more often a choice between two courses of action neither of which is provably more nearly right than the other.

Most books on decision-making tell the reader: "First find the facts." But managers who make effective decisions know that one does not start with facts. One starts with opinions. These are, of course, nothing but untested hypotheses and, as such, worthless unless tested against reality. To determine what is a fact requires first a decision on the criteria of relevance, especially on the appropriate measurement. This is the hinge of the effective decision, and usually its most controversial aspect.

But also, the effective decision does not, as so many tests on decision-making proclaim, flow from a "consensus on the facts." The understanding that underlies the right decision grows out of the clash and conflict of divergent opinions and out of the serious consideration of competing alternatives.

To get the facts first is impossible. There are no facts unless one has a criterion of relevance. Events by themselves are not facts.

Only by starting out with opinions can the decision-maker find out what the decision is all about. People do, of course, differ in the answers they give. But most differences of opinion reflect an underlying—and usually hidden—difference as to what the decision is actually about. They reflect a difference regarding the question that has to be answered. Thus to identify the alternative questions is the first step in making effective decisions.

Conversely, there are few things as futile—and as damaging—as the right answer to the wrong question.

The effective decision-maker also knows that he starts out with opinions anyhow. The only choice he has is between using opinions as a productive factor in the decision-making process and deceiving himself into false objectivity. People do not start out with the search for facts. They start out with an opinion. There is nothing wrong with this. People experienced in an area should be expected to have an opinion. Not to have an opinion after having been exposed to an area for a good long time would argue an unobservant eye and a sluggish mind.

People inevitably start out with an opinion; to ask them to search for the facts first is even undesirable. They will simply do what everyone is far too prone to do anyhow: look for the facts that fit the conclusion they have already reached. And no one has ever failed to find the facts he is looking for. The good statistician knows this and distrusts all figures—he either knows the fellow who found them or he does not know him; in either case he is suspicious.

The only rigorous method, the only one that enables us to test an opinion against reality, is based on the clear recognition that opinions come first—and that is the way it should be. Then no one can fail to see that we start out with untested hypotheses—in decision-making, as in science, the only starting point. We know what to do with hypotheses. One does not argue them; one tests them. One finds out which hypotheses are tenable, and therefore worthy of serious consideration, and which are eliminated by the first test against observable experience.

The effective decision-maker therefore encourages opinions. But he insists that the people who voice them also think through what it is that the "experiment"—that is, the testing of the opinion against reality—would have to show. The effective executive, therefore, asks, "What do we have to know to test the validity of this hypothesis?" "What would the facts have to be to make this opinion tenable?" And he makes it a habit—in himself and in the people with whom he works—to think through and spell out what needs to be looked at, studied, and tested. He insists that people who voice an opinion also take responsibility for defining what factual findings can be expected and should be looked for.

Perhaps the crucial question here is "What is the measurement appropriate to the matter under discussion and to the decision to be reached?" Whenever one analyzes the way a truly effective, a truly right, decision has been reached, one finds that a great deal of work and thought went into finding the appropriate measurement.

## The Need for Dissent and Alternatives

Unless one has considered alternatives, one has a closed mind. This, above all, explains why the Japanese deliberately disregard the second major command of the textbooks on decision-making and create discussion and dissent as a means to consensus.

Decisions of the kind the executive has to make are not made well by acclamation. They are made well only if based on the clash of conflicting views, the dialogue between different points of view, the choice between different judgments. The first rule in decision-making is that one does not make a decision unless there is disagreement.

Alfred P. Sloan, Jr., is reported to have said at a meeting of one of the GM top committees, "Gentlemen, I take it we are all in complete agreement on the decision here." Everyone around the table nodded assent. "Then," continued Mr. Sloan, "I propose we postpone further discussion of this matter until our next meeting to give ourselves time to develop disagreement and perhaps gain some understanding of what the decision is all about."

Sloan was anything but an "intuitive" decision-maker. He always emphasized the need to test opinions against facts and the need to make absolutely sure that one did not start out with the conclusion and then look for the facts that would support it. But he knew that the right decision demands adequate disagreement.

Every one of the effective presidents in American history had his own method of producing the disagreement he needed in order to make an effective decision. Washington, we know, hated conflicts and quarrels and wanted a united Cabinet. Yet he made quite sure of the necessary differences of opinion on important matters by asking both Hamilton and Jefferson for their opinions.

There are three reasons why dissent is needed. It first safeguards the decision-maker against becoming the prisoner of the organization. Everybody always wants something from the decision-maker. Everybody is a special pleader, trying—often in perfectly good faith—to obtain the decision he favors. This is true whether the decision-maker is the president of the United States or the most junior engineer working on a design modification.

The only way to break out of the prison of special pleading and preconceived notions is to make sure of argued, documented, thought-through disagreements.

Second, disagreement alone can provide alternatives to a decision. And a decision without an alternative is a desperate gambler's throw, no matter how carefully thought through it might be. There is always a high possibility that the decision will prove wrong—either because it was wrong to begin with or because a change in circumstances makes it wrong. If one has thought through alternatives during the decision-making process, one has something to fall back on, something that has already been thought through, studied, understood. Without such an alternative, one is likely to flounder dismally when reality proves a decision to be inoperative.

Both the Schlieffen Plan of the German Army in 1914 and President Franklin D. Roosevelt's original economic program in 1933 were disproved by events at the very moment when they should have taken effect.

The German Army never recovered. It never formulated another strategic concept. It went from one ill-conceived improvisation to the next. But this was inevitable. For twenty-five years no alternatives to the Schlieffen Plan had been considered by the General Staff. All its skills had gone into working out the details of this master plan. When the plan fell to pieces, no one had an alternative to fall back on. All the German generals could do, therefore, was gamble—with the odds against them.

By contrast, President Roosevelt, who, in the months before he took office, had based his whole campaign on the slogan of economic orthodoxy, had a team of able people, the later "Brains Trust," working on an alternative—a radical policy based on the proposals of the old-time Progressives, and aimed at economic and social reform on a grand scale. When the collapse of the banking system made it clear that economic orthodoxy had become political suicide, Roosevelt had his alternative ready. He therefore had a policy.

Above all, disagreement is needed to stimulate the imagination. One may not need imagination to find the *one right* solution to a problem. But then this is of value only in mathematics. In all matters of true uncertainty such as the executive deals with—whether his sphere be political, economic, social, or military—one needs creative solutions which create a new situation. And this means that one needs imagination—a new and different way of perceiving and understanding.

Imagination of the first order is, I admit, not in abundant supply. But neither is it as scarce as is commonly believed. Imagination needs to be challenged and stimulated, however, or else it remains latent and unused. Disagreement, especially if forced to be reasoned, thought through, documented, is the most effective stimulus we know.

The effective decision-maker, therefore, organizes dissent. This protects him against being taken in by the plausible but false or incomplete. It gives him the alternatives so that he can choose and make a decision, but also ensures that he is not lost in the fog when his decision proves deficient or wrong in execution. And it forces the imagination—his own and that of his associates. Dissent converts the plausible into the right and the right into the good decision.

## The Trap of "Being Right"

The effective decision-maker does not start out with the assumption that one proposed course of action is right and that all others must be wrong. Nor does he start out with the assumption "I am right and he is wrong." He starts out with the commitment to find out why people disagree.

Effective executives know, of course, that there are fools around and that there are mischief-makers. But they do not assume that the man who disagrees with what they themselves see as clear and obvious is, therefore, either a fool or a knave. They know that unless proven otherwise, the dissenter has to be assumed to be reasonably intelligent and reasonably fair-minded. Therefore, it has to be assumed that he has reached his so obviously wrong conclusion because he sees a different reality and is concerned with a different problem. The effective executive, therefore, always asks, "What does this fellow have to see if his position were, after all, tenable, rational, intelligent?" The effective executive is concerned first with *understanding*. Only then does he even think about who is right and who is wrong.*

Needless to say, this is not done by a great many people, whether executives or not. Most people start out with the certainty that how they see is the only way to see at all. As a result, they never understand what the decision—and indeed the whole argument—is really all about.

The American steel executives have never asked the question "Why do these union people get so terribly upset every time we mention the word 'featherbedding'?" The union people in turn have never asked themselves

*This, of course, is nothing new. It is indeed only a rephrasing of Mary Parker Follett (see her *Dynamic Administration,* ed. by Henry C. Metcalf and L. Urwick [Harper & Row, 1941]), who in turn only extended Plato's arguments in his great dialogue on rhetoric, the *Phaedo.*

why steel managements make such a fuss over featherbedding when every single instance thereof they have ever produced has proved to be petty, and irrelevant to boot. Instead, both sides have worked mightily to prove each other wrong. If either side had tried to understand what the other one sees and why, both would be a great deal stronger, and labor relations in the steel industry, if not in U.S. industry, might be a good deal healthier.

No matter how high his emotions run, no matter how certain he is that the other side is completely wrong and has no case at all, the executive who wants to make the right decision forces himself to see opposition as *his* means to think through the alternatives. He uses conflict of opinion as his tool to make sure all major aspects of an important matter are looked at carefully.

## Is a Decision Necessary?

There is one question the effective decision-maker asks: "Is a decision really necessary?" *One* alternative is always the alternative of doing nothing.

One has to make a decision when a condition is likely to degenerate if nothing is done. This also applies with respect to opportunity. If the opportunity is important and is likely to vanish unless one acts with dispatch, one acts—and one makes a radical change.

Theodore Vail's contemporaries agreed with him as to the degenerative danger of government ownership; but they wanted to fight it by fighting symptoms—fighting this or that bill in the legislature, opposing this or that candidate and supporting another, and so on. Vail alone understood that this is the ineffectual way to fight a degenerative condition. Even if one wins every battle, one can never win the war. He saw that drastic action was needed to create a new situation. He alone saw that private business had to make public regulation into an effective alternative to nationalization.*

At the opposite end there are those conditions with respect to which one can, without being unduly optimistic, expect that they will take care of themselves even if nothing is done. If the answer to the question "What will happen if we do nothing?" is "It will take care of itself," one does not interfere. Nor does one interfere if the condition, while annoying, is of no importance and unlikely to make much difference.

It is a rare executive who understands this. The controller who in a financial crisis preaches cost reduction is seldom capable of leaving alone

*See also Chapter 13.

minor blemishes, elimination of which will achieve nothing. He may know, for instance, that the significant costs are in the sales organization and in physical distribution. And he will work hard and brilliantly at getting them under control. But then he will discredit himself and the whole effort by making a big fuss about the "unnecessary" employment of two or three old men in an otherwise efficient and well-run plant. And he will dismiss as immoral the argument that eliminating these few semipensioners will not make any difference anyhow. "Other people are making sacrifices," he will argue. "Why should the plant people get away with inefficiency?"

When it is all over, the organization will forget that he saved the business. They will remember, though, his vendetta against the two or three poor devils in the plant—and rightly so. *De minimis non curat praetor* (The magistrate does not consider trifles) said the Roman law almost two thousand years ago—but many decision-makers still need to learn it.

The great majority of decisions will lie between these extremes. The problem is not going to take care of itself; but it is unlikely to turn into degenerative malignancy either. The opportunity is only for improvement rather than for real change and innovation; but it is still quite considerable. If we do not act, in other words, we will in all probability survive. But if we do act, we may be better off.

In this situation the effective decision-maker compares effort and risk of action to risk of inaction. There is no formula for the right decision here. But the guidelines are so clear that decision in the concrete case is rarely difficult. They are:

—act if on balance the benefits greatly outweigh cost and risk; and
—act or do not act; but do not "hedge" or compromise.

The surgeon who takes out only half the tonsils or half the appendix risks as much infection and shock as if he did the whole job. And he has not cured the condition, has indeed made it worse. He either operates or he doesn't. Similarly, the effective decision-maker either acts or he doesn't act. He does not take half-action. This is the one thing that is always wrong.

## Who Has to Do the Work?

When they reach this point, most decision-makers in the West think they can make an effective decision. But, as the Japanese example shows, one essential element is still missing. An effective decision is a commitment to action and results. If it has to be "sold" *after* it has been made, there will be no action and no results—and, in effect, no decision. At the least, there may be so much delay as to obsolete the decision before it has become truly effective.

The first rule is to make sure that everyone who will have to do something to make the decision effective—or who could sabotage it—has been forced to participate responsibly in the discussion. This is not "democracy." It is salesmanship.

But it is equally important to build the action commitments into the decision from the start. In fact, no decision has been made unless carrying it out in specific steps has become someone's work assignment and responsibility. Until then, there are only good intentions.

This is the trouble with so many policy statements, especially of business: they contain no action commitment. To carry them out is no one's specific work and responsibility. No wonder that the people in the organization tend to view these statements cynically if not as declarations of what top management is really not going to do.

Converting a decision into action requires answering several distinct questions: "Who has to know of this decision?" "What action has to be taken?" "Who is to take it?" "And what does the action have to be so that the people who have to do it *can* do it?" The first and the last of these are too often overlooked—with dire results.

A story that has become a legend among management scientists illustrates the importance of the question "Who has to know?" A major manufacturer of industrial equipment decided to discontinue one model. For years it had been standard equipment on a line of machine tools, many of which were still in use. It was decided, therefore, to sell the model to present owners of the old equipment for another three years as a replacement, and then to stop making and selling it. Orders for this particular model had been going down for a good many years. But they shot up temporarily as former customers reordered against the day when the model would no longer be available. No one had, however, asked, "Who needs to know of this decision?" Therefore nobody informed the clerk in the purchasing department who was in charge of buying the parts from which the model itself was being assembled. His instructions were to buy parts in a given ratio to current sales—and the instructions remained unchanged. When the time came to discontinue further production of the model, the company had in its warehouse enough parts for another eight to ten years of production, parts that had to be written off at a considerable loss.

Above all, the action must be appropriate to the capacities of the people who have to carry it out.

A chemical company found itself, in the early sixties, with fairly large amounts of blocked currency in two West African countries. To protect this money, it decided to invest in local businesses which would contribute to the local economy, would not require imports from abroad, and would, if successful, be the kind that could be sold to local investors if and when currency remittances became possible again. To establish these businesses, the company developed a simple chemical process to preserve a tropical fruit which is a staple crop in both countries and which, up until then, had suffered serious spoilage in transit to its markets.

The business was a success in both countries. But in one country the local manager set the business up in such a manner that it required highly skilled and, above all, technically trained management of the kind not easily available in West Africa. In the other country the local manager thought through the capacities of the people who would eventually have to run the business and worked hard at making both process and business simple and at staffing from the start with nationals of the country right up to the top.

A few years later it became possible again to transfer currency from these two countries. But though the business flourished, no buyer could be found for it in the first country. No one available locally had the necessary managerial and technical skills. The business had to be liquidated at a loss. In the other country so many local entrepreneurs were eager to buy the business that the company repatriated its original investment with a substantial profit.

The process and the business built on it were essentially the same in both places. But in the first country no one had asked, "What kind of people do we have available to make this decision effective? And what can they do?" As a result, the decision itself became frustrated.

All this becomes doubly important when people have to change behavior, habits, or attitudes if a decision is to become effective action. Here one has to make sure not only that responsibility for the action is clearly assigned and that the people responsible are capable of doing the needful. One has to make sure that their measurements, their standards for accomplishment, and their incentives are changed simultaneously. Otherwise, the people will get caught in a paralyzing internal emotional conflict.

Theodore Vail's decision that the business of the Bell System was service might have remained dead letter but for the yardsticks of service performance which he designed to measure managerial performance. Bell managers were used to being measured by the profitability of their units, or at the least, by cost. The new yardsticks made them accept rapidly the new objectives.

If the greatest rewards are given for behavior contrary to that which the new course of action requires, then everyone will conclude that this contrary behavior is what the people at the top really want and are going to reward.

Not everyone can do what Vail did and build the execution of his decisions into the decision itself. But everyone can think through what action commitments a specific decision requires, what work assignment follows from it, and what people are available to carry it out.

## The Right and the Wrong Compromise

The decision is now ready to be made. The specifications have been thought through, the alternatives explored, the risks and gains weighed. Who will have to do what is understood. At this point it is indeed reasonably clear what course of action should be taken. At this point the decision does indeed almost "make itself."

And it is at this point that most decisions are lost. It becomes suddenly quite obvious that the decision is not going to be pleasant, is not going to be popular, is not going to be easy. It becomes clear that a decision requires courage as much as it requires judgment. There is no inherent reason why medicines should taste horrible—but effective ones usually do. Similarly, there is no inherent reason why decisions should be distasteful—but most effective ones are.

The reason is always the same: there is no "perfect" decision. One always has to pay a price. One has always to subordinate one set of *desiderata.* One always has to balance conflicting objectives, conflicting opinions, and conflicting priorities. The best decision is only an approximation—and a risk. And there is always the pressure to compromise to gain acceptance, to placate strong opponents of the proposed course of action or to hedge risks.

To make effective decisions under such circumstances requires starting out with a firm commitment to what is right rather than with the question "Who is right?" One has to compromise in the end. But unless one starts out with the closest one can come to the decision that will truly satisfy objective requirements, one ends up with the wrong compromise—the compromise that abandons essentials.

For there are two different kinds of compromise. One kind is expressed in the old proverb "Half a loaf is better than no bread." The other kind is expressed in the story of the Judgment of Solomon, which was clearly based on the realization that "half a baby is worse than no baby at all." In the first instance, objective requirements are still being satisfied. The purpose of bread is to provide food, and half a loaf is still food. Half a baby, however, is not half of a living and growing child. It is a corpse in two pieces.

It is, above all, fruitless and a waste of time to worry about what is acceptable and what one had better not say so as not to evoke resistance. The things one worries about never happen. And objections and difficulties no one thought about suddenly turn out to be almost insurmountable obstacles. One gains nothing, in other words, by starting out with the question "What is acceptable?" And in the process of answering it, one loses any chance to come up with an effective, let alone with the right, answer.

## The Feedback

A feedback has to be built into the decision to provide continuous testing, against actual events, of the expectations that underlie the decision. Few decisions work out the way they are intended to. Even the best decision usually runs into snags, unexpected obstacles, and all kinds of surprises. Even the most effective decision eventually becomes obsolete. Unless there is feedback from the results of a decision, it is unlikely to produce the desired results.

This requires first that the expectations be spelled out clearly—and in writing. Second, it requires an organized effort to follow up. And this feedback is part of the decision and has to be worked out in the decision process.

When General Eisenhower was elected president, his predecessor, Harry Truman, said: "Poor Ike; when he was a general, he gave an order and it was carried out. Now he is going to sit in that big office and he'll give an order and not a damn thing is going to happen."

The reason why "not a damn thing is going to happen" is, however, not that generals have more authority than presidents. It is that military organizations learned long ago that futility is the lot of most orders and organized the feedback to check on the execution of the order. They learned long ago that to go oneself and look is the only reliable feedback.* Reports—all an American president is normally able to mobilize—are not much help. All military services have long ago learned that the officer who has given an order goes out and sees for himself whether it has been carried out. At the least he sends one of his own aides—he never relies on what he is told by the subordinate to whom the order was given. Not that he distrusts the subordinate; he has learned from experience to distrust communications.

One needs organized information for the feedback. One needs reports and figures. But unless one builds one's feedback around direct exposure to reality—unless one disciplines oneself to go out and look—one condemns oneself to sterile dogmatism and with it to ineffectiveness.

In sum: decision-making is not a mechanical job. It is risk-taking and a challenge to judgment. The "right answer" (which usually cannot be found anyway) is not central. Central is understanding of the problem. Decision-making, further, is not an intellectual exercise. It mobilizes the vision, energies, and resources of the organization for effective action.

*This was certainly established military practice in very ancient times—Thucydides and Xenophon both take it for granted, as do the earliest Chinese texts on war we have—and so did Caesar.

# 38

## Managerial Communications

*More Talk; and Less Communication—What We Have Learned—The Fundamentals—Communication Is Perception—Communication Is Expectation—Communication Makes Demands—Communication and Information Are Different—Information Presupposes Communication—Why Downward Communications Cannot Work—The Limitations of "Listening"—The Demands of the Information Explosion—What Can Managers Do?—Management by Objectives, Performance Appraisal and Management Letter as Communications Tools—Communications, the Mode of Organization*

We have more attempts at communications today, that is, more attempts to talk to others, and a surfeit of communications media, unimaginable to the men who, around the time of World War I, started to work on the problems of communicating in organizations. Communications in management has become a central concern to students and practitioners in all institutions—business, the military, public administration, hospital, university, and research. In no other area have intelligent men and women worked harder or with greater dedication than psychologists, human relations experts, managers, and management students have worked on improving communications in our major institutions.

Yet communications has proven as elusive as the Unicorn. The noise level has gone up so fast that no one can really listen any more to all that babble about communications. But there is clearly less and less communicating. The communications gap within institutions and between groups in society has been widening steadily—to the point where it threatens to become an unbridgeable gulf of total misunderstanding.

In the meantime, there is an information explosion. Every professional and every executive—in fact, everyone except the deaf-mute—suddenly has access to data in inexhaustible abundance. All of us feel—and overeat—very much like the little boy who has been left alone in the candy store. But what has to be done to make this cornucopia of data redound to information, let alone to knowledge? We get a great many answers. But the one thing clear so far is that no one really has an answer. Despite information theory and data processing, no one yet has actually seen, let alone used, an "information system," or a "data base." The one thing we do know, though, is that the abundance of information changes the communications problem and makes it both more urgent and even less tractable.

There is a tendency today to give up on communications. In psychology, for instance, the fashion today is the T-group with its sensitivity training. The avowed aim is not communications, but self-awareness. T-groups focus on the "I" and not on the "Thou." Ten or twenty years ago the rhetoric stressed "empathy"; now it stresses "doing one's thing." However needed self-knowledge may be, communication is needed at least as much (if indeed self-knowledge is possible without action on others, that is, without communications).

Despite the sorry state of communications in theory and practice, we have learned a good deal about information and communications. Most of it, though, has not come out of the work on communications to which we have devoted so much time and energy. It has been the by-product of work in a large number of seemingly unrelated fields, from learning theory to genetics and electronic engineering. We equally have a lot of experience—though mostly of failure—in a good many practical situations in all kinds of institutions. We may indeed never understand "communications." But "communications in organizations"—call it *managerial communications*—we do know something about by now.

We are, to be sure, still far away from mastery of communications, even in organizations. What knowledge we have about communications is scattered and, as a rule, not accessible, let alone in applicable form. But at least we increasingly know what does not work, and, sometimes, why it does not work. Indeed we can say bluntly that most of today's brave attempts at communication in organizations—whether business, labor unions, government agencies, or universities—is based on assumptions that have been proven to be invalid—and that, therefore, these efforts cannot have results. And perhaps we can even anticipate what might work.

## What We Have Learned

We have learned, mostly through doing the wrong things, four fundamentals of communications.

1. Communication is perception.
2. Communication is expectation.
3. Communication makes demands.
4. Communication and information are different and indeed largely opposite—yet interdependent.

1. *Communication is perception.* An old riddle posed by the mystics of
many religions—the Zen Buddhists, the Sufis of Islam, and the Rabbis of
the Talmud—asks: "Is there a sound in the forest if a tree crashes down and
no one is around to hear it?" We now know that the right answer to this
is no. There are sound waves. But there is no sound unless someone perceives it. Sound is created by perception. Sound is communication.

This may seem trite; after all, the mystics of old already knew this, for
they too always answered that there is no sound unless someone can hear
it. Yet the implications of this rather trite statement are great indeed.

First, it means that it is the recipient who communicates. The so-called
communicator, the person who emits the communication, does not communicate. He utters. Unless there is someone who hears, there is no communication. There is only noise. The communicator speaks or writes or
sings—but he does not communicate. Indeed, he cannot communicate. He
can only make it possible, or impossible, for a recipient—or rather, "percipi-
ent"—to perceive.

Perception, we know, is not logic. It is experience. This means, in the first
place, that one always perceives a configuration. One cannot perceive single
specifics. They are always part of a total picture. The "silent language,"*
that is, the gestures, the tone of voice, the environment altogether, not to
mention the cultural and social referents, cannot be dissociated from the
spoken language. In fact, without them the spoken word has no meaning
and cannot communicate.

It is not only that the same words, e.g., "I enjoyed meeting you," will be
heard as having a wide variety of meanings. Whether they are heard as
warmth or as icy cold, as endearment or as rejection depends on their setting
in the "silent language," such as the tone of voice or the occasion. More
important is that by itself, that is, without being part of the total configuration of occasion, value, "silent language," and so on, the phrase has no

---

*As Edward T. Hall called it in the title of his pioneering work (Doubleday, 1959).

meaning at all. By itself it cannot make possible communication. It cannot be understood. Indeed it cannot be heard. To paraphrase an old proverb of the human-relations school: "One cannot communicate a word; the whole man always comes with it."

But we know about perception also that one can perceive only what one is capable of perceiving. Just as the human ear does not hear sounds above a certain pitch, so does human perception altogether not perceive what is beyond its range of perception. It may, of course, hear physically, or see visually, but it cannot accept it. It cannot become communication.

This is a fancy way of stating something the teachers of rhetoric have known for a very long time—though the practitioners of communications tend to forget it again and again.

In Plato's *Phaedo* which, among other things, is also the earliest extant treatise on rhetoric, Socrates points out that one has to talk to people in terms of their own experience, that is, that one has to use carpenters' metaphors when talking to carpenters, and so on. One can communicate only in the recipient's language or in his terms. And the terms have to be experience-based. It, therefore, does very little good to try to explain terms to people. They will not be able to receive them if they are not terms of their own experience. They simply exceed their perception capacity.

The connection between experience, perception, and concept formation —that is, cognition—is, we now know, infinitely subtler and richer than any earlier philosopher imagined. But one fact is proven and comes out strongly in the most disparate work, e.g., that of Piaget (in Switzerland), that of B. F. Skinner, and that of Jerome Bruner (both at Harvard). Percept and concept in the learner, whether child or adult, are not separate. We cannot perceive unless we also conceive. But we also cannot form concepts unless we can perceive. To communicate a concept is impossible unless the recipient can perceive it, that is, unless it is within his perception.

There is a very old saying among writers: "Difficulties with a sentence mean confused thinking. It is not the sentence that needs straightening out, it is the thought behind it." In writing we attempt, first, to communicate with ourselves. An "unclear sentence" is one that exceeds our own capacity for perception. Working on the sentence, that is, working on what is normally called communications, cannot solve the problem. We have to work on our own concepts first to be able to understand what we are trying to say—and only then can we write the sentence.

In communicating, whatever the medium, the first question has to be "Is this communication within the recipient's range of perception? Can he receive it?"

The "range of perception" is, of course, physiological and largely (though not entirely) set by physical limitations of man's animal body. When we speak of communication, however, the most important limitations on perception are usually cultural and emotional rather than physical.

That fanatics are not being convinced by rational arguments, we have known for thousands of years. Now we are beginning to understand that it is not "argument" that is lacking. Fanatics do not have the ability to perceive a communication which goes beyond their range of emotions. First their emotions would have to be altered. In other words, no one is really "in touch with reality," if by that we mean that he has complete openness to evidence. The distinction between "sanity" and "paranoia" does not lie in the ability to perceive, but in the ability to learn, that is, in the ability to change one's emotions on the basis of experience.

That perception is conditioned by what we are capable of perceiving was realized forty years ago by the most quoted but probably least heeded of all students of organization, Mary Parker Follett (e.g., especially in her collected essays, *Dynamic Administration,* Harper's, 1941). Follett taught that a disagreement or a conflict is likely not to be about the answers, or indeed about anything ostensible. It is, in most cases, the result of incongruity in perceptions. What A sees so vividly, B does not see at all. And, therefore, what A argues, has no pertinence to B's concerns, and vice versa. Both, Follett argued, are likely to see reality. But each is likely to see a different aspect of it. The world, and not only the material world, is multidimensional. Yet one can see only one dimension at a time.

One rarely realizes that there could be other dimensions, and that something that is so obvious to us and so clearly validated by our emotional experience has other dimensions, a "back" and "sides," which are entirely different and which, therefore, lead to entirely different perceptions. The story I mentioned earlier about the blind men and the elephant in which each one, encountering this strange beast, feels one of the elephant's parts, his leg, his trunk, his hide, and reports an entirely different conclusion, and holds to it tenaciously, is simply a metaphor of the human condition. There is no possibility of communication until this is understood and until he who has felt the hide of the elephant goes over to him who has felt the leg and feels the leg himself. There is no possibility of communications, in other words, unless we first know what the recipient, the true communicator, can see and why.

2. *Communication is expectation.* We perceive, as a rule, what we expect to perceive. We see largely what we expect to see, and we hear largely what we expect to hear. That the unexpected may be resented is not the important thing—though most of the work on communications in business and government thinks it is. What is truly important is that the unexpected is usually not received at all. It is not seen or heard, but ignored. Or it is misunderstood, that is, mis-seen or mis-heard as the expected.

On this we now have a century or more of experimentation. The results are unambiguous. The human mind attempts to fit impressions and stimuli into a frame of expectations. It resists vigorously any attempts to make it "change its mind," that is, to perceive what it does not expect to perceive or not to perceive what it expects to perceive. It is, of course, possible to alert the human mind to the fact that what it perceives is contrary to its expectations. But this first requires that we understand what it expects to perceive. It then requires that there be an unmistakable signal—"this is different," that is, a shock which breaks continuity. A gradual change in which the mind is supposedly led by small, incremental steps to realize that what is perceived is not what it expects to perceive will not work. It will rather reinforce the expectations and will make it even more certain that what will be perceived is what the recipient expects to perceive.

Before we can communicate, we must, therefore, know what the recipient expects to see and hear. Only then can we know whether communication can utilize his expectations—and what they are—or whether there is need for the "shock of alienation," for an "awakening" that breaks through the recipient's expectations and forces him to realize that the unexpected is happening.

3. *Communication makes demands.* Many years ago psychologists stumbled on a strange phenomenon in their studies of memory, a phenomenon that, at first, upset all their hypotheses. In order to test memory, the psychologists compiled a list of words to be shown to their experimental subjects for varying times as a test of their retention capacity. As control, a list of nonsense words, mere jumbles of letters, was devised. Much to the surprise of these early experimenters almost a century ago or so, their subjects (mostly students, of course) showed totally uneven memory retention of individual words. More surprising, they showed amazingly high retention of the nonsense words. The explanation of the first phenomenon is fairly obvious. Words are not mere information. They do carry emotional charges. And, therefore words with unpleasant or threatening associations tend to be suppressed, words with pleasant associations retained. In fact, this selective retention by emotional association has since been used to construct tests for emotional disorders and for personality profiles.

The relatively high retention rate of nonsense words was a greater puzzle. It was expected that no one would really remember words that had no meaning at all. But it has become clear over the years that the memory for these words, though limited, exists precisely because these words have no meaning. For this reason, they make no demand. They are truly neutral. With respect to them, memory could be said to be truly "mechanical," showing neither emotional preference nor emotional rejection.

A similar phenomenon, known to every newspaper editor, is the amazingly high readership and retention of the "fillers," the little three- or five-line bits of irrelevant incidental information that are used to "balance" a page. Why should anybody want to read, let alone remember, that it first became fashionable to wear different-colored hose on each leg at the court of some long-forgotten duke? Or, when and where baking powder was first used? Yet there is no doubt that these little tidbits of irrelevancy are read and, above all, that they are remembered, far better than almost anything else in the daily paper except the screaming headlines of the catastrophes. The answer is that the fillers make no demands. It is their total irrelevancy that accounts for their being remembered.

Communication is always "propaganda." The emitter always wants "to get something across." Propaganda, we now know, is both a great deal more powerful than the rationalists with their belief in "open discussion" believe, and a great deal less powerful than the myth-makers of propaganda, e.g., Dr. Goebbels in the Nazi regime, believed and wanted us to believe. Indeed the danger of total propaganda is not that the propaganda will be believed. The danger is that nothing will be believed and that every communication becomes suspect. In the end, no communication is being received. Everything anyone says is considered a demand and is resisted, resented, and in effect not heard at all. The end results of total propaganda are not fanatics, but cynics—but this, of course, may be even greater and more dangerous corruption.

Communication, in other words, always makes demands. It always demands that the recipient become somebody, do something, believe something. It always appeals to motivation. If, in other words, communication fits in with the aspirations, the values, the purposes of the recipient, it is powerful. If it goes against his aspirations, his values, his motivations, it is likely not to be received at all or, at best, to be resisted. Of course, at its most powerful, communication brings about "conversion," that is, a change of personality, of values, beliefs, aspirations. But this is the rare, existential event, and one against which the basic psychological forces of every human being are strongly organized. Even the Lord, the Bible reports, first had to strike Saul blind before he could raise him up as Paul. Communications aiming at conversion demand surrender. By and large, therefore, there is no communication unless the message can key in to the recipient's own values, at least to some degree.

4. *Communication and information are different and indeed largely opposite—yet interdependent.* Where communication is perception, information is logic. As such, information is purely formal and has no meaning. It is impersonal rather than interpersonal. The more it can be freed of the human component, that is, of such things as emotions and values, expectations and perceptions, the more valid and reliable does it become. Indeed it becomes increasingly informative.

All through history, the problem has been how to glean a little information out of communications, that is, out of relationships between people, based on perception. All through history, the problem has been to isolate the information content from an abundance of perception. Now, all of a sudden, we have the capacity to provide information—both because of the conceptual work of the logicians (especially the symbolic logic of Russell and Whitehead, which appeared in 1910), and because of the technical work on data processing and data storage, that is, especially because of the computer and its tremendous capacity to store, manipulate, and transmit data. Now, in other words, we have the opposite problem from the one mankind has always been struggling with. Now we have the problem of handling information per se, devoid of any communication content.

The requirements for effective information are the opposite of those for effective communication. Information is, for instance, always specific. We perceive a configuration in communications; but we convey specific individual data in the information process. Indeed, information is, above all, a principle of economy. The fewer data needed, the better the information. And an overload of information, that is, anything much beyond what is truly needed, leads to information blackout. It does not enrich, but impoverishes.

At the same time, information presupposes communication. Information is always encoded. To be received, let alone to be used, the code must be known and understood by the recipient. This requires prior agreement, that is, some communication. At the very least, the recipient has to know what the data pertain to. Are the figures on a piece of computer tape the height of mountaintops or the cash balances of Federal Reserve member banks? In either case, the recipient would have to know what mountains are or what banks are to get any information out of the data.

The prototype information system may well have been the peculiar language known as *Armee Deutsch* (Army German) which served as language of command in the Imperial Austrian Army prior to 1918. A polyglot army in which officers, noncommissioned officers, and men often had no language in common, it functioned remarkably well with fewer than two hundred specific words—"fire," for instance, or "at ease," each of which had only one totally unambiguous meaning. The meaning was always an action. And the words were learned in and through actions, i.e., in what behaviorists now call "operant conditioning." The tensions in the Austrian Army after many decades of nationalist turmoil were very great indeed. Social intercourse between members of different nationalities serving in the same unit became increasingly difficult, if not impossible. But to the very end, the information system functioned. It was completely formal; completely rigid; completely logical in that each word had only one possible meaning; and it rested on completely pre-established communication regarding the specific response to a certain set of sound waves. This example, however, shows also that the effectiveness of an information system depends on the willingness and ability to think through carefully what information is needed by whom for what purposes, and then on the systematic creation of communication among the various parties to the system as to the meaning of each specific input and output. The effectiveness, in other words, depends on the pre-establishment of communication.

Communication communicates the more levels of meaning it has and the less it lends itself to quantification.

Medieval esthetics held that a work of art communicates on a number of levels, at least three if not four: the literal; the metaphorical; the allegorical; and the symbolic. The work of art that most consciously converted this theory into artistic practice was Dante's *Divina Commedia*. If by "information" we mean something that can be quantified, then the *Divina Commedia* is without any information content whatever. But it is precisely the ambiguity, the multiplicity of levels on which this book can be read, from being a fairy tale to being a grand synthesis of metaphysics, that makes it the overpowering work of art it is and the immediate communication which it has been to generations of readers.

Communications, in other words, may not be dependent on information. Indeed the most perfect communications may be purely "shared experiences," without any logic whatever. Perception has primacy rather than information.

This summary of what we have learned is gross oversimplification. It glosses over some of the most hotly contested issues in psychology and perception. Indeed it may well brush aside most of the issues which the students of learning and of perception, would consider central and important.

But the aim has not been to survey these big areas. My concern here is not with learning or with perception. It is with communications, and in particular, with communications in the large organization, be it business enterprise, government agency, university, or armed service.

This summary might also be criticized for being trite, if not obvious. No one, it might be said, could possibly be surprised at its statements. They say what "everybody knows." But whether this be so or not, it is not what "everybody does." On the contrary, the logical implication for communications in organizations of these apparently simple and obvious statements is at odds with current practice and indeed denies validity to the honest and serious efforts we have been making to communicate for many decades now.

## Why Downward Communications Cannot Work

What, then, can our knowledge and our experience teach us about communications in organizations, about the reasons for our failures, and about the prerequisites for success in the future?

For centuries we have attempted communication "downward." This, however, cannot work, no matter how hard and how intelligently we try. It cannot work, first, because it focuses on what *we* want to say. It assumes, in other words, that the utterer communicates. But we know that all he does is utter. Communication is the act of the recipient. What we have been trying to do is to work on the emitter, specifically on the manager, the administrator, the commander, to make him capable of being a better communicator. But all one can communicate downward are commands, that is, prearranged signals. One cannot communicate downward anything connected with understanding, let alone with motivation. This requires communication upward, from those who perceive to those who want to reach their perception.

This does not mean that managers should stop working on clarity in what they say or write. Far from it. But it does mean that how we say something comes only after we have learned what to say. And this cannot be found out by "talking to," no matter how well it is being done. "Letters to the Employees," no matter how well done, will be a waste unless the writer knows what employees can perceive, expect to perceive, and want to do. They are a waste unless they are based on the recipient's rather than the emitter's perception.

But "listening" does not work either. The Human Relations School of Elton Mayo, forty years ago, recognized the failure of the traditional approach to communications. Its answer* was to enjoin listening. Instead of starting out with what "we," that is, the executive, want to "get across," the executive should start out by finding out what subordinates want to know, are interested in, are, in other words, receptive to. To this day, the human relations prescription, though rarely practiced, remains the classic formula.

Of course, listening is a prerequisite to communication. But it is not adequate, and it cannot, by itself, work. Listening assumes that the superior will understand what he is being told. It assumes, in other words, that the

---

*Especially as developed in Mayo's two famous books, *The Human Problems of an Industrial Civilization* (Harvard Business School, 1933) and *The Social Problems of an Industrial Civilization* (Harvard Business School, 1945).

subordinates can communicate. It is hard to see, however, why the subordinate should be able to do what his superior cannot do. In fact, there is no reason for assuming he can. There is no reason, in other words, to believe that listening results any less in misunderstanding and miscommunications than does talking. In addition, the theory of listening does not take into account that communications is demands. It does not bring out the subordinate's preferences and desires, his values and aspirations. It may explain the reasons for misunderstanding. But it does not lay down a basis for understanding.

This is not to say that listening is wrong, any more than the futility of downward communications furnishes any argument against attempts to write well, to say things clearly and simply, and to speak the language of those whom one addresses rather than one's own jargon. Indeed, the realization that communications have to be upward—or rather that they have to start with the recipient rather than the emitter, which underlies the concept of listening—is absolutely sound and vital. But listening is only the starting point.

More and better information does not solve the communications problem, does not bridge the communications gap. On the contrary, the more information, the greater is the need for functioning and effective communication. The more information, in other words, the greater is the communications gap likely to be. The information explosion demands functioning communications.

The more impersonal and formal the information process in the first place, the more will it depend on prior agreement on meaning and application, that is, on communications. In the second place, the more effective the information process, the more impersonal and formal will it become; the more will it separate human beings and thereby require separate, but also much greater, efforts, to re-establish the human relationship, the relationship of communication. It may be said that the effectiveness of the information process will depend increasingly on our ability to communicate, and that, in the absence of effective communication—that is, in the present situation—the information revolution cannot really produce information. All it can produce is data.

The information explosion is the most compelling reason to go to work on communications. Indeed, the frightening communications gap all around us—between management and workers; between business and government; between faculty and students, and between both of them and university administration; between producers and consumers, and so on—may well reflect in some measure the tremendous increase in information without a commensurate increase in communications.

## What Can Managers Do?

Can we then say anything constructive about communication? Can we do anything? We can say that communication has to start from the intended recipient of communications rather than from the emitter. In terms of traditional organization we have to start upward. Downward communications cannot work and do not work. They come *after* upward communications have successfully been established. They are reaction rather than action; response rather than initiative.

But we can also say that it is not enough to listen. The upward communications must be focused on something that both recipient and emitter can perceive, focused on something that is common to both of them. They must be focused on what already motivates the intended recipient. They must, from the beginning, be informed by his values, beliefs, and aspirations.

Management by objectives is thus a prerequisite for functioning communication. It requires the subordinate to think through and present to the superior his own conclusions as to what major contribution to the organization—or to the unit within the organization—he should be expected to perform and should be held accountable for.

What the subordinate comes up with is rarely what the superior expects. Indeed, the first aim of the exercise is precisely to bring out the divergence in perception between superior and subordinate. But the perception is focused, and focused on something that is real to both parties. To realize that they see the same reality differently is in itself already communication.

Management by objectives gives to the intended recipient of communication—in this case the subordinate—access to experience that enables him to understand. He is given access to the reality of decision-making, the problems of priorities, the choice between what one likes to do and what the situation demands, and above all, the responsibility for a decision. He may not see the situation the same way the superior does—in fact, he rarely will or even should. But he may gain an understanding of the complexity of the superior's situation and of the fact that the complexity is not of the superior's making, but is inherent in the situation itself.

And these communications, even if they end in a "no" to the subordinate's conclusions, are firmly focused on the aspirations, values, and motivation of the intended recipient. In fact, they start out with the question "What would you *want* to do?" They may then end up with the command "This is what I tell you to do." But at least they force the superior to realize that he is overriding the desires of the subordinate. It forces him to explain, if not to try to persuade. At least he knows that he has a problem—and so does the subordinate.

A performance appraisal based on what a man can do and has done well; or a discussion on a man's development direction, are similarly foundations for communications. They start out with the subordinate's concerns, express his perception, and focus his expectations. They make communications his tool rather than a demand on him.

These are only examples, and rather insignificant ones at that. But perhaps they illustrate the main conclusion to which our experience with communications—largely an experience of failure—and all the work on learning, memory, perception, and motivation point: communication requires shared experience.

There can be no communication if it is conceived as going from the "I" to the "Thou." Communication works only from one member of "us" to another. Communication in organization—and this may be the true lesson of our communication failure and the true measure of our communication need—is not a *means* of organization. It is the *mode* of organization.

# 39

## Controls, Control, and Management

*Controls and Control—The Characteristics of Controls—Controls Are Goal-Setting and Value-Setting—Controls Needed for Measurable and for Nonmeasurable Events—The Specification for Controls—Economy— Meaning—Controls Follow Strategy—Appropriateness—Congruence— Timeliness—Simplicity—Controls Must Be Operational—The Ultimate Control of Organizations—Controls and the Spirit of an Organization*

---

In the dictionary of social institutions the word "controls" is not the plural of the word "control." Not only do more controls not necessarily give more control, the two words, in the context of social institutions, have different meanings altogether. The synonyms for controls are measurement and information. The synonym for control is direction. Controls pertain to means, control to an end. Controls deal with facts, that is, with events of the past. Control deals with expectations, that is, with the future. Controls are analytical, concerned with what was and is. Control is normative and concerned with what ought to be.

We are rapidly acquiring great capacity to design controls in business and in other social institutions, based on a great improvement in techniques, especially in the application of logical and mathematical tools to events in a social institution, and in the ability to process and analyze large masses of data very fast. What does this mean for control? Specifically, what are the requirements for these greatly improved controls to give better control to management? For, in the task of a manager, controls are purely a means to an end; the end is control.

Ordinary language and its use make abundantly clear that here is a problem. The man in a business who is charged with producing the controls is the controller. But most, if not all executives, including most controllers themselves, would consider it gross misuse and abuse of controllership were this controller to use his controls to exercise control in the business. This, they would argue, would actually make the business be "out of control" altogether.

The reasons for this apparent paradox lie in the complexity both of human beings and of the social task.

If we deal with a human being in a social institution, controls must become personal motivation that leads to control. Instead of a mechanical system, the control system in a human-social situation is a volitional system. That we know very little about the will is not even the central point. A translation is required before the information yielded by the controls can become grounds for action—the translation of one kind of information into another, which we call *perception*.

In the social institution there is a second complexity, a second "uncertainty principle." It is almost impossible to prefigure the responses appropriate to a certain event in a social situation.

We can, and do, build controls into a machine which slow down the turning speed whenever it exceeds a certain figure. And we can do this either by mechanical means or by instrumentation which shows a human operator what the turning speed is, and which gives him the specific, unambiguous instruction to turn the speed down when the indicator reaches a certain point. But a control-reading "profits are falling" does not indicate, with any degree of probability, the response "raise prices," let alone by how much; the control-reading "sales are falling" does not indicate the response "cut prices," and so on. There is not only a large number of other equally probable responses—so large that it is usually not even possible to identify them in advance—there is also no indication in the event itself which of these responses is even possible, let alone appropriate, not to mention its being right. The event itself may not even be meaningful. But even if it is, it is by no means certain what it means. And the probability of its being meaningful is a much more important datum than the event itself—and one which is almost never to be discerned by analyzing the event.

Social situations require a decision based on assumptions—and essentially assumptions not with respect to the recorded event but to the future, that is, expectations which know no probability but can only be judged according to plausibility. For there are no "facts" regarding the future in a social universe in which periodicity—at least on our minuscule time scale —cannot be assumed, must indeed be considered quite unlikely.

## The Characteristics of Controls

There are three major characteristics of controls in business enterprise.

1. *Controls can be neither objective nor neutral.* When we measure the rate of fall of a stone, we are totally outside the event itself. By measuring we do not change the event; and measuring the event does not change us, the observers. Measuring physical phenomena is both objective and neutral.

In a perceptual situation of complexity, that is, in any social situation of the kind we deal with in business enterprise, the act of measurement is, however, neither objective nor neutral. It is subjective and of necessity biased. It changes both the event and the observer. For it changes the perception of the observer—if it does not altogether create his perception. Events in the social situation acquire value by the fact that they are being singled out for the attention of being measured. No matter how "scientific" we are, the fact that this or that set of phenomena is singled out for being "controlled," signals that it is being considered to be important.

Everybody who ever watched the introduction of a budget system has seen this happen. For a long time—in some companies forever—realizing the budget figures becomes more important than what the budget is supposed to measure, namely economic performance. Managers, upon first being exposed to a budget system, often deliberately hold back sales and cut back profits rather than be guilty of "not making the budget." It takes years of experience and a very intelligent budget director to restore the balance. And there are any number of otherwise perfectly normal research directors who act on the conviction that it is a greater crime to get research results for less than the budgeted amount than not getting any research results at all while spending all the "proper" budget money.

*Controls in a social institution such as a business are goal-setting and value-setting.* They are not "objective." They are of necessity moral. The only way to avoid this is to flood the executive with so many controls that the entire system becomes meaningless, becomes mere "noise."

From that point of view maybe the gross abuse of our new data-processing capacity, namely as a tool for grinding out huge quantities of totally meaningless data—an abuse of which every early computer user is guilty —may be a blessing after all.

But to render controls harmless by rendering them meaningless is hardly the right way to use our capacity to provide controls. This must start out with the realization that controls create vision. They change both the events measured and the observer. They endow events not only with meaning but with value. And this means that the basic question is not "How do we control?" but "What do we measure in our control system?"

2. *Controls need to focus on results.* Business (and every other social institution) exists to contribute to society, economy, and individual. In consequence *results* in business exist only on the outside—in economy, in society, and with the customer. It is the customer only who creates a "profit." Everything inside a business—manufacturing, marketing, research, and so on—creates only costs, is only a "cost center."

In other words, the managerial area is concerned with costs alone. But results are entrepreneurial.

Yet we do not have adequate, let alone reliable, information regarding the "outside." It is not only by far the hardest to get—to the point where no organization for the acquisition and collection of meaningful outside information could really be set up—the job is much too big. Above all we still lack necessary entrepreneurial concepts. The job itself has never been thought through—at least not so far. And the century of patient analysis of managerial, inside phenomena, events and data, the century of patient, skillful work on the individual operations and tasks within the business, has no counterpart with respect to the entrepreneurial job.

We can easily record and therefore quantify efficiency, that is, efforts. We have very few instruments to record and quantify effects, that is, the outside. But even the most efficient buggy-whip manufacturer would no longer be in business. It is of little value to have the most efficient engineering department if it designs the wrong product. The Cuban subsidiaries of U.S. companies were by far the best run and, apparently, the most profitable—let alone the least "troublesome"—of all U.S. operations in Latin America. This was, however, irrelevant to their expropriation. And it mattered little, I daresay, during the period of IBM's great expansion in the fifties and sixties how "efficient" its operations were; its basic entrepreneurial idea was the right, the effective one.

The outside, the area of results, is much less accessible than the inside. The central problem of the executive in the large organization is his—necessary—insulation from the outside. This applies to the president of the United States as well as to the president of United States Steel. What today's organization therefore needs are synthetic sense organs for the outside. If modern controls are to make a contribution, it would be, above all, here.

3. *Controls are needed for measurable and nonmeasurable events.* Business, like any other institution, has important results that are incapable of being measured. Any experienced executive knows companies or industries which are bound for extinction because they cannot attract or hold able people. This, every experienced executive also knows, is a more important fact about a company or an industry than last year's profit statement. Any logical positivist who were to tell an executive that this statement, being incapable of unambiguous definition, is a "nonstatement" dealing with a

"nonproblem," would be quickly—and correctly—dismissed as an ass. Yet the statement cannot be defined clearly let alone "quantified." It is anything but "intangible"; it is very "tangible" indeed (as anyone ever having to do with such a business quickly finds out). It is just nonmeasurable. And measurable results will not show up for a decade.

But business also has measurable and quantifiable results of true meaning and significance. These are all those that have to do with past economic performance. For these can be expressed in terms of the very peculiar measurement of the economic sphere, money.

This does not mean that these are "tangibles." Indeed most of the things we can measure by money are so totally "intangible"—take depreciation, for instance—that they outdo any Platonic Idea in that nothing corresponds to them in any reality whatever. But they are measurable.

To this comes the fact that the measurable results are things that happened; they are in the past. There are no facts about the future. To this comes, second, the fact that the measurable events are primarily inside events rather than outside events. The important developments on the outside, the things which determine that the buggy-whip industry disappears and that IBM becomes a big business—let alone that Cuban subsidiaries of American companies are confiscated—are not measurable until it is too late to have control.

A balance between the measurable and the nonmeasurable is therefore a central and constant problem of management and a true decision area.

Measurements which do not spell out the assumptions with respect to the nonmeasurable statements that are being made—at least as parameters or as restraints—misdirect therefore. They actually misinform. Yet the more we can quantify the truly measurable areas, the greater the temptation to put all-out emphasis on those—the greater, therefore, the danger that what looks like better controls will actually mean less control if not a business out of control altogether.

## Specifications for Controls

To give the manager control, controls must satisfy seven specifications:

—they must be economical;
—they must be meaningful;
—they must be appropriate;
—they must be congruent;
—they must be timely;
—they must be simple; and
—they must be operational.

1. *Control is a principle of economy.* The less effort needed to gain control, the better the control design. The fewer controls needed, the more effective they will be. Indeed, adding more controls does not give better control. All it does is create confusion.

The first question the manager therefore needs to ask in designing or in using a system of controls is "What is the minimum information I need to know to have control?"

The answer may vary for different managers. The company's treasurer needs only to know the total amount invested in inventories and whether it is going up or down. The sales manager needs to know the half a dozen products and product lines which together account for 70 percent of inventory, and those in considerable detail. But total inventory amount is not of primary importance to him. And both the treasurer and the sales manager do not, as a rule, need complete inventory figures except once or twice a year; a fairly small sample should give them all the information they need in between. But the warehouse clerk needs daily figures—and in detail.

The capacity of the computer to spew out huge masses of data does not make for better controls. On the contrary, what gives control is first the question "What is the *smallest* number of reports and statistics needed to understand a phenomenon and to be able to anticipate it?" And then one asks, "And what is the minimum of data regarding this phenomenon that gives a reasonably reliable picture?"

2. *Controls must be meaningful.* That means that the events to be measured must be significant either in themselves, e.g., market standing, or they must be symptoms of at least potentially significant developments, e.g., a sudden sharp rise in labor turnover or absenteeism.

Trivia should never be measured. One has control by controlling a few developments which can have significant impact on performance and results. One loses control by trying to control the infinity of events which are marginal to performance and results.

Controls should always be related to the key objectives and to the priorities within them, to "key activities" and to "conscience areas" (see Chapter 42). Controls should, in other words, be based on a company's definition of what our business is, what it will be, and what it should be.

## Controls Follow Strategy

Whatever is not essential to the attainment of a company's objectives should be measured infrequently and only to prevent deterioration. It should be strictly controlled by "exception," that is, a standard should be set, measurement should be periodical and on a sample basis, and only significant shortfalls below the established standard should even be reported, let alone paid attention to.

That we can quantify something is no reason for measuring it. The question is "Is this what a manager should consider important?" "Is this what a manager's attention should be focused on?" "Is this a true statement of the basic realities of the enterprise?" "Is this the proper focus for control, that is, for effective direction with maximum economy of effort?"

If these questions are not being asked in designing controls, we will end up by making business essentially uncontrolled—for then we will simply have no remedy except to proliferate control information to the point where it does not register at all.

3. *Controls have to be appropriate to the character and nature of the phenomena measured.* This may well be the most important specification; yet it is least observed in the actual design of controls.

Because controls have such an impact it is not only important that we select the right ones. To enable controls to give right vision and to become the ground for effective action, the measurement must also be appropriate. That is, it must present the events measured in structurally true form. Formal validity is not enough.

Formal complaints, that is, grievances, coming out of a work force are commonly reported as "five grievances per thousand employees per month." This is formally valid. But is it structurally valid? Or is it misdirection? The impression this report conveys is, first, that grievances are distributed throughout the work force in a random manner. They follow, the report seems to say, a U-shaped Gaussian distribution. And second—a conclusion from the first impression—they are a minor problem, especially if we deal with five grievances per thousand employees per month. This, while formally valid, completely misrepresents and misinforms, let alone misdirects.

Grievances are a social event. Physical nature knows no such phenomena. And social events are almost never distributed in the "normal distribution" we find in the physical world. The normal distribution of social events is almost always exponential—with the hyperbola the typical curve. In other words, the great majority of departments in the plant, employing 95 percent of the work force, normally does not have even a single grievance during one year. But in one department, employing only a handful of men, we have a heavy incidence of grievances—so that the "five per thousand" may well mean (and in the actual example from which I took these figures, did mean) a major grievance per man per year. If this department is then the final assembly through which all the production has to pass, and if the workers in this department go out on strike when their grievances are being neglected by a management which has been misled by its own controls, the impact can be shattering. It bankrupted the company, which is no longer in existence.

Similarly, 90 percent of the volume of a business is usually represented by 2 to 5 percent of the number of its products. But 90 percent of the orders by number cover, typically, only 4 or 5 percent of the volume—but account for 90 percent and more of the costs. A modern strategic bomber may have a million parts. But 90 percent of its cost is represented by a very small number of parts, maybe fifty or so—and so is 90 percent of the upkeep it needs, though, unfortunately, the 90 percent of the dollars and the 90 percent of the upkeep needs rarely comprise the same parts.

Practically all the innovations in a research laboratory, no matter how large, come out of the work of a very small percentage of the research people. And invariably, 80 percent of a company's distributors move, at best, 20 percent of its output, while 10 percent or fewer of the distributors move two-thirds to three-quarters of total sales.

Most measurements of sales performance, whether of the entire sales force or of the individual salesman, report sales in total dollars. But in many businesses this is an inappropriate figure. The same dollar volume of sales may mean a substantial profit, no profit at all, or a sizable loss—dependent on the product mix sold. An absolute sales figure not related to product mix, therefore, gives no control whatever—neither to the individual salesman, nor to the sales manager, nor to top management.

These are elementary things. Yet few managers seem to know them. The traditional information systems, especially accounting, conceal appropriateness rather than highlight it. (In particular the allocation of overhead tends to obscure the true distribution of economic and social phenomena.)

Without controls that bring out clearly what the real structure of events is, the manager not only lacks knowledge. He will tend to do the wrong things. For all the weight of the daily work pushes him toward allocating energies and resources in proportion to the *number* of events. There is a constant drift toward putting energies and resources where they can have the least results, that is, on the vast number of phenomena which, together, account for practically no effects.

4. *Measurements have to be congruent with the events measured.* Alfred North Whitehead (1861–1947), the distinguished logician and philosopher, used to warn against the "danger of the false concreteness." A measurement does not become more "accurate" by being worked out to the sixth decimal when the phenomenon measured is at best capable of being verified within a range of, say, 50 to 70 percent (and that, presumably, with an error of plus or minus 20 percent). This is "false concreteness," gross inaccuracy in reality, and misleading.

It is an important piece of information that this or that phenomenon cannot be measured with precision but can be described only within a range or as a magnitude. To say "we have 26 percent of the market" sounds reassuringly precise. But it is usually so inaccurate a statement as to be virtually meaningless. What it really means, as a rule, is "we are not the dominant factor in the market, but we are not marginal either." And even then the statement is no more reliable than the definition of the market which underlies it.

It is up to the manager to think through what kind of measurement is congruent to the phenomenon it is meant to measure. He has to know when "approximate" is more accurate than a firm-looking figure worked out in great detail. He has to know when a range is more accurate than even an approximate single figure. He has to know that "larger" and "smaller," "earlier" and "later," "up" and "down" are quantitative terms and often more accurate, indeed more rigorous, than any specific figures or range of figures.

5. *Controls have to be timely.* The time dimension of controls is very similar to their congruence. Again frequent measurements and very rapid "reporting back" do not necessarily give better control. Indeed they may frustrate control. The time dimension of controls has to correspond to the time span of the event measured.

It has lately become fashionable to talk of "real time" controls, that is, of controls that inform instantaneously and continuously. There are events where "real time" controls are highly desirable. If a batch of antibiotics in the fermentation tank spoils as soon as temperature or pressure deviate from a very narrow range for more than a moment or two, "real time" monitoring on a continuous basis is obviously needed. But few events need such controls. And most cannot be controlled at all by them. "Real time" is the wrong time span for real control.

Children planting a garden are so impatient, it is said, that they tend to pull out the radishes as soon as their leaves show, to see whether the root is forming. This is "real time" control—misapplied.

When a new product is being first introduced, the product manager may want and need daily reports from the test markets, and as close to "real time" as possible. Six months later, when he has worked out his promotion and selling strategy, daily reports in "real time" can only lead him into "pulling up the radish to see whether the root is forming." He then needs to think through at what periods of time and in what areas he has to attain what results to be able to achieve his objectives. And then he has to pay the greatest attention to the measurement of results at their crucial moments in time. If he, however, worries about "real time" daily measurements, he is almost bound to confuse himself and his associates and to muddle even the best strategy.

Similarly, the attempt to measure research progress all the time is likely to confound research results. The proper time span for research is a fairly long one. Once every two or three years research progress and research results should be rigorously appraised. In between an experienced manager keeps in touch. He watches for any indication of major unexpected trouble, and, even more, for any sign of unexpected breakthroughs. But to monitor research in "real time"—as some research labs have been trying to do—is pulling up the radishes.

However, there is also the opposite danger—that of not measuring often enough. It is particularly great with developments that (a) take a fairly long time to have results, and (b) have to come together at a point in the future to produce the desired end result.

6. *Controls need to be simple.* Every major New York commercial bank worked in the sixties on developing internal controls, especially of costs and of allocation of efforts. Everyone spent a great deal of time and money on the task and came up with voluminous control manuals. In only one of the banks are the manuals being used, to the best of my knowledge. When the executive in that bank was asked how he explained this, he did not (as his interviewer expected him to) credit a massive training program or talk about his "philosophy." He said instead, "I have two teen-age daughters. They know nothing about banking and are not terribly good at figures. But they are bright. Whenever I had worked out an approach to controlling an activity, I took my intended procedure home in draft form and asked my girls to let me explain it to them. And only when I had it so simple that they could explain back to me what the procedure intended to accomplish and how, did I go ahead. Only then was it simple enough."

Complicated controls do not work. They confuse. They misdirect from what is to be controlled toward attention on the mechanics and methodology of the control. But if the user has to know how the control works before he can apply it, he has no control at all. And if he has to sit down and figure out what a measurement means, he has no control either.

Indeed, the bank executive's method is a pretty good one. Training sessions in using a new control rarely accomplish much. Ask the intended user to explain its purpose and its use. And when he stumbles over complexities, ambiguities, or subtleties, redesign for simplicity.

7. *Finally, controls must be operational.* They must be focused on action. Action rather than information is their purpose. The action may be only study and analysis. In other words, a measurement may say, "What goes on we don't understand; but something goes on that needs to be understood." But it should never just say, "Here is something you might find interesting."

This then means that controls—whether reports, studies, or figures—

must always reach the person who is capable of taking controlling action. Whether they should reach anyone else—and especially someone higher up —is debatable. But their prime addressee is the manager or professional who can take action by virtue of his position in the flow of work and in the decision structure. And this further means that the measurement must be in a form that is suitable for the recipient and tailored to his needs.

Workers and first-line supervisors should, as said earlier (Chapter 18) receive measurements and control information that enable them to direct their own immediate efforts toward results they can control. Instead, typically, the first-line supervisor receives each month a statement of the quality control results for the entire plant—and the worker receives nothing.

And top management usually receives the information and measurements operating middle managers need and can use, and little or nothing of pertinence to their own top-management job.

The reason for this is largely a confusion between control as domination of others and control as rational behavior. Unless controls are means toward the latter, and this means toward self-control, they lead to wrong action. They are "mis-control."

## The Ultimate Control of Organizations

There is one more important thing to be said. There is a fundamental, incurable, basic limitation to controls in a social institution. This lies in the fact that a social institution is both a true entity and a fiction. As an entity it has purposes of its own, a performance of its own, results of its own— and survival and death of its own. These are the areas of which we have been speaking so far. But a social institution is comprised of persons, each with his own purpose, his own ambitions, his own ideas, his own needs. No matter how authoritarian the institution, it has to satisfy the ambitions and needs of its members, and do so in their capacity as individuals but through *institutional* rewards and punishments, incentives, and deterrents. The expression of this may be quantifiable—such as a raise in salary. But the system itself is not quantitative in character and cannot be quantified.

Yet here is the real control of the institution, that is, the ground of behavior and the cause of action. People act as they are being rewarded or punished. For this, to them, rightly (as said earlier in Chapter 36), is the true expression of the values of the institution and of its true, as against its professed, purpose and role.

A system of controls which is not in conformity with this true, this only effective, this ultimate control of the organization which lies in its people decisions will therefore at best be ineffectual. At worst it will cause never-ending conflict and will push the organization out of control.

In designing controls for an organization one has to understand and analyze the actual control of the business, its people decisions. Otherwise one designs a system of controls which does not lead to control. One has to realize that even the most powerful "instrument board" complete with computers, operations research, and simulation, is secondary to the invisible, qualitative control of any human organization, its systems of rewards and punishments, of values and taboos.

# 40

# The Manager and the Management Sciences

*Management Sciences: Promise and Performance—Why Management Sciences Do Not Yet Perform—How the Management Sciences Originated —Why They Tend to Be Unscientific—The Basic Postulates—The First Need of the Management Sciences—The Fear of Risk-Taking—What Managers Should Expect—Testing Assumptions—Right Questions, Not Answers—Alternatives, Not Solutions—Understanding, Not Formulae— What the Management Sciences Should Work On—From Potential to Performance*

The first management scientist was that long-forgotten Italian who, very early in the Renaissance, invented double-entry bookkeeping. No other management tool designed since can compare with it in simplicity, elegance, and utility. Double-entry bookkeeping and all its offsprings and variations is still the only truly universal "management science," the only tool of systematic analysis that every business, and indeed every institution, uses every day.

But no one ever talked of double-entry bookkeeping as management science. That term made its appearance after World War II.* The very term was a manifesto. "Management," it proclaimed, "was to be made rigorous, scientific, quantitative." The new tools, with operations research in the van, would substitute certainty for guesswork, knowledge for judgment, "hard facts" for experience.

*TIMS*, The Institute of Management Sciences, which is the professional society of the management scientists, was founded in 1953 and held its first meeting in Pittsburgh, Pennsylvania, in 1954.

These were, of course, the heady days when it was widely predicted that the computer would replace the manager. And a good many of the management scientists, awed by their new shiny tools, similarly saw themselves "taking over" decision-making control.

Most managers have long learned that the computer will not replace managers (see Chapter 35, "From Middle Management to Knowledge Organization"). Most have learned that the computer is a tool—very useful if properly employed, but a tool nonetheless. Most managers also know by now that the management sciences are tools. Indeed it would have been more prudent—let alone a little more modest—to speak of "management analysis" rather than of "management sciences."

Still, the management sciences are tools with high potential for contribution. There is no more reason for a manager to be a management scientist than there is reason for a physician to be a blood chemist or a bacteriologist. But a manager needs to know what to expect of the management sciences and how to use them as managerial tools, just as the physician needs to know what to expect of blood chemistry and bacteriology and how to use them as diagnostic tools.

For this the manager first needs to understand what the management sciences try to do—and what they should be doing. He next needs to know what contributions to expect of them. Few managers, so far, have acquired the skill of making the management sciences contribute to their managerial work. Few, so far, are putting these new tools to effective work.

## Promise and Performance

Most managers know that they need better tools. Most have learned by bitter experience that intuition is unreliable, if not downright treacherous, if used as the only basis for decision. Indeed, most experienced managers have long suspected what a leading management scientist of today, Jay W. Forrester of M.I.T., brilliantly demonstrated in two books:* complex systems actually behave "counter-intuitively"; the plausible tends to be wrong. And markets, technologies, and businesses are very complex systems indeed. There is nothing very startling in this insight; there is nothing more plausible, after all, than that the earth is flat or that the sun revolves around the earth.

When management science first appeared it was therefore hailed by managers with glad cries. Since then, a whole new profession has come into being: the management scientists, with their own professional associations, their own learned journals, their own departments in universities, business

*Urban Dynamics (M.I.T. Press, 1969) and World Dynamics (Wright-Allen Press, 1971).

schools, and schools of technology, and with good jobs in large numbers within industry.

And yet, management science has been a disappointment. It has not lived up, so far, to its promise. It certainly has not revolutionized the practice of management. Few managers, indeed, pay much attention to it.

The widening gap between the claims and promises of management science and its use by business is recognized—and deplored—by both management scientists and managers. Not unexpectedly each blames the other. Managers complain that management scientists concern themselves with trivia and "reinvent the wheel." Management scientists, in turn, tell horror stories of "resistance by reactionary managers."

There is a good deal to both complaints. But the truth is more complex —and far more important than who is to blame.

## Why Management Science Fails to Perform

There is one fundamental insight underlying all management science. It is that the business enterprise is a *system* of the highest order: a system the parts of which are human beings contributing voluntarily of their knowledge, skill, and dedication to a joint venture. And one thing characterizes all genuine systems, whether they be mechanical, like the control of a missile, biological like a tree, or social like the business enterprise: it is interdependence. The whole of a system is not necessarily improved if one particular function or part is improved or made more efficient. In fact, the system may well be damaged thereby, or even destroyed. In some cases the best way to strengthen the system may be to weaken a part—to make it less precise or less efficient. For what matters in any system is the performance of the whole; this is the result of growth and of dynamic balance, adjustment, and integration rather than of mere technical efficiency.

Primary emphasis on the efficiency of parts in management science is therefore bound to do damage. It is bound to optimize precision of the tool at the expense of the health and performance of the whole. (That the enterprise is a social rather than a mechanical system makes the danger all the greater, for the other parts do not stand still. They either respond so as to spread the maladjustment throughout the system or organize for sabotage.)

But when we look at the actual work done by management scientists in business, we find little that lives up to the basic insight with which management science starts out.

The bulk of the work done so far concerns itself with the sharpening of already existing tools for specific technical functions—such as quality control or inventory control, warehouse location or freight-car allocation, machine loading, maintenance scheduling, or order handling. A good deal of the work is little more than a refinement of industrial engineering, cost accounting, or procedures analysis. Some, though not very much, attention has been given to the analysis and improvement of functional efforts—primarily those of the manufacturing function but also, to some extent, of marketing and of money management.

But there has been little work, little organized thought, little emphasis on managing an enterprise—on the risk-making, risk-taking, decision-making job. Throughout management science—in the literature as well as in the work in progress—the emphasis is on techniques rather than on principles, on mechanics rather than on decisions, on tools rather than on results, and, above all, on efficiency of the part rather than on performance of the whole.

Technically this is all excellent work. But therein lies its danger. The new tools are so much more powerful than the old tools of technical and functional work—the tools of trial and error and of cut and fit—that their wrong or careless use must do damage.

There are a few significant exceptions. At the General Electric Company almost twenty years of effort have led to the development of genuine models of whole businesses showing their basic economic characteristics and principal interrelationships. Similar work has been done at the British Coal Board. The potential is there, in other words.

But most of the actual work has concerned itself with doing a little better what we already know how to do. We did control inventories, after all, or allocate freight cars, well before the advent of management science. And it is unlikely that any business will survive rather than die, or prosper rather than languish, because we now know how to do these things better—even significantly better.

What explains this underuse—or misuse—of such potentially powerful tools?

The first clue lies, perhaps, in the origin of the management sciences—and the origin is an unusual one indeed. Every other discipline of man began with a crude attempt to define what its subject was. Then people set to work fashioning concepts and tools for its study. But the management sciences began with the application of concepts and tools developed within a host of other disciplines for their own particular purposes. It may have started with the heady discovery that certain mathematical techniques, hitherto applied to the study of the physical universe, could also be applied to the study of business operations.

As a result, the focus of much of the work in the management sciences has *not* been on such questions as "What is the business enterprise?" "What is managing?" "What do the two do, and what do the two need?" Rather, the focus has been "Where can I apply my beautiful gimmick?" The emphasis has been on the hammer rather than on driving in the nail, let alone on building the house. In the literature of operations research, for instance, there are several dissertations along the lines of "155 applications of linear programming," but I have not seen any published study on "typical business opportunities and their characteristics."

What this indicates is a serious misunderstanding on the part of the management scientist of what "scientific" means. Scientific is not—as many management scientists naively seem to think—synonymous with quantification. If this were true, astrology would be the queen of the sciences. It is not even the application of the scientific method. After all, astrologers observe phenomena, derive the generalization of a hypothesis therefrom, and then test the hypothesis by further organized observation. Yet astrology is superstition rather than science because of its childish assumption that there is a real zodiac, that the signs in it really exist, and that their fancied resemblance to some such earthly creature as a fish or a lion defines their character and properties (whereas all of them are nothing but the mnemonic devices of the navigators of antiquity).

In other words, "scientific" presupposes a rational definition of the universe of the science (that is, of the phenomena which it considers to be real and meaningful) as well as the formulation of basic assumptions or postulates which are appropriate, consistent, and comprehensive. This job of defining the universe of a science and of setting its basic postulates has to be done, however crudely, *before* the scientific method can be applied. If it is not done, or done wrongly, the scientific method cannot be applied. If it is done, and done right, the scientific method becomes applicable and indeed powerful.

Management science still has to do this job of defining its universe. If it does this, then all the work done so far will become fruitful—at least as preparation and training ground for real achievement. The first task for management science, if it is to be able to contribute rather than distort and mislead, is therefore to define the specific nature of its subject matter.

This might include as a basic definition the insight that the business enterprise is made up of human beings. The assumptions, opinions, objectives, and even the errors of people (and especially of managers) are thus primary *facts* for the management scientist. Any effective work in management science really has to begin with analysis and study of them.

Starting, then, with this recognition of what there is to be studied, management science must next establish its basic assumptions and postulates.

It might first include the vital fact that every business enterprise exists in the economy and in society; that even the mightiest is the servant of its environment, by which it can be dismissed without ceremony, but that even the lowliest affects and molds the economy and society instead of just adapting to them; in other words, that the business enterprise exists only in an economic and social ecology of great complexity.

The basic postulates might further include the following ideas:

1. The business enterprise produces neither things nor ideas but humanly determined values. The most beautifully designed machine is still only so much scrap metal until it has utility for a customer.

2. Measurements in the business enterprise are such complex, not to say metaphysical, symbols as money—at the same time both highly abstract and amazingly concrete.

3. Economic activity, of necessity, is the commitment of present resources to an unknowable and uncertain future—a commitment, in other words, to expectations rather than to facts. Risk is of the essence, and risk-making and risk-taking constitute the basic function of enterprise. And risks are taken not only by the general manager, but right through the whole organization by everybody who contributes knowledge—that is, by every manager and professional specialist. This risk is something quite different from risk in the statistician's probability; it is the risk of the unique event, the irreversible qualitative breaking of the pattern.

4. Inside and outside the business enterprise there is constant irreversible change; indeed, the business enterprise exists as the agent of change in an industrial society, and it must be capable both of purposeful evolution to adapt to new conditions and of purposeful innovation to change the conditions.

Some of this is often said in the prefaces of books on the management sciences. It generally stays in the preface, however. Yet for the management sciences to contribute to business understanding, let alone become "sciences," postulates like the foregoing ought to be the fabric of its work. Of course we need quantification—though it tends to come fairly late in the development of a discipline (only now, for instance, can scientists really quantify in biology). We need the scientific method. And we need work on specific areas and operations—careful, meticulous detail work. But above all, we need to recognize the particular character of business enterprise and the unique postulates necessary for its study. It is on this vision that we must build.

*The first need of a management science is, then, that it respect itself sufficiently as a distinct and genuine discipline.*

## The Fear of Risk-Taking

The second clue to what is lacking in the management sciences as applied today is the emphasis throughout its literature and throughout its work on "minimizing risk" or even on "eliminating risk" as the goal and ultimate purpose of its work.

To try to eliminate risk in business enterprise is futile. Risk is inherent in the commitment of present resources to future expectations. Indeed, economic progress can be defined as the ability to take greater risks. The attempt to eliminate risks, even the attempt to minimize them, can only make them irrational and unbearable. It can only result in that greatest risk of all: rigidity.

The main goal of a management science must be to enable business to take the right risk. Indeed, it must be to enable business to take *greater* risks —by providing knowledge and understanding of alternative risks and alternative expectations; by identifying the resources and efforts needed for desired results; by mobilizing energies for contribution; and by measuring results against expectations, thereby providing means for early correction of wrong or inadequate decisions.

All this may sound like mere quibbling over terms. Yet the terminology of risk minimization does induce a decided animus against risk-taking and risk-making—that is, against business enterprise—in the literature of the management sciences. Much of it echoes the tone of the technocrats of a generation ago. For it wants to subordinate business to technique, and it seems to see economic activity as a sphere of physical determination rather than as an affirmation and exercise of responsible freedom and decision.

This is worse than being wrong. This is lack of respect for one's subject matter—the one thing no science can afford and no scientist can survive. Even the best and most serious work of good and serious people—and there is no lack of them in the management sciences—is bound to be vitiated by it.

*The second requirement for a management science is, then, that it take its subject matter seriously.*

## What Managers Need to Know

But managers too share in the blame for the gap between the potential and the actual contribution of the management sciences. And by and large, the manager's share may be the greater one, and the contribution he needs to make—and has not made—the truly crucial need of management science and management scientist.

However, the management scientist's typical complaint about the manager is, bluntly, nonsense. It is the complaint that the manager does not bother to learn management science and remains ignorant. To demand of any tool user that he understand what goes into the making of the tool is admission of incompetence on the part of the tool maker. The tool user, provided the tool is made well, need not, and indeed should not, know anything about the tool.

The basic problem is much more serious than the unwillingness of managers to learn a few mathematical techniques. Managers, by and large, have failed to take managerial responsibility for management scientists and management sciences. They have refused to accept the fact that the management scientist, like any other high-grade specialist, depends on the manager for his direction and his effectiveness. They have left the management sciences unmanaged—and are therefore largely responsible for their degenerating into a box of tricks, a "management gadget bag" of answers to nonexisting questions in many cases.

Managers, despite all their apparent enthusiasm for the management sciences when they first made their appearance, have not, as a rule, thought through what the management sciences should or could contribute.

We know, by and large, what managers need: a systematic supply of organized knowledge for the risk-making and risk-taking decisions of business enterprise in a complex and rapidly changing technology, economy, and society.

Tools for the measurement of expectations and results: effective means for common vision and communication among the many functional and professional specialists, each with his own knowledge, his own logic, and his own language, whose combined efforts are needed, however, to make the right business decisions, to make them effective, and to produce results.

Managers need something teachable and learnable if only because our world needs far too many people with managerial vision and competence to depend on the intuition of a few "natural-born" geniuses; and only the generalizations and concepts of a discipline can really be learned or taught.

This becomes clear when one looks at the few places where management sciences have produced results. In every single case this is not because the management scientists have done anything they are not doing every place. It is because managers have asked the right questions and have managed the management sciences.

One example is a large manufacturer with a broad product line, selling directly to the public through thousands of outlets, such as department stores, discount chains, and hardware stores. Its executives came to their management scientists and said, "Everybody in this industry knows that extending credit to wholesalers and retailers is the way to get sales. And everybody also knows that there is a point where the additional credit risks outbalance the additional sales. Are these the right assumptions on which to base our selling and credit policies?" The management scientists came back six months later and said, "No, these are the wrong assumptions. What everybody knows is, as so often happens, not true. What is true is that in our industry you can get additional sales by extending credit to the biggest and best customers who are also good credit risks, and to the smallest and worst customers who are also the poorest credit risks. You cannot get additional sales by extending credit to the 'average' customer who is also an 'average' credit risk." As a result, the company completely changed its policy. It cut off credit from the small accounts—and while it lost some sales, it greatly improved its selling and credit performance. And it extended credit to its big and best accounts. The total amount of credit it now extends is actually less than what it used to extend when it had a very tight credit policy. But it now has a rational understanding of the relationship between credit, sales, and credit risk.

Even more instructive perhaps is the case of one large big-city hospital which asked its management scientists, "Can you find any pattern in the patient load which would enable us to schedule basic services of the hospital and to plan ahead for the utilization of services, facilities, and staff? This is our basic problem. But we do not even know whether we are asking the right questions." The management scientists, after about two years of hard work, could show that there are predictable patterns, both long range and short range. It is possible to predict, with high probability, the use of scarce facilities, such as X-ray rooms, X-ray technicians, medical laboratories, operating rooms, and so on, as well as the length of stay of patients and thereby utilization of room and bed capacity. But they also said, "In one area you are not asking the right questions: what kind of beds do we need and how many of them? All the beds in the hospital are beds for seriously sick people, that is, beds requiring high capital investment; yet no more than one-third of the patients at any one time require this kind of a bed and this kind of facility. Another third require what, in effect, are convalescent beds, with a capital investment no more than half that of the acute-sickness bed; and yet another third require probably nothing but a motel room with a minimum of service and a minimum of capital investment."

What managers, in other words, need to do to make management science capable of contribution is to think through the areas in which they need to have basic assumptions tested.

Managers expect management scientists to come up with answers where nobody has asked them the right question. They expect the management scientist, that is, a technical specialist, to know better than a manager what the needs, the problems, the questions of a business are.

Above all, they expect final answers. But the great strength of management science—whether its methods be those of the physical sciences, of economics, or of the social sciences (and a good management scientist needs to be at home in all three areas)—is its capacity for asking questions. The manager himself will have to give answers. For answers in business are always judgment, always choice between alternatives of different and yet uncertain risks, always a blend of knowledge, experience, and hopes.

To make the management sciences capable of contribution, the manager has to demand of them that they identify the right questions to ask.

Managers, as a rule, expect the management sciences to come up with one best solution. But what the management sciences should be able to contribute are the alternatives available to the manager. They should be expected to say, "Here are four or five different courses of action. Not one of them is perfect. Each has its own risks, its own uncertainties, its own limitations, and its own costs. Each of them, however, satisfies at least some of the major specifications. You, the manager, will have to choose between them. You will have to decide on one of them, at least as the lesser evil. Which one you choose is *your* decision. It is your judgment regarding the risks the company can take. It is your judgment with respect to the things you can sacrifice and the things you have to insist on. But at least you now know what choices are available to you."

There are no "solutions" with respect to the future. There are only choices between courses of action, each imperfect, each risky, each uncertain, and each requiring different efforts and involving different costs. But nothing could help the manager more than to realize what alternatives are available to him and what they imply. And this the management scientist can supply with varying degrees of precision.

Finally the manager should expect his management scientists to provide understanding rather than formulae. The formulae are the tools of the management scientist and are of little interest to the manager. If he cannot assume that the management scientist knows his craft, he better get himself another management scientist. But understanding, that is, insight into what a decision is really about, is something he should hold the management scientist accountable for. What the management sciences can contribute— and should be expected to contribute—is understanding that a certain decision, while it looks like a decision on manufacturing, is really a decision on marketing. It is a decision on what customers will want, will be willing to pay for, will buy. What a manager should expect from his management scientists is to hear, "Look, the problem you assigned us is the wrong problem. *This* is the problem we ought to be working on."

The greatest contribution a group of management scientists made to the pharmaceutical company which employed them was not solutions. It was to say to management, "All your efforts, all your energies, all your attention are focused on the new products. But three-quarters of your income today and for the foreseeable future will come from drugs that have been in the inventory at least three years. Nobody manages them, nobody sells them, nobody knows what to do with them. In fact, nobody has the slightest interest in them. The only thing we know is that the way to keep old drugs in the market is completely different from what is needed to introduce new ones. But what managing an existing product line of old and established drugs requires we do not know. This, however, is what we should be studying."

These four demands and expectations:

—that the management scientists test assumptions;
—that they identify the right questions to ask;
—that they formulate alternatives rather than solutions;
—that they focus on understanding rather than on formulae

are the keys to making the management sciences productive. They all are based on the assumption that the management sciences are not methods of computation but tools of analysis. They all assume that the purpose of the management sciences is to help with diagnosis. They are insights and not prescription, let alone wonder drugs.

But they all require also that the manager take responsibility for the management sciences. They all require that the manager manage these tools. They all require of the manager that he decide, in close working relationship with the management scientists, what the management scientists should go to work on. They should not go to work on the things that are interesting to the management scientists and easily amenable to their tools. They should go to work on the areas in which a manager needs understanding. And if these areas are areas in which the tools are not particularly appropriate, areas, for instance, in which quantification is difficult or perhaps even impossible, this should not deter manager or management scientists. Insight, understanding, ranking of priorities, and a "feel" for the complexity of an area are as important as precise, beautifully elegant mathematical models—and in fact usually infinitely more useful and indeed even more "scientific." They reflect the reality of the manager's universe and of his tasks.

It is up to the manager to convert the management sciences from potential to performance. To do this he has to understand what the management sciences are and what they can do. He has to understand the peculiar limitations which are inherent in the management sciences largely as a result of their origin and history. But above all he has to understand that the management sciences are the manager's tools, and not the tools of the management scientist. And it is up to the manager to focus these tools on managerial tasks and direct them toward managerial contributions.

# Managerial Organization

Organization structure is the oldest and most thoroughly studied area in management. But we face new needs in organization which the well-known and well-tested structural designs of "functional" and "decentralized" organization cannot adequately satisfy. New structural designs are emerging: "the task force team"; "simulated decentralization"; "the systems" structure. We have learned that organization does not start with structure but with building blocks; that there is no one right or universal design but that each enterprise needs to design around the key activities appropriate to its mission and its strategies; that three different kinds of work, operating, innovative, and top-management, require being structured and lodged under the same organizational roof; and that organization structure needs to be both task-focused and person-focused and to have both an authority axis and a responsibility axis.

# 41

# New Needs and New Approaches

*The Emphasis on Organization Structure in the Management Boom—And the Reasons for It—The Danger of the Wrong Structure—The Importance of Organization for the Small Business—Yesterday's Final Answers—Fayol's "Functions" and Sloan's "Federal Decentralization"—Traditional Assumptions and Current Needs—What We Have Learned—The First Step: Identifying the Building Blocks—"Structure Follows Strategy"—The Key Activities—The Three Kinds of Work: Operations, Top Management, Innovation—What We Need to Unlearn—"Task Focus" versus "Person Focus"—"Hierarchy" versus "Free Form"—"Constitutional Lawyer" versus "Educator"—From "Simple-Axis" to "Multi-Axis" Organization—"There Must Be One Final Answer"*

"Of the making of organization studies there is no end"; this might well be the plaint of a modern Psalmist. For organization studies leading to reorganizing companies, divisions, and functions has been one of the more spectacular "growth industries" of the last few decades. Everybody, whether government department or armed service, research laboratory, Catholic diocese, university administration, or hospital—in addition to countless businesses—seems forever to be engaged in reorganizing and being reorganized. Management consultants, thirty or forty years ago, concerned themselves mainly with work study, production flow, and sales training. In the sixties they got the bulk of their assignments and revenues from organization studies, especially of large companies and government departments.

Even the Bank of England, which had admitted no outsiders through its doors for almost three hundred years, was finally reorganized by one of the large American consulting firms; and to add insult to injury, it was a Labour government that, violating the privacy of the "Old Lady of Threadneedle Street," forced an organization study on it.

There are reasons for this interest in organization and for the underlying conviction that inherited organization structures or structures that "just grew" are unlikely to be appropriate to the needs of the enterprise. Above all, we have learned the danger of the wrong organization structure. The best structure will not guarantee results and performance. But the wrong structure is a guarantee of nonperformance. All it produces are friction and frustration. The wrong organization puts the spotlight on the wrong issues, aggravates irrelevant disputes, and makes a mountain out of trivia. It accents weaknesses and defects instead of strengths. The right organization structure is thus a prerequisite of performance.

The small enterprise needs right structure just as badly as the big one—and may find it more difficult to work it out.

Only a few short decades ago, such interest as there was in organization was to be found only in very large businesses. The earlier examples, e.g., the example of Alfred P. Sloan's organization structure for General Motors in the early twenties, were all examples of large businesses.

Today, we know that organization becomes critical, above all, when a small business grows into a medium-sized one, and a simple business into a complicated one. (See Chapter 53.) The small business that wants to grow, even into only a medium-sized business, therefore has to think through and work out the right organization which enables it at one and the same time to function as a small business and to be able to grow into something bigger. Similarly, the simple one-product, one-market business faces crucial organization problems the moment it adds even a little diversity or complexity.

As recently as the early or middle fifties, managers still had to be convinced that they need to pay attention to the organization of work and the design of organization structure.

The most stubborn opposition to the reorganization of the General Electric Company in the early fifties did not come from those who objected to the seemingly radical proposals. It came from GE managers who did not see the need for doing anything about organization. They admitted that the inherited structure was a crazy, shapeless jumble which the business had long outgrown. "But why waste time on organization?" they asked. "We make and sell turbines, so why bother about who does what?" Ten years later this was still the reaction of many managers when Paul Chambers, as new chief executive of England's Imperial Chemical Industries, tackled the organization structure of another giant that had "just grown."

Today one often needs, on the contrary, to convince managements not to rush into organization studies and not to become enamored of reorganization as an end in itself—or as a substitute for strategic planning and business decisions.

## Yesterday's Final Answers

But while we have accepted that organization and management structure are crucial, we are outgrowing yesterday's "final answers."

Twice in the short history of management did we have the "final answer" to organization. The first time was around 1910 after Henri Fayol, the French industrialist, had thought through what, to this day, are the functions of a manufacturing company. At that time the manufacturing business was, of course, the truly important organizational problem.

A generation later one could again say that we "knew." Fayol had given "the answer" for the single-product manufacturing business. Alfred P. Sloan, Jr., in organizing General Motors in the early twenties, made the next step. He found "the answer" for organizing the complex and large manufacturing company.* The Sloan approach, which used Fayol's functional organization for the subunits, the individual "divisions," but organized the business itself on the basis of "federal decentralization," that is, on the basis of decentralized authority and centralized control, became after World War II the organization model worldwide, especially for larger organizations.

Another generation later, that is, by the early seventies, it had become clear that the General Motors model was no more adequate to the realities, or at least to the most important challenges in organization, than Fayol's model was adequate to the realities of a very big business which Alfred P. Sloan, Jr., faced when he tackled the task of making General Motors manageable and managed.

Where they fit the realities that confront designer and architect of organization structure, Fayol's and Sloan's models are still unsurpassed. Fayol's functional organization is still the best way to structure a small business, especially a small manufacturing business. Sloan's federal decentralization is still the best structure for the big multiproduct company. Indeed (see Chapters 45 through 48) none of the new design structures that have emerged in the decades since World War II are nearly as close to fulfilling the design specifications of organization structure as are functional organization and federal decentralization *if and when they fit.* But more and more of the institutional reality that has to be structured and organized does not

---

*Sloan drew heavily on Pierre du Pont's slightly earlier work at the Du Pont Company. On this see the two books by Alfred D. Chandler listed in the Bibliography.

fit. Indeed, the very assumptions that underlay Sloan's work—and that of Fayol—are not applicable to major organization needs and challenges.

## Traditional Assumptions and Current Needs

The best way, perhaps, to bring out the current needs of organization structure is to contrast the basic characteristics of the General Motors Company which Sloan so successfully structured with current needs and realities of organization and structure.

1. General Motors is a manufacturing business, producing and selling highly engineered goods. And Fayol too was concerned with a business producing physical goods; his model was a fair-sized coal-mining company. Today we face the challenge of organizing the large business that is not exclusively or even primarily a manufacturing business. There are not only the large financial institutions and the large retailers. There are worldwide transportation companies, communications companies, companies which, while they manufacture, have their center of gravity in customer service (such as most computer businesses). Then there are, of course, all the nonbusiness service institutions with which Chapters 11 through 14 dealt. These nonmanufacturing institutions are increasingly the true center of gravity of any developed economy. They employ the most people. They both contribute and take the largest share of gross national product. They are the fundamental organization problems today.

2. General Motors is essentially a single-product, single-technology, single-market business. More than four-fifths of its sales are automotive. The cars which General Motors sells differ in details, such as size, horsepower, and price, but they are essentially one and the same product. Indeed, most U. S. "made by GM" cars, regardless of nameplate, are now assembled in the same plants and under one assembly manager. A man who came up the line in, say, the Pontiac Division, will hardly find Chevrolet totally alien— and even Opel in Germany will not hold a great many surprises for him.

By contrast, the typical businesses of today are multiproduct, multitechnology, and multimarket businesses. They may not be "conglomerates." But they are "diversified." And their central problem is a problem General Motors did not have: the organization of complexity and diversity.

3. General Motors is still primarily a U. S. company. It looms very large on the international automobile market. But the foreign markets do not loom very large for GM (though perhaps they should). In America General Motors dominates the automobile industry. But only in Australia—a secondary market—does General Motors dominate any non-U. S. market. In Europe it is at best number four. Organizationally the world outside the United States is still, for GM, "separate" and "outside." Organizationally

GM is still an American company, and its top management is primarily concerned with the American market, the American economy, the American labor movement, the American government, and so on.

By contrast, the most rapid growth in the last twenty-five years has been the multinational company, that is, the company for which a great many countries and a great many markets are of equal importance, or at least are of major importance.

4. Because GM is a one-product and one-country company, information is not a major organizational problem and need not be a major organizational concern. Everyone in GM speaks the same language, whether by that we mean the language of the automotive industry or American English. Everyone fully understands what the other one is doing or should be doing, if only because, in all likelihood, he has done a similar job himself. GM can therefore be organized according to the logic of the marketplace, and the logic of authority and decision. It need not, in its organization, concern itself a great deal with the logic and the flow of information.

By contrast, multiproduct, multitechnology, and multinational companies will have to concern themselves in their organizational design and structure with organization according to the flow of information. At the very least they will have to make sure that their organization structure does not violate the logic of information. And for this GM offers no guidance —GM did not have to tackle the problem.

5. Four out of every five GM employees are production workers, either manual workers or clerks on routine tasks. GM, in other words, employs yesterday's, rather than today's, labor force.

But the basic organization problem today is knowledge work and knowledge workers. They are the fastest-growing element in every business. In the service institutions, they are the core employment.

6. Finally, General Motors has been a "managerial" rather than an "entrepreneurial" business. The strength of Sloan's approach lay in its ability to manage, and manage superbly, what was already there and known. General Motors has not been innovative—altogether the automobile industry has not been innovative since the days before World War I. (There was innovation at General Motors. But it was essentially the contribution of one man, Charles Kettering, who was indeed an innovative genius of the first order. But GM itself did not have to organize for entrepreneurship and innovation.)

But the challenge is going increasingly to be entrepreneurship and innovation. What we need is the innovative organization—in addition to the managerial one. And for this, the General Motors model offers no guidance.

The need for new approaches is therefore again as great in the field of organization as it was when Fayol and Sloan each did his pioneering work. The period when federal decentralization could be considered the universal model—as it largely was in the quarter century of the management boom —is at an end.

But of course we have learned a great deal in the three-quarters of a century since Fayol's generation first tackled organization. We know what the job is. We know the major approaches. We know what comes first. We know what will not work—though not always what will. We know what organization structure aims at and therefore what the test of successful organization design is.

## What We have Learned

1. The first thing we have learned is that Fayol and Sloan were right: organization structure will not just "evolve." The only things that evolve in an organization are disorder, friction, malperformance. Nor is the right —or even the livable—structure "intuitive"—any more than Greek temples or Gothic cathedrals were. Traditions may indicate where the problems and malfunctions are but are no help in finding solutions to them. *Organization design and structure require thinking, analysis, and a systematic approach.*

2. We have learned that the first step is not designing an organization structure; that is the last step. The first step is to identify and organize the *building blocks* of organization, that is, the activities which have to be encompassed in the final structure and which, in turn, carry the "structural load" of the final edifice.

This is, of course, what Fayol did in his functions. But the trouble is not only that these functions fit only a manufacturing company. Above all, Fayol tried to design his functions according to *the work* they did.

We now know that building blocks are determined by the kind of *contribution* they make. And we know that the traditional classification of the contributions—e.g., the "staff and line" concept of conventional American organization theory—is more of a hindrance to understanding than a help.

Designing the building blocks is, so to speak, the "engineering phase" of organization design. It provides the basic "materials." And like all materials, these building blocks have their specific characteristics. They belong in different places and fit together in different ways.

3. *"Structure follows strategy."* Organization is not mechanical. It is not "assembly." It cannot be "prefabricated." Organization is organic and unique to each individual business or institution. For we now know that structure, to be effective and sound, must follow strategy.*

Structure is a means for attaining the objectives and goals of an institu-

---

*The fundamental work on this was done by Alfred D. Chandler in his book, *Strategy and Structure* (M.I.T. Press, 1962), a depth study of the design of modern organization in pioneering American companies, such as Du Pont, General Motors, and Sears.

tion. Any work on structure must therefore start with objectives and strategy. This is perhaps the most fruitful new insight we have in the field of organization. It may sound obvious, and it is. But some of the worst mistakes in organization building have been made by imposing a mechanistic model of an "ideal" or "universal" organization on a living business.

Strategy, i.e., the answers to the questions "What is our business, what should it be, what will it be?", determines the purpose of structure. It thereby determines what the key activities are in a given business or service institution. Effective structure is the design that makes these key activities capable of functioning and of performance. And in turn the key activities are the "Load-bearing elements" of a functioning structure. Organization design is, or should be, primarily concerned with the key activities; the rest are secondary.

## The Three Kinds of Work

It was a misunderstanding to define the building blocks as different kinds of work. But there are different kinds of work in every organization, however small and simple.

There is, first, operating work, that is, the work of managing what is already in existence and known, building it, exploiting its potential, taking care of its problems.

There is always top-management work. And (as will be discussed in Chapers 49 through 52) it is different work, with its own tasks and requirements.

Finally, there is innovative work—and it too (see Chapter 61) is different work, requiring different things with respect to both operations and top management.

As will be seen in the subsequent chapters of this section, no one of the available design principles can be used for organizing all three different kinds of work. Yet they need to be organized. They need to be integrated into one overall organization.

## What We Need to Unlearn

There are also a few things we need to unlearn. Some of the noisiest and most time-consuming battles in organization theory and practice are pure sham. They pose an "either/or"; yet the right answer is "both—in varying proportions."

1. The first of these sham battles which better be forgotten fast is that between task-focus and person-focus in job design and organization structure. To repeat what has been said already (Chapter 32), *structure* and *job design* have to be task-focused. But *assignments* have to fit both the person

and the needs of the situation. There is no point in confusing the two as the old and tiresome discussion of the nonproblem insists on doing. Work, to say it once more, is objective and impersonal; the job itself is done by a person.

2. Somewhat connected with this old controversy is the discussion of hierarchical versus free-form organization.

Traditional organization theory knows only one kind of structure applicable alike to building blocks and whole buildings: the so-called scalar organization, that is, the hierarchical pyramid of superior and subordinates. Traditional organization theory considers this structure suitable for all tasks.

Today another—equally doctrinaire—organization theory is becoming fashionable. It maintains that shape and structure are what we want them to be—they are, or should be, "free-form." Everything—shape, size, and apparently tasks—derive from interpersonal relations. Indeed the purpose of the structure is to make it possible for each person to "do his thing."

The first thing to say about this controversy is that it is simply not true that one of these forms is regimentation and the other freedom. The amount of discipline required in both is the same; they only distribute it differently.

A hierarchy does not, as the critics allege, make the superior more powerful. On the contrary, the first effect of hierarchical organization is the protection of the subordinate against arbitrary authority from above. A scalar or hierarchical organization does this by defining carefully the sphere within which the subordinate has the authority, the sphere within which the superior cannot interfere. It protects the subordinate by making it possible for him to say, "This is *my* assigned job." Protection of the subordinate underlies also the scalar principle's insistence that a man have only one superior. Otherwise the subordinate is likely to find himself caught between conflicting demands, conflicting commands, and conflicts of interest as well as of loyalty. "Better one bad master than two good ones," says an old peasant proverb.

The first organization structure of the modern West was laid down in the canon law of the Catholic Church eight hundred years ago. It set up a strictly scalar organization. But most of the provisions in the canon law that deal with the structure and organization of the Catholic Church define those things which *only* the parish priest, i.e., the bottom man in the pyramid, can do in his parish. The bishop appoints him; and, within clear procedural limits, the bishop can remove him. But within his parish only the parish priest can discharge the parish priest's canonical functions, e.g., dispense the sacraments of baptism and matrimony or hear confession. Even the Pope has to be formally invited by the individual priest before he can officiate in a priest's parish.

At the same time, the hierarchical organization gives the most *individual* freedom. As long as the incumbent does whatever the assigned duties of his position are, he has done his job. He has no responsibility beyond it.

There is much talk these days about the individual's "doing his thing." But the only organization structure in which this is remotely possible is a hierarchical one. It makes the *least* demands on the individual to subordinate himself to the goals of the organization or to gear his activities into the needs and demands of others. Altogether, the more clearly a structure defines work, authority, and relationships, the fewer demands does it make on the individual for self-discipline and self-subordination.

Free-form organization is, of course, a misnomer. What is meant is organization designed for specific tasks rather than for supposedly "eternal" purposes. In particular, what is meant is organization of work in small groups and teams.

This (as will be discussed in some detail in later chapters of this section) demands, above all, very great self-discipline from each member of the team. Everybody has to do "the team's thing." Everybody has to take responsibility for the work of the entire team and for its performance. Indeed, Abraham Maslow's criticism* of Theory Y as making inhuman demands on that large proportion of people who are weak, vulnerable, timid, impaired, applies with even greater force to free-form organization. The more flexible an organization is, the stronger do the individual members have to be and the more of the load do they have to carry.

But also, hierarchy is needed in any structure by both individual members and the entire organization. There has to be someone who can make a decision; or else the organization deteriorates into a never-ending bull session. The knowledge organization in particular needs extreme clarity with respect to decision authority and specific, designated "channels" (see Chapter 35). Every organization will find itself in a situation of common peril once in a while. And then all perish unless there is clear, unambiguous, designated *command* authority vested in one person.

The hierarchy versus free-form argument is simply another version of the oldest and stalest argument in political theory: the argument between the constitutional lawyer who—rightly—insists that there have to be good and clear laws, and the educator who—equally rightly—insists that the best constitution fails unless there are upright rulers.

And just as statesmen learned long ago that both good laws and good rulers are needed, so organization builders (and even organization theorists) will have to learn that sound organization structure needs *both* a hierarchical structure of authority, decision-making, and pyramid, and the capacity to organize task forces, teams, and individuals for work both on a permanent and a temporary basis.

*See Chapter 19.

Both the advocates of hierarchical and those of free-form organization assume, if only unconsciously, that an organization must have one axis. It must be either hierarchical or "free-form." But this is a mechanistic assumption—and organization is a social phenomenon.

The classical organization structure was, indeed, presumed to have only one axis: that of formal authority downward and "reporting" upward. But the first studies of actual organization in the early work of the "human relations school" in the twenties* brought out immediately a second structure present in every work group studied. The human relations people called it—misleadingly—"informal" organization ("unwritten" organization would have been better; there is nothing informal about an informal organization which, being based on custom rather than explicit rules, tends to be more formal and, above all, to be far less flexible than the written rules of the formal organization chart). Still, the belief persists that organization structure should be "single-axis" structure.

But every system higher than the simplest mechanical assemblage of inanimate matter is a "multi-axis" system. An animal body such as that of man has a skeletal-muscular system, a number of nervous systems, an ingestive-digestive-eliminating system, a respiratory system, sense organs each a system, a procreative system, and so on. Each is autonomous. Yet all interact. Each is an "axis of organization."

No business could or should be as complex as a biological organism. Yet the organizations we need to design and to structure—the organizations of business enterprise and public-service institution—have a number of axes: decision-authority but also information; the logic of the task but also the dynamics of knowledge. That individual jobs have to be designed and positioned in contemplation of a number of axes—task and assignments; decision-responsibility; information and relations—has been discussed earlier (in Chapter 32).

The same applies to organization design and structure.

3. At bottom these sham battles—between task focus and person-focus and between scalar and free-form organization—reflect the belief of traditional organization theory that there must be "one best principle" which alone is "right" but which is also always "right." There must be *one final answer*.

Perhaps; but if so, we do not know it.

Instead of the "one right" principle, *three* new major design principles have emerged in the twenty-five years since World War II ended, to join Fayol's functions and Sloan's federal decentralization. These three—the team, simulated decentralization, and systems management—do not supersede the older designs. None of them could lay claim to being a "universal"

*Especially by Elton Mayo, on whom see Chapter 2.

principle; indeed, all three have both serious structural weaknesses and limited applicability. But they are the best answers available for certain kinds of work, the best structures available for certain tasks, the best approaches to such major organization problems as top management, innovation, the structure of comparison in the materials, transportation and financial industries or the multinational corporation.

The final tradition we will have to unlearn therefore is that "there must be one final answer." The right answer is whatever structure enables people to perform and to contribute. For liberation and mobilization of human energies—rather than symmetry or harmony—is the purpose of organization. Human performance is its goal and its test.

# 42

## The Building Blocks of Organization . . .

*The Four Tasks of the Organizer—Finding the Key Activities—Key Vulnerabilities—Values—When Key Activities Have to Be Reanalyzed—The Contributions Analysis—Revenue-Producing Activities—Result-Producing Work—Support Work—The "Conscience" Areas—Making Service Staffs Effective—The Two Faces of Information—Information: An Unanswered Organization Problem—Hygiene and Housekeeping—Contribution Determines Function*

---

In designing the building blocks of organization four questions face the organizer.

1. What should the units of organization be?
2. What components should join together, and what components should be kept apart?
3. What size and shape pertain to different components?
4. What is the appropriate placement and relationship of different units?

From the earliest beginnings of work on organization, well over a century ago, these were the tasks to which the organizer had to address himself before he could design structure.

We therefore now have a considerable amount of experience. There are no prescriptions for the design of the building blocks or for the design of the structure itself. But one can clearly indicate what the right approaches are and what approaches are unlikely to work.

The traditional approach to the identification of the basic units of organization has been to analyze *all* the activities needed for performance in the enterprise.* This then results in a list of typical functions of a manufacturing business or of a retail business.

This approach to the typical functions sees organization as mechanical, as an assemblage of functions. But organization has to be "organic." Organizations will indeed use typical activities—though not necessarily all of them. But how the structure is to be built depends on what results are needed. Organizing has to start out with the desired results.

## The Key Activities

What we need to know are not all the activities that might conceivably have to be housed in the organization structure. What we need to know are the load-bearing parts of the structure, the *key activities*.

Organization design, therefore, starts with these questions:

In what area is excellence required to obtain the company's objectives?

In what areas would lack of performance endanger the results, if not the survival, of the enterprise?

Here are some examples of the kind of conclusions these questions lead to.

Sears, Roebuck in the United States and Marks & Spencer in England are in many ways remarkably similar, if only because the founders and builders of Marks & Spencer consciously modeled their company on Sears, Roebuck. But there is a pronounced difference in the organizational placement and organizational role of the "laboratory" in these two companies. Sears, which defines its business as being "the buyer for the American family," uses its laboratory to test the merchandise it buys. Accordingly, the laboratory, while large, competent, and respected, is organizationally quite subordinate. Marks & Spencer, on the other hand, defined its business as mentioned earlier (Chapter 8), as "developing upper-class goods for the working-class family." As a result, the laboratory is central to Marks & Spencer's organization structure. The laboratory rather than the buyer decides what new products are desirable, develops the new merchandise, designs it, tests it, and then gets it produced. Only then does the buyer take over. As a result, the head of the Marks & Spencer laboratory is a senior member of management and, in many ways, the chief business planner.

Any company that shows outstanding success will be found to have made the key activities—and especially those in which excellence is needed to attain business performance and business objectives—the central, load-carrying elements in its organization structure.

But equally important are the questions "In what areas could malfunc-

*I still followed this approach in *The Practice of Management* in 1954.

tion seriously damage us? In what areas do we have major vulnerability?" They are questions, however, that are much less often asked.

The New York brokerage community, by and large, did not ask it. If it had, it would have realized that malfunction of the "back office," where customer orders, customer accounts and securities are handled, could seriously endanger the business. Failure to organize the back office as a key activity was the single most important cause for the severe crisis that overtook Wall Street in 1969 and 1970 and destroyed a good many of the best-known and apparently most successful firms. The one Wall Street firm, however, that had asked those questions, Merrill Lynch, and had organized the back office as a load-bearing key activity in its structure, emerged from the crisis the giant of the brokerage business.

Finally, the question should be asked "What are the *values* that are truly important to *us* in this company?" It might be product or process safety. It might be product quality. It might be the ability of the company dealers to give proper service to the customer and so on. Whatever the values are, they have to be organizationally anchored. There has to be an organizational component responsible for them—and it has to be a key component.

These three questions will identify the key activities. And they in turn will be the load-bearing, the structural elements of organization. The rest, no matter how important, no matter how much money they represent, no matter how many people they employ, are secondary. Obviously, they will have to be analyzed, organized, and placed within the structure. But the first concern must be those activities that are essential to the success of a business strategy and to the attainment of business objectives. They have to be identified, defined, organized, and centrally placed.

An analysis of key activities is needed in the business that has been going for some time, and especially in the business that has been going well. In such a business the analysis will invariably reveal that important activities are either not provided for or are left hanging in midair to be performed in a haphazard fashion. It will almost invariably bring out activities that, once important, have lost most of their meaning but continue to be organized as major activities. It will demonstrate that historically meaningful groupings no longer make sense but have, instead, become obstacles to proper performance. And it will certainly lead to the discovery of unnecessary activities that should be eliminated.

The new business needs such thinking. But the greatest need for key-activity analysis is found in the business that has been growing fast (see Chapter 60). Rapid growth is both a disorganized and a disorganizing process. The enterprise that starts out, so to speak, in a lowly but functional two-room cottage, puts in, as it grows, a new wing here, an attic there, a partition elsewhere, until it is housed in a twenty-six-room monstrosity in which all but the oldest inhabitants need a St. Bernard to bring them back from the water cooler. To reorganize mechanically in such a situation—the usual approach—will make things worse. To copy the "GM organization" in such a situation will put on a tremendous superstructure of "staff" and "coordinators" without remedying the basic structural defects. Only a key-activities analysis starting out from objectives and strategy can provide the organization structure the business really needs.

A business should always analyze its organization structure when its strategy changes. Whatever the reason—a change in market or in technology, diversification or new objectives—a change in strategy requires a new analysis of the key activities and an adaptation of the structure to them. Conversely, reorganization that is undertaken without a change in strategy is either superfluous or indicates poor organization to begin with.

## The Contributions Analysis

From the earliest days of concern with organization, a hundred years ago, the most controversial question has been "What activities belong together and what activities belong apart?" A number of answers have been given over the years.

Perhaps the earliest one was the German division of a business into two major areas: the "technical," embracing research, engineering, and production, and the "commercial," embracing sales and finance. Somewhat later came "line" and "staff," which tried to distinguish "operating" and nonoperating "advisory" activities. Finally there was Henri Fayol's analysis of functions, defined (too narrowly) as "bundles of related skills," which still underlies the typical organization of most businesses.

All of these have merit. But a more searching analysis is needed which groups activities by the *kind of contribution* they make.

There are, by and large, four major groups of activities, if distinguished by their contribution.

There are, first, *result-producing activities*—that is, activities which produce measurable results which can be related, directly or indirectly, to the results and performance of the entire enterprise. Some of these activities are directly revenue-producing. Others contribute measurable results.

There are, second, *support activities* which, while needed, and even essential, do not by themselves produce results but have results only through the use made of their "output" by other components within the business.

There are, third, activities which have no direct or indirect relationship to the results of the business, activities which are truly ancillary. They are *hygiene and housekeeping activities.*

Finally, and different in character from any of these, is the *top-manage-*

*ment activity* (which will be discussed separately in Chapters 49 through 52).

Among the result-producing activities, there are some that directly bring in *revenues* (or, in service institutions, directly produce "patient care" or "learning"). Here belong innovating activities, selling and all the work needed to do a systematic and organized selling job, such as sales forecasting, market research, sales training, and sales management. Here also belongs the treasury function, that is, the supply and management of money in the business.

In a commercial bank, all lending operations, the fiduciary activities of managing other people's money, and, of course, the money-making operation of the bank itself, that is, the management of its own liquid funds, are revenue-producing activities. In a department store buying and selling are always revenue-producing operations (and at Marks & Spencer innovation has also been a revenue-producing activity). In a life insurance company selling is obviously revenue-producing. But so is the actuarial activity insofar as it develops new types of policy; and finally, investment is an important —in many insurance companies the most important—revenue-producing activity.

The second group of result-producing activities are those which do not generate revenue but can still be directly related to the results of the entire business, or of a major revenue-producing segment. I call them *result-contributing* rather than result-producing.

Manufacturing is typical of these activities. But training of people belongs here too, as does their original recruitment and employment, that is, the activities concerned with the supply of qualified and trained people to the enterprise. Purchasing and physical distribution are result-contributing but not revenue-producing activities. "Engineering," as the term is normally understood in most manufacturing businesses, is a result-contributing but not a revenue-producing activity. In a commercial bank "operations," that is, the handling of data and papers, belong here; in a life insurance company, claims settlement. Labor negotiations and many other similar "relations" activities are result-contributing though not revenue-producing.

The third group of result-producing activities are information activities. They do produce a "finished product" that is needed by everyone in the system. Information performance can also be defined and measured, or at least appraised. Yet information, by itself, does not produce any revenue. It is "supply" to revenue and cost centers alike.

First among the "support" activities which do not by themselves produce a "product" but are "input" to others stand the "conscience" activities. These activities set standards, create vision, and demand excellence in *all* the key areas where a business needs to strive for excellence.

Conscience activities tend to be slighted in most organizations. But every company—and every service institution—needs to provide itself and its managers with vision, with values, with standards, and with some provision for auditing performance against these standards.

There are indeed in all larger businesses people who are supposed to do this job, usually the executives who head up major "service staffs." But their first duty is not to be the organization's conscience but to be servant of, and advisor to, operating managers. As a result they rarely get around to doing the conscience job systematically. Instead they run departments.

Another support function is advice and teaching, i.e., the traditional service staffs. The contribution is not in what the activity itself does or can do, but the impact it has on the ability of others to perform and to do. The "product" is an increased performance capacity of the rest of the organization.

A good many of the "relations" activities are also "support"—as is the legal staff, or the patent department.

The last group of activities defined by their contribution are the hygiene and housekeeping activities, ranging from the medical department to the people who clean the floor, from the plant cafeteria to the management of pension and retirement funds, from finding a plant site to taking care of all the manifold record-keeping requirements imposed on business by government. These functions contribute nothing directly to the results and performance of the business. Their malfunction, however, can damage the business. They serve legal requirements, the morale of the work force, or public responsibilities. Of all activities they are the most diverse. And of all activities they tend to get the shortest shrift in most organizations.

This is a very rough classification, and far from scientific. Some activities may be put into one category in one business, into another one in another, and in a third company will be left fuzzy and without clear classification at all.

In some manufacturing companies, manufacturing is a cost center. It contributes results but does not generate revenue. But there are some true manufacturing businesses, i.e., businesses whose revenue is generated by manufacturing sans research, sans engineering, sans selling. There are businesses where licensing, selling, and buying of patents are major revenue producers.

Purchasing, while normally a support activity, can also be defined as part of a result-contributory activity: "materials management," which includes manufacturing and physical distribution, all three managed together to minimize costs of goods and money needs, and maximize quality, delivery, and customer satisfaction.

Why classify then? The answer is that activities that differ in contribution have to be treated differently. Contribution determines ranking and placement.

Key activities should never be subordinated to nonkey activities.

Revenue-producing activities should never be subordinated to nonrevenue-producing activities.

And support activities should never be mixed with revenue-producing and result-contributory activities. They should be kept apart.

## The "Conscience" Activities

Activities that are the conscience of an organization must never be subordinated to anything else. They also should never be placed with any other activity; they should be clearly separate.

The conscience function of giving vision, of setting standards, and of auditing performance against these standards is basically a top-management function. But it has to work with the entire management group. Every business, even a small business, needs this function. In a small business, it need not be set up as a separate function but can be discharged as part of the top-management job. In any business of more than medium size, however, the function has usually to be set up and staffed separately.

However, there should be very few people actually doing the conscience job. It is a job for a single individual rather than a staff. It is a job for a man whose performance has earned the respect of the management group. It is not a job for a "specialist." It is best discharged by a senior member of the management group with proven performance record who has manifested concern, perception, and interest in the area for which he is supposed to act as the conscience.

Only those few areas that are vital and central to a company's success and survival should become areas of conscience. Objectives and strategy determine what conscience activities are needed. Managing people is always a conscience area, and so is marketing. The impact of a business on its environment, its social responsibilities and basic relations with the outside community, are also basic conscience areas. Innovation (whether technological or social innovation) is likely to be a conscience area for any large business.

Beyond these, however, there is no formula.

Conscience work is incompatible with operating and with giving advice.

The only activity that should "report" to a man in charge of a conscience activity is auditing the actual performance of managers. For it is not enough to have vision and to set standards. Performance of the organization against these standards needs to be appraised regularly.

"Conscience," many people will argue, is a very strong, in addition to being a rather strange, term. But it is the right term. The task of the conscience activities is not to help the organization do better what it is already doing. The task is to remind the organization all the time of what it should be doing and isn't doing. The task is to be uncomfortable, to hold up the ideal against the everyday reality, to defend the unpopular and to fight the expedient.

This requires, however, self-discipline on the part of the conscience executive and acceptance of his competence and integrity on the part of the organization.

The tenure of the few conscience executives should be limited as a rule. No matter how greatly a conscience executive may be respected, and no matter how successful he has been, he will eventually wear out either his integrity or his welcome. This is a good place for a senior man to end a distinguished career. A younger man in the job should be moved out after a few years—preferably back into a "doing" job.

## Making Service Staffs Effective

There are similarly stringent rules with respect to advisory and teaching activities, that is, with respect to service staffs.

There should be very few of them. They should be set up only in key activity areas. It is counterproductive to have a service staff in every function. The secret of effective service work is concentration rather than busyness.

Advisory and teaching staffs should never try to do a little bit of everything. They should zero in on a very small number of crucial areas. Rather than serve everybody they should select "targets of opportunity," i.e., areas within the organization where the managers are receptive and do not have to be "sold," and where achievement generates "multiplier impact" throughout the whole company.

The staffs and their activities should be kept lean.

The supply of men of the right temperament for this kind of work is not very large. To do a decent job in an advisory and teaching capacity requires a man who genuinely wants others to get the credit. It requires a man who starts out with the aim of enabling others to do what *they* want to do, provided only that it is neither immoral nor insane. It requires further a man who has the patience to let others learn rather than go and do the work himself. And finally, it requires a man who will not abuse his position in headquarters close to the seat of power to politick, to manipulate, and to play favorites. People who possess these personality traits are rare. Yet people without them in services work can do only mischief.

One basic rule for advisory and teaching staffs is that they abandon an old activity before they take on a new one. Otherwise they will soon start to "build empires" or to produce "canned goods," that is, programs and memoranda, rather than develop the knowledge and performance capacity of the operating men whose job it is to produce. They will also otherwise be forced to use second-raters rather than men of outstanding competence. Only if they are being required to abandon an old activity before taking on a new one will they be able to put on the job the really first-rate people in the group.

Advisory and teaching activities should never "operate." A common weakness of personnel staffs is that they operate. They run the labor negotiations, they do a lot of housekeeping chores such as managing the cafeteria, or they train. As a result the advisory and teaching work does not get done. The "daily crisis" in "operations" takes precedence over the work of advice and teaching which can always be postponed. Mixing advice and operations means building large staffs rather than building performance.

Other service staffs are just as guilty of mixing "doing" work in with advice and teaching—and thereby shifting either the one or the other.

A company may have need for acoustics engineering while no division, however, has enough work in the area to justify its own acoustics engineers. It seems logical therefore to put a few good acoustics engineers into "manufacturing services" or "engineering services." The acoustics people, however, are not service staff but result-producers who go to work wherever, in a given division, an acoustics job is to be done. They are not expected to give advice or to teach, but to do. If placed into a services component the unit will rarely produce. The good people in it will become frustrated and are unlikely to stay long.

If "joint-operating work" is needed—and it often is—there might be a separate central operating pool under one manager for all such work, regardless of technical area. The management problems in all joint operating work are the same: relations, assignments, priorities, and standards.

Advisory and teaching activities are service institutions, as discussed in Chapters 11 through 14. They should be required to impose on themselves the self-discipline of setting objectives, of setting targets, of determining priorities and measuring their results against them. They should not have a monopoly. If consulting or teaching work has to be done other than in their areas of concentration somebody from the outside should be brought in to do it. And insofar as possible, their "customers," the managers of the various units, should have the choice between using the internal advisory and teaching staff, going on the outside, or not using any staff at all.

Advisory and teaching work should not be a career. It is work to which a manager or career professional should be exposed in the course of his growth. But it is not work which a man should, normally, do for long. As a career it corrupts. It breeds contempt for "those dumb operating people," that is, for honest work. It puts a premium on being "bright," rather than on being right. It is also frustrating work because one does not have results of one's own but results only at secondhand.

But it is excellent training, excellent development, and a severe test of a man's character and of his ability to be effective without having the authority of command. It is an experience everyone should have had who rises to the top of an organization. But it is an exposure no one should suffer for more than a limited period of time.

There is constant discussion these days whether this kind of work requires a high degree of specialized knowledge or whether a good "generalist" can rapidly acquire enough of a "smattering of ignorance" to be effective in advisory and teaching work. The debate rages forever in any consulting practice. There is no answer to the question—indeed, it is probably the wrong question. In some areas, clearly, professional and highly specialized competence is a requirement. If a company, for instance, needs advice and teaching in advanced areas of polymer chemistry or in structuring highly complex and risky international capital transactions, somebody with a background in marketing or in purchasing need not apply, no matter how good and perceptive a teacher he is. But in many areas of advice and teaching the generalist who is willing to learn, who will think through the relationship with his "client," and who takes responsibility for his contribution, is likely to do a better job than the highly specialized expert who refuses to make himself understood and is contemptuous of the "laity" who do not possess his advanced expertise. Indeed, in most successful advisory and teaching activities, the expert is the "inside" man who furnishes the tools for the consultants, but who is not himself active, let alone effective, in advising and teaching work.

## The Two Faces of Information

Information activities present a special organizational problem. In the terms the chemist uses, they are "bi-valent"; they have two faces, two dimensions, and require two different "bonds." Unlike most other result-producing activities, they are not concerned with one stage of the process but with the entire process itself. This means that they have to be both centralized and decentralized.

Information-producing activities, whether accounting work or operations research, resemble the nervous system of a biological organism which is also both centralized and decentralized down to the smallest and most remote cell in the body.

Information activities therefore have two organizational homes rather than one.

The traditional organization chart expresses this in the two different lines that connect an information activity to "bosses": a solid line to the head of the unit for which it is the information provider, and a dotted line to the central information group, for instance, the company controller. One conclusion from this is that information work should be kept separate from other kinds of work.

American business has typically violated this rule by putting accounting, i.e., a traditional information activity, into one component with the treasurer, i.e., the result-producing operating work of supplying capital and managing money in the business. The justification has been that both "deal with money." But, of course, accounting does not deal with money; it deals with figures. The consequence of the traditional approach has been the slighting of financial management. As long as money was—or seemed— cheap this could be excused; but the excuse no longer holds.

The tough question with respect to information activities is which of them belong together and which should be kept apart. There is much talk today about "integrated total information systems." This of course implies that all—or at least most—information activities should be in one component. Insofar as this means that new and different information activities, e.g., operations research or a computer system, should not be subordinated to traditional accounting, the point is well taken. But should they be coordinated? Or should they be separate?

There is, so far, no clear answer and no satisfactory way to organize information work—though it is clearly a key activity. Nobody has yet seen a total information system. No one may ever see one. But as we develop information capacity we will have to grapple with the organizational problem and will have to find answers, or at least approaches.

## Hygiene and Housekeeping

The last group of activities according to their contribution are hygiene and housekeeping activities. They should be kept separate from other work, or else they will not get done. The problem is not that these activities are particularly difficult. Some are. Many others are not. The problem is that they are not even indirectly related to results. Therefore, they tend to be looked down upon by the rest of the organization. They are "donkey work" because they are neither result-producing nor professional work.

One reason for the tremendous increase in health-care costs in the U.S. is managerial neglect of the "hotel services" by the people who dominate the hospital, such as doctors and nurses. They all know that the hotel services are essential and that patients do not get well unless they are reasonably comfortable, are being fed, have their beds changed and their rooms cleaned. But these are not professional activities for a medical man, for a nurse, or for an X-ray technician. They are not willing to yield an inch to make it possible for the people in charge of the hotel services to do their jobs. They are not willing to have these activities represented on the upper levels of hospital management. As a result, no "respectable" manager in a hospital wants to have anything to do with these activities. They are left unmanaged. And this means they are done badly and expensively.

There rarely is such a problem with the medical department within a company—if only because our value system respects the doctor and places him high in our social hierarchy. But even so important a function as the selection of a plant site, or the construction of a plant are often considered "extraneous" by the people within a business. Activities where less seems to be at stake, whether the parking lot, the cafeteria, or maintenance in general, tend to be slighted and neglected.

This extends even to activities in which a great amount of money is at stake. Very few companies in the United States for instance have done even an adequate job of managing the pension funds of their employees, despite the enormous amount of money involved and the serious impact on the company's future. It is an activity which does not, it seems, have any relationship to results and therefore it is an activity which tends to be relegated to somebody else.

One way out is to turn hygiene and housekeeping activities over to the work community to run (see Chapter 21). They are activities "for" the employees and they are therefore best managed by the employees. Or, such activities may be farmed out to somebody whose business it is to run a pension fund or to manage a cafeteria.

But insofar as a company's management has to do these things itself— and picking a plant site and building a factory is something a company has to do for itself, or at least has to participate in actively—hygiene and housekeeping activities ought to be kept separate from all others. They require different people, different values, different measurements—and should require little supervision by business management itself.

One example are the autonomous real estate management companies which large businesses have created to handle everything concerned with the procurement of real estate, the construction of a building or a factory, and the management and maintenance of buildings. Another example is the General Services Administration of the U.S. Government, which handles all housekeeping tasks for all government agencies. For the senior soil scientist in the Department of Agriculture, managing the automotive fleet for his unit is a chore for which he has neither interest nor respect. Yet there obviously is a good deal of money at stake—and cars need organized, systematic purchasing and organized, systematic maintenance. For the General Services Administration the administration of the government automotive fleet is its business and can be organized as such.

There is one overall rule. Activities that make the same kind of contribution can be joined together in one component and under one management, whatever their technical specialization. Activities that do not make the same kind of contribution do not, as a rule, belong together.

It is entirely feasible—indeed, it often is the best way—to put all advising and teaching activities, in personnel, in manufacturing, in marketing, or in purchasing, in one "services" group under one manager. Similarly, in any but large companies, one man might well be the company's conscience in major conscience areas. Contribution rather than skill determines function.

# 43

## . . . And How They Join Together

Identifying key activities and analyzing their contributions defines the building blocks of organization. But to place the structural units which make up the organization requires two additional pieces of work: an analysis of decisions and an analysis of relations.

### Decision Analysis

What decisions are needed to obtain the performance necessary to attain objectives? What kinds of decisions are they? On what level of the organization should they be made? What activities are involved in, or affected by them? Which managers must therefore participate in the decisions—at least to the extent of being consulted beforehand? Which managers must be informed after they have been made? The answers to these questions very largely determine where certain work belongs.

It will be argued that it is impossible to anticipate what kinds of decisions will arise in the future. But while their content cannot be predicted their kind and subject matter have a high degree of predictability.

In one large company well over 90 percent of the decisions that managers had to make over a five-year period were found to be "typical," and fell within a small number of categories. In only a few cases would it have been necessary to ask, "Where does this decision belong?" had the problem been thought through in advance. Yet, because there was no decision analysis, almost three-quarters of the decisions had to "go looking for a home," as the graphic phrase within the company put it, and most of them went to a much higher level of management than was needed. The company's components had been placed according to the size of their payroll rather than according to their decision responsibility so that the activities that should have made key decisions were placed so low as to be without authority and also without adequate information.

To place authority and responsibility for various kinds of decisions requires first that they be classified according to kind and character. Such standard classifications as "policy decisions" and "operating decisions" are practically meaningless, however, and give rise to endless debates of a highly abstruse nature. Not much more helpful is classification according to the amount of money involved.

There are four basic characteristics which determine the nature of any business decision.

First, there is the degree of *futurity* in the decision. For how long into the future does it commit the company? And how fast can it be reversed?

The buyer at Sears, Roebuck has practically no limit as to the amount to which he can commit the company. But no buyer or buying supervisor can either abandon an existing product or add a new one without the approval of the head of the entire buying operation who, traditionally, is the number two or number three man in the entire Sears, Roebuck organization. Similarly, the foreign exchange trader in a major commercial bank traditionally has only the loosest limit on the amounts to which he can commit the bank. But he cannot start trading in a new currency without approval from high authority in the bank. And he cannot carry a "position" regardless of amount, beyond a fixed and short period of time.

The second criterion is the *impact* a decision has on other functions, on other areas, or on the business as a whole. If it affects only one function, it is of the lowest order. Otherwise it will have to be made on a higher level, where the impact on all affected functions can be considered; or it must be made in close consultation with the managers of the other affected functions. To use technical language, "Optimization" of process and performance of one function or area must not be at the expense of other functions or areas; this is undesirable "suboptimization."

One example of a decision which looks like a purely "technical" one affecting one area only, but which actually has impact on many areas, is a change in the methods of keeping the parts inventory in a mass-production plant. This affects all manufacturing operations. It makes necessary major changes in assembly. It affects delivery to customers—it might even lead to radical changes in marketing and pricing, such as the abandonment of certain designs and models and of certain premium prices. And it may require substantial changes in engineering design. The technical problems in inventory-keeping—though quite considerable—pale into insignificance compared to the problems in other areas which any change in inventory-keeping will produce. To "optimize" inventory-keeping at the expense of these other areas cannot be allowed. It can be avoided only if the decision is recognized as belonging to a fairly high order and handled as one affecting the entire process: either it has to be reserved for management higher than the plant; or it requires close consultation among all functional managers.

The consideration of the impact of a decision and the need to prevent "suboptimization" may shift the focus of a decision decisively, as the following example shows.

In the early days of the Du Pont Company, when it was still solely an explosives manufacturer, the company was by far the world's largest buyer of nitrate, without, however, owning any nitrate fields. Yet the purchasing department was given a completely free hand in buying nitrate. It did so, indeed, most successfully—from the point of view of purchasing. It bought nitrate when the market prices were low and succeeded in obtaining the vital raw material for the company at prices far below what the competitors usually had to pay. Yet this was suboptimization. For the low prices for nitrate and the resulting competitive cost advantage were paid for by tying up large sums of money in inventory. This, in the first place, meant that a good deal of the cost advantage of low nitrate prices was illusory and offset by high interest payments. More serious, it also meant that the company, in the event of a downturn in business, might find itself in a liquidity crisis. The decision to balance cheap raw material prices against the cost of money and the danger of illiquidity was therefore properly made as a top-management decision. But after the new limits for inventory had been established, the buying decisions again became exclusively the task of the purchasing people.

The character of a decision is also determined by the number of *qualitative factors* that enter into it: basic principles of conduct, ethical values, social and political beliefs, etc. The moment value considerations have to be taken into account, the decision moves into a higher order and requires either determination or review at a higher level. And the most important as well as the most common of qualitative factors are human beings. (This, of course, underlies the strong recommendation in Chapter 36 for top-management people to play an active part in the decisions on promotion to upper levels of middle management.)

Finally, decisions can be classified according to whether they are periodically *recurrent* or *rare*, if not unique, decisions. The recurrent decision requires the establishment of a general rule, that is, of a decision in principle. Since suspending an employee deals with a person, the rule has to be decided at a fairly high level in the organization. But the application of the rule to the specific case, while also a decision, can then be placed on a much lower level.

The rare decision, however, has to be treated as a distinct event. Whenever it occurs, it has to be thought through.

A decision should always be made at the lowest possible level and as close to the scene of action as possible. However, a decision should always be made at a level insuring that all activities and objectives affected are fully considered. The first rule tells us how far down a decision *should* be made. The second how far down it *can* be made, as well as which managers must share in the decision and which must be informed of it. The two together tell us where certain activities should be placed. Managers should be high enough to have the authority needed to make the typical decisions pertaining to their work, and low enough to have the detailed knowledge and the first-hand experience, "where the action is."

## Relations Analysis

The final step in designing the building blocks of organization is an analysis of relations. It tells us where a specific component belongs.

With whom will a manager in charge of an activity have to work, what contribution does he have to make to managers in charge of other activities, and what contribution do these managers, in turn, have to make to him?

The basic rule in placing an activity within the organization structure is to impose on it the *smallest possible number of relationships*. At the same time, it should be so placed that the crucial relations, that is, the relationship on which depend its success and the effectiveness of its contribution, should be easy, accessible, and central to the unit. *The rule is to keep relationships to a minimum but make each count.*

This rule explains why functions are not, as traditional organization theory would have them be, "bundles of related skills." If we followed that logic, we would, for instance, put production planning into a planning component in which all kinds of planners would work together. The skills needed in production planning are closely related to all other operational planning skills. Instead we put the production planner into manufacturing and as close as possible both to the plant manager and to the first-line supervisors. This is where he belongs according to his relationship.

There is often a conflict between placement according to decision analysis and placement according to relations analysis. By and large, one should try to follow the logic of relations as far as he can.

If organization design has to follow the logic of decisions in order to avoid suboptimization (as is usually the case with respect to the accounting function) the work itself should be planned according to relations analysis, that is, as close as possible to the scene of action. The direction of the work, the setting of rules, of standards, but also the appraisal and evaluation of the work should be placed according to decision analysis in a central component which can see the entire business and think through the impacts.

The four analyses—of key activities, of contributions, of decisions, of relations—should always be kept as simple and as brief as possible. In a small enterprise they can often be done in a matter of hours and on a few pieces of paper. In a very large and complex enterprise, though, such as General Electric, the First National City Bank, or Unilever (not to mention the Department of Defense) the job may well require months of study and the application of highly advanced tools of analysis and synthesis. But these analyses should never be slighted or skimped. They should be considered a necessary task and one that has to be done well in every business.

## Symptoms of Malorganization

There is no perfect organization. At its best an organization structure will not cause trouble. But what are the most common mistakes in designing the building blocks of organization and joining them together? And what are the most common symptoms of serious flaws in organization?

1. The most common and the most serious symptom of malorganization is multiplication of the number of management levels. A basic rule of organization is to build the *least possible* number of management levels and forge the shortest possible chain of command.

Every additional level makes more difficult the attainment of common direction and mutual understanding. Every additional level distorts objectives and misdirects attention. Mathematical "information theory" has a law that any additional relay in a communications system halves the "message" and doubles the "noise." Any "level" in an organization is a "relay." Every link in the chain sets up additional stresses and creates one more source of inertia, friction, and slack.

Every additional level, especially in the big business, adds to the difficulty of developing tomorrow's managers, both by adding to the time it takes to come up from the bottom and by making specialists rather than managers out of the men moving up through the chain.

In some large companies there are today twelve or even fifteen levels between first-line supervisor and company president. Assuming that a man gets appointed first-line supervisor at age twenty-five, and that he spends only five years on each intervening level—both optimistic assumptions—he would be eighty or ninety before he could even be considered for the company's presidency. And the usual "cure"—a special promotion ladder for hand-picked young "geniuses" or "crown princes"—is as bad as the disease.

How few levels are really needed is shown by the example of the oldest, largest, and most successful organization of the West, the Catholic Church. There is only one level of authority and responsibility between the Pope and the lowliest parish priest: the bishop.

The second most common symptom of malorganization is recurrence of organizational problems. No sooner has a problem supposedly been "solved" than it comes back again in a new guise.

A typical example in a manufacturing company is product development. The marketing people think it belongs to them, the research and development people are equally convinced that it belongs to them. But placing it in either component simply creates a recurring problem. Actually both placements are wrong. In a business that wants innovation, product development is a key activity and a revenue-producing activity. It should not be subordinated to any other activity. It deserves to be organized as a separate innovative component.*

The recurrent organization problem indicates unthinking application of traditional "organization principles" such as that of the "typical function" or that of "staff and line." The answer lies in making the right analyses—the key activities analysis, the contributions analysis, the decisions analysis, and the relations analysis. An organization problem that comes back more than a couple of times should not be treated mechanically by shuffling little boxes on a piece of paper. It indicates lack of thinking, lack of clarity, and lack of understanding.

Equally common and equally dangerous is an organization structure that puts the attention of key people on the wrong, the irrelevant, the secondary problems. Organization should put the attention of people on major business decisions, on key activities, and on performance and results. If, instead, it puts attention on proper behavior, on etiquette, on procedure, let alone on jurisdictional conflict, organization misdirects. Then organization becomes a bar to performance.

Again, this is the result of mechanical rather than organic organization building. It is the result of slapping on so-called principles, instead of thinking through what organization the strategy of the business demands. It is the result of focusing organization on symmetry rather than on performance.

No organization chart is likely ever to be displayed in a major art mu-

---

*On this see Chapter 61, "The Innovative Organization."

seum. What matters is not the chart but the organization. A chart is nothing but an oversimplification which enables people to make sure that they talk about the same things in discussing organization structure. One never makes organizational changes for the sake of the chart. This always results in malorganization.

There are a number of common symptoms of poor organization which, usually, require no further diagnosis. There is, first, the symptom of *too many meetings* attended by too many people.

There are, especially in large organizations, managerial organs which do their work in and by meetings. The top committees in General Motors are examples. And so are the boards of directors composed of the top officers which govern both Standard Oil of New Jersey and Du Pont. But these are exceptions—deliberative organs which do not have operating functions and, as a rule, do not have decision-making functions either. They are organs to guide, to reflect, to review—and perhaps their most important function is to compel the operating top managers who sit down with the committee to think through their own direction, their own needs, and their own opportunities.

But apart from such deliberative bodies, which discharge their functions in meetings, meetings should be considered as a concession to organizational imperfection. The ideal is the organization which can operate without meetings—in the same sense in which the ideal of the machine designer is to have only one moving part in his contraption. In every human organization there is far too much need for cooperation, coordination, and human relations to have to provide for additional meetings. And the human dynamics of meetings are so complex as to make them very poor tools for getting any work done.

Whenever executives, except at the very top level, spend more than a fairly small fraction of their time—maybe a quarter or less—in meetings, there is *prima facie* a case of malorganization. An excess of meetings indicates that jobs have not been defined clearly, have not been structured big enough, have not been made truly responsible. Also the need for meetings indicates that the decisions and relations analyses either have not been made at all or have not been applied. The rule should be to minimize the need for people to get together to accomplish anything.

An organization in which people are all the time concerned about feelings and about what other people will like or will not like is not an organization that has good human relations. On the contrary, it is an organization that has very poor human relations. Good human relations, like good manners, are taken for granted. Constant anxiety over other people's feelings is the worst kind of human relations.

An organization that suffers from this—and a great many do—can be said unequivocally to suffer from overstaffing. It might be overstaffed in terms of activities. Instead of focusing on key activities, it tries to do a little bit of everything—especially in advice and teaching activities. Or the individual activities are overstaffed. It is in crowded rooms that people get on each other's nerves, poke their elbows into each other's eyes, and step on each other's toes. Where there is enough distance they do not collide. Overstaffed organizations create work rather than performance. They also create friction, sensitivity, irritation, and concern with feelings.

It is a symptom of malorganization to rely on "coordinators," "assistants," and other such *whose job it is not to have a job*. This indicates that activities and jobs have been designed too narrowly, or that activities and jobs, rather than being designed for one defined result, are expected to do a great many parts of different tasks. It usually indicates also that organizational components have been organized according to skill rather than according to their place in the process or according to their contribution. For skill always contributes only a part rather than a result. And then one needs a coordinator or some other such nonjob to put pieces together that should never have been separated in the first place.

## "Organizitis" as a Chronic Affliction

Some, indeed a good many, businesses, especially large and complex ones, suffer from the disease of "organizitis." Everybody is concerned with organization. Reorganization is going on all the time. At the first sign of any trouble, be it only a spat over a specification between a purchasing agent and the people in engineering, the cry goes up for the "organization doctors," whether outside consultants or inside staff. And no organizational solution ever lasts long, indeed few organizational arrangements are even given enough time to be tested and worked out in practice, before another organization study is put in train.

In some cases this does indeed suggest malorganization. "Organizitis" will set in if organization structure fails to come to grips with fundamentals. It is, especially, the result of not rethinking and restructuring the organization when there is a fundamental change in the size and complexity of a business or in its objectives and strategy.

But just as often "organizitis" is self-inflicted and a form of hypochondria. It therefore should be emphasized that organizational changes should not be undertaken often and should not be undertaken lightly. Reorganization is a form of surgery; and even minor surgery has risks.

The demands for organization studies or for reorganization as a response to minor ailments should be resisted. No organization will ever be perfect. A certain amount of friction, of incongruity, of organizational confusion is inevitable.

The last two chapters have dealt with the "engineering" aspects of organization: the building blocks, their placement, and their relationships. But organization also needs "architecture"; it needs structural logic and structural principles. It also calls for understanding of the requirements organization structure needs to satisfy, i.e., of "design specifications."

# 44

# Design Logics and Design Specifications

*The Five "Design Principles"—Is an Additional One Still Unknown?—*
*Limitations and Requirements—Formal Specifications—Clarity—*
*Economy—The Direction of Vision—Understanding of Task—Decision-*
*Making—Stability and Adaptability—Perpetuation and Self-Renewal—*
*Operating, Innovative, Top-Management Structures*

The "organization architect" has available today *five design principles,* i.e., five distinct organization structures for the placement of activities and the ordering of the relationships. Two of them are traditional and have been known as principles of organization design for many years: Henri Fayol's functional structure, and Alfred P. Sloan's federal decentralization.

Three are new, are indeed so new that they are not generally known, let alone recognized as design principles: team organization; "simulated" decentralization; and the "system" structure.

Each of these five was developed empirically and for specific needs. The first impression is therefore that they represent expediency rather than design, let alone logic.* But, in reality, these designs express different *design logics.* Each takes one generic dimension of managerial organization and builds the structure around it.

---

*This was expressed most cogently by one of the most respected organization theorists, Harold Koontz, in his article, "The Management Theory Jungle," *Journal of the Academy of Management,* December, 1965.

## Design Logics

*Work and task* are surely a generic dimension of management. And two of the available design principles are structured around work and task: the functional principle and the team.

These two differ in the way they balance "static" and "moving" parts. In the functional organization "stages of the work," e.g., manufacturing and marketing, and "skills," e.g., accounting, are designed as static; the "work" moves from one to the others. In team structure the work is conceived as static with "skills," that is, individual manufacturing, marketing, and accounting experts moving to form the specific team which a specific piece of work, i.e., a "task," requires.

Functional organization and team organization are commonly assumed to be antithetic, with the "modern" team being opposed to the "old-fashioned" function.

That the team is not "free-form" but a highly disciplined and highly structured form has been said earlier (in Chapter 41). But the belief that these two are opposite is largely misunderstanding. In fact, they are not even alternatives. For a number of design problems one of the two is the only appropriate design principle. For the biggest organization problem, the structure of knowledge work, the two are complementary.

*Results and performance* are as much a true dimension of management as work and task. The two "decentralization" principles available, "federal decentralization" and "simulated decentralization," are built around this dimension. They are "result-focused" designs.

Unlike functional and team structures they are, however, not complementary. They are not even alternatives. Federal decentralization is an "optimum," simulated decentralization a "lesser evil" to be resorted to only when the stringent requirements of federal decentralization cannot be met.

*Relationships* are also a generic dimension of management. The last of the available design principles, "systems designs," is relations-focused.

Relations are inevitably both more numerous and less clearly definable than either work and task, or results. A relations-focused structure will therefore, of necessity, be both highly complex and lacking in clarity. It will present greater difficulties than either work-focused or result-focused design. But there are, as we shall see, organizational problems where the very complexity of relationships makes "systems design" the only appropriate design principle.

This rough classification indicates that at least one additional design principle might yet be developed. *Decision* is as much a dimension of management as are work and task, results and performance, and relations. Yet so far we know no decision-focused design principle of organization structure.* So far we have only theoretical speculation. But a decision-focused design principle is at least a theoretical possibility. If it were to be developed into an operationally usable structure, it might have considerable impact.

Because each of the available design principles structures around one dimension of a multidimensional entity, management, each must have limitations. Each must be the best available design principle for certain structural tasks; usable, though with increasing inefficiency, for others; and just plain wrong for yet a third group. Each must also have its own requirements and make its own demands on management and enterprise.

## Formal Specifications

Any "structure," by definition, has to satisfy requirements that have nothing to do with the purpose of the structure but are grounded in the nature of structure itself. Structures are "forms"; and forms have to satisfy "formal" specifications.

Organization structure specifically needs to satisfy minimum requirements with respect to: clarity; economy; the direction of vision; understanding by the individual of his own task and the task of the whole; decision-making; stability and adaptability; and perpetuation and self-renewal.

1. *Clarity*. Each managerial component, and each individual within the organization, especially each manager, needs to know where he belongs, where he stands, where he has to go for whatever is needed, whether information, cooperation, or decision, and how to get there. Clarity is by no means the same thing as simplicity. Indeed, structures that look simple may lack clarity. And seemingly complex structures may have great clarity.

The Gothic cathedral has great clarity; the modern office building has practically none. In the Gothic cathedral everyone knows, without being told, where he stands and where to go. Even someone ignorant of the mysteries of the Christian religion would know immediately what the purpose of the building is and how to relate to it. Yet the Gothic cathedral is exceedingly complex, an expression of highly abstract principles of metaphysics and esthetics, and endowed with a wealth of adornments, allusions, and symbols. By contrast, the modern office building is as simple as a structure can be: an assemblage of cubes. Yet no one in the modern office building can find his way without instructions—and even then it is easy to become confused.

A structure in which no one knows without an elaborate organization

*Herbert A. Simon and his school have been attempting to develop one. At least this is how I read H. A. Simon, *Administrative Behavior* (Macmillan, 1957) and J. G. March and H. A. Simon, *Organizations* (John Wiley & Sons, 1958).

manual where he belongs, where he has to go, and where he stands, creates friction, wastes time, causes bickering and frustration, delays decision, and is altogether an impediment, rather than a help.

2. *Economy.* Closely related to clarity is the requirement of economy. The minimum effort should be needed to control, to supervise, and to coax people to perform. Organization structure should make possible self-control and should encourage self-motivation. And the smallest possible number of people, especially of people of high-performance capacity, should have to devote time and attention to keeping the machinery going, i.e., to "management" and "organization," to "internal control," "internal communications," and "personnel problems."

In any organization some of the effort has to be directed inward, some of it has to be used to keep the organization running and in good repair. In organization as well as in physics, perpetual motion is not possible; some "friction" is inevitable. But the less of the input of the organization has to be used to keep it going or to lubricate the friction points, the more of the input can become output, the more economical the organization will be, and the more of its "inputs" can become performance.

3. *The direction of vision.* Organization structure should direct the vision of individuals and of managerial units toward performance rather than toward efforts. And it should direct vision toward results, that is, toward the performance of the entire enterprise.

Performance is the end which all activities serve. Indeed, organization can be likened to a transmission belt that converts activities into the one "drive"—performance. Organization is the more efficient the more "direct" the transmission is, that is, the less it has to change the speed and direction of individual activities to make them result in performance. The largest possible number of managers should perform as businessmen rather than as "experts" or "bureaucrats," should be tested against business performance and results rather than primarily by standards of administrative skill or professional competence.

Organization structure must not misdirect vision toward the wrong performance. It should not encourage managers to give major attention to the old and easy, but tired, products and businesses while slighting the new and growing, though perhaps difficult, products. It must discourage the tendency to cling to unprofitable products and businesses by letting them ride on the coattails of the profitable lines. It must not make effort more important than results and craftsmanship an end in itself. It must, in brief, make for willingness and ability to work for results rather than for the sake of the work itself, to work for the future rather than rest on the achievements of the past, and to strive for strength rather than to put on fat.

4. *Understanding one's own task and the common task.* An organization

should enable each individual, especially each manager and each professional—but also each managerial component—to *understand his own task*. This, of course, means that the work itself has to be specialized. Work is always specific. And one can understand only a task that can be defined, a task in which what is needed to accomplish it is inherent in the task itself.

But at the same time, an organization should enable everyone to *understand the common task, the task of the entire organization*. Each member of the organization, in order to relate his efforts to the common good, needs to understand how his task fits in with the task of the whole and, in turn, what the task of the whole implies for his own task, his own contribution, his own direction. Communications therefore need to be helped rather than hampered by organizational structure.

5. *Decision-making*. None of the available design principles is primarily structured around a "decision model." Yet decisions have to be made, made on the right issues and at the right level, and have to be converted into work and accomplishment. An organization design, therefore, needs to be tested as to whether it impedes or strengthens the decision-making process.

A structure that forces decisions to go to the highest possible level of organization rather than be settled at the lowest possible level is clearly an impediment, and so is a decision structure that obscures the emergence of the need for crucial decisions, or focuses attention on the wrong issues, such as jurisdictional disputes.

A decision is only good intention until it has been carried out in work and action and has become accomplishment. No organization structure by itself can make sure of this. But different structures can make it more or less difficult for decisions to become organizational commitment and individual work.

6. *Stability and adaptability*. An organization needs a substantial degree of *stability*. It must be able to do its work even though the world around it is in turmoil. It must be able to build on its performance and achievement of yesterday. It needs to be able to plan for its own future and continuity.

The individual needs also a "home." Nobody gets any work done in a railroad station waiting room; no one gets much work done as a transient. The individual needs to belong to a "community" in which he knows people, in which he is known by them, and in which his own relationship is anchored.

But stability is not rigidity. On the contrary, organization structure requires a *high degree of adaptability*. A totally rigid structure is not stable; it is brittle. Only if the structure can adapt itself to new situations, new demands, new conditions—and also to new faces and personalities—will it be able to survive. Adaptability is a major requirement therefore.

7. *Perpetuation and self-renewal*. Finally, an organization needs to be

able to *perpetuate itself.* It needs to be able to *provide for its self-renewal.* These two needs entail a number of demands.

An organization must be capable of producing from within tomorrow's leaders. One minimum requirement for this is, as said in the preceding chapter, that it must not have so many levels of management that an able man, getting into a management job early, say at age twenty-five, cannot normally reach the top rungs of the promotion ladder while still young enough to be effective.

What matters are not the number of levels at the very top. Once a man has been promoted to general officer in the armed services, he is "at the top," even though there are three or four different "ranks" of generals. What matters is the number of "levels" to be traversed until a man reaches what in his organization is considered "top management."

But more important than the number of levels are the experience and exposure the organization structure provides or desires. Organization structure should help each man *learn* and *develop* in each job he holds; it should be designed for continuous learning.

One self-renewal specification is the ability of an organization structure to prepare and test a man on each level for the next level above, and especially to prepare and test today's junior and middle managers for senior and top-management positions. For perpetuation and self-renewal it is further necessary for an organization structure to be *accessible to new ideas* and to be willing and able to do new things.

## Operating, Innovative, Top-Management Structures

These " formal" specifications apply to any organization structure: of the small business and the large one; of the simple business and the complex one; of business enterprise and of nonbusiness service institutions.

They also apply to the three different kinds of management that have to be structured and organized: operating management responsible for performing the work and for producing the results of today's business; innovative management responsible for creating the company's tomorrow; and top management capable of directing, of giving vision, and of setting the course for the business of today and the business of tomorrow.

These are clearly conflicting specifications. No design principle could fully satisfy all of them. Any organization structure that is to be capable of performance and continuity will however have to satisfy all these specifications to some degree. This means, inevitably, compromises, trade-offs, balancing. It also implies that several design principles rather than one are likely to have to be used even for simple organization. For if any one of these specifications goes totally unsatisfied, the enterprise will not perform. Organization building therefore requires understanding of the available design principles, their requirements, their limitations, and their "fit" against the design specifications.

# 45

## Work- and Task-Focused Design: Functional Structure and Team

*The Three Ways of Organizing Work and Task—The Functional Structure—Its Strengths and Its Limitations—Can the Weaknesses Be Offset?—Vail's "Bogeys"—GE's "Functional Objectives"—Their limited Scope—Where Functionalism Works—The Team—Examples: The Hospital; the Plastic-Mold Company—Their Lessons—Requirements for Effective Teams: Continuing Mission; Clear Objective; Leadership; Group Responsibility—The Team Leader's First Job: Clarity—The Limitations of the Team Principle—How Large Can a Team Be?—The Scope of Team Organization—Top-Management Teams—Innovating Teams—Team Design and Functional Structure—Team Design and Mass-Production Work—Team Design and Knowledge Organization*

---

All work, physical as well as mental, can be organized in three ways.

It can be organized by stages in the process. In building a house we first build the foundation, then the frame and the roof, and finally the interior.

It can be organized so that the work moves where the skills and the tools are for each of the steps required. The traditional metalworking unique-product plant has batteries of reamers and lathes in one aisle, stamping machines in another, heat treating equipment in a third, with the pieces of metal moving from one group of tools and their skilled operators to another. Or, to give another example, the student at the university—the "raw material" of the educational process—moves from classroom to classroom, from professor to professor, from course to course. Each professor in each course teaches only the subject of his specialized skill, with the student emerging at the end as an "educated man," or at least as a diploma holder.

Finally, we can join together in a team workers with different skills and different tools and move them to the work, which itself is stationary. A movie-making crew—the director, the actors, the electricians, the sound engineers—"goes on location." Each does highly specialized work; but they work as a team.

"Functional organization" is commonly described as organizing work into "related bundles of skill." Actually it uses both the stage organization and the skill organization of work. Such traditional functions as manufacturing or marketing comprise a very wide variety of unrelated skills, viz., the machinist's skill and the production planner's skill in manufacturing, and the salesman's skill and the market researcher's skill in marketing. But manufacturing and marketing are distinct stages in the process. Other functions, such as accounting and personnel, are, however, organized by skills. But in any functional organization the work is moved to the stage or the skill. The work moves, while the position of the worker is fixed.

In the team structure, however, work and task are, so to speak, "fixed." Workers with different skills and different tools are brought together in a team or a task force and assigned to a piece of work or a job whether this is a research project or the architectural design of a new office building.

Both functional structures and team are very old designs. The Irrigation Cities of Mesopotamia and the Egyptian pyramid builder organized work functionally. And the organized and permanent team of the "hunting band" goes back even further, to the last Ice Age.

But as conscious, deliberate, *designed* structures, both are new. Functional organization was defined and designed by Henri Fayol in the early years of this century. The team is only now being recognized as a design principle.

Work and task have to be structured and organized. Any organization has to apply one or both of the design principles for work and task, i.e., functional structure and team. Many, as will be discussed later in this chapter, should apply both. And all organizations need to understand both.

## The Functional Structure

Functional design has the great advantage of *clarity*. Everybody has a "home." Everybody *understands his own task*. It is an organization of high *stability*.

But the price for clarity and stability is that it is difficult for anyone, up to and including the top functional people, *to understand the task of the whole* and to relate their own work to it. While stable, the structure is *rigid* and resists adaptation. It does not prepare people for tomorrow, does not *train and test* them, and on the whole, tends to confirm them in the desire to do a little better what they already do, rather than to be receptive to new ideas and new ways of doing things.

The strengths and the limitations of the functional principle give it peculiar characteristics with respect to the *economy* specification. At its best, functional organization works with high economy. Very few people at the top need to spend much time on keeping the organization running, that is, on "organizing," "communications," "coordination," "conciliation," and so on. The rest can do their work. But at its fairly common worst, functional organization is grossly uneconomical. As soon as it approaches even a modest degree of size or complexity, "friction" builds up. It rapidly becomes an organization of misunderstandings, feuds, empires and Berlin-Wall building. It soon requires elaborate, expensive, and clumsy management crutches—coordinators, committees, meetings, troubleshooters, special dispatchers—which waste everybody's time without, as a rule, solving much. And this degenerative tendency prevails not only with respect to relations between different "functions." The large functional unit with its subdivisions and subfunctions is equally prone to rapid internal inefficiency and equally requires more and more managerial effort devoted to its own internal running.

Another way of saying the same thing is that functional design, *where it applies,* makes the least psychological demands on the people. They are highly secure both in their work and in their relationships. When it, however, is being used beyond fairly narrow limits of size and complexity it creates emotional tensions, hostilities, and insecurities. People will then tend to see themselves and their functions belittled, besieged, attacked. They will come to see it as their first job to defend their function, to protect it against marauders in other functions, to make sure "it doesn't get pushed around." "Nobody here realizes that the company is being kept alive by us engineers" (or "us salesmen" or "us accountants") is a common complaint. And besting the "wicked enemies" within will become sweeter victory than making the business prosper. Precisely because functional design demands from functional people little responsibility for the performance and success of the whole, a poorly working—or overextended—functional structure is likely to make people both insecure and parochial.

The basic strength as well as the basic weakness of functional organization is its *effort-focus.* Every functional manager considers his function the most important one. This results in high emphasis on craftsmanship and professional standards. But it also makes people in the functional unit prone to subordinate the welfare of the other functions, if not of the entire business, to the interests of their unit. There is no real remedy against this tendency in the functional organization. The lust for aggrandizement on the part of each function is the price paid for the laudable desire of each manager to do a good job.

*Communications* are fairly good in the small functional organization. They break down once the functional organization reaches even moderate size. Even within the individual functional unit, e.g., the marketing department, communications weaken if the unit becomes large or complex. People are then increasingly specialists and interested primarily in their own narrow specialty.

The most extreme example is the largest and most highly specialized functional organization around: the large university. But a large manufacturing department or the commercial-loan department of a big bank also resembles that well-known description of a large university faculty as "a collection of anarchists held together by a common parking lot."

As a decision-making structure functional organization—even if fairly small—works poorly. For decisions cannot, as a rule, be made except at the highest level of a functional organization. No one except the man at the top sees the entire business. As a result, decisions are also easily misunderstood by the organization and are poorly implemented. They are seen as "who is right" rather than as "what is right." And because a functional organization has high stability but low adaptability, the challenge to do something truly new and truly different is likely to be suppressed rather than brought out in the open and faced up to.

*Functional organization* also does poorly in *developing, preparing, and testing men.* Functional organization of necessity puts the major emphasis on a man's acquiring the knowledge and competence that pertain to it. Yet the functional specialist may become narrow in his vision, his skills, and his loyalties. In a functional organization there is a built-in emphasis on not showing "unbecoming curiosity" about the work of other functions or specialties, that is, on narrow departmentalization.

Moreover, functional organization tends to make a man unfit for management—precisely because most of the emphasis is on functional skill rather than on results and performance. Indeed the more highly skilled functionally an organizational unit is, the less will it value management, the less well will it prepare a man to be a manager.

French businesses tend to be most rigidly functional in their structures. It is therefore perfectly logical that top management in large French companies does not, as a rule, come out of the business itself and tends to consider that a career in the company unfits a man for a top-management position (see Chapter 35). But the fault is not in the men; it is in using functional organization far beyond the size and complexity for which it is appropriate.

## Can the Weaknesses Be Offset?

These limitations and weaknesses of functional organization were apparent from the very first. A good deal of thought has therefore been given to attempts to offset them, and to offset in particular the greatest weakness: the tendency of functional organization to misdirect the vision of functional people from contribution and results to efforts and busyness.

The first attempt was made by Theodore Vail of the Bell Telephone System (see Chapter 13). His "bogeys," that is, the specific goals and measurements which were developed for functional work, were derived from his overall business definition and from the business objectives of the Telephone Company. While far from perfect and confusing by their sheer number, they served for many years to direct the efforts of functional managers toward performance and to give functional managers an immediate "reading" of their contribution to key results.

But it is doubtful that anything like Vail's system could be designed for a functional system that is faced with complexity. A telephone system, after all, has only one product. Until very recently it has had only one market —and no competition. And while there have been great and constant technical changes in telecommunications, what the customer bought did, until recently, not change at all.

Vail's feedback controls for a functional structure work, in other words, for a monopoly, whether private or governmental, with a single product and one known market. There they are indeed the model—and this is the situation of a good many, if not of most, nonbusiness service institutions, e.g., the hospital.

In the typical business, however, these conditions are not present. And that a similar system of feedback controls for functional work can be designed for the complex business enterprise seems unlikely; at least no one has yet been able to do it.

The most comprehensive attempt so far has been made by GE which, for the last several decades, has been working on developing performance objectives for functional work. Yet all that has been accomplished, by and large, is to work out "standards of good manufacturing work" or "standards of good accounting work," that is, standards focused on the function itself rather than on its contribution to the whole.

## Their Limited Scope

Even where functional organization applies, its scope is limited to operating work. Top management is specific "work" (see Chapter 50), but it is not "functional" work. And functional organization is the wrong organization for it. Wherever applied, it has made for a weak top management.

The large German company after 1900 tended to structure its top management functionally; in many German companies this is still being done.

There was indeed a top-management team, the *Vorstand* of German company law. But only one man, the General-Director, was concerned with top-management work. The other members were the heads of the major functions and concerned primarily with their areas. As a result, the General-Director became an autocrat, and the *Vorstand* team degenerated into legal fiction. Or there was no top management at all, with each function going its own way.

The functional principle is even less applicable to innovating work (see Chapter 61, "The Innovative Organization"). In innovation, we try to do something we have not done before, that is, something we do not yet know. We do need the individual skills of the various disciplines in innovation. But we do not know where and when they will be needed, for what time, in what degree, or in what volume. The innovative task therefore cannot be organized on the basis of functional organization. It is incompatible with it.

## Where Functionalism Works

Functionalism works—and exceedingly well—in the kind of business for which it was designed. The model for Henri Fayol's functional design early in this century was the coal-mining company he ran. It was a fairly large business at that time but would be considered a fairly small business today. Except for a few engineers it employed only manual workers who did one kind of work. A coal mine has only one product; only sizes vary for different customers. Coal requires no treatment beyond simple washing and sorting. Coal had, at least at that time, only three markets—steel mills, power plants, and homeowners. And while the technology of mining coal was changing fairly fast in Fayol's day—when he started out, explosives had not yet come into use and when he retired mechanical coal cutters were already at work—the process itself did not change at all. And all one can ever get out of a coal mine is coal. There is not much scope for innovation.

Fayol's company is the kind of business which the functional design principle organizes well. Anything more complex, more dynamic, or more entrepreneurial demands performance capacities which the functional principle does not possess. If used beyond the limits of Fayol's model, functional structure rapidly becomes costly in terms of time and effort, and runs a high risk of misdirecting the energies of the organization away from performance and toward mere busyness. In businesses that exceed Fayol's model, in size, in complexity, in innovative scope, functional design should be used only as *one* principle and never as *the* principle. And even in businesses that fit Fayol's model, top-management design and structure require a different design principle.

## The Team

A team is a number of people—usually fairly small—with different backgrounds, skills, and knowledge, and drawn from various areas of the organization (their "home") who work together on a specific and defined task. There is usually a team leader or team captain. His is often a permanent appointment for the duration of the team's assignment. But leadership at any one time places itself according to the logic of the work and the specific stage in its progress. There are no superiors and subordinates; there are only seniors and juniors.

Every business—and every other institution—has been using teams all along for ad hoc nonrecurrent tasks. But we have only recently recognized what our nomadic Ice Age ancestors knew—the team is also a principle for permanent, structural design. The mission of the team is a specific task: the hunting expedition or product development. But the team itself can be permanent. Its composition may vary from task to task; its base remains, however, fairly constant even though individual members may scatter between tasks or belong, at one and the same time, to a number of teams.

## Some Examples

Teams have become very popular and are indeed in danger of being damaged by becoming fashionable. Countless books are being written on "task forces," "project teams," "free-form organizations," "small groups," and so on. A few examples will, however, show better than any theoretical discussion what a team is, how it works, what its requirements are, and what it cannot do.

The hospital may be the simplest example. The structural component in the hospital is a team mobilized ad hoc from the "services" for the needs of the individual patient as defined by the team captain, the physician, with the nurse as the executive officer of the group.

In the hospital everyone directly concerned with patient care, that is, everyone on the team, is supposed to take personal responsibility for the success of the whole team's effort. The doctor's orders are law in a hospital. Yet a physical therapist who is told, for instance, to give rehabilitation exercises to a patient is expected to notice if the patient seems to run a fever, to stop the exercises, and to notify the nurse immediately and ask for a temperature reading. He will not hesitate to countermand a doctor's orders within his own sphere. The doctor may order an orthopedic patient to be measured for crutches and taught how to use them. The physical therapist may take one look and say, "You don't need crutches; you'll be better off using a cane right away or just walking on your walking cast without any support."

A business parallel to the example of the hospital is the organization of a medium-sized European company which designs, makes, and services plastic molds for several hundred customers, mostly large companies such as the big automobile plants in the Common Market. In this company, the work of making the molds is organized on strictly functional lines. It is highly skilled but self-contained work. But mold design, selling, and customer service, while shown on the organization chart as functions, do not work as such. The individual mold designer works as a member of a team—or of several teams—which is responsible collectively for an individual customer or a number of customers. The team leaders may come from any function—selling, service, or mold design.

Performance responsibility rests with the team. Each team leader draws on the resources of the whole organization as needed. At one stage he brings in mold designers, at another, salesmen, at another stage, customer-service people, and so on. Not even salesmen are assigned permanently to customers; they are assigned to product lines. But the team leader who carries primary account responsibility will tend to work again and again with the same three or four men in each functional area. Each of them, in turn, considers himself as being "close" to three or four of the teams—though a team leader often also calls on a specialist whom he never before put on his team to handle a rare or new problem.

"It's my job to decide that one of my accounts needs this or that kind of service engineering," said one account leader, himself a mold designer. "Then it's my job to bring in the right service engineer—a man I know, trust, and can recommend to my customer. It's then the service engineer's job to decide what needs to be done. And if he decides that we have to redesign molds for the customer, then I have to go to work and redesign molds until they satisfy the specifications for mold design the service man lays down—he then becomes my 'boss.' "

The same mold designer, in addition to heading the "account team" for the company's biggest and most profitable account, also considered himself —and was considered by all the others—a member of two or three other account teams. "They call me in, maybe half a dozen times a year, when they have design problems that for them are fairly uncommon but are daily occurrences on the account where I head the team," the man explains it. "And then I go to work for their team as a fairly junior member and do whatever designing they need."

## Their Lessons

These two examples show that what characterizes a team is not "free form" or the absence of regimentation. Teams at the plastic-mold company are indeed highly flexible and without a rigid chain of command within the team. Team leadership moves with the task. But few social organizations around are as rigid as the hospital; a "rod" of command rather than a chain of command characterizes hospital structure. Yet both, the plastic-mold company and the hospital, form and use genuine teams.

Team design requires a continuing mission in which the specific tasks change frequently, however. If there is no continuing mission, there might be an ad hoc temporary task force—but not an organization based on the team as a permanent design. If the tasks do not change, or if their relative importance or sequence remain unchanged, there is no need for team organization, and no point to it.

A team needs a clear and sharply defined objective. It must be possible all the time to feed back from the objectives to the work and performance of the whole team and of each member.

A task force needs leadership. It can be a permanent leader—physician and nurse on the patient-care team in the hospital, or the recognized head man on a top-management team. Or leadership can shift with each major phase. But then, as in the mold-making company, one man needs to be clearly designated to decide, at a given stage, who takes team leadership for a particular phase of the task. It is not leadership responsibility for making the decision and giving the command. It is leadership responsibility for deciding who among the team members has, for a particular phase and a particular challenge, the decision and command authority (on this see also the discussion of the Japanese approach to decision-making in Chapter 37). A team is therefore not "democratic" if by that is meant that decisions are taken by vote. It emphasizes authority. But the authority is task-derived and task-focused.

It is always the team as a whole that is responsible for the task. The individual contributes his particular skill and knowledge. But, every individual is always responsible for the output and performance of the entire team rather than only for his own work. The team is the unit.

Team members need not know each other well to perform as a team. But they do need to know each other's function and potential contribution. "Rapport," "empathy," "interpersonal relations" are not needed. Mutual understanding of each other's job and common understanding of the common task are essential.

An example is the team used to produce advertising or educational movies.

In contrast to the teams used for TV programs or for large-scale entertainment movies, crews for advertising or educational films are usually composed of "free-lancers" hired for one production, that is, for anything from a few hours to a few weeks. Every director knows a dozen technicians in each category—electricians, sound engineers, cameramen, lighting people—with whom he has worked before and whom he trusts. He knows of another half dozen men in each category and has heard good things of them. Every one of the technicians, in turn, knows a number of directors who meet his standards. But who is hired for a given assignment depends on who is available at the time, and usually on very short notice. As a result, the crew members often meet each other for the first time a few minutes before production gets under way. Sometimes they never learn each other's names and address one other as "sound engineer" or "lights" all the way through the assignment. And yet they immediately form a team. The director "calls the shots." But the sound engineer can and will stop the director and say, "I get a noise," and everything stops until the source of the noise is found and eliminated. The cameramen can and will say, "I get a reflection off the wall," and everything stops until the lighting is adjusted. When the assignment is over, the crew members go their own separate ways and may not meet again for years. Yet while they belong to the same crew, they work closely together as a team.

It is therefore the team leader's first job to establish clarity: clarity of objectives and clarity with respect to everybody's role including his own.

## The Strengths and Limitations of the Team Principles

The team has obvious strengths. Everybody always knows the work of the whole and holds himself responsible for it. It is highly receptive to new ideas and new ways of doing things. And it has great adaptability.

It also has great shortcomings. It does not possess clarity unless the team leader creates it. It has poor stability. Its economy is low; a team demands continuing attention to its management, to the relationships of people within the task force, to assigning people to their jobs, to explanation, deliberation, communication, and so on. A large part of the energy of all the members goes into keeping things running. Although everybody on the team understands the common task, he does not always understand his own specific task. He may be so interested in what others are doing that he pays inadequate attention to his own assignment.

Teams are adaptable. They are highly receptive to experimentation, to new ideas, and to new ways of doing things. They are the best means available for overcoming functional insulation and parochialism. Any career professional should serve on a few teams during his working life.

Still, teams do only a little better than straight functional organization in preparing men for higher management responsibilities or in testing them in performance. A team makes neither for clear communications nor for clear decision-making. The whole group must work constantly on explaining both to itself and to managers throughout the rest of the organization what it is trying to do, what it is working on, and what it has accomplished. The team must constantly make sure that the decisions that need to be made are brought into the open. There is real danger otherwise that teams will make decisions they should not make—decisions, for instance, that irreversibly commit the whole company.

In the plastic-mold company, for example, the "account teams" tend all the time to make pricing decisions without telling anyone about them. Yet, while meant for one customer only, these decisions immediately affect the entire business.

Teams fail—and the failure rate has been high—primarily because they do not impose on themselves the self-discipline and responsibility that are required precisely because of the high degree of freedom team organization gives. No task force can be "permissive" and function. This is the reason why the same young educated people who clamor for team work tend so often in reality to resist it. It makes tremendous demands on self-discipline.

But the greatest limitation of the team structure is size. Teams work best when there are few members. The aboriginal hunting band had seven to fifteen members. So do the teams in team sports such as football, baseball, and cricket. If a team gets much larger it becomes unwieldy. Its strengths, such as flexibility and the sense of responsibility of the members, attenuate. Its limitations—lack of clarity, communication problems, overconcern with the internal mechanism and internal relationship—become crippling weaknesses.

## The Scope of Team Organization

Its size limitation determines the scope of applicability of the team principle of organization.

It is the best available design principle for top-management work. Indeed (as will be discussed in Chapter 51) it is probably the *only* appropriate design principle for top management. Similarly, the team is the preferred design principle for innovative work (see Chapter 61).

But for most operating work the team is not appropriate *by itself and alone* as the design principle of organization. It is a complement—though a badly needed one. It may well be that it is team organization that will make the functional principle fully effective and will enable it to do what its designers had hoped for.

This may turn out to be the case with respect to mass-production work (see Chapter 21). Mass production, especially "rigid" mass production, is an extreme application of functional organization. Each man is a "unit" with a specific function; and the work moves from one of these human units of function to the next. Encouraging men to form teams within the mass-production system—as IBM has done for many years and as some automobile plants are doing now—promises to result in both productive work organized on the functional principle and in achieving workers working in teams.

## Team Design and Knowledge Organization

But the area where team design as a complement to functional organization is likely to make the greatest contribution is in knowledge work. The knowledge organization (see Chapter 35) is likely to balance "function" as a man's "home" with "team" as his "place of work."

Knowledge work by definition is specialized work. The shift from middle management to knowledge organization therefore brings into the management group a host of specialists not as staff but as operating people. The traditional pattern of typical functions is being replaced by an enormous number of new functions. Of course many of them can, and should, be grouped together. Still, while the tax specialist will often be put together with other "financial" people, either in accounting or in the treasurer's department, his work is different and separate. This also applies to product managers or market managers, who are equally related to, and part of, the traditional marketing function, the traditional research and development function, and the traditional manufacturing function.

This requires better functional management. What specialties are needed has to be decided or else the organization will drown in useless and unused learning. There is need to think through what the key activities are in which a high degree of specialized knowledge is needed and to make sure that knowledge work in the key areas is provided for in depth and with excellence. It also demands that knowledge work in other areas either not be done at all or be kept in low key.

There is need to manage a specialty to make sure that it makes the contribution to the enterprise for the sake of which it has been established. There is need to anticipate today the new specialties that will be needed tomorrow and the new demands that will be made tomorrow on existing specialties. There is need, in other words, for functional concern with what (in Chapter 33) I called *management development*.

There is great need for concern with, and for management of, the specialists themselves. Do they work on the truly important things, or do they fritter away their time? Do they do over again what they already know how to do, or do they work on creating new potential and new performance capacity? Are they being used productively, or are they just being kept busy? There is need also for concern with their development as professionals and as persons.

These are crucial questions which cannot be answered by checking how many hours a man works. They require knowledge of the functional area and genuine functional management.

A good deal of knowledge work will undoubtedly be organized on a strictly functional basis. A good deal will also be done by individuals who, in effect, are an "organizational component" by themselves.

The tax expert is an example. He has a "home," that is, he is usually housed in some financial or accounting staff. But he really has no boss except the company, and no customer except the company. And he has little concern with what the other people in the accounting department are doing. In fact, he is actually an outside consultant on the permanent payroll.

But these isolated individuals—tax expert and company lawyer, medical director and government-relations counsel—rarely create organizational or structural problems.

An increasing number of knowledge workers, however, will have a "functional" home but do their work in a team with other knowledge workers from other functions and disciplines. The more advanced the knowledge worker's knowledge the more likely it is that he will do his work and make his contribution in cross-functional teams rather than in his own functional component. For the more advanced knowledge is the more specialized it has to be. And specialized knowledge is a fragment, if not mere "data." It becomes productive only if put together with other people's knowledge. It becomes effective only as input to other people's decisions, other people's work, other people's understanding. It becomes "results" only in a team.

Knowledge organization will therefore increasingly have two axes: a functional one, managing the man and his knowledge; another one the team, managing work and task. Seen one way, this undermines the functional principle and destroys it. Seen another way, it saves the functional principle and makes it fully effective. It certainly requires strong, professional, effective, functional managers and functional components.

The team is clearly not the panacea advertised by a good deal of the discussion of the "small group" and "free-form organization." It is a difficult structure requiring very great self-discipline. It has severe limitations and major weaknesses.

But it is also not, as many managers still believe, a temporary expedient for dealing with nonrecurring "special problems." It is a genuine design principle of organization. It is the best principle for such *permanent* organizing tasks as top-management work and innovating work. And it is an important and perhaps essential complement to functional structure—in mass-production work, whether manual or clerical, and above all, in knowledge work. It is the key, in all probability, to making functional skill fully effective in the knowledge organization.

# 46

## Result-Focused Design:
## Federal and Simulated Decentralization

*Decentralization and Functional Organization—The Strengths of Federal Decentralization—Federal Decentralization and Manager Development—Its Application to Nonbusiness Organizations—The Requirements of Federal Decentralization—A Strong Top Management Doing Top-Management Work—The "Reserved" Areas—The Need for Centralized Controls and Common Measurements—The Demands on the Autonomous Business —Size Requirements—What Is Too Big and What Is Too Small?—The Role of Service Staffs—What Is a "Business"?—The Innovative Component —Simulated Decentralization—The "Materials" Business—IBM—The Commercial Bank—The Problems of Simulated Decentralization—Its Limited Scope—Simulated Decentralization a Last Resort—Its Future*

In "federal decentralization"* a company is organized in a number of autonomous businesses. Each unit has responsibility for its own performance, its own results, and its own contribution to the total company. Each unit has its own management which, in effect, runs its own "autonomous business."

Federal decentralization (as has been mentioned earlier, in Chapter 41) was first worked out, though only crudely, by Pierre S. du Pont in 1920 in the reorganization of the family-owned Du Pont Company, which had outgrown, during World War I, an older functional structure. When Pierre S. du Pont, shortly thereafter, took over the presidency of General Motors,

---

*The commonly used term is "decentralization" ("divisionalization" in Japan). But this is confusing as there are other forms of "decentralization." It is also misleading. The best name for this design principle would be the "federal principle."

which was then in desperate trouble, he found that Alfred P. Sloan, then GM's executive vice-president, had arrived at a similar, though far more polished version. Sloan's "decentralized operations with centralized policy control"—put into effect during 1921–22—became the prototype of decentralization. Among the many imitations and adaptations, the one made in 1950–52 for the reorganization of the General Electric Company became, in the years of the "management boom," the standard model worldwide.*

Federal decentralization presupposes that the activities *within* an autonomous business are organized on the functional principle—though, of course, the use of teams is not excluded. The autonomous businesses of a decentralized structure are designed to be small enough to put to work the strengths of a functional structure while neutralizing its weaknesses.

But the starting point of decentralization is different. Functional and team organization start with work and task. They assume that the results are the sum total of the efforts. "If only efforts are organized properly, the right results will follow" is the underlying premise. Decentralization, by contrast, starts out with the question "What results do we aim for?" It tries to set up the right business first, that is, the unit that will have optimal capacity for results and especially for results in the marketplace. Then the question is asked "What work, what efforts, what key activities have to be set up and organized *within* the autonomous business?"

It is desirable, of course, to set up the same or, at least, a similar functional structure for all or most of the autonomous businesses within a company. All Sears stores, regardless of size or location, have, for instance, a store controller, an operations manager, and department heads for major merchandise areas such as appliances. All GM manufacturing divisons have the same seven key functions: engineering, manufacturing, master-mechanic, purchasing, marketing accounting, and personnel, with the head of each reporting directly to the division's general manager.

But care should be taken lest this desirable unity become stifling uniformity.

The GE reorganization of 1950–52 provides an example of what not to do. GE decided that the "typical manufacturing business" has five key functions: engineering, manufacturing, marketing, accounting, and personnel. That this did not fit nonmanufacturing businesses such as the General Electric Credit Corporation, everyone saw, of course. But two things were not seen—with resulting high damage. First, it was not realized that some manufacturing businesses needed additional and different key functions, or at least a different arrangement of the same functional work. One example was the computer business, where product development and customer ser-

---

*For Sloan's prototype see my book, *Concept of the Corporation*.

vice were far too important to be subordinated to engineering and marketing. GE's failure in the computer business had many causes, but the imposition of the functional structure of a typical manufacturing business was probably a major contributor. Second, there were some businesses that looked like manufacturing businesses but were, in effect, innovative businesses. These units were genuine businesses and result centers, but they had no "product"; they were set up to develop one. They had no "market," but a research and development contract, mostly from the U.S. government. They did not "manufacture"; at most they had a model shop to build a few prototypes. Yet the functions of a typical manufacturing business were imposed on them. Some of these innovative development businesses managed to survive by quiet sabotage of the official structure. The others were seriously damaged—some irreparably—by having to carry a heavy load of functions they did not need and, above all, by misdirection of vision and efforts.

This is misuse of the true strength of federal decentralization: the focus on results. In using federal decentralization, the first question should always be "What is the business of this 'autonomous' business? What will it be? What should it be?" Then the key activities emerge and can be organized effectively on functional or team lines.

## The Strengths of Federal Decentralization

Of all design principles available so far, federal decentralization comes closest to satisfying all design specifications. It also has the widest scope. Both operating work and innovative work can be organized as decentralized autonomous businesses. And while top management can obviously not be set up as an autonomous business, federal decentralization of the business, if done properly, makes for strong and effective top managements. It frees top management for the top-management tasks.

Federal decentralization has great *clarity* and considerable *economy*. It makes it easy for each member of the autonomous business to *understand his own task* and to understand *the task of the whole business*. It has high *stability* and is yet *adaptable*.

It focuses the *vision* and efforts of managers directly on business performance and results. The danger of self-deception, of concentrating on the familiar but old and tired rather than on the difficult but new and growing, or of allowing unprofitable lines to be carried on the backs of the profitable ones, is much lessened. Reality is not easily obscured by overhead or hidden in the figures for total sales.

With respect to *communications* and *decisions*, the federal organization is the only satisfactory design principle we possess. Since the entire management group, or at least the upper ranks within it, share a common vision and a common perception, they tend to communicate easily. And usually, for that reason, communication between people in different kinds of work is encouraged all the way down the line rather than frowned upon. Decision-making is also likely to be placed at the optimal level without great effort. The focus tends to be on the right rather than the wrong issue, and on the important rather than the trivial decision.

The greatest strength of the federal principle is, however, with respect to *manager development*. It alone of all known principles of organization prepares and tests people for top-management responsibility at an early stage. This by itself makes it the principle to be used in preference to any other.

In a federally organized structure, each manager is close enough to business performance and business results to focus on them. He is close enough to results to get immediate feedback from business performance on his own task and work, even though he himself may be purely functional in his job. The federal principle therefore enables us to divide large and complex organizations into a number of businesses that are small and simple enough so that managers know what they are doing and can direct themselves toward the performance of the whole instead of becoming prisoners of their own work, effort, and skill.

Because *management by objectives* and *self-control* becomes effective, the number of people or units under one manager no longer is limited by the span of control; it is limited only by the much wider span of managerial responsibility.

A Sears, Roebuck vice-president may have three hundred stores under him—each an autonomous unit, responsible for marketing and for profits. Each store manager may have thirty section managers under him, each running his own autonomous unit and also responsible for marketing and profitability goals. As a result, there are only two levels in Sears between the lowest management job, section manager in a store, and the president: the store manager and the regional vice-president.

Above all, the general manager of the decentralized business, if only in charge of a small business, is truly top management. He faces most of the challenges of the top-management job in an independent company—the one exception being, as a rule, the responsibility for financial resources and their supply. He has to make decisions. He has to build a team. He has to think about markets and processes, people and money, today and tomorrow. As a result, he is being tested in an autonomous, albeit not an independent, command. Yet he is being tested fairly early in his career, and at a reasonably low level. A mistake can, therefore, be unmade without too much damage to the company, and, equally important, without too much damage to the man. No other known principle of organization, whether in business or in any other institution, satisfies the need to *prepare* and *test* men for tomorrow's leadership positions nearly as well as the federal principle does.

The search for a system which will prepare and test tomorrow's leaders is the oldest problem of political theory and political practice. No political system has ever solved it adequately. The principle of federal decentralization, of course, does not solve it fully. The autonomous manager of a decentralized business is still not faced with the full responsibility, let alone with the full loneliness, of the top position. But the federal principle comes closer to a solution than any other known design.

The principle of federal decentralization was developed for business purposes. But it is just as applicable to nonbusinesses, that is, to service institutions.

The hospital of tomorrow may be reorganized in autonomous federal units. One such unit might, for instance, take care of the fairly small number of hospital patients—about a quarter to one-third at any one time in a general hospital—who need intensive care or clinical care. Another unit might take care of the large load of ambulatory or short-stay patients who require neither intensive clinical care nor surgery. Yet another unit might take care of the large number of surgical patients who require no hospitalization or only a short stay of a day or two in a "hotel" bed rather than the far more expensive "hospital" bed. Another autonomous component might be a mental health unit, again mostly for ambulatory patients. Another unit might be the convalescent unit. There might further be a "hotel" unit—which in effect is all the healthy mother and her healthy baby need two days after the delivery of the child. All these units would, of course, share common services—laboratories, dietitians and the kitchen, social and maintenance workers, psychiatric case workers, physical therapists, and so on. But these services are organized as central services anyhow today.

The federal principle is equally adaptable to the organizing of subunits within autonomous federal businesses.

Each of the autonomous departments which Pierre du Pont set up in 1920 has grown so much that it split itself internally into a number of autonomous businesses—in Du Pont they are called divisions—each with its own general manager, who has profit and loss responsibility and runs an entire business with all its functions (except accounting, which is a departmental function if not a corporate one). In some of these sub-businesses there are even smaller autonomous units, each with its own product lines, its own market, and its own business responsibility.

## The Requirements of Federal Decentralization

Federal decentralization has stringent requirements. It also makes very substantial demands for responsibility and self-discipline.

Decentralization must not create a weak center. On the contrary, one of the main purposes of federal organization is to *strengthen* top management and to make it capable of doing its own work rather than be forced to supervise, coordinate, and prop up operating work. Federal decentralization will work only if the top-management job is clearly defined and thought through.

The crucial question in any federal system is "What are the tasks of top management, and how can top management get the time, the thought, the perspective to discharge them?" Federalization, if properly applied, makes top management capable of doing its own job precisely because it does not have to worry about operations, but can concentrate on direction, strategy, objectives, and key decisions for the future.

"Decentralization" is therefore a misleading term—though it is by now far too popular to be discarded.

The test of effective federal decentralization is top-management strength. Top management in a decentralized company must first accept its responsibility for thinking through "what our business is and what it should be." It must accept the responsibility for setting the objectives for the entire company and for working out the strategies for obtaining these objectives. It must, in other words, accept the responsibility for its own job. If a federal structure is the best-functioning of all structures if properly managed, it is a shambles if top management abdicates and does not live up to the responsibilities of its own tasks

Top management must think through carefully what decisions it reserves for itself. For there are decisions which have to do with the entire company, its integrity, and its future. It does not necessarily follow that every such decision has to be made on "overall considerations." On the contrary, most of them should be made on the basis of what is good for an individual autonomous business. But these decisions can be made only by somebody who sees the whole and is responsible for the whole.

At General Electric, for instance, only corporate top management can make the decision to abandon a business or go into a new one. At General Motors, top management at the central office sets the price ranges within which each automobile division's products have to fall, and thus controls the competition between the major units of the company. At Sears, Chicago headquarters decides what kinds of goods—hard goods, appliances, fashion goods, and so forth—each store must carry.

In other words, there must be a kind of "supremacy clause" reserving to central management the decisions that affect the business as a whole and its long-range future welfare, and allowing central management to override, in the common interest, local ambitions and pride.

Specifically, there must be *three reserved areas* if the business is to remain a whole rather than splinter into fragments. Top management, and top management alone, can make the decision what technologies, markets, and products to go into, what businesses to start and what businesses to abandon, and also what the basic values, beliefs, and principles of the company are.

Second, top management must reserve to itself the control of the allocation of the key resource of capital. Both the supply of capital and its investment are top-management responsibilities which cannot be turned over to the autonomous units of a federal organization.

The other key resource is people. The people in a federally organized company, and especially managers and key professionals, are a resource of the entire company rather than of any one unit. The company's policies with respect to people and decisions on key appointments in the decentralized autonomous businesses are top-management decisions—though of course, autonomous business managers need to take an active part in them. And a decentralized company needs to have a strong, respected, and senior executive in top management who is the company's conscience with respect to people.

Top management in a decentralized structure has to be separate. It cannot also run any of the autonomous businesses no matter how big or important they are. Even in a small company that is organized on the federal design at least one man (and preferably more—on this see Chapters 50 and 51) needs to be charged exclusively with responsibility for the top-management task for the entire business.

The traditional English system in which the "executive directors" of the board, i.e., the full-time members of top management, tend to be the heads of the major divisions and subsidiaries, therefore results in there being neither top management nor decentralization. Basic decisions are either not made at all or they are made by "swapping" between division heads concerned—properly—with their own divisions rather than with the company.* This may well be one of the main reasons for the often-reported tendency of English companies to allocate capital and other resources according to past history and size of a division rather than according to opportunity, thus starving tomorrow.

---

*On this see the case studies in David Granick, *Managerial Comparisons of Four Developed Countries, France, Britain, United States and Russia* (M.I.T. Press, 1972).

Federal decentralization requires centralized controls and common measurements. Indeed, wherever a federal organization gets in trouble (wherever, for instance, layers of central management staffs are being heaped on top of a federal structure), the reason is always that the measurements at the disposal of the center are not good enough, so that personal supervision has to be substituted. Both the managers of the autonomous businesses and top management must know what is expected of each business, what is meant by "performance," and what developments are important. To be able to give autonomy one must have confidence. And this requires controls that make opinions unnecessary. To be able to manage by objectives one must know whether goals are being reached or not; and this requires clear and reliable measurements.

The need for what Sloan called "centralized controls" is illustrated by the experience of one of the world's largest and fastest-growing multinationals, Philips of Holland. Between 1959 and 1972, Philips's worldwide sales increased almost fivefold: from $1.3 billion to $6 billion. But profits all but disappeared. The company had a strong top-management team. It had technical and product leadership in a number of major areas, from household appliances to electronics to light bulbs. It represented an extreme in decentralization, with hundreds of subsidiary companies in sixty countries, each traditionally with its own autonomous management. But it had virtually no control system such as central planning, and no common measurements. The result was fragmentation instead of decentralization, excessive and uncontrolled inventories, unplanned capital investment, and overstaffing. Philips, in terms of sales, is only two-thirds the size of the General Electric Company, but in capital investment and number of employees it matches GE—while its profits are barely a fifth of those of GE. It was only when Philips in several years of hard work injected centralized controls, common measurement, and coordinated planning that the company began to reap the rewards of its technical and marketing achievements. And only then did the "autonomous business managers" of the various Philips companies really acquire autonomy; only then could they plan for their businesses, set objectives, and organize their own work.

The converse of this is that the federal principle demands great responsibility from the operating units, the autonomous businesses. They are given the maximum of autonomy; and this requires that they assume the maximum of responsibility.

Above all, it is their job to make top management capable of doing the top-management job. It is the duty of the head of each autonomous business to think through what top management has to know of the autonomous business in his care, its markets, products, potentials, opportunities, and problems. He has to ask himself, "What are the fundamental factors which make for performance or failure in *my* business? What does top management have to understand so that it can know where the business is going and what the real opportunities and problems are?" Autonomous managers in a federal structure cannot be content with "reports." They must think through what top management needs to understand. And they must accept the responsibility for educating their top management.

A federal structure requires common vision. A federal unit of a company is autonomous, but it is not independent and should not be. Its autonomy is a means toward better performance for the entire company. Its managers should regard themselves all the more as members of the greater community, the whole enterprise, for being given broad local autonomy.

## Size Requirements

Federal decentralization was designed as an answer to a problem of size: the deterioration that sets in in functional structures when they reach more than medium size. But federal decentralization also has size requirements. When the federal unit becomes so large that the components within it, that is, the functional subunits (e.g., manufacturing) exceed the size at which they function, the whole autonomous business becomes unwieldy, sluggish, and too big to perform. The "brain," that is, the top management of the autonomous unit, may still perform. But the "members," that is, the functional components, turn rigid and bureaucratic and will increasingly serve themselves rather than the common purpose.

Du Pont has been counteracting this in part by splitting autonomous businesses in two as they grow bigger, in part (as said earlier) by setting up small autonomous decentralized businesses within large autonomous decentralized businesses. Another approach is that of Johnson & Johnson, the very large, multinational producer of health-care products ranging from absorbent cotton to birth-control pills. J & J for many years tried to limit the size of each business to 250 employees, each run as a separate company with its own complete management and its own board of directors, and each "reporting" directly to a small, central parent-company top-management team. While J & J, with worldwide sales of over a billion dollars and 40,000 employees, has been forced to accept individual businesses a good deal larger than 250 employees, it still limits the size of each business and will split it rather than permit it to grow large. As a result, functional units are still quite small in every J & J business.

But breaking up or subdividing autonomous businesses as they grow to large size is not always possible; or at least it is not always done. And the result is then the emergence of "functional empires."

The Chevrolet division of General Motors, for instance, has grown so large that it would by itself be the world's third or fourth largest manufacturing company if it were independent. It is a decentralized autonomous product business. But internally it is functionally organized and highly centralized. GM tries to counteract the resulting insulation of the large—very large—functional units by frequently moving functional managers from Chevrolet into the other and smaller (though still large) automotive divisions and moving functional managers from other divisions into Chevrolet. But when GM in the early seventies took responsibility for final assembly away from Chevrolet and moved it into a separate assembly division organized on the "simulated decentralization" principle (see below), one explanation given for this move was the need to restore "result-focus" to a large assembly operation that was becoming "effort-focused." And a good many, especially of the younger, GM executives apparently believe that Chevrolet should long ago have been split up into a number of separate divisions, one, for instance, in charge of the large truck business; another one, perhaps, in charge of the smaller cars such as "compacts" and "subcompacts," with the original Chevrolet division confined to "standard-sized" passenger automobiles. (See below, Chapter 55.)

Ralph Cordiner, the architect of GE's reorganization in the fifties, used to say that an autonomous business in a decentralized structure should be so small that "a good man can get his arms around it." This is hardly a precise quantitative term. But it would imply that an autonomous business should be no more than "fair-sized" to get the full benefits of federal decentralization. This means (as discussed in Chapter 54) that a small group of men at the top—four or five maybe—can still tell without having to consult charts, records, or organization manuals, who the key people are in the unit, where they are, what their assignments are and how they perform, where they came from and where they are likely to go. If autonomous businesses get much larger federal decentralization may still be the best alternative. But it is then the "lesser evil" rather than the optimum.

## How Small Is Too Small?

But the decentralized autonomous unit also needs to be big enough to support the management it needs.

How small is too small depends on the business. A Sears store, or a Marks & Spencer store, can be quite small and yet support adequate management. All a small store needs is one manager and a few department heads who actually manage on the selling floor.

In the U.S., mass-production metalworking industry, a truly autonomous product business, is rarely capable of supporting adequate management and its own engineering, manufacturing, and marketing work unless it sells twenty to thirty million dollars' worth of merchandise a year. Businesses with a significantly lower sales volume are in danger of being understaffed, or staffed with inadequate people.

When such very small units are organized as autonomous businesses, their internal structure should be team design rather than functional structure. This is the way in which all but the largest of the individual Sears stores actually work.

The decisive criterion is not size but the scope and challenge of the management job. A federal unit should always have enough scope so that a good man can show his ability. It should have enough challenge so that the management group in the unit truly has to manage: that is, to think through objectives and plans, to build human resources into an effective team, to integrate the work, and to measure its performance. It should have enough challenge so that management will have to work on all major phases of a business, but also enough challenge so that it can really develop a market, a product or service—and, above all, can truly develop people. The true criterion of size for an autonomous business unit is not economics. It is managerial scope and challenge, and managerial performance.

The autonomous businesses of a decentralized organization should not have to depend on central service staffs, that is, on advisory and teaching activities operating out of headquarters.

A decentralized organization needs effective "conscience" work. It needs, especially if large and diversified, organized thinking and planning for top management, that is, the "secretariat" or "business research" group discussed in Chapter 51. It needs strong central information and unified controls and measurements. It will have some "common operating work," e.g., the supply and management of money, research, legal counsel, relations with the public, organized labor, and government, and perhaps purchasing. It may have to organize company-wide work on the kind of "social R & D" discussed in Chapter 25 and on innovation in key activities whether marketing or managing people.

But it should neither need nor use central service staffs to "advise" the operating managements of the decentralized units. These units should be strong enough to stand on their own feet. If they are not, service staffs will not cure their weakness but compound it. Such service staffs are, of necessity, focused on their functional area rather than on business performance and business results. Being located at the central office, they inevitably have the inside track to top management. In decentralized companies where service staffs are big and busy pleasing the staff people thus becomes more important than running the business for performance.

The pioneers of federal decentralization knew this and kept service staffs small and lean. Many of the companies that adopted federal decentralization in the fifties or sixties have, however, built massive central service staffs. They may have had little choice. Setting up these central services in functional areas was, in many cases, the only *politically feasible* thing to do. Otherwise, the strong traditional functional structures would have blocked the shift to federal decentralization, which of course, threatened their power and prominence. Even the rhetoric used to justify these large staff services —e.g., "the need for excellence" or "for professionalism" in functional areas—was often a necessary political price. But at least this should be recognized. Service staffs created to placate powerful functional barons should be phased out as the people in them retire. New people should not be brought in. New work should be sanctioned only if old projects and activities are being sloughed off. And, after a transition period of a few years, that part of the budget of such staffs that goes for "service" to autonomous businesses might be limited to what the "customers," i.e., the people in the autonomous businesses, voluntarily "buy" rather than be raised by a compulsory levy.

Dependence on central staff services can only impose on a decentralized organization the weaknesses and vulnerabilities, without giving it the benefits and strengths, of functional design.

## What Is a "Business"?

Federal decentralization is applicable only where a company can truly be organized into a number of genuine "businesses." This is its basic limitation.

But what is a "business"? Ideally, of course, a federal unit should be a complete business in its own right.

This idea underlay Alfred P. Sloan, Jr.'s, organization of General Motors in the early 1920s. Each of the automotive divisions did its own design, its own engineering, its own manufacturing, its own marketing, and its own sales. The divisions were limited as to the price range in which they could offer automobiles but totally autonomous otherwise. GM's accessory divisions sold a large share of their output to the automotive divisions of their own company. But they were organized to sell an even larger share directly to the outside market and indeed, very often, to General Motors's own competitors. They too were "businesses" in every sense of the word. And so are the autonomous companies into which Johnson & Johnson has organized itself. Each has its own product lines, its own research and development, its own markets and marketing.

But how much of the reality of a genuine business does there have to be for federal decentralization to work effectively? As a minimum the unit must contribute a profit to the company rather than merely contribute to the profit of the company. Its profit or loss should directly become company profit or loss. In fact, the company's total profit should be the sum total of the profits of the individual businesses. And it must be a genuine profit— not arrived at by manipulating accounting figures, but determined by the objective judgment of the marketplace.

Perhaps even more important—and the genuine touchstone of autonomy —is that the federal unit must have a market of its own. The market may be only a geographic entity—as in the Sears or the Marks & Spencer stores, or in the case of the "regional companies" into which several large American life insurance companies have divided themselves. But still there has to be a distinct market within which the unit is, so to speak, *the* company.

In some industries there may be more than one distinct market for the same product lines in the same geographic area, and therefore scope for two distinct businesses with similar products.

Institutional buyers of chairs—hospitals, schools, restaurants, hotels, large offices—are a different market from homeowners. They may buy the same or very similar merchandise. But they use different distributive channels, pay different prices, buy in different ways. One fair-sized furniture company attributes its growth largely to having set up retail furniture and institutional furniture as separate product businesses.

As long as a business can have full market responsibility and objective comparability of results, it can obtain its products from another autonomous unit or from a centralized company-run manufacturing source, and yet be an autonomous business.

Neither the Sears store nor the Marks & Spencer store are true "businesses." They do not do their own buying, do not even decide what merchandise to carry and what prices to charge. Yet in its geographic area each store stands on its own. And because all Sears or Marks & Spencer stores get the same merchandise at the same cost from the same central buying office, they can be compared meaningfully to one another. Within the system, the Sears store manager is autonomous and can be measured by performance and results.

Where, however, no genuine market test exists, we should not speak of an autonomous business. Federal decentralization then does not work.

GE had had one big autonomous business, the apparatus sales division, to sell and supply turbines, switch gear, and transformers to the electric-power companies. This division worked closely with the individual power companies on the overall design of power stations and transmission lines, and then assembled from the various GE plants, as well as from outside, whatever equipment was needed to satisfy an individual customer. Under the GE reorganization of 1952 the "product departments," i.e., switchgears or transformers, were given "business responsibility," and the apparatus sales division became a "distributor." This did not work. The product departments could not truly assume business responsibility. And the apparatus sales division, while the only real "business," no longer had the needed authority. Confusion instead of clarity was created; friction instead of responsibility. Eventually most of the old structure had to be restored, even though the apparatus sales division is far bigger than what "one man can get his arms around."

So far we have been discussing federal decentralization of operating work, that is, of existing and known businesses. A decentralized unit for innovative work is structured and measured differently (see Chapter 6). But federal decentralization is also the most effective design principle for such work—on condition, however, that its performance and results can be objectively measured. A decentralized innovative unit also has to be a business—or must be capable of becoming one.

## Simulated Decentralization

Whenever a unit can be set up as a business no design principle can match federal decentralization. We have learned, however, that a great many large companies cannot be divided into genuine businesses. Yet they have clearly outgrown the limits of size and complexity of the functional or of the team structure.

These are the companies that are increasingly turning to "simulated decentralization" as the answer to their organization problem.

Simulated decentralization forms structural units which are not businesses but which are still set up as if they were businesses, with maximum possible autonomy, with their own management, and with at least a "simulation" of profit and loss responsibility. They buy from and sell to each other using "transfer prices" determined internally rather than by an outside market. Or their "profits" are arrived at by internal allocation of costs to which then, often, a "standard fee" such as 20 percent of costs, is added.

The prime examples are companies in the chemical and "materials" industries.

An integrated chemical company runs on three axes or on three different logics: the logic of research, the logic of process, and the logic of the market. In research and development, the categories that inform organization are given by knowledge definitions, such as "polymers," "bonding," and "surface phenomena." The process, in turn, tends to be raw-material determined. No process can conceivably turn sulfuric acid into petrochemicals or petrochemicals into sulfuric acid. The market, finally, has a logic all its own. It buys neither "inorganic" chemicals nor "organic" chemicals. It buys adhesives, glue, coatings, reagents, cleansers. It buys, in other words, what a product will do rather than chemical formula or process technology.

And most customers buy a bewildering variety of different chemicals for all kinds of purposes. The logic of the market is "end-use" logic.

Yet the large chemical company, whether Du Pont and Monsanto in the U.S., ICI in Britain, Pechiney in France, or Badische in Germany, must be able to:

—develop new products across a wide range of chemical disciplines and technologies;

—produce a wide variety of products from a large number of raw materials; and

—supply a wide variety of end users with the chemicals they need for their own manufacturing process.

The same applies, in somewhat lesser degree, to glass, steel, aluminum, and paper manufacturers. These "materials" businesses were the success stories before World War I. They were still leaders in the period between the two wars. Their growth in terms of sales and volume since World War II has been even faster than in earlier periods. But results have been increasingly disappointing. And the reason, as more and more have come to realize, is that they have outgrown functional organization. They have lost the ability for effective communications, for flexibility, for making decisions fast, and for carrying out decisions once made.

It has been often said of such major American materials companies as Aluminum Company of America that they make the right decisions, but make them nine months too late and then take another nine months before putting them into action—and the same criticism has been leveled against the chemical giants, whether in the U.S., in Britain, or in Germany. It simply takes too long for a decision to travel the way it has to travel in a large functional structure; all the way up to the top and then all the way down again. And both the problems to be decided and the decisions reached are likely to be garbled out of all recognition on their way through countless levels.

Simulated decentralization is the one available design principle that copes with the structural problems of the big materials business.

Many chemical manufacturers have, for instance, organized their business in three sets of units, each based on simulated decentralization. A research and development corporation is set up and organized by major fields of study and inquiry. Some companies, e.g., Monsanto, have set up separate marketing components and separate manufacturing components, both with profit and loss responsibility.

The Japanese steel companies market through separate "trading companies," both at home and abroad. In the Aluminum Company of America and in Republic Steel production is organized in geographic manufacturing units, each considered a profit and loss center. Marketing, however, is organized in end-use units, that is, by major industrial buyers of aluminum or steel, such as the automobile industry and the construction industry. Corning Glass, one of the world's largest manufacturers of glass, is similarly organized by manufacturing units and by marketing units, each set up on the basis of simulated decentralization.

Simulated decentralization is equally applicable in single-product companies of similar size and complexity. IBM may be the leading example.

IBM, by and large, has one main product: computers. Only one of the markets can be split off as autonomous, the government and defense market. The great bulk of IBM's business, some 80 percent or so, supplies one product to one market, i.e., computers to business, both in the United States and abroad. Yet the computer business, with its many billions of dollars of sales and its great complexity is much too big to be organized by functions. Accordingly, IBM has split its data processing (for which read "computer") business into two key units, each considered an autonomous business, on the basis of simulated decentralization. Marketing and services is one, and development and manufacturing is the other. Each unit is considered a profit and loss center.

The most interesting attempts to apply simulated decentralization to very large businesses which cannot apply federal decentralization were the reorganizations of major New York commercial banks in the 1960s.

Both the First National City Bank and the Chase Manhattan Bank, respectively New York's first and second banks in deposits, have reorganized themselves into simulated decentralized structures. City Bank split itself into five autonomous units, each headed by a "president": retail (i.e., the individual depositor and borrower), commercial (i.e., small and medium-sized businesses), corporate (i.e., large businesses), international, and fiduciary services such as investment management. Each unit has its own objectives, its own plans, and its own profit and loss statements. The Chase organization, though developed independently, is roughly similar.

These bank examples also show clearly some of the major problems of simulated decentralization. In both banks it is the large branch, such as the Rockefeller Center branch of each bank, or the branch in London, which is the geographic focus of the bank's business. Sometimes the branch acts merely as the landlord and facilities manager for the representatives of each of the five "autonomous banks" that occupy space in the branch. Sometimes the branch is the "banker." At different times it is both. Clearly, the large branch is also a "business" and a profit and loss center. And who coordinates the different "banks" and focuses them on the individual customer who often is—or should be—a "retail," a "commercial," a "fiduciary," and even a "corporate" customer all at once? The head of a small business, for instance, will use the bank which finances his firm for his personal banking business and for his savings account, will expect it to act as executor of his will, to be the manager for his investments and the trustee for his firm's pension fund. He does not want to deal with four different banks. Whose customer is he, and who gets the credit for his business?

Simulated decentralization is obviously difficult and full of problems. Yet it will be used even more in the future. For the growth areas of economy and society—process industries and private and governmental service institutions—are the sectors in which simulated decentralization has its greatest potential of application. In these sectors neither functional organization nor federal decentralization can do the organizing job. Managers therefore need to know the requirements and limitations of simulated decentralization. What problems can be expected in an organization built on it?

## The Problems of Simulated Decentralization

Simulated decentralization is a poor "fit" with respect to *all* design specifications. It is not clear. It does not make for an easy focus on performance. It rarely satisfies the specification that everyone should be able to know his own task. Neither does it satisfy the demand that managers and professionals should be able to understand the job of the whole.

Least satisfactory in simulated decentralization are *economy, communications,* and *decision authority*. These weaknesses are inherent in the design. Because the unit of simulated decentralization is not truly a business, its results are not truly determined by market performance. They are, in large measure, the results of internal management decisions. They are decisions on "transfer prices" and "cost allocations."

What should a market component of a chemical company pay for the products it "buys" from a manufacturing component inside the company which is also considered a business and expected to make a profit on its own investment? There is no "market price." There is, therefore, no objective basis, such as the prices the accessory divisions of General Motors obtain for their product outside of GM. The only possible basis is cost. And the only way to show a profit is to impose an arbitrary charge on top of the manufacturing unit's cost. The marketing unit, however, could not obtain the products it sells on the outside—either because they are not obtainable at all except from competitors, because the volume needed is too great to depend on outside suppliers, or because quality is crucial (as in the "intermediates" for pharmaceutical products). At the very best, the profit and loss of both, the manufacturing and the marketing, are *approximations* of genuine results.

*Communications* therefore are likely to carry more "noise" than message.

A tremendous amount of managerial time and energy is spent on working out the demarcation lines between different units which supposedly are autonomous; on making sure that they cooperate; on adjudicating disputes between them; or on settling priorities between two marketing divisions within the same company, both of which want the same scarce product from the same autonomous manufacturing unit, and in the shortest possible time. The smallest adjustment becomes a top-management decision, a trial of strength, and a matter of honor and sacred principle.

Simulated decentralization makes high human demands: on self-discipline, on mutual toleration, on subordinating one's own interest, including the interest in one's own compensation, to arbitration by higher authority; demands to be a "good sport" and a "cheerful loser"; demands that are far more difficult and, above all, far more divisive than the high demands which federal decentralization makes on people.

I once heard a candidate for a very senior position in a big bank turned down because his unit was doing too well at the bank's expense. "He puts the performance of his own unit before everything else." The next man was turned down because "he is too willing to subordinate the performance of his unit to the needs and requirements of other units and, therefore, does not show a good enough performance." Everyone admitted to confusion when I asked, "Are there any guidelines for behavior? Is there any way in which you can tell a man ahead of time what you consider 'excessive concern' for performance and what you consider 'excessive cooperation'?" Everyone also admitted that this was the greatest worry of his own subordinates. "You have to play it by ear," the ranking officer finally concluded. But then he stopped himself and added, "But by whose ear?"

In its *scope*, simulated decentralization is limited to operating work. It clearly has no applicability to top-management work. And if innovative work cannot be set up as a federal decentralized unit, it requires either functional or team structure.

## Rules for Using Simulated Decentralization

The main rule is to look upon simulated decentralization as a *last resort* only. As long as a functional structure—with or without the complement of teams—works, that is, as long as a business is small or fair-sized, simulated decentralization is to be shunned. And beyond such size, federal decentralization is vastly preferable.

Even in the materials company, federal decentralization might be tried first. One example of an adaptation of genuine federal decentralization to a materials business is Owens-Illinois in Toledo, Ohio, a very large manufacturer of glass bottles. After World War II, when plastic bottles came into wide use, Owens-Illinois had to go into plastics to retain its leadership position in the bottle market. The company decided, after long soul-searching, to set up both the glass-bottle business and the plastic-bottle business as separate autonomous "product" businesses, competing with each other for the same customers and in the same markets.

The Owens-Illinois strategy was a brilliant success; the company's growth has been very rapid. And yet, fifteen years later, in the early seventies, Owens-Illinois changed over to simulated decentralization. It retained the two divisions but confined them to manufacturing. Marketing of all bottles, glass and plastic, was put into a new marketing division. The reason given was that the customers demanded one source of supply for all their bottles. "Glass" and "plastics" were not meaningful terms for them; they buy bottles and not materials.

With all its limitations, weaknesses, and risks, simulated decentralization may therefore be the best available principle where constituent parts of the same large business have to work together and yet have to have individual responsibility. This applies especially where the logic of market is incompatible with that of technology and production.

Indeed, we may have to learn how to extend its scope. It is the most promising approach to the organization of large and complex "monolithic" businesses (and nonbusiness service institutions). The leading examples here are the large transportation companies, especially railroads and airlines, but also the typical government agency.

A railroad or an airline has by definition no purely "local" business. Hence, businesses like this have so far no choice but to organize themselves according to functions with, at best, a regional coordinator who intervenes between the functions, mediates, and insures liaison. The decisions which affect performance of a transportation system can only be taken centrally. They are, above all, decisions on capital utilization, on the assignment of airplanes, locomotives, and freight cars, for instance. Yet transportation businesses, while incapable of being decentralized except for relatively unimportant tasks, are also clearly far too large to work well under functional organization.

This means, in effect, that there are businesses—and nonbusiness service institutions—for which we do not possess an adequate principle of organization.

In simulated decentralization we at least know what to expect. It is therefore a major task of organization theory and organization practice to develop for these large and overcentralized functional structures, such as a railroad system or most government agencies, an organization design that works no worse for them than simulated decentralization works, for instance, for the large materials companies and the large commercial banks. This will probably have to be some application of the principle of simulated decentralization.

# 47

# Relations-Focused Design:
# The Systems Structure

*NASA—The Japanese Systems Designs and the "Multinational"—Diversity of Cultures and Values—The Difficulties of the Systems Structure—Its Requirements—Its Importance*

---

Of the design principles of organization, only one, Fayol's functions, can be said to have started in a theoretical analysis. The others—the team, federal decentralization, and simulated decentralization—grew out of ad hoc responses to specific challenges and needs of the moment. This applies also to the systems structure. It was developed as a design principle for one apparently unique management problem: that of the American space effort in the 1960s.

Systems organization is an extension of the team design principle. But instead of individuals comprising a team, the systems organization builds the team out of a wide variety of different organizations. They may be government agencies and any number of private businesses, large and small; universities and individual researchers; organizations that are part of the central organization charged with the task and directly controlled by it, others who may be wholly or partly owned by it but run autonomously, and yet others which stand only in a contractual relationship to the parent organization and are in no way controlled by it or even controllable. Systems design uses *all* the other design principles as the task demands: functional organizations and teams, federal and simulated decentralization.

Some of the members of the systems structure may have a specific task which does not change throughout the entire life of the venture. Others may have various tasks according to the stage of the program. Some will be permanent members. Others may be brought in only for one specific assignment, after which they sever their relationship with the systems structure.

The "model" which first made the systems structure visible as a principle of organization design was the National Aeronautics and Space Administration (NASA) in its organization of the U. S. space program in the 1960s.* But while our awareness of the existence of such a structure is fairly recent, it has been in existence a long time. While the large systems structure emerged as a design principle in a huge governmental program, it actually was first developed as a structure for businesses; and major future application is probably in business.

Though Sayles and Chandler may not have realized it, their book on NASA describes a system used in Japan for a century. The Japanese large company and its suppliers and distributors work in a very similar relationship to that in which NASA worked with its suppliers, subcontractors, and partners. The Japanese large company sometimes owns its suppliers. More often it has little or no ownership stake in them. Yet the suppliers are integrated into the "system." Similarly, the Japanese large company usually depends upon a trading company which is both independent and integrated. The relationships among the large companies which constitute one industrial group (Zaibatsu) are also comparable to the relationships which NASA developed for its own needs.

It is becoming clear that something very much like the systems structure will have to be developed for the multinational corporation. Indeed, many of the approaches worked out for the multinational corporation are truly (though not consciously) systems management concepts. And the typical problems of the multinational corporation are also the typical problems of a systems structure.

One example is the structure the Chase Manhattan Bank has developed for its worldwide banking system. In contrast to the traditional approach, Chase decided not to rely exclusively or even primarily on wholly-owned branches abroad. Instead, it has been expanding worldwide through acquiring minority interests in well-established, medium-sized, local banks. These banks are not owned or controlled by the Chase. Nor is the top management usually furnished by the Chase. But they are part of the "Chase system." They are integrated into the worldwide banking facilities and services of the bank while, at the same time, they keep strong local roots in their own community. They are both independent and integrated.

Another example is the multinational advertising agency. The headquar-

---

*And the only description of systems management we have so far are studies of NASA: James E. Webb (NASA Administrator from 1961 to 1968), *Space Age Management* (McGraw-Hill, 1968) and, especially, Leonard R. Sayles and Margaret K. Chandler, *Managing Large Systems* (Harper & Row, 1971).

ters of the firm may be in New York, and the branches in England or Germany may be wholly owned subsidiaries. The structure may look, at first glance, like federal decentralization. But the needs of multinational clients demand that these federal autonomous businesses work together in a systems relationship. To service a client whose headquarters is outside of the United States—Unilever in London and Rotterdam, for instance, Nestle in Switzerland, or Sony in Tokyo—the overall responsibility for the account has to be lodged where the client is, that is, in England, Switzerland, or Japan. Yet there have to be relationships with every one of the subsidiaries of the clients wherever they might be. There is need, therefore, for a network of local account executives who work out of a local autonomous decentralized business and yet work closely together. All the worldwide facilities of the advertising agencies, whether market research, media research, or media buying, have to be available to these account executives, wherever the experts are. While an advertising campaign may be worldwide, it has to be adapted in every single country to the products the multinational client produces and markets in the country, to the specific needs and demands of the local market, to local habits, tastes, and consumer preferences, and to the media available in each market and effective in it.

And a worldwide accounting practice—legally one huge multinational partnership—is also a true systems structure.

What all these organizations have in common is the need to integrate diversity of cultures and values into unity of action. Each of the components of the system has to work in its own way, be effective according to its own logic and according to its own accepted norm of behavior. Or else it will not be effective at all. Yet all components have to work toward a common goal. Each has to accept, understand, and carry out its own role. This can be achieved only by direct, flexible, and tailor-made relationships among people or groups of people in which personal bond and mutual trust bridge wide differences in ways of behavior, point of view, and in what is considered "proper" and "appropriate."

NASA, for instance, faced the problem of the divergent values and cultures of a large government agency some major units of which were organized by, and heavily staffed with, men used to the ways of U. S. military services while others were built and run by German-born and German-trained space scientists like Wernher von Braun in the tradition of the German *Herr Professor* with his helpers and assistants. Businesses, some very large (e.g., Pan American Airways), some quite small, were "partners" on the "team" rather than "subcontractors." They did not make and deliver a part to preset specifications but planned, designed, and operated the "nervous systems" of the entire space effort, e.g., the huge launch complex at Cape Kennedy. Other "team members" were individual university scientists working by themselves in their own laboratories.

That the multinational faces similar problems of cultural and value diversity needs little explanation. (See also Chapter 59.) But to talk of the large Japanese company as "multicultural" may at first glance seem surprising. But Japan has had—and in large measure still has—what the Japanese call the "double economy": the "pre-modern" economy of (mostly small) workshops and of wholesalers and retailers, and a "modern" economy of (mostly large) manufacturing, banking, and marketing businesses. They represent very different structures, are organized and run quite differently, and define objectives and performance quite differently. The systems design has enabled Japan to maintain those two economies in parallel and in partnership for a century and to avoid—or at least to cushion—the disruption of traditional society by "modernization" which has occurred in every other non-Western country. And there has been a second "cultural" problem for the large, modern Japanese business: its relationship with and integration into the international economy and business world, as a source of supply of materials, machinery, and technology; as a market; and as an investor and partner. Both the trading company and the "joint venture" are cultural bridges, and systems design.

## The Difficulties and Problems of the Systems Structures

Systems design is a very poor "fit" with respect to all design specifications. It lacks *clarity*. It lacks *stability*. People neither find it easy to know what *their job* is, nor to understand the *job of the whole* and their relationship to it. *Communications* are a continuing problem, and one not capable of lasting solution. It is never clear where a certain decision should be made, nor indeed what the basic decisions are. *Flexibility* is great and receptivity to *new ideas* is almost too great. Yet the structure does not, as a rule, *develop people* and test them for top-management positions. Above all, the systems structure violates the principle of internal *economy*.

When NASA first started, the scientists who dominated it then believed that controls, and especially, of course, computer-based information, would run the system. They were soon disabused. One constant theme of the Sayles-Chandler book is the crucial importance of face-to-face personal relationships, of constant meetings, and of bringing people into the decision-making process, even on matters that are remote from their own assignments. The key executives at NASA spent something like two-thirds of their time in meetings, and mostly in meetings on matters that, at first sight, were not directly related to their own tasks.

Personal relationships are the only thing that prevents breakdown in the systems structure. There is constant need for arbitration of conflicts between various members of the system, for adjudication of disputes or jurisdiction, on direction, on budgets, on people, on priorities, and so on. The most important people, regardless of their job descriptions or assigned tasks, spend most of their time keeping the machinery running. In no other organizational structure is the ratio between output and effort needed for internal cohesion as unfavorable as in the systems structure.

At the same time, the requirements for the systems structure to work at all are exceedingly stringent. It demands absolute clarity of objectives. The objectives themselves may well change, and change rapidly. But at any one time they must be clear. And the objective for the work of each of the members of the system must be derived from the objective of the whole and directly related to it. In other words, the systems structure can function only if the job of thinking through "what is our business and what should it be" is taken seriously and performed with excellence. And then it requires that *operational* objectives and strategy be developed with great care from the basic mission and purpose.

"Get a man on the moon by 1970" is the kind of clear objective which enables a systems structure to work. But so was "Build an economically strong Japan." The multinational still has to develop objectives that enable each of its constituent units to direct its behavior toward some such a common goal—which is one of the main problems of the multinational corporation.

Another requirement is a demand for universal communications responsibility. Every member of the systems structure, but especially every member of every one of the managing groups, has to make sure that mission, objective, and strategies are fully understood by everyone, and that the doubts, questions, and ideas of every member are heard, listened to, respected, thought through, understood, and resolved. This is how Sayles and Chandler phrased it:

One conclusion is clear: the communications requirements in these projects [i.e., NASA] are overwhelming compared to those of more traditional manufacturing processes. The impact of a newly identified problem or discovery, or the search for the source of an unexplained difficulty demands that a number of people in a variety of organizations be involved almost simultaneously.*

The one multinational manufacturing business that has tackled the problem reports exactly the same extreme emphasis on constant communications.

The reorganization of Philips of Holland (discussed in the preceding chapter) was based on federal decentralization. But because of the diversity of Philips in geography, in technologies, and in products, top management is largely a "system" of interlocking teams—a ten-man board of manage-

*Sayles and Chandler, *op. cit.,* p. 8.

ment, thirteen worldwide product groups, and top-management groups in up to sixty countries. And "management" at Philips means nonstop communication, consultation, negotiation. Most of the key people throughout Philips are Dutchmen who have come up in the company; yet the diversity of their specific concerns, assignments, and environments creates so much cultural diversity that only constant relationships can establish common vision, common effort, and effective decision.

A third requirement is that each member of the team, i.e., each managerial unit, take responsibility far beyond its own assignment. Each member must, in effect, take top-management responsibility. To get any results requires, from each member, a "high order of responsible autonomy and the opportunity to innovate and even to change plans."* At the same time, each member must make efforts to know what goes on throughout the entire system.

More than anything else the executives within a large-scale endeavor must be able, one by one, and altogether, to see and to understand the totality of the job that the end result was designed to do. Each must see and understand the relationship of his evolving and changing individual assignment, and of the functions and people involved in that assignment, to the whole job and its requirement. This requires more than knowing his place and his responsibility within the organization itself, or knowing the organization "upside down." It requires an awareness between the total job as he sees it at the time, and his own particular job within the total framework, including the elements of the environment that are so much a part of the total.†

No wonder that the systems structure has not, on the whole, been an unqualified success. For every NASA with a successful moon shot (but also with an almost unlimited budget to support it) dozens of systems structures have failed miserably to perform or have done so only through budgetary irresponsibility such as no private business could survive (e.g., the Concorde and various "weapons systems," in Europe as well as in the U.S.). The attempt to use systems management to tackle major social problems—the much-touted promise of the sixties—is almost certain to be a total failure. Social and political complexities that are encountered whenever we move from outer space (where, after all, there are no voters) into the inner city and its problems, into economic development, or even into something seemingly so purely technical as mass transit, are almost certain to overwhelm the precarious cohesion of a systems structure.

And yet the Japanese have been running complex and large systems structures for a century. They have not avoided the difficulties nor found

*Sayles and Chandler, *op. cit.*, p. 6.
†James E. Webb, *Space Age Management*, pp. 135–137.

a way around them. Indeed all the obvious inefficiencies of the Japanese system—the fact, for instance, that top-management people spend endless time in meetings and in building personal relationships and communications—are, we now understand, built-in characteristics of the systems structure. But the Japanese experience also shows that the system can be made to work and can indeed be highly productive.

It needs, however, clear goals, high self-discipline throughout the structure, and a top management that takes personal responsibility for relationships and communications.

For the majority of managers, the systems structure is not of direct personal concern—though any manager in a multinational business will have to learn to understand it if he wants to function effectively himself. The systems structure will never be a preferred form of organization; it is fiendishly difficult. But it is an important structure, and one that the organization designer needs to know and needs to understand—if only to know that it should not be used where other, simpler and easier structures will do the job.

# 48

## Organization Conclusions

*"Ideal Organization" or "Pragmatism"?—The Need to Test Assumptions—The Need for Simplicity—Focus on Key Results and Key Activities—The Test: The Performance of People*

Organization theorists have argued for years whether organization design should start out with an "ideal organization" or whether it should be "pragmatic." Should "principles" come first? Or should the first consideration be "fit" to the special needs, the exceptional situations, the habits and traditions of an organization?

Our discussion of organizational building blocks, of design specifications, and of design principles leads to the conclusion that the argument is pointless. Both approaches are needed and have to be used in parallel. Organization design has to be grounded in an "ideal organization," that is, a conceptual framework. There has to be careful work on defining and delineating the structural principles. This work, in turn, must be grounded in the mission and purpose of the business, its objectives, its strategies, its priorities, its key activities. But there is no universal design principle. There is not even a best design principle. Each principle makes stringent demands and has severe limitations. Each has only limited scope; none embrace operating work, top-management work, and innovation work in one design.

Reality, in all its complexity, therefore has to be probed in designing organization. It has to be understood. The assumptions that are being made, and especially the assumptions that underlie the "ideal organization design" have to be tested and validated. These assumptions are always eminently plausible to the people within a company. They are often held subconsciously—but their hold is all the stronger for that. As long as one could assume that organization design meant one basic principle or a combination of two (i.e., functional and federal structures), development of an ideal organization could be considered the logical first step. Everybody knew of course that no ideal organization could ever be achieved in reality; reality always demands concessions, compromises, and exceptions. But one could hope to come close to the ideal—with exceptions truly "exceptional," that is, infrequent and confined to purely local situations.

One can no longer assume this. The testing of basic assumptions regarding organizational reality has to proceed parallel to the conceptual thinking about organization. Otherwise one ends up with an ideal organization that, while "conceptually pure," is inappropriate and stultifies.

Two examples, both from the same major organizing task, illustrate this:

In the GE organization of the early fifties, it was "obvious" to everyone that any unit charged with "product responsibility" was actually a "manufacturing business." Yet as said before, there were quite a few units that manufactured nothing but had been set up to develop a new process or a new product line. These units had a "customer"; they had "revenue"—usually a governmental research and development contract; they had "performance responsibility." But they were not manufacturing businesses but innovative organizations. To set them up on the functional design of the typical manufacturing business stifled them. This would have been clear to everyone had the ideal design been tested. But it was far too obvious for that.

The other GE assumption was that the general manager of a product business would be an operating manager, as are the heads of the automotive divisions of General Motors on which GE modeled its design. But all GM automotive divisions are alike. GM, while a multimarket business, is, in effect, a single-product business. GE, however, is one of the most diversified companies in the world, in its technologies, its processes, its products, and its markets. And most of GE's product businesses are the leaders in separate, distinct, large industries. The GE general manager, therefore, is top management rather than operating management (on this see Chapter 51). Again, testing the assumptions would have shown this at once. But without such a test GE set up general managers, who did not have the team they needed to do their top-management work, and autonomous businesses far too small in volume and scope to support the top management they needed. That GE has been constantly reorganizing its supposedly "definitive" organization structure—in sharp contrast to the stability of Alfred Sloan's design for GM—is in large measure the result of failure to test plausible assumptions.*

The approach to organization design through the ideal organization structure, i.e., through a conceptual model, is not "theory." It is eminently practical. But the pragmatic approach through explicit definition of assumptions and their testing in the reality of the organization is not "muddling through" or "patchwork." It is theoretically sound in a situation in which there are conceptual alternatives. Organization design is both concept and experimental validation—or it is faulty design.

## The Need for Simplicity

The simplest organization structure that will do the job is the best one. What makes an organization structure "good" are the problems it does not create. The simpler the structure, the less that can go wrong.

But there is neither a perfect nor a universal design principle. All of them have limitations. Even the simplest business—a small- to medium-sized company with one major product line for one major market—will use at least two design principles: functional design and teams, the latter for top-management and innovative work and as a complement to functionally organized work.

And to use, for the sake of simplicity or symmetry, a design principle beyond its inherent limits is asking for trouble.

To use functional structure for tasks for which team structure is needed, in knowledge work or for genuine innovation, for instance, makes for a "clean" structure. But it also makes for nonperformance. Conversely, to use teams as the structural units for unchanging, large-scale functional work causes only confusion. *Jobs,* in such work, can then be—and often should be—done in teams; but the work itself always has to be specific and specialized. And to set up a federally decentralized unit that is not a genuine business will only confuse; for all its limitations simulated decentralization will have to be used.

Some design principles are more difficult and problematical than others. But none is without difficulties and problems. None is primarily people-focused rather than task-focused; none is more "creative," "free," or "more democratic." Design principles are tools; and tools are neither good nor bad in themselves. They can be used properly or improperly; and that is all. To obtain both the greatest possible simplicity and the greatest "fit," organiza-

---

*Since these remarks may be read as criticism of the work at GE, it needs to be said that the author was closely connected with it; and what seems so obvious now had yet to be learned in the early fifties.

tion design has to start out with a clear focus on *key activities* needed to produce *key results*. They have to be structured and positioned in the simplest possible design. Above all, the architect of organization needs to keep in mind the purpose of the structure he is designing.

Organization is a means to an end rather than an end itself. Sound structure is a prerequisite to organizational health; but it is not health itself. The test of a healthy business is not the beauty, clarity, or perfection of its organization structure. *It is the performance of people.*

# PART THREE

# TOP MANAGEMENT: TASKS, ORGANIZATION, STRATEGIES

———

*Top Management is the directing, vision-setting, standard-setting organ. As such it has specific tasks. It requires its own organization. And it faces specific top-management challenges of structure and strategy with respect to size and complexity, diversity and diversification, growth, change, and innovation.*

# 49

## Georg Siemens and the Deutsche Bank

*Top Management: Rank or Function—Georg Siemens and the "Universal Bank"—Top-Management Tasks—Top-Management Team—The "Secretariat"—The Lessons*

Top management is a fact. But is its essence power? Is "top management" simply another term for the "bosses"? Or is there a specific top-management function? And if so, what is it and how should it be structured?

Management theory is generally silent on the function and structure of top management. But in management practice this was the very first area tackled systematically—long before Frederick W. Taylor tackled the organization of work, and long before Henri Fayol developed the first systematic organization design in his functional structure. Top management as a function and as a structure was first developed by Georg Siemens (1839–1901) in Germany between 1870 and 1880, when he designed and built the Deutsche Bank and made it, within a very few years, into continental Europe's leading and most dynamic financial institution. (On Siemens, see also Chapters 1 and 29.)

The management books usually mention that the emergence of the transcontinental railroad in the U.S. during the 1870s first created need for, and awareness of, management. The books fail to mention—and their authors usually do not know—that at the same time there emerged on the continent of Europe an institution, the "universal bank," which, while totally different from the large railroad, equally posed a problem of managing a large and geographically dispersed organization. The railroads' problem was organization and coordination of *operations;* the universal bank's problem was organization and coordination of *top management.*

The universal bank grew out of the *banque d'affaires,* the entrepreneurial bank which was intended, in accordance with the doctrines of the French economists and sociologists from J. B. Say to Saint-Simon, to be the motor of economic and social development by directing the capital resources of the economy into tomorrow's productive growth industries. The first *banque d'affaires,* the Crédit Mobilier, which the Pereire Brothers founded in Paris in 1850, proved the theory.* But as a bank it was a failure. It lacked the deposit base and the commercial banking business to sustain itself while its industrial investments matured and therefore had to go into "growth situations" and "go-go stocks," that is, into speculation rather than industrial development.

The lesson was heeded across the Rhine, in Germany, where economic development was just starting in the 1860s. The Germans proceeded to start banks which would be industrial-development banks (that is, *banques d'affairs)* but which would, like the older English "commercial" banks, also have a broad deposit base and a commercial-banking business—hence the name universal bank.

Of the many such banks started in Germany at that time, Deutsche Bank had the most pretentious title. Actually, there was as yet no *Deutschland* when it was founded early in 1870; Bismarck's unification of Germany was still a year in the future. But despite its grandiose title and its avowed intention of becoming the first truly "national" bank in Europe, the new Deutsche Bank was the smallest, the most poorly capitalized, and the most precariously backed of the new German banking ventures. It was indeed so unpromising that no experienced and established banker could be found to head it. The founders had to turn for the leadership of their new business to a thirty-year-old and virtually unknown government lawyer without banking or business experience: Georg Siemens.

Within ten years Siemens had built the Deutsche Bank into Germany's leading financial institution. Within another five years, by the mid-eighties, the Deutsche Bank had become the giant among the credit institutions of the European continent.

## Building a Top-Management Team

What Siemens did was to build a top management—the first such organ in economic and business history. Siemens himself, many years later, summed up his approach in an epigram: "A bank without an effective top-management is so much office furniture, fit only to be auctioned off."

*On the Pereire Brothers and the Crédit Mobilier, see my books, *Managing for Results* and *The Age of Discontinuity.*

The old merchant firms of Hamburg and Bremen, which were the "modern" businesses of a still predominantly pre-industrial Germany, were, of course, family partnerships as a rule, with a team of brothers or of father and son at the head. Siemens transformed this partnership of co-owners into a top-management team of professionals.

He analyzed the *key activities* of the bank and made sure that each of them was an assigned responsibility of one member of the team. He analyzed the key relations of the bank, with major investments and major customers, or with such major outside factors as governments, and again made sure that one member of the top-management team was responsible for each of them. There was, of course, a captain of the management team —Siemens himself for many years filled that position. But whichever member of the team had designated responsibility for a key activity (e.g., underwriting) or for a key relationship (e.g., with one of the major industrial investments) was in charge, was directly and primarily responsible, and made the decisions. Even Siemens, while chairman of the "board of management" and clearly first man on the team, was, in many areas, the number two man who served as alternate to the colleague in charge.

Who did what, and who was responsible for what, was decided on the basis of a man's personality, his interests, his qualifications, and his load. The job had to fit the man. At the same time, great care was taken to have every key activity and every key relationship "covered," that is, assigned as a primary responsibility to one of the team members.

So far Siemens may be said to have done little but define the functions of the board of management of German company law. But Siemens soon went far beyond this and organized a top-management team grounded in function rather than in law.

Unlike France, where the *banque d'affaires* had its origin, Germany did not have then, and does not have today, one major city in which governmental and economic activities are centralized. Even in the 1920s, when Berlin was at its peak, most of the large German industrial companies did not have their headquarters there. Only the electrical industry was dominated by Berlin-based companies.

Such centers as Hamburg, Frankfurt, and Munich were much older than Berlin. They had been capital cities when Berlin was still a fishing village. Their citizens, and especially their leading businessmen, had intense civic pride and were not at all willing to be controlled from Berlin. Yet the Deutsche Bank, if it wanted to carry out its function as the German entrepreneur, had to become a national rather than remain a regional or a local bank. Also the new industrial business of the rapidly growing German economy soon began to be national, with plants, branches, and customers throughout the country.

Hence Siemens had to work out a national top-management team of which the bank's leading executives in major centers outside of Berlin could be members. These men were not legally members of the top management, that is, of the board of management *(Vorstand)*. But internally they were members of the *top-management teams.* They were responsible for the bank's relations with the major businesses in their area. With industry largely outside of Berlin these men often carried the responsibility for the bank's major industrial investments and major business relationships. As late as 1926, when the German chemical industry merged into the I. G. Farben, and established its corporate headquarters in Frankfurt, the Deutsche Bank's top man in Frankfurt assumed, for instance, primary responsibility for the relationship with what then was Germany's largest and most important industrial corporation.

As a result, outstanding men in the various communities were willing to serve the bank in local leadership positions when they would neither have moved to Berlin nor have been content with subordinate jobs. And strong local banks were willing to merge with the Deutsche Bank for the same reason.

## The "Secretariat"

Such a large, widely dispersed, and dynamic team created at once a major communications problem. How to keep all the members informed (their number may have reached twenty-five or thirty-five at times)? How to keep control of the business of the bank once it had grown beyond financing a few companies and had actually become the national entrepreneur its founders had expected it to be? How to keep control of the allocation of the bank's resources of capital and key people? How altogether to prevent under this top-management system a breakup of a unified bank into a series of semi-independent fiefdoms? Georg Siemens's answer to this was the creation of the executive secretariat *(Direktions-Sekretariat).* *

Siemens assembled a small professional staff and charged it with the responsibility for keeping all members of the top-management teams informed of each other's activities and decisions, for thinking ahead for the bank as a whole, and for staying in close touch with every major investment and commitment.

---

*Without any knowledge of Siemens's work, the National Aeronautics and Space Agency (NASA) almost a hundred years later, in the 1960s, arrived at the same solution of an executive secretariat to maintain communication, information, and cohesion in a systems structure. On this see Sayles and Chandler, *op. cit.*

## Georg Siemens's Lessons

This example teaches, first, that there is a top-management function. There are a number of tasks which are top-management tasks, not because top management is the "top"—that is, because it has the legal authority or the power—but because they are tasks that can be discharged only by people who are capable of seeing the whole business and of making decisions with respect to the whole business.

Secondly, the story of the Deutsche Bank under Georg Siemens demonstrates that top management requires a specific structure. It is a different organ from any other organ of management and has to have a different design.

Finally, the story shows that top management requires its own organ of input, its own organ for the supply of stimulation, information, and thought.

# Top-Management Tasks and Organization

Top-Management tasks differ fundamentally from the tasks of the other management groups. They are multidimensional. They are recurrent but intermittent. They make different and often conflicting demands on personality and temperament. There is, therefore, need so to structure the top-management job that both the objective tasks to be accomplished and the personalities of the people available are taken care of. And there is need for providing top management with the stimulation and information it needs for its specific tasks.

# 50

## Top-Management Tasks

*The Dimensions of the Top-Management Task—Specific Needs in Specific Businesses—To "Operate" or Not to "Operate"—The Rules—Recurrent but Intermittent Tasks—Required: A Diversity of Capabilities and Temperaments—Top-Management Tasks and Chief-Executive Styles—The Top-Management Work Plan*

Every managerial unit other than top management is designed for one specific major task—whether the organization is structured on functional lines, in teams, on the basis of decentralization, or on the systems approach. Every building block of organization is defined by a specific contribution.

The one exception is top management. Its job is multidimensional. There is no top-management task; there are only top-management *tasks*. And this is just as true for public-service institutions as it is for businesses.

Since each of the management tasks has been identified earlier in this book, what follows is mainly recapitulation.

1. There is, first, the task of thinking through the mission of the business, that is, of asking the question "What is our business and what should it be?" This leads to the setting of objectives, the development of strategies and plans, and the making of today's decisions for tomorrow's results. This clearly can be done only by an organ of the business that can see the entire business; that can make decisions that affect the entire business; that can balance objectives and the needs of today against the needs of tomorrow; and that can allocate resources of men and money to key results.

2. There is need for standard setting, example setting, i.e., for the conscience functions. There is need for an organ of the enterprise which con-

cerns itself with the gap—always a big one—between what the organization stands for and what it actually does. There is need for an organ concerned with vision and values in the key areas. Again this can only be an organ of the enterprise that sees and comprehends the entire business.

3. There is the responsibility to build and maintain the human organization. There is need for work on developing the human resources for tomorrow, and especially for work on providing tomorrow's top management. The spirit of an organization is created by the people at the top. Their standards of conduct, their values, their beliefs, set the example for their entire organization and determine its self-respect.

There is need also for thinking through organization structure and organization design. This requires someone, or a group of people, who can see the entire business and can make decisions in contemplation of the entire business.

4. Equally important are major relations which only the people at the top of a business can establish and maintain. They may be relations to customers or major suppliers. They may be industry relations or relations with bankers and the financial community. They may be relations to governments or other outside institutions. These relations crucially affect the capacity of the business to perform. And they are relations that can be made, again, only by somebody who represents the entire business, speaks for it, stands for it, commits it.

Out of these relations emerges a host of top-management policy decisions and actions—on the environment and on the social impact of a business; on its employment policies and on its position on proposed legislation.

5. There are countless "ceremonial" functions—dinners, civic events, etc. —that are actually more time-consuming and less easy to avoid for the top people in a small or medium-sized business that is prominent in its local community than they are for the heads of the very big companies.

As the head of a fair-sized company said, "As long as the president of General Electric sends a check he can be represented by one of his vice-presidents—and he has sixty-five of them. I have to go myself; we are the largest employers in the place."

6. There is also need for a "stand-by" organ for major crises, for somebody who is available to take over when things go seriously wrong. Then it is the most experienced, the wisest, the most prominent people in an organization who have to roll up their sleeves and go to work. They are legally responsible. But there is also a responsibility of knowledge—and it cannot be abdicated.

This is still a partial list only. It should prove, however, that the top-management task will not get done unless it is recognized as a distinct function, a distinct kind of work, and organized as such.

But this list also shows that while there is a genuine top-management function there is no general formula for the top-management tasks.

Every business, indeed every institution, needs a top-management function. But every one has specific top-management tasks. The elements of the job are the same. But the specific top-management tasks are particular to an individual business. They have to be developed out of a specific analysis of the mission and purpose of the institution, its objectives, its strategies, and the key activities. The question to ask is not "What is top management?" The question is "What are the specific things to be done in *this* business which are of crucial importance to the success and survival of the business and which can be done only by top management?" "What are the specific things which can be done only by people who see this business whole; who can balance the present needs of the business against the needs of the future; and who can make final and effective decisions?"

It therefore makes little sense to talk of an "ideal" top-management structure—as a good many of the books on the subject do. The ideal top management is the one that does the things that are right and proper for its enterprise here and now. We need, to be sure, a theory of top management. But the specific application must be developed concretely, indeed pragmatically. It must be tailored to the individual enterprise. It must be developed from an analysis of the specific enterprise. It must, above all, follow the strategies of the enterprise and be in harmony with them.

## To "Operate" or Not to "Operate"

Only the analysis of the individual business (or public-service institution) will bring out what key activities are properly top-management responsibilities.

The management texts agree that top management should not "operate." And most informed observers of top management agree that the most common reason why the top-management job doesn't get done is that top executives "operate" and, in consequence, do not tackle the top-management tasks.

Yet Georg Siemens in his top-management design included a good deal of "operating work." He did not confine his top management to directing others, to planning, to reviewing, to setting the direction of his Bank. On the contrary, the first job of the members of his top-management team was specific work on the major industrial and financial investments the bank had decided to develop. It was not "directing" the work of others but "doing." Far from isolating themselves from the "nuts and bolts," Siemens's top men were supposed to take direct personal responsibility for finding the right investment opportunities and for developing them into successful, well-managed businesses. Clearly this was one of the secrets of the success of the Deutsche Bank.

Effective top managements tend to follow the Siemens practice rather than the theorist's and consultant's preachings.

Here are some examples. A medium-sized French producer of branded and nationally advertised consumer goods has gained, within the last decade or two, a strong position in the European markets. One of the reasons is that the head of the company is also the company's advertising and promotion manager. He himself writes most of the company's advertisements and designs the company's promotions. He also has assigned to himself direct responsibility for relations with the dealers throughout Europe, and especially throughout France. He personally visits about thirty of the larger dealers in the course of a year, listens to them, studies their businesses, and altogether manages the company's relationship with them. "Our business is a promotion business. Our business, above all, depends on the willingness of the dealers to work hard at selling our merchandise. Our business, therefore, depends on our knowing the dealers and their knowing us, and on our willingness and ability to design products they want to sell and can sell, to deliver them the way they need them delivered, and to price them in line with the price preferences of their customers." Yet the same man flatly refuses to have anything to do with manufacturing—even though his own background is manufacturing engineering.

Work on major innovations may be such an "operating" top-management task at a given stage of a company's development.

A large pharmaceutical company, for instance, decided to broaden its base. It had long held leadership in one major area but decided that its product base was too narrow. It identified several new areas in which it expected to become an important factor, each requiring the development of new drugs. In each of the three areas it selected one of the members of top management moved in as a member—but not the leader—of the "project team" formed to develop the new products and to develop the new business. In the early stages leadership in the task force rested, of necessity, with the research scientists. But even then the top-management member of the project team actively worked, thinking through the marketing strategies, working on medical testing and on obtaining approval from the government regulatory agencies involved; planning the changes necessary in the sales force to enable the company to move into fields in which it had no acceptance by the medical profession as a reliable supplier.

This work, it was felt, and rightly so, was so crucial to the future of the company and, at the same time, involved so many basic and difficult decisions, that a member of top management had to gain direct working experience in the field for the whole group to be able to make the necessary decisions and take the necessary action.

Another example: Sears, Roebuck is a company which, from its early days, has insisted on keeping top management out of operations, and confined to top-management tasks. No one believed in this more firmly than General Wood. Yet when Wood systematized the top-management job and organized a three-man top-management team, he assigned to top management as a "doing" responsibility the selection of sites for new major retail stores. This decision, he argued, had long-range and irreversible impact on the company's ability to sell and to make money. Once the site has been selected and a store has been built, there is a twenty-year commitment. A decision like this, though clearly an operating decision, has to be made by top management. And to be able to make the decision intelligently, a member of top management has to work on the project from the beginning.

These are clearly dangerous precedents. If operating work can be legitimately included in the top-management job, then chief executives who open all the incoming letters or who themselves do the final inspection of the company's products—and I have seen both done, and in fairly large businesses—can claim that they are doing top-management work (as indeed both did).

The rules are simple:

1. It is not top-management work if someone else can do it. Of course, most operating work will be eliminated as top-management work by the analysis of key activities; for top management should never be involved in any other activities. But key activities should then be subjected to the question "Could anyone else in the organization do them just as well—or nearly as well? At least, should there be someone capable of doing them?" If the answer is yes, it is not top-management work.

2. People who move into top-management work should, further, give up the functional or operating work they did earlier. That should always be turned over to someone else. Otherwise they are likely to remain functional or operating people.

But it is not in itself a final argument against inclusion of this or that task in the top-management function to say, "This is operating work." The many executives who, despite all the exhortations in the books, continue to operate, have a sound instinct. But if they do not subject the top-management job to a searching analysis of key activities, they will do the wrong operating work. They will do the things they are familiar with and like to do. They will do the things they have always done. And they will slight the "operating" work that actually belongs in the top-management job.

## The Characteristics of Top-Management Tasks

The top-management function is singularly difficult to organize. Every one of the tasks is a recurrent task. It needs to be done over and over again.

But very few of them, if any, are *continuous* tasks. Very few of them have to be done every day from nine to five. When they arise, they are of crucial importance to the enterprise. They are the true "life and death" decisions. But it would be foolish to "plan" five days a week fifty-two weeks a year. Key personnel decisions also arise fairly infrequently. But then they require a great deal of time; few things are less likely to succeed than hasty personnel decisions. And the same applies to most of the other top-management tasks.

But individuals require a continuing day-to-day job. They do little work, as a rule, unless they work steadily.

Another peculiar characteristic of top-management tasks is that they require a diversity of capabilities, and, above all, of temperaments. They require the capacity to analyze, to think, to weigh alternatives, and to harmonize dissent. But they also require the capacity for quick and decisive action, for boldness and for intuitive courage. They require being at home with abstract ideas, concepts, calculations, and figures. They also require perception of people, a human awareness, and empathy and altogether a lively interest in people and respect for them. Some tasks demand that a man work by himself, and alone. Others are tasks of representation and ceremonial, outside tasks, that require the politician's enjoyment of crowds and protocol; the ability to represent and to make a good impression by saying nothing.

The top-management tasks require at least four different kinds of human being: the "thought man," "the action man," the "people man," and the "front man." Yet those four temperaments are almost never found in one person.

Failure to understand these characteristics is a main reason why the top-management task is so often done poorly or not at all.

Because the tasks, while continuing, are not continuous, the top-management job itself is often seen, even by people running sizable businesses, as something that will be done if and when the need arises. But in the meantime, that is, day by day, the people at the top feel the need to do a continuing job. That, of course, means that they do functional work. For there is day-to-day work in manufacturing and marketing, in accounting and engineering, in advertising and in quality control. And the top-management tasks will not get done at all. There are simply too many of them to be done that way. While each individual task within the top-management function may require only a comparatively limited amount of time in the smaller and less complicated business, the totality of the top-management function, even in the small business, is far too large to be handled on the side and in additon to functional work. Day-by-day operating work always has urgency—and many top-management jobs are for the long pull and look as if they can wait until the "tomorrow" that never comes.

In addition, the top man, even in the large business, tends to see only those parts of the top-management function which are congenial to him. They will then constitute for him *the* top-management job—and it will get done. The top man is right when he assigns to himself those top-management tasks that fit his personality, his temperament, his experience. He is wrong, however, in believing, often without conscious thought, that this takes care of the top-management function. It actually makes the business unbalanced and likely to be out of control.

The first requirement of effective top management, as Georg Siemens saw a century ago, is to identify objectively all the key activities and key tasks of top management in the business. The old saw that "every chief executive has his own style and decides what top management is" is nonsense. Every chief executive—indeed, every person—has his own style and is entitled to it. But what decides what top management is or should be is an objective decision. It depends no more on individual style than the law of gravity depends on what the physicist had for breakfast.

The fact that the top-management tasks, or at least a good many of them, while continuous tasks, are not continuous work and the fact that the top-management tasks demand a diversity of qualifications, skills, and temperaments make it essential that every top-management task be clearly assigned to someone. Otherwise, important tasks will be overlooked. In fact, there should be a *top-management work plan*—especially in the small business—which spells out in considerable detail who is responsible for what; what the objectives and goals are with respect to each task; and what the deadlines are. Precisely because the top-management function differs in basic character from practically every other kind of work within the enterprise, it has to be made specific and has to be clearly assigned.

# 51

## Top-Management Structure

Top-management work is work for a team rather than for one man. It is quite unlikely that any one man will, in his own person, unite the divergent temperaments which the job requires. Moreover, it will be found, when the top-management tasks are analyzed, that there is more work to be done than any one man can do. The tasks require, except in the smallest business, at least one full-time man who does nothing else, and then one or two, at least for a major part of their time, who take on part of the task in which they are then the "leaders" and have primary responsibility.

There are additional reasons why the one-man top management tends to malfunction. Every top-management succession in a one-man top management is a "crisis" and a desperate gamble. No one in the business except the former top man has really done the top-management work and proven himself in it.

To recognize the team nature of the top-management job is particularly important in the small business. The one-man top management is a major reason why businesses fail to grow. (On this, see Chapter 60.)

But the job itself is a team job to begin with. Whatever the titles on the organization chart, the top-management job in a healthy company is almost always actually done by a team.

Henry Ford, as has been said (in Chapter 29, "Why Managers?"), did not believe in managers at all, and this, in large part, explains the decline and near-collapse of his company in his latter years. But, as recent studies have brought out (especially Allan Nevins's *Ford, the Times, the Man, the Company* [Scribner, 1954]), the Ford Motor Company at the time of its growth and success, that is, from 1907 through the early twenties, was in effect run by a true top-management team with James Couzens co-equal to Ford and the final authority in a great many and clearly assigned top-management areas. After Couzens left—he later entered politics and became a greatly beloved liberal senator from Michigan in the New Deal days—Henry Ford became a one-man top management. It is hardly coincidence that from that day on the Ford Motor Company began to go downhill.

On paper the top management of a company may look like a one-man job. But if the company is healthy, a closer look is likely to disclose that other people carry clearly assigned top-management responsibilities as well. The controller often takes on a part of the top-management function— usually the analytical, the planning, the objective-setting aspects. Or it is the manufacturing man who takes on responsibility for the human organization in addition to his functional duties.

This works reasonably well as long as the business is simple and small. The larger and more complex business needs a clearly structured top-management team.

This team may be organized, as has become the fashion, as a "president's office," in which a number of people serve as equals, each with his own assigned area of primary responsibility within which he has final say. This is the structure Siemens designed; and for the large and complex business it is probably the best one—though it is not an easy one.

It is essentially the structure which the organization builders of the twenties at Du Pont, Standard Oil of New Jersey, Royal Dutch/Shell, and Unilever evolved—probably without ever having heard of Georg Siemens.

But it is also possible to have one man only, a president or a chairman, who carries the title of chief executive officer. He has then affiliated with him a small number of colleagues, perhaps with some such title as executive vice-president, each of whom has clearly assigned authority and responsibility for a part of the top-management task, and no other duties.

Or, to cite another fairly common structure, there may be a three- or four-man top, with each man carrying clearly assigned top-management responsibilities even though one man is definitely number one. This is the structure which General Motors has had for fifty years—a chairman, a vice-chairman, a chairman of the executive committee, a president. What assignments each of these four men carries is then worked out to fit their personalities. But the four positions are permanent.

And there are many variations on these themes.

But just because the organization chart shows a top-management team does not necessarily mean that there is one. There is need for safeguards against the danger of dictatorships disguised as a top-management team.

The best proof is what happened to Siemens's own concept in Germany. The German Company Law, enacted in 1887, largely as a result of Siemens's work, provided for a *Vorstand,* i.e., a top-management team. But many German companies, especially in the period between 1900 and World War II, were run by an autocratic *Generaldirektor* because the other members of the *Vorstand*—contrary to Siemens's rule—had full-time functional assignments. Few of these companies were well-managed or did well.

The only effective safeguard is to have every top-management task clearly lodged in a man with direct and primary responsibility for it. And in the larger company no one who carries any top-management responsibility should carry any responsibility that is not part of the top-management job.

The same lesson is being taught by a more recent and perhaps less serious top-management malfunction, the operating "group executive" who is supposed to "give part of his time" to the top-management job.

The group executive in charge of a number of divisions who has become popular in large companies is supposed to be the operating head of his group but give some of his time—a common figure is 30 percent—to the company's top-management tasks. This sounds plausible—but it has not worked out. The group executive is far too busy to have clearly assigned responsibility for a top-management task. As a result, he makes no top-management contribution.

One company that has recognized this is IBM. IBM has group executives for major areas (research, engineering, and manufacturing; domestic marketing and service; international; and noncomputer businesses). But it also has a four-man management committee composed of the chairman, the president, and two senior officers, none of whom operates. Each of the four has clearly assigned top-management responsibilities and no other function.

And yet the group executive is a member of a top-management team. Only it is not the top-management team of the parent company. It is the top-management team of the divisions in his group, each a major and important autonomous business in its own right, and each therefore requiring its own top management.

This was largely the way GE managers worked their way out of the mistaken designation of the general manager of a product business as an operating manager (see Chapter 46). The group executive became, in effect, the leader of a top-management team for his group, and a member of the top management of every one of the product businesses. But he never functioned as a member of GE's top management—which is what the job had been designed to be.

## How Many Top Managements?

In the large and complex business—and even more in the multinational company—there are *always* several top managements rather than one. The company as a whole is a business. But the autonomous division of a federally organized company is also a business. It requires its own top management, has its own top-management tasks, and its own key activities.

Again Georg Siemens realized this a century ago. His *Vorstand* in Berlin was one top-management group. Another one was composed of members of the Berlin *Vorstand* and the key men in the major branches. But every one of the major branches outside of Berlin had also a small top-management team of its own. The Berlin team was, so to speak, the first team. But every one of the provincial teams had responsibilities in which it was "first," and with respect to which Berlin was "support" or "understudy."

Indeed, it is one of the characteristics of complexity in a business that it requires more than one top-management team—with clear recognition of which of the teams has primary responsibility in what area and with what limitations.

We can now summarize the basic specifications for a functioning top-management structure:

The starting point is an analysis of the top-management tasks.

Each top-management task must be clearly assigned to someone who has direct and full responsibility for it.

This requires a top-management team, with responsibilities assigned to fit the personalities, qualifications, and temperaments of the members.

Whoever has assigned responsibility for a top-management activity is "top management" whatever his title.

Except in the small and simple business no one who has top-management responsibilities does any but top-management work.

The complex business requires more than one top-management team, each structured according to these rules.

## Teamwork in Top Management

A top-management team has to satisfy stringent requirements to be effective. It is not a simple structure. It will not work just because its members like each other. Indeed whether the members like or dislike each other is beside the point. A top-management team must function no matter what the personal relationships between its members are.

1. First, whoever has primary responsibility in a given area has, in effect, the final say. To have a functioning top management requires further that no subordinate can appeal a decision by one member of the team to another. Every member speaks with the full authority of top management.

To deviate from this and to allow an appeal from one member of the top-management group to another invites politicking. It undermines the authority of the entire top-management group.

2. No member will make a decision with regard to a matter for which he does not have primary responsibility. Should such a matter be brought to him, he will refer it to the colleague whose primary responsibility it is. Indeed it is a wise precaution for members of the top-management team not even to have an opinion on matters that are not within their own areas of primary responsibility.

Alfred P. Sloan, Jr., was the undoubted head of General Motors with moral authority within GM's general management such as has rarely been equaled. Yet Sloan said again and again, "I think you'd better take this matter up with Mr. Brown or with Mr. Bradley or with Mr. Wilson"—at that time (the late forties) his colleagues in the top-management group. "I would be interested to hear what they decide; perhaps you'll let me know." After the caller had left—and the callers were usually high GM executives —Sloan would sometimes take the telephone and quietly call up Mr. Brown and ask him to come to the office to discuss the matter. Sloan usually had very definite opinions and fought for them. But he had disciplined himself never to express an opinion outside the top group, unless he himself had direct responsibility in the matter under discussion.

3. Members of the top-management team need not like each other. They need not even respect each other. But they must not agitate against each other. In public, that is, outside top management's conference room, they have no opinions on each other, do not criticize each other, do not belittle each other. Preferably they do not even praise each other.

To enforce this rule is the team captain's job—and he better be strict about it. Even the most "temperamental" (i.e., undisciplined) man must not be allowed, as a member of top management, to express in public criticism, dislike, or contempt for any other member.

4. A top-management team is not a committee. It is a team. A team needs a captain. The team captain is not the "boss"; he is a leader.

There are several ways of determining the role of the team captain.

The president of Du Pont traditionally has just one vote and depends primarily on his moral authority. At Standard Oil of New Jersey the chairman traditionally did not even have this much legal power; for many years votes, whenever taken, required unanimity. Alfred P. Sloan at General Motors had the legal power to overrule his colleagues on the management team. But he almost never used it. He made a decision after he had made sure that he knew where every colleague on the top-management team stood and that each, in turn, had fully grasped where the chairman and chief executive officer stood. In other top-management teams the senior man has the power of final decision, or at least a veto power. In yet others, it is the team captain's main role to designate the member of the team who, in a particular situation, makes the final decision, which is then accepted by everybody.

But there has to be a team captain. And in times of extreme crisis he has to be willing and able—and has to have the legal power—to take over. In times of common peril there has to be unity of command.

5. Within his assigned sphere, a member of top management is expected to make decisions. But certain decisions should be "reserved." There only the team itself can make the decision. At least the decision has to be discussed with the team before it can be made. It is desirable to think through in advance what these areas are or should be.

Defining "what is our business and what should it be" clearly belongs here. Abandoning major product lines or adding new ones belongs here too, as do major capital appropriations. But key personnel decisions are of this kind too.

Key personnel decisions are made neither by acclamation nor by taking a vote. They do require careful thought, careful discussion, and the pooling of the experience of different people within the organization. They are, properly, matters which top management considers as a group, even though it will then often leave the actual decision to one of its members.

6. The top-management task requires systematic and intensive work on communications among the members of the top-management team. It requires this precisely because there are so many different top-management tasks, each, however, with decisive impact on the welfare of the entire organization. It requires it, above all, because each member of top management should be able to operate with the maximum of autonomy within his own sphere—and that can be granted him only if he makes every effort to keep his colleagues fully informed.

Philip Young and Gerald Swope, who largely built the General Electric Company in the twenties and thirties, formed a singularly effective top-management team. Swope, headquartered in Schenectady, was concerned with engineering, production, and selling; Young was in charge of finance, government relations, international affairs, and public responsibilities. The two men, legend has it, disliked each other and rarely talked to each other. But they took great care to keep each other informed of all their actions and activities—everything that went on in one office was known at the other office within a day or two. There are some old-timers in GE who maintain that this impersonal but highly organized system worked better than the constant meetings and the close personal association of the top-management teams that have succeeded Swope and Young since World War II.

Respect for the task, and clear understanding of what it is and who has responsibility, are, in other words, the foundations for an effective top management.

## How to Nourish the Brain

Siemens's most distinct innovation in organizing the top management was the "executive secretariat." It may have been his most important contribution.

The human brain absorbs almost half of all the oxygen and all the energy in the body. The five sense organs work directly for the brain and supply it with stimuli. Altogether, the human body, it may be said, is organized first, and above all, to nourish the brain, to supply it with stimulus and energy.

One cannot expect a social body to equal the performance of a biological organism, let alone of that marvel of flexibility, precision, and economy, the functioning human body. But still one might wonder whether the "brain" of the business enterprise, its top management, does not need its own organ of nourishment, of stimulation, and of information.

In most businesses all the world over there is a surfeit of data. There are constant reports, there are studies, there are researches of all kinds, there are presentations and meetings. Most of them are intended for operating management and for its use. The staff services within the typical business are set up to support the operating people. Indeed, it is the theory of staffs that their job is to support, service, and educate operating managers. Who then nourishes the brain, who then serves top management?

What top managements get, by and large, are the same data, the same information, the same stimuli that operating managers get. Yet there are specific top-management tasks and specific top-management needs. Top management's needs are different in kind from those of the operating people, if only because it is largely concerned with the future rather than solely with the present, and with the whole business rather than with any of its parts.

The questions "What is our business?" and "What should it be?" imply a very different look at the present enterprise from the look on which present objectives, present structure, present assignments, and therefore present information are being based. Genuine innovations never fit existing organization structures, but fall outside and beyond any existing organization scope. And tomorrow's key people should always be picked for reasons different from those for which one yesterday picked the key people of today.

A simple but telling example is that of a major manufacturer of electrical apparatus. Traditionally the company had been in the steam-turbine business, in which it long held a leadership position. During World War II, it went into jet engines, which at first were seen only as engines to power aircraft, even though a jet engine, that is, a gas turbine, is just as much a producer of electrical energy as a steam turbine. Then the company went into the atomic energy field. Because each of these three means of producing electricity had a different technological origin, and at first also a different market, each was organized as a separate business. However, for the customer, the power company, the three are simply alternative ways of producing electricity. Any two of them together will give an electric utility a complete power supply. But none of the existing service staffs of the manufacturing company saw this, or could have seen this. Their job, after all, was to service the operating managements of each of the three divisions—the steam turbine, the jet engine, and the atomic power divisions. The people who ran these divisions saw their own product as the prime generator and expected to get for it the lion's share of the growth in electric-power generation. A task force organized specifically to supply top management with new thinking about tomorrow's markets finally pointed out that these three divisions were in the same business. By that time the company's standing in one of its major markets had already been seriously eroded by the failure to supply information and thinking for the top-management job.

Georg Siemens's specific solution, the German "executive secretariat," will not suit every company and every cultural tradition. Yet every company, beyond the very small and simple one, needs a specific organ to supply top management with thinking, with stimulation, with questions, with knowledge and, above all, with information. Top management work is a specific kind of work. Any kind of work requires the right tools; and the tools for the top-management job are information, stimulation, analysis, and questions.

Georg Siemens's "secretariat" was set up as a distinct career. Great pains were taken to find the ablest, most brilliant, most intelligent young men in the bank's employ or to recruit such men from the universities or from government service. Then they stayed, as a rule, in the secretariat. Very few of them were ever moved out into operating work in the bank. A few made it into top management—but their number was small too. As a result, the secretariat tended to become insulated.

This is still a weakness of the secretariat as it is being used in Germany. But it is an unnecessary weakness and one that can be remedied. The rule should be that no one gets into such a secretariat, that is, into a group the purpose of which is to support top management with information, stimulation, and questions, unless he first has shown real performance in actual work. A secretariat assignment should be considered as a major training position for men who, at a fairly early age, have shown high capacity to perform.

No one should stay in the secretariat for more than a few years—five to eight might be the upper limit. Then he should be moved back into a position where he has to perform, that is, into an operating position with direct and measurable responsibility for contribution and results.

The secretariat should always be kept small. It should be kept on key activities rather than attempt to cover everything. It should be expected to focus on the major needs of the business. Indeed its first—and perhaps its most important—assignment is to identify and to think through the major factors that affect the performance and results of the business, the major factors that underlie the question, "What is our business and what should it be?" It should always ask, "What information does top management need to make its decisions?"

In countries in which "secretariat" has the connotation of low-level paper-pushing clerks (as it has in English-speaking countries) the function might well be called "business research." But the function should be clearly defined as an organ *to serve* top management. Its job is to provide top management with the information it needs to work as an effective team, and with the information and knowledge to prepare itself today for the major decisions it has to face tomorrow.

No business can do better than its top management will permit; the "bottleneck" is, after all, always "at the head of the bottle." Of all the jobs in the enterprise the top-management job is the most difficult one to organize. But it is also the most important one to organize.

# 52

## Needed: An Effective Board

*The Board: Legal Fiction and Impotent Reality—The Push to "Politicize" the Board—The Board in Germany, Sweden, and the U. S.—The "Euroboard"—Why Top Management Needs a Board—The Three Functions of the Board—The Board as Review and Appeals Organ—The Board as Safeguard Against Incompetent Management—The Public and Community Relations Function—What Is Needed—Objectives and a "Work Plan" for the Board—Who Belongs on the Board—The "Professional" Director—Designing and Building an Effective Board as a Top-Management Task*

Different countries have different names for the organ that supervises top management, counsels it, reviews its decisions, and appoints men into top-management positions—board of directors, supervisory board, and *conseil d'administration*. Different countries provide for different membership.

Members of management, for instance, cannot sit on the German supervisory board but are permitted to do so under American, British, and Japanese law. In France the top-management function is conceived as delegated by the board of directors to one or several of its members so that board membership is almost obligatory for membership in top management. And there are other variants. Outside of countries of the German-type company law, where this is forbidden, it is not uncommon to find boards in which membership is restricted to full-time members of management. In Japan, for instance, the board is usually another name for the top-management committee. In Great Britain there is a distinction between "executive" members of the board, that is, top-management people, and "nonexecutive" members, that is, outsiders who hold no official position in the company.

But there is one thing all boards have in common, regardless of their legal position. *They do not function.* The decline of the board is a universal phenomenon of this century. Perhaps nothing shows it as clearly as that the board, which, in law, is the governing organ of a corporation, was always the last group to hear of trouble in the great business catastrophes of this century.

This happened in the collapse of the Austrian Credit Anstalt, the leading Austrian bank, which in 1931 triggered the first worldwide monetary crisis and, within a few weeks, brought down the English pound. It was equally true in the big German business failures of the early thirties which led to the collapse of the German banking system and which had a good deal to do with Hitler's ascent to power. It was true in the business collapses of the post-World War II period—Rolls-Royce in England, the Penn-Central Railroad in the United States, and the catastrophic decline of Italy's leading chemical company, Monticatini, in the mid-sixties. Only at the very last minute, if even then, did the boards of these companies find out that things were not going well.

Whenever one of the "scandals" breaks, the board's failure is blamed on stupidity, negligence of board members, or on failure of management to keep its board informed. But when such malfunction occurs with unfailing regularity, one must conclude that it is the institution that fails to perform rather than individuals.

The board, whatever its name and whatever its legal structure, has become a fiction. The law may still treat it as the sovereign organ of the corporation—but, then, English legal rhetoric still treats the Queen as an Absolute Monarch whose every whim is a command. The reality, however, is that boards are either simply management committees, or they are ineffectual. Rather than decry the failure of individuals, we therefore better ask "Why have boards, regardless of their legal structure, lost their capacity to perform?"

In Georg Siemens's day they apparently did perform. In fact, their performance could be taken for granted—as it was by Siemens, who himself served on quite a few boards and who, at the same time, worked closely with the board of his own bank and treated it as an integral part of his own top management.

One reason for the malfunction of the board is, of course, the development of the large publicly held corporation. The original board, whether American, English, French, or German, was conceived as representing the owners. This was reality in the nineteenth century when stock ownership, by and large, was concentrated among a few people or a few groups, each holding a substantial share of the total. Each board member had a sizable stake in the enterprise. Each was able to devote a good deal of time and attention to the company. Each sat on only a few boards.

But large companies in advanced countries are no longer owned by a small group. Their legal ownership is held by many thousands of "investors." The boards no longer represent the owner, or indeed anyone in particular. As a result, board membership has lost its rationale. People are invited to sit on boards because of their name. Or worse, board members are recruited from people who do business with a company, such as the company's bankers or the company's lawyers. Above all, board members are being recruited from among successful corporate executives—and in return for the president of Company A accepting board membership at Company B, the president of Company B accepts board membership at Company A. These busy people do not have a large enough stake in the company to justify their spending much time on it. Or, if they are doing business with the company, they are understandably reluctant to probe into its affairs, to ask inconvenient questions, or to appear critical. They go through the motions. And they are likely to sit on so many boards that they cannot really do their homework.

Another reason is that the board cannot be what the law in most countries (other than those that followed the German law, e.g., Austria and Switzerland) says it is. It cannot be the *governing* body of the company. That is a full-time job. To try to do it on a part-time basis means that only trivia will even be looked at, let alone discussed.

A final factor in the steady decline of the board has surely been that top management, by and large, does not want a really effective board. An effective board demands top-management performance and removes top executives who do not perform adequately—this is its duty. An effective board asks inconvenient questions. An effective board insists on being informed *before* the event—this is its legal responsibility. An effective board will not unquestioningly accept the recommendations of top management but will want to know why. It will not rubber-stamp the personnel decisions of top management but will want to know, indeed to get personally acquainted with, alternative candidates for senior appointments. An effective board, in other words, insists on being effective. And this, to most top managements, appears to be a restraint, a limitation, an interference with "management prerogatives," and altogether a threat.

## Why Top Management Needs an Effective Board

Many top managements will argue that there is nothing wrong with the decline of the board. They are perfectly content to see the board become a legal fiction. Indeed they would be perfectly willing to see the board disappear altogether (and where the board is completely an "inside" board, that is, controlled entirely by members of top management, the board as such *has* disappeared).

But this is exceedingly shortsighted. It is becoming increasingly clear that top management will not—and in the large corporation must not—be permitted to operate without an effective and strong board. The alternative to top management's developing an effective board for its own needs and those of the enterprise, is the imposition by society of the wrong kind of board, especially on the large corporation. Such an imposed board will attempt to control top management and to dictate direction and decision. It will indeed become the "boss." It must consider itself an adversary of top management. It will not, indeed, cannot, act in the interest of the enterprise. The first signs of this are clearly around us—indeed, it may already be too late to reverse the trend.

The malfunction of the board first became apparent in the Germany of the Weimar Republic. And it is Germany also where the first outside control has been imposed on the boards of large companies, in the form of "co-determination," that is, of legally required worker representation on the board, first for companies in the coal and steel industries and then for all large businesses. Of course, no worker representative sits on German company boards; the members are trade union officials. But this does not alter the fact that the large-company board in Germany today has become a battleground for contending factions.

A different development, but one pointing in the same direction, is under way in Sweden, where government now appoints members to boards of the major banks. So far, people of stature and known integrity have been selected by and large. But once there are political appointees on the boards of individual companies, politics cannot be kept out of such appointments for very long. As soon as this happens, the board ceases to be able to work effectively as the review organ, the confidant, the advisor, and guide of top management. It becomes a regulator, an adversary. (Sweden, since 1972, also requires that employee representatives be elected to the boards of large companies, including banks.)

The proposed statutes for the "European" company combine the German and the Swedish approaches and call for boards controlled by government and employee representatives.

In the United States in the last few years there has been mounting pressure to make boards "relevant," that is, to appoint as board members representatives of all kinds of groups: Blacks, women, the poor, and so on. These appointees, no matter how distinguished the individual, cannot function as board members. Their role is to represent this or that outside group, this or that special interest. Their role must be to make demands on top management and to push special projects, special needs, and special policies. They cannot be concerned with, or responsible for, the enterprise. Nor should they be expected to hold in confidence what they hear at board meetings; in fact their trust is not to the enterprise but to their constituents outside.

These developments demonstrate that society will not allow top management, and especially top management of large and visible businesses, to exercise its power without an appropriate and effective board. The board, as it has been conceived originally—well over a century ago—has indeed outlived its usefulness. This, however, makes it an urgent top-management job to think through what kind of a board the enterprise and its top management need. The decay of the traditional board has created a vacuum. It will not remain unfilled.

## The Three Functions of the Board

There are actually three different tasks for which a company, and especially a large one, needs a functioning board.

1. The enterprise, first, does need a review organ. It needs a group of experienced people, people of integrity and stature, people of proven performance capacity and proven willingness to work, who counsel, advise, and deliberate with top management. It needs people who are not part of top management but who are available to it, and who can act with knowledge and decision in a crisis.

The big company is too important to society not to have a "control" in its own structure. Somebody has to make sure that top management thinks through what the company's business is and what it should be. Somebody has to make sure that objectives are being set and strategies are being developed. Somebody has to look critically at the planning of the company, its capital-investment policy, and its managed-expenditures budget. Somebody has to monitor people decisions and organization problems and has to be the "supreme court." Somebody has to watch the organization's spirit, has to make sure that it succeeds in utilizing the strengths of people and in neutralizing their weaknesses, that it develops tomorrow's managers and that its rewards to managers, its management tools and management methods strengthen the organization and direct it toward objectives.

Without such an organ of review, top management has no way to control itself. It has no true legitimacy. But management also needs someone to talk to. Everybody within a company always wants something from top management. And no outsider knows enough about the company, its business and its people.

To have someone to talk to is, above all, a top-management need in the small company where top management otherwise tends to be isolated. Small company managements, without easy, continuous access to outside advisors such as experienced lawyers and consultants, need to have available to them a few people who are experienced, who understand the business, and who are not yet part of it. Small-company top managements need, therefore, a true board of directors—yet small companies, as a rule, have even less of a functioning board than the large ones.

2. An effective and functioning board is needed to remove a top management that fails to perform.

A board capable of removing incompetent or nonperforming top managements has, of course, real power. But only a weak top management is afraid of it. And no society can tolerate top-management incompetence in its large businesses. If top managements do not build boards that will remove weak and incompetent chief executives, government will take over the job.

There is another alternative: the "takeover" by the "financial raider." Management experts and economists have been telling us for a long time that the top managements of large publicly held companies have become immune to stockholder control and that only coronary thrombosis or bankruptcy can dislodge a top management once it has established itself. This no longer holds.* Top managements—most of them seemingly all-powerful, seemingly deeply entrenched, seemingly in complete control—have been toppled by stockholder revolts organized by the financial raiders and their "takeover bids." The raiders did not aim at companies in trouble. They aimed in the main at companies that did not live up to their potential, companies the top managements of which did not perform adequately.

Unless top management builds into the company's structure an effective organ for its removal in case of nonperformance, the raider and his takeover bid will become an ever-present threat. A jackal is better than no scavenger.

Top executives are paid for performance. Their compensation is high because it includes a "risk premium." In any large company, especially where ownership is so widely diffused that there is no controlling interest, it is the duty of the board to review top-management performance regularly and in depth, and to remove top executives who do not measure up to very high demands. And this requires both a board familiar with the company, and a strong board.

3. Finally, the enterprise needs a "public and community relations" organ. It needs easy and direct access to its various "publics" and "constituents." It needs to hear from them and to be able to talk to them. The need is readily apparent for the big company, of course. But it may be even greater for the small or fair-sized company which is a major employer in a small or medium-sized community.

---

*For an analysis of the "takeover wave" and its meaning, see the essay "The New Markets and the New Entrepreneurs" in my book, *Men, Ideas and Politics*; English title *The New Markets*.

The central fact is that the modern enterprise has a multiplicity of constituencies. The shareholders are one. But they are no longer *the* one, as traditional legal theory has it. Instead of being "owners" they have become "investors." The employees are clearly also such a constituency, but they are not, as the German trade unions (or the "industrial community" laws in various Latin-American countries) assert, *the* constituency. There are also the communities where a major company has its plants. There are consumers, suppliers, and distributors. All of them need to know what goes on in a major business, what its problems, its policies, and its plans are. The business needs to be understood by them. Top management needs to be known by them, respected by them, accepted by them. Top management needs even more, perhaps, to understand what these constituencies want, understand, misunderstand, see, question.

Big companies are spending enormous sums on public relations. Yet the evidence is clear that they fail to make themselves understood by their publics and, worse, that they fail to understand their publics. Public relations as top-management press-agentry has failed. But this makes all the more important genuine public and community relations, aimed at understanding the public rather than at making it "love" a company and its top management. This requires that top management have access to, and can work with, people from these publics and constituencies whom it respects, but who are independent—people who, in turn, respect top management and know what it is trying to do. This means a public and community relations board that is built into the enterprise's structure and functions as an integral organ of top management.

The German trade unionist or the American consumer advocate has a point when he pushes for board representation for his constituency. He is wrong only in believing that his constituency is *the* constituency; it is one of many.

The governing board of directors must be a board that represents no one except the basic long-term interests of the enterprise. It must be capable of discharging its function as the review organ and as the supervisor of top-management performance.

But the enterprise also needs a board that is, in effect, an organ of information, advice, consultation, and communication—that is, the public and community relations board. If the enterprise and its top management do not create this board, it will be imposed on them in wrong and harmful form, that is, as an organ of antagonism, control, and restraint—which is what worker representation on the German board, government representation on the Swedish board, and minority-group representation on the American board are. That this will further undermine the board may be a minor matter. It will, however, also undermine the authority of company and top management, impair their integrity, and reduce their capacity to perform.

## What Is Needed

Clearly, two different organs are needed. One is the executive board which gives top management somebody to talk to, a review organ, a conscience, a counselor, an advisor—but also an informed and prepared "stand-by" in case there is "power failure," that is, failure of a company's top management or need to find successors to today's top management.

The other organ is the public and community relations board which gives a company, and especially a large one, access to its various publics.

There is no reason why these two could not legally be one body. But they have to operate differently. With its public and community relations board, top management needs to discuss what the various publics want, need to know, and need to understand. With its executive board top management needs to discuss what top management itself needs to discuss, what top management itself needs to think through, needs to decide, needs to understand. One way to satisfy the need for two boards is to have the executive board operate as a special committee—an executive committee—of a big board.

There are effective boards in existence. None so far fulfills adequately all three of the board's functions. Even so, however, they demonstrate the importance of an effective board and the contribution it can make.

One example is the small but exceedingly effective boards of the Wallenberg Companies, affiliated with Stockholm's Enskilda Bank in Sweden. Marcus Wallenberg, who led the Enskilda Bank in the period after World War II, insisted on clear definition of top management's place and functions in the companies in which the bank played a leading role. This then enabled him to build strong boards, which made a major contribution to the affairs of each company. The tremendous economic growth of Sweden—and especially of the Wallenberg Companies—in the post-World War II period, is in no small measure the result of Wallenberg's insistence on an effective board based on a clear definition of the top-management job.

Another example is the rise of Merck & Company, a small and fairly obscure drug house before World War II, to leadership in the American pharmaceutical industry. In large part this was brought about by one member of the board of directors, Vannevar Bush. Bush, who had been a distinguished scientist at M.I.T. and then chief scientific administrator in America's World War II effort, joined the Merck board as a part-time chairman with the specific assignment to think through what the top management of the company should be and should do. One of his conclusions was the need for an effective board which could both review and guide top management, and could create access for it to major publics such as the scientific community. And this, in turn, led to a long-range strategy for Merck which, within a decade, gave a company that had started far behind the old pros in its industry worldwide leadership in an extremely competitive industry.

What is needed for an effective board is first careful thinking through of the top-management function and of the function and work of the board. It requires objectives and a work plan for the board. Unless the board is set up to discharge specific functions with clear objectives, it will not perform.

## Who Belongs on a Board?

This requires thinking through who belongs on the board. Some of the people who today are being put on boards—e.g., the company's bankers and underwriters—belong on the public and community relations board. The financial community is a constituent. Management needs to have access to it, be understood by it, and understand it. But very few other people who today sit on boards should be considered eligible for membership on either the public and community relations board or the review and appeals board.

Neither, for instance, should contain former company officers who have retired. It will be argued that to exclude former senior managers from board membership is to deprive the company of a great deal of knowledge and wisdom. But the right way to keep available to a management the knowledge and wisdom of one of its retired elder statesmen is the Japanese practice of retaining such a man as a "counselor." Similarly, no one who sells anything to the company, whether goods or services, such as suppliers, lawyers, or consultants, should be a member of the board.

Who, then, should be a board member? So far we can answer this question only for membership on the review and appeals board.

The first requirement is competence. Board members should have proven their ability as senior executives—whether in a business, in government service, or in other institutions. Ideally, the board member of the future will be in his (or her) mid-fifties and willing to step out of operating to become an advisor, a guide, a conscience.

Second, board members should have time for the job. In fact, no one can really do the job well if he sits on more than a small number of boards—maybe four or five at the most.

Georg Siemens, a century ago, knew this. He limited himself to a few boards and promptly stepped down when he considered that he had accomplished the mission for which he had originally joined a board. His successors, however, forgot this—one of the more recent chief executives of the Deutsche Bank sat on well above a hundred boards. No matter how brilliant and how well supported by a secretariat, no man can possibly do his homework sitting on more than four or five boards.

This then clearly means that the effective board member has to be a "professional director." Indeed, board membership should be recognized as a full-time profession for a really first-rate man. And it should be paid as such, i.e., by a fee and not by stock options or a share in the profits.

Finally, board members should be independent of management. This probably implies election for a limited period of years after which a man would not be eligible for re-election. If a man knows that he will not be re-elected after five years, no matter how well he gets along with the management whom he serves as a board member, he is unlikely to find it necessary to be subservient. At the same time, board members should be elected for definite periods and should have reasonable security of tenure during that period.

How to build the communications and community relations board we do not yet know. But it is just as urgent. Politically—as witness the German, Swedish, American, and "Euroboard" developments—it may be more urgent. Surely the traditional attitude of management, i.e., to resist any development that would introduce the public and community relations function into the board can no longer be maintained. However justified it may have been, it will not work any longer.

The choice is no longer between having a nonboard, which is what we are having today, by and large, and an effective board. It is between a board imposed on enterprise and both hostile and inappropriate to it and a board that is an effective organ of the enterprise and appropriate to its needs.

# Strategies and Structures

The job, task, and responsibilities of worker and foreman in the plant, key-punch operator and secretary in the office, metallurgist in the engineering lab, field salesman and branch manager of a bank or insurance company are little affected by size, complexity, growth, or diversity. Even innovation has an effect on most people in an organization only after it has become accomplished fact. But the structure, the behavior, the tasks, and the strategies of top management are profoundly molded by changes in size and complexity, by diversification, growth, and innovation. And, in turn, top management—and only top management—can make the strategic decisions that lead to growth, diversification, or innovation. The managerial strategies that relate to a company's basic structure have received almost no attention. They may, however, be of greater importance than strategies with respect to finances, product-development, or marketing on which the discussion has focused. Size, diversity, complexity, growth, and innovation are, above all, *managerial* challenges and opportunities to top management and make *managerial* demands on it.

# 53

## On Being the Right Size*

*The Law of Surface and Mass—Size and Complexity—Why Changes in Size Are "Quantum Jumps"—Size and Strategy—Size and Complexity as Top-Management Tasks*

The surface of any object increases with the square of its diameter, the mass with the diameter's cube. As the diameter goes from 2 to 3 to 4, the mass goes from 8 to 27 to 64, while the surface increases only from 4 to 9 to 16.

This elementary law of geometry is of profound importance to management. It means that size, structure, and strategy are closely related. Different sizes require different structures, different policies, different strategies, and different behaviors. There are right sizes and wrong sizes for different businesses. The law implies that there is a finite limit to size beyond which an organization declines in productivity and ultimately ceases to be manageable. It finally implies that changes in size are not continuous but that, at a point in growth, there has to be an "evolutionary leap," a genuine transformation.

For biological organisms, the implications of the law of surface and mass were worked out by a British biologist.† Thompson proved that beyond a point in size—and a fairly early one at that—the hardened skin of the insect can no longer support the mass. A skeleton is required. Thompson also proved that there are finite limits to size. If the elephant were to grow much

*With apologies to J.B.S. Haldane, whose 1928 essay of the same title on biological organisms remains the most perceptive discussion of the relationship between size, function, and structure.

†D'Arcy Thompson, *On Growth and Form* (Cambridge, 1917).

larger, legs sturdy enough to support the animal's weight would be too massive to be lifted.

Social organisms may be far too complex to allow neat quantitative formulae for their sizes.* But in a social organism, too, "mass" always increases much faster than "surface." "Weight," too, therefore goes up faster than the supporting structure. As a result, changes in size are not merely quantitative. They are changes in quality. There are, as a result, "right" and "wrong" sizes; that is, sizes which require a structure that is appropriate to performance and function, and sizes in which the structure needed to support the mass is inadequate or inappropriate and becomes an impediment. And there is a finite limit to size. There are organizations that are simply too big to function (as Gallant and Prothero tried to demonstrate for the giant university).

The law of surface and mass implies an inescapable relationship between size and complexity. The bigger the organism grows, the further away will be the bulk of its mass from the outside environment. The more will it therefore need specialized and complex organs to supply it with the essentials of life. Again, there is a finite limit to complexity. Beyond a certain point the complexity becomes more than structure, no matter how designed, can support.

The human body, for instance, has reached the limit of its evolution with respect to brain size. Were the brain to become bigger or more complex, the oxygen supply needed to sustain it would require such high blood pressure as to kill man in order to keep him alive.

In social organization, such as a business, growth in size soon requires disproportionate increase in complexity and more and more specialized organs. Soon organs have to be developed that take care of the "inside," that is, organs that inform and direct the increasing mass and "feed back" to it from the increasingly remote outside the results of its own "inside" activities. The larger any body, physical or social, becomes, the more of its energy will be needed to keep the "inside" that is, its own mechanisms, alive and functioning. Again, mere quantity soon becomes a change in quality.

The reciprocal relationship also holds. The more complex the organization, the more does it have to be organized on the structural principle of larger size. Size determines complexity. But complexity, in turn, determines size. The law of surface and mass implies that change from one kind of size to another, or from one kind of complexity to another, is not continuous.

---

*The first attempt to work out a "law of size" for social structures is an article, "Weight Watching at the University: The Consequence of Growth," by J. A. Gallant and J. W. Prothero (*Science*, Vol. 175, No. 4020, January 28, 1972). The authors concluded that a university becomes too large to educate students and to be manageable once it grows beyond 15,000 to 20,000 students in enrollment.

It is a "threshold" phenomenon. There is a point at which a transformation has to take place.

The skeleton of the higher animals did not evolve out of the insect's hard skin. And the early hominoids, our remote ancestors, had to develop a brain a good deal larger than their own needs required before they could make the next evolutionary step to walking upright, to making tools, or to using fire.

Beyond a point in size or complexity quantity demands a "quantum jump," a transformation in quality rather than a mere addition.

This is what Henry Ford failed to understand when he believed that he could continue to run his company without management and managers despite its giant size. For management is an "evolutionary leap." It did not evolve from the single proprietor any more than the skeleton evolved from the insect's hard skin.

This is what people usually do not understand when they talk of "delegation," that is, when they imply that managers do their job as part of the job of top management or as part of the job of the board of directors. "Delegation" always implies that the delegator can take back the delegated task. But the cells of the higher animals cannot take back the function of the brain. It is not delegated, but is an autonomous function of its own.

Similarly, every managerial job, if properly designed, is not delegated but is a function of its own with its own authority. It is the result of an evolutionary leap rather than an extension of what is already being done.

## Size and Strategy

Size by itself has major impact on strategy. And strategy, in turn, has major impact on size. The small organization can do things the large ones cannot do. Its simplicity and its small size should give it fast response, agility, and the ability to focus its resources. But the large organization, in turn, also can do things the small organization cannot do. It can commit resources for a much longer time, for instance, to long-term research projects which are beyond the staying power of the small business. The question "What strategies befit different sizes?" is thus of crucial importance to top management.

But, in turn, different strategies also require different sizes. A business that aims at a leadership position in a major, let alone a worldwide, market, clearly has to be a large business. But even in a big market, a business which aims at filling a special and limited niche better remain small.

One example of such a business would be Rolls-Royce, which in one of the world's largest markets, the automobile market, has carved out for itself a small but exceedingly profitable niche where it is practically without competition, but where it also cannot grow beyond modest size.*

The relationship between size and strategy is further complicated by the fact that the "big" business may actually be a confederation of fair-sized or even of small businesses, each with its own strategies and its own markets. Then the business needs to think through in effect two strategies, a number of "small-business strategies" for each of its constituent units, and a "big-business strategy" for the business overall. Complexity then becomes a major factor.

The individual employee, whether rank-and-file or managerial, is not primarily affected by the questions of size and complexity. The worker on the machine, the key-punch operator, the billing clerk, the heat-treating specialist, or the plant manager do the same job whether the company is small or huge, simple or complex. Size and complexity become problems, first, in the upper reaches of middle management and especially for senior professionals. They affect their work, yet they, in turn, have little impact on, and practically no responsibility for, the decisions on size and complexity.

Size and complexity are above all top-management problems and require top-management decisions.

Public-service institutions also stand under the laws of size and complexity. For them too (as mentioned earlier with respect to the university) there is a right size and a wrong size. The also applies to "service staff" within a business. That a "conscience activity" requires small size, and preferably a one-man staff, was argued earlier (Chapter 42). A staff that is supposed to teach and to innovate in a functional area—marketing, for instance, or the management of people—had better be small, otherwise its internal complexity will force its ablest people to become "administrators" instead of being teachers and innovators. And in a staff service within an organization, size and structure should always be adjusted to fit the needs of the desired strategy and to serve the objectives of the work. In a staff service, above all, size and complexity must be managed—or strategy and objectives suffer.

Top management needs to know, first, what size its company is. Top management needs to know what size its business should be. It needs to

*This refers, of course, only to the Rolls-Royce automobile business. The Rolls-Royce aircraft business, which caused the company's bankruptcy in 1971, is, however, also an example of the relationship between size and strategy. For here, Rolls-Royce suffered from being far too small in size and resources for the leadership role it aimed at in the world's jet-engine business. In the aircraft-engine market Rolls-Royce was the "wrong size."

know whether its business is the right size or the wrong size. It needs to know whether the structure is appropriate to the company's size and complexity. It needs to know what top management's own job is in companies of different sizes and complexities.

And it needs to relate size and complexity to company strategy. It might have to decide that the company, as it now stands, is not capable of carrying out its strategy. It may even have to decide that the company, as it now stands, is not viable because it is of an incurably wrong size. And top management needs to know what follows from such findings and what alternatives of strategy and behavior are available to the company. For, unlike biological organisms, a social organization such as a business does not have a size entirely determined by forces over which it has no control.

There are minimum sizes below which a business in a given industry or market is simply not viable. There are maximum sizes beyond which a business, no matter how well managed, will not, in the long run, prosper. But in between—and the range is very wide indeed—size and complexity have to be considered as "business objectives." Like all other objectives they are not "under the control" of management in the sense that what is desirable is also, therefore, attainable, let alone already achieved. Like all other business objectives, attaining the right size requires hard thinking and serious, consistent work.

Specifically, there are five major areas to be considered:

1. Managing smallness and bigness—that is, the management requirements of size by itself. "How big is big?" "What are 'right' sizes and what are 'wrong' sizes?" "What are the limits beyond which further growth is degenerative?" And, "What are the implications of size for business strategy?"

2. The second major area is the management of complexity and diversity. "How complex is complex?" "How complex is too complex?" And, "What requirements does complexity make?"

A separate problem in complexity that deserves some discussion is that of the limits on the family-owned business. "Can it perpetuate itself?" "Can it grow beyond small size?" And, "What are its limits in time and size?"

3. A special case of complexity, so important as to deserve a separate chapter, is the most complex of business organizations, the multinational corporation. For here is added to complexities of size, markets, products, and technologies, the complexities of cultures and the complexities of multiple political and governmental relationships and restraints.

4. Managing change and growth is the next major topic. "At what point in change and growth does management have to change its characteristics, its structure, its behavior?" And, "How can it prepare itself so that it is ready for change and for growth without, at the same time, overloading the

company with functions and complexities which, at the present state of the business, it does not require and can ill afford?"

5. Managing innovation is a topic in itself.

"Man is the only animal capable of purposeful evolution; he makes tools." This insight of Alfred Russel Wallace, co-discoverer with Darwin of the principle of evolution, means that man and his social organizations can innovate. They can create, so to speak, a different animal. Indeed, in a changing environment their survival depends on their capacity to innovate. What does an innovative organization have to be and how does it have to be structured and managed?

It is with these topics that the next chapters will concern themselves.

# 54

## Managing the Small, the Fair-Sized, the Big Business

*How Big Is Big?—No Measurement Truly Adequate—Size Is a "Configuration"—Management Structure, the One Criterion of Size—The Three Categories: Small, Fair-Sized, and Big—Managing the Small Business—The Need for a Distinct Niche—Structuring the Top-Management Tasks—Making the Top Man Effective—Control and Information in the Small Business—The Fair-Sized Business—The Three Types—Their Specific Requirements—The Danger of Becoming Flabby—The Need for Self-Discipline—The Big Business—An Impersonal Business—The Need for Structure—The Need for Clarity—Organizing "Disorder"—The Role of the "Old Boy Network"—The Role of the Task Force Team—The Danger of Becoming Inbred—The Danger of Exclusive "Promotion from Within"—Size as a Top-Management Challenge*

### How Big Is Big?

Nothing would seem simpler than to know how big a business is. Everybody, after all, knows that the corner grocery store is "small" and that the General Electric Company or the Deutsche Bank is "big." But things are by no means so simple.

In 1966, the Small Business Administration, an agency of the U.S. Government, ruled that the American Motors Company was a small business and therefore entitled to borrow on special and highly advantageous terms. At that time, American Motors was sixty-third in size among all American manufacturing companies and was among the world's one hundred largest manufacturing companies. It had sales of a billion dollars and about 30,000 employees. Yet the government ruling was not entirely irrational. In the

American automobile industry, American Motors was indeed a midget. Its sales were no more than one-twentieth of that of the industry's leader, General Motors. Even Chrysler, next to American Motors smallest U.S. auto maker, had seven times the sales of American Motors. With no more than 3 or 4 percent of the American automobile market, American Motors was so small as to be in danger of collapse.

American Motors was, of course, not a small business at the time, nor is it today. It was something quite different—a big business that is the wrong size. Yet the example shows that size is not mere quantity and that indeed it is far from obvious in many cases what size a business really is.

The traditional measurement of business size is the number of employees. For many years the U.S. Department of Commerce in its industry analyses defined a small business as one that has fewer than a certain number of employees—originally around 300 to 500. The number of employees is important. Once the number of employees goes beyond 1,000, for instance, systematic personnel administration becomes necessary. A business employing over 1,000 people requires policies and procedures which are not normally considered as pertaining to a small business. Yet there are businesses that are very modest in total employment and yet are quite clearly fair-sized, if not big businesses. And there are businesses that are quite small in their basic management requirements and yet have many more then 1,000 employees.

A management consulting firm with 300 or 400 professional consultants working out of a dozen offices is, in terms of employees, a small business. In terms of its management requirements, it is a very big business indeed. A worldwide accounting firm, such as Price Waterhouse, with 4,000 or 5,000 professional employees working in thirty countries—or one of the multinational advertising agencies which grew so rapidly during the 1960s —is actually a giant business. It may well be at, if not beyond the limit of manageability, even though in terms of employees it is medium-sized.

But there are also such examples as a multinational manufacturing company, headquartered in one of the small European countries which manufactures and sells highly engineered precision equipment for the heavy apparatus and machinery industry. The entire company has only 1,800 employees working in about ten countries, with no office or plant having more than 300 or 400 people. Manufacturing employment is almost minuscule—a total of 400 men in five plants. The rest are design engineers, service engineers, metallurgists, and so on. This company, despite its small employment, is a fairly big business and has to be run as such; it is complex beyond its size.

In contrast, there are businesses employing a great many people which are essentially small or, at best, fair-sized companies.

One example is a highly specialized American company which, in a major region of the country, has leadership position in one branch of insurance. There are 4,000 or 5,000 people on the payroll, most of them salesmen and claims adjusters. In its basic characteristics, however, this is still a fairly small business. There are no more than two levels of management, the management at the headquarters of the company, and the general managers of each of the fourteen districts. The "feel" of the company is clearly "small business."

Rolls-Royce, in its automotive business, is also a small business turning out a few thousand cars a year, with a handful of major distributors throughout the world and with a management structure of the utmost simplicity.

No other yardstick does any better than employment as a measurement of size. Sales, for instance, while used widely, is quite misleading. A chemical company with $30 million of sales may be a fairly big business. A metalworking company with the same sales volume may be actually so small as to be hardly viable.

Most of the sales volume of the typical chemical company is "value added." But the typical metalworking company tends to be an assembler rather than a manufacturer. Two-thirds or more of its sales volume may actually be represented by parts and supplies which it buys from others.

Businesses may be very much larger and rank high in terms of sales and yet be small or, at best, fair-sized.

American Home Products Company, in the 1950s, was already, in terms of its sales, a very large company, selling then about a half a billion dollars' worth of goods a year. Yet the company's top management consisted of four men who worked practically without staff: a chairman, a president, a financial vice-president, and a personnel vice-president. The company had six to eight divisions, each a sizable business in its own field, but all engaged in the same basic business, the manufacturing, promotion, and distribution of branded products through retail stores. It could be run as a simple, and indeed almost as a small, business, and was run successfully in that fashion.

Another similar example—also from the 1950s—was the automotive business of A. O. Smith in Milwaukee, the leading supplier of passenger-car frames to the American automobile industry. Sales of this business, then the main division of the company, were around $200 million, with employment well above 20,000. Yet in its "feel," but also in its strategy and structure, this was a fair-sized business. It required excellence in cost control, in manufacturing, and in scheduling deliveries to the customers and their many plants scattered around the country. But, being a single-product business with one technology, one market, and with only a handful of customers, the business could be managed by one chief executive with all the rest of his people functional managers or specialists. It required neither elaborate controls nor central staffs, nor any of the appurtenances of bigness.

Even for companies in the same industry sales figures are not always a reliable indicator of size. One of the large American rubber companies, for instance, used to sell the bulk of its output through its own wholly owned retail stores. The sales figure, therefore, was based on the retail value of its products, and especially of automobile tires. Another leading American rubber company, however, sold practically nothing directly to the public. It either sold tires to the automobile companies as original equipment for new cars, or it sold tires under "private labels" to the large petroleum companies for distribution through their service stations. Its sales volume, therefore, represented manufacturer's value, which in the rubber industry is a good deal less than half of what the final consumer pays. According to its sales figures, the second company was much smaller than the first company, whereas in actual output, but also in return on investment, it was by far the larger business.

But even "value added" is not an adequate measurement. For it can be applied only to manufacturing companies. "Value added" is a meaningless concept for a retail business, for a bank, for a life insurance company, and for any other business which is not primarily engaged in manufacturing.

In sum: size is a configuration rather than a single aspect of a business. To determine whether a company is small or big, one needs to look at a number of factors: employment, sales, value added (where applicable), the complexity and diversity of its product range, the number of markets it is engaged in, the complexity of its technology, and so on. But one also has to look at the structure of the industry in which it operates, and at its share of its markets, and a number of other factors, none of them by itself decisive.

The one true expression of this configuration which is size is management and management structure. A small business is a business which requires *at most* one man who does nothing but top-management work and who is not engaged in any of the functional work required.

This, however, tells us what ought to be, rather than what is. A business is not necessarily small because the entire top-management task is vested in one man. It may very well be a big business that is structured the wrong way; Henry Ford's company was one example. In turn, a business that has a big top-management structure may still be a small business in which the top-management job has been misorganized. Examples abound.

There is only one criterion which, with fair reliability, indicates whether a business is small, fair-sized, or big. In a genuinely small business, the man at the top knows who the few people are in the organization in whom responsibility for key results rests without having to consult the records or any of his associates. He knows what their assignments are. He knows their backgrounds, their previous assignments, and how well they have performed in them. He knows what they can do. He also knows their limitations—or at least he thinks he does. And he knows, as a rule, what their next assignment is likely to be. This, of course, means that the key group is a small one. Regardless of title and position, it can hardly exceed twelve to fifteen men, which is about the largest number one man can really know and can really be familiar with.

In a fair-sized business—the next and in some ways the most important category of business—the one man at the top can no longer by himself identify and really know every one of the truly important men in the organization. This requires a group of three or four men together. Typically, in the fair-sized organization, the top man, when asked to name his key people, will bring in a few of his closest associates and will answer the question with them collectively rather than individually. In a fair-sized organization the number of key people who are known to be crucial to the performance and results of the organization may run to forty or fifty.

Any business in which even a small group at the top no longer knows, without consultation with others or without consulting charts or records, who the crucial people are, where they are, where they have come from, what they are doing, and where they are likely to go, is a big business.

It is this test which shows that the management consulting firm with 300 or 400 professionals on its staff is a big business. It is this test which shows that American Home Products in the 1950s was a fair-sized company despite its $500 million of sales. And it is this test which also shows that the multinational precision-engineering company mentioned above, despite its very small employment, is close to being a big business and has to be run as such.

This test is neither infallible nor precise. But it focuses on the one and only genuine characteristic of size: the management structure it requires.

## Managing the Small Business

For a hundred years we have been told by eminent authorities that small business is being gobbled up by the "giants" and is about to disappear. For a hundred years this has proven to be nonsense. The small business is doing just as well as it did a hundred years ago. The figures show clearly that proportionately neither the importance nor the number of small businesses —but also of big businesses—has changed very much since 1900, despite all the dire prophecies of monopoly, and all the fears of "undue concentration of economic power."

Small business and big business are not alternatives. They are complements. The big business depends on small and medium-sized businesses, who in turn depend on a big business. (This seems to be just as true in communist economies in which all businesses are owned and managed by the government as it is in free-enterprise economies.) Typically, there is, for instance, a big manufacturer, say, an automobile company such as General Motors, Volkswagen, or Toyota. But this company depends on a host of suppliers and subcontractors who are mostly small or fair-sized. It depends on a host of dealers, who again are small or fair-sized. The large retailers such as Sears, Roebuck, Marks & Spencer, and the department store chains in Japan, depend on a host of small manufacturers, who in turn depend on the big stores for access to the market. There is no economic chain in a modern economy that is composed entirely of big businesses, but also no economic chain that is composed entirely of small businesses. Businesses of different sizes are interdependent, with the small ones often requiring a large one, and the large one in turn dependent on small ones.

## What the Small Business Needs

Not so long ago it was widely believed that the small business needed little or no attention to management. Management was then thought to be for the "big boys." One still hears people in a small business saying, "Management? That's for General Electric; we are small and simple enough to do without attention to management." But this is delusion. The small business needs organized and systematic management even more than the big business. It does not need, to be sure, large central staffs. It does not need elaborate procedures and techniques in many areas. In fact, it can afford neither large staffs nor elaborate procedures. But it does need management of a high order.

In the first place, it needs *strategy*. The small business cannot afford to become marginal. Yet this is its perennial danger. It must therefore think through a strategy which gives it distinction. It must, to speak in biological terms, find its specific ecological niche in which it has an advantage and can therefore withstand competition. This specific niche may be leadership in a distinct market, whether it is defined by geography, consumer needs, or consumer values. The strategy may lie in a specific excellence, such as a capacity to give service. Or it may lie in a specific technology.

An example of such an ecological niche is a small pharmaceutical company in the United States which has more than held its own in an industry led by multinational giants. By concentrating on the need of the opthalmologist in the treatment of his patients, and especially on the needs of the ophthalmological surgeon, the company has carved out an ecological niche in which, while not without competition, it has established strong leadership.

And there is also the Checker Cab Company, which does nothing but manufacture taxicabs for major American cities. Checker produces only 4,000 cars a year. But while American Motors with eighty times that volume is marginal, Checker Cab is a leader.

The strategy of a small business may also focus on excellence in a small but vital area of service. In a period in which the large supermarket chains in the United States did, by and large, rather poorly, a small number of regional chains, some in the East and some on the West Coast, showed extraordinary results. In every case this rested on a decision on the part of their managers to concentrate and to build excellence in one area. Typically, one of them decided that in the vast array of processed branded foods, it could not offer anything the giants could not do just as well. But it could offer what the giants, by virtue of their size, would find very difficult to offer: really first-rate meat and truly courteous service. And these are exactly what supermarket customers value the most.

But businesses that are even smaller also need a strategy and can develop one.

The suburban areas surrounding the major cities of the United States are, as a rule, oversupplied with real estate agents, most of whom just eke out a living. But in one area, one real estate agent has developed a small but exceedingly profitable business by thinking through a strategy for leadership. When he first started out around 1950, this man took a close look at his area and found that its leading "industry" was higher education. While many of the residents commuted into the big city nearby, a sizable and affluent group consisted of the teachers in twenty-odd universities and colleges, most of them small, but a few quite large. Of all occupational groups in the United States, young college faculty may have the highest turnover. Typically, the young college professor takes a job for a few years, after which he moves to another institution elsewhere. In total, the twenty colleges and universities in the area hire each year more than five hundred new people, while an equal number leave. The young real estate man decided to concentrate on this market and developed for it the services it needs. He also realized that he could get direct access to his market with a minimum of cost. For, of course, the names of all the new teachers hired as well as the names of those who will be leaving at the end of the academic year are known to the colleges many months before they actually move. And each college is only too happy to hand over the difficult and irritating job of finding housing for new faculty to a reliable man. As a result this real estate agent does almost three times the business that an office of his size usually handles and with a minimum of expense. His total volume, about 500 to 1,000 houses a year, is still modest, but his net profit is almost four times that of the typical suburban realtor.

These, to be sure, are highly atypical examples. For the typical small business has no strategy. The typical small business is not "opportunistic," it is "problematical"—it lives from problem to problem. But the typical small business is also, as a result, not a successful business.

The first requirement in managing a small business is therefore to ask and answer the question "What is our business—and what should it be?"

The second requirement is that small business organize and structure the *top-management tasks.* A small business is defined as a business which requires at most one full-time top manager who does nothing else. In fact, in most small businesses, the top man also carries some functional responsibility and usually should do so. But this makes it all the more necessary for the small business to identify the key activities which are needed to attain the objectives of the business and to make sure that they are being assigned to somebody who is accountable. Otherwise key activities will not be done at all.

Most small businesses think that they know what the key activities are. Most small businesses also believe that they take care of the key activities. But even superficial analysis usually reveals that they deceive themselves. Everybody may talk about the key activities but nobody pays much attention to them. They are seen but not perceived—and as a result usually neglected. The need is rarely for more staff. The need is for a little thought, a little organization, and a simple reporting and control system—no more than a checklist, perhaps—to make sure that the work is actually being done.

This also means, in effect, that even a small business needs a top-management team. Most of its members will be engaged on top-management tasks part-time. Their primary duties are likely to be functional. But the small business, as much as any other—and perhaps more than most—needs to make sure that its entire management group knows what the key activities are, what the goals in each are, and who is responsible for getting the work done.

Everybody in a small and highly specialized business supplying lawn-care products, such as grass seeds, fertilizers, and pesticides, to the suburban homeowner, "knew" what the key activities were: manufacturing and selling, obviously. But the first time that someone asked the question, it turned out that the key activities were different—they were research on how the consumer in the American suburb looks at the lawn, and does the work on the lawn. It was research on what the consumer expects and considers value. It was promotion both to the dealer and to the consumer. It was packaging to make it possible for dealers to move the company's products without having to "sell" them, and so on. Nobody was surprised—in fact, it was all "obvious." But nobody up to that time had actually taken the trouble to put down the obvious. As a result, no one was responsible for any of the key activities. It took little time to identify the key activities and not much more time to make sure that each was lodged in the existing structure and made the responsibility of someone already in management. The company itself credits its rapid growth and success, in the years since, to its identifying the key activities and building them into the management structure.

The small business has limited resources, above all, of good men. Concentration is therefore essential to it. And unless the key activities are clearly identified and assigned as responsibilities, there will be diffusion of resources rather than concentration.

The small business needs to pay special attention to making the top man effective. Even if he is free from functional work and can devote all his time to the top-management tasks, the load on him is likely to be heavy. He is certain to be under relentless pressure from all kinds of demands—from major customers and from employees; from suppliers and from banks. Unless he takes responsibility for his own job, his energies will not be used properly.

The first questions to ask are "What is the top man really good at?" "What is it that he can do better than anybody else in the business?" And, "What, among the things he is really good at, are crucial and are essential to the survival and success of the business?" In the top-management team, the specific job assignment to any one member should, as has been said before (Chapter 50) reflect personality. The small business needs to ask: "Which of the key activities are the ones the top man himself should take?" Analysis of the key activities should be impersonal and objective; but assignments, and especially the assignment of that part which the top man himself handles, has to be based on what the individual excels in.

In many small, and especially in small and growing, businesses, the top man is criticized by his associates for spending his time on the wrong things. If by that they mean that the key activities of the business are not being taken care of, their criticism is well taken. But often they mean that he is using his strengths and tackling the activities he is particularly good at, whereas other and equally important key activities are not being done by him. Then the answer is not to talk a man who, for instance, is not very good at handling people but excellent at finance into letting the controller do the finance work, while he himself takes on the management of people. The answer is to recognize that a top man gifted in the financial area is a major asset. But then, somebody else better take over the people responsibility which is a key activity and has to be discharged.

The top man in a small business has to structure his job so as to have time for two tasks which nobody else can carry. He has to have time for the key people in the company. And, he has to have time for the "outside," that is, for the market, the customer, the technologies. He has to make sure that he does not become desk-bound.

A major strength of small business is the ability of the man at the top to know every one of the key people, their ambitions, their aspirations, their way of thought and action, their strengths and their limitations, their performance record, and their potential. This requires time. Above all, it requires unstructured time; that is, time without a specific agenda, time not spent on a "problem."

The same goes for the time needed for the outside. A small business needs a strategy for leadership in a small but defined area. This requires intimate acquaintance with the outside. If the business aims at leadership in supplying taxicabs, as the Checker Cab Company does, it requires time to spend with the licensing authorities of the major cities whose specifications create the market for the company. It requires time with the owners of taxi fleets. It perhaps even requires time with taxicab drivers and passengers.

Most top men in small businesses will protest that they already spend too much time outside the office. They are forever on the road. They themselves often handle the big accounts, for instance. They usually have to negotiate whatever loans they need from the bank. But they need outside time of a different kind. They need time to keep themselves informed on their market, on new opportunities, on changes that affect the business. They need time to be able to answer the question "And what should our business be?" Again, this does not require many hours. But it does require systematic, purposeful work that is different in character from the daily operating routine.

Finally, the small business needs its own control and information system. Its resources are limited, in both men and money. It has to make sure that its resources are deployed where they bring in results. Its ability to get additional resources is equally limited. It therefore needs to make sure that it will not outrun its financial base. It needs to know well in advance when and where its financial needs will increase. The small business cannot afford to find itself in a liquidity squeeze and with a sudden demand for more money. Even if the business prospers, it takes time, as a rule, to provide additional financing.

The small business also needs to know major changes in its environment. It depends for its success on its preferred position in a small ecological niche. It therefore needs to know any possibility of changes in this niche.

The usual accounting information, while needed, is not enough. The small business needs to know where each of its key people is positioned and whether he is assigned to "results" or to "problems." It needs to know the productivity of its scarce resources—the productivity of people; the productivity of capital; and the productivity of raw materials and supplies. It needs to know how its business is distributed among its customers: does it, for instance, depend for its business on two or three large customers with the rest of its business splintered among many hundred small ones? And to what extent is it therefore vulnerable?

Special mention should be given here to the financial and economic information the small business needs and usually does not have. To be sure, small businesses today are likely to have the conventional accounting figures. Few, however, know their cash flow, and even fewer are in a position to forecast tomorrow's cash needs. They all know, or should know, their receivables. But they do not, as a rule, know whether their customers, their distributors and dealers, are building up their inventories of the company's products. They need, therefore, a little information about the ultimate market for their goods, that is, consumer purchases from dealers.

Again, a small business needs very few figures. And most of the figures it needs are easy to obtain, especially as precision is rarely needed. But the figures the small business needs the most to be managed are not, as a rule, figures the ordinary accounting model provides. They are figures which relate the present condition of the company and the present deployment of its key resources to anticipated future developments, both to identify opportunities and to ward off danger.

The small business cannot afford "big management," if by that is meant an abundance of staff, of procedures, and of figures. But it needs first-rate management. It needs to structure the top-management job precisely because it cannot afford an elaborate top-management structure.

## The Fair-Sized Business

In many respects the fair-sized business is the ideal business. It should enjoy the advantages both of being small and of being big. People still know each other and can easily get together. Teamwork organizes itself and should require no special effort. Everybody should understand what his job is and what he is expected to contribute. At the same time, resources are already adequate to support key activities and to obtain excellence in those areas where excellence is required and produces results. And the fair-sized business is big enough to obtain whatever economies of scale there are. The fair-sized business is the "middle class" in the Aristotelian sense: the position in business society which is most secure, most enjoyable, and most productive.

The fair-sized business should also be the easiest business to manage. In fact, observance of the simple rules that make a small business manageable should be enough. Yet the fair-sized business also has its own challenges and its own problems. It needs its own management rules.

There are actually three different types of fair-sized businesses. One is exemplified by the automotive division of the A. O. Smith Company, mentioned above, as it was in the 1950s: a fair-sized business with a narrow product range, one technology, and one major market. This, in many ways, is basically a small business but one with a larger key personnel group than any one man can really know.

The second type is also typified by an example already given: that of the American Home Products Company of twenty years ago in which a fair-sized—almost a big—business is composed of a number of autonomous small businesses, each with its own product lines and its own markets, but with the same basic economic characteristics.

And then there is a third fair-sized business in which there are separate businesses with separate markets which, however, are mutually dependent on each other.

The best example is a Japanese one. The privately owned electric railroad —known as the Hankyu Line—which Ichizo Kobayashi built around 1910 to connect Osaka and Kobe was a small business. But then Kobayashi started a real estate company which developed commuter suburbs along the railroad's right of way, both as a business in itself and to generate traffic for the railroad. Then Hankyu started big restaurants in its two main terminals. The next venture was popular theaters, especially the famous Girls' Opera at the terminus of one of the branch lines. A big department store on top of the Osaka station came next, and finally hotels. Each of these ventures was an independent, and highly successful, business. And each fed off the business generated by the others and provided customers for them. All exploited and, at the same time, increased the company's basic "franchise."

This last category is perhaps the one line of business to which the much-abused term "synergetic" should be applied. Each unit of such a company is a true business. But the businesses are also interdependent and comprise together one system, which is a business in its own right and has to be managed and measured as such.

All three of these types are fair-sized by the yardstick given above. In each of them, in other words, a small top-management group can and does know, without consulting organization charts and records, who the key people in the business are, what their assignments are, where they came from, what their strengths and limitations are, and where they are likely to go. But otherwise, they have different problems.

The central problem of the fair-sized one-product or one-market business, the A.O. Smith type of business, is organization structure. Such a business is, as a rule, already too large and too complex to be served adequately by the traditional functional organization. The symptoms of malorganization to look for in this kind of business are the symptoms of overextended functionalism: poor communication; functional parochialism; a long response time to new stimuli; the tendency to "solve problems" rather than to make decisions; and the tendency to tackle business challenges in terms of functional specialties rather than in terms of the direction and performance of the entire business.

Yet such a business cannot be organized in terms of federal decentralization. There are no autonomous profit and loss centers within it. This business has to apply simulated decentralization to what are, in effect, cost centers: e.g., manufacturing. Such a business also often should use the task force team as a supplementary organizational principle.

But top-management structure also is a problem in such a business. For such a business requires a top-management team. Yet it is usually organized in such a way that only one man is working full-time on the top-management job. The fair-sized, one-product or one-market, business will therefore have to build a top management in which a number of people are exclusively, or at least primarily, engaged in top-management work.

This is particularly true for what I call "conscience" work. The fair-sized business needs to think through the areas in which it requires excellence. In these areas—and only in them—it should, as a rule, have a few, a very few men whose job it is to think, to plan, to advise, and not to operate. Otherwise there is danger that the business will lose its excellence in key areas and will decline into middle-aged mediocrity.

The federally organized fair-sized business is the easiest to organize. It need not, as a rule, use any organization principles other than the functional principles for the individual businesses and the principle of federal decentralization for the overall company design. Teams, to be sure, will be used. But they are not essential within the individual units, except for innovation.

But top management in such a business has to be based on the team design, and on a fairly complex one. For such a business needs a number of top-management teams. And its key people will have to play on several of these teams at the same time. Such a business needs a small corporate top management which does not engage in any work except top-management work.

But each autonomous business unit also needs a top management. The top management of the unit should be small. The man who heads each unit is "top management" for it. But he needs to think through the key activities of the unit and to lodge them within his own group. But at the same time, the top-management team of his unit also includes the top management of the company. At American Home Products, for example, each of the four members of corporate top management was, at the same time, a member of the top-management team of one or more of the operating businesses.

For the areas which are "corporate," such as what the business is and what it should be; what new businesses to enter and what old ones to go out of; the supply and allocation of capital; and the placement of key people, corporate top management is the top-management team. It will, of course, consult with the heads of the individual units. But the decision has to be made in contemplation of the entire business.

For his individual unit, however, it is the general manager of the unit rather than the chief executive officer of the corporation who is the leader and who should be expected to take full business responsibility for his unit. The corporate top-management group is, in effect, "support" to the heads of the individual businesses.

"We sometimes replace the president of one of our divisions," one of the top men at American Home Products explained in the early fifties. "But we never overrule him. He is expected to consult us; to ask for our opinions; and to keep us informed. But when it comes to a decision with respect to his own business, he makes it. If he is not willing to do this and wants us to make the decisions for him, we have no choice but to replace him, no matter how effective he may be in day-to-day operations. Otherwise we cannot do our top-management job."

This means that the people who run the individual units have to take the responsibility for keeping corporate top management informed regarding their own business. Corporate top management is their team—and they owe to it the information and education which a team leader always owes to his team members.

The "synergetic" fair-sized business, finally, has to be organized on two axes. It is a unified business, a system, and as such requires strong, unified top management, and especially unified planning. But its individual units are both autonomous and interdependent.

Corporate top management must see—and manage—the company as one unit. Yet each unit is a business of its own. Each has to be able to stand on its own feet; no business in such a synergetic system can ever be allowed to be merely a cost center, justified by its contribution to its sister businesses rather than by its own results. Each has to be a leader in its field, have clear business objectives, understand its key activities, and be organized to perform them. But each business also depends on the other. The head of each unit, therefore, has to know what goes on in all others, and has to be concerned with them.

There are, therefore, three kinds of top-management teams in the synergetic fair-sized business—and they better make sure that they play according to the rules that govern each of these three different teams. There is, first, of course, a top-management team for the entire group—very similar to the top-management team required by the business based on true federal decentralization. Then, there has to be a top-management team for each unit, again similar to what each American Home Products division required several decades ago.

But the heads of each division are also of necessity, together with corporate top management, a distinct top-management team. They have to work out the relationships among the different ventures. They have to think through how each of these ventures affects the others. They have to think through in what form they have to make their contribution to each other. They have, in other words, to look upon themselves as being responsible both for their own unit and for the health and performance of all the others.

All three types of fair-sized businesses are prone to the same degenerative disease: flabbiness. In a fair-sized business, great care is required to make sure that fat is not mistaken for muscle and business volume for business performance.

The fair-sized business is particularly susceptible to marginal ventures. A well-managed fair-sized business is a business of high competence within its area. It usually does with great ease, indeed without apparent effort, what many other businesses find hard to do and often cannot do at all. It is therefore likely to have great self-confidence. At the same time, it is a business that, precisely because of its competence, does not offer great excitement. "Crises" are comparatively rare. Everybody knows what he is expected to do and does it. And there is often, therefore, in the fair-sized business a strong desire for doing new and "exciting" things; a strong push for adventure.

And it seems so easy then to tackle things to which one's competence, one's knowledge, one's expertise, would be applicable. Indeed the management people in a well-run fair-sized business always wonder why other businesses, in what to them seem closely related areas, are not doing better. They always think that if they only went into this new product line, or that new market, they could easily establish leadership there.

Yet few things are harder to predict than the extent to which knowledge and expertise in one area can be transferred to another.

The secret of success for a fair-sized business is concentration of effort. Sony in Japan has refused to go beyond its specific ecological niche and to engage in ventures beyond it. At the same time, it clearly has a policy of doing nothing marginal. Each product line, each market, apparently has to stand on its own feet and has to meet high performance standards of its own. This policy of concentration made Sony, within fifteen years, into one of the world's best known fair-sized companies. A few years later, in the early 1970s, Sony then grew from being fair-sized to being a genuinely big business.

In those areas in which excellence is required to obtain objectives, a fair-sized business better behave as if it were a big business. These areas need strength. They need resources. They need high demands and insistence on performance. But in all other areas, only the minimum—or less—should ever be done. A fair-sized business is a business which has leadership in a fairly narrow but already visible and important area. To maintain this leadership position is the secret of success in a fair-sized business. To dilute it is to court failure.

The fair-sized business is, perhaps, best suited of all business sizes for successful innovation. But the innovative efforts should strengthen the basic unity of the business rather than dilute it. They should capitalize on the strengths of the business. Particularly in the fair-sized business that is a configuration of autonomous small businesses—e.g., the American Home Products of the early 1950s—innovation should be directed toward developing new small businesses with high growth potential but with the same basic characteristics; that is, businesses in which the skill and knowledge of the fair-sized business can have full play. For a fair-sized business is strong precisely because it has excellence in a clearly defined area or a clearly defined market.

In a synergetic fair-sized business, innovation should aim at exploiting the "franchise" of the company, its acceptance by a segment of the market, or its special knowledge in one area.

A fair-sized business requires, in sum, great managerial self-discipline. It requires the willingness to support, with full resources, the efforts and areas on which the success of the business has been built. It requires self-restraint and almost austerity in all other areas. The well-managed fair-sized business is a business that knows what its business is and what it should be, and that purposefully and systematically concentrates its resources—and especially its resources of performing key people—toward the attainment of its basic mission.

## The Big Business

The small and the fair-sized business belong essentially in the same category. The group on the performance of which the success of the business depends is still small enough and cohesive enough to know each other personally and to be in continuing personal contact with each other. The aim of management in these businesses is to make these direct, close, intimate personal relationships fully effective through direction, system, and structure.

The definition of a big business is that the top-management group, no matter how large, no longer knows personally every key performer, no longer works with each of them directly, no longer constitutes a self-disciplining team. The big business has to be impersonal.

Once the business has reached the point at which the top-management group can no longer know the key people personally and directly, it has, in effect, reached the final stage in size. From there on, additional managerial needs and demands are caused by increasing complexity rather than by increasing size.

A big business has to organize properly the formal, the objective structure. Relationships, information about people, and mobilization of individual energies have to be built into a structure which, of necessity, has to be impersonal, based on policies, on objectives, on abstract definitions of jobs and of contributions, and on the routines of procedures. The big business requires clarity.

People in the big business no longer easily know each other. They no longer know from daily experience what the other man's job is and how he goes about performing it. They no longer have immediate access to final results and therefore cannot easily direct their own work and efforts toward contribution and performance. They need to know the objectives of the business and its priorities; its strategies and its goals; their own position within the structure and their relationship to others. Otherwise a big business degenerates into bureaucracy where observing the proprieties becomes more important than results, and procedure is mistaken for productivity.

The big business, almost by definition, needs to employ a number of organization structures. It is far too big to be organized on the functional principle. Wherever possible, therefore, it needs to employ federal decentralization. And where this is not available to it, e.g., in a process industry or a commercial bank, it needs to experiment wth simulated decentralization. But it also needs teams. Indeed it is in the big business where the function becomes the man's "home" rather than his "place of work," and where the professional is most likely to make his greatest contribution as a member of one or several teams.

This, however, also requires clear thinking about the manager's job. It requires that the job be defined in terms of contribution and assignment, but also in terms of its position in decision strategy, in the flow of information, and in terms of relationships. And in the big business, both the development of management and the development of managers become crucial.

A big business requires, practically without exception, a number of top-management teams. It requires, therefore, that top-management activities become clearly identified, clearly defined, and firmly assigned. And in a big business the key activities will always include a number of conscience areas.

The big business also needs the "executive secretariat" or the "business research group" discussed in Chapter 51, to make its top management effective. Otherwise the top-management teams will lose cohesion. Or else they will spend far too much of their time on "coordinating," far too much time on jurisdictional conflicts and on clearing up misunderstandings. Top management in the big business is too complex a function not to have its own organ of information, stimulation, thinking, and communications.

Big business is therefore, of necessity, highly structured, complex, formal —and not very fast.

This implies that big business should not, as a rule, engage in small-business ventures. At least it should not engage in any venture which, if reasonably successful, will not develop into a fair-sized business. Small businesses cannot afford the overhead of a big business, its formal management structure, its job descriptions and administration, its staffs, or its formal planning and budgetry. Big business cannot do without these tools.

Big business management also lacks the "feel" for small business. It is unlikely to understand it and it will therefore make the wrong decisions. Yet, to innovate, big business needs to start small ventures; for the new always starts small. Big business therefore needs to be able to set up and tolerate the innovative team (see Chapter 61, "The Innovative Organization") as both part of, and outside of, its structure at one and the same time. But big business also needs systematic attempts to introduce flexibility and even "disorder" into what otherwise easily becomes a straitjacket of rules and procedures.

Top management, in particular, needs to work on direct face-to-face relationships with people throughout the organization and especially with the younger professional contributors. It needs to organize itself to sit down with people throughout the organization, to listen to them, to help them focus their vision on the objectives and opportunities of the business rather than on their own functional or technical work, and above all, to get to know them.

But the personal relationships which give flexibility to the big business and establish the habit of cooperation between what otherwise might well become rigid bureaucrats cannot be left to top management alone—though they will not develop unless top management works at them. Management development within big business has as one of its major duties the creation of personal bonds and relationships throughout the organization.

The best way to do this is for managers and professionals to grow up together and to get to know each other in their work. When they reach positions of responsibility, they should know enough people in all areas of the company to be able to go directly to the "right" man if something needs to be done in a hurry and "outside of channels." Teams in a big business are therefore a good deal more than organizational designs for specific tasks, such as innovation or special studies. In the big business the team in which people from various areas and from various kinds of work join together in a common effort and as colleagues is "management development." It is building the capacity for tomorrow.

### The Danger of Becoming Inbred

A big business needs to guard against the danger of becoming insular and inbred. Most of its managers and professionals are not, in their daily work, in direct contact with the outside world. They work inside. It is in the big business where the law of surface and mass creates the need for special organs but also dictates that these special organs will further insulate an already insulated inside.

The members of the top-management teams in the big business, therefore, have a particular responsibility for becoming the "sensing" organ for the outside, the eyes and ears of the organization. If they remove themselves from market and customer and come to rely on reports and inside information, they will soon lose their ability to sense and anticipate changes in the market and to perceive, let alone to appreciate, the unexpected.

If they insulate themselves from knowledge other than that peculiar to the industry or to the company, they will soon lose their capacity for technological or social understanding and insight. If they confine their working contacts to people inside the organization, or to people from other businesses who do exactly the same work—as most top-management people are prone to do—they will soon become unable to understand how ordinary human beings behave. They will soon fall into the old fallacy of saying, "There is a right way and a wrong way and our way." They need to organize themselves for productive working time outside of their own business, and indeed outside their own industry.

But the new, the different, the outside view also has to be injected into the organization itself. The big business which relies exclusively on promotion from within breeds complacency, rigidity, and blind adherence to custom. The big business needs a systematic policy for bringing in outsiders to fill positions of substantial responsibility.

It is an admission of bankruptcy for a big business to have to go on the outside to recruit into top management. It is also a desperate gamble. There is no certainty, indeed, not even high probability, that the newcomer will "take." But if he is not the right man, it is difficult and indeed risky—and at the least most painful—to get rid of him again. At the same time, the outsider who comes in in a junior position has no power and little chance of being heard. And by the time he reaches a position of influence and responsibility, he has of course, become an insider.

Upper-middle management positions are the positions into which people from the outside should be brought with fair regularity. It might be company policy to fill a small proportion of such positions with people who have not come up in business but have made their careers in other institutions.

New work should, preferably, be filled from the inside unless it requires such special talents or such special technical and professional background as to make going on the outside absolutely necessary. New work, by definition, is difficult and certain to run into trouble. There is therefore a premium on staffing it with people whose capacity to perform is proven and known —and that one only knows of the insider. New work always requires acceptance on faith on the part of the organization. For it takes always a good long time before any new work produces results. In the beginning therefore all new work will be received with skepticism within the organization, will tend to be considered a "fad," will be controversial. And then the insider whose capacity to perform has been tested will be accepted because he is known and trusted.

The outsider should, as a rule, be brought into work that is known and, by and large, already done. But he should be brought in with the express understanding that it is his job to take a critical look at the way the work is being performed and to suggest new and different ways of doing it. He should be brought in with the understanding that he is to ask questions, suggest changes, and be altogether a "disorganizer." This is an uncomfortable role. It is also one that an organization tolerates only if it is being done on a fairly regular basis and is not a "sensation" every time.

Top management needs to know what size its top-management group actually is and needs to adopt a strategy and build a structure appropriate to the size of the business. For size is not, as most managements seem to believe, intuitively obvious. On the contrary, a great many businesses do not know what size they are and know even less what the right strategies and the right structures are for their size. There are countless small businesses which load themselves down with expensive staffs in areas which have little to do with the performance and results of the business. There are countless fair-sized businesses which fritter away their strengths on marginal activities, marginal products, and marginal markets. There are countless big businesses whose top managements suffer from the delusion that they are really "one small happy family." There are indeed many big businesses in which top management is the victim and prisoner of its own inanities, such as "I still know every man in the plant by his first name," or, "My door is always open." There are countless big businesses which, as a result, are essentially unmanaged. But there are also a great many big businesses which believe that formal structure and rules are all that is needed and which, as a result of neglecting direct human relationships and the development of management and managers, become byzantine, rigid, and riddled with bureaucracy, protocol, and intrigue.

Management needs to know what size its business is. But management also needs to know whether its business is the right size or the wrong size.

# 55

## On Being the Wrong Size

*Being the Wrong Size—A Serious and Common Disease—Many Causes—But Always the Same Symptoms—What Works and What Doesn't—Changing the Character of the Business—American Motors and Volkswagen—Courtaulds and Celanese—Merger and Acquisition to Cure "Wrong" Size—Sale, Divestment or Systematic Shrinkage—Can a Company Be Too Big to Be Manageable?—The Unmanageable Service Institution—Multinational Business Services—Unmanageably Big Service Staffs—The Optimum Point—The Company That Is Too Big for Its Environment—Why General Motors Should Have Split Itself—The Company That Is Too Big for Its Community—The Company That Is Too Big for Its Economy—Wrong Size Requires Top-Management Action*

Being the wrong size is a chronic, debilitating, wasting—and a very common—disease.

Being the wrong size is curable in the majority of cases. But the cure is neither easy nor pleasant. Managements of companies afflicted with the disease usually resist taking the right medicine. The cures most managements prefer instead are quackery and almost certain to aggravate the disease and to make it permanent.

There are many causes for being the wrong size.

In certain industries the minimum viable size for a business is very large. It is almost as impossible, under conditions of present-day technology, to be a "small steel company" as it is to be a "small army." It is almost impossible to be a "small petroleum company," or to be a small company and successful in petrochemistry. In fields like these, a small or even a fair-sized business can survive only if it occupies a distinct ecological niche that removes it from competition with the industry's giants.

In some industries it is the big business that is apparently not viable. One example may be trade book publishing in the United States. Publishing houses which publish books for the general reader, whether fiction or nonfiction (which are known as "trade books" in the publishing industry), apparently are not likely to be successful unless small or fair-sized. Trade book publishers that exceed fair size rapidly build up such overhead expenses, require so much administration, so much promotion expense, and so large a selling staff as to become marginal. No such restriction on size seems to apply to publishers of textbooks, technical books, or of "near-books," such as encyclopedias and reference books.

There are industries in which a big business and a small business can prosper. But the in-between businesses, the fair-sized business, is the "wrong size." One such industry seems to be the domestic airlines in the U.S. The trunk lines, that is, the very big airlines such as American Airlines and TWA, are viable. And so are some "feeder" or commuter lines, such as PSA on the Pacific West Coast, which give frequent service to a local, or at least a narrowly circumscribed, territory. The regional carriers, a Western Airlines or Northeastern, apparently are not viable. They are too small to have the revenues of the large trunk carriers, and too large to have the economics of the small local lines.

What is the right or the wrong size may well change from one period of time to another. Since the end of World War II the size needed to be an effective competitor in the world economy has changed, for instance. The middle size is becoming the wrong size. What was a respectably large international business of perfectly adequate size thirty or even twenty-five years earlier had, by the early 1970s, become the wrong size. At the same time, many businesses that are small or, at best, fair-sized have shown themselves capable of establishing a distinct leadership position in a distinct ecological niche in the world economy. The successful multinational company apparently is either very big or fairly small.

But many more companies are the wrong size because of something that *they* themselves do or fail to do. Typical of the company that is the wrong size is the fair-sized business, perhaps with $60 to $80 million in sales, of which about three-quarters are in products and in markets in which the company has a leadership position while 25 percent of total sales are in marginal products or in marginal markets in which the company has, in effect, no business to be. At the same time, three-quarters or more of the efforts and resources of the company go toward these marginal products and markets. The company, because of its earlier achievements, still has a strong position in its main market. But whatever profit it derives therefrom is swallowed up by the marginal 25 percent, and so are the company's resources, especially strong people. As a result, the company's leadership position in its original market and product line is being steadily eroded and will not last very long.

Or, typically, there is the company which, in order to obtain orders for its main product, has to give away, as "market promotion," efforts or products which far exceed in value what the customer pays.

The school furniture division of a well-known American company in the 1950s and 1960s was recognized throughout the industry as the quality "leader." It had almost 60 percent of the school furniture market, at least for new school buildings; and its products commanded a substantial premium over the products of its competitors. Yet the company lost money year after year, and the more it increased its sales and market position, the bigger were its losses. In order to get the contract for supplying the furniture for a new $2 million school—a contract worth, maybe, $60,000 or $70,000 —the company's sales people had to work with the school board, the architectural firm, or the state engineers, from the moment the plans for the school first emerged until the school was finished, four or five years later. The $70,000 contract on furnishing a new school produces at best a gross profit of $15,000. In order to obtain it, however, the company had to give free consulting services which, however conservatively priced, cost more than any profit it could possibly realize from getting the final sale.

But even what looks at first sight like a problem of industry or market structure may well be one of managerial mistake or managerial failure to understand what the "right size" implies for a given business. American Motors, for instance, is clearly the wrong size in the American automobile market with an annual sales volume of 300,000 passenger cars. But at the very time at which American Motors with a billion dollars in sales and a sales volume of 300,000 cars a year was declared a small business and deserving of special financial subsidies, Volkswagen had become perfectly viable, indeed a highly successful competitor in the American automobile market with then still substantially lower volume.

While the causes of being the wrong size may be obscure, the diagnosis is simple. The symptoms are clear and are always the same. In a business that is the wrong size, there is always one area, activity, function, or effort —or at most a very few—which is out of all proportion and hypertrophied. This area has to be so big, requires so much effort, and imposes so much cost on the business as to make economic performance and results impossible. No matter how much revenue the business can produce, the hypertrophied area will always absorb more. It is of a magnitude, weight, or complexity out of all proportion to any achievable results. And yet it is needed, is indeed still too small, in the typical business of the wrong size to satisfy the demands and to support the volume, the product line, or the market standing of the company.

American Motors's basic problem is its weak distribution system. It simply does not have enough dealers. And outside of a few regions where American Motors is firmly entrenched such as the Northeast and California, the dealers are too small and do not do a good enough job, whether in sales or in service. Yet it is the cost burden of its distribution system which cripples American Motors. Being in direct competition with the Big Three—General Motors, Ford, and Chrysler—and offering essentially the same lines of automobiles in the lower and middle price ranges, American Motors is forced, by the structure of the distribution system for automobiles in the United States, to maintain a nationwide selling and servicing network. This requires costs which could be borne only if American Motors had twice the sales volume. To maintain its competitive position, it has to change its models as often as the Big Three do and has then to furnish its dealers with all the parts for all the models on the market so as to give a minimum of service. Yet the dealers do not have enough volume to build strong service departments in many areas. Hence, American Motors does not attract or hold dealers with sufficient capital and sufficient selling ability to build leadership positions in their communities. American Motors, in other words, is caught in a vicious circle. To obtain the sales volume which would make it viable, it has to incur distribution expenses way out of proportion to revenues and has actually to increase its distribution expenses disproportionately just to stay in its market. But at the same time, it does not generate the revenue that would make such distribution costs economically bearable.

Another example is a company which is in serious trouble even though it has leadership position in its field and adequate sales volume. But all its sales are concentrated in a very small period of time each year, either a few weeks or, at most, a few months. Yet to obtain this sales volume, the company needs substantial research and development work and, above all, continuous high-quality technical service in the field. These technical services have to be maintained at a level adequate to support the peak sales volume. They have to be maintained and paid twelve months in the year to obtain six weeks of sales. The company is justly proud of its technical excellence. But it cannot afford the cost burden this imposes. The disproportion between income obtainable in six weeks and the cost of maintaining service excellence all year round is simply too great.

These examples illustrate the basic problem of the business that is the wrong size. The expenses of such a business are always proportionate to the size of the hypertrophied activity or function. Efforts and costs are always, and in any structure, whether biological or social, determined by the largest part or the largest organ. But the revenue is, of course, determined by the actual performance, the actual results. It is therefore never adequate to support the business of the wrong size. The hypertrophied function, while absolutely necessary—or so it always seems—constitutes a permanent drain on the business. It saps its energies and deprives it of resources. And, like a cancer, it is insatiable and always demands "more." This makes being the wrong size a degenerative disease. Radical action is needed to cure it and to re-create a business that is of the right size, a business in which attainable revenues can support the needed activities.

## What Works and What Doesn't

The normal response of management in a business of the wrong size is to try to bring the sales of the business up to the size required to support the hypertrophied function. It is to plan for "growth" which, it is hoped, will bring about balance.

Again American Motors furnishes the example. Since the late fifties, the company has tried several times to raise its sales volume. In the spring of 1972 American Motors announced once more a plan aggressively to recruit new and strong dealers and to push its sales up to 600,000 cars a year, almost twice its then current volume. It again decided to increase its distribution expenses to produce the needed volume. Such a strategy might conceivably work, but the odds are against it. In order to obtain the sales volume that would give the business a viable size, the expenses which make the business nonviable have to be increased—as the American Motors example shows. And this is precisely what the business cannot afford. The great probability is that such a strategy will have to be abandoned, and often just when it is beginning to bear results.

A company may have no choice but to attempt such a strategy. But it is a strategy of despair. It should be considered only as a last resort. Unfortunately most managements consider it the only available strategy and the one to use, and to use again, whether it shows results or not.

There are, however, three strategies available which come to grips with the problem.

The first, the most difficult, but also potentially the most rewarding, is to attempt to *change the character of the business*. A business that is the wrong size is a business which does not have the right ecological niche to survive and prosper. The first strategy to think through is changing the character of the business so as to give it distinction.

A comparison between American Motors and Volkswagen shows the difference between being the wrong size as a result of lack of distinction, and being the right size by occupying a distinct ecological niche. In sales volume in the American market American Motors still had a substantial edge in the mid-sixties. But American Motors, offering the same cars as the Big Three to the same American buyer, engaged in direct, head-on competition with the products of General Motors, Ford, and Chrysler, and had to bear the same costs of an annual model change. Volkswagen, however, at that time offered only the "Beetle" and the Minibus. Neither was in competition with Detroit. Neither was aimed at the choice customers for new cars. The Beetle was bought by people who otherwise would have bought a second-hand car. And there was then no car on the American market in competition with the Minibus. Volkswagen did not offer an annual model change but rather emphasized that its models remained the same year after year—which enabled Volkswagen to offer excellent service to its American customers with a minimum of parts inventory and therefore of dealer capital.

But how does one turn oneself from being an "American Motors" into a "Volkswagen"?

Two lessons, both from the same industry, but each of a different strategy, are contained in the conversion of the "artificial silk" companies into different businesses when the petrochemical textile fibers, beginning with nylon, made them the "wrong size" after World War II.

Until then the "artificial silks," such as rayon, had enjoyed distinction. The major chemical companies, by and large, lacked scientific and technical knowledge to enter the field; the artificial silks were based on wood pulp, which is a material the chemical companies know nothing about. And the petroleum companies had no incentive before the late 1940s to enter a field which did not utilize any of their products. With the advent of the petrochemical fibers this changed drastically. The chemical companies now suddenly had the technical expertise, and they had also the means to mount massive research efforts. For the petroleum companies, petrochemical fibers became a highly attractive way to bring their product, crude oil, to the market. They also had the cash flow to support massive investments. The old artificial silk companies could not compete with the much larger chemical companies in massive research. Nor could they compete with the cash flow of the large oil companies. Yet, the artificial silk companies had to become producers of the new petrochemical fibers or perish.

The two leading artificial silk companies in Great Britain and the United States, respectively, Courtaulds and Celanese Corporation of America, reestablished themselves as viable businesses within distinct ecological niches in which they again had leadership positions. Both restored themselves to the right size. But they followed different strategies.

Courtaulds integrated forward, mainly through the acquisition of major customers for textile fibers, that is, fabric producers. It thereby assured itself of a market for its own petrochemical fibers, but also of the ability to use other producers' fibers and to make a profit on them.

Celanese Corporation of America remained essentially a producer of textile fibers rather than a producer of textile fabrics (even though it too made some acquisitions among textile converters). But it developed a strategy of becoming the preferred channel through which other—and particularly non-American—companies would bring their synthetic petrochemical fibers into the American market. Celanese, in other words, built its strategy on its marketing strength, which then offered such non-American giants as Imperial Chemicals of Great Britain a vehicle for obtaining market position and leadership in the U.S. for their research results, which otherwise would have been very expensive to obtain.

Both companies essentially exploited their knowledge of the market in a manner suited to their economy. The Courtaulds strategy would not have worked in the United States, where the textile industry is too big and too diversified for any one outside supplier to obtain by acquisition a dominant position. In Great Britain, on the other hand, the Celanese strategy would not have worked. For the major non-British producers of petrochemical fibers, especially the Americans, prefer marketing their own products worldwide and would not have been receptive to the licensing strategy which Celanese developed and exploited successfully.

These two examples show that the strategy of changing the economic characteristics of one's business to overcome the problem of the wrong size is an exceedingly difficult one. It is highly risky. Not only is failure of the effort risky. There is an even greater risk, that of making a successful effort only to find out that it has not really changed anything. It is most difficult indeed to say in advance what strategy will produce a business that has different economic characteristics and what strategy will work only in the short run, no matter how successful, and might, in the long run, make things even worse.

American Motors again supplies a clear illustration. The first attempt to cure its size problem was the design of the "compact" in the early fifties. The compact car was a smaller version of what up till then had been the Detroit "standard" car; cheaper, but also more adapted to heavy traffic and to parking in congested cities, and yet a full-service car, giving the American family the space to which it had become accustomed. It was an instantaneous success and produced substantial results for American Motors for a few years. But it was a pyrrhic victory and in the end made American Motors' position worse than it had been before. For there was nothing to the compact which the Big Three could not easily do just as well. It fitted their dealer system, their design and engineering expertise, and their production facilities far better than it did American Motors's. And so American Motors, in effect, achieved little except to create a market for the Big Three, a market in which again it found itself to be the wrong size.

In retrospect it is easy to see that the compact was the wrong strategy for American Motors. But it is also easy to see why, in the 1950s, the compact appeared to be the solution to American Motors's management and the means for transforming the business into the right size.

Any company contemplating the transformation of its business as a cure for its size problem needs to ask itself not only, "How likely is success?" It needs to ask itself also, "Will success be the answer?" "Or is it only likely to put us into an even worse position in the end?" "Will it, in other words, really give us lasting distinction?"

## Merger and Acquisition

The second strategy, and one that is much less risky, is to try to cure the size problem by *merger or acquisition.* Indeed, being the wrong size is one of the few cases where serious thought about merger or acquisition is a must. The problem cannot, to repeat, be cured by growth from within as a rule. It requires a "quantum jump." And this, of course, merger and acquisition can provide.

The aim of such a merger or acquisition must not, however, be volume, as such. To pile additional volume on the wrong foundation is asking for trouble. The aim is to try to find the missing piece that, put together with what one has, will result in a genuine whole. The aim is to find a business that also suffers from being the wrong size—but for the opposite reasons. If a company needs to have an oversized distribution system or an oversized research effort to stay in business, it needs to look for a business which has too large a product line for its distribution system or its research capacities. At the same time, to make it the right fit, the product lines of the two businesses should be compatible; that is, should be able to use the same distribution system or the same research capacity.

The merger and acquisition strategy therefore requires understanding of the reasons why one's business is the wrong size. But if they are clearly understood and if the proper match can be arranged, the cure is likely to be rapid and complete.

## Sale and Divestment

The final strategy for the business that is the wrong size is *sale, divestment, or systematic shrinkage.* It is a strategy managements as a rule find so distasteful that they rarely even consider it. Yet it is by all odds the one most likely to succeed. Wherever applicable, it should be adopted.

It should always be followed if the wrong size is the result of expanding from the strong and secure foundation of leadership into a lot of marginal areas. The fair-sized business which dilutes its strength by building a lot of "beachheads" without ever securing a beach should withdraw its forces and cut back on its efforts. It should admit that it has made a mistake. This is not just a strategy for the small and fair-sized business. It is equally important to the big business which, for whatever reason, finds itself in a marginal area in which it is the wrong size.

In the early seventies, General Electric sold off its computer business to Honeywell. It had proven to be the wrong size. It was much too big to do anything but compete head-on in the major computer markets. Yet it was much too small to be a serious challenger to IBM. Combined with Honeywell, which by that time had already established itself as a successful computer manufacturer of small to medium-sized computers, the new company had enough business to support the massive research effort, the tremendous sales effort needed in the computer business, and the capital investment. Had General Electric not acted when there was still someone to sell its computer business to but waited only a year or two longer, it would, like its closest competitor in the computer market, RCA, have had to close out the computer business and take a tremendous loss.

In his essay "On Being the Right Size," J.B.S. Haldane in 1928 concluded that "small" and "large" were meaningless terms for biological organisms. The right size mattered, whether that was being small like the termite, or large like the elephant, both being highly successful species. The same can be said for a business. Absolute size by itself is no indicator of success and achievement, let alone of managerial competence. Being the right size is.

## Can a Company Be Too Big?

Whether a company can be too big to be manageable is an old question. There can be little doubt that a company can become too complex. Indeed some of today's multinational conglomerates are clearly at the very bounds of manageability. But mere bigness by itself seems so far not to have reached proportions which exceed manageability. Our capacity to structure and to organize the management job has so far kept pace with bigness in business.

This does not, however, mean that there is no limit beyond which size will become unmanageable. It only means that the typical business, whether manufacturing or service business, has not yet reached it. Other institutions, however, clearly have.

## The Unmanageable Service Institution

One example is today's defense establishment of a major power such as that of the United States. It was right in the late forties to unify the American armed services, or at least to put them under unified command. There was essentially no alternative. But the resulting monster is so big that it defies control. Indeed, what the first Secretary of Defense, James Forrestal, is reported to have said of the unified armed services of the United States in the late forties, only half in jest, has been proven to be true: "The peacetime mission of the armed services of the United States is to destroy the Secretary of Defense."

We know that a hospital becomes increasingly less manageable when it exceeds 1,000 beds or so. And the very large hospitals—for instance, those monsters among New York City hospitals, Bellevue and Kings County with 3,000 to 4,000 beds apiece—are clearly too big for effective management and decent patient care.

But there are also businesses which are too big, or at least so big as to bump clearly against a limitation on their manageability. They are to be found among the business service businesses, such as consulting, auditing, and advertising.

The large multinational auditing firm with 5,000 or 6,000 professionals spread over 120 offices in thirty or forty countries is not manageable. More and more of the top people spend more and more of their time trying to coordinate, administer, and hold together this vast mess of professionals, each of whom supposedly has to do his own work in his own way and yet to exacting professional standards. The same may be true of the very large management-consulting firms or of the advertising agencies with offices in thirty or forty countries serving multinational as well as local clients.

Business services depend on the ability of the top people to give personal example and at the same time to know what goes on. But one cannot give personal example to 6,000 professional people spread out over many countries. One cannot have direct knowledge of 400 to 500 consulting assignments or "assignment teams," each of which has to be able to do its own work without much supervision and yet with high professional standards of quality.

In business service firms, therefore, the question of the absolute limit should be taken most seriously. And long before this limit is being approached, the business service firm is well advised to split itself into a number of independent and competing firms. Each of these "daughters" is likely to do better than the overweight parent.

Service staffs within a business or within a public-service institution can also—and easily—become too large to be manageable and to function. Like the business service firm, they depend on the competence, knowledge, and attention of a limited number of high-grade professionals. A service staff that gets big either dilutes this personal quality or it becomes so busy running itself, worrying about its own internal machinery and its own "inside" concerns, that it ceases to give service.

An example is the big service staffs which some of the conglomerates have built up to supply expertise and leadership in specific areas—manufacturing, for instance—"across the board" to a multitude of subsidiaries and affiliates each engaged in a different business and supplying a different market. One such conglomerate has, for instance, around 300 different "businesses," ranging from quite small to very large, from near-commodity businesses (e.g., bakeries making bread) to highly technological businesses and to businesses engaged entirely in such service operations as shipping or hotels. The manufacturing services staff of the company has 900 members —far too many for each of them to be a truly first-rate man, capable of directing and managing himself. Indeed, of the 900 almost one-third do not do any "services" work but administer the staff itself. Yet, the staff is too big to be manageable—there is endless confusion, constant friction, and ceaseless meetings to debate what work to do, when, where, and how—and very little time for the work. Yet the staff is too small to serve a client effectively. In such work one has first to know a fair amount about the specific manufacturing process the client uses— and no one can master 300 processes. But also to serve a client with any impact one has to be able to give a few days a year exclusively to his problems. There are 300 clients. Manufacturing, as the company understands the term, is broken down into almost twenty "subdisciplines" from assembly operations to production scheduling. To be able to give five days a year to one of the client businesses —probably the minimum needed—would therefore require a staff at least three times its present size—and an overhead burden to match. As it is, the staff can only grind out memoranda, make "formal presentations," and write theoretical treatises on the "principles of production scheduling" which duplicate what is available in the management literature at a tiny fraction of the cost.

Institutions, in other words, can well be too big. But as far as individual *businesses* are concerned there has, so far, been no example of a company that outgrew its manageability—the way the U.S. Department of Defense, the giant hospital, the multinational auditing firm, and the service staff in the conglomerate have outgrown manageable size. Especially where federal decentralization (see Chapter 46) can be applied, even very large businesses are apparently still within the limits of manageability.

## The Optimum Point

There is, however, also an optimum point—and it may well have been reached by some of the giants—beyond which additional size no longer improves performance capacity but begins to impede it. The optimum size may, in other words, be well below maximum size. And such a business would be well advised to consider splitting itself.

The prime example has for three-quarters of a century been U.S. Steel, the giant of the American steel industry. Consistently it has done far worse than its smaller competitors. The optimum size in the American steel industry, judging by performance—whether this be defined as profitability or as leadership in innovation—seems to be that of companies such as Armco, Republic, or Inland Steel which, while very big businesses indeed, are no more than a third the size of "Big Steel."

Very big companies should test themselves to find the point beyond which further size no longer produces economies of scale but on the contrary produces dis-economies. Where in terms of size is the point of diminishing returns for a given business? At that point the management owes it to its trust—it owes it to employees, shareholders, the community—not to grow but rather to think through how to give birth to new independent businesses that then have the capacity for growth and can benefit again from the economies of scale.

One public-service institution has done this successfully. The University of Toronto in Canada decided around 1960 that it would not grow beyond 15,000 students. At the same time, it also realized that there was need for university growth in the province of Ontario. It therefore embarked on a systematic program of starting new universities, supplying them with faculty and staff for the first few years, subsidizing and guiding them for a short time, but cutting them loose as soon as they were graduating their first class. The new institutions, such as York University (also in Toronto though in a different part of the city), have shown remarkable vigor. They very rapidly developed into institutions with their own profile, their own personality, and their own educational philosophy, thus offering students in Ontario a choice between different approaches to higher education.

In business, however, such strategies are so far very rare.

The closest is the strategy of Johnson & Johnson in New Brunswick, New Jersey. This manufacturer of medical and sanitary supplies has long had a policy of starting a "new company" as soon as any new product or new market reaches appreciable size. By this method it has kept businesses reasonably small and highly manageable. And yet Johnson & Johnson itself has been able to grow into a truly big multinational company, and one of the most productive and profitable ones.

## Too Big for the Environment

But the major problem of bigness in business is not internal. It is not manageability. It is the company that is too big in relation to its environment.

Any company is too big when it no longer can make business and management decisions in the interest of the company, its stockholders, and employees, because its size impairs its freedom of action. It is too big if, out of concern for the community, or for fear of the reaction of the community, it is forced into doing the wrong things, the things that management itself knows will damage the business.

One example is General Motors. Internally GM is clearly eminently manageable. But since the mid-twenties or so, that is, since it became the leader of the American automobile industry and acquired a market share of 50 percent or more of the total U.S. market, GM management has known that the company cannot get a larger market share without running into antitrust problems. This is largely the reason why GM, though fully cognizant, one assumes, of the risk it ran, decided not to compete against the small foreign imported automobile when it first appeared in the 1950s and 1960s. There was no point for GM in trying to expand its market share. In fact, there was every reason for keeping market share where it was, that is, well below 60 percent (and this was already a good deal higher than earlier GM managements would have considered prudent). As a result, GM abandoned the "lower end" of the market to the foreign imports. It concentrated on the middle and upper ends which, of course, are the far more profitable segments of the market. But this also meant that there was no leadership to keep the American-made automobile truly competitive even in its own domestic market. By the early seventies, when the imports had become a challenge to Detroit, and a threat to the American balance of payments and therefore to the American position in the world economy, so much of the market had been ceded to the imports—first the Germans with Volkswagen and then the Japanese—that the counteroffensive had become a formidable undertaking.

This is not just hindsight. A good many people, even within GM, saw clearly in the forties that GM, with 50 percent or more of the market, had become too big for its own good. Some of the younger staff men in GM headquarters seriously discussed spinning off Chevrolet and setting it up as a separate company. And Chevrolet, by itself, would have been a very big company with something like 25 percent of the American market; that is, larger than Ford or Chrysler.

Yet GM top management considered even the mere mention of a Chevrolet spin-off to be outright treason. In the company that is too big pride always gets in the way of management vision.

There are quite a few companies of far smaller size than GM which are still too big for their community. There are many companies which cannot do the things they and their own management know to be the right things to do for the business because they are restrained by their size in relation to their community.

The typical example is the company, perhaps even a fairly small one, which is the dominant employer in an area. Any company which is the mainstay of its community is too big. It can no longer move with freedom. It has only two choices: either to become "father and mother" to the community and to take over control of its welfare, its cultural life, and its community organization; or, it can become the "ugly," the tyrant, the autocrat, the bully. And the line between the two is blurred. Yesterday's benefactor becomes today's bully very fast. It is indeed debatable whether the "benefactor" is harmed more by being too big than the bully. Neither has freedom of action any more.

Any company which finds itself arguing, "We cannot do this no matter how badly we need it because of the impact on the community," is too big. If it persists in expanding in the community, it sacrifices the best interests of the business, but also the best interests of the community, to the vanity and lust for power of its management. And this is betrayal of management trust. The company may be quite small; what matters is its relative size. The one-company, one-employer community is healthy neither for the company nor for the community.

The least such a company needs to do is not to expand any further in its community. The least it needs to do is not to aggravate the situation. This is not "social responsibility." This is business responsibility.

A company exploiting a natural resource, such as copper or petroleum, has little choice. It has to establish itself where the resource is. If this then means that it will be too big, the question is only how to mitigate the impact. The situation itself cannot be remedied. Anaconda has little choice but to be "too big" in Butte, Montana. This is where the copper is. The petroleum companies have little choice but to be "too big" in the Arab countries along the Persian Gulf. This is where the oil is. But companies in other industries, in manufacturing, in distribution, in financial and other services, have no such excuse. As soon as such a company finds that its community has become so dependent on it that the company's freedom of business action and business decision is seriously impaired, it owes it to itself, but also to the community, to stop getting bigger and to try to reduce, if only gradually, the mutual dependence between business and community. It has to take effective action to reduce itself to a size which is manageable. For being too big for one's environment is, in effect, to be unmanageable.

A company can also be too big for a particular economy. Both the Japanese and the French governments have been forcing companies within their own countries—in steel, for instance, and in chemicals—to merge to be able to compete in the world economy and to hold their own against the multinationals. The results are companies that are still not big enough to compete on even terms in the world economy. Yet these companies are too big for their own national economies. So many jobs depend on them that no government could afford to see them disappear or even to allow them to become smaller and to reduce their employment. Yet if there is one thing predictable in business life, it is that every business goes through a period of trouble sooner or later. If and when this happens, the French and Japanese governments will have no choice but to subsidize and eventually to take over these creatures of their own policies. This, needless to say, will not improve their position or save the companies. It will only convert an economic problem into a major political problem. Again the villain is pride, though governmental rather than managerial pride.

The business that is the wrong size—whether too small for its market or for key activities needed; or too big for environment, community, or economy—is one of the toughest problems a top management can face. But it is not a problem that will cure itself. It requires courage, integrity, hard thinking, and purposeful action.

# 56

## The Pressures for Diversity

Shoemaker, stick to your last! The old cliché is still sound advice. The less diverse a business, the more manageable it is. Simplicity makes for clarity. People can understand their own job and see its relationship to results and to the performance of the whole. Efforts will tend to be concentrated. Expectations can be defined, and results can easily be appraised and measured.

The less complex a business is, the fewer things can go wrong. And the more complex a business is, the more difficult it is to figure out what went wrong and to take the right remedial action. Complexity creates problems of communications. The more complex a business, the more layers of management, the more special "coordinators," the more forms and procedures, the more meetings, and the more delays in making decisions.

Yet for a long time the belief has been held widely that the business that "diversifies" into many areas is likely to do better than the business that concentrates on one area. The belief is sheer myth and is contradicted by all evidence.

Never was the belief in diversification as a panacea more widely held than in the 1950s and 1960s. Yet the success stories of these years were not the businesses that diversified, let alone the "conglomerates." They were IBM and Xerox in the U.S., Sony, Honda, and Toyota in Japan, Fiat and Volkswagen, Pilkington Glass in England, and the Swiss pharmaceutical companies—all businesses with one central product or product line, one central market, one central technology. The success story of Swedish manufacturing industry was Atlas Copco, a company that has one main business: drilling hard rock. Concentration rather than diversification also characterizes the outstanding business successes outside of manufacturing. Here the success stories are Sears, Roebuck in the U.S., Marks & Spencer in Great Britain, Donaldson, Lufkin & Jenrette, specializing in the institutional investor among the New York Stock Exchange firms, and the Enskilda Bank in Stockholm, concentrating on the development of a few major Swedish industries. Sotheby, the London-based art auctioneer, and such publishing houses as Bertelsmann in Germany and Prentice-Hall in the United States, all major "growth" companies, are all businesses with one clear mission and one focus, and with excellence in one area, one market, and essentially one product line.

Indeed the experience of the fifties and sixties indicates that complexity is competitive disadvantage. Complex businesses, despite their size and large resources, have again and again shown themselves exceedingly vulnerable to competition by a small but highly concentrated single-market or single-technology business.

Among the "long-pull" performers the "stars" are also the highly concentrated, single-market or single-technology businesses, e.g., Eastman Kodak, GM, and the Swiss pharmaceutical companies.

The outstanding public-service institutions similarly tend to be single-mission institutions rather than diversified. In the United States in the last thirty or forty years the examples of public-service achievement are the Port of New York Authority, the Tennessee Valley Authority (TVA), Rural Electrification, or the Social Security Administration in its earlier and relatively uncluttered days. Each of these agencies tried to do one thing at a time. But the "diversification craze" hit public-service agencies as hard in the fifties and sixties as it hit businesses. It led to the emergence of the "multiversity," willing, indeed eager, to tackle any job anyone was willing to give a professor a contract for; to the "conglomerate agencies" of the War on Poverty tackling simultaneously all social ills known to mankind; or to the agencies of the Environmental Crusade, concerned with every problem of environment, pollution, and technology. These newer agencies dispose of vastly bigger budgets. They engage in scintillating intellectual debates—whereas the earlier ones tended to be rather dull and concerned with such boring matters as getting things done. But the new diversified or conglomerate public-service institutions have not accomplished much.

The same thing applies to service staffs within businesses. The performers are single-purpose staffs, trying to do one thing, and one thing only. Few of the highly diversified research labs which try to "cover all the basic sciences" have research results; those seem to emerge mostly from labs that focus on one area, whether antibiotics or power metallurgy.

Engineers speak half-jokingly of Murphy's Law: "If anything can go wrong, it will." But complexity stands under a second law as well. Let me call it Drucker's Law: "If one thing goes wrong, everything else will, and at the same time." And if anything goes wrong, then there is a premium on knowing one's business, on understanding it, on being close to it. Diversity and complexity, however, mean that one cannot know one's businesses, cannot understand them, cannot be close to them.

There is a point of complexity beyond which a business is no longer manageable. When top management has to depend totally on abstractions, such as formal reports, figures, and quantitative data, rather than be able to see, know, and understand the business, its reality, its people, its environment, its customers, its technology, then a business has become too complex to be manageable. A business is manageable only if top management is capable of testing against concrete reality the measurements and information it receives, that is, its abstract figures, data, and reports.

The information system can be as well designed as possible, as complete as possible, and as much in "real time" as possible. Yet it only answers questions which top management has already asked. It can only report what had already had impact—that is, what is already yesterday. For one can only codify the past. And every report is codification.

The new developments that really matter are always by definition outside any possible reporting system. By the time they show up in the figures, it is very late—and may well be too late. Unless one understands what is truly relevant, unless one has the ability to hold the actual reality against one's expectations, one will be overtaken by events. One will become aware of problems only when they have become "trouble." One will see opportunities only when they have already been missed.

Litton Industries in the United States was the pioneer of all the post-World War II conglomerates. It was built and led by exceedingly able men with wide industrial experience, who had earlier built Hughes Aircraft into leadership in military electronics. Litton was the first of the conglomerates to preach the gospel of management by "controls," that is, by reports, data, and organized information. Yet Litton was the first of the conglomerates to stub its toes, and to prove the vulnerability of complexity and diversification. By the time the Litton top management found out that its office-equipment business was in serious trouble, it was very late.

## The Fallacy of "Asset Management"

The greatest fallacy of them all, but also the one that was most popular in the heady days of the merger and acquisition boom of the 1960s, is the fallacy of "asset management." There is such a business. But it is strictly a financial one—it is, for instance, how Donaldson, Lufkin, & Jenrette have come to define their financial business, which embraces securities research, securities advice, portfolio management, and mutual fund management. There is also an asset management function within each business. Every business needs to make sure that assets are being managed and are being employed where the results are. But asset management as it relates to nonfinancial businesses is a function and not the definition of the business.

The asset managers who acquired operating businesses performed a useful function when they closed down or sold off parts that were tying down large chunks of assets without producing returns. But once they had done this, they did not know what to do. They did not know how to manage a business—and the boom of asset management ended in predictable failure.

## "Investor" vs. "Asset Manager"

There is indeed a way to do what the asset managers promised to do, but it is long-term industrial investment rather than sleight-of-hand asset management.

One example is the group built in England by Lord Cowdray around his family firm of S. Pearson & Son. The Cowdray group holds interests in the original business of the firm, construction. It controls Lazards, one of London's leading merchant banks. It controls newspapers and magazines, such as the London *Economist.* Yet each of these businesses is managed separately, by its own management team. Each has its own mission, its own objectives, its own strategy—and its own results. Lord Cowdray and his associates sit on the board of directors. They make sure that the board does its own task; that is, that it reviews the basic plans and strategies of each company and puts in a top-management team that is doing its job and performs. But they do not "manage" the businesses. Above all, they do not pretend that they own or manage one conglomerate company. They are investors. Cowdray, for instance, identifies himself in *Who's Who* as an "investment company executive."

Similarly, Friedrich Flick in Germany (died 1972) was an "investor," controlling Mercedes-Benz, Feldmuehle, a major paper and chemical company, a large manufacturer of specialty machinery, and a steel company. While Flick's influence on these companies was great, he did not manage them. He was a major outside investor and hard-working board member.

The Mellons in Pittsburgh, similarly, have been large and influential long-term investors in a number of companies ranging from Gulf Oil to the Aluminum Company of America, but never "managers." And both the Mellons and the "Mellon companies" have greatly benefited from the relationship.

The investment company which looks for the right business to invest in, takes a substantial position in it, and then provides counsel and effective hard-working board members is indeed a viable business of its own. But it is a financial business.

Just as fallacious as the belief in asset management is the belief in a "superman" who can do what other people cannot do, and who therefore can somehow keep manageable a business that is in dozens—or, as in one case, in several hundred—different fields, from insurance to electronics—from rental cars to convenience foods—from computers to hotels. Supermen may actually exist in the executive suite—though the evidence is hardly convincing. But despite everything their press agents say, even supermen are mortal. And one cannot replace them once they are gone. What only supermen can do is always unsound; it cannot be perpetuated.

Nothing succeeds like concentration on the right business. And if the company is not in the right business, diversification will no more make it a "growth company," than a man with a broken hip will be restored to health, by being taken on a twenty-mile forced march with an eighty-pound pack on his shoulders.

## Why Diversification?

All this should be fairly obvious. What, then, explains the persistent allure of this managerial *Lorelei,* the quest for diversity and complexity, and the worship of diversification?

The record provides a clue. For while the best-performing group of businesses is always found to comprise highly concentrated, single-market, or single-technology companies, the worst-performing group also always includes a goodly number of such highly concentrated, single-market, or single-technology companies. The railroads—since the end of World War II if not since the end of World War I—belong here.

So do the "traditional materials" businesses—steel in the U.S. and Western Europe, coal everywhere, copper and aluminum, and so on.*

There are internal as well as external reasons and pressures for diversification. Management needs to understand them, to be able to manage them —and to manage such diversification as might be needed in, and indeed desirable for, a business.

First, the *internal pressures:*

1. One major pressure for diversification is psychological. People get tired of doing the same things over and over again. They want to do something different. Otherwise work becomes a bore.

In a pharmaceutical business one hears again and again, "Our customers, the physicians, are getting tired of the same drug. They have been using it now for three years. They need something different."Judging by the prescriptions the physicians write for the drug, there is no loss of interest. It is the salesmen who are getting tired of repeating the same story again and again every time they call on a physician. It is the salesmen who want "something different."

This is not altogether frivolous. Indeed it is highly desirable that any company remain flexible and practice doing something new and different. Otherwise its capacity for change may atrophy. And when the need for change arises, as it always does sooner or later, the company will be unable to make even small and minor changes.

This is shown by the contrast between the two largest European automobile companies of the post-World War II period, Volkswagen and Fiat. Volkswagen scored phenomenally with its "Beetle" for fifteen years, from 1950, when the company got going, until the late sixties. Volkswagen knew, of course, of the ultimate collapse of Ford's earlier "universal car" of the World War I period, the Model T. Yet it kept the "Beetle" unchanged until it showed fairly advanced symptoms of old age in the late sixties. Then Volkswagen poured enormous amounts of money into developing a multitude of new models. But not one of them has so far proven successful in the market.

Fiat too had the "universal car" for the early stages of automobilization in its famous Model 500, the *Topolino.* But Fiat, from the beginning of the European automobile boom, systematically built up a full product range

*A statistical study that relates diversification strategy to business performance will be published shortly after the publication of this book. Entitled *Organizational Strategy: Analysis, Commitment, Implementation* (Irwin, 1974) and authored by Professor William Guth of the Graduate Business School of New York University, it reports the results of many years of work on diversification strategies and their results. Guth's analysis fully bears out the conclusions reached independently by me and presented in this and the two subsequent chapters. Guth's analysis is, to my knowledge, the first fully documented study of this important subject.

from the low-price "universal car," the almost unchanged successor to the *Topolino,* to cars that extend well into the medium-price range. For the ten or fifteen years during which the "Beetle" enjoyed its phenomenal success, Fiat seemed in danger of being overtaken by Volkswagen. But when the "Beetle" began to falter, Fiat forged ahead. All along it had maintained its capacity to innovate and at the same time had given its customers the choice of upgrading themselves to a bigger and better car as their incomes and their appetites increased.

The advantages of concentration always carry with them the danger of overspecialization. Every product, every process, every technology, every market eventually become old. The sales volume may still be there, may indeed still go up. But the profitability disappears. Then yesterday's specialist is in danger of becoming extinct.

Like any habit, the habit of doing the new and different has to be kept alive by practice. Otherwise the capacity for doing the different will not be developed or—as in the case of the once highly innovative textile industry —it will wither away. Diversification is not only a psychological necessity. To keep one's ability to diversify is an economic survival need.

But care has to be taken lest this kind of diversification degenerate into splintering. The need to give the pharmaceutical company salesman something new to talk about may easily degenerate into meaningless product proliferation which then not only confuses the customer but annoys him. The product proliferation in which a good many of the American pharmaceutical companies indulged for the sake of "doing something new" explains, in large measure, why the U.S. medical fraternity has come to be so highly critical of the drug companies.

The right rule was developed many, many years ago by the musician. An accomplished and well-established concert pianist will, as a matter of course, add one new major piece to his repertoire each year. Every few years he will pick for his new piece something quite different from the repertoire through which he has made his name. This forces him to learn again, to hear new things in old and familiar pieces, and to become a better pianist altogether. At the same time, concert pianists have long known that they slough off an old piece as they add on one new major one. The total size of the repertoire remains the same. There are only so many pieces of music even the greatest painist can play with excellence.

How to apply this to a business has been demonstrated by the one American pharmaceutical company that has, for many years, followed a systematic plan for research and for the introduction of drugs, Merck & Co.

Merck is as conscious as any other pharmaceutical company of the need of salesmen to have "something new." But it will not spend much time or effort on the modification of existing products. It focuses its energies on producing each year a small number of genuinely new and different drugs which represent a major improvement in the treatment of disease. As a result, its salesmen really have something new to talk about. But as a result also there is genuine diversification rather than mere product proliferation. And Merck also then quietly withdraws effort and support from older drugs which no longer have leadership. This strategy, adopted in the late 1940s, has made Merck, which originally was an insignificant and almost marginal distributor of patent medicines, into the largest and most successful of American drug manufacturers, and also into a most innovative one.

## Backward and Forward Integration

2. Another factor pressing for diversification has already been discussed in a preceding chapter: being the wrong size. Diversification, that is, extension of the business into new areas which balance the vulnerabilities and weaknesses of one's own wrong size, is not the only remedy. But it is one of the remedies. And where it is appropriate, it is the right remedy. Diversification in this situation becomes the best strategy for a business.

Closely related to the problem of the business that is the wrong size is the need to integrate either "backward" into earlier stages of the economic chain, e.g., manufacturing for a distributor or mining for a manufacturer, or integration "forward," that is, toward the marketplace.

Sears, Roebuck with $10 billion in sales is by far the largest American retailer. But it is also one of the largest American manufacturers. More than half of what Sears sells is made by manufacturers in which Sears has an ownership stake, and sometimes even full ownership. This "backward integration" of Sears is usually explained as a result of Sears's desire to "control" its sources of supply. But the more probable answer might be that Sears found in the twenties and early thirties, when it first emerged as a retail giant, that suppliers would not commit themselves to Sears unless assured of the permanence of the relationship. For most Sears suppliers, and certainly for the successful ones, Sears becomes rapidly their major customer, and their main, if not eventually their sole, channel to the market. A supplier would be very foolish if he did not insist on more assurance of a permanent relationship than even a long-term contract provides. Without such evidence of Sears's commitment, he would, for instance, find it difficult to obtain capital or credit from the outside. An intelligent supplier would have balked at being tied to Sears unless Sears were also tied to him. The major impetus to Sears's backward integration was surely that without it Sears was the "wrong size."

The same largely applies to integration backward into raw materials. The traditional explanation for backward integration is the fear of a loss of supply. A manufacturer of petroleum products, of paper, or of aluminum, integrates backward because he sees the danger of a shortage in his basic material, i.e., crude oil, timber, or bauxite. But this explanation is suspect. For such fears of scarcity have so far always been disproven.

Successful backward integration creates a more profitable business.

The oil refinery which has a substantial distribution system in the form of gas stations, but which lacks crude oil reserves, may decide to integrate backward and to acquire supplies of crude oil, because otherwise it is the wrong size to be profitable. The profitable link in the economic chain that leads from the oil well to the automobile's gas tank may be crude oil production. Or it may turn out that only the combination of oil production and oil distribution is truly profitable; each alone is a fragment rather than a business.

This, for instance, seems to have been the thinking that led one of the large American marketers of petroleum products, Atlantic Refining, into integration backward through merger with a crude oil producer who in turn lacked refining and marketing capacity, the Richfield Oil Company. Forward integration should be based on the same thinking. Courtaulds (see the preceding chapter), which solved its problem of being the wrong size by forward integration into textile production, is a good example.

Only integration—backward or forward—that remedies a problem of the wrong size works out, as a rule. Integration is complexity. Even though a company that integrates forward or backward stays in the same industry, it moves into areas in which it has little or no previous experience. It diversifies its activities. It requires new skills. It assumes new risks. This is justified if it remedies gross disparity between the cost and rewards of certain phases of the economic process of which the company is a part. Decisions concerning integration should therefore always start out with an understanding of cost structure and revenue streams for the entire economic process. That combination of stages in the economic process which will give over the long term the most favorable ratio between cost and revenues, and between opportunities and risks, is the best integration balance for a business.

3. Another internal pressure for diversification is the understandable—and indeed laudable—desire to convert an internal cost center into a revenue producer.

J. Lyons & Company started out as caterers to an exhibition held in London in the 1890s. The firm then branched out rapidly into building popular chain-restaurants serving decent food at low prices. By 1914, its "tea shops" had become a London landmark. It then diversified further, still within the same market, into building large restaurants, the famous Corner Houses; into building popular-priced hotels; and into manufacturing foodstuffs, first for its own restaurants and hotels and then increasingly for the British consumer. It became a major manufacturer of baked goods, of tea, and of ice cream. In order to support these activities, Lyons very early had to build its own laundry—laundry service for tea shops, restaurants, and hotels could not be obtained on the outside in the quality and, above all, in the quantity needed. And it had to develop its own trucking fleet. For many years now these two ancillary businesses have been run as profit-making businesses of their own, offering laundry and trucking services to a wide variety of commercial and industrial customers.

But even a profitable business that is developed out of a cost center should be kept only if it fits in. It should be kept only if it is compatible with one's own mission, and one's own strategy, and if it serves one's own market or exploits one's own technology. Otherwise it leads to a diffusion of efforts.

Indeed it might be advisable to separate such a business developed out of a cost center and to set it up independently, even though it does fit into the overall frame. One example of this is offered by Heineken, the leading Dutch brewery, which for reasons that closely paralleled those underlying the Lyons diversification, went into financing and then owning restaurants and cafés, then into investments in hotels and also into trucking. Heineken, however, has put these outside interests, which are not directly a part of the business of making and selling beverages, into a separate investment company which Heineken owns but which Heineken does not manage.

## External Pressures

More important and more pervasive are a number of external pressures toward diversity.

1. There is first the pressure of an economy which is so small and confined that the individual business cannot grow beyond small size. At the same time, the economy is so small that an individual management can know it in all its facets and dimensions. At that stage in the development of an economy, technology is likely to be available from the outside; the market is still too small to appear promising to major companies elsewhere. Capital at this stage of development is likely also to have to come from the outside. And the foreign investor tends to prefer working with people who have already established themselves in the market and have proven their entrepreneurial and managerial competence. Under these circumstances business growth will tend to become growth through diversification.

This is indeed a major stage in economic development.

Belgium, which in the early nineteenth century was the most highly industrialized of all countries on the European continent, became the proto-type. The pattern then established has persisted until now: one entrepreneurial and managerial group diversifies into a substantial number of different industries, all producing for the same limited national market. This same pattern was then repeated half a century later in the industrialization of Japan. Three or four Zaibatsu groups were the managerial foci. Their ability to obtain technology from abroad enabled them to go into a large number of different industries, each of them for a long time quite small and producing for what, until well into this century, was a limited home market. In Brazil the same pattern emerged when industrialization started after World War I. The Mattarazzos, for instance, began around World War I with a noodle factory—perhaps the first industrial business in Brazil that was purely domestic rather than a branch of a foreign company. Thirty years later, by the early 1950s, the Mattarazzos controlled a vast industrial empire composed of fairly small companies in a variety of businesses. India still exhibits very much the same pattern with the two business empires of Tata and Birla, both engaged in a large number of quite different businesses. The same pattern of the one management group engaged in a large number of businesses within a small market characterizes industry in such countries as Peru and Venezuela today.

But the same pattern also ruled California until World War II even though politically California had of course long been part of a continental economy, that of the United States. Yet until World War II, geography and distance provided a measure of isolation which made California in many ways a protected and at the same time a small market.

In many cases of economic development the diversified company in the small economy may indeed be the best pattern. It is, however, not an "inevitable stage" in development. Neither Switzerland nor Holland—both at that stage poorer and less populous than Belgium—followed it. Both overcame the limitations of their home market by early expansion abroad.

And diversification within the confined economy should always be considered a transitory place.

Many of the Californian businesses that were started, mostly after World War I, to supply a limited West Coast market—and which were often based on technology bought or licensed from the big companies of the East and Middle West—have by now grown into national businesses, some of them (e.g., Avery Products, a leader in adhesive labels and other paper products) into very sizable businesses. Others went "national" by merging with companies from the East. The other "regionals" have either disappeared or shrunk into insignificance.

For diversification within the small and confined economy becomes the wrong pattern when the market grows. Japan had outgrown the pattern even before the American Occupation dissolved the Zaibatsu. Brazil has outgrown it since the end of World War II. The dominant Brazilian businesses of today are highly concentrated, e.g., Volkswagen do Brazil, or Sanbra, the leading Brazilian producer of edible oil products.

Where the pattern is not being sloughed off as an economy develops it is likely to become a straitjacket, stunting growth, both of the economy and of the economy's businesses. The pattern of diversification within the small market which served Belgium so well in Victorian days was clearly one of the reasons for the stagnation of the country in this century and for its difficulty in generating new growth businesses.

2. Quite different is business diversification based on market expansion. The most visible and most important example today is the multinational company. It will be discussed in Chapter 59.

3. Equally important as a force pushing business toward diversification is technology. Technology by its very nature tends to branch. What starts out as a technology for one product, product line, or market soon becomes a whole family of technologies generating a multitude of different products for a great number of different markets.

Both the electrical and the chemical industries were founded in the third quarter of the nineteenth century on two or three processes leading to two or three products for two or three markets. The electrical industry was based on the dynamo and on the electric light bulb, to which shortly thereafter the electric streetcar was added. The modern chemical industry has three roots: explosives for mining and railroad building; chlorine, largely for the paper and textile industries; and dyestuffs for the textile industry.

Within twenty-five years these technologies branched out into a multitude of different products and product lines for different markets. By 1900, General Electric and Siemens, Hoechst in Germany and Brunner Mond (one of the forerunners of Britain's Imperial Chemical Industries), had already become conglomerates in the fullest meaning of the word. By now the major electric-apparatus and chemical companies are the most conglomerate of all the conglomerates, exceeding even an ITT in the number of different businesses, different processes, different product lines, and different markets they are engaged in.

This diversification was not planned; it grew out of what happened in a test tube in the laboratory or on the drawing board of a machine designer. Technology begat new technology—and business diversification then followed.

These dynamics of technology are at work not only in material, i.e., "technical" areas, but equally in social technology and services.

Today's American commercial bank is truly a conglomerate in the services it offers. It is diversified perhaps beyond easy manageability. Yet each of the services developed out of the others. Each developed as a result of a new capacity to provide a financial service fashioned out of existing knowledge, to meet a new need of an old customer, or to make old services suitable for new customers.

4. Another extraneous factor, and one that is rarely taken into account by economists, is the thrust of modern tax legislation.

In practically every developed country the tax laws put a high premium on a company's reinvesting capital in its business rather than paying it back to the investors. Capital paid out is not considered repayment but a distribution of profits and taxed accordingly. It is therefore far more economical for the investors—and for the company as well—to diversify with capital that is no longer needed in a company's original business.

A perfect example is the origin of the diversification which converted W. R. Grace & Co. from a fairly small business engaged in shipping, trade, and a little manufacturing in the small countries along South America's west coast into one of the major chemical companies of the United States.

Latin America has traditionally found itself with a tremendous cash surplus whenever there is war in Europe. The raw materials and foodstuffs which Latin America produces then command very high prices, while the money earned cannot be spent on manufactured goods from the developed countries. W. R. Grace found itself therefore with cash on its hands at the end of World War II. Diversification was the only way to keep the money out of the clutches of the tax collector.

This is probably an extreme case. But on a smaller scale the same tax considerations underlie a great many diversification moves, especially of older companies in stable or declining industries where investment of excess funds in the existing business would make little or no sense.

The tax laws of the developed countries which, in one way or another, penalize the return of excess capital to the investors—the American tax laws, for instance, allow this only if the whole business is being liquidated —are a powerful engine of diversification. That GM did not spin off Chevrolet is in some degree also the fault of the tax system. The tax laws were not, of course, designed for that purpose. On the contrary. But altogether the effect of present-day tax laws on industrial concentration, on the emergence of conglomerates, and on bigness has been in every country almost the exact opposite of what tax policy professes to believe in and to work for.

5. Finally as the last major pressure toward diversification there is the emergence of what I call the "new markets," the markets for investment and capital as a "mass market," and the emergence of the market for jobs and careers as another mass market (on this see the essay, "The New Markets and the New Entrepreneurs," in my book, *Men, Ideas and Politics*.

The mass-market investor—and he is quite different from the old-style capitalist—is also a "customer." The "product" that is "value" for him in terms of a company's securities must fit his expectations. Similarly the young educated people today are customers in the mass market for jobs and careers. And the "product," that is, the jobs and career opportunities which an employer offers, also have to fit their expectations and be "value" to them. And both of the new mass markets put high value on diversification. Indeed, the growth of the conglomerate, and the take-over fever of the late sixties, were in large measure first responses to the demands and expectations of these new mass markets. As first responses to new problems usually are, they were the wrong responses. But the demands of these new mass markets will remain and will have to be satisfied. And both, in large measure, will be satisfied only by diversification.

Diversification, in fine, is a complex phenomenon. No matter how preferable the purity of concentration may be, all businesses need to think through whether they need to diversify and how.

Some of the pressures that make for diversification may be opportunities for a company. Others are threats. Some, such as the tax laws, reward the wrong and punish the right behavior. In some stages of a company's development, diversification, in other words, may be a necessity. In others it may be highly desirable. In others yet, it may be a temptation that should be sternly resisted.

### Right and Wrong Diversification

The record shows clearly that there is *right diversification* and there is *wrong diversification.* * The right diversification produces businesses whose performance capacity almost equals that of the top performers among highly concentrated, single-market or single-technology companies. Wrong diversification produces businesses performing as poorly as a single-market or single-technology firm that is highly concentrated in the wrong business. And the difference is always that the performing diversified company has a *common core of unity* to its business or businesses.

This, however, implies that diversification is not something that can be either condemned or recommended as such. It is therefore a major task of top management to decide what diversification and how much a particular company needs to make the most of its strengths and to get the best results from its resources.

One starting point must be the question "What is the *least* diversification this business needs to accomplish its mission, obtain its objectives, and continue to be viable and prosperous?" But at the same time the question "What is the *most* diversification we can manage, the most complexity this

*The study by Professor William Guth cited earlier also bears this out.

business can bear?" should also be asked. The optimum will lie, as a rule, between the two extremes. The closer it can come to the minimum needed, the more easily manageable will the business be. The burden of proof always lies on those who want more diversification rather than on those who want more concentration.

No matter how desirable concentration is, it may have to be harmonized with diversification. Otherwise it could become overspecialization. But no matter how desirable—or indeed inescapable—diversification is, it has to make possible concentration. Otherwise it becomes splintering and diffusion. Simplicity and complexity are both genuine needs. They pull the business in opposite directions. Yet they must not be allowed to become conflicts. They must instead be synthesized. To manage diversity by embedding it in a common core of unity is a top-management task—and equally pressing in the small, the fair-sized, and the big business.

# 57

# Building Unity Out of Diversity

*The Two Cores of Unity: Market and Technology—A Caveat: Customers, Not Manufacturers, Define the Market—The Risks of the Market Definition—The Need for a Business Strategy—GM and British Leyland—Technology as a Common Core of Unity—Some Basic Rules—Technology Must Be Specific—Technology Must Be Distinct—Technology Must Be Essential —Strategies for Technology-Based Diversification—The "Extended Technological Family"—Is It Outmoded?—Its Limitations—What Does Not Work—Two-Axes Diversification—"Countercyclical" Diversification—The Illusion of "Financial Synergism"—Diversification for the Sake of Diversification—Diversification to Cure Weakness—The Need for "Temperamental Fit"*

————

There are only two ways in which diversity can be harmonized into unity. A business can be highly diversified and yet have fundamental unity if its businesses and technologies, its products and product lines, and its activities are embraced within the unity of a common *market*. And a business can be highly diversified and have fundamental unity if its businesses, its markets, its products and product lines, and its activities are held together in a common *technology*. Both a common market and a common technology provide the first requirement for unity: a common language throughout the entire organization. They make possible mutual understanding.

Of the two, unification in and through the market is more likely to be successful.

Pepsi-Cola stayed in its own market when it bought Fritolay, a manufacturer of snack foods—for a bottled soft drink is, of course, also a "snack."

And Coca-Cola stayed within its market when it bought Minute Maid, the pioneer of frozen orange juice. Unilever and Nestle, the two giant multinationals of the European consumer goods industry, are in many phases of packaged and processed products in a large number of countries. But for all their products, the customer is the grocery store or the supermarket. Similarly, Procter & Gamble stayed within its market when it bought a large regional coffee blender. Michelin, the world's oldest rubber tire manufacturer and, in fact, the pioneer in pneumatic tires of the 1890s, diversified within the same market, the automobilist, when it went into travel guides.

Provided there is true unity in the market, technology can be very diverse indeed and yet not lead to the kind of diversification that is splintering and complex.

One major pharmaceutical company has successfully added a chain of medical laboratories and a line of advanced diagnostic instruments to its business. The technologies are totally different. But the customers are the same—the practicing physicians who are in private practice or on a hospital staff. They consider very much the same things "value" with respect to prescription drugs, to medical tests, and to instruments.

There are two caveats to diversification within market unity. First, the customer decides what the market is rather than the manufacturer. It is not enough that a diversification appears to the manufacturer to constitute another approach to the same and familiar market. The customer must also see the new diversification as part of the same market. Otherwise there is high risk of failure.

RCA, in the late 1940s, was probably the leading brand in the United States for radios and phonographs. From the point of view of manufacturing industry, these are "appliances." It therefore must have seemed logical to RCA to diversify into the rapidly growing market for kitchen appliances such as ranges and refrigerators. RCA clearly had the engineering competence. It also had the distributor network. Yet RCA, despite its resources, and despite the acknowledged high quality of its products, did not succeed in the kitchen business. To the customer, the housewife, the kitchen and the living room are different. Living room appliances are not appliances. They are "furniture." RCA's famous trademark did not, as the company confidently expected, create customer acceptance. After a few years of struggle, RCA was forced to sell its kitchen appliance business to an appliance manufacturer whose trademark was established in the kitchen market, the Whirlpool Corporation, which had long been supplying refrigerators and ranges to Sears, Roebuck.

This holds true for services as well as goods. And it holds true in industrial markets too. Despite the prestige of General Electric as a manufacturer of advanced electrical and electronic equipment, the buyers of computers did not accept GE as a "superior" computer maker. The GE computers were technically fully competitive. Yet GE could not establish itself in the computer business and finally gave up.

Technical expertise is altogether unlikely to lead to a correct definition of a "common market." It is far more likely to work as the foundation of unity for diversification into different markets.

For the customer is very likely *not* to consider as one market what to the manufacturer or supplier appear as closely related products. He is also quite likely to aggregate as one market what to the manufacturer or supplier are clearly very different products or services, and even quite different end uses and end users.

Sears, Roebuck carries, as do, of course, many retailers, a staggering number of different products in its stores and catalogs. It also has developed a successful casualty insurance company which has become a leader in the competitive automobile insurance field. It has launched a mutual fund. It has the largest chain of automotive repair centers. And it has, at various times, organized book clubs and travel services. What all these have in common is that these goods and services are being bought by the American middle-class family and as part of its normal "budget." They fit into Sears's definition of its business as buyer for the American family. Technically there is a world of difference between refrigerators and automobile insurance. But the same customer buys them, very much the same way, and with the same value expectations.

The basic risk of the market definition is implied in these examples. Foresight and analysis are highly unreliable tools to define a common market. It is not easy to predict whether a given product or service will actually fit into one's market or not. It is not even easily determined by market research. Only in the blinding light of hindsight is it always obvious why this or that product that seemed such a perfect fit did not succeed in what "should have been" its market.

No amount of market or consumer research, it is safe to say, would have brought out the fact that the American housewife does not consider kitchen appliances and living room radios part of the same product category. After all, several companies were at that time successful in both markets, e.g., General Electric, GM, and Westinghouse. And Sears too had established itself successfully in both. After the RCA debacle the reason for it became crystal clear. But by then it was too late.

## The Need for a Business Strategy

The second caveat is that unity of the market will work on a basis of diversification only if there is a true business strategy. It will not work if diversification is mere aggregation.

A strategy always defines both what to include within the definition of one's business and what to exclude. One of the earliest and most successful diversification policies based on market unity was the "transportation company" which the Canadian Pacific Railroad built in the early years of this century. Canadian Pacific built, on its railroad foundation, a sizable chain of hotels across Canada and a large steamship company operating both on the Atlantic and the Pacific (to which was added, after World War II, a fair-sized international airline). But the market that gave unity to CP's businesses was not transportation. It was the passenger. While the railroad, of course, carried goods as well as people, the diversification strategy focused on the traveling public.

A diversification strategy should include a plan which defines the role of each business within the entire enterprise. Diversification strategy—like any other strategy—must serve as the basis for specific goals, specific targets, specific assignments to specific businesses.

Diversification strategy explains the success of General Motors after it had been reorganized—and in effect re-founded—around market unity by Alfred P. Sloan, Jr., in the early 1920s. The GM which Sloan inherited was diversified on the basis of market unity but without any strategy. It included half a dozen automobile businesses, each with its own nameplate, its own engineering, its own policies, and its own distribution network, but none with clear mission or identity. It had been built by financial acquisitions and was essentially a conglomerate even though its businesses were all primarily automotive. What made GM effective is that Sloan revamped this structure on the basis of a systematic strategy. Despite tremendous opposition from within, he took the grave risk of moving an established nameplate, Oldsmobile, out of its market segment and into a new and more logical one. He completely changed the basic policy of Chevrolet and focused it on the market which Chevrolet had been trying to avoid till then: the mass market where Ford seemed to hold an impregnable position. He replaced Oakland with an entirely new nameplate, Pontiac, to which he gave, from the beginning, a clear position in the market and a clear strategy.

In contrast to Sloan, the men who merged the bulk of the British-owned automobile companies into British Leyland Motors in the sixties have kept a miscellany of nameplates, some with a clear market of their own, some without much identity or personality. They went apparently much further than Sloan did in internal rationalization of manufacturing facilities, interchangeability of parts and processes, and effective cost control—things General Motors tackled only much later. But they did not, as far as an outsider can discern, develop a business strategy for a unified business, or a market strategy based thereon.

General Motors emerged as the leader in the American automobile industry within two or three years after Sloan's reorganization. British Leyland, five years after the merger that created it, had not significantly improved its market position or its performance. It had remained a conglomerate.

Each business within a diversified company, indeed each product line and each distribution channel, needs its own plans, goals, and strategies. Each needs to set clear objectives and to measure results against expectations. Each needs, in other words, to be managed as an autonomous business. But, at the same time, to obtain the results of diversification, there has to be a unified strategy, an overall design, a common mission for the entire business. There has to be diversity in unity. Otherwise even a common market will not provide unity. A common market makes unity possible. It is management that makes it reality.

## Technology as a Common Core of Unity

The second axis of successful diversification is technology. A common technology can be used as the foundation for diversification into a substantial number of quite different markets.

It seems to be more difficult to build market diversification on common technology than it is to build technological diversification on market unity. Psychologically, the manager is likely to be respectful of, and attentive to, different demands of different technologies. They are "rational." But that different markets behave differently he is far more likely to resist—indeed, to resent—as "irrational." Expertise in technology is readily identified. It can be acquired systematically, though not always in a "course." Expertise in a market is experience. It is "feel" rather than "fact." It is understanding rather than information.

For one major group of industries, technology-based diversification is *the* only way to conduct their business. These are the materials or process industries: steel, glass, aluminum, paper, and copper. They are "process-determined." The only thing that can come out of a glass kiln is glass. Yet these products go into every conceivable market.

The experience of the materials industries shows that technology-based diversification is not easy. By and large these industries have performed indifferently, at least since World War II—and some have been among the poorest performers. They have all put great emphasis on "marketing." Many (as pointed out earlier in Chapter 46) have used the design principle of simulated decentralization to create near-autonomous units for specific markets. But they have found this no royal road to success.

The materials industries were the leaders in nineteenth-century industrial development. In terms of volume—let alone of capital investment—they are still growing vigorously. But their products have become "commodities," earning not much more than their costs. The cause is clearly the built-in diversity in the market which their technology imposes on them.

The one exception seems to be petroleum. But petroleum is the one materials industry with market concentration. The great bulk of the industry's output are fuels for a very small number of end uses: gasoline and diesel fuel for motor vehicles on land, sea, and air, and fuel for power plants. Economically the petroleum industry is a "marketing industry" that has integrated backward into raw material supply.

Even among the genuine materials companies, a few have done very well. They exemplify both what can be done and how to do it.

An outstanding example may well be an American glass manufacturer, Corning Glass Works. Corning Glass is in a multitude of markets, from special glasses for the most advanced scientific uses, to tableware for the mass market sold through hardware stores and supermarkets, to receiving tubes for television sets and many others—all based on one common technology: glassmaking.

With $600 million in sales in 1971 and some 30,000 employees, Corning is still a fairly small company compared to the materials giants of petroleum, steel, and copper. But it is a very large company in its own materials field. And it is both far more profitable and has shown far faster growth than the great majority of materials businesses.

Outside of the materials field there are also examples of successful technology-based diversification. Tateisi Electronics in Kyoto is not as well known in the West as Sony but is in its own way as successful. The company grew as a maker of industrial equipment such as control instruments and switches. It built first on licenses from foreign, and mostly from American, electronic companies. It then developed its own technological competence in the electronics field. It has successfully diversified into medical technology, first into the design and production of highly sophisticated diagnostic tools, and then into the design and production of electronically controlled artificial limbs. It also has moved into the office equipment market with a line of desk calculators, and so on. The markets for its products are diverse. The technology is common.

"Technology" does not necessarily mean "science and engineering." *Techne,* the Greek word from which "technology" derives, means, after all, "useful knowledge," or "organized skill," rather than "engineering."

The bank credit card, such as BankAmericard, was not "invented" by the commercial banks and is surely not science or engineering. But it required learning new and difficult skills. It represents genuine diversification based on new techne.

A common technology provides a common language. It provides a competitive edge. It gives advantage in the marketplace. And it makes possible diversification which does not splinter a business but unites it.

## Some Basic Rules

Technology-based diversification, to be successful, requires observance of some basic rules.

1. The technology must be specific. It must be a "skill," a techne, rather than a theory. Clichés such as communications or transportation are not a common technology. The large broadcasting chains in the U.S. are undoubtedly in communications. They have not covered themselves with glory in managing book publishers. Nor, one suspects, would they do well publishing trade magazines. The large American university floundered miserably when it took on government contracts in urban and social problems, or in international development, as an extension of its competence in "knowledge" and in "teaching."

Academic disciplines are not a "common technology," if only because they are theory-focused rather than skill-focused. Nor is competence in "problem solving." One can build a successful practice on problem solving, e.g., as a consultant in operations research who applies his tools to the problems of a client. One cannot say, "We know how to solve problems and therefore can make or market any product or science where 'problems' exist."

Most managements tend to define "market" too narrowly. They tend to see it as "the market for what *we* make" rather than as "the value the *customer* pays for." But many managements tend to define "technology" much too broadly. They think it means "what we can intellectually grasp." What it really means is "what we can *do* with great skill and high distinction."

2. The technology must be distinct. It must be able to endow a company's product with leadership characteristics.

It is observance of this rule which explains why Corning Glass has high performance while so many other materials companies produce undifferentiated commodities and show only mediocre results. Corning has stayed away from ordinary glass tableware, even though it has both the technical and the productive capacity to make it. But in glass tableware there are no requirements above the ordinary glass technology. The tableware and kitchenware which Corning makes and sells are based on advanced or proprietary technology, such as making glass heat-resisting or chip-proof. And when Corning went into an area of glass exploitation in which the premium was on design and artistry rather than on glass technology; that is, when it decided to go into the production of specially designed and hand-blown art objects made from glass but meant for collection rather than for use, it set this up as a completely separate business, under its own name, Steuben Glass, with its own management and its own marketing. Steuben has been highly successful—but it is not managed as a part of Corning Glass, even though it is wholly owned.

3. The technology in which a company has distinction must be central rather than incidental to the product or service into which a company diversifies. To disregard this rule invites frustration.

The bank credit card seemed a logical extension of "retail banking." Yet it turned out that the major skills of the commercial banker were only incidental to the credit card business. New and very different skills are required—mail selling, for instance, which has a highly specialized technology, and credit control. As a result, the banks did not do well for a long time. They signed up the customers all right—but then lost their shirts. The Chase Manhattan Bank in New York, which had pioneered the bank credit card, abandoned the field after a few disastrous years, as did the major banks in Chicago. The Bank of America, which took over when the Chase gave up, then spent five years or more to learn the new skills.

The American paper industry presents good examples of both the right way and the wrong—or at least, unduly risky—way of using technology as a base for diversification. A few, mostly medium-sized, companies extended the standard and well-known technology of papermaking into new consumer markets, making and selling, for instance, facial tissues. They were highly successful (though a non-papermaker, Procter & Gamble, has been equally successful in parts of this field, e.g., disposable diapers, where it used its knowledge of consumer marketing to diversify in technology and product beyond its original oil, soap, and fat-based business).

By contrast, many, especially the very large, paper companies have unsuccessfully spent millions of dollars and years of effort on establishing themselves in the market for "technical" papers—paper for photographic or inkless reproduction; heat-conducting or heat-reactive paper; light reactive or electricity-conducting paper, and many others. They were right in their assumptions: the market for technical paper has been growing very fast and has high profit potential. But the paper companies, it turned out, were wrong in their belief that paper technology is a central element in making technical paper. The central technologies are surface physics and surface chemistry; the paper is merely a—rather incidental—carrier.

The paper industry example—but also the bank credit card—shows that it is not easy to predict whether a given technology will be central to a new market or a new product line or service. It may indeed be even more difficult to predict the applicability of technology than to predict whether a given new product or service will fit into one's old market and market understanding.

4. Finally, technological-based diversification needs basic strategy as much as does market-based diversification. And the strategy is more complex and more difficult.

The examples given so far of technology-based diversification all dealt with new and additional products, services, or businesses. But technology can be productively exploited in a number of ways of which doing it oneself is only one. "What is the best way to exploit our technology" should always be asked in considering diversification of one's techne.

One of the leading pharmaceutical companies has a firm rule. Whenever research comes up with a new development that seems to have high promise, top management sits down with the research and marketing people and asks, "For which of our competitors would this be an ideal development? Into whose product line, whose market, whose expertise would this development fit the best, provided it really works out?" "We do not ask this question," says one of the firm's senior executives, "because we prefer to sell a development, least of all to a competitor. We ask this question in the first place to force ourselves to think through what the development will require from us to live up to its promise, what strategy we should work out, what resources will be needed, and what we can eventually expect. But in almost half the cases, this question has led us not to go ahead, ourselves and alone.

"Occasionally, as a result of this question, we have decided to abandon what at first seemed to be a highly promising development. It turned out not to be so promising after all. Instead of a major new addition to the physicians' arsenal of disease-fighting drugs, it would have been a nice scientific curiosity, with little therapeutic differentiation. But more often, we have come to the conclusion that the development, while indeed highly promising, is not for us. It may be a development that, if successfully carried to conclusion, will result in a drug with significant disease-fighting properties, but for a very narrow range of diseases or for a very limited segment of the medical practice. Then the drug fits better into the product line of a small company which specializes in the area, a company for which this drug is really a major product, where for us it would be a complication requiring marketing efforts that lie essentially outside our business and our market. In other cases, while the development seemed to lead to a product line with substantial sales potential, we still sometimes have come to the conclusion that we might as well license it, and either become one company among many that produce the product or let others do it altogether. We have done this, for instance, with a few drugs mainly applicable to tropical diseases where we have very little marketing strength. We have licensed developments where the end result was likely to be a single drug in a market, e.g., pain-killers, in which we have no other drugs in the line so that we would have had to mount a major marketing effort to sell just one drug where the physician needs half a dozen to choose from.

"In a few cases, we decided to use the development to build on it a joint venture with other companies, usually with chemical companies which have production expertise which was needed for this particular drug category and which we do not possess. I cannot recall a single case where we abandoned, sold, licensed, or joint-ventured a development we should have held on to. If we made a mistake, it is by holding on to too many of our own developments, by being too reluctant to accept the fact that the development of our own research, no matter how exciting and promising, could still not be the right thing for us, or that we could not be the right company to do the development and marketing job."

Yet, this company is known above all for the breadth of its product line and for its leadership position, domestic as well as international, in the major end-use markets of the pharmaceutical industry. For its policy has enabled it to focus on the developments of major significance. It has, at the same time, enabled it to derive maximum benefit from its technological resources. It derives almost one-third of its income from drugs and chemicals that it pioneered but does not make itself, but has sold, licensed, or joint-ventured.

Another strategy requirement is to identify and define what additional or new technology is needed to put existing technology into new products, services, or markets.

This was the question the large American commercial banks did not ask when they originally went into bank credit cards. They saw the skills that "fitted," but not the ones they lacked.

And a corollary is the question "And what old technology do we need to abandon or play down because it does not fit the new products, services, or markets?"

A small company had for many years based its business of blending and marketing grass seed throughout the U.S. on highly developed technical competence in testing soils and supplying a custom-blended seed mixture based on the test. When it decided to diversify into "lawn-care products" —that is, into fertilizers, weed controls, pesticides, and herbicides based on its knowledge of the *techne* of lawn making and lawn maintenance—it decided that it had to abandon the very expertise on which its earlier business had largely been based: the expertise in soil testing. To make its fertilizers, pesticides, and herbicides truly distinctive and effective they had to be able to produce good results with any seed package bearing the company's label. And this, of course, meant uniform seed blends, at least for major climatic zones. This entailed major work on developing and testing new seed blends. It also was a highly risky thing to do. Yet it explains, in large measure, the success of the company's fertilizers and weed controls which, within a decade, made it into a fair-sized business and gave it leadership position in a market many times as large as its original seed market.

Finally, technology-based diversification often requires new marketing knowledge and new marketing strategy.

GM succeeded in diversifying into diesel locomotives because it recognized this. It failed in aircraft engines because it did not recognize this. Its Electromotive Division was based on a technological development: the re-engineering of the diesel engine. But it succeeded—to the point of having a virtual monopoly position in the market—because of a clear recognition that the railroads were a very different market and required hard, consistent work and new marketing strategies. GM also acquired a small aircraft engine maker, Allison, as a vehicle for technology-based diversification. Despite substantial technological achievements, at least in the early years before the jet engine, Allison has never amounted to much. It took for granted that the aircraft market was not much different from the markets GM knows, understands, and is active in.

### The "Extended Technological Family"

The most challenging problem in technology-based diversification is what one might call "the extended technological family": the business that is being pushed into diversification through the inherent dynamics of technology and its tendency to "branch." In their origin, these businesses have a common technological ancestor: electricity or chemistry. But then technology "branched."

The electrical giants of today, Siemens and AEG in Germany, the American and British General Electric Companies, Westinghouse, Philips, and Hitachi, all grew out of what was, a hundred years ago, the common technology of "electricity." But step by step they have diversified into an almost infinite number of different businesses with different markets, from nuclear generators to toasters. All of them have something to do with electricity. But in many of them, electricity is a minor rather than the essential factor.

Similarly, the chemical giants grew out of what a century ago was a unified discipline and, step by step, branched into a multitude of different technologies, processes, and markets. The ancestors of I. G. Farben in Germany, Du Pont, Monsanto, and Union Carbide in the United States, and Imperial Chemical in England all grew out of narrow technologies. The descendants are in scores of markets and in as many technologies: in industrial products and consumer goods, in textile fibers and in explosives, in dyestuffs, in pharmaceuticals, and in food additives.

Are these "natural conglomerates" viable? Are they manageable? Are they optimal? A short time ago such questions would have seemed preposterous. These technology-linked natural conglomerates were so clearly the major success stories of the nineteenth and early twentieth centuries. But while they still dominate the industrial landscape these extended technological famiies no longer possess the clear advantages they seemed to enjoy not so long ago. All around them there are businesses which, concentrating on one field within these extended technologies, are doing very well indeed and are, in many cases, steadily increasing their market shares.

It is perhaps even more ominous that the major innovations within their own technology no longer seem to come from these giants—even though they are the companies with the large research labs and lavish research budgets. Pharmaceutical sales of U.S. companies grew from $100 million in 1945 to some $6 billion in 1970—most of it in products that did not exist in 1945. Practically none of these products were developed by the chemical giants, whether American or European. It is not GE or RCA who have the computer but companies that started small and were innocent of electronic technology such as IBM, Remington Rand (Univac), an old typewriter manufacturer, or Honeywell, which had grown as a manufacturer of switches and simple controls. Even in electronics, the most successful firms are specialists such as Texas Instruments or Sony, which make a very small corner of the electronics technology their province rather than attempt to diversify into all the possible businesses in which electronics play a role.

It may well be that the extended technological family is becoming outmoded as a business strategy. It may represent a transition phase in the development of a technology similar to that of diversification into many different businesses within a small, confined economy discussed in the preceding chapter. In the early stages of a new major technology there is sometimes not enough scope for the full exploitation of new knowledge and skill within one area or a few areas. Simultaneous development into many areas to which the new technology applies is optimal. Beyond a certain stage —characterized as much by the size of the markets as by the proliferation or branching of the technology into many directions—"electricity" or "chemistry" or "electronics" ceases to provide a "common technology." But so probably do "banking" or "retailing." Beyond this stage diversification becomes splintering and counterproductive.

That this might be the case is indicated by the fact that most of these giant extended technological families have a few areas in which they have strength and maintain their leadership position: GE and Westinghouse in heavy electrical apparatus, Philips in consumer electronics, Union Carbide in metallurgical chemistry, Du Pont in textile fibers and so on. In these areas they also maintain their innovative capacity. The reason for the relative sluggishness and vulnerability of these companies is not "poor management" but "spotty management." It is not that they are in too few "good" businesses but that they are in too many that do not "fit."

Only the General Electric Company among the major extended technological families seems so far to have faced up to these questions. At least GE in the sixties and early seventies quietly went out of a number of businesses—in the consumer goods as well as the industrial products areas —in which electricity had become an incidental, rather than an essential, factor.

The extended technological family is at the limit of manageable diversification. What holds it together is common history rather than common task.

## What Does Not Work

Attempts to diversify without either a foundation in common market or in common technology are doomed to frustration. They result essentially in unmanageable businesses; that is, in businesses that do well in fair weather but flounder when the wind starts blowing.

The most nearly manageable of these is the business that diversifies simultaneously along both axes—that of market and that of technology.

One of the leading multinational companies started out a century ago with a process to extract starch from corn (maize). Out of this basis of a common technology, it grew steadily into industrial products such as adhesives, glues, and coatings, and into a whole range of consumer products. For the last thirty years or so, the emphasis has been on the development of consumer products. To the original corn-based products, a whole list of other product lines, condensed soups, for instance, and mayonnaise, were added—all aimed at the processed foods market, that is, at the grocer or supermarket. Yet the industrial products business was continued. The company's performance, whether measured by growth or by profits, has been outstanding in processed foods where corn-based products now account for a fairly small share of sales. The industrial products business, by contrast, has not done so well. It has not developed new products out of the original cornstarch technology. And it has not been able to move into new technologies, that is, into synthetic glues, adhesives, or coatings based on petrochemicals and polymerization. It produces volume and grinds up a great deal of corn. But it no longer achieves market standing, let alone substantial profits.

The reason is probably not that cornstarch is an "old technology." A number of smaller (but still sizable) competitors who have stayed with the corn-based technology and have made it the foundation for their diversification are doing well. The reason is that market-based diversification and technology-based diversification require different management thinking, different management attitudes, different strategies, and raise different questions. Either management, especially top management, will be divided, or one attitude and point of view will prevail to the neglect of the other. It is perhaps not impossible to develop and manage a diversified business that has both axes of diversification. But it is certainly difficult.

## "Countercyclical" Diversification

Diversification to make a business "countercyclical," e.g., by balancing cyclical strengths and risks of a capital goods business against the different cyclical strengths and risks of a consumer goods business, rarely works.

It is not true that these two kinds of businesses tend to behave radically differently in cyclical fluctuations. Or rather they do so only in the kind of cyclical fluctuation that matters the least; that is, the relatively mild and relatively short downturn, which is the classical "recession" of business cycle theory. Then sometimes some consumer goods do indeed show greater strength than capital goods. But where it really matters—that is, both on the upside and the downside of a major business cycle—the two businesses behave pretty much the same way. What the consumer goods business may gain in a severe downturn in terms of sales volume, it is likely to lose through higher credit losses and lower margins.

## The Illusion of "Financial Synergism"

Equally fallacious is the attempt to diversify by marrying a business with a high demand for capital to a business with a high cash throw-off. A healthy and growing business rarely produces cash surpluses for very long.

The one exception to this, the acquisition by manufacturing companies with substantial cash needs of investment businesses such as insurance companies, for instance, is pernicious on other grounds. An investment company, such as an insurance company, a savings bank, or a commercial bank, is a fiduciary. Its first duty is to invest the money entrusted to it in the best interests of its policyholders and depositors, and to be totally unswayed by any other consideration. If it is part of an industrial company, it may subject itself to pressures to invest its funds which are incompatible with its first duty to its depositors or policyholders. And a fiduciary owes it to its trust not to expose itself even to the most unfounded suspicion that there exists such a conflict of duties and interests.

Financial "synergy" is a will-o'-the-wisp. It looks good on paper, but it fails to work out in practice. For two and two to make more than four—indeed for two and two in business even to add up to four—a great deal more "fit" is needed than money alone. Money is universal in that every effort requires it and every economic value can be expressed in it. But for that reason money by itself is symbol rather than economic value and reality. Yet in diversification, economic realities and economic values have to fit—and this means market, productivity, technology, and management.

The "financial strategy" that was most popular in the sixties in the U.S.

and England, that is, "acquisition by price/earnings ratio" is even unsound as a purely financial maneuver. It is, in fact, not much more than a confidence game. To buy a business not because it makes sense as a business but because the accident of stock-market valuation makes it possible to acquire it and obtain an immediate increase in the buyer's per share earnings—i.e., by paying for a stock with a low price/earnings ratio with a share with a high price/earnings ratio—is financial sleight-of-hand. It creates "leverage," that is, raises apparent earnings per share and with it stock prices in a rising economy and a rising market. But leverage always works in both directions. In a sagging economy and a sagging stock market such acquisition policy therefore creates at the slightest setback sharply lower per share earnings and collapsing stock prices. Such an "acquisition policy" is simply another variation of the old game of "pyramiding" that was so popular in the U.S. in the twenties and—deservedly—was outlawed in the thirties, in which companies sold bonds to buy up the shares of other companies. The people who fell for it and sold their companies to the financial manipulators and their "takeover bids" usually found this out fairly soon—unless they immediately sold the securities they got in the merger.

To diversify for the sake of diversification rather than because it is the best thing to do for the business and for its performance and growth is always a mistake. Yet the grass always tends to be greener on the other side of the fence. It is always easy to say, "We break our backs in this business for a 6 percent return on capital; look at this or that industry where they make 20 percent—and then let's find a cheap company in that industry and buy it." But there are almost always very good reasons why a company is available, let alone why it can be bought cheaply. Second, the acquired company will not retain its profitability very long. The management that knew how to run it is unlikely to stay. And the management that has bought the company does not understand the business and is unlikely to make the right decisions or to put in the right people.

Equally, diversification will fail if its aim is to cure the weaknesses and vulnerabilities of a business by going into other and different businesses. It is obviously unsound to say, "Because we are not competent to manage our own business, we better go into another one of which we know even less." Yet this is, in effect, what a company says which, in order to cure a weakness of its own, acquires another business which supposedly has the needed strengths.

The same multinational cornstarch-based company mentioned above, aware of its weakness in chemical technology outside of the milling of cornstarch, bought a small company in the polymer-chemical field to obtain its apparently highly knowledgeable management. Within two years the polymer chemists had left—as managements of acquired companies will do under such circumstances. And then the cornstarch company found that it could not manage a business of which it understood neither the technology nor the markets.

In diversification one has to build on strength. Diversification will be successful only if it promises a greater return on what one can do, and do well. It has to be an extension of one's proven performance capacity. Whenever management contemplates diversification, whether through grassroots growth or through acquisition, it should ask, "If this new business got into trouble, would we know how to fix it?" If the answer is no, one better stay away from it. For any business, and especially a new one or a newly acquired one, will predictably get into trouble sooner or later, and usually sooner. And then it is the parent company and the parent company's top management who have the responsibility for knowing what action to take and for taking it.

## The Need for "Temperamental Fit"

One more thing remains to be said about the management of diversity and complexity. There is one absolute requirement for successful diversification: "temperamental" unity. Even if the diversity is embedded in the common unity of the market or in the common unity of a technology, it will not work if the diversified businesses, product lines, markets, or technologies are not compatible in their values. There must be a common "personality." There must be what I would call a "temperamental fit."

Many of the major pharmaceutical companies diversified into cosmetics and perfumes. Not one of them has been successful. No one in a pharmaceutical business really respects cosmetics and perfumes. To people who see themselves as engaged in a humanitarian, a serious, a scientific task, cosmetics are "frivolous."

One of the major electrical companies found itself in the years after World War II suddenly a pioneer in an important area of chemistry. In order to provide better materials for such uses in its own products as insulation in electrical apparatus and appliances, or tops for ranges, the company had gone into chemical research and had, much to its surprise, come up with some major inventions and technical breakthroughs. It decided to build on this a specialty chemicals business—and has been totally unsuccessful. "We have the basic patents but the chemical companies have the market," commented one of the senior executives of the company. "We should have licensed our patents right away rather than try to become ourselves a major chemical producer." The company has invested more capital in its chemical businesses than chemical companies would have done for the same sales volume. It has put good men into chemical management and it has continued productive research work. But a chemical business in its basic "temperament" is so different from the mechanical businesses with which an electrical apparatus manufacturer is familiar that decisions and timing were always "a little off."

It took Sears, Roebuck almost twenty years to learn to market high-fashion merchandise. Sears's top management, from General Wood down, insisted on the need to become a leader in high-fashion merchandise. But no one at Sears, from General Wood down, really respected high fashion. To Sears, basic "values" were utility, wearing quality, durability, washability—all sterling virtues, to be sure, but not what the fashion buyer considers "value." It was not until a whole management generation at Sears had passed out of the picture that Sears was able to develop a successful high-fashion business.

That a business has to "fit" temperamentally and in its values is the fundamental reason why the conglomerates cannot really work. Their trouble is not only that they try to manage a diversity of markets, of technologies, of products beyond what any one management can truly know and can truly understand. Their basic problem is that they try to manage businesses that cut across a wide range of "temperaments," of "values," of "personalities." This by itself guarantees that in making the crucial decisions, the conglomerate will make the wrong decisions.

# 58

## Managing Diversity

*Managing Successful Diversification—What to Do with the "Misfit"?—The Temptation of the "Partial Fit"—The Four Tools of Diversification—Grass-Roots Development vs. Acquisition—The Question of Temperament—The Difference in Approach—What Contribution Can We Make?—Grass-Roots-Acquisition Strategy—Divestment of the Misfit: A Marketing Problem—Joint Venture—The Various Kinds—The Gound Rules—The Danger of Success—Who Shall Manage?—When Joint Ventures No Longer Make Sense—A Note on the Family Business*

---

Even the most soundly based diversification strategy cannot avoid an occasional "misfit." It is, after all, not truly predictable whether extension either of the market or of the technology will "fit." And there are bound to be occasional "partial fits"—diversifications that are successful but exceed a company's ability to manage, or diversifications that might be successful if only the company could do something it cannot or should not do.

Managing diversification requires that one knows what to do if a product, service, or business that looked like a logical extension of one's own market turns out not to belong in that market, e.g., because the consumer defines the market differently from the way the producer does. It requires knowing what to do with developments that come, so to speak, organically, out of one's own business or technology but do not fit into a frame of common unity. The development may be too promising to be given up. Yet to try to fit it within one's business structure is likely to create splintering and to diffuse. Managing diversification requires that one know what to do if a business that has had original unity finds its technology branching increasingly into different directions that have less and less in common with one another. Sometimes it is the most successful new development that turns out to go out of bounds and to threaten, by its very success, to make the whole company unmanageable.

What every management would like to hear is that it can have its cake and eat it too, that is, that it can hold on to the misfit and yet somehow continue to have a manageable and performing business. Unfortunately, this is unlikely to happen. Managements that attempt this feat will soon find themselves in the proverbial position of the bird that has hatched the cuckoo's egg. The changeling in the nest will end up by pushing out the legitimate brood.

If the misfit is a failure, the course of action is clear: one gets rid of it, one way or another.

But what about the misfit that, viewed by itself, is highly promising or even apparently successful?

The classic case is GM's development, in the twenties, of tetraethyl lead to cure the "knocking" problem of the gasoline engine. This was not only a scientific achievement. It also was a business achievement. For "knocking" was a major obstacle to consumer acceptance of the high-performing but economical automobile on which Sloan had based GM's entire strategy. Yet tetraethyl lead was clearly a misfit for GM. It was a chemical product, rather than a mechanical one. And it had to go to market as part of the gasoline and thus required a gasoline distribution system.

The legend persists at GM that the developers of tetraethyl lead proposed that GM buy a fair-sized oil company and its gas stations to market tetraethyl lead. But Sloan was wiser. Instead he teamed up in a joint venture—Ethyl Corporation—with Standard Oil of New Jersey, which had the distribution system. This produced more profit for GM than even owning a large oil company could have yielded. Instead of being a competitor to the large oil companies, Ethyl became their supplier worldwide. GM, in effect, made money on almost every gallon of gasoline sold anyplace by anyone. Yet it not only had a minimal capital investment. It maintained the essential unity and manageability of GM. Ethyl was a separate business under its own management of chemical engineers and chemical marketers.

The joint venture is, of course, only one way to handle the promising or successful misfit. But whatever the way chosen—joint venture, outright sale, licensing, or spin-off into a separate business—the way should always lead to a clear managerial divorce. If the misfit is to succeed, it requires its own management. For what makes it a misfit is that it does not fall into the market unity or technological unity which the company's management knows, understands, can manage. In turn, the misfit, if promising or successful, needs its own management—and deserves it.

Misfits like tetraethyl lead are comparatively rare. Far more common are "partial fits." The usual case is the new product or technology that does not fit because its success demands its own market and its own customers, but which also constitutes an important supply to the originating business or an important customer for one of its own products.

GM had a need for tetraethyl lead to be available to its customers. Yet not one drop of the stuff went into a GM product. The situation was quite different with respect to the—equally sizable—achievement in chemical technology mentioned in the preceding chapter: the development of a whole family of new plastic compounds by one of the major electrical manufacturers. These new plastics promised to have uses across a very wide range of industries and products. Indeed, without such large markets the research and capital investment required would have been uneconomical. Something like 90 or 95 percent of their potential markets lay totally outside the originating company's business. But something like 5 to 10 percent—and of course the most immediately realizable 5 to 10 percent—of the market was in their use as components for some of the company's own products. The company decided to develop the new chemicals itself. But while the new technology has been a major success, the company did not reap the harvest—chemical companies did who very rapidly ran around the inventor's original patents. It would have been better—for the company and for its promising "child"—if the new technology had been licensed out or at least been made the basis for a joint venture with a major chemical producer.

If the new development that requires diversification is a product or service which promises to provide a profitable and new access to market for an existing product or service, that is, if it promises to become an important customer, one asks, "Is the contribution our product, our service, our market makes to the new development the essential, the central contribution? Or is it incidental?" If the former, then it is likely to be sound and manageable. If the latter, the new development better be on its own.

The partial fit is the most dangerous temptation in diversification. The half-understood is always more dangerous than the totally unknown; it is only too easy to deceive oneself into believing that one really understands it. It is also so easy to deceive oneself into believing that one can really make a crucial contribution to its development and success. But what one does not understand about it is likely to turn out to be critical, if not decisive.

The pharmaceutical companies that went into perfumes and cosmetics all believed that their chemical and compounding knowledge would be a major contribution. But the key to perfumes and cosmetics is fashion-marketing, promotion, and image-creation—all three well beyond the ken, let alone the values, of a pharmaceutical manufacturer.

Whether contemplating diversification or managing diversification that has already become part of the business, top management should always start out with the question of the successful pharmaceutical company reported in the preceding chapter: "Could this product, process, service, technology, or market fit better elsewhere?" If the answer is yes—or even if it is only "maybe"—one asks, "What would we have to be able to do to make it fit our business—and how likely are we to learn it?" One also asks, "What would be the most desirable divorce—desirable for us and for the misfit or partial fit?"

Diversification that results in misfits or partial fits, that is, diversification that damages or destroys a company's core of unity, is another form of being, or becoming, a business of the wrong size. The very least that is required is that it not be allowed to endanger managerial unity, managerial clarity, and managerial concentration on one's own business and its opportunities. The minimum action is setting up such a partial fit as a fully separate though wholly-owned business. At least one no longer manages the partial fit. This is, however, an investment decision. As such it should always be judged by the same criterion as any other decision to invest *outside* of one's own business: "Is this the best investment of the capital available to us?" Otherwise, it is splintering of scarce resources.

And if not the best—or a very good—investment opportunity, divestment, either in whole or in part—sale, licensing, or joint venture—is preferable. This will not only bring greater direct returns. Freeing management for what it can and should do is likely to bring even greater indirect results.

## The Tools of Diversification

To manage diversification, management has available four tools.

Two are tools to diversify: development from the beginning (often called "grass-roots development") and acquisition.

One is a tool to cure unsound diversification: divestment of misfit or partial fit.

One is a tool both to diversify and to get out of unsound diversification: the joint venture.

Grass-roots development and acquisition as royal roads to diversification and growth each have vocal partisans. But it is not either/or. These are alternatives; and for one important problem, these two are complements.

It is often said that acquisitions cost more money than grass-roots developments, but telescope time. This is not necessarily true. Many grass-roots developments cost more money than acquisition would have required. At the same time, many acquisitions take longer to produce results than an energetically pursued grass-roots venture.

One rarely can buy an exact fit whether in markets, products, or people. To make an acquisition truly serve the purpose for which it was made may take a long time. Until then it is unlikely to produce the results it was purchased for.

It is often said that an acquisition, while more expensive than grass-roots development, is less risky. This is not true either. The proportion of acquisitions that turn out to be expensive mistakes or at least disappointments, is substantial. I would put it close to 50 percent. And while the failure rate of grass-roots development is higher—perhaps two-thirds—most of them can be recognized as mistakes and liquidated early, before the investment has become substantial.

One can never be sure of a grass-roots development, it is said. There are always surprises—and few of them are pleasant surprises, true. But I have never seen an acquisition or heard of one in which there were not unpleasant surprises too. Indeed, the one absolute certainty in acquisitions is that the day after the contract has been signed, skeletons of all sizes and shapes start tumbling out of all kinds of cupboards.

What is true is that grass-roots development and acquisition require different approaches and different temperaments, pose and require different questions, and run into different kinds of problems. Both have in common, however, that they must be grounded in a diversification strategy. "We want to grow, let's do something different," is unlikely to produce results in either approach. "What is our business and what should it be?" is the starting point for both successful diversification from the grass roots and successful diversification through acquisition.

But thereafter the two differ in essentials.

They are indeed so different that few companies are likely to do well in both grass-roots development and acquisitions. A company that is constantly "unlucky" with acquisitions should stop making them. It is not unlucky. It lacks the temperament for making them. It is not prepared for the difficulties, troubles, and problems which inevitably follow the most harmonious and most logical acquisition. Similarly, a company that is consistently "unlucky" with grass-roots development is not unlucky. It does not understand the problems of the new and the growing. It does not have the innovative capacity (on this, see Chapter 61). Neither company will find it easy to acquire what it lacks.

The two American companies that exemplify this—and that also seem to understand this—are General Motors and General Electric. GM has not for decades developed anything from the ground up. But GM has an enviable record for developing into star performers successful businesses it acquires, such as the small and quite successful diesel manufacturer which GM developed in a few years into the Electromotive Division and the giant of the railroad locomotive business. GE, on the other hand, has not done particularly well with any acquisition since its early days. But it has a highly successful record as a developer of new successful businesses out of technical or market innovations.

Every management needs to be able to do one or the other: grass-roots development or acquisition. For each company, or at least each company beyond small size, may need to diversify. But a management also needs to know which of these two tools of diversification fits its temperament, its way of doing things, its abilities. And then it should probably work at what it can do and finds congenial. It is better to have great skill and strength in one hand than to be ambidextrous but skilled in neither hand.

The basic approaches to grass-roots development and to acquisition are different to begin with. In deciding to initiate or to go ahead with a grass-roots development the key question is "What can it contribute to us? What new capability, what new strength, what new market or technology does it promise to produce for us? And altogether what will it do for us?"

But in acquisition the key question is always "What contribution can we make to the new acquisition?" Unless the acquiring company can make a contribution that significantly raises the capacity of the acquired business to perform and to produce results, it is unlikely to be a successful acquisition.

It is because GM has, it appears, always understood this that it has been so successful with the businesses it bought. But one need not be a giant like GM to have a successful acquisition strategy based on the question "What can we contribute?"

A company in the American Midwest has grown in fifteen years from tiny to fair—and almost big—size, and to outstanding profitability, by an acquisition strategy based on careful analysis of what it can contribute. All the company's businesses make parts and supplies for manufactured products, either mechanical or electronic. And the company does have substantial manufacturing ability. But it sees itself primarily as an industrial marketer with proven ability to build market and distribution for industrial products. It constantly looks for *successful* small to medium-sized companies which have engineering and manufacturing leadership in products of this kind but which are being run as manufacturing, rather than as marketing businesses. When it finds such a company it proposes a joint study to the company's management. If the study shows to the satisfaction of management in both companies that a systematic marketing approach would indeed result in substantial increases, an acquisition bid is made—usually at a generous price. So far, every such bid has been accepted. And in all but one of the eleven acquisitions the company made within fifteen years results have come up to the expectations, usually within a fairly short time.

There is one compelling reason for basing an acquisition on one's ability to make a contribution. One cannot take for granted that the management of the acquisition will stay—even if one wants it to stay. The odds, based on experience, are strongly against its staying on. And when the acquiring company has to provide management—and the time for this is usually when there is trouble—one better lead from strength and be able to contribute what the acquisition needs.

That this is not usually a problem in grass-roots development is the strongest argument for it. There one can acquire in the course of the development what abilities, skills, competences are needed. One can learn. In an acquisition one has to possess these abilities, skills, and competences when one goes in.

## The "Grass-Roots-for-Acquisition" Strategy

New Deal legislation in the thirties split into two the banking firm of J. P. Morgan and Co. One of the two parts, Morgan Stanley, took over underwriting and venture banking—that is, the areas in which the original firm had been pre-eminent. The firm that continued under the original name inherited commercial banking, which had been little more than a sideline. The new J. P. Morgan & Co. had the name. It had the clientele of the country's biggest businesses. But it lacked the deposit base to be a major factor in commercial banking. It also lacked commercial banking knowledge. And it lacked seasoned commercial bankers. Everybody expected J. P. Morgan to drift into well-heeled oblivion. But not much more than a decade after the split-up J. P. Morgan took over the Guaranty Trust Company, which, while one of the country's oldest and largest commercial banks, had also become one of the sleepiest. The new Morgan Guaranty Trust Company at once became aggressive and energetic and emerged as New York's leading "big business" bank. Though it has only a handful of branches—each a very big bank in itself—it now ranks fourth among New York banks in deposits and ranks much higher in trust and investment business. This was brought about by deliberate diversification strategy which practiced grass-roots development to make possible successful acquisition.

It seems plausible that Henry Alexander, the Morgan partner who headed the commercial-banking torso after the split-up, realized that his firm was the wrong size for successful commercial banking. He lacked the deposit base. He also probably realized that this could not be cured by growth, but only by merger or acquisition. He certainly must have realized that he lacked the strength to make a major contribution to an acquisition. He therefore went in for systematic grass-roots development. Specifically, he brought in a fairly large number of bright young men and trained them in commercial banking. There was much joking in New York banking circles in those years about "Alexander's Kindergarten." But when Alexander finally moved and took over Guaranty Trust he could fill every key spot in a bank ten times as large as his own with an experienced, seasoned Morgan executive, and could revitalize every key activity with new but carefully tested ideas and policies.

Precisely because the key to successful acquisition is the contribution the acquiring company can make to the business it acquires, grass-roots development can provide the foundation for acquisition. And because a grass-roots development often runs into an "awkward stage," or "wrong size" where it needs to make a quantum jump—to a bigger distribution system, a bigger deposit base, or a broader technology—acquisition is often the best way to make productive a grass-roots development. But this requires first the rare ability to perform both grass-roots development and acquisition. It requires purposeful business strategy even more.

## Divestment of the Misfit

The unsuccessful misfit of diversification should be put out of its misery as fast as possible. Otherwise it becomes a drain on a company's resources and a crushing burden on its management. A diversification strategy— whether pursued through grass-roots development or through acquisition —needs a systematic and purposeful policy for abandoning the misfit. The successful misfit or partial fit should not be let go. But it should be moved out of the managerial system. It should be divested.

Sears has done this with the most successful of the manufacturing companies it owned and developed: Whirlpool. As long as Whirlpool's entire output of appliances was bought and distributed by Sears, Sears owned the company. When it was then decided that Whirlpool would also sell appliances directly to the public under its own brand name, Sears took the company public and retained only a controlling majority interest in it. And gradually Sears has sold off its Whirlpool shares as the company grew and prospered.

One reason for this strategy is that a growing and successful business both needs capital and can obtain it itself. But such a business also needs genuine managerial independence. It is unlikely that it will realize its full potential if dominated by another management whose interests, vision, and preoccupations are—and should be—focused on its own business. Such a business is no longer a "child" but an "adult." And adults do better standing on their own two feet.

Whirlpool is still the sole supplier of major appliances for Sears. It has indeed taken over supplying a lot of additional appliances for Sears, e.g., home heating furnaces. It was, until 1972, managed at the top by former Sears executives. But the growth that has made it the hundredth largest company among U.S. industrial corporations has primarily been in sales directly to the consumer, through its own dealers and under its own brand name. It began only after Sears had ceased to be in control. And it was financed directly in the capital and credit markets.

For the majority of successful misfits or partial fits financial as well as managerial divorce is the right thing from the start. Like grown children, they need their own "home."

Divestment is a "marketing" rather than a "selling" problem. The question is not "What do we want to sell and for how much?" It is "For whom is this venture 'value' and under what conditions?" It is, of course, a financial transaction. But the salient point is finding the potential buyer for whom what is misfit to the seller is perfect fit, the buyer to whom the venture to be sold offers the best opportunity or solves the worst problem. This is then also the buyer who will pay the most.

A major printing company decided that a mass-circulation magazine it owned was at best a partial fit and should be sold. The magazine had been bought originally to hold its printing contract. Then it had been in difficulties. Under the printing company's management it had been turned around and was now moderately successful. But the printing company executives knew that it required new directions and new strategy. They themselves neither were, nor intended to become, publishing experts. Indeed they had concluded that they already spent far too much of their time on a business which they did not really understand. What the magazine needed, they realized, was publishing management of a high order. Then they asked, "What is value to a magazine publishing company?" "If it is a growing magazine company," they answered, "its greatest need is cash. For a growing magazine requires heavy cash investments in building circulation for several years." "How can we supply this need of the potential buyer to our own advantage?" was the next question. And the answer was, "By giving him ninety days rather than the customary thirty days to pay his print and paper bill to our printing plants." For next to investment in circulation, printing and paper make the largest cash demands on a magazine. The printing company then rapidly found a publishing group that filled their requirements. The group gladly bought the magazine, paying more for it than the seller had expected to get. They could, however, well afford to do so. By getting cash financing for their own needs, they still came out with substantial cost advantages. The seller almost doubled what to him mattered most: his magazine printing business, as he got the printing contracts for the buyer's other magazines. He did so at minimal risk. And within two years the buyers had increased the magazine's circulation and advertising revenues by 50 percent.

"In looking for a husband for your daughter," says an old proverb, "don't ask: 'Who'll make the best husband for her?' Ask instead: 'For which kind of a man would she make a good wife?' " This is the right rule for the divestment of a successful or promising misfit or partial fit.

## The Joint Venture

The joint venture is the most flexible instrument for making fits out of misfits. It will become increasingly important. It is at the same time the most demanding and difficult of all tools of diversification—and the least understood.

There are several kinds of joint ventures, each of which serves different purposes and has different characteristics. There is, first, the joint venture in which the strengths of two different and independent businesses are pooled together in a jointly owned new business. Each parent contributes what he can do. The resulting whole is—and should be—different from the sum of its constituent parts.

The Ethyl Corporation was an early example. A more recent and much smaller one is the joint venture set up in 1972 by BOAC, a major airline, and Leasco, a computer-leasing company, to supply to smaller airlines a reservations system for airline travelers. This venture combines the programs and process data which BOAC has developed for its own reservation needs with the computer expertise and the financing capability of a major computer-leasing company. BOAC saw the opportunity of converting a cost center into a profit center. But it also realized that except as a joint venture, that is, as an independent company, this would be the wrong diversification. It would require the financial strength which BOAC does not have. And it would detract from BOAC's own efforts to run its own business in a highly competitive industry.

The second kind of joint venture attempts to make a viable whole out of several misfits which by themselves cannot survive. It attempts to provide a quantum jump from the wrong size to the right size, and from the nonviable to the viable. Here all partners make essentially the same contribution, though in varying proportions. The whole, however, should be greater than the sum of its parts—simply because by itself each part is well below the threshold of effectiveness. One might call this "aggregation by joint venture."

Here belong the "consortium" banks that have been formed, mostly in London, in the late sixties and early seventies, to engage in medium-term lending. The partners are major European banks, American banks, and in some cases Japanese and even Latin American banks. The banks are all big and powerful in their own right. But none of them has the financial strength and, above all, the market to develop a medium-term loan business that could compete with American giants such as Bank of America, Chase Manhattan, and First National City, which have used their medium-term expertise to establish themselves as leaders in multinational banking. Each of the parent banks of the consortium banks would have had to invest resources and efforts way out of all proportion to the results it could possibly hope to achieve had it decided to compete directly. Yet each could also not have withdrawn from the medium-term market without losing important customers altogether.

Very similar are the joint ventures in raw material supply. The Arabian American Oil Company (Aramco) is a joint venture of three U. S. oil giants —Jersey Standard, California Standard, and Mobil—to explore, produce, and refine petroleum in Saudi Arabia. When Aramco was set up in the forties, the oil field in Saudi Arabia was already known to be so large as to produce far more than even a very big worldwide petroleum company could hope to market by itself. Bringing together the marketing systems of three major companies, the Saudi Arabian oil fields were converted from a threat to oil marketing into a major opportunity.

Finally, there is the joint venture that is created to provide what might be called "dual nationality." This is a joint venture created primarily to harmonize political or cultural obstacles.

The best-known examples, the many joint ventures between Japanese companies and Western partners set up since World War II, are usually explained, especially by the Japanese, as harmonizing the Westerner's technical and product knowledge with a Japanese company's knowledge of its market, language, and culture. By themselves, the Japanese argue, the Westerners could not manage in so alien a culture. But there are enough Western companies successfully operating wholly-owned Japanese subsidiaries—for instance, Singer, IBM, Coca-Cola, and some Swiss pharmaceutical firms—to disprove this argument. There is little doubt that most Western companies would have greatly preferred building or buying their own wholly-owned Japanese subsidiaries. The reasons why they went into joint ventures are political rather than economic.

The joint venture in Japan is something more important than an economic marriage of convenience. It is a way to reconcile the conflicting realities of an economy that is worldwide and of a political system based on the nation-state. It is a way to make productive the tension between two different kinds of power: economic power and political power. It is therefore crucial to the relationship between the multinational corporation and the small, but especially the developing, nation. (On this, more in Chapter 59, "The Multinational Corporation.")

## Ground Rules for Joint Ventures

Whatever the reason for a joint venture, the rules which all of them need to observe are pretty much the same. They have to be known *before* a company engages in a joint venture. Otherwise, no matter how successful the joint venture, there will be grief. Indeed the more successful a joint venture, the more trouble there will be unless all the partners—and their child, the joint venture company—fully understand the ground rules.

Joint ventures can, of course, get into trouble because they fail. But then it is reasonably clear what to do. And then the interests of both parents are identical. Both want to straighten out the problem. And if the joint venture cannot be saved, they want to get out with minimum loss. But when a joint venture succeeds, it becomes problematical. For then it always becomes clear that the interests of the parents are not identical and are, usually, barely compatible.

The first rule, therefore, is to spell out in complete detail and candor three sets of objectives: the two sets of objectives of the respective parents, and the objectives of the joint venture. It is crucial to bring out, in advance, the basic differences in objectives which the two parents can be assumed, with very high probability, to hold. To say "We want our joint venture child to grow, to prosper, and to be profitable," and leave it at that, is simply asking for trouble a few years hence.

Several joint ventures which large German chemical companies, e.g., Hoechst, set up with large American chemical companies in Brazil in the middle and late fifties failed because they were successful. Then the two partners began to disagree as to the direction and the policies the joint venture should follow. Neither understood that the objectives of the other had been different from the start. Indeed both assumed that the objectives had to be the same for both. The Germans, for good and valid reasons of their own, looked upon the Brazilian company primarily as a user of German-developed technology against license fees, and as a buyer of German-produced raw materials and intermediates. They did not even want the Brazilian joint venture to grow very fast, since the parent company in the early fifties was under severe cash pressure to finance its own growth in Europe and did not want to have to divert scarce cash into financing the expansion of a Brazilian subsidiary. The Americans, on the other hand, looked upon the Brazilian joint venture as a "growth company," which, in the shortest possible time, should develop the largest possible business and become both a producer of its own technology and a producer of its own raw materials and intermediates. And cash in those years was no problem at all for the large American chemical companies. In fact, they suffered from excess liquidity. When, therefore, the Brazilian companies began to grow fast, the two partners found themselves in such irreconcilable conflict that these joint ventures had to be liquidated with one or the other of the two partners taking over.

Even when the objectives have been spelled out in advance, there is danger of disagreement among the partners—and again, especially in case of success. And both being equal—and usually equally stubborn as well—there is no one to resolve it. A way to make a decision in case of disagreement or deadlock should be built into the joint venture from the start.

I consider it necessary to provide in advance, for instance, for an arbitrator, an outsider, who is respected by both parties and to whom conflicts and disagreements will be brought. His verdict is to be considered as final and binding. One disease to which a joint venture is particularly prone is politicking in which the people within the joint venture try to play off the parent companies against each other. This can poison the atmosphere to the point where the joint venture ceases to be viable. To provide in advance for settlement of disputes is therefore elementary hygiene.

The joint venture has to have autonomy. The reason for forming a joint venture is that a business, a product line, a market, an activity, does not fit into the structure of either parent company. Then the joint venture must be set up so that it can develop its own business, its own mission, its own objectives, its own strategy, its own policies, in true autonomy.

This, of course, leads to the question "Who manages a joint venture?"

In all but the "dual-nationality" joint ventures the answer is clear. The joint venture needs its own management. It is not part of the business of any of its parents, but a separate business. But the dual-nationality joint venture is part of the business of both parents. It is still preferable for it to have its own management. Otherwise it should be managed in its entirety by one of the parents. Joint management will not work and will only lead to frustration.

In the successful ventures between Japanese and Western companies in Japan, management is usually in the hands of the Japanese. The Japanese in the management of the joint venture are de facto executives of the Japanese parent company, on loan to the joint venture, who retain their position in the seniority and promotion structure of the Japanese parent company. In these companies there are also Americans—or other Westerners—who are supposedly part of the joint venture's management. But in effect they are technical advisors and usually badly frustrated ones. Conversely, there are a few Japanese-Western joint ventures in Japan where the Western partner has management responsibility. And then the representatives of the Japanese parent in the joint venture's management feel frustrated and are "outsiders."

Finally, if the joint venture succeeds, and especially when it gets to be a big business, it should be spun off. It should cease to be a joint venture. Maybe the parents still retain an investment. But the business then becomes independent for all intents and purposes. It should acquire at least a minority of outside shareholders where capital markets permit. It should finance itself, or at least be capable of self-financing. Otherwise it will be stunted. General Motors and Jersey Standard sold Ethyl in the fifties precisely because it had become too big and too successful to be a joint venture any longer.

Sometimes a joint venture, especially if it is of the aggregation type, may be split up and divided between its parents. This is bloody and painful. But it might be the right thing to do.

Standard Vacuum was set up around the time of World War I as a joint venture by Standard Oil of New Jersey and Mobil Oil to produce, refine, and market petroleum products in the Far East. When it started, the market in Southeast Asia was both already too large to be left unattended, and yet still too small to give much scope. By the 1950s, this was clearly no longer true. And the two partners also were in fundamental disagreement on objectives and strategies. They therefore decided to split Standard Vacuum, with each parent taking half of what had been a unified company. Despite the severe trauma inflicted on a very proud management team by such major surgery, both Jersey Standard-Southeast Asia and Mobil Oil-Southeast Asia were within ten years larger than Standard Vacuum as a joint venture had been projected to become.

To keep Standard Vacuum as a joint venture after it had become a big and successful company retarded its growth. Even if objectives are clear and management autonomous, a joint venture will still, in the last analysis, be looked upon by its parents as a tool for their objectives rather than as a business on its own. And once a business has become established and successful, this is wrong policy and wrong posture.

Diversification will, it is fair to predict, be of even greater importance in the years and decades to come. The pressure of "the new markets"—the mass market for investment and capital, and the mass market for jobs and success; the emerging world economy; the dynamics of technology, will all push companies toward diversifying. It will, therefore, be of utmost importance for a top management to understand what pressures to accede to and what pressures to resist; to distinguish between sound diversification that strengthens unity and manageability, and diffusion that splinters; and to be able to manage diversification and diversity.

## A Note on the Family Business

The complexities and diversities discussed so far are complexities of business, its products, markets, technologies. But there is also an important case where the complexity is not a function of business structure but of management structure: the family business.

The family business used to be the norm. And there are still many around—even big ones. But in developed countries, at least, where there is a supply of professional managers and where availability of capital is not limited to inherited wealth and family fortunes, the large family business is clearly on the wane. What are its needs? What does it have to do to survive? What are its limits of size and time span?

There is little doubt that beyond a certain size a business can no longer reserve management to family members and remain viable. Beyond a certain size—and that usually means beyond being fair-sized—the management burden increasingly has to be borne by professional managers with little or no ties to the family that founded the business. Ownership may still be in the hands of these families. In Japan, for instance, ownership of the Zaibatsu groups remained in the hands of the founding families till the end of World War II, despite the giant size and complexity of each group. But even though Japanese families can—and do—adopt freely, Zaibatsu management had long before 1900 become professional non-family management in all of the groups.

In the major European and American family companies, family also often remained important beyond the fair-sized stage. At Siemens in Germany, for instance, the family was powerfully represented in management until after World War II, that is, for a hundred years. At the Du Pont Company in the United States, the family is still powerful in management, seventy years after two Du Pont brothers and a cousin took over, in 1902, some floundering old black-powder mills and started building today's Du Pont Company. But both at Siemens and at Du Pont, professional managers long ago became equal members of the top-management group, in authority, influence, and decision-making powers (though not necessarily in official myth and in the proprieties of protocol).

Beyond a certain size, the family can perpetuate itself only if it succeeds in attracting and holding first-rate men who are not members of the family—not even by adoption (which the American Du Ponts have practiced, perhaps even more successfully than the Japanese—even though, unlike the Japanese, the "adopted" Du Ponts, who have married Du Pont daughters, do not change their names). The family business, if it wants to perpetuate itself, better think through, and fairly early, what needs to be done to make living and working with a "ruling family" acceptable to the outsider.

The rules are fairly simple—both Du Pont and Siemens worked them out many years ago. Only those members of the family who, on their own merit, qualify for a top-management position are allowed to stay in the business. A family member in a family business has a position of authority and power, regardless of his title and rank, even regardless of his job. He has the inside track to the top—as a son, a brother, a brother-in-law. No matter what his rank, he is top management. If he cannot command the respect due a member of top management on his own merit and on the basis of his performance, he should not be allowed to stay on the payroll.

Cousin Paul may indeed have to be supported by the family. But if he is not of top-management caliber, he better be paid a stipend to stay away from the office. Outside of the company he costs only his stipend. If he is allowed to work in the company, he costs a great deal more: respect for the family, ability to attract and hold good people, and career opportunities for those who truly deserve them.

A family member who lacks ability but is willing to work hard may still be tenable. People will accept, though not very willingly, his right to a job. The family member who is not willing to work, no matter how able, must not be allowed in a family company. He destroys morale and breeds both resentment and cynicism.

And, as Pierre du Pont realized when he restructured the Du Pont Company in 1920 and made it capable of becoming a truly big and successful business, the professional nonfamily members in the top-management group must be given rewards and incentives that make them feel like "owners." Pierre du Pont invented the first stock-option plan in American business, over the strenuous opposition of the other members of his family. But he felt strongly and, as events proved rightly, that without such a plan first-rate nonfamily members would feel discriminated against. It is not the money that matters; it is the status.

Even if the family company succeeds in attracting the professional management it needs once it has grown beyond a certain size, it is unlikely to perpetuate itself forever. The family's entrepreneurial qualities may not weaken. The Rothschilds have maintained theirs for close to two hundred years, which is quite a bit longer than any other dynasty on record—business or nonbusiness—has kept its genetic vigor. But family members become increasingly independent as the family company grows and prospers. They can afford other pursuits and will be attracted to them. Fewer and fewer of the members of the family, and especially fewer and fewer of the truly able ones, will be willing to devote themselves to the business and to give it hard work and dedication. Eventually, the family company becomes a professionally managed business in its entirety. Such members of the family as may still remain in the business then become the exception rather than the rule. The Rothschilds, it is well known, vie in pride of family with any royal family anywhere. But even the Rothschild banks now have non-Rothschild partners. Once this happens, the family business has ceased to be a "family business."

To run a successful family business therefore demands planning for the day when the very success of the business makes necessary changing its character. Within two generations—and with growth to fair size—the family becomes the beneficiary rather than the boss of such a business. If the planning is well done—as, for instance, by Pierre du Pont in the early twenties—careers in the business still remain a challenge for the ablest and hardest-working members of the family. The others should much earlier have become outside investors.

# 59

## The Multinational Corporation

*The Major Social Innovation Since World War II—The Testing Period Still Ahead—What Explains the Multinational?—Not an American Development—Not Confined to Big Business—Not Confined to Manufacturing—Not the Response to Protectionism—The Emerging Common World Market—The New Demands—From "Multinational" to "Transnational" Company—The Split Between Economy and Sovereignty—The "Multicultural" Corporation—Integrating Political and Cultural Diversity into Managerial Unity—The Internal Forces—The Need for Business Strategy and Strategies—The Need to Concentrate—The Top-Management Teams—The Need for Systems Management—The Individual Manager—His Organizational Placement—A Man Needs a Home—How to Pay?—The Multinational and Its Environment—Its Position in Its Host Country—Its Position in Its Home Country—Not an Economic but a Political Problem—The Multinational in the Developing Countries—The Folly of "Import Substitution"—The Wholly-Owned Subsidiary—The Canadian Example—The Problems of Success—The Petroleum Concession—The Multinational Tomorrow*

---

The multinational corporation raises diversity and complexity to new levels and makes new and unprecedented demands on top management with respect to business strategy as well as structure and behavior.

The multinational corporation is the outstanding social innovation of the period since World War II—a period otherwise lacking in social innovation and in social imagination. It has become the foremost non-nationalist institution in a world torn asunder by paroxysms of nationalist fever and an organ of integration in a world of political fission. This makes the multinational corporation important beyond its service as a business institution. But this also makes the multinational corporation a difficult and problematical institution. Indeed, the testing period is still ahead for the multinational corporation. If it cannot resolve the contradictions it has created, both internally and externally, as a result of being multinational in a nationalistic world, it is unlikely to prosper. For the multinational corporation is both cause and result—but also symbol—of a most profound event of the post-World War II period—the split between economy and sovereignty.

Multinational public-service institutions are lacking so far. There are "international agencies," but they are, for the most part, coordinating, rule-making, or research organizations rather than actors and performers. The only truly multinational public-service agencies capable of action in their own right rather than as agents of governments are the World Bank and the International Monetary Fund (the latter, especially, since International Drawing Rights were introduced as a supplementary "key currency" in 1971) and both, of course, reflect the same reality of a *world economy* distinct from political sovereignties that underlies the rise of the multinational corporation.

However, just as the economy is in the process of splitting off from sovereignty, so is the ecology. Truly transnational *environmental* organizations capable of acting and performing in their own right and without regard to national boundary lines are urgently needed. "Pollution" may be a local phenomenon, comparable with (and indeed closely linked to) production. But environment is becoming worldwide—just as the economy is in the process of becoming. In dealing with oceans and ocean beds, air resources and climate, soil and raw material resources, "sovereignties," even those of the biggest and largest nations, are increasingly coming to be seen as restraints rather than as the carriers of effective action. The multinational corporation may therefore well become the prototype and forerunner of a truly multinational public-service agency of tomorrow—just as, domestically, the management of business can now be seen to have been the forerunner and prototype of "management" for public-service institutions. And the multinational environmental agency of tomorrow will, predictably, encounter all the problems and questions of the multinational corporation of today, both internally and in its relationships to the multitude of political sovereigns, i.e., nation-states, their governments, but also their cultures and values.

This chapter discusses *businesses* and uses only business examples and business illustrations—it is all we have so far. But everything said in it should be applicable to the multinational public-service institution if and when it emerges.

If multinationalism is the most dramatic economic development since World War II, it is also the least understood. Myths abound regarding the multinational corporation. It is commonly believed to be something radically new and indeed unprecedented. But it is also the revival of an old trend. There were multinationals galore in the nineteenth century. And the fear of the multinationals is nothing new either. The most articulate outcry against being "taken over by the Americans" can be found in English books and magazine articles of 1900.

Both in the United States and in Europe, major scientific and technical inventions of the nineteenth century led almost immediately to the emergence of multinational corporations; that is, of companies that were making and selling goods in many countries. This was the case with Siemens in the 1850s; the English subsidiary was founded almost immediately after the German parent company, as was a subsidiary in Russia; for long years these subsidiaries almost overshadowed the German parent. McCormick's harvester and the reaper-thresher of his English rival, Fowler, also went multinational in the nineteenth century. So did Singer's sewing machine and the Remington typewriter within a few years after the original patents had been issued. The trend accelerated in the early twentieth century when, for instance, the Swiss chemical and pharmaceutical companies became multinational. Fiat and Ford both established subsidiaries abroad within a few years of their founding. In the 1920s such prototypes of the multinational businesses of today as Unilever and Royal Dutch/Shell were established.

The surge of the multinationals in the fifties and sixties represented in large measure a resumption of the pre-World War I trend rather than a totally new development. It expressed a return of the economic vitality and capacity to grow which World War I had paralyzed. Even in form, the multinationals of the present closely resemble the pre-World War I development: a parent company with wholly-owned subsidiaries and affiiliates in other countries. Unilever and Royal Dutch/Shell—the Anglo-Dutch companies with two parent companies in two countries and with top management and headquarters in two countries—are far more truly multinational in their structure than the new multinationals of the recent past.

In some areas, indeed, there was more multinationalism in the nineteenth and early twentieth centuries than there is today. Before World War I, for instance, two insurance companies domiciled in Trieste—then part of Austria-Hungary—were writing large amounts of life insurance through subsidiaries in thirty to forty countries all over the world, in Europe, in Latin America and Africa, on mainland China, and in Russia.

Another myth about the multinational corporation is that it is entirely or primarily an American development. To be sure, when the development got going in the fifties, it did so under the leadership of American companies. The reason for this was in part American economic and financial strength during this period. More important, however, were the economic policies of European governments. Despite the Common Market, the governments of Europe for a long time were unwilling to let their businesses become European businesses. Mergers or even "communities of interest" across the national boundaries of Europe were discouraged and frowned upon by most European governments (the British being the exception). It was therefore left to the Americans to avail themselves of the opportunities which the Common Market created. It is not too much exaggeration to say (as Servan-Schreiber did in *The American Challenge*, 1968) that it is largely the American initiative which converted the Common Market from good intentions into economic reality.

But the phase in which the leadership in the development of multinational corporations was in American hands came to an end in the mid-sixties. Since then, non-American businesses have taken the lead. By the early 1970s a little more than half of the business done by the multinationals was still done by companies headquartered in the United States. The other half was done by companies headquartered in many other places and managed as Dutch, Swiss, German, Swedish, French, English, Japanese—and, in a few cases, Latin American—companies.

By the mid-1960s the movement toward multinationalism had become general. The growth of the non-American multinationals since has been far faster than that of the American-based ones. And it promises to be faster still. The Pan-European company, in particular, is likely to emerge as a major factor in the world economy.

Another prevailing myth is that multinational business development is confined to big business. A prediction widely quoted in the early seventies asserted that by the mid-eighties of this century the entire manufacturing of the world would be in the hands of three hundred large multinational world companies, each doing business worldwide, and each doing many billion dollars in sales.

Actually multinational companies come in as many sizes as national companies do. The concentration of economic power is not necessarily greater in the multinational sector than it is within any national economy. Small multinational businesses may even have proportionately grown faster all along and may have done better. They just do not make the headlines.

Such small to medium-sized companies are building a multinational business on excellence and leadership in one small ecological niche. Here are some examples:

A Swiss-based company doing precision mechanics employs 1,800 people all over the world for a total sales volume of less than $50 million. It operates in almost fifty countries and manufactures in almost a dozen countries. It has grown from fifty employees in 1960; that is, it has grown more than thirtyfold in a dozen years.

There is, similarly, an American-based company of about the same size. When it started to go multinational, it employed only about one hundred people in Southern California. Ten years later it did business in some thirty countries with manufacturing plants in half a dozen: Great Britain, Germany, Sweden, Brazil, and, in joint ventures, Japan and Yugoslavia. It also built on the basis of leadership in a very small but highly demanding branch of technology on the boundary between chemistry and metallurgy.

There is the company which supplies spare parts for aircraft to most of the smaller airlines of the world, with warehouses and maintenance facilities from Accra to the Fiji Islands and Warsaw. There is the small New York Stock Exchange firm specializing in research for institutional investors which has offices and partners in London, Brussels, and Hong Kong, and which serves as many institutional investment clients outside of the United States as it does within the United States.

These are still small businesses and likely to remain so. Yet they have become as fully multinational as the big companies.

The idea that it is manufacturing that has gone multinational is a misunderstanding. The fastest growth has been in finance, where the large American commercial banks went multinational before their clients did.

The most dramatic development on the multinational front are the new "consortium" banks in which large and medium-sized commercial banks pool their resources in a joint venture to become multinational "universal banks." One example is CCB, the group formed by the German Commerz Bank, the French Crédit Lyonnais, and the Italian Banco di Roma. Other consortium banks have British, American, Canadian, Brazilian, Belgian, Dutch, Japanese, Australian, Austrian, and Scandinavian partners.

The management consultants, the auditors, and the advertising agencies have also moved well ahead of the American-based manufacturing companies. And Sears, Roebuck started to go multinational in the late 1940s when it moved simultaneously into Canada and into Latin America, and later on, in the 1960s, into a number of European countries. In fact, the Sears, Roebuck store may have had greater impact on economy and society of Latin America, in Peru, in Colombia, and in Brazil, than any of the manufacturing companies that established subsidiaries in Latin American countries. And when Britain decided in 1972 to join the Common Market, retailers such as Lyons and Marks & Spencer moved much faster to become "European" than did manufacturers.

Even less valid than the common beliefs about the nature of multinationalism are the popular explanations of its causes. One sees in it a response to protectionism. Companies build factories abroad, it is being argued, because they can no longer export. But this explanation, while plausible, simply does not fit the facts.

The period of most rapid growth of multinationals—the fifties and sixties —was the period of the most rapid growth of international trade. Indeed, during this period the world trading economy grew faster—at an annual rate of 15 percent or so in most years—than even the fastest growing domestic economy, i.e., that of Japan. And the Japanese clearly could not have grown at the rate they did if protectionism had made impossible economic expansion based on exports abroad. It is not in the most heavily protected industries where multinationalism has forged ahead the fastest. It came late, for instance, in the chemical industry, which is very heavily protected. But pharmaceuticals, where protection plays a minor role, was a leader from the start. And there has been almost no multinationalism in the heavily protected steel industry.

But the best proof that protectionism is not at the bottom of the multinational trend is the European development. The rise of the multinationals began when continental Europe abolished protection and joined in a common market.

The common belief that the growth of the multinational companies has to do with trade restrictions will not hold up. The multinationals create export markets for their country's products. The multinational's subsidiary abroad is the best market for its home country's machinery, its chemical intermediates, and so on.

This shows clearly in American trade figures. Neither the export markets which America has been losing nor the markets in which imports have become important in the U.S. are those in which American multinationals are active. The American textile companies are still almost completely domestic. So are the American producers of chinaware, of flat glass, and of shoes. The foreign automobiles which have taken an increasing share of the American market are not those the overseas subsidiaries of the American automobile companies make. They are Volkswagens, Renaults, and Toyotas. But of the American exports, an increasing share, perhaps amounting to as much as one-third of the exports of manufactured goods in the late sixties and early seventies, were exports by the same companies that vigorously expanded multinationally, and were, above all, exports to the subsidiaries of such companies abroad. Very much the same thing applies to the Dutch, Swiss, Swedish, German, and Italian balances of trade.

Multinationalism and expanding world trade are two sides of the same coin. And far from being a cause of multinationalism, protectionism is incompatible with it. Indeed, an emergence of protectionism would be the greatest threat to the multinational corporation.

## The Common World Market

The true explanation of the explosive upsurge of the multinational corporation is something far more important than either American economic strength or protectionism. It is the emergence of a genuine world market, that is, a market which is not limited or defined by national, cultural, or even ideological boundaries, but transcends them. The market is no longer even international but increasingly "non-national," and based on common worldwide demands and expectations.

Any market is defined by demand. It is demand which creates the supply. It is demand which determines, indeed, what is "supply." And it is demand that determines the opportunities, the needs, the characteristics which make the market.

The great and unprecedented event of the post-World War II period is the fact that country after country, as its income and, above all, its information, increased, developed the same or similar demand patterns. This was unexpected. When World War II came to an end, it was "known" that the European countries and Japan, should they ever regain economic health, would develop different demand patterns. No one then doubted that an economically recovered France would surely have appetites and demands totally different from the United States, but also from Japan, from the Soviet Union, from Germany, or probably even from neighboring Belgium. This certainty—a certainty grounded in the reality of nineteenth- and early-twentieth-century experience—explains why such different people as De Gaulle and Khrushchev considered the emergence of a common demand, that is, of a genuine worldwide market, as "abnormal" and proof of some sort of "conspiracy."

By now we know that all the talk in the 1950s about the "Coca-Cola-ization" of Europe was nonsense. It was not that Europe became "Americanized." It was simply that the mass market, the "post-industrial" market, to use a slogan of the sociologists, had first become visible and overt in the United States. But when conditions appeared that were similar to those in the United States—not so much, however, higher incomes as greater mobility and a wider horizon of information—the demand pattern all over the world proved to be the same.

This does not necessarily mean that the same goods and services have a worldwide market, and that what sells in one area will sell in another.

A cautionary tale is the failure of one of the big multinational food processors to introduce dehydrated soups into the American market. In Europe these soups had become a main pillar of the company's success, had become immensely popular and were growing fast. When introduced into the U.S., they failed. It turned out that what is high convenience for the European housewife means nothing to the American housewife. The light weight of a dehydrated product as against a heavy can means little to a woman who goes shopping by car. And the small bulk of a dehydrated product has little appeal to a woman who has ample space in her kitchen, as the American housewife has. Its longer preparation time and its shorter shelf life, carrying with it a danger of rancidity, make the dehydrated soup less convenient than the canned soup despite the latter's weight and bulk.

But housewives—American, European, Japanese, and all the others— want convenience and are willing to pay for it.

The demand pattern that has emerged in the world economy is not the demand pattern the economists expected. The customer proved again that he knew better than the experts what he wanted.

The great demand has been for a little mobility—and a little power—that is, for such satisfactions as the automobile gives; earlier they had been inaccessible to any but a few very rich and very powerful. Another common demand is for a little health care so that a child has a fair chance to live to adulthood in a reasonable state of physical health and unscarred by disease or crippling deformation. It is demand for a little education. It is demand for access to a big world, which is what the news media, the movie, the radio, the television set offer to the masses who for millennia were limited in their knowledge, their horizon, and their vision, to the confining valley around them and to the small town in which everybody knew everybody else and in which everybody lived exactly the same life. And then there is the desire for the "small luxuries," for the things that are, in effect, assertions of personality over the confinement of poverty—the lipstick, the candy bar, the soft drink, and the ballerina slipper.

These have emerged as the universal demands. They are not based on affluence. They are based on something far more potent: information. If the world has not, as Marshall McLuhan announced, become a "global village," it surely has become a "global shopping center."

One effect of the change in the world economy is that every business from now on, even a purely local one, will in effect have to be managed as if it operated in a worldwide economy, even though it sells only in a small district. It will have to be international in its vision, just as a business operating in, say, southwest Bavaria has long had to be "German" in its vision, or a business operating in northern Michigan "American" in its vision. Just as that German business in Bavaria or the Michigan business in America has to understand and know its own national economy even though it does not operate in any but a small corner thereof, so will any business henceforth have to understand the major currents and trends of the world economy.

This development cannot be undone. Protectionism could indeed make the world economy poor and impede its functioning to the point of near-collapse. But it cannot destroy the common demands. It cannot undo the worldwide horizon and vision. The fundamental change has happened irrevocably. The question is not whether it will remain. The question is whether it can be turned to advantage—for society, for the individual, and for the business enterprise.

And the multinational corporation is both the response to the emergence of a common world market and its symbol.

## The World Market as Integrator

A market integrates. It converts "resources" into "factors of production." The national markets—the great achievement of the "commercial revolution" of the seventeenth and eighteenth centuries—integrated "factors of production" within a national economy. The common world market, as it is emerging now, integrates the same factors of production within a world economy.

The traditional theory of the international economy still sees countries having "comparative advantages" with respect to their "factorial costs." And insofar as they produce those things in which they have the greatest advantage, everybody's resources will be optimized. The guiding example is still Adam Smith's exchange of English wool against Portuguese wine. In this theory the individual country is the market that integrates the factors of production. And what is being traded are finished goods. Goods are mobile. The factors of production stay put.

But with a common world economy as the integrator, it is no longer a country that is the unit of production. The goods are the same everywhere —or pretty much so. The mobility is in the factors of production. Whereas international trade meant trade in goods or services, it now increasingly means trade in the factors of production.

To be specific, the most advanced multinational of the nineteenth century was probably Singer Sewing Machines with big, ultramodern plants in Scotland, France, Russia, Japan, and many other places, in addition to the original plant in Bridgeport, Connecticut. The Scottish plant at Clydeside near Glasgow was probably a more efficient plant with lower costs than the Bridgeport plant; it was also the bigger plant. It produced the same machines Bridgeport produced; and it produced the full range of Singer machines. But even though tariff walls were minimal in those days, Clydeside produced only for the British market; at the same time it produced everything Singer sold in Britain.

Compare this to the multinational of today. A major pharmaceutical company sells drugs in more than eighty countries of the world. In each of these countries it sells its entire product line. It has manufacturing plants in eleven countries: the U.S., Canada, Mexico, and Brazil in the Americas; in Britain, France, Germany, and Italy in Europe; in South Africa, Japan, and Australia. Only a few of the main drug products in the company's line are made by all eleven plants. Most of the company's drugs are made in only one plant, a few in two or three. Even the U.S. plants do not turn out the full product line. As a result, each of the plants sells some drugs to every one of the eighty-odd sales companies; and every one of these sales companies buys some drugs from each of the eleven manufacturing plants. Pharmaceutical drugs are made from chemical intermediates, e.g., from citric acid, which is the chemical base for many antibiotics. The company manufactures intermediates in seven countries: U.S., Mexico, Ireland, Great Britain, France, Australia, and Japan. Again, no country makes all the intermediates—each specializes. Each therefore supplies all eleven manufacturing plants. But each also sells a good part of its output—in some cases, more than half—directly on the outside to other competing pharmaceutical companies and to a wide range of chemical manufacturers. Research, finally, is being carried on in four countries—the U.S., Britain, France, and Japan, with a fifth research lab, in Brazil, to open in the mid-seventies. Again, each lab is specialized. The French lab, for instance, does all the company's research on central-nervous-system drugs but also all the work to convert drugs originally designed for the treatment of human diseases into drugs suitable for the veterinarian. And a drug developed by any one of these four research labs may be put into chemical testing and market introduction first in any one of the eighty countries in which the company operates.

But it is not only the—admittedly complex—pharmaceutical industry that integrates factors of production rather than trade in goods.

The most successful Detroit-designed "small" car, Ford's Pinto, gets its engine from Ford's German company, its transmission from Ford's British company, and much of its electrical system from Ford's Canadian company —but is sold exclusively in the U.S. and by Ford's American company. Similarly, major components for the Volkswagen sold in the U.S. are being made by Volkswagen do Brazil in São Paulo.

When it was announced in the spring of 1972 that all British government agencies would henceforth buy their computers from the one British computer company, ICL, the British subsidiary of the American Honeywell company pointed out in protest that its computers, though made by an American-owned company, contained a larger proportion of British-made components than the computers of British-owned ICL.

In the services areas, this integration of the factors of production within a common world market has gone even further.

A major U.S. bank arranged a $15 million, five-year loan for a Japanese manufacturing company in early 1971. The deal was initiated in Tokyo and by the bank's Japanese representative. The deal was worked out by the bank's offices in London and Frankfurt. The syndicate that advanced the money contained eight banks, one each from the U.S., Japan, Great Britain, Holland, Sweden, France, Switzerland, and Latin America. Most of the money was raised in Germany, where interest rates at the time were favorable. And the purpose of the loan was to finance a manufacturing subsidiary of the Japanese company in Latin America. Yet this was a routine transaction such as each of the participating banks engages in every week.

So far, most multinationals are still cast in the nineteenth-century, Singer-Sewing-Machine mold—that is, each subsidiary makes products or furnishes services for its own discrete national market. But the trend is toward the integration of the factors of production for a common worldwide market. It is the trend that follows from the logic of the market itself.

The term multinational is of very recent coinage: it was unknown even twenty years ago. It fits the nineteenth-century structure—Singer Sewing Machine—much better than it fits the development to which it is being applied. Singer Sewing Machine was truly "multinational." But the pharmaceutical company that integrates eleven drug-manufacturing plants, seven intermediate plants, and four research labs into sales of many drug products in eighty countries is not multinational. It is "transnational." And so is the automobile company that integrates plants in Germany, Britain, Mexico, and Canada for a sale in the U.S., or the commercial bank that integrates banking resources in eight countries to raise money in a ninth country to finance a development in a tenth country. National boundaries are no longer determinants. They are restraints, obstacles, complications. What determines is the reality of a non-national common market.

The term multinational, in other words, obscures reality rather than explains it. It is by now, however, probably too deeply entrenched. Even though it will have to be used, it should never be forgotten that the opportunities—but also the problems—of the so-called multinational lie not in its being multinational, that is, in its doing business in many countries. They lie in its being *transnational*, that is, based on the reality of a common world market—common in its demands, in its vision, and in its values.

This means that it is not factors of production that explain the new multinational, inform its strategy, and explain its behavior. It is factors of demand. It is demand that exerts the pull. The multinational business is in every case a marketing business.

## The Split Between Economy and Sovereignty

The development of a common world market has not been paralleled by the development of a world political community. The years during which the world economy created a demand for multinational business were years of continuing splintering in the world political system. The world political system is still based on the concept of the national sovereign state. For the first time, therefore, in three hundred years economy and sovereignty are becoming divorced from each other.

Such divorce was normal until the seventeenth century. Indeed, no one up to that time conceived a unity of economic entity and political entity. The unit of economic activity was first and foremost a local agricultural community, such as the medieval manor, producing most of the things it consumed. And the other unit was long-distance trade, totally divorced from any political system and carried out by merchants of trading cities who, in effect, constituted a transnational and closely integrated trading society. The bankruptcy in 1557 of the Spanish Crown, Europe's leading political power of the time—a traumatic event without precedent—brought the intercity merchant society crashing down in financial ruin from which it never recovered. But it also demonstrated to the emerging national rulers that to have political sovereignty, they had to take control of their own money and credit system and with it of their own economy. (See also the discussion of mercantilism in Chapter 27.)

The idea of a "national economy" as it emerged in the seventeenth century conceived for the first time of the political sovereign as engaged in economic as well as in political and military competition. The last remnants of the old separation of political sovereignty and economy, the international gold standard, then disappeared in the aftermath of World War I.

But while the victory of the national state as the economic sovereign seemed complete—and became indeed the major tenet of Keynesian economics in the interwar period—the postwar period has seen an abrupt reversal of what for three hundred years seemed a law of nature. It has seen the emergence of an autonomous world economy which is not just the sum of national economies.

The clearest symptom of this is to be found in the financial sphere. When the U.S. government, in 1967, tried to stop the multinational expansion of American companies and restricted the investment of U.S. funds abroad (a move prompted as much by pressure from America's allies, such as De Gaulle's France, as by concern for the U.S. balance of payments), the world economy successfully nullified the decree of the world's most powerful government. It immediately created the Eurodollar market (see also Chapter 7) which took over the financing of the multinationals—a market which essentially made European funds available to the American companies for their expansion in Europe.

Few governments, even during the heyday of mercantilism, have suffered from the delusion that they are truly "independent" economically. It always had to be recognized that the outside world exerts powerful influence on the domestic economy even of the strongest country, and that it sets very real limits on the freedom of action of the political sovereign. "Autarky," most governments knew, was a delusion (though the United States government, and especially the U.S. Congress, have frequently been victims of the delusion that their economy is, so to speak, on a separate planet and that U.S. policy, U.S. regulations, and U.S. fiat can operate independent of outside economic realities). But it has been for three hundred years the basic aim of national policy to keep this outside force and restraint to a minimum; to do so constituted the essence of national sovereignty. The emergence of the multinationals, while an effect rather than a cause of a fundamental change, is therefore a direct challenge to deeply rooted convictions, to deeply entrenched political institutions, and to habits of the mind, now three hundred years old. It is not only that the emergence of businesses which are multinational contradicts the doctrine—by now considered axiom by most—of the national state as the "natural" unit of organization for every sphere of human and social activity. It also contradicts the doctrine—heresy three hundred years ago, but by now a comfortable article of faith—that every institution of society must, ultimately, base its legitimacy and derive its constitution from the governing organ of the sovereign state, the national government.

What makes the multinational business so important is precisely that it challenges these axioms.* It is the first non-national institution—at least it is the first modern institution of importance which considers national boundaries an incident and a restraint rather than part of its own definition and identity. And this, in a world that threatens to be destroyed by nationalist passions, is an important institution. But it is by that token also a problematical and endangered one.

So far we have no theory, whether political, social, or economic, to account for the reality of the world economy and therefore for the behavior of the multinational corporation. The only theories we have are those of the "national economy," that is, the seventeenth-century theories of national sovereignty. This need not surprise anybody. Theories follow events. One can only codify what has already happened.

But it means that the multinational corporation has to grope its way, has to improvise as it goes along, has to experiment and test rather than proceed along clearly understood lines and on the basis of firmly grasped principles.

It means also that the multinational corporation is an extraordinarily difficult structure. It presents difficulties internally, with regard to its basic business strategy, its management structure, and its managerial relation-

*One of the best books on the multinational corporation is *Sovereignty at Bay* by Raymond Vernon, (Basic Books, 1971): this may be exaggeration—but sovereignty is being challenged.

ships. It represents new problems with regard to its external existence in its environment, and with regard to its relationship to the national state in which it does its business and into whose political jurisdiction it inevitably falls—there being no other political jurisdiction available.

Even if, as some people suggest, multinational corporations could incorporate with some international or supranational agency, the United Nations, for instance, or a European Parliament, they would still be multicultural. For it is not only political sovereignty that is national. Different peoples have different cultures, beginning with their language. This is bound to become more of a problem as the world economy becomes more universal. The more homogeneous economically the world becomes—in its appetites, at least, if not in its actual economic conditions—the more will local and cultural roots be needed. People need a home—and even the most luxurious 2,000-room hotel is not a "home." Managing the multinational corporation is therefore largely a problem of integrating political and cultural diversity into managerial unity.

## The Problems of Strategy

What distinguishes the multinational corporation from any other business is that it faces both internal and external diversity. It has to create unity within its own managerial organization and yet do justice to the diversity of peoples, nationalities, and loyalties within it. And it has to create a unified business that can optimize factorial costs and factorial advantages within a common world market and yet live in peace—or at least without constant conflict—with a multitude of separate political sovereignties

The pharmaceutical company mentioned earlier needs a strategy for the company as a whole. But each of the eighty-odd national companies needs one as well. So do the manufacturing units, the units making intermediates, and the research laboratories. Each has to be managed as an autonomous business with its own objectives, its own priorities and plans, its own profit and loss responsibility.

But at the same time, none of these units is truly autonomous. All are interdependent. It may, for instance, seem to be purely a concern of the subsidiary in a given Latin American country whether to accept an offer from the country's national health service of a contract that guarantees a sizable market for a drug for five years but at a 25 percent reduction in price. Yet such a price concession may set off demands for lower prices from the health services of other Latin American countries—and without any five-year purchase guarantee. It may appear purely a matter for one of the intermediate plants within the system whether it decides to expand its facilities because outside customers, that is, other pharmaceutical manufacturers, are increasing their uses of a substance it makes. But this immediately raises the question whether the company's own plants for finished products are to be considered preferred customers whose orders will be given priority, or whether the new outside customers are to be considered as preferred customers, or at least as equals. If the first line is taken, the company decides in effect to optimize its own manufacturing unit's results at the expense of suboptimizing the results of the intermediate unit. If the second alternative is taken, the company decides, in effect, that being an intermediate manufacturer is more advantageous than being a drug manufacturer.

These are strategic decisions. They have long-term—and often irreversible—impact. They cannot be made by "the top" alone. They require local knowledge. But they cannot be made locally either. They affect the whole company and must be made at the top. A multinational strategy which takes into account only the overall company is condemned to futility. Unless it can be translated into specific strategy for individual markets, it cannot succeed. But the multinational strategy which is decentralized, that is, a strategy which considers each unit and each market as an autonomous business, is equally condemned to futility. And it is impossible—theoretically as well as practically—to predict in advance whether the company-wide, overall approach to strategy or the market-by-market approach to strategy will be appropriate to a given situation.

The large-scale commercial banks have a similar problem. It is their very strength—it is indeed the reason for their existence as multinationals—that they can give financial service anyplace in the world. Equally it is their strength that they can offer one-stop banking—that is, that they can satisfy the major financial needs of a customer, whether for short-term money or for long-term loans, and even for equity capital, whether in dollars, in German marks, or in Japanese yen. This, however, requires one strategy which focuses on the needs of a major customer, such as, for instance, one of the big international companies, wherever they might arise. Whoever is in charge of this particular area, e.g., the major airlines, therefore has to look upon the entire bank as one business, as one resource, as one pool of capital, and as one pool of services. But at the same time, the bank's manager in any one particular market needs a strategy for his business. He needs to think through which companies in, for instance, Japan, are potential customers and for what services of the bank. He needs to be able to mobilize the resources of the bank worldwide for their needs. But he also needs to build up a purely local business. For the multinational customers of today are, as a rule, yesterday's satisfied local customers. Again, neither one global, bank-wide strategy nor local strategies can suffice. The bank needs both—and can never say in advance which of the two should come first, or which of the two actually govern a particular business relationship.

Few multinationals have thought through business strategy so far. One exception might be Unilever, which, for many years, has systematically planned both for the entire Unilever group, for major product lines within, such as edible oils and fats (margarine), soaps and detergents or fish, and for each major country. Fiat, in its deliberate policy of encouraging government-owned but Fiat-built automobile plants in communist Eastern Europe may be another example. A more recent and so far not yet truly tried case is Philips in Holland, with business strategies both for major product groups —of which Philips has sixteen—and for each of the countries in which Philips does business. No American company, to my knowledge, has so far done anything comparable.

But every multinational company faces the complexity of business strategy, precisely because it has to be both unified for the entire company and specific for each major product category as well as for each major market. This means that the multinational has complexity built into its very structure. It is multicultural, it is multinational, it is multimarket, and also multimanagement.

Adding to this a diversity of businesses makes the company unmanageable.

The successful multinationals are in effect single-market or single-technology companies. There is IBM, which has only one product. There are the pharmaceutical companies which have only one customer, the physician. There are the multinational commercial banks which have only one technology: financing business. There is Sony, which is the most multinational of all Japanese companies with almost half of its sales and profits coming from outside of Japan—yet concentrated on consumer electronics, and on a fairly small range at that. There is ADELA, the multinational venture banker in Lima, Peru, which concentrates on Latin America. And the multinational business services—the management consultants, the public accountants, and the advertising agencies which may have grown even faster than the multinational businesses themselves—are also, of course, highly concentrated in what they "make" and in what they "sell."

Without such fundamental business unity, the multinational company splinters into fragments. Management people lose the ability to understand each other, even with the help of an interpreter. The company then rapidly degenerates into a bureaucracy which adds more layers the less it truly directs and controls. The temptation to diversify, no matter how great in any given case, should be firmly resisted in a multinational corporation. The multinational conglomerate is an abomination.

## The Top-Management Teams

Of necessity, the multinational has not one but many top-management teams. It has as many top-management teams as it has business strategies. Corporate top management is one such team. But for each country, region, or product line there is another team. Insofar as members of the corporate top management also sit on a top-management team for a country or a market they are members thereof, rather than the team leader.

No one so far has found a satisfactory answer to the problem of top-management structure in the large multinational corporation. One thing, however, is clear. The traditional pattern is not the answer.

The traditional pattern constructs towering hierarchies in which levels are heaped on levels. The head of a national company typically reports to a regional executive who reports to another regional level—such as a European or a Latin American executive—who in turn reports to an international vice-president who in turn then reports to corporate top management. This not only denigrates the man who has to make the actual decisions, that is, the head of a business in a given country, it also creates a cumbersome bureaucracy, the main achievement of which is to delay decisions.

Some alternatives to this pattern can already be seen, and they do offer advantages.

The most satisfactory structure is perhaps that which Unilever has been developing. There each company in any country reports to one of the two head offices of the parent company, that is, either to London or to Rotterdam. But for each of the major product groups, e.g., soaps or fish or retail trade, there is a coordinating committee at headquarters, usually composed of people who have successfully operated businesses in the particular area. And within each major country, such as Germany, where Unilever has a number of companies, there is a "national board" composed of former senior executives of the companies in the country and chaired, as a rule, by a distinguished citizen of the country. This is cumbersome enough. But at least the head of a Unilever company, wherever he might be, has direct access to top-management people who can make a decision. Normally he will not use the right of access. He will rather work with his national board or with the committee in his product area. But organizationally he reports directly to top management. And this status within the company gives him status outside, within the industry in his country, with the country's government, with labor unions, and so on.

But even within Unilever the balance between the need to look upon each company as an autonomous business, the need to look upon each major product area as a unified business in its own right, and the need to look upon the whole company as a unit, in terms of capital appropriation or of key personnel, for instance, is difficult, precarious, and easily upset. At the very least, far too much time is spent on working out organizational relationships and on keeping the system going.

There are other alternatives.

One of the leading American multinationals, CPC (formerly Corn Products), has organized itself into five distinct companies: two American ones (consumer goods and industrial products), a European one, a Latin American one, and a Far Eastern one. Each is headed by its own president whose headquarters are within his territory. The company's top-management team of three or four men constitutes the board of each of these companies. It spends equal time working with the presidents of each of these companies and their senior men, at *their* locations, acting as the presidents' advisors, review organ, and resource.

Only one organizational conclusion has emerged clearly. In the multinational, the top-management team of the overall company must not, at the same time, be the top-management team of any of the operating companies, and least of all of the operating company where the headquarters are located. As soon as more than a very small fraction of a company's business is multinational, top management has to divorce itself from running any one national or regional component on any product area. Otherwise, it will spend all its time on its own immediate management job and will neglect the other businesses.

This, in other words, means that the traditional organization in which top management is both the top management of the overall company and that of its largest single—and usually the domestic—company, while all the rest of the business is under an international division, is the wrong structure. Wherever it persists—and it is still fairly common—it does damage or weakens the company's performance.

It was long ago proven that a central government cannot be ambulatory. A multinational organization needs a headquarters.

The best example of a "multinational government" in Western history, that of the government of Charlemagne, proved this point in the ninth century. Charlemagne's court moved from imperial castle to imperial castle. This was the only way in which the Emperor could keep contact with his representatives in the various parts of the empire. But in a pre-monetary age, the court could also support itself only by living off the land. This dependence on ambulatory headquarters was a major reason why, almost immediately after Charlemagne's death, the empire fell apart and split up into manageable pieces; that is, pieces that a ruler could govern from one place of residence. And yet Charlemagne's court did not even suffer from "jet fatigue," though "ox-cart fatigue" must have been severe.

A fixed place of business is a necessity for managing. Work requires time, continuity and rhythm and schedule. One needs the organized, systematic support which one can build up only over long years in one place. Imperial chancellors can perhaps travel all the time, as can executive vice-presidents. Market research men, accountants, personnel people, that is, people paid to think—not to mention secretaries or computer experts—have to stay put if they are to produce.

But at the same time, local decisions have to be made at the scene of action. The local decision has to be made within the framework of corporate strategy. But it has to be a local rather than a corporate decision if it is to be effective. The headquarters for the local business—and this may be European or it may be Swedish—has to be where the decision is to be effective. It has to be made with full knowledge of local conditions. It has to be made in cooperation with people on the spot and in relationships with local institutions. It has to fit local laws, local expectations, local habits. It has to be, above all, comprehensible to the people who have to carry it out, that is, to local people whose knowledge of the overall company is of necessity limited. The factory manager in Spain or the manager of the branch bank in Hong Kong achieves his results through his local knowledge, his local contacts, his local action.

Yet the pharmaceutical company manager in a Latin American country, the manufacturing manager in Ford's engine plant in Germany, or the Chase Bank branch manager in Frankfurt must know enough about the objectives, strategies, and needs of the entire company not to make the wrong decisions. He must know enough not to make decisions that optimize his own business but suboptimize the whole company.

There is another important problem in top-management structure for the multinational. Top-management structures are not mechanical; they are, above all, cultural. The top-management structure which an American management group accepts as right and proper may appear decidedly odd and uncomfortable to a French, a Japanese, or a German management group. Yet these French, Japanese, or German managers have to understand their own local top-management group, have to feel comfortable with it, have to work with it. To be successful, the top-management teams in a multinational have therefore to be different in their structure in different countries, or else they will not make local sense. Yet they have to be compatible at least throughout the company, or else various top-management teams cannot work together.

Top-management structure in the multinational, therefore, has to be built on the most complex and most difficult of all design principles: systems management. (This will be discussed in more detail later in this chapter.)

## The Individual Manager

Even more perplexing than top-management structure in the multinational is the design of the individual manager's job and of his function.

The man who heads the subsidiary of a major pharmaceutical company —whether the company be American, Swiss, Dutch, British, or German— in, say, a medium-sized Latin American country, e.g., Colombia, has to be a big man in his own country. He may head the largest pharmaceutical company in his country and be one of the largest employers, especially of educated people. With health care a major political and governmental matter in such countries—as it should be—he better be a man of considerable standing. Among the heads of pharmaceutical subsidiaries in such Latin American countries are, for instance, several men who were deans of the leading medical schools in their countries before they went into industry, and several who had served as ministers of health.

Drugs are the one part of modern medicine which a developing country can use effectively. It is easier and cheaper to obtain modern drugs than to educate and pay physicians, build hospitals, or develop health services in poor rural areas and in urban slums. Drugs, therefore, are likely to play a far more important part in the health-care system of such a country.

Yet in terms of sales, the country does not account for much more than a fair-sized sales district in one of the major developed countries, such as Kansas City in the United States or Manchester in England. How then should the executive be structured within the overall organization?

This is a problem which conventional organization theory cannot solve. The Unilever structure described earlier comes closest to solving it. But again, the only solution is to say that the head of the Colombian subsidiary is *both* manager of a fair-sized sales district and a member of company top management. Which of the two he is depends on the situation. In fact, it must largely be left to him to decide which role the situation demands. He should always have immediate access to the company's very top. But he should rarely use it. Yet he should also be the kind of man whom corporate top management looks to for leadership, guidance, advice, and counsel on major policy matters, e.g., on relationships with governments throughout Latin America, on long-range strategy in Latin America, and so on. He surely should not report to a Latin American vice-president in Basel or New York. He also should not have to "clear" the great bulk of his day-to-day problems with people who are even more junior.

Again, only systems-management concepts, nebulous though they are, are truly pertinent. Ordinary organization charts are likely to confuse rather than to clarify.

## A Man Needs a Home

Equally difficult are the problems of management personnel policy, of opportunities, status, pay.

The ablest man, by common consent, in the entire management group of one of the major American-based multinationals was the head of the Italian company, Dr. Manzoni. Manzoni had first become known to the company as the lawyer representing the Italian owners of a medium-sized business the American company acquired. The American president was so impressed by him that he asked Manzoni to take over when the Italian subsidiary ran into trouble a few years later. Manzoni restored the Italian subsidiary to health and rapidly built it into the leading Italian business in its industry. When the Common Market came into being, Manzoni planned and spearheaded the company's expansion throughout Western Europe, found the right acquisitions and partners, found management people for the new companies, trained and developed them, and, to all intents and purposes, ran the European companies of the group from his Italian headquarters. When finally replacement for the company's aging chief executive in the United States had to be found, everybody at once thought of Manzoni. But Manzoni turned the job down flat. "My sons are in high school, and I do not want them to become expatriates. My wife has old parents whom she cannot leave alone. And frankly, I myself see little that would make me feel at home in a small Midwestern town, and few attractions there that could compare with those of Rome. I know that I could do the job you want me to do—and the job is a fascinating one and far more than I would ever have dared aspire to in my wildest dreams. But, still, it is the wrong job for me."

People need roots. They need a home. They have a right to be concerned with the education of their children. They have a duty to aging parents. And they are probably more realistic than the company's personnel vice-president when they argue that they are unlikely to "transplant" well. Yet the company better find a way to put to work the talents of a Manzoni. If (as this company did, by the way) it concludes that the man is no longer "promotable" and relegates him to second-class citizenship, it cuts off its nose to spite its face. Such a man will leave—as Manzoni did within a year or two.

How then can one build a management structure which recognizes and indeed respects the roots of a man and yet builds a truly multinational team?

It is clear that one requirement is equal opportunity regardless of passport. A Manzoni must have the opportunity to get to the top according to his abilities. To deny the opportunity and to reserve senior management positions to people of a given nationality is to deprive the multinational corporation of its ability to attract capable people in every country in which it works.

Companies domiciled in small countries, such as Holland, Switzerland, and Sweden, confine, by and large, senior management positions in all their subsidiaries and affiliates to nationals of the parent company who have been trained and who have started their careers in the parent company. (The only exception to this rule is the United States, where the major Dutch and Swiss companies have, for many years, promoted Americans into their top management. But the American subsidiary of these companies is usually the largest unit within the entire group and has to be managed as a truly separate entity.) There are advantages to this—communications obviously are much easier. And some of the disadvantages which companies domiciled in large countries, such as the United States or Great Britain, would suffer if they followed this practice are not incurred by companies headquartered in smaller, neutral countries. No one worries much about Swiss imperialism.

But even in these cases, the policy is clearly not in the company's best interest. With competition for first-rate management people intense, good young men will not come to work in a company—or will not stay—unless they have equal opportunities. A company which, no matter what its professions, promotes only nationals of the mother country into senior positions, in its subsidiaries and affiliates or at home, is unlikely to obtain or to hold the managerial resources it requires.

The multinational corporation needs to offer the able young people in any country in which it operates *more* opportunities than a purely domestic one does. It needs, in other words, to make a virtue out of its being transcultural. Otherwise it will be less attractive than a well-managed purely domestic company. Yet a man's national roots, national loyalties, national culture, and his need for a "home" must be respected.

## How to Pay?

There are also serious compensation problems of the multinational executive. Should executives around the world be paid the same salary in line with their position? Or should salaries fit the widely varying local standards? Should the American or Dutchman who is sent from his parent company into the management of a subsidiary be paid on the local scale—which, for instance, in Japan would mean a salary far too low for an expensive place like Tokyo—but also receive substantial "benefits," e.g., in the form of housing or an unlimited expense account? And what about the man who heads what is in effect a small business within the corporate structure—the president of a pharmaceutical subsidiary in Colombia, for instance, who in terms of the size of his business is a middle-level executive, but who in terms of his position in the country is a top man?

Again, the requirements are not easily compatible. It is highly desirable to make it possible for a man to move and not to be penalized by a promotion. Yet if people are being paid according to the prevailing standards in the country in which they work, being promoted very often will mean that they are being asked to take a cut in pay.

The most extreme cases of this are the Japanese executives who are sent to work in the United States or in Europe. Even though what Japanese executives in New York and Düsseldorf receive is low by American or German standards, it is unheard of by Japanese standards. When, after five years or so, the successful Japanese executive is transferred back to a much bigger job at home, he often has to take a cut of 50 percent of income or more.

But, to have one member of a management group, and especially a member from abroad who is also a foreigner, paid quite differently from the rest of the group is disruptive.

By far the most serious compensation problem arises out of the fundamental business strategy of the multinational. For the multinational manager needs to be both a member of the top-management team of the whole company and of the top-management team of the unit for which he works. Traditional compensation plans, especially plans with big bonuses geared to the results of the unit which the manager manages directly are therefore likely to be both unfair and destructive. They penalize teamwork, just where teamwork is needed the most.

This can be seen in its most acute form in the multinational commercial bank. In the teacher example, the New York bank's representative in Japan, who initiated the business and produced a new and major client for the bank, had nothing to show for it in his profit and loss statement. The London branch, which did all the work, showed in its books only a liability. The Frankfurt branch, simply because it had a German mark surplus available, showed all the income from the deal. The typical bonus policy would highly reward Frankfurt, penalize London, and leave Tokyo out altogether.

To tie a man's compensation to the results of his own branch or territory will therefore make him slight the very opportunities that might produce the greatest results for the bank—opportunities where the actual transaction might be done by another branch or by headquarters. To pay him on any other basis, however, or to rely on personal and subjective judgment rather than on impersonal and objective yardsticks, is equally undesirable. But what *is* desirable is by no means clear yet—let alone how it can be achieved.

In almost every area throughout this book examples of successful approaches could be given. But I have not been able to find yet a successful and working compensation policy for managers in multinational business. American companies profess the same frustration and confusion as European or Japanese ones. And every compensation policy in multinational corporations I know of is forever being restudied, reorganized, revised. The most successful policy may well be that of a major Swiss pharmaceutical company which frankly says, "We know that whatever we do will at best take care of symptoms for a few months; but at least we try to make our management people understand that there is no solution and that day-to-day accommodations to the worst problems of the moment is the best they —and we—can expect."

A true multinational which completely transcends in its management structure, in its managerial jobs, and in its personnel policies, national and cultural boundaries is neither likely nor perhaps desirable. What is needed is a floating balance between conflicting needs and conflicting demands. A multinational must be able to use a Dr. Manzoni as a member of the top management of an American-based company and yet respect his legitimate desire to remain a resident in his own country and a member of his own culture. It must be able to have both an overall company strategy and local strategies for a given unit. It must be able to pay for performance and yet encourage teamwork. It must be able to be both centralized and decentralized, and to know when to be one or the other.

This requires a great deal of formal structure and policy. But it requires, even more, a great deal of mutual knowledge, mutual trust, and shared experience. Above all, it requires tremendous self-discipline throughout the entire managerial group.

## The Multinational and Its Environment

Practically every argument against the multinational corporation advanced in any country is by itself a fallacy. It can be disproven easily. And yet the disproof is not going to convince the critics and enemies of multinationalism. They may be using the wrong arguments. But their hostility is directed toward a reality. They are formulating the problem wrongly. But there is a real problem.

In its host countries, even highly developed ones with substantial economic strength of their own, the multinational is attacked as being impervious to the country's economic, social, and financial policies, and as undermining the country's sovereignty and its government. It is attacked as having a power of decision over what will be produced, over jobs, over industrial and economic policy, which is illegitimate and beyond proper control. Decisions, rather than rest in the country's legitimate authority, such as its parliament or government, are exercised in a shadowy and indefinable way, someplace far away, by faceless men who neither know the country nor care for it.

But in the multinational's home country it is also attacked—and in strong countries, including the United States, as well as in weak ones. Here too, the multinational is seen as a means to evade, if not to subvert, political authority and of creating a superpower, not accountable to anyone and yet in control of economic policy, of jobs, and even, to a large extent, of policies in noneconomic areas. The American-based multinational is accused in the United States of "exporting jobs" but also of using its subsidiaries abroad to evade U.S. policies such as the former ban on trading with Red China. And it has been attacked with equal bitterness in host countries abroad because the subsidiaries in these countries, by not being willing to trade with Red China, defied and subverted the host country's, e.g., Canada's or Sweden's, own policies in international affairs.

The counterargument of the multinational companies is a perfectly valid one. No business, no matter how rich and big it may be, has any power against a national government. In any clash between economic and political power, at least in this century, economic power has come out a very poor second. The multinational exists, like any business, at the sufferance of national government.

But this argument does not go to the heart of the matter. The real problem is that the multinational by its very nature must look upon the economy in non-national terms. It must look upon resources, such as manufacturing plants, as part of a transnational economic system rather than as national assets. It must try to optimize in accordance with the market rather than in accordance with national boundaries.

This is the true difference between the twentieth-century multinational and its predecessors before World War I.

It is the function of the multinational in a common world market to allocate production and markets according to economic logic; that is, to optimize production and distribution across very large areas, if not the entire world. But "production and distribution" is simply another term for jobs, for imports and exports, that is, for balances of trade and balances of payment, for wage levels—and altogether for economic conditions and economic policies.

It is simply not true that the economic optimization of the multinational "exports jobs." Every study has shown that it creates jobs. The goods its subsidiaries abroad produce and market would not otherwise have been made in, and bought from, the multinational's home country. But the subsidiary buys equipment and supplies from the multinational's home country. Indeed the multinational, by moving production to people, may be a major force in preventing dislocation and turbulence. The alternative—large-scale migration of low-skill and low-income peoples—whether Blacks into Harlem, Algerians into France, Turks into Germany, sharecroppers from Brazil's Northeast into São Paulo, or Sicilians into Torino—creates, we now know, unbearable tensions. The economist—almost any economist—would therefore conclude that all the criticism of, and resistance to, the multinational, is misinformed.

But this misses the point. The multinational is a problem precisely because its decisions are based on economic rationality and divorced from political sovereignty.

There is no solution. The multinational is a political problem not because of anything it does or does not do. It is a problem because political sovereignty and economic reality no longer coincide. It does the multinational no good to protest that it and each of its subsidiaries are "good corporate citizens" of the country in which each operates. Of course, it and each of its subsidiaries observe the laws—at least to the same extent to which the country's nationals observe it. But if the phrase is meant to imply—as it usually does—that the multinational in every country in which it operates thinks and acts in terms of that country's national economy and market, it is nonsense. To do so would deny the whole logic of the multinational corporation, which is to optimize resources within the world market reality.

But to reassert against the multinational the reality of national sovereignty is also futile. This is what De Gaulle tried to do. The only result was a rapid decline in the competitive position of the French economy in the world. It is no accident that the French have become the strongest advocates of the proposed law for a "European transnational company."

There is indeed a real need for new international law to come to grips with this tension.* Such law will not only have to define under what conditions countries accept multinationals and what limitations they may impose on ownership, on remittance of profits and repayments of capital, and on freedom of movement of goods, people, and capital from one subsidiary of a multinational to another.

It will, above all, have to "depoliticize" the multinational. Insofar as this means that the multinational will be forbidden to try to use the political strength of its home government for its own ends, beyond what it is entitled to under the new international law, this should present relatively little problem. As far as relations between developed countries are involved, such use of political power for corporate ends has long ceased to be feasible. And

*As has been argued for many years and with great cogency by Jack N. Behrman, former Assistant Secretary of Commerce of the U.S. under President Kennedy, and now Professor of International Economics at the University of North Carolina.

as far as relations between the developed and economically strong home country of a multinational and an economically weak developing country are concerned, it is by now abundantly clear that "multinational imperialism" is futile.

After the electoral victory of the Left in Chile in 1970, an officer of ITT suggested to the Nixon Administration that it foment economic and political chaos in Chile to prevent the inauguration of a Marxist president and to save ITT's Chilean telephone company from expropriation. The officer only ensured that the Nixon Administration—despite its hostility to the new Chilean government—would do nothing and remain scrupulously uninvolved. Still the Chileans seized upon this to attack all foreign business, and business altogether.

Any future international law regarding the multinational must outlaw any action of this kind. In whatever country it operates, the subsidiary or affiliate of a multinational is clearly entitled to no more political support from its home government than a private citizen.

Far more difficult will be the legal resolution of the question of preference given by governments to their own national businesses. To what extent should it be permitted? To what extent, for instance, should the universal practice of giving limited or absolute preferences to national producers in public works or government purchases be legalized? And who is a national producer in the age of the multinationals?

In the example cited earlier of the British government ruling to have British government departments give preference in buying computers to British-owned ICL, "national" was defined by ownership. British Honeywell's protest against the ruling, in effect, asked that nationality be defined by the number and location of jobs. Both companies are, of course, British in terms of their incorporation and location. And with respect to many other products even the British government accepts the logic of the Honeywell argument.

The thorniest issue is that of the reach of the home country's jurisdiction. It is also the one which the U.S. will find the most difficult.

Traditional U.S. legal—or at least governmental—doctrine has held that any subsidiary or affiliate of an American company abroad is subject to American jurisdiction, with respect to antitrust, for instance, but also with respect to restrictions on trade with certain countries. But American antitrust ideas are by no means universally accepted as sound or even as moral. Compulsory cartels, for instance, are in most continental countries (and in Japan) considered normal instruments of economic policy. And competition is seen as more of a vice than a virtue.

Resolving these problems by a common code of behavior is the only way to make the multinational what it should and could be: a powerful instrument for economic strength and political harmony. The problems are largely political and legal. But they are problems which it is the duty—and the opportunity—of top management in the multinationals to think through. Otherwise, it is safe to predict, political solutions will be imposed on the multinationals which can only damage them and the world economy.

Few of the multinationals even seem to be aware of the task. They seem to assume that the problems will go away if only no one talks about them —which is neither intelligent nor responsible.

## The Multinationals and the Developing Countries

Some 80 percent of multinational investment and business—after taking out as not truly multinational the plantation and extractive industries (such as crude oil production or iron-ore mining)—is in developed countries. And so is some 80 percent of world trade, again subtracting agricultural products and raw materials.

But both the greatest contributions and the greatest problems of multinationalism lie in the developing countries.

On the one hand, there are few things a developing country needs as much as the multinational corporation. There are few contributions from which it can benefit so much as from those only the multinational corporation can make. A developing country needs capital. It needs access to technology even more. It needs access to markets for whatever goods its one surplus resource—labor—can produce.

The greatest contribution the American multinationals have made to countries like Taiwan, Hong Kong, and Singapore, has been neither capital nor technology. It has not even been entrepreneurial and managerial skill —these countries, being ethnically Chinese, have adequate supplies of both. It was a guaranteed market in the U.S. for the textiles, the Christmas ornaments, and the radio sets which these countries manufacture.

Most of all, a developing country needs a way to acquire skills—industrial skills, managerial skills, entrepreneurial skills. And no other institution has so far proven capable of providing the transfer of skills, on which rest all hopes for the economic and social development of a developing country.

But at the same time, a developing country, almost by definition, has a balance of payments problem. The more capital it imports, the more foreign exchange will it have to produce to service the capital. Even more important, a developing country, almost by definition, has a severe problem of national identity. It may be—and usually is—"nationalist." But it rarely has a tradition of nationhood. And the multinational company in which a country's ablest, or at least its most affluent, people are subordinate to "bosses" elsewhere—in London or New York, Rotterdam or Tokyo—

creates a problem of national loyalty and allegiance, at least in the minds of people who are desperately struggling to define their own national identity. It also creates a "brain drain"—the ablest people go to work for a foreign employer. This creates a feeling of dependence, if not of helpless impotence, in the face of concentrations of economic power compared to which a poor country looks puny indeed.

It is not just paranoia that makes a Peruvian or, for that matter, an Indian minister feel that a big multinational, domiciled elsewhere in a developed country, is a threat. He knows perfectly well that no matter how important the company's subsidiary may be to his own national economy, it matters little to the treasurer of the multinational at headquarters. For Peru or India, a given subsidiary of a multinational—the pharmaceutical subsidiary of an American company in Peru or Hindustani Lever in India—may be a giant on which the national economy heavily depends. But it produces at best a small percent of the total revenue of the pharmaceutical multinational or of Unilever. In its decisions, the central management of the multinational cannot possibly subordinate the interest of the total company to the interests of Peru or India. It may not willfully do damage—indeed there is no reason why it should. But it must treat as trivial the very concerns which are central and essential to the Peruvian or to the Indian cabinet minister or politician.

And then the very qualities which make it an economic asset to the developing country also make it a powerful competitor to the local entrepreneur, the local business establishment. Both in Brazil and in India, the local businessmen, while themselves deeply engaged in joint ventures with multinationals based in Europe and in the United States, have also been most vocal in their demand for "protection" from the multinational, for majority ownership, or at least controlling ownership to be in the hands of local investors, or for closing whole sectors of the economy to the multinationals.

The ambivalence of the developing countries was shown dramatically by the very different reaction of the countries along the north and west coasts of South America to the so-called Andean Pact which proposes, in effect, that multinationals be strictly limited, and confined to narrow sectors of the economy and to minority holdings.

Chile and Peru demanded even more stringent provisions which, in effect, would have banished the multinationals within ten or fifteen years. Colombia signed the pact—but with severe reservations and indeed with the clear and declared intention of not carrying it out. Venezuela long refused to sign at all.

The reason for these differences in attitude is not ideology—the Venezuelan government was more leftist than was the Chilean at the time (around 1968) the pact was drafted. The reason is that each country has different multinationals. In Chile and Peru the foreign company was still nineteenth century, as a rule: extractive industries such as copper mining and petroleum, and "infrastructure" utilities such as power and light, and telephone companies. In both countries foreigners largely manage these businesses, and local businessmen are kept out of both management and ownership. In Colombia, the multinational did not make its appearance until after World War II. It is active mostly in manufacturing, both for the home market and for export. The Colombia subsidiaries of the multinationals are, almost without exception, managed by Colombians. And many are partnerships with Colombian entrepreneurs. Venezuela, finally, eagerly wants multinational manufacturing companies to offset its industrial oligarchy—the few families who, as local representatives and confidants of the big international petroleum companies, have come to dominate whatever industry there is in the country. Venezuela—in part because of its oil revenues—has a large number of highly trained young men who find opportunities seriously limited in the family-run companies of the country and who, highly nationalist though they are, would welcome the coming of the foreign multinationals with their career opportunities for the able man regardless of family background.

These examples show that it is up to the multinational and its top management to structure the right relationship with a developing country. The tension cannot be eliminated. But it can be assuaged.

An intelligent multinational management will, for instance, refrain from going into businesses that will, inevitably, become a burden on the slender foreign-exchange resources of a developing country or into businesses that cannot exist unless so heavily protected as to become a burden on the country's consuming masses.

It is clearly undesirable to build a manufacturing facility where the costs —of raw materials, of labor, or of capital—are so high as to make economic operations highly problematical. It is foolish to depend on promises of governmental protection in such a case.

Many companies have built manufacturing plants in the smaller Latin American countries despite high factorial disadvantages and based on promises of government protection alone. These governments, in the 1950s and 1960s, were willing to promise almost anything to obtain "import substitution." By now most of these companies have learned that they made a mistake. They may show the profits which a prohibitive tariff guarantees them, but they cannot remit them. For this would damage the country's precarious balance of payments. A plant which can be justified only with import substitution makes the country, as a rule, actually more import-dependent—on raw materials or on machinery. At the same time it creates a demand for foreign exchange to service the capital investment without creating the exports to produce the foreign exchange. Furthermore these companies stand in danger of seeing their investment wiped out should there be any move toward economic integration such as the proposed Latin American free trade area.

Any investment made anywhere should be capable of survival in a competitive market. If there is little reason to hope that within a few years a new plant or a new business will gain competitive strength, at least adequate to survival without protection, it should not be started in the first place.

This, of course, has been known since the first protectionist theory was developed—in the early decades of the nineteenth century, by Henry Clay in the United States, and by his disciple, Friedrich List, in Germany. "Infant industries" may need protection, may indeed deserve it. But the purpose of such protection is to enable them to grow into "adults" who can stand on their own feet. If that is not accomplished, the industry will sooner or later be in trouble, no matter how great the protectionist subsidy.

It can also be said that the traditional nineteenth-century pattern of the wholly-owned subsidiary does not fit the developing countries. It discourages rather than encourages what the country needs the most: native investment and capital formation, and native managers and entrepreneurs. Yet the local subsidiary must be capable of being part of an integrated worldwide economic and business strategy. It must be capable, for example, of specializing in making one major component for the multinational's plants and markets everywhere but of importing, from the other plants of the multinational, whatever components it is not suited to make.

Ford's Mexican subsidiary, as mentioned before, specializes in making electrical assemblies for the Pinto. But it probably should not make engines at all but get them from Ford's Canadian, German, or English plants.

But this then raises the very difficult problem of harmonizing the interests of the local partners—let alone those of the local governments—and those of the multinational system. Who makes the optimization decisions?

In many developing countries the traditional congruence of capital investment and management control needs to be re-examined. Some developing countries can—and should—generate their own capital. Brazil is one example. But so are, to a large extent, the Chinese territories of Taiwan, Hong Kong, and Singapore. What they need is technology, management, and access to markets. Here management contracts rather than ownership of subsidiaries may be needed.

Other developing countries need the capital as well but need also either provision for eventual participation in ownership by nationals or, from the beginning, financing other than investment by the multinational. Otherwise the relationship will become unbearable when the country develops.

The key case is, of course, Canada. That Canadian industry is so heavily owned by foreign, and especially by U.S. companies, is the result of

*Canadian* decisions and actions, and especially of the deliberate policy of the Liberal governments of Canada in the thirty years after the Great Depression of the thirties, to channel Canadian capital into "infrastructure" investments such as public works and leave industrial investment to the foreigner. The result, in economic terms, has been a brilliant success. Canada which, in 1930, was a poor and largely pre-industrial economy is by now one of the world's most highly developed and wealthiest economies. Politically the result has, however, been undesirable. A major economic power, which is what Canada has become, cannot be "owned" abroad.

The only large company that has understood this is the American Telephone Company. At the end of World War II it owned practically all of the two telephone companies in Canada's most populous provinces, Ontario and Quebec. Then it began systematically to divest itself of share ownership to the point where these companies are now almost entirely Canadian-owned. Yet, technically and in terms of operations, they have remained members of the Bell System.

Finally, the multinational needs to think ahead and solve the problems which its own success will create in a developing country. As a result of such success the country will no longer be a developing country but, like Canada, become a developed one. At the least it will change to the point where the old relationship becomes untenable.

The petroleum concession becomes untenable as it succeeds. For this first means that a formerly dirt-poor country becomes oil-rich. It means also that nomadic Bedouins become skilled mechanics, geologists, and chemical engineers. The concession made sense in the beginning, if only because of the enormous costs and high risks of exploration. The petroleum-producing country still needs the international oil company—perhaps more than ever. For it needs a complex and highly expensive transportation and marketing system worldwide. But the concession as a relationship has outlived its usefulness and becomes a millstone around the neck of both producing country and oil company.

That not one international petroleum company, at least to public knowledge, faced up to the problem and thought through a new relationship is a severe indictment of top management.

## The Multinational Tomorrow

One thing is clear: the multinational tomorrow will be different from the multinational of today.

We still, substantially, have the nineteenth-century multinational but use it to do the twentieth-century task of the transnational. We are, in other words, in a transition period.

About the relationship between the multinational and its political environment, it is easier to say what will not work than what will.

1. What will not work is clearly what might be called the Canadian pattern. Somehow the multinationals must be built into the political reality of their host countries so that political sovereignty becomes a support of multinationalism.

Seen in this perspective, the Japanese policy has been realistic despite its obvious parochialism and despite the fact that it is based on fear of the outsider, and on aversion to him rather than on any conscious and systematic thought regarding Japan's position in the world economy. Japan's policy has attempted to obtain the benefits of economic integration without the resultant dependence on, let alone domination by, outside business. It has attempted to find new forms of integration, e.g., the joint venture and the technical partnership, without relinquishing ultimate decision-making power.

But the Japanese policy is still focused on nineteenth-century realities rather than on those of today. It also, for this reason, is no longer adequate, even though in many important respects, it may more closely foreshadow the structures of tomorrow than the monolithic company, owned, controlled, and directed throughout the entire economic world from one decision-making center.

2. Also untenable is the nineteenth-century pattern of foreign domination and control of the infrastructure businesses, such as electric power, transportation, and telephone. One reason is that the foreigner cannot afford these investments in an inflation-prone world. These are capital-intensive businesses. Yet they are also politically very sensitive businesses, the prices of which are everywhere under government control. In an inflation, a foreign company will not be allowed to raise telephone rates—only a government can get away with this. And in an inflation a foreign company cannot raise the capital to maintain, let alone expand, service—only a government with the power of taxation can do this.

3. A position such as IBM has in the world's computer industry is not a tenable one and goes beyond the limits that will be allowed to any one multinational company. IBM has a near-monopoly on the vital new social function of information technology. The IBM dominance may be overcome gradually as other businesses in the computer and information industry grow more rapidly than IBM. This would be the most desirable solution. Or governments in other areas, such as Western Europe and Japan, may succeed in their attempts to organize their own effective competitors to IBM. Finally, IBM may be deprived of its dominant position by governmental fiat.

There might even be a totally new way to resolve the IBM problem. IBM might become the first truly transnational public utility. It might continue as a company enjoying worldwide leadership, if not near-monopoly position, and yet be anchored in the economic and even political structure of the host countries, through partnership with local governments, local part ownership, and local regulation.

But one way or another the IBM dominance on a key necessity of modern society will be curbed.

4. Finally, multinationals will not be permitted to operate in developing countries without thinking through the consequences of their success as developers of the local economy and without planning ahead for the change in the relationship that is mutually desirable.

But as to what will be, one can only say that top management has the responsibility to develop the relationships that will work—and especially the relationships with developing countries.

## Tomorrow's Management Structures

Tomorrow's management structure of the multinational will also be different from today's.

Even within the developed countries the multinational will have to be able to harmonize, in one structure, the need for "polycentric" management with the need for a common business strategy. One reason for this is the need to have the necessary corporate flexibility to exploit whatever capital markets are most advantageous in the form preferred by each capital market.

The American-based multinational is already heavily owned by Europeans. But the European investor has long preferred a convertible debenture to outright equity investment. As a result, up to 20 percent of the equity capital of large American-based multinationals is already in the form of convertible debenture, often in European currencies and owned mainly by European institutions and investors.

But this might mean also the creation of European subsidiaries and affiliated companies with direct European stock ownership, of a similar Brazilian subsidiary and affiliated companies with shares in the hands of Brazilians, of joint ventures and similar partly owned partnerships in Japan and other places, and so on. Organizationally what is required—and evolving—is systems management.

The multinational cannot hope to solve its internal problems or the problems of its relationship to its political environment unless it organizes itself as a highly disciplined, centrally directed, but flexible, federation of equals. This is the only way in which the president of the Colombian subsidiary of the worldwide pharmaceutical company can be both top management and a regional sales manager. It is the only way in which he can operate in two different roles according to the logic and the needs of different situations. It is the only way in which the multinational can adopt and turn to its own advantage very different forms of relationships with different hosts and environments: joint ventures here; partnerships there; ownership of substantial minorities in regional or local subsidiaries by local investors; partnership with governments in the many countries where government enterprises are important and indeed central factors in the economy; management contracts rather than ownership in certain developing countries, and many others.

At the same time, it is equally clear that the multinational company needs to be structured so as to be able to manage common resources for one world common market. One such resource is capital. Another one is knowledge. The most important and most difficult one is managers and professionals. Unless managers and professionals can be both "full citizens" within the overall company and important leading members of their own communities, the multinational companies will not be able to attract and hold the kind of people they need. They will fail to capitalize on what is their greatest asset: the desire of the young to be part of a bigger world, to travel and to live in different cultures, and to have a wide range of choices. The multinational company offers this in a way yesterday's domestic company could never do. At the same time, it must be able to offer to the same young people, and especially to the able young people in the developing countries, the opportunity to make a contribution to their own country, their own society, their own economy.

It is also reasonably clear that tomorrow's multinational company will have to be able to embrace within one and the same corporate framework, and within one and the same management group, different managerial traditions. In Japan it will have to be able to make productive the Japanese traditions of structure, of promotion, of management. But in Germany it will have to be a German company. It will not only have to build its top management the way Germans expect their top managements to be built —that is, as a team under a presiding officer—it will also have to satisfy German notions of the proper qualifications for management, for instance, the German valuation of an engineering career as a preeminent preparation for top management (a valuation which no other country shares, at least not to anything like the same extent). In France, whether it approves of it or not, it will have to be able to accept the French emphasis on the graduate of the Grandes Écoles, such as the École Polytechnique, as an elite corps, and even the French tradition under which a *polytechnicien* starts his career in government service—in which he usually does not use the technical education he has received—then around age forty-five or fifty, when at the top of the government ladder, switches directly into the top management of major business enterprise. And in America—as most multinational Europeans operating in this country learned long ago—top management will have to bear the American top-management stamp.

But at the same time the multinational company will have to be unified. Its management people, even in middle management, will have to be able to understand these differences, will have to be willing to accept them, will have to learn to respect them. Where today the tendency in most multinationals is to say, "This is how we do it in Chicago (or Munich, or Osaka, or Eindhoven)," they will have to learn tomorrow to say, "This is what we want to achieve; how does one get it done in Peoria (or Munich, or Osaka, or Amsterdam)?"

The multinational of tomorrow will inevitably have to have more than one management team. Its corporate top management will be such a team. But at the same time, it will be a member of a great many other top-management teams. And in the other top managements, somebody who is not necessarily corporate top management will have to be the team leader.

CPC, the American-based company already mentioned, is a first example. Corporate top management is a team of about four or five people. But it is also a member of top management of each of its five companies. The president of each of these companies is the presiding officer for the top-management team of his company, of which his own corporate top management are members. They can, of course, replace him. They certainly make the decision whom to appoint into the presidency of each of the five companies. But with respect to his own area, he "sits at the head of the table." Each president, and especially the presidents of the European, Latin American, and Far Eastern companies which preside over a large number of autonomous companies in different countries, is in turn a member of the top-management team of each of these companies, with the head of that company "in the chair."

This is a complex and difficult structure. It requires not only that corporate top management free itself from all operating responsibility. It requires that management think through clearly what its business—or businesses—are and should be. It requires management by objectives and self-control. It requires that conscience functions are organized and made effective. It requires the highest degree of self-discipline on the part of managers and willingness to take upward responsibility to keep higher management, and especially the corporate top management, informed, knowledgeable, and educated. It also requires the "executive secretariat" or "business research staff" (Chapter 51).

And there is need for highly effective boards of directors, both for the overall company and for major parts, and functioning both as review and control boards and as public and community-relations boards (see Chapter 52).

But multinational management, like all systems management, also demands personal contact, vigorous efforts on the top to create and to maintain communications, and willingness both to learn and to teach. It cannot be run by "systems," though it requires a high degree of it. Like its prototype in the NASA "systems management" (Chapter 47), top management in such a structure has to be free to spend time with people, and not only with the top people. It has to make sure that every decision-maker in the structure knows what goes on and not only within his own unit. It has to make sure that people pretty far down the line understand and that they in turn help top management understand. This requires that the people in New York or in Basel have enough time to sit down with their associates in São Paulo or Sydney—not with a problem, not with their own concerns, but as learners, as listeners, as resource. It similarly requires that the top-management people, the members of the corporate top-management team as well as the members of all other top-management teams down to the smallest local company, have time for direct personal relationships with important groups in their environment: the government people, the political leadership, the opinion-makers, whether in the communications media or in the universities. They cannot hope to reconcile the cleavage between the reality of a world economy and the reality of national sovereign states. But it is their job to make it bearable.

The multinational company is surely the most important economic instrument in today's world. It is important precisely because it reflects the new reality of a world market and of a world economy. It is important because it is the most effective tool for optimizing the economic resources available. But precisely because it reflects a new reality rather than the extension of yesterday's business, it also requires new structures, new methods of integration, and new relationships. The multinational company is still new enough to be crippled. If so, the world would be the poorer. And the greatest sufferers would be precisely those developing countries which are, at the same time, most afraid of the multinational company, most conscious of the disparity between its strength and their own weakness, most in need of psychological, but also of economic, security and identity. But to make the multinational corporation live up to its promise requires innovative work of high quality from its top managements.

# 60

## Managing Growth

*IBM's Near-Miss—Ford, Siemens, AT&T & Sears, Roebuck—The "Identity Crisis"—Why Growth Is Not Automatic—Is Growth Necessary—The Growth Craze of the Fifties and Sixties—Myths about "Growth Companies" and "Growth Industries"—The Turbulence of Zero Growth—Growth in the Public Service Institution—Growth as a Minimum Need—Preparing for Growth—Top Management: The Controlling Factor—Staffing Key Activities—The Symptoms of the Need for Change—The Top Man's Personal Decision—And His Responsibility.*

Growth is not automatic. It does not follow from success. Of course it requires having the right products or services for the right markets at the right time. But this is a prerequisite for growth, a necessary condition, rather than growth itself.

Growth of a social organism such as a business is as much stress and strain as growth is in a biological organism. It is discontinuity. At one stage a business must change itself. And at that stage there is usually the kind of identity crisis of which the modern psychologists speak when they analyze the transition from adolescence to adulthood. As with human beings, the ablest, the brightest, the most highly motivated seem to suffer the worst identity crisis.

The best example is the story of IBM's "near-miss."

### IBM's Near-Miss

In retrospect, IBM's rise from a fair-sized $100 million business around 1950 to the $8 billion computer colossus of the early 1970s seemed smooth, trouble-free, and all but preordained. Actually, IBM went through a severe identity crisis. It almost missed the computer opportunity. It became capable of growth only through a palace coup which overthrew Thomas J. Watson, Sr., the company's founder, its chief executive, and for long years the prophet of "data processing."

Yet, if any company should have been able to grow smoothly and without trouble, it was IBM. No other company in American business history was so carefully prepared for growth, trained for growth, and directed toward growth. And it was, from the beginning, to be growth in data processing.

Thomas J. Watson, Sr., started before World War I by buying the patents for the punch card, to which he added later patents for a time clock. To convert the patents into a business proved painfully slow and difficult. When World War II started, IBM was still a small and struggling company, occupying a limited niche in the business equipment field.

But long before IBM had established itself even in this small niche Watson had begun to prepare the company for growth and for becoming a big, indeed a very big, enterprise. He adopted a grandiose name, International Business Machines, at a time when IBM was neither international nor truly business machines. Long before any other American company thought of such things—even before Adriano Olivetti, having inherited a small typewriter company in northern Italy, adopted a similar course— IBM created a company image through distinctive design and distinctive typography for its products, its publications, and its communications inside and outside the company. Watson invented the slogan "THINK" and distributed hundreds of thousands of "THINK" posters and stickers to employees and customers.

From very early days Watson developed and trained a human organization that would look upon itself as an elite corps and be prepared to manage a very much bigger business. As has already been related (in Chapter 20) he insisted that his workers take responsibility for their own work and thus trained a whole cadre of proud and competent men who became the skeleton around which the much bigger IBM work force of later years was built.

Above all, Watson trained, and trained, and trained. All employees were expected to continue to learn while on the job. But for the men who were considered "IBM's business"—that is, for salesmen, servicemen, and sales managers, continuous training was a way of life.

The district sales managers, in particular, were trained to be top executives. Not one of these men had technical education or technical background. Yet when in the fifties and sixties the company switched to advanced electronics from a mechanical appliance, the punch-card sorter— in many cases still operated by hand or at the most by the simplest of electrical motors—these technically unschooled men became the management that built the world's leading computer company. Having grown up in continuous training, they had learned to learn. Into the 1970s, IBM's top management was primarily staffed with former punch-card district managers.

From early days Watson saw the future of IBM in what he may have been the first to call data processing. He was convinced all along that the day would come when a machine would take over the tedious job of handling large masses of data speedily, reliably, and at low cost.

Watson therefore saw at once what no one else at the time realized: that the computer market would be in business. He saw that the key to the computer business was not technology but marketing. He saw that what mattered was not what the computer could do but what the user could get from it. On these basic insights IBM's rise to dominance in the computer field essentially rests—and they were Thomas J. Watson, Sr.'s insights.

There is little doubt that Watson was an autocrat. He has been harshly criticized for the conformity he imposed on his organization, for his heavy-handed paternalism, and for his narrow prejudices. Yet, as subsequent events showed, he did not stifle, let alone break, the managerial people in his organization. Whatever his shortcomings—and they were great—he had, from early days, a clear vision of the goal, and the ability to think through what policies, what basic attitude, what strategy would be required.

And yet Thomas Watson, Sr., almost destroyed the very opportunity he had waited for, worked for, and built for. When the computer finally arrived, and with it the realization of Watson's dreams, he suddenly did not want growth. He began to dither. He was afraid of doing anything that might hurt the company's punch-card business. And of course the computer threatened—or seemed to threaten—the punch-card business altogether. He began to sabotage manufacturing developments and selling efforts that might replace existing or potential punch-card installations; and that, of course, meant that he sabotaged all computer development and all computer selling. He had been almost sinfully proud of his key people, and especially of his elite group, the district sales managers. Now he suddenly felt that not one of them was "ready" for a bigger or different job.

Above all, he refused to change his own behavior. He did not want to become the chief executive officer of a big business. He was determined to remain the owner of a small one. He did not want to let other people, including his own two sons, take on any responsibility of their own or make any decisions. He resisted anything that would have impaired in the slightest degree his direct personal control of every aspect of the business, or that would have made it difficult for him to know in great detail everything that was going on. He stubbornly and with great determination held on to a relationship to his company as his "own child" and as an extension of his own personality.

Judging by the experience of other companies, Watson would have destroyed IBM's opportunity for growth had he remained at the head of the company much longer. Even a few years' delay would have been fatal. By then, that is, in the early fifties, the first important customers would have bought computers and would have thereby designated the leading companies. The first major new technical developments would have had to be made beyond the early crude models. Considering how innocent of technology Thomas Watson's IBM was—the first engineer was not even hired until the late thirties, and then for production engineering and not for design—IBM could hardly have leap-frogged directly into the "second generation" computers of the early fifties in which transistors replaced vacuum tubes and electronic switches replaced mechanical drives. If Watson had been permitted to stay for a few years, IBM would at best have become an "also ran" in the computer business—and probably not even that. It surely would not have become the leader in data processing, for which he had prepared the company.

But then providence intervened in the highly improbable guise of the Anti-Trust Division of the U.S. Department of Justice. At the very moment when punch cards were losing their importance, the Anti-Trust Division brought suit against IBM for allegedly monopolizing the punch-card field. The one thing of which Watson was mortally afraid was an antitrust suit. When still a young man, in the early years of the century, an antitrust suit had almost destroyed him. Having been made a scapegoat for serious antitrust violations of his earlier associates at the National Cash Register Company, he had been sentenced to a stiff term in jail and was rescued only by a presidential pardon. His panic made it possible for his closest associates, led by his two sons, to force him to abdicate. The sons at once built a top-management team. They concentrated the key resources, and especially the men Watson had trained, on their new business. And within three years IBM emerged as the leader.

The only thing that is atypical about the IBM story is the happy ending. In the great majority of cases, the growing company that runs into an identity crisis succumbs to it. In the great majority of cases it loses its opportunity, no matter how badly it wants to grow—or says it wants to grow. In the great majority of cases, the business then remains stunted. Money is spent. Plans are made. But there are no results. Instead of growth there is frustration.

And few companies manage to escape such an identity crisis.

At the Ford Motor Company the point where the company had to become a big business arose during World War I. At that time Henry Ford's closest associates, his partner James Couzens and his brother-in-law and financial advisor Ernest Kanzler, urged Ford to change the structure of the company and the way in which he himself ran it. But Ford pushed both men out of the company. Almost immediately the Ford Motor Company began to decline. Five years later it had been overtaken by GM, and another five years later, toward the end of the twenties, it lost even its number two position to a brash newcomer, Walter P. Chrysler, who, apparently on Alfred Sloan's advice, had organized his fledgling company as a big business from the start.

Siemens (as was told in Chapter 29) went through a similar crisis after the death of the founder when his sons refused to adopt the structure, management, and policies appropriate to the big company Siemens had become. Had they been allowed to go on, Siemens might well not have survived, at least not as a major and important business.

AT&T, the Bell Telephone Company, went through a similar trauma. By the late 1890s, AT&T had reached the point when it could no longer be run as a financial holding company for a large number of small and local telephone businesses. It had to become a large and national company. Theodore N. Vail saw this clearly. He was then about fifty and the company's general manager, with the title of president. But the company's chief executives were a small group of Boston investment bankers. When Vail came to them with his plans and proposals, they refused to listen and forced him into early retirement. Ten years later, however, their refusal to build the management the company required had so weakened AT&T that nationalization seemed almost inevitable. The Bostonians then ate humble pie and implored Vail to come back and take over, this time with full power. Within a few years Vail built the new structure of a big company which enabled the Bell Telephone System to become the world's biggest privately owned business.

The most instructive example might, however, be Sears, Roebuck. Richard Sears, whose name the company still bears, had pioneered many of the fundamental policies on which the success of Sears is based to this day. But when the company grew from a very small to a fair-sized business, Sears refused to change the company and to change himself. As a result, in the early years of the century, he nearly went bankrupt and was forced to sell to a total outsider, Julius Rosenwald, a Chicago clothing merchant. Rosenwald immediately organized a top-management team and structured a big company. And Sears, Roebuck, almost moribund under its founder, started to grow. Twenty years later Rosenwald himself realized that the company and its management needed to make another quantum jump. Sears, already a big company, had to be ready to become a very much bigger one. He turned to a total outsider, General Robert E. Wood, who had proven his administrative capacity as quartermaster in charge of supply for the American Army during World War I, and had then become merchandising vice-president at Sears's arch-rival, Montgomery Ward. For a year or two Rosenwald watched from the sidelines. Then he turned over the top job to Wood and withdrew, taking his own management group with him.

In order to grow, as these stories show, there is need for strategy. There is need for preparation. There is need for establishing an ideal of behavior focused on what one wants to become. But none of this is of much avail unless top management is willing to make the change. Even great vision and high resolve will otherwise lead only to frustration and futility.

## Is Growth Necessary?

The 1950s and especially the 1960s indulged in a veritable "growth craze" in economy as well as in business. Growth was what the investor was looking for to put his money in. Growth—on the order of "10 percent growth in sales and 10 percent growth in profit each year"—was what managements promised. And growth also was the focus of economics, both in the developing and in the developed countries.

In large measure this was a reaction to the stagnation that had characterized world economy and business in the period between the two World Wars. Then growth seemed to have stopped. The best anyone could hope for was protection against debilitating depression and decline. When the black mood of frustration lifted after World War II, it was a tremendous relief. The zest with which economy after economy and company after company rediscovered growth was very healthy.

But the growth craze soon went too far. And where, before 1940, we had believed the myth of stagnation, we soon began to believe myths about growth. It is simply not true that an exponential rate of growth can be maintained for long periods, let alone forever. A business that grows at an exponential rate—let alone at so high a rate as the much-proclaimed 10 percent each year—would soon gobble up the world and all its resources. Growth at a high rate and for an extended period is also anything but healthy. It makes a business—or any institution—exceedingly vulnerable. It makes it all but impossible to manage it properly. It creates stresses, weaknesses, and hidden defects which, at the first slight setback, become major crises.

Even from the purely financial point of view of the investor interested in capital gains, the growth company is not a sound investment. Such a company sooner or later—and usually sooner—runs into real difficulties. Sooner or later it runs into tremendous losses, has to write off vast sums, and becomes, in effect, unmanageable. It takes years then for such a company to regain its health and its capacity to grow again and to produce profit. There are few exceptions to the rule that today's growth company is tomorrow's problem.

The same vulnerability characterizes the "growth industry." Indeed the dynamics of a growth industry are perfectly well known—and they make the growth industry a poor investment except for the most knowledgeable. In the growth industry there is first the opening up of a new major area of economic activity which promises to offer tremendous opportunities. Any entrant into this new area of activity seems to be doing very well. As a result, a great many new entrants clamor to get into the act. Soon the industry is overcrowded. Inevitably there is then a "shake-out." Where there were thirty or forty entrants, only five or six, maybe seven or eight, remain. Of these, three or four assume leadership and retain it for many decades. Another three or four manage to become respectable fair-sized businesses, occupying small but distinct niches. The rest disappear.

But which companies will emerge as leaders in this process and which will disappear is unpredictable. Even the insider has little chance to guess correctly. The decisive factor is well hidden. It is, above all, the capacity of a company's management to manage for growth and to develop the strategy that will give it leadership position in the shake-out.

One example is the U.S. chemical industry in the period of its most rapid growth, that is, in the twenties, when it first emerged as a major American industry. Anyone who then tried to pick a winner would have chosen Allied Chemical, which emerged from World War I as a very big company with an almost impregnable patent position in the major areas. It would have been a very rash man indeed at that time who picked either Du Pont or Dow. These were, at best, minor companies in fringe areas such as explosives or metallurgy. Yet Allied Chemical never succeeded in building on its strengths. It had neither management nor strategy, and floundered. Du Pont and Dow emerged as leaders.*

Similarly, few people in the early stages of the growth of the American pharmaceutical industry in the late 1940s and 1950s would have been likely to pick the two companies that emerged as the winners and as leaders in the industry, Merck and Pfizer. The former was marginal, with no apparent strength in pharmaceutical research and limited to a few rather unexciting patent medicines. The latter was not even in the pharmaceutical industry

---

*Even the Du Pont management did not consider its company to be a growth company at that time. The decision to invest a large part of the profits the company had made during World War I in General Motors—which then, a few years later, led to GM's reorganization and subsequent rise—was made because the Du Pont top management (and especially Pierre du Pont, the company's chief executive) did not see much growth opportunity for their company in their own industry.

but had been, for all of its long and up till then undistinguished history, a local manufacturer of yeast for the New York breweries. In retrospect—but only in retrospect—it is clear that these two companies had a strategy for growth, and a management willing to structure a big company and change its own behavior.

The securities market would be well advised to put a discount on growth stocks and growth industries rather than a premium. For growth is a risk.

The idea that growth is by itself a goal is altogether a delusion. There is no virtue in a company's getting bigger. The right goal is to become better. Growth, to be sound, should be the result of doing the right things. By itself, growth is vanity and little else.

## Growth in the Public-Service Institution

Growth crazes in the business world are a recurrent disease; in the last century they have swept America, for instance, three times (in the 1870s, in the 1920s—at a time when Europe was in the grip of a "stagnation craze" —and in the 1960s.) In public-service institutions, and especially in government agencies, the growth craze is, however, endemic and permanent. This (as discussed in Chapter 12) is in large part the result of dependence on a budget which makes the large staff and the large budget the one generally accepted measurement of performance, success and importance.

But bigger is also not necessarily better in a service institution, whether a hospital, a government agency, a university—or in the personnel staff in a business, or in its research laboratory.

The best example of the lack of any correlation between size and performance in service institutions may be the two American philanthropic foundations which respectively were first in size in the decades before and the decades after World War II: the Rockefeller Foundation and the Ford Foundation. By present-day standards the resources of the pre-World War II Rockefeller Foundation were quite modest—well below one billion dollars. Ford, by contrast, had almost three billions to spend. But its limited resources forced the Rockefeller Foundation to keep its staff small and to concentrate. Its impacts, as a result, were very substantial—both in the field of medicine and in the sciences. Ford, by contrast, was almost forced by the heavy weight of all the sums it had to spend to look for projects that would absorb the most money—and how much impact *any* Ford Foundation project has had so far is a matter of considerable controversy.

But growth is also just as demanding and difficult in the public-service institution as it is in a business. The larger budget may make possible taking on new and important tasks—though often enough it means only doing more of the things that need not be done at all. It always, however, also means taking in people who have to be trained, directed, supervised, and managed. It means additional complexities. Above all, growth in the public-service institution—including the service staffs in businesses—also means that top management has to change.

The public-service institution needs to pay the greatest attention to "weight control" (as said earlier, in Chapters 13 and 14). It is particularly prone to mistake fat for muscle, weight for importance, and busyness for achievement. But it also needs to know how to manage growth. And the approaches to managing growth are essentially the same whether the growing institution is a business or a service institution. For managing growth is a top-management challenge and a top-management task and requires, therefore, top-management strategy and top-management organization.

## Growth as a Survival Need

The growth craze had to come to an end like every mania. And yet growth will continue to be a desirable and indeed a necessary business objective. Even if the economy, as so many were predicting in the early seventies, would turn to zero growth—thus returning, in effect, to the stagnation of the twenties and thirties—there would be need for management to understand how to manage growth. For, as the example of the twenties and thirties clearly shows, a period of zero growth in the economy is not one of stability. It is one of turbulence.

In a growing economy there is plenty of room. Industries that have passed their peak decline slowly and are being held up by the overall buoyancy of the economy. New industries can grow fast. But there is still room for those that do not know how to grow well and grow more by accident than by management.

But when the economy as such does not grow, changes in the economy are bound to be abrupt and sharp. Then indeed a company or an industry that does not grow will decline. Then there is even more need for a strategy that enables a management to plan for growth and to manage growth.

Whether we are at the end of economic growth and will have to learn to live in a "solid state economy"—if only because of the limitations of the environment and of its resources—is not within the scope of this book to discuss. It is not the most probable forecast, given the fact that two-thirds of mankind still live in abject poverty. But growth in the future may well mean different things. It may mean using fewer resources, that is, a shift to growth in knowledge industries rather than in manufacturing. Costs will be different; what we considered free goods, such as air and water, will be anything but free and will have a high cost attached to them. The pattern of development in tomorrow's fast-developing countries may well differ significantly from the traditional nineteenth-century pattern with its emphasis on steel, which still underlay the explosive growth of Japan after World War II and the growth of Brazil in the sixties. Undoubtedly there will be increasing need to guard and maintain the balance between what man takes out of his environment and what he puts back. This alone will make growth opportunities different in the future from what they have been in the past.

But there will also be new factors pressing for growth. One that is usually overlooked is the expectation of the young, educated people.

A company that is not able to attract, motivate, and hold men of talent and competence will not survive. Increasingly, this will mean attracting, motivating, and holding the knowledge worker. Unlike the manual worker of yesterday, the knowledge worker does not, however, look just for a job. He looks for a career. He looks for an opportunity. Even under conditions of zero population growth, that is, under conditions in which each age group in the population is of the same size (which means in effect that the center of gravity is in middle age rather than among the young) the pressure of the educated, young knowledge workers for career opportunities will persist beyond what can be satisfied by the opportunities opened up by the retirement of older men. Even zero population growth demands opportunities for younger people to achieve. The advent of the knowledge worker creates pressure for at least some, and in many cases, for considerable, growth.

## The Need for Growth Objectives

But the collapse of the growth craze of the sixties showed that it is not enough for a management to say, "We want growth." A management needs a *rational growth policy*. A management needs objectives that are based on more solid grounds than the desire to grow or the promise to grow.

Management needs to think through the *minimum* of growth which its company requires. What is the minimum of growth without which the company would actually lose strength, vigor, and ability to perform, if not to survive?

A company needs a viable market standing. Otherwise it soon becomes marginal. It soon becomes, in effect, the wrong size. And if the market expands, whether domestically or worldwide, a company has to grow with the market to maintain its viability. At times a company therefore needs a very high minimum growth rate.

In the pharmaceutical market or in the computer market in the fifties and sixties, when the total market expanded at a fast clip, to stay even meant very fast growth. In the textile industry in the developed countries, there was little net overall growth of the market in the same period (though more than is commonly believed). Here minimum growth consisted primarily of identifying the most promising market segments and of concentrating on them.

In GE's strategic business planning (see Chapter 10) the first question is not "What markets have the *greatest* growth potential?" It is rather "What is the *minimum* growth of each market? Can we expect to keep up with it? What market segments (even in the slow-growth markets) offer the best opportunities for us?"

Growth in the context of a business is an economic rather than a physical term. Volume, by itself, is irrelevant. To use up more wood each year may be a rational objective for the Gypsy Moth. It is an inane objective for a paper company. What matters in a business—whether it operates in a market economy or in any other economic system—is economic performance, as measured by contribution to economy and society; by productivity of resources—men, capital, materials; and by profitability. A business grows if it grows in economic performance and economic results. To want to be a "billion-dollar company" is not a rational growth objective. Growth objectives have to be economic objectives rather than volume objectives.

This is particularly important as the most dangerous mistake is to confuse growth with putting on fat. A business actually grows if it sloughs off activities which do not contribute. Such activities only drain. They impede the true growth potential. The second step, therefore, in GE's strategic business planning is to ask whether this or that activity of the company should be closed down, sold, or at least de-emphasized. When GE began to ask this question in the late sixties it regained its capacity to grow after long years of relative stagnation.

The second growth objective needed is an *optimum* objective. What is the combination of activities, products, and businesses that promises to produce the best balance between risk and return on resources? What is the point, in other words, at which increased market standing can be obtained only at a cost in productivity of every major resource and of all resources altogether? What is the point beyond which greater profitability could be obtained only by a steep increase in risk? But what also is the point below which a decrease in risk is likely to sharply curtail productivity and profitability—and also to endanger market position?

It is this optimum point, rather than a maximum, which determines the upper range of a company's growth goals. Growth should be at least the minimum growth. But it should, as a rule, not exceed the optimum. Indeed, growth that exceeds the optimum, that is, growth that purchases market position at the price of lower productivity, or growth that purchases higher productivity at a price in market position, is basically unsound and cannot be sustained. It is the growth that leads to the costly "surprises" in the "growth company." It is the growth that creates vulnerabilities, flaws, overextension, lack of control and, fairly soon, a major, if not a fatal, setback.

A growth policy, in other words, is a business policy. It does not differ from any other business policy. It requires objectives, it requires priorities, it requires strategy. Above all, it requires that growth goals be rational and grounded in the objective reality of a business, of its markets, of its technologies, rather than in financial fantasy.

## The Need to Prepare for Growth

Growth requires internal preparation. Because IBM had prepared for growth for many years, it was able to take off as soon as the dead hand of the past had been removed. Without such preparation even the desire to grow, even the understanding of what was needed for growth in the new computer industry, would hardly have sufficed to turn, almost overnight, a maker of simple products without much engineering content into the leader in a technically advanced industry.

When the opportunity for rapid growth will come in the life of a company cannot be predicted. But a company has to be ready. If a company is not ready, opportunity moves on and knocks at somebody else's door.

The IBM story shows that a company, to be able to grow, must, within itself, create an atmosphere of continuous learning. It must be managed in such manner that all its members—down to the lowest-ranking employees —are willing and ready to take on new, different, and bigger responsibilities as a matter of course, and without trepidation. A company can grow only to the extent to which its people can grow.

Of course—at least in the West—one can bring in this or that expert, this or that specialist, this or that capacity, competence, or talent. But fundamentally growth, even growth by acquisition (as has been said earlier) has to come from within and has to be based on the strengths of a company. A growth policy requires that a human organization establish the atmosphere of continuous learning and acquire the readiness to do different and bigger things.

Financial planning for the demands of a bigger business is also needed. Otherwise, when growth comes, the company will find itself in a financial crisis that is likely to frustrate growth. This applies to the small, but also to the fair-sized, business (see Chapter 54 on the needs of the small and the fair-sized company). For even fairly moderate growth soon outruns the financial foundations of a business. It soon creates financial demands in areas to which no one, as a rule, has paid much attention. It soon makes obsolete capital structure or existing arrangements for obtaining short-term loans and working capital. Financial strategy is essential to growth—as essential as product strategy, technological strategy, or market strategy.

But the key to the ability to grow is a human organization that is capable of growth.

## Top Management: The Controlling Factor

The controlling factor in managing growth is top management—again a lesson of the IBM story. For a company to be able to grow, top management must be willing and able to change itself, its role, its relationship, and its behavior.

This is easily said—and very hard to accomplish. The very people—and usually, the very man—of whom such change is demanded are also as a rule the people to whom the success of the company so far can be attributed. Now, when success is within their grasp, they are asked to abandon the behavior that has produced it. They are asked to give up the habits of a lifetime. They are asked—or so it seems to them—to abdicate their leadership position. They are asked, above all, to hand over their "child" to others. For growth always requires that the management of one man—or of a small handful of men—be replaced by a genuine top-management team.

Most top-management people in the growth company which somehow does not seem to be growing—that is, in the great majority of small and fair-sized companies with growth potential—know rationally what is needed. But, like Watson, they lack the will to change.

Top management therefore has to start preparing itself for growth at a very early stage. Specifically, it has to take three steps:

—It has to define the key activities and build, in effect, a budding top-management team to take care of them.
—It has to be aware of the symptoms of the need for change in basic policy, structure, and behavior so that it knows when the time for change has arrived.
—It has to be honest with itself and decide whether it really wants to change or not.

IBM worked for long years on making itself look like a big company, internally as well as externally. It worked on its appearance to the outside world, in the design of its products and in the design of all the graphics with which it communicated to its own people and to the outside world. It did not spend a great deal of money on advertising and promotion. But when it did, it tried to make a "big splash."

But at the same time, IBM was run internally on a basis of managerial austerity. There were no staffs. There was no research and development. There were no vice-presidents of this and that. There was a top man— Thomas Watson. There was a strong field sales organization. And there was, as the only staff officer, an educational director. Even engineering was unknown until the late thirties—which seems almost unbelievable today.

IBM, in other words, had analyzed its key activities. It supplied them with resources far in excess of what seemed appropriate to the small company IBM still was in the late thirties and early forties. But it did not do anything else.

There is a paradox to growth. "If you want to be a big company tomorrow, you have to start acting like one today" is said to have been Thomas Watson's favorite aphorism. The company that wants to be able to grow has to support the key activities on the level on which they will be needed *after* the growth has taken place. Otherwise it will lack competence, ability, and strength in the areas in which it needs them the most. But at the same time, such a company does not have the resources. Only by starving all but the truly essential can it balance the conflicting requirements of the present business, i.e., a business with very limited resources, and those of the business of tomorrow, i.e., a business that will demand fairly heavy support in major areas.

One way in which the chief executive of a small or fair-sized business that has growth ambitions can prepare himself for the day when the company will have outgrown management by one man is to build a top-management team at the earliest possible moment. The one way in which he himself can learn to be a true manager, rather than "the boss," is by analyzing first the key activities the business needs and his own personality. There will always be key activities that do not fit the top man, key activities which others can do better—and then others should do them.

When Rosenwald took over Sears he analyzed the key activities and built a top-management team of three people. As long as he stayed in the company, he was the undisputed leader and chief executive. But from the beginning, decisions on the location, organization, and layout of the mail-order plants—a key activity for Sears in those days—were made by Otto Doering and not by Julius Rosenwald. Basic decisions on finance and personnel were made by Albert Loeb. Rosenwald was close to every decision. He did not hesitate to express his opinion and occasionally to overrule his associates. But these men, even in the fairly small company which Sears was in the early days, were "associates" and not "subordinates."

Similarly, the first thing George Merck of Merck & Co. did when, at the end of World War II, he decided that the pharmaceutical industry would grow very rapidly and that his company would be a major factor in it was to bring in Vannevar Bush as chairman of the board, and as an associate.

Merck knew that he and his company were innocent of basic scientific knowledge and organized research. But he also knew that this was a key activity.

The top man—or the top men—in a company that has ambitions to grow has to know when the time for a change has come. He has to know the symptoms that indicate that a company has outgrown its traditional structure, its traditional management behavior, and, above all, the traditional role of the top man.

There is *one* reliable symptom.

The top man in a company—especially in a small or fair-sized company that has been growing fast—is typically exceedingly proud of the men who work with him. And yet—and this is the infallible symptom of the need for change—not one of the "boys" is "quite ready yet." When the time for change comes, he always finds good reasons for not moving this man to that bigger responsibility, for not turning over a key area to another man, and so on. He always says "so and so is the best man—but he is not quite ready." This is a clear indication that the top man himself is not ready.

The chief executive, the top man, in the small and fair-sized—but also in the big—company that wants to grow has to impose on himself a change in his own role, behavior, and relationships.

The resistance of the top man to change is often blamed on his age. Ford and Thomas Watson, Sr., were indeed well along in years when their companies outgrew the way they were managing them; Ford was in his sixties, Watson in his seventies. But the resistance to the change in behavior, goal, and relationship which growth elicits from the top man can be just as great among younger men. The Siemens sons were young men, for instance; and so were the Boston bankers who blocked Vail at the Bell Telephone System in the 1890s. On the other hand, many older men are capable of imposing change on themselves. Julius Rosenwald was past sixty when he decided to bring in General Wood and step down. So was George Merck when he decided his own role had to change.

A company may even be fortunate to have an old or aging chief executive when the time for change in his role and behavior arrives. It is much easier to get a man in his sixties or seventies to step down gracefully than to force out a man in his prime who is unwilling to change.

What is demanded of the top man is indeed a great deal. He has to accept that he no longer can be the virtuoso performer. Instead he has to become the "conductor." Where he prides himself, as did Thomas Watson, Sr., on knowing everybody in the company, on knowing every customer, on knowing everything that went on, and on making every decision and solving every problem, he now has to manage by objectives for managers and through their self-control. Where formerly he was the court of last resort

—and very often the court of first resort as well—he now has to have a management structure. Where he "knows how to do everything," he now has to let people do it their own way.

To expect of anybody that he can make such a change suddenly is to expect the miracle of conversion. And even conversions in retrospect always have a long history of preparation. The top man who wants his business to grow has to accept the role which he will have to play in the bigger business long before it becomes a necessity.

First, he has to think through whether he really wants his company to grow, and whether it is really capable of growth. A great deal can be said for the "middle class" in business as well as in society. Not to be a big company is often more enjoyment, more satisfaction, and certainly, for the people at the top, a great deal more personal achievement and personal freedom. There is no reason to believe that Luxembourg or Switzerland is less happy, less achieving, or less valuable to humanity than today's super-power.

No company needs to strive to be "bigger" beyond the minimum growth needed to stay abreast of its market. Growth beyond this must be based on capacity to contribute. But a company that decides that it is happy in its niche, satisfied with the contribution it makes and the market it serves, and content with doing a good job is not, by this token, a "less good" or a "less valuable" company. In economic terms it may well be—and often is—a far more productive company than the giant. Growth as a goal, to repeat, is delusion. William James, the American philosopher, talked of the "bitch goddess success." A philosopher of business today might well talk of the "bitch goddess growth."

But even if the top man decides that his company needs growth, he still has a second question—and a more difficult one: "Do *I* want growth of the business for myself?"

Thomas Watson apparently knew that he did not want to work in a big company, even though his whole life was spent in building one. He lacked, however, the wisdom or the strength of character to face the consequences. Julius Rosenwald apparently did not. He realized that he did not want to run a giant company. He also knew that Sears could and should become one—and he knew the correct conclusions for himself.

The top man who concludes that his company needs to grow but who also then realizes that he does not want to change himself and his behavior has, in conscience, only one line of action open to him. *He has to step aside.* Even if he legally owns the company, he does not own the lives of other people. A company is not a child—and even with a human child, the time comes when the parent has to accept that the child has grown up and needs to be independent and on his own.

A business is a human achievement. And a business, no matter what its legal ownership, is a trust. The top-management man who realizes that he does not want to change also realizes that he will stifle, stunt, and throttle the very thing he has loved and built, his business. If he cannot face up to the demands of his own achievement, he owes it to himself and to his company to step aside.

# 61

## The Innovative Organization

The need to innovate is mentioned—indeed emphasized—in every book on management. But beyond this the books, as a rule, pay little attention to what management and organization need to be and need to do to stimulate, to direct, and to make effective innovation. Most discussions stress, almost exclusively, the administrative function of management, that is, the task of keeping going and of improving what is already known and what is already largely being done. Little thought or space is normally devoted to the entrepreneurial function of creating effectively and purposefully the new and the different.

In this neglect of the management of innovation, the books only mirror business reality. Every management stresses the need to innovate. But few, in the large as well as the small businesses, organize innovation as a distinct and major task. To be sure, since World War II, "research" has become fashionable. Large sums of money are being spent on it. But in many companies the outcome has been improvement rather than innovation.

This is even more true of the public-service institutions.

There were good reasons in the past for the focus on the administrative function to the neglect of innovation. When management first became a concern, in the early years of this century, the great and new need was to learn how to organize, structure, and direct the large-scale human organization which was suddenly coming into being. Innovation insofar as it received attention was seen as a separate job, a job done by the individual by himself, by the "inventor" of the nineteenth century. Or it was seen as a predominantly technical job, that of research.

Moreover, there was not too much scope for innovation in the years from 1920 to 1950 when most of the basic work on management was being done. For contrary to common belief, these were not years of rapid change, either in technology or in society. They were (as was stressed in Chapter 3) years in which, by and large, technology built on foundations that had been laid before World War I. And while they were years of tremendous political turbulence, social and economic institutions were stagnant. Indeed, the same can be said for social and economic ideas. The great revolutionary ideas which have been at work in the last fifty years are those of thinkers living, or at least rooted, in the nineteenth century, such as Marx, Darwin, and Freud. Even Keynes, no matter how innovative he was, built on foundations which such economists of the late nineteenth century as Léon Walras and Alfred Marshall had already put securely in place.

Now, however, we may be entering a period of rapid change more comparable in its basic features to the closing decades of the nineteenth century than to the immediate past with which we are familiar. In the late nineteenth century, as we need to remind ourselves, a new major invention, leading almost immediately to the emergence of a new major industry, surfaced every few months on average. This period began in 1856, the year that saw both Siemens's dynamo and Perkins's aniline dye. It ended with the development of the modern electronic tube in 1911. In between came typewriter and automobile, electric light bulb, man-made fibers, tractors, streetcars, synthetic drugs, telephone, radio, and airplane—to mention only a few. In between, in other words, came the modern world.

By contrast, no truly new major industry was started after 1914 until the late 1950s, when computers first became operational.

Between 1870 and 1914 the industrial geography of the world was in rapid change. A new major industrial area emerged on average every decade or so: the U.S. and Germany between 1860 and 1870, western Russia and Japan during the next twenty years, Central Europe (that is, the western part of the old Austria-Hungary and northern Italy) by 1900. Between World War I and World War II, however, no major new industrial area joined the "industrial club."

Now, however, there are signs of rapid change, with Brazil and China, for instance, approaching "the takeoff point"—Brazil may well have reached it. Now, in other words, there are signs that fundamental economic relationships will be in rapid change and flux. And while Bretton Woods in 1944 attempted to restore the monetary world as it had existed before 1914—and almost succeeded for twenty-five years—the Eurodollar of the sixties, followed by the "paper gold" of the Special Drawing Rights a few years later, and finally by the abandonment of the dollar as the key currency, ended the period in which yesterday was the norm and clearly ushered in a period of great and rapid change and of major innovation in international economy, international currency, and international credit.

But the need for innovation will be equally great in the social field. And the public-service institutions too will have to learn how to manage innovation.

Just as the late nineteenth century was a period of tremendous innovative activity in technology, so also was it in social and economic institutions. And just as the fifty years after World War I were years of technological continuity rather than of rapid change and innovation, so also were they years of continuity in social and economic institutions. Government as we know it today had largely been created by the time of World War I. The Local Government reform in Great Britain which began in the middle of the nineteenth century created new institutions, new relationships, and, above all, established new tasks for government. Building the modern welfare state began shortly thereafter in Bismarck's Germany. At about the same time—the 1880s—the United States made a major contribution to the arts and practice of government: the regulatory commission. Every one of the New Deal reforms of the 1930s had been discussed, worked out, and in many cases put in practice on the local or state level twenty years earlier, that is, in the Progressive Era just before World War I.

The great American university was the innovative creation of half a dozen brilliant university presidents between 1860 and 1900 (on this, see Chapter 13). The modern hospital was essentially designed between 1900 and 1920. Armed services took their present shape in the two major conflicts of the mid-nineteenth century, the American Civil War and the Franco-Prussian War of 1870. Since then, the development has been linear—larger armies, more firepower, more armor, but fundamentally the same strategies and tactics and indeed even the same stress on "hardware technology." Even such radical technical innovations as the tank and the airplane were largely integrated into traditional command structures and traditional military doctrines.

Now the need for social and political innovation is becoming urgent again. The modern metropolis needs new governmental forms. The relationship between man and his environment has to be thought through and restructured. No modern government governs effectively anymore. The crisis of the world is, above all, an institutional crisis demanding institutional innovation.

The business enterprise, its structure and organization, the way in which it integrates knowledge into work and work into performance—and the way in which it integrates enterprise with society and government—are also areas of major innovative need and innovative opportunity. Surely there is need in the social and economic sphere for another period of innovative activity such as we last lived through in the second half of the nineteenth century.

In sharp contrast to the nineteenth century, however, innovation from now on will have to be built into existing organizations. Large businesses —and equally large public-service institutions—will have to become increasingly capable of organizing themselves for innovation as well as for administration.

In the first place, they command access to manpower and capital to a degree undreamed of a hundred years ago. But also the ratio between invention or research and the efforts needed to convert the results of research or invention into new businesses, new products, or new institutions had changed significantly. It is by now accepted, if only as a rule of thumb, that for every dollar spent on generating an idea, ten dollars have to be spent on "research" to convert it into a new discovery or a new invention. For every ten dollars spent on "research," at least a hundred dollars need to be spent on development, and for every hundred dollars spent on development, something between a thousand and ten thousand dollars are needed to introduce and establish a new product or a new business on the market. And only after a new product or a new business has been established in the market is there an "innovation."

Innovation is not a technical term. It is an economic and social term. Its criterion is not science or technology, but a change in the economic or social environment, a change in the behavior of people as consumers or producers, as citizens, as students or as teachers, and so on. Innovation creates new wealth or new potential of action rather than new knowledge. This means that the bulk of innovative efforts will have to come from the places that control the manpower and the money needed for development and marketing, that is, from the existing large aggregation of trained manpower and disposable money—existing businesses and existing public-service institutions.

This may be particularly true with respect to the public-service institution. A hundred years ago there were few of them and they were small. The task then was largely to create new institutions where none existed. Today these institutions are massive and dominate the social, political, and economic landscape. They represent existing bureaucracies, existing concentrations of expertise, existing assignments, and ongoing programs. If they cannot become innovative, the new we need has little chance of becoming effective innovation. It is likely to be smothered by muscle-bound giants of big government and big armed service, big university and big hospital, and many others.

This does not mean that the small business, or even the lone entrepreneur, will not continue to play an important role. Nothing is further from the truth than the hoary myth of the Populists that the small man is being squeezed out of the marketplace by the giants. The innovative growth companies of the last twenty-five years all started as small businesses. And by and large the small businesses have done far better than the giants.

In every single industry, except those where monopoly is protected by government (e.g., in railroading), small upstarts which a few short years ago were unknown have acquired major market positions and have proven themselves more than capable of competition with the giants. This is particularly true, as has been said before, where the giants, through natural growth or deliberate policy, grew into conglomerates. In the chemical industry, in the electrical apparatus industry, and in many others, the traditional giant, a GE or an Imperial Chemical, has lost market position and market share in many markets—and largely to small or medium-sized newcomers with an innovative bent.

An established company which in an age demanding innovation is not capable of innovation is doomed to decline and extinction. And a management which in such a period does not know how to manage innovation is incompetent and unequal to its task. Managing innovation will increasingly become a challenge to management, and especially to top management, and a touchstone of its competence.

## Innovative Examples

While in a minority, especially among big businesses, innovative companies do exist. One might mention Renault in France and Fiat in Italy, Marks & Spencer in England, ASEA in Sweden, Sony in Japan—or, between the two World Wars, the publishing house of Ullstein in Germany. In the United States 3M (Minnesota Mining and Manufacturing, St. Paul, Minnesota), the Bell Laboratories of the Telephone Company, or the Bank of America come to mind. These firms apparently have no difficulty innovating and no difficulty getting change accepted in their organizations. Their managements, one would expect, rarely have occasion to ask, "How can we keep our organization flexible and willing to accept the new?" These managements are much too busy finding the manpower and the money to run with the innovations their own organizations force on them.

Innovative organizations are not confined to business. Both the Manhattan Project in the United States, which developed the atomic bomb during World War II, and CERN (*Conseil Européen pour la Recherche Nucleaire*) in Geneva under its first Director-General, Victor Weisskopf, furnish examples of innovative organizations. This is all the more remarkable, as these two institutions were heavily staffed with university professors who, in their natural habitat, are remarkably resistant to change and notoriously slow to innovate.

These examples indicate that an organization's ability to innovate is a function of management rather than of industry, size, or age of the organization, let alone to be explained with that common excuse of poor managers, a country's "culture and traditions."

Nor can the explanation be found in research. Bell Laboratories—perhaps the most productive industrial research laboratory—has indeed been stressing for many years fundamental inquiries into the laws of nature. But Renault and Fiat are not particularly distinguished for their research; what makes them innovative organizations is ability to get new designs and new models rapidly into production and on the market. The Bank of America, finally, innovates mainly in its customers' businesses, and in terms of financial structure and credit, inventory and marketing policies.

These examples imply that the innovative organization institutionalizes the innovative spirit and creates a habit of innovation. At the beginning of these organizations there might well have been an individual, a great innovator. He might have succeeded in building around him an organization to convert into successful business reality his new ideas and inventions—as did Werner von Siemens in Germany a hundred years ago, A. P. Giannini in building the Bank of America seventy years ago, and as Edwin H. Land of Polaroid has been doing since World War II. But no such founding genius presided over Bell Laboratories, over 3M, or over Renault. The innovative organization manages to innovate as an organization, that is, as a human group organized for continual and productive innovation. It is organized to make change into norm.

These various innovative organizations are very different indeed in their structures, their businesses, their characteristics, and even their organization and management philosophies. But they do have certain characteristics in common.

1. Innovating organizations know what "innovation" means.
2. Innovative organizations understand the dynamics of innovation.
3. They have an innovative strategy.
4. They know that innovation requires objectives, goals, and measurements that are different from the objectives, goals, and

measurements of a managerial organization, and appropriate to the dynamics of innovation.

5. Management, especially top management, plays a different role and has a different attitude in an innovative organization.

6. The innovative organization is structured differently and set up differently from the managerial organization.

## The Meaning of Innovation

Innovation organizations first know what "innovation" means. They know that innovation is not science or technology, but value. They know that it is not something that takes place within an organization but a change outside. The measure of innovation is the impact on the environment. Innovation in a business enterprise must therefore always be market-focused. Innovation that is product-focused is likely to produce "miracles of technology" but disappointing rewards.

The outstanding innovators among the world's pharmaceutical companies define their goal as new drugs that will make a significant difference to medical practice and to patient health. They do not define innovation in terms of research, but in terms of the practice of medicine. Similarly, Bell Laboratories always starts out with the question "What will make a difference to telephone *service*?"

Not surprisingly, however, it is precisely the most market-focused innovator who has come up with some of the most important technical or scientific advances. Bell Labs, for instance, created the transistor, produced the basic mathematics of information theory, and is responsible for some of the fundamental discoveries underlying the computer.

To start out with the consumer's or client's need for a significant change is often the most direct way to define new science, new knowledge, and new technology, and to organize purposeful and systematical work on fundamental discovery.

## The Dynamics of Innovation

Innovating businesses are aware of the dynamics of innovation. They do not believe that innovation is determined—or at least they know that there are so many factors in whatever causal patterns may exist that no one can possibly unravel them. Neither, however, do they share the common belief that innovation is haphazard and incapable of being predicted or foreseen.

They know that innovation follows a probability distribution. They know that it is possible to say what kind of innovation, if successfully brought about, is likely to become a major product or process, a major new business, a major market. They know how to look systematically for the areas where innovative activity, if it produces results, is likely to enjoy success and to be rewarding.

One such heuristic guide to what one could call "the innovation-prone" is basic *economic* vulnerability of a process, a technology, or an industry. Wherever an industry enjoys growing market demand without being able to turn the demand into profitability, one can say, with high probability, that a major innovation which changes process, product, distributive channel, or customer expectations will produce high rewards.

Examples abound. One is the paper industry, which, all the world over, has enjoyed rapidly expanding consumer demands—on the order of 5 to 10 percent a year, year in and year out—without being able apparently to earn a decent return on its capital. There is the steel industry, which is in a very similar position. But there is also life insurance, which is one of the few "products" a customer is ready to buy—one of the few products, by the way, in which the interests of producer and consumer are completely identical—and which yet has to be sold through "hard-sell" methods and against apparently very high buyer resistance.

Similarly, innovative opportunity exists where there is glaring disparity between various levels of an economy or of a market.

The major growth industry in Latin America in the 1960s, for instance, was not manufacturing. It was retail distribution. Huge masses of people flocked into the cities and from a subsistence economy into a money economy. Individually they were, of course, mostly very poor. But collectively they represented large new purchasing power. Yet the distribution system in most Latin American countries remained in the pre-urban mold —small shops, undercapitalized, undermanaged, poorly stocked, and yet with very slow turnover. Wherever an entrepreneur moved in to offer modern distribution—Sears, Roebuck was the first to recognize the opportunity—success was instantaneous.

Another area of innovative opportunity is the exploitation of the consequences of events that have already happened but have not yet had their economic impacts. Demographic developments, i.e., changes in population, are among the most important. They are also the most nearly certain. Changes in knowledge are less certain—the lead time is difficult to predict. But they too offer opportunities. And then, most important, but least certain, are changes in awareness, changes in vision, changes in people's expectations.

The pharmaceutical industry, for instance, earned its success largely because it anticipated the impact of fundamental changes in awareness. After World War II health care every place became a "good buy." And drugs are the only way to health care easily accessible to poor and poorly educated rural countries. Where physicians and hospitals are scarce, drugs can still be dispensed and will be effective for a great many health problems. The pharmaceutical company which understood this and went into the developing countries found that, with respect to drug purchases, they are "fully developed."

Finally, of course, there are the innovations which are not part of the pattern, the innovations that are unexpected and that change the world rather than exploit it. They are the innovations in which an entrepreneur sets out to make something happen. They are the truly important innovations. They are the innovations of a Henry Ford, who envisioned something that did not exist at the time, namely a mass market, and then set about to make it happen.

These innovations lie outside of the probability distribution—or, at least, they place so far toward the extreme as to be grossly improbable. They are also clearly the most risky ones. For every one such innovation that succeeds, there must be ninety-nine that fail, ninety-nine of which nothing is ever heard.

It is important for the innovating business to realize that these atypical innovations exist and that they are of supreme importance. It is important to keep watching for them. But, by their very nature, they cannot be the object of systematic, purposeful organized activity within the business enterprise. They cannot be managed.

And they are sufficiently rare to be treated as exceptions, despite their overreaching importance. The business that focuses on the probability pattern and organizes its innovation strategy to take advantage of it will innovate. And it will in the process become sensitive to the exceptional, the great, the truly historic innovation, and equipped to recognize it early and to take advantage of it.

To manage innovation, a manager need not be a technologist. Indeed, the first-rate technologist is rarely good at managing innovation. He is so deeply engrossed in his specialty that he rarely sees development outside of it. It is not a metallurgist who is likely to recognize the importance of basic new knowledge in plastics even though it may, within a reasonably short time, obsolete a good many of his proudest products. Similarly, the innovative manager need not be an economist. The economist, by definition, can concern himself with the impact of innovations only after they have become massive. The innovating manager needs to anticipate vulnerabilities and opportunities—and this is not the economist's bent. The innovative manager needs to study innovation as such and to learn its dynamics, its pattern, its predictability. To manage innovation, a manager has to be at least literate with respect to the dynamics of innovation.*

## Innovative Strategy

Like all business strategies, an innovative strategy starts out with the question "What is our business and what should it be?" But its assumptions regarding the future are different from the assumptions made with respect to the ongoing business. There the assumption is that present product lines and services, present markets and present distribution channels, present technologies and processes will continue. The first objective of a strategy for the ongoing business is to optimize what already exists or is being established.

The ruling assumption of an innovative strategy is that whatever exists is aging. The assumption must be that existing product lines and services, existing markets and distribution channels, existing technologies and processes will sooner or later—and usually sooner—go down rather than up.

The governing device of a strategy for the ongoing business might therefore be said to be: "Better and More." For the innovative strategy the device has to be: "New and Different."†

The foundation of innovative strategy is planned and systematic sloughing off of the old, the dying, the obsolete. Innovating organizations spend neither time nor resources on defending yesterday. Systematic abandonment of yesterday alone can free the resources, and especially the scarcest resource of them all, capable people, for work on the new.

Unwillingness to do this may be the greatest obstacle to innovation in the existing large business. That the General Electric Company did not succeed in establishing itself as a computer producer is, within the company itself, explained in large part as the result of unwillingness or inability to make available managers and professionals of the high quality and proven performance capacity needed. To be sure, GE assigned a great many good people to its computer group. But few of them were allowed to stay there long. No sooner were they gone from their original post in a research lab or a large division, than the cry went up "we cannot do without them," and back they went to their old assignments of improving what was already known and what was already done.

---

*For a more extended discussion of this topic, see my book, *Managing for Results*, especially Part II.

†This point has been made with great force by Michael J. Kami, who served successively as head of long-range planning for IBM and Xerox. See his essay, "Business Planning and Business Opportunity," in Peter F. Drucker, ed., *Preparing Tomorrow's Business Leaders Today*.

The new and especially the as-yet unborn, that is, the future innovation, always looks insignificant compared to the large volume, the large revenue, and the manifold problems of the ongoing business. It is all the more important, therefore, for an existing business to commit itself to the systematic abandonment of yesterday if it wants to be able to create tomorrow.

Second in a strategy of innovation is the clear recognition that innovation efforts must aim high. It is just as difficult, as a rule, to make a minor modification to an existing product as it is to innovate a new one.

Michael J. Kami, the author of the essay cited above, states as a rule of thumb that the projected results of innovative efforts should be at least three times as large as the results needed to attain company objectives. This is probably an underestimate. In improvement work—adding a new product, upgrading a product line, broadening the market, and so on—one can assume a success rate of 50 percent. No more than half the projects should be total failures.

This is not the way innovation works. Here the assumption must be that the majority of innovative efforts will not succeed. Nine out of every ten "brilliant ideas" turn out to be nonsense. And nine out of every ten ideas which, after thorough analysis, seem to be worthwhile and feasible turn out to be failures or, at best, puny weaklings. The mortality rate of innovations is—and should be—high.

Innovative strategy therefore aims at creating a new business rather than a new product within an already established line. It aims at creating new performance capacity rather than improvement. It aims at creating new concepts of what is value rather than satisfying existing value expectations a little better. The aim of innovating efforts is to make a significant difference. What is significantly different is not a technical decision. It is not the quality of science that makes the difference. It is not how expensive an undertaking it is or how hard it is to bring it about. The significant difference lies in the impact on the environment.

"Success" in innovating efforts is a batting average of one out of ten. This is, of course, the reason for aiming high in innovative efforts. The one winner has to make up for the nine losers and has to produce its own results.

Bernard Baruch is mostly remembered today as the head of the U.S. war economy in World War I and the friend, confidant, and advisor of presidents from Woodrow Wilson to Harry Truman. But before Baruch became America's elder statesman, he had amassed a very sizable fortune as a venture capitalist. While other financiers of his era, the thirty years before World War I, speculated in real estate and railroad bonds, Baruch looked for new and innovative businesses. He knew apparently little about technology—or at least affected ignorance. He invested in the man rather than in the idea. And he invested at the very early stage at which the budding business, as a rule, did not need much money beyond a few years' support for a man with an idea. He invested on the principle that eight out of every ten investments would turn out failures and would have to be written off. But he maintained—and his own record proved him right—that if only two out of ten turned out to be successful, he would reap a far larger harvest than the shrewdest investor in already existing businesses could possibly attain.

An innovation does not proceed in a nice linear progression. For a good long time, sometimes for years, there is only effort and no results. The first results are then usually meager. Indeed, the first products are rarely what the customer will eventually buy. The first markets are rarely the major markets. The first applications are rarely the applications that, in the end, will turn out to be the really important ones.

The discussion of the social impacts of new technology (Chapter 25) pointed out that the impacts of new technology are very difficult, and sometimes impossible, to predict. But this difficulty extends to everything connected with the truly new—as demonstrated by the example (also given in Chapter 25) of the gross miscalculation of the size of the computer market in the thorough market-research study conducted around 1950. But even more difficult to predict than the eventual success of the genuinely new is the speed with which it will establish itself. "Timing is of the essence" —above all in innovation. Yet timing is totally incapable of being predicted. There are the computer, the antibiotics, the Xerox machine—all innovations that swept the market. But for every successful innovation that has results faster than anyone anticipates, there are five or six others—in the end perhaps, equally successful ones—which for long years seem to make only frustratingly slow headway. The outstanding example may be the steam-driven ship. By 1835 its superiority was clearly established; but it did not replace the sailing ship until fifty years later. Indeed, the "golden age of sail" in which the great clippers reached perfection began only after the steamship had been fully developed. For almost half a century, in other words, the steamship continued to be "tomorrow" and never seemed to become "today."

But then, after a long, frustrating period of gestation, the successful innovation rises meteorically. It becomes within a few short years a new major industry or a new major product line and market. But until it has reached that point it cannot be predicted when it will take off, nor indeed whether it ever will.

## Measurements and Budgets

Innovation strategy requires different measurements and a different use of budgets and budgetary controls from those appropriate to an ongoing business.

To impose on innovating efforts the measurements, and especially the accounting conventions that fit ongoing businesses, is misdirection. It cripples the innovative effort the way putting a one-hundred-pound pack would cripple a six-year-old going on a hike. And it also fails to give true control. Finally, it may become a threat when the innovation becomes successful. For then it needs controls that are appropriate to rapid growth, that is, controls which show what efforts and investments are needed to exploit success and prevent overextension.

The successfully innovating businesses learned this long ago.

The oldest, best-known, and most successful managerial control system is probably that of the Du Pont Company, which, as early as the 1920s, developed a model for all its businesses focused on return on investment. But innovations were not included in that famous model. As long as a business, a product line, or a process was in the innovating stage, its capital allocation was not included in the capital base on which the individual Du Pont division in charge of the project had to earn a return. Nor were the expenses included in its expense budget. Both were kept separate. Only after the new product line had been introduced in the market and had been sold in commercial quantities for two years or more were its measurements and controls merged into the budget of the division responsible for the development.

This made sure that division general managers did not resist innovation as a threat to their earnings record and performance. It also made sure that expenditures on, and investments in, innovative efforts could be tightly controlled. It made it possible to ask at every step, "What do we expect at the end, and what is the risk factor, that is, the likelihood of nonsuccess?" "Can we justify continuing this particular innovative effort or not?"

Budgets for ongoing businesses and budgets for innovative efforts should not only be kept separate, they should be treated differently. In the ongoing business, the question is always "Is this effort necessary? Or can we do without it?" And if the answer is "We need it," one asks, "What is the minimum level of support that is needed?"

In the innovative effort the first and most serious question is "Is it the right opportunity?" And if the answer is yes, one asks, "What is the maximum of good people and key resources which can productively be put to work *at this stage?*"

A separate measurement system for innovative effort makes it possible to appraise the three factors that determine innovative strategy: the ultimate opportunity, the risk of failure, and the effort and expenditure needed. Otherwise, efforts will be continued or will even be stepped up where the opportunity is quite limited while the risk of nonsuccess is great.

Examples are the many broad-spectrum antibiotics produced with great scientific ingenuity by pharmaceutical companies in the late sixties. By then the probability of synthesizing a new broad-spectrum antibiotic with properties significantly better than those already on the market had become fairly small. The risk of nonsuccess was high, in other words. At the same time the opportunity had become much more limited than ten years earlier. Even an antibiotic with significantly better performance than the existing ones would have to compete against perfectly good products with which the physicians were familiar and which they had learned to use. Even a scientific breakthrough would in all likelihood have produced a "me-too" product. At the same time, the expenditure and effort needed to find anything really new in a field that had been worked over so thoroughly were rising fast. Traditional market thinking, that is, thinking that looks at the size of the market and deduces therefrom great success for a new product that is "better," would have been totally misleading—as indeed it misled a substantial number of companies.

Nothing is therefore as inimical to successful innovation as a goal of "5 percent growth in profits" every year. Innovations for the first three or five years—some for longer—show no growth in profits. They do not show any profits at all. And then their growth rate for five to ten years should be closer to 40 percent a year than to 5 percent a year. It is only after they have reached relative maturity that they can be expected to grow year by year by a small percentage. But then they are no longer innovations.

Innovative strategy, therefore, requires a high degree of discipline on the part of the innovator. He has to operate without the crutch of the conventional budget and accounting measures which feed back fairly fast and reasonably reliable information from current results to efforts and investments. The temptation is to keep on pouring people and money into innovative efforts without any results. It is therefore important in managing innovation to think through what one expects, and when. Inevitably, these expectations are changed by events. But unless there are intermediate results, specific progress, "fallouts" to actual operation along the way, the innovation is not being managed.

When Du Pont engaged, in the late twenties, in the polymer research that eventually led to nylon more than ten years later, no one was willing or able to predict whether mastery of polymer technology would lead to synthetic rubber, to textile fibers, to synthetic leathers, or to new lubricants. (In the end, of course, it led to all of them.) It was not until fairly close to the end of the work that it became clear that synthetic fibers would be the first major commercial product. But from the beginning Du Pont, together with Dr. Carrothers, the research scientist in charge, systematically laid out a road map of what kind of findings and results could be expected and when. This map was changed every two or three years as results came in. But it was always redrawn again for the next stages along the road. And only when he came up with polymer fibers, which then made large-scale development work possible, did Du Pont commit itself to massive investment. Until then, the total cost was essentially the cost of supporting Carrothers and a few assistants.

## The Risk of Failure

A strategy for innovation has to be based on clear acceptance of the risk of failure—and of the perhaps more dangerous risk of "near-success."

It is as important to decide when to abandon an innovative effort as it is to know which one to start. In fact, it may be more important. Successful laboratory directors know when to abandon a line of research which does not yield the expected results. The less successful ones keep hoping against hope, are dazzled by the "scientific challenge" of a project, or are fooled by the scientists' repeated promise of a "breakthrough next year." And the unsuccessful ones cannot abandon a project and cannot admit that what seemed like a good idea has turned into a waste of men, time, and money.

But a fair number of innovative efforts end up in near-success rather than in success or failure. And near-success can be more dangerous than failure. There is, again and again, the product or the process that was innovated with the expectation that it would "revolutionize" the industry only to have it become a minor addition to the product line, neither enough of a failure to be abandoned nor enough of a success to make a difference. There is the innovation which looks so "exciting" when work on it is begun, only to be overtaken, during its gestation period, by a more innovative process, product, or service. There is the innovation which was meant to become a "household word" that ends up as another "specialty" which a few customers are willing to buy but not willing to pay for.

It is therefore particularly important in managing innovation to think through and to write out one's expectations. And then, once the innovation has become a product, a process, or a business, one compares one's expectations to reality. If reality is significantly below expectations, one does not pour in more men or more money. One rather asks, "Should we not go out of this, and how?"

Bernard Baruch knew this seventy years ago. When asked whether there were not investments in innovations that were neither great successes nor great failures, he is reported to have answered, "Of course—but those I sell as early as possible and for whatever I can get." He then added, "In my early days those were the ventures on which I spent all my time. I always thought I could turn them around and make them the success we had originally expected. It never worked. But I found that I missed the real opportunities and that I misallocated my money by putting it into 'sound investments,' rather than into the big opportunities of the future."

## The Innovative Attitude

Resistance to change, by executives and workers alike, has for many years been considered a central problem of management. Countless books and articles have been written on the subject. Countless seminars, discussions, and courses have been devoted to it. Yet it is questionable that much progress has been made in resolving the problem.

Indeed, it is incapable of being resolved as long as we talk of "resistance to change." Not that there is no such resistance, or that it is not a major obstacle. But to focus on resistance to change is to misdefine the problem in a way that makes it less, rather than more, tractable. The right way to define the problem so as to make it capable of resolution is as a challenge to create, build, and maintain the innovative organization, the organization for which change is norm rather than exception, and opportunity rather than threat. Innovation is, therefore, attitude and practices. It is, above all, top-management attitude and practices. The innovative organization casts top management into a different role and embodies a different concept of top management's relationship to the organization.

In the traditional managerial organization such as management texts discuss, top management is *final judge.* This means, in effect, that management's most important power is the veto power, and its most important role is to say no to proposals and ideas that are not completely thought through and worked out. This concept is caricatured in that well-known jingle composed many years ago by a senior Unilever executive.

> Along this tree
> From root to crown
> Ideas flow up
> And vetoes down.

In the innovative organization, the first and most important job of management is the opposite: it is to convert impractical, half-baked, and wild ideas into concrete innovative reality. In the innovative organization, top management sees it as its job to listen to ideas and to take them seriously. Top management, in the innovative organization, knows that new ideas are always "impractical." It also knows that it takes a great many silly ideas to spawn one viable one, and that in the early stages there is no way of telling the silly idea from the stroke of genius. Both look equally impossible or equally brilliant.

Top management in the innovative organization, therefore, not only "encourages" ideas, as all managements are told to do. It asks continuously, "What would this idea have to be like to be practical, realistic, effective?" It organizes itself to think through rapidly even the wildest and apparently silliest idea for something new to the point where its feasibility can be appraised.

Top management in the innovative organization is the major "drive" for innovation. It uses the ideas of the organization as stimuli to its own vision. And then it works to make ideas a concern of the entire organization. Top management in the innovative organization fashions thought and work on the new into both organizational energy and entrepreneurial discipline.

This, however, presupposes restructuring relations between top management and the human group within the enterprise. The traditional organization, of course, remains. Indeed, on the organization chart there may be little to distinguish the innovative organization from the most rigidly bureaucratic one. And an innovative organization need not be "permissive" or "democratic" at all. But the innovative organization builds, so to speak, a nervous system next to the bony skeleton of the formal organization. Where traditional organization is focused on the logic of the work, there is also an additional relationship focused on the logic of ideas.

In innovative companies (as has been mentioned before) senior executives typically make it their business to meet with the younger men throughout the organization in scheduled (though not necessarily regular) sessions in which there is no "agenda" for top management. Rather, the seniors sit down with the younger men and ask, "What opportunities do *you* see?"

In the period of its greatest growth and development, the 3M Company was anything but a permissive company. It was tightly run by two or three men at the top who made all the decisions. But even the most junior engineer was encouraged, indeed practically commanded, to come to the top-management people with any idea, no matter how wild. And again and again he would be told, "The idea makes no sense to me; but are you willing to work on it?" If the engineer said yes, he would then be asked to write up his idea, together with a budget request—and more often than not he would be freed from his other responsibilities, given a modest sum of money for a year or two, and told to go ahead. As a result, the company grew from a small and obscure producer of abrasives into one of America's largest businesses.

Yet the young engineers at 3M were held strictly accountable. Not all of them succeeded, of course. Indeed, only one or two out of every ten did. And failure of an idea was not held against them—at least, not the first time. But failure to take responsibility, to organize the task, to work at it, and to appraise progress realistically—let alone to keep top management fully informed of the progress of the project—was not tolerated.

The innovative organization requires a learning atmosphere throughout the entire business. It creates and maintains continuous learning. No one is allowed to consider himself "finished" at any time. Learning is a continuing process for all members of the organization.

Resistance to change is grounded in ignorance and in fear of the unknown. Change has to be seen as opportunity by people—and then there will be no fear. It is seen as opportunity by the Japanese because they are guaranteed their jobs and are not afraid of putting themselves or their colleagues out of work by proposing something new (see Chapter 20). But fear and ignorance are also overcome in Japan by making continuing change the opportunity for personal achievement, for recognition, for satisfaction. The man who in a Japanese training session comes up with a new idea receives no monetary reward, even if his idea is a big and profitable one. But even if it is a very small improvement, he derives stature, recognition, intense pleasure.

We need not go to Japan to learn this. Every one of the "suggestion systems" that are so widely used in American business teaches the same lesson. The suggestion system in which the reward is recognition, achievement, participation, is the successful system. And in those departments in a plant where the suggestion system is being run this way, there is very little resistance to change, despite fears for job security and union restrictions. Where this does not prevail—as in the great majority—the suggestion system is not a success, no matter how well it pays for successful suggestions. It also has none of the effect on worker behavior and attitude which the proponents of the suggestion system promise.

## Structure for Innovation

The search for innovation needs to be organized separately and outside of the ongoing managerial business. Innovative organizations realize that one cannot simultaneously create the new and take care of what one already has. They realize that maintenance of the present business is far too big a task for the people in it to have much time for creating the new, the different business of tomorrow. They also realize that taking care of tomorrow is far too big and difficult a task to be diluted with concern for today. Both tasks have to be done. But they are different.

Innovative organizations, therefore, put the new into separate organizational components concerned with the creation of the new.

The oldest example is probably the development department at E.I. du Pont de Nemours in Wilmington, founded in the early twenties. This unit is concerned exclusively with the making of tomorrow. It is not a research department—Du Pont has a separate, big research lab. The job of the development department is to develop new businesses; production, finance, and marketing are as much its concern as technology, products, and processes. 3M, too, has set up a separate business development lab in parallel with, but separate from, its research labs.

This was not understood in 1952 when the General Electric Company embarked on its massive reorganization which then became the prototype for major organization changes in large businesses around the world. Under the GE plan the general manager of every "product business" was to have responsibility for both the ongoing business in his charge and the innovative efforts for tomorrow's new and different business. This seemed plausible enough. Indeed it seemed an inescapable conclusion from the idea that the general manager of a product business should, as much as possible, behave like the chief executive of an independent business. But it did not work— the general managers did not innovate.

One reason was the press of ongoing business. General managers had neither the time nor the motivation to work on obsoleting what they were managing. Another, equally important reason was that true innovation is rarely an extension of the already existing business. It rarely fits into the scope, objectives, goals, technologies or processes of today. But, of course, one can define only the scope, products, technologies, processes—even the markets—of today. The most important innovative opportunities always fall outside existing definitions—and thereby outside the "assigned scope" of an existing decentralized product business. After ten years or so GE began to draw the proper conclusions from its frustrations and began to organize major innovation separately and outside of existing product departments and product divisions—and very similar to the way innovative efforts had been organized at Du Pont for many years, that is, in a separate organizational "business development" unit.

Experience in public-service institutions also indicates that innovative efforts best be organized separately and outside of existing managerial organization.

The greater innovative capacity of the American university as compared to the universities of continental Europe has often been remarked upon. The main reason is clearly not that American academicians are less resistant to change. It is the ease with which the American university can set up a new department, a new faculty, or even an entirely new school to do new things. The European university, by contrast, tends to be compelled by law and tradition to set up a new activity within an already existing department or faculty. This not only creates immediately a "war of the ancients against the moderns" in which the new is fought as a threat by the established disciplines. It also deprives the new, as a rule, of the resources needed to innovate successfully. The ablest of the young scholars, for instance, will be under great pressure to stick to the "safe" traditional fields which still control the opportunities for promotion. For significant innovation to move fast in the European academic setting usually requires "break-away institutions." The great age of English physics and chemistry in the late seventeenth century was ushered in by setting up the Royal Academy outside the established university system. More than two hundred years later, a similar break-away institution, the London School of Economics, created the opportunity for genuine innovation in teaching—and learning—in the economic and social fields. In France Napoleon systematically set up the *grandes écoles* such as the École Polytechnique and the École Normale outside the university system as vehicles for innovation in learning and research, e.g., to make effective the then brand-new idea that teachers needed training and could actually be trained. And one of the main reasons why the Germans, in the decade before World War I, set up the separate scientific research institutes of the Kaiser-Wilhelm Gesellschaft (now Max-Planck Gesellschaft) was to gain freedom to develop new disciplines and new approaches in old disciplines, that is, to gain freedom for innovation.

Similarly the Manhattan Project, which developed the atomic bomb, as well as CERN, the European nuclear-research facility, were set up outside the existing academic and governmental structures precisely because their purpose was to be innovation.

## Innovation as a "Business"

At the same time, the innovative organizations realize that innovation needs from the beginning to be organized as a "business" rather than as a "function." In concrete terms, this means setting aside the traditional time sequence in which "research" comes first, followed by "development," followed by "manufacturing," with "marketing" at the very end. The innovative organizations consider these functional skills as part of one and the same process, the process of developing a new business. When and how each of these tools is to be put into play is decided by the logic of the situation rather than by any preconceived time sequence.

A project manager or business manager is therefore put in charge of anything new as soon as it is decided to pay attention to it. He may come from any function—or from no function at all. And he can draw on all the functions right from the beginning; use marketing, for instance, before there is any research; or work out the financial requirements of a future business before he even knows whether he will have products.

The traditional functions organize work from where we are today to where we are going. The innovative function organizes work from where we want to be, back to what we now have to do in order to get there.

The design principle for innovation is the team, set up outside of existing structures, that is, as an "autonomous unit." It is not a "decentralized business" in the traditional sense of the word, but it has to be autonomous and separate from operating organizations.

One way to organize innovative units within a large business might well be to group them together into an innovative group, which reports to one member of top management who has no other function but to guide, help, advise, review, and direct the innovating team at work. This is, in effect, what the Du Pont development department is. Innovation has its own logic, which is different from the logic of an ongoing business. No matter how much the innovative units may themselves differ in their technologies, their markets, their products, or their services, they all have in common that they are innovative.

Even such autonomous team organization may be too restricted for the kind of innovation that will increasingly be needed, innovation in fields that are quite different from anything that business has done so far. We may need to set up the innovating unit as a genuine entrepreneur.

Several large companies in the United States, e.g., GE and Westinghouse —and also several large companies in Europe—have set up innovative efforts in the form of partnerships with the "entrepreneurs" in charge. The innovative effort is organized as a separate company, in which the parent company has majority control and usually a right to buy out the minority stockholders at some prearranged price. But the entrepreneurs, that is, the people who are responsible directly for developing the innovation, are substantial shareholders in their own right.

One advantage of such a relationship is that it eases the compensation problem. Innovative people can command substantial salaries in the managerial organization, as senior research scientists or as senior marketing people. Yet it is highly undersirable to saddle an innovative venture with high salary costs—it cannot afford them. At the same time, it is highly desirable to compensate the entrepreneurs for results. But results in the innovative effort are unlikely to be known for a good many years. A method of compensation which induces these entrepreneurs to work for modest salaries until results are achieved, while promising substantial rewards in case of success, is therefore appropriate. A "partnership" makes this possible. It also—and this is no small advantage—lessens (although it never completely eliminates) the friction which setting up separate innovative organizations within the company structure otherwise creates.

The same results, however, can also be achieved without a partnership —provided the tax laws permit it (which, in many countries, they no longer do). 3M, for instance, never organized a partnership with its young engineers heading a project team. It never set up a separate corporation in which the entrepreneurs became shareholders. Still, the salaries of the entrepreneurs were kept low until the innovation had proven itself and had become successful. And then the entrepreneurs not only had the opportunity to stay on and manage what they had created, at salaries commensurate to the size and performance of the business they had built, they also received handsome bonuses.

Whether these "confederations" in which the entrepreneurs become partners and shareholders will become general will depend as much on tax laws as on economics or organization structure. The principle, however, is important: compensation of the innovators should be appropriate to the economic reality of the innovating process. This is a process in which the risks are high, the lead time long, and the rewards, in case of success, very great.

Whether the innovating team is a separate company or simply a separate unit, an innovating company is likely to apply some of the design principles of systems management. There will be managerial units engaged in managing what is already known and what is already being done. And there will be innovative units, separate from them, working with them but also working on their own, and charged with their own responsibility. Both will have to report independently of each other to the top-management group and work with top-management people. To innovate within existing organizations will require acceptance of a hybrid and rather complex organization design. It is neither centralized nor decentralized. Within such a company, functional organization, federal decentralization, simulated decentralization, and teams may all be found next to each other and working together.

The innovative organization, the organization that resists stagnation rather than change, is a major challenge to management, private and public. That such organizations are possible, we can assert with confidence; there are enough of them around. But how to make such organizations general, how to make them productive for society, economy, and individual alike, is still largely an unsolved task. There is every indication that the period ahead will be an innovative one, one of rapid change in technology, society, economy, and institutions. There is every indication, therefore, that the innovative organization will have to be developed into a central institution for the last quarter of the twentieth century.

CONCLUSION

# THE LEGITIMACY
# OF MANAGEMENT

———

In this century society has become a society of organizations. Every major social task in this society is being performed in and through large, managed institutions. As a result, the great majority of people in developed countries work as employees. They work as members of managed institutions and within a managerial structure and organization.

In this century society has become a knowledge society. More and more of the members of developed society make their living by putting knowledge to work. More and more acquire their qualifications through long years of formal education. More and more of them are managers themselves or work as knowledge professionals with direct responsibility for performance and results.

The two developments are interrelated. Because of the emergence of the society of organizations, one can now make a living through knowledge work. And because of the availability of large numbers of people with substantial formal education, large institutions are possible and can be managed.

Management is both the carrier and the result of these two developments. It is the organ through which the institutions of the society of organizations can be made to function and to perform their mission. And management itself is such a "knowledge." It is a discipline with its own subject matters, its own skills, its own expertise. Above all, the managers of these institutions in a society of organizations form the leadership groups of the society.

Unless this society of organizations destroys itself, managers as a leadership group and management as a discipline and challenge will remain with us. To repeat the *leitmotiv* of this book, we are moving from management boom to management performance. It is the task of *this* management generation to make the institutions of the society of organizations, beginning with the business enterprise, perform for society and economy; for the community; and for the individual alike.

This requires, first, that managers know their discipline. It requires that they know management.

We hear a great deal today about the manager of the future. But the important man is the manager of today. And the first requirement is that the manager know his craft, his tools, his task and responsibility. The first requirement is that he be able to function.

## The Limits of Technocracy

The management boom focused on management skills and management competence. But it largely defined the management job as internal. It was concerned with organization and motivation, with financial and other controls, with the management sciences, and with manager development. It was, to use a fashionable term, technocratic in its orientation. This was understandable. It was also right. One has to know one's own craft. There are few things as useless as the man who wants to set right the world because he does not know his own job.

But if the years of the management boom have taught us anything, it is that the technocrat as manager is not enough. It is precisely because in the society of organizations there is no leadership group other than the managers that more is required than technocracy.

The first task of the manager is indeed to manage the institution for the mission for which it has been designed. The first task of the business manager is, therefore, economic performance. But at the same time he faces the tasks of making the work productive and the worker achieving, and of providing for the quality of life for society and individual. And this goes well beyond technocracy.

President Kennedy's administration was the peak of a great wave of technocracy. It was also its tragedy. And Robert McNamara, President Kennedy's Secretary of Defense, personified both the strength and the limitations of the technocrat. In the final analysis McNamara was a failure —not because of Vietnam but because "managing" to him was focus on the internal and excluded the external, the value, the people, the social dimensions.

But General Motors also can be seen as the triumph and the failure of the technocrat manager. Indeed the book which the builder of General Motors, Alfred P. Sloan, wrote* shows both the strength of the truly accomplished technocratic manager and his limitations. General Motors has stayed with Sloan's legacy. And in Sloan's terms i.e., in terms of sales and profits, it has succeeded admirably, at least in the North American

*My Years with General Motors (Doubleday, 1964).

market. But it has also failed abysmally—in terms of public reputation, of public esteem, of acceptance by the public.*

There is great temptation here—the temptation for the manager to become a philosopher, the temptation to become "cosmic." Hence it cannot be said too often that the foundation for "doing good" is "doing well." Good intentions are no excuse for incompetence. And the manager who believes that social consciousness is a substitute for managing his business—or his hospital or his university—so that it produces the results for the sake of which it exists, is either a fool or a knave or both.

## The Need for Legitimacy

But a leadership group needs not only to function. It needs not only to perform. It also has to have legitimacy. It has to be accepted by the community as "right."

"Legitimacy" is an elusive concept. It has, in effect, no real definition. Yet it is crucial. Authority without legitimacy is usurpation. And the leadership groups of a society—and this means the managers today—have to have authority to perform their functions.

At the same time, none of the traditional grounds of legitimacy will do for the managers. Birth or magic are just as unsuitable for them as popular election or the rights of private property. They hold office because they perform. And yet performance by itself has never been sufficient grounds for legitimacy.

What managers need to be accepted as legitimate authority is a principle of morality. They need to ground their authority in a moral commitment which, at the same time, expresses the purpose and character of organizations.

Almost three centuries ago the English pamphleteer Mandeville in a didactic poem "The Fable of the Bees" laid down what became, a century later, the principle of capitalism. "Private vices make public benefit." Blind and greedy profit-seeking, Mandeville laid down, advances the public good through the "invisible hand." In terms of performance, history has proven Mandeville remarkably right. But morally his principle was never acceptable. And the fact that capitalism has become the less acceptable the more it succeeded—as the great Austro-American economist Joseph Schumpeter pointed out repeatedly—has been the basic weakness of modern society and modern economy.

*On General Motors's triumph and failure, see also the Epilogue to the new (1972) edition of my book, *Concept of the Corporation*.

This, by the way, is why the rhetoric of "profit maximization" and "profit motive" are not only antisocial. They are immoral.

Although we still talk in De Mandeville's terms, we have long ago shifted to a very different base. We long ago learned that it is the job of the business manager to convert public needs into business opportunities. It is his task to anticipate, identify, and satisfy the needs of market and individual, the needs of consumer and employee.

But these are still inadequate grounds of legitimacy. They explain business activity rationally, but they do not supply it with the justification for authority. To maintain an autonomous management, a management that in serving its institution serves society and community, a principle of morality has to be grounded in the purposes and the characteristics of organization and in the nature of the institution itself.

There is only one such principle. It is the purpose of organization and, therefore, the grounds of management authority: *to make human strength productive.* Organization is the means through which man, as an individual and as a member of the community, finds both contribution and achievement.

The invention of organization as society's tool for accomplishing social purposes may well be as important to the history of man as was the invention of the specialization of labor for individuals ten thousand years ago. And the principle underlying it is not "private vices make public benefits." It is *"personal strengths make social benefits."* This can serve as grounds for legitimacy. This is a moral principle on which authority can be based.

To maintain management as autonomous, and indeed as "private," is an essential need of society. It is essential for keeping society free. It is essential for keeping society performing. The alternative, the "totalitarian" structure in which all activities, all individuals, and all organizations monolithically repeat the same pattern, are managed by one and the same governing group, and express the same values, the same doctrine, and the same orthodoxy, is not only death to the human spirit, it is grotesque. It is also wasteful, rigid, stifling. It is not, above all, business that needs the autonomy of the markets for goods and services, for capital, and for jobs and careers, that is, autonomous and accountable management of autonomous institutions. It is (as Chapter 27 pointed out earlier), the economy, the society, and government itself which require managerial autonomy and "free enterprise."

Yet to have a society of organizations with autonomous managements, each a decision-maker in its own sphere, requires that managers, while private, also know themselves to be public. They are private in that they are not subservient to a central political authority which, in turn, is uncontrolled, uncontrollable, and despotic as inevitable result. But they are public in that they consciously, knowingly, openly, strive to make a public need into a private opportunity of their autonomous self-governing institution.

The old fights are still being fought and the old slogans still reverberate. Yet even the Soviet Union has had to accept "profit" as a necessary condition of economic activity and as a means to build the "capital fund" without which no economy can survive, let alone advance. Indeed, the profit requirement of a totally planned and therefore rigid economy is, of necessity, many times greater than that of a "market economy." "Ownership" is becoming a secondary issue, especially as the "workers" increasingly are also becoming the "owners" in the most highly developed countries. This does not mean that we cannot be killed by these old fights and issues. The scars fester and are toxic. But nothing can be "solved" by the remedies of the nineteenth century.

What is needed to break out of the straitjacket of old slogans and old issues is management performance. This first requires performance as a technocrat. It requires performance that makes the manager's organization capable of supplying to society and economy the contribution for the sake of which it exists, such as economic goods and services and the capital fund for tomorrow. But it also requires performance beyond the immediate mission, beyond technocracy: performance in making work productive and the worker achieving and performance with respect to the quality of life. But above all, it has to be performance with respect to the role and function of the manager. If he is to remain—as he should—the manager of an autonomous institution, he must accept that he is a public man. He must accept the moral responsibility of organization, the responsibility of making individual strengths productive and achieving.

# Bibliography

Management literature has become so voluminous that no one can hope to keep up with it. Even to pick out the "best" books is a fruitless attempt. What I have tried to do is to prepare a list—admittedly overlong—of the books which a fairly large number of friends, experienced managers in a number of countries around the world, have found to be stimulating, readable, and worthwhile. Even so, the list suffers from being heavily biased toward American authors.

To make the list more useful, I have divided the books into major categories and have not hesitated to list a title more than once if it seemed to me to deserve mention in several categories.

Most management books take Western, and especially American, management for granted. For this reason, I have included a small list of six titles on Japanese management. They will not only help the Western reader to understand the one non-Western managerial system in a highly developed country, but will also give him a better insight into the cultural and historical roots of his own system.

I. *Origins, Foundations, and Tasks of Management*

Chandler, Alfred D., Jr. *Strategy and Structure.* Cambridge, Mass.: M.I.T. Press, 1962.

Chandler, Alfred D., Jr., and Salisbury, Stephen. *Pierre S. Du Pont and the Making of the Modern Corporation.* New York: Harper & Row, 1971.

Drucker, Peter F. *The Future of Industrial Man.* New York: John Day, 1942.

Drucker, Peter F. *Concept of the Corporation.* New York: John Day, 1946; revised edition, 1972. Title of British edition: *Big Business.* London: Heinemann, 1946.

Drucker, Peter F. *The New Society.* New York: Harper & Row, 1950.

Eells, R.S.F. and Walton, C.C. *Conceptual Foundations of Business.* Homewood, Ill.: Irwin, 1961.

Emmet Boris, and Jeuck, John C. *Catalogues and Counters; A History of Sears, Roebuck & Co.* Chicago: University of Chicago, 1950.

Galbraith, John Kenneth. *The New Industrial State.* Boston: Houghton Mifflin, 1967.

Landes, David S. *The Unbound Prometheus; Technological Change and Industrial Development in Western Europe from 1750 to the Present.* Cambridge University Press, 1969.

Nevins, Allan, and Hill, Frank E. *Ford: Decline and Rebirth 1933–1962.* New York: Scribner's, 1962/3.

Reader, W. J. *Imperial Chemical Industries: A History,* vol. 1, 1870–1926. Oxford University Press, 1970.

Schumpeter, Joseph. *The Theory of Economic Development.* Cambridge, Mass.: Harvard University Press, 1934; Original German Edition, 1911.

Schumpeter, Joseph. *Capitalism, Socialism and Democracy.* New York: Harper Bros., 1942.

Siemens, Georg. *Der Weg der Elektrotechnik; Geschichte des Hauses Siemens.* Freiburg: Alber, 1961.

Sloan, Alfred P., Jr. *My Years with General Motors.* Garden City, N. Y.: Doubleday, 1964.

Woodruff, Philip. *The Men Who Ruled India,* 2 vols. New York: St. Martin's Press, and London: Macmillan, 1954.

## II. *Management as a Process and a Discipline*

Drucker, Peter F. *The Practice of Management.* New York: Harper & Row, 1954.

Gantt, Henry. *Gantt on Management.* Edited by Alex W. Rathe. New York: American Management Association, 1961.

Koontz, Harold, and O'Donnell, Cyril. *Principles of Management.* New York: McGraw-Hill, 1972.

Merrill, Harwood, ed. *Classics in Management.* New York: American Management Association, 1960.

Urwick, Lyndall F., and Brech, E.F.L. *The Making of Scientific Management.* London: Sir Isaac Pitman & Sons, 1952.

Urwick, Lyndall F., ed. *The Golden Book of Management.* London: Newman Neame, 1956.

## III. *Management in Japan*

Abbegglen, James. *The Japanese Factory.* Glencoe, Ill.: Free Press, 1958.

Hirschmeier, Johannes. *The Origins of Entrepreneurship in Meiji Japan.* Cambridge, Mass.: Harvard University Press, 1964.

Kobayashi, Shigeru. *Creative Management.* New York: American Management Association, 1971.

Nakane, Chie. *Japanese Society.* Berkeley, Calif.: University of California Press, 1970.

Tobata, Seiichi, ed. *The Modernization of Japan.* Tokyo: Institute of Asian Economic Affairs, 1966.

Yoshino, M. *Japan's Managerial System: Tradition and Innovation.* Cambridge, Mass.: M.I.T. Press, 1968.


## IV. *Managing for Performance*

Crozier, Michael. *The Bureaucratic Phenomenon.* Chicago: University of Chicago Press, 1964.

Dean, Joel. *Managerial Economics.* Englewood Cliffs, N. J.: Prentice-Hall, 1951.

Drucker, Peter F. *Managing for Results.* New York: Harper & Row, 1964.

Penrose, Edith T. *The Theory of the Growth of the Firm.* London: Oxford University Press, 1959.

Schumpeter, Joseph. *The Theory of Economic Development.* Cambridge, Mass.: Harvard University Press, 1934.

Shackle, G.L.S. *Decision, Order and Time in Human Affairs.* Cambridge University Press, 1961.


## V. *Work and Worker*

Herzberg, Frederick. *Work and the Nature of Man.* Cleveland: World, 1966.

Herzberg, Frederick; Mausner, B.; and Snyderman, B. B. *The Motivation to Work.* New York: Wiley, 1959

Homans, J. G. *The Human Group.* New York: Harcourt, Brace, 1950.

Likert, Rensis. *The Human Organization.* New York: McGraw-Hill, 1967.

Maslow, A. H. *Motivation and Personality.* New York: Harper & Row, 1954.

Mayo, Elton. *The Social Problems of an Industrial Civilization.* Boston: Harvard Business School, 1945.

Mayo, Elton. *The Human Problems of an Industrial Civilization.* Boston: Harvard Business School, 1946.

McGregor, Douglas. *The Human Side of Enterprise.* New York: McGraw-Hill, 1960.

Taylor, F. W. *The Principles of Scientific Management.* New York: Harper's, 1912, and many editions since.

Wiener, Norbert. *The Human Use of Human Beings.* Boston: Houghton Mifflin, 1950.

Woodward, Joan. *Industrial Organization; Theory and Practice.* Oxford University Press, 1965.


## VI. *Social Impacts and Social Responsibilities*

Bowen, H. R. *The Social Responsibility of the Businessman.* New York: Harper & Row, 1953.

McGuire, J. W. *Business and Society.* New York: McGraw-Hill, 1963.

Steiner, George A. *Business and Society.* New York: Random House, 1971.

### VII. *The Manager's Work and Job*

Barnard, Chester I. *The Functions of the Executive.* Cambridge, Mass.: Harvard University Press, 1938.

Drucker, Peter F. *The Effective Executive.* New York: Harper & Row, 1966.

Follett, Mary Parker. *Dynamic Administration; The Collected Papers of Mary Parker Follett.* Edited by Henry C. Metcalf and L. Urwick. New York: Harper's, 1941.

McGregor, Douglas. *The Professional Manager.* New York: McGraw-Hill, 1967.

Simon, Herbert A. *Administrative Behavior.* New York: Macmillan, 1957.


### VIII. *Managerial Skills and Managerial Tools*

Anthony, R. N. *Planning and Control Systems.* Boston: Harvard Business School, 1965.

Beer, Stafford. *Decision and Control.* New York: Wiley, 1966.

Churchman, C. W.; Ackoff, R. L.; and Arnoff, E. L. *Introduction to Operations Research.* New York: Wiley, 1957.

Ewing, D. W., ed. *Long-Range Planning for Management.* New edition. New York: Harper & Row, 1972.

Forrester, Jay W. *Industrial Dynamics.* Cambridge, Mass.: M.I.T. Press, 1961.

Solomon, Ezra, ed. *The Management of Corporate Capital.* Glencoe, Ill.: Free Press, 1959.

Solomon, Ezra. *The Theory of Financial Management.* New York: Columbia University Press, 1963.

Steiner, George A. *Top Management Planning.* New York: Macmillan, 1969.


### IX. *Organization Design and Structure*

Dale, Ernest. *The Great Organizers.* New York: McGraw-Hill, 1960.

Drucker, Peter F. *Concept of the Corporation.* New York: John Day, 1946; revised edition, 1972. Title of British edition: *Big Business.* London: Heinemann, 1946.

Fayol, Henri. *General and Industrial Management.* New York and London: Pitman, 1949.

March, James G., and Simon, Herbert A. *Organizations.* New York: Wiley, 1958.

Sayles, Leonard R., and Chandler, Margaret K. *Managing Large Systems: Organizations for the Future.* New York: Harper & Row, 1971.

Sloan, Alfred P., Jr. *My Years with General Motors.* Garden City, N.Y.: Doubleday, 1964.

Urwick, Lyndall F. *Notes on the Theory of Organization.* New York: American Management Association, 1953.

Webb, James E. *Space Age Management.* New York: McGraw-Hill, 1969.

## X. *The Top-Management Job*

Bower, Marvin. *The Will to Manage.* New York: McGraw-Hill, 1966.
Chandler, Alfred D., Jr., and Salisbury, Stephen. *Pierre S. Du Pont and the Making of the Modern Corporation.* New York: Harper & Row, 1971.
Holden, Paul E. and others. *Top-Management Organization and Control.* New York: McGraw-Hill, 1951.
Sloan, Alfred P., Jr. *My Years with General Motors.* Garden City, N.Y.: Doubleday, 1964.
Woodruff, Philip. *The Men Who Ruled India.* 2 vols. New York: St. Martin's Press, and London: Macmillan, 1954.

## XI. *Strategies and Structures*

Chandler, Alfred D., Jr., and Salisbury, Stephen. *Pierre S. Du Pont and the Making of the Modern Corporation.* New York: Harper & Row, 1971.
Dale, Ernest. *The Great Organizers.* New York: McGraw-Hill, 1960.
Guth, William. *Organizational Strategy: Analysis, Commitment Implementation.* Homewood, Ill.: Irwin, 1974.
Sayles, Leonard R., and Chandler, Margaret K. *Managing Large Systems: Organizations for the Future.* New York: Harper & Row, 1971.

## XII. *The Multinational Corporation*

Brooke, M. Z. *The Strategy of Multinational Enterprise.* New York: Elsevier, and London: Longman, 1970.
Dunning, John J. *The Multinational Enterprise.* London: Longman, 1971.
Eells, Richard. *Global Corporations.* New York: Interbook, 1973.
Rolfe, Sidney E., and Damon, Walter, eds. *The Multinational Corporation in the World Economy.* New York: Praeger, 1970.
Vernon, Raymond. *Sovereignty at Bay: The Multinational Spread of Private Enterprise.* New York: Basic Books, 1971.

## XIII. *The Innovative Organization*

Argyris, Chris. *Organization and Innovation.* Homewood, Ill.: Richard D. Irwin, Inc., 1965.
Bennis, W. G. *Changing Organizations.* New York: McGraw-Hill, 1966.
Gardner, John W. *Self-Renewal: The Individual and the Innovative Society.* New York: Harper & Row, 1964.

XIV. *The Manager of Tomorrow*

Boulding, Kenneth E. *The Organizational Revolution.* Ann Arbor: University of Michigan Press, 1953.

Boulding, Kenneth E. *The Image.* New York: Harper & Row, 1956.

Drucker, Peter F. *The Age of Discontinuity.* New York: Harper & Row, 1969.

Drucker, Peter F., ed. *Preparing Tomorrow's Business Leaders Today.* Englewood Cliffs, N.J.: Prentice-Hall, 1969.

# Index

Iron Law of, 24
Japan, 250–3
as living, 188–92
as motivation, 196, 237–41
*see also* benefits
Walker, Charles R., 260*n*, 273*n*, 277*n*
Wallenberg Co.'s, 635
Walton, Richard E., 275*n*, 283
War on Poverty, 680
Watson, Thomas J., Sr., 74, 260–1, 264–5, 275–6, 340, 766–8, 779–80
*Wealth of Nations* (Smith), 22
Webb, James E., 593*n*, 597*n*
*Weight Watching at the University: The Consequence of Growth* (Gallant and Prothero), 639*n*
West Africa, 14
West Germany, 370
Westinghouse, 696, 704–5, 802
West Virginia, 320–2, 345
"What We Already Know About Tomorrow's Schools" (Drucker), 134*n*
Whirlpool, 718–19
White, Andrew W., 150–1
Wilson, Charles, 172–3
Wood, Robert E., 12, 25, 53–6, 58, 615, 710, 769–70, 779
Woodruff, Philip, 404
Woodward, Joan, 273–4
Woolf, Leonard, 404
*Work and the Nature of Man* (Herzberg), 196*n*, 446*n*
work and working, 24, 128, 168–9, 180–97
analysis, 182–3, 199–203, 247
assignments, 101, 524–5
changes in and, 179
community, 281–4, 307, 326, 328
dimensions of working, 183–97
dominant-dimension fallacy, 194–7

economic dimension, 188–94, 194–5
economic shares and authority, 192–4
ethic, 179, 185–6
groups, 272–4
job design, 202, 247, 262
job enrichment, 260–2, 274–7
management of, 27, 199
organization, managerial, 524
physiology and, 183–4, 194–5
power relationships, 192–5
as process, 182–3, 198ff.
productive (*see also* production; productivity), 27, 41, 182–3, 199
psychology and (*see also* industrial psychology; motivation), 184–6, 194–5, 202, 231–45
simplification, 202*n*, 271
social dimension, 187–8, 194–5
studies of, 181–2, 199
synthesis, 182–3, 199, 202, 247
workers, *see* employees; labor; knowledge workers and work; personnel management; specific subjects
*Work Organization and Job Design of Saab-Scandia in Södertalje* (Norstedt), 275*n*
World Bank, 729
*World Dynamics* (Forrester), 507*n*

Xerox Corp., 84–5, 124, 680

York University, 675
Yugoslavia, 13, 19, 156, 190, 194, 196, 293, 361, 732

Zaibatsu, 7, 386, 593, 689, 725
*see also* names
Zeiss, Carl, 258
Zeiss, Optical Works, 207, 209, 258–60, 263–5, 268, 276–7, 284, 286, 291, 294, 301–2, 341

## About the Author

With the publication of his first book, *The End of Economic Man*, in 1939 Peter F. Drucker established himself as a trenchant, unorthodox and independent analyst of politics, economics and society. Today, he is considered the founding father of the discipline of management, and is the most influential and widely read thinker and writer on modern organizations and their management.

The author of seventeen books on the subject (as well as two novels and a spirited memoir), Drucker has achieved both national and international bestsellerdom as his works have been translated into more than twenty languages. He also has been a frequent contributor to magazines for many years and is an editorial columnist for *The Wall Street Journal*.

Drucker has had a distinguished career as a teacher—of economics and statistics (at Sarah Lawrence), of politics, history and philosophy (at Bennington), and for more than twenty years as professor of management at the Graduate Business School of New York University. Since 1971 he has been Clarke Professor of Social Science at Claremont Graduate School in Claremont, California.

For more than thirty years Peter Drucker has been adviser and consultant on basic policies and long-range trends to businesses, public and private institutions, and government agencies in the United States and abroad. He has received ten honorary doctorates from universities in five countries.

Peter Drucker is married and has four children. He was born in 1909 in Vienna, and was educated there and in England. He took his doctorate in public and international law while working as a newspaperman in Frankfurt, Germany. A mountaineer and hiker and a student of Japan and Japanese art, he lives with his wife in Claremont, California.

*Peter F. Drucker Books Available in Paperback Editions*

## MANAGEMENT: TASKS, RESPONSIBILITIES, PRACTICES

"He joins vast erudition and experience with responsible, usable, and convincing wisdom . . . totally comprehensive."    —*Business Week*


## MANAGING IN TURBULENT TIMES

"His breadth of vision, his internationalism and his sober realism combine to make his analysis of the present and predictions about the future gripping."                                   —*The Economist*


## THE EFFECTIVE EXECUTIVE

"An intelligent, authoritative, and original guide."
                                            —*Washington Post Book World*


## THE AGE OF DISCONTINUITY

"[This] book has tremendous scope. . . . It is a useful, stimulating survey of the political and economic realities that may shape the next few decades."                              —*Wall Street Journal*